Just As I Am
A Unique Memoir

Roy W. Lilley

© 2018 Roy Lilley
All Rights Reserved
Fort Collins, Colorado
ISBN # 13: 978-1983607721

Lynette McClain and Allen Peacock, Editors
McClain Productions
www.mcclainproductions.com
Longmont, CO

I dedicate this book to my children:
Elizabeth Ruth, Shaun Ilene,
Brendan Christopher, and Jennifer Dawn
and to the memory of my parents.

Denver 028427, 028428 and 028571

4—1007.

The United States of America,

To all to whom these presents shall come, Greeting:

WHEREAS, a Certificate of the Register of the Land Office at Denver, Colorado,
has been deposited in the General Land Office, whereby it appears that, pursuant to the Act of Congress of May 20, 1862,
"To Secure Homesteads to Actual Settlers on the Public Domain," and the acts supplemental thereto, the claim of
Charles W. Lilley
has been established and duly consummated, in conformity to law, for the Lots one and two and the northwest quarter of the southwest quarter of Section twenty, the southeast quarter of Section twenty-two and the north half of the northeast quarter and the west half of Section twenty-six in Township twelve north of Range seventy-one west of the Sixth Principal Meridian, Colorado, containing six hundred three acres and three hundredths of an acre,

according to the Official Plat of the Survey of the said Land, on file in the GENERAL LAND OFFICE:

NOW KNOW YE, That there is, therefore, granted by the UNITED STATES unto the said claimant the tract of Land above described; TO HAVE AND TO HOLD the said tract of Land, with the appurtenances thereof, unto the said claimant and to the heirs and assigns of the said claimant forever; subject to any vested and accrued water rights for mining, agricultural, manufacturing, or other purposes, and rights to ditches and reservoirs used in connection with such water rights, as may be recognized and acknowledged by the local customs, laws, and decisions of courts; and there is reserved from the lands hereby granted, a right of way thereon for ditches or canals constructed by the authority of the United States. Excepting and reserving, however, to the United States all the coal and other minerals in the lands so entered and patented, together with the right to prospect for, mine, and remove the same pursuant to the provisions and limitations of the Act of December 29, 1916 (39 Stat., 862).

IN TESTIMONY WHEREOF, I, Calvin Coolidge,
President of the United States of America, have caused these letters to be made Patent, and the seal of the General Land Office to be hereunto affixed.
GIVEN under my hand, at the City of Washington, the FOURTH
day of MAY in the year of our Lord one thousand
nine hundred and TWENTY-SEVEN and of the Independence of the
United States the one hundred and FIFTY-FIRST

By the President: *Calvin Coolidge*

By *Viola B. Pugh*, Secretary.

M. P. LeRoy
Recorder of the General Land Office.

RECORDED: Patent Number 1001156

Grant signed by Calvin Coolidge to Dad for 603 acres
homesteaded by him on the north side of Table Mountain in 1927.

Contents

	Acknowledgments	*i*
	Foreword	*v*
	Introduction	1
1	Mom and Dad	3
2	Kate and Harry	10
3	Early Memories	15
4	Ranch Life	23
5	Fort Collins	27
6	Denver	32
7	Lakewood	35
8	Driving a Team	46
9	Eighth Grade Memories	54
10	Basketball and School Politics	57
11	Summer Cabin	62
12	Sophomore Basketball	71
13	First Summer Job	77
14	New School - Old Friend	82
15	Questionable Behavior	89
16	Trail Creek Dude Ranch	98
17	State Basketball Finals	107
18	Taking Responsibility	125
19	College Freshman	132
20	Round Corral Rodeos	142
21	First National College Rodeo Finals	149
22	Gintsie	158
23	Second Rodeo Finals	172
24	Senior Year	181
25	Last and Best Rodeo Finals	191
26	Dick Peters	209
27	Reflections of a Korean War Draftee	219
28	Adjusting After Korea	225
29	Great Job Opportunity	244
30	Learning the Ropes	259
31	Farm and Horses	268
32	Learning Job	275
33	Sprinkler System	280

34	Deer Hunt and Convention Chores	284
35	Swift Trip	290
36	Cattle Industry Issues	297
37	Rad	303
38	Major Issues	311
39	Ingrid	323
40	J. Edgar Dick	332
41	New Mexico	343
42	Domestic Problems	355
43	Washington D. C. Trip	367
44	Jesse Dowdy	374
45	Maxine	381
46	Moving the Office	393
47	Brink's Brangus	406
48	Tight Budget	414
49	Foreign Marketing	424
50	Software Disaster	435
51	Paid Vacation	443
52	Nebraska	456
53	Feeders	469
54	Farm Crisis	479
55	Merger	488
56	Our Little Farm	503
57	Tom Scott	512
58	4-H Fiasco	519
59	Sarah	529
60	Bad Year	538
61	Reprieve	548
62	Cleaning Up Messes	555
63	Retirement	563

Acknowledgments

I particularly wish to recognize three people who encouraged me to "keep on writing" as I worked on this book. They are the only ones who saw all of the unedited final draft. Mary Ridder who worked for me as Communications Director at the Nebraska Stock Growers Association in the early 1980s and has remained a friend was the first person I called when my thoughts of putting together a family history evolved into writing a memoir instead. I also forwarded chapters to my eldest nephew, Charles Lilley, in Africa, who had retired from his law firm and joined the Peace Corps after his wife died of ALS (Lou Gehrig's disease). Responding to his request to give an informal presentation on the Lilley family history at a family reunion in the summer of 2014 just before Jan succumbed to the horrible affliction I had prepared a summary of my remarks that I subsequently expanded. About a year ago I called Chuck Schroeder who was Director of the Nebraska State Department of Agriculture when I worked for the cattle industry there during the agricultural depression of the mid eighties. I mentioned I was writing a memoir and sent him a couple of chapters. He offered to read them all and was kind enough to write the introduction.

Charles Lilley shared a few chapters of the book with his siblings and his youngest brother, Mark who is a graphic artist, offered to design the cover and their elder sister, Karen, was kind enough to take the picture of the entrance to the Table Mountain Ranch that is part of it. I am so grateful for their help and was glad to get some of my talented kin folk involved.

I made a lot of phone calls over the last two years and wish to thank those who so kindly took time out from their busy lives to visit with me. They include: the staff at the Intercollegiate Rodeo Association who combed through their records trying find the missing records of the June, 1952 Intercollegiate Rodeo during the Portland Rose Festival; Oscar Lilley, the grandson of my late brother Frank, who helped me wade through the records of the American National Cattlemen's Association that are stored at the University of Wyoming American Heritage Center; Oscar's mom, Shirley, who was always available to help jog my memory on family matters and provided some pictures; my daughter, Jennifer Applequist who helped me recall our escapades at the Box Butte County Fair in Hemingford, Nebraska during her 4-H days; and my eldest daughter Elizabeth for sending thepictures of her and her mom.

Others include: Burton Eller, Executive Vice President of the National Cattlemen's Association when it changed its name from ANCA; Tom Cook, Vice President of Government Affairs under Eller; Bill Helming, founder of ANCA's marketing service that later became CattleFax; Billy Gatlin, Executive Vice President of the California Cattlemen's Association; Caren Cowan, Executive Director of the New Mexico Cattle Growers Association; Tommy Perkins, Executive Vice President of the International Brangus Breeders Association; Peyton Waldrip, IBBA Communications Coordinator; Ludwig Brand past IBBA President; Sammy Pierce, a successful Brangus sales manager who gave me valuable first hand information about Clear Creek Ranch in Oklahoma (he worked there right after he left college) which was so important in developing the Brangus breed; and Chris Shivers, Executive Vice President of the American Brahman Breeder's Association.

I have a special place in my heart for the late Bob Howard who was both an employee and mentor. Bob who was the Executive Secretary of the Nebraska Stock Growers Association and Editor of the Nebraska Cattleman for years was the source of most of the information about the early days of the organization. I also owe a debt of gratitude to the current Editor of the Nebraska Cattleman, Mike Fitzgerald who was a friend and supporter through some trying times. He made a special effort to help me find records I wanted covering my seventeen years in Nebraska. Also a special thanks to Paul Johnson a competitor, co-worker and good friend as we worked to help unite the Nebraska cattle industry.

Finally I want to salute the twenty five presidents and other volunteers I worked with during my forty five years of cattle association employment who gave their time and treasure to serve their industry.

***

    This book might never have been published if I hadn't stumbled on to Lynette McClain through a neighbor who knew someone who knew her. She did the work necessary to prepare this book for reproduction in the digital age. The technology is amazing, but daunting for some one whose relationship with computers is somewhat strained.

    My daughter Jennifer Applequist who teaches school in Farson, Wyoming did the final proof reading on the last draft of the book as soon as school left out and ferreted out a good many errors we had missed earlier. My thanks to her for dropping everything and taking this on.

View of home place on Table Mountain Ranch from Wyoming.

Foreword

My mother and father, dad and mom, were and continue to be a most important influence on me long after their passing. They were always in full agreement on matters concerning their children. The three Lilley boys differed a great deal in personality and disposition and our parents gave each of us the discipline we needed and deserved and unconditionally loved all of us for the children we were and the adults we grew into. Each member of my immediate family always had the luxury of taking for granted the love and support of every other.

My mother often said that I was a compulsive talker. She was right of course and it has only gotten worse as I have aged. One of my good rodeo buddies once said, " Lilley, you talk a lot but at least you always have something to say". My nephew Clay Lilley may have put it best when he remarked after I finished answering a question: "Boy, Uncle Roy you sure told me a lot more about that than I really wanted to know". I have always been endlessly curious and even though I pestered them constantly with questions my parents always patiently answered them.

I wrote regular columns for the magazines published by organizations I worked for during my career and occasionally wrote articles for other publications. I tended to put off finishing writing assignments till the last minute, but when I decided to write a book three years ago at the age of eighty five I realized that the deadline I faced would be enforced by the Grim Reaper and got to work.

I have had three wives and I loved each of them. All made significant contributions to my life. Without Ingrid I wouldn't have my precious Liz, who in addition to being her mother's pride and joy was also much loved by Maxine and is in turn by Donice. Maxine came into my life at a time I felt I was losing my way. When I married her and adopted her seven-year-old daughter and three-year-old son I found the stability of a loving family that I badly needed.

When I retired on January 1, 1996 I had been a widower for five years and had no thought of getting married again; then I had the good fortune to re- discover and good sense to marry Donice with whom I used to enjoy dancing at country dances when we were in our teens. She encouraged me to tackle this memoir, but suggested I end it with my retirement. We have had twenty-one happy years sailing through the Golden Years together and are warily approaching old age.

"Just As I Am" is a hymn written in 1835 and was famous for being played while people came forward at the conclusion of Billy Graham's crusades. It has always appealed to me. I surely first heard it as a child when we sang it at the little white church in Virginia Dale, Colorado.

****

Since I never kept a diary I likely remembered things differently than some readers might and would be happy to hear from anyone that wishes to share their version of events. Contact me at tripa123@gmail.com or on the Facebook page my daughter Jennifer Applequist is setting up and managing for me.

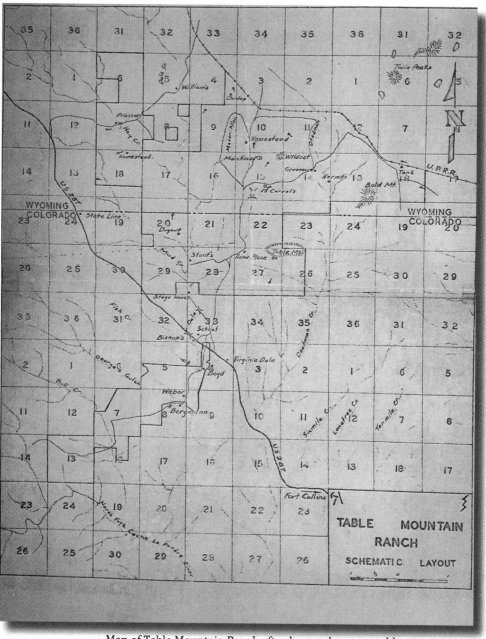

Map of Table Mountain Ranch after lower place was sold and Weber Ranch Purchased

Julia Frances Williams Lilley at age 20.

Introduction

This is the story of an uncommon man whose character was formed in challenging times and exercised firmly through the twisting trails of his life. For those readers who know Roy Lilley, it will be an opportunity to revisit their intersections with him and this era of history. But, this is not just a story of interest to Roy's pals. It is an important story of big changes in the livestock industry; it is an important story of providing leadership for colleagues swimming through difficult straits; it is an important story of understanding one's self in order to make life-forming decisions at critical junctures. Indeed, it is a "unique memoir."

Roy W. Lilley was raised and loved by a strong family, buffeted by difficult circumstances, and compelled to make choices at vital moments based in personal values, not societal expectations. Roy's life, from childhood through his career of service to the beef cattle industry, included full immersion in very disparate environments. They say that scents and odors spur some of our most powerful memories. When I read his fascinating story, I find myself catching the smell of short grass pastures, hay fields in harvest, and a damp creek bank where little boys lie on their bellies looking for critters; I sniff sweaty saddle blankets and oiled leather, bucking chutes and county fair food, board rooms and convention halls, gun powder and wet wool, printers ink and mail rooms, hospital wards and bunkhouses, country cafés and cowboy beer joints, pickup trucks and jet planes. These images do not reflect a life of ease and privilege. They arise from hard, sometimes dirty work, pursuit of adventure, risking love, indulging strong intellectual curiosity and a youthful sense of wonder, and responding consistently to a commitment to duty.

"Let me offer you this piece of advice: Never be surprised when people remain in character." Roy and I were driving late at night from a Nebraska Stock Growers Association meeting when he offered me this nugget. It was shortly after I announced I was leaving the ranch to work for Gov. Bob Kerrey during the tumultuous Ag Crisis of the 1980's. Roy had already become a trusted friend and mentor, so we were talking about this major transition on which I was about to embark with no insignificant chance of failure. As is referenced often in his memoir, Roy is "verbal." But, I always found him worth my listening, and this, as expected, was no cotton candy platitude. It was a rich and profound handful of guidance to which I still return thirty five years later. And that is Roy. His concern for his friends is never superficial and he is willing to invest his treasure of life's lessons in them.

This is a story filled with influential relationships. Though Roy and I are nearly a generation apart in age, we have intersected with an interesting cohort of common characters. Hugh Bennett and Cotton Rosser in the rodeo realm, Jack Maddux and Pat McGinley among many others from the NSGA, NLFA, NCBA adventure, Lloyd Brinkman, Wayne Pruett, Glen LeDioyt, Bill McMillan – all left marks on my life, as well. So, I know firsthand the nature of prominent figures in this account. Roy is not casual about relationships with family, friends, colleagues, people in authority or people in need. You will see that reflected throughout this story. He measures character, values trust, offers his best and risks disappointment. He gives others a chance, and often a second. But, he is not a fool and is willing to make choices when his trust is violated. He is likewise loathe to stand by when he see others abused.

There are many audiences to whom I would commend this book. Young adults launching their careers will find lessons in choices, determination and sensitivity to not only your own character, but that of your closest associates in business and life. Those who have spent their lives and careers in and around the livestock industry will find familiar passages of history and insights to some of its big issues. Those who have been in challenging leadership roles will read an intimate account of one who had to reach deep into his own soul to determine direction for not only himself, but his trusted subordinates. For the casual reader who doesn't fit any of the above, you will find an intriguing, entertaining, emotional real-life account of a man who experienced wars, droughts, bucking horses and head slinging bulls, colorful women and beloved children, courageous decisions and broken trust, scrapping for survival and enjoying the rewards of thoughtful perseverance. Roy Lilley is an uncommon man.

Chuck Schroeder

1
Mom and Dad

I had the good fortune to live the first ten years of my life on the Table Mountain Ranch in Virginia Dale, Colorado. I was born May 14, 1930 at the Poudre Valley Hospital in Fort Collins, as were my two older brothers. Charles W. Lilley, Jr. was born July 1, 1925, shortly after the hospital was built, and Frank was born December 20, 1926.

In 1930, Virginia Dale consisted of a community of cattle ranches covering roughly 400 square miles, with a post office, a filling station (with hand operated pumps) and a store. In the store was an old-fashioned switchboard, which the postmistress tended. It served a dozen or so battery-powered phones scattered across the community. A single strand of steel wire, sometimes strung on fence posts, connected all these phones, making for one large party line. A series of long or short rings was assigned to each customer. Our number was three long rings. If you called a neighbor you simply turned the hand crank the correct number of longs and shorts. To reach the operator at the post office for long distance calls, you cranked one good long ring and she connected you to Livermore, a community about fifteen miles to the north, which had a full-time operator, who then connected you to Fort Collins, which in turn connected to the national phone network, AT&T. The Virginia Dale post office and store are long since closed and the local telephone system built before World War I lasted until shortly after World War II.

We got our mail, including the Fort Collins daily 'Express Courier,' three times a week at the post office. On Sundays, often on the way home from Sunday school, we picked up the Sunday 'Denver Post.' When I was old enough to read the funnies, I couldn't figure out why we got the Post all the way from Denver before we got the Fort Collins paper. The postmistress and switchboard operator was a formidable woman named Mable Bashor. She and her husband, Burt, also owned and operated the store and let you pump your own gas by hand five gallons at a time (about twenty-five cents a gallon). They carried a limited stock of groceries, ammunition for the most commonly used ranch guns, kerosene for the lamps that lit nearly every area home and a few other staples. For a penny, you could buy a Hershey bar that was nearly as large as one that costs over a dollar at a modern convenience store—but even pennies were hard to come by then!

It is generally accepted that this beautiful foothill community was named Virginia Dale after the wife of Jack Slade, the notorious but efficient employee of the Wells Fargo Company, which operated the Overland Stage line through this community for a period of time around the Civil War.

My mother, Julia Frances (Williams) Lilley, was born in Cheyenne, Wyoming on May 7, 1902, and my father, Charles Weston Lilley, was born on April 30, 1902 in Littleton, Colorado. Dad was the youngest son of Harry and Katherine (Bergen) Lilley, who had purchased the Table Mountain Ranch in 1917. Mom, the second of three daughters born to Frank Perry Williams and Edith Mae (Jenks) Williams, was born in Cheyenne and raised on the Windy Hollow ranch about twenty miles northeast of the Table Mountain ranch.

My grandfather, Harry Lilley, owned a ranch in Brush, Colorado, which he sold when he and Grandma Lilley purchased the Virginia Dale property in 1917. He continued to use the reversed LIL brand, which he had registered in 1913 and is now in my name. A neighboring rancher, Axel, the brother of Olie Moen, whose family homesteaded in the area in the 1880's, mentioned in his diary that he was visiting the Table Mountain Ranch in 1917 and met H. H. Lilley and his son Charles who were also at the ranch that day looking to possibly purchase it.

My dad, who was very close to his father, had often traveled to the Brush ranch with him before it was sold and the Table Mountain Ranch was purchased, so he soaked up a lot of valuable information about ranch management at a very young age.

Dad spent his summers on the ranch with his parents during high school and his one year of college, and on Saturday nights he attended dances in the neighborhood—any place within driving distance in the Model T Ford he borrowed from his parents. One of these was in a barn close to Granite Canyon, Wyoming, which was on the Lincoln Highway. Charles, or Charlie, as most people called him, took note of a pretty girl (my mother) and asked her to dance.

She sized him up too, thinking this good looking, cocky young man, who already had a dark beard and smoked, was too old for her and not her type; anyway, she wasn't that interested in boys. Dad, who was interested in girls, learned she lived at the Windy Hollow Ranch not far away. Although she looked a bit young, he decided to keep his eye on her. Actually they were both 15.

For the next few years mom and dad may have seen each other occasionally, but their lives took separate turns. Dad went to high school in Fort Collins, attending the School of Agriculture, which was referred to as "Horn School" by the students. This was a prep school at what is now Colorado State University attended by many farm and ranch boys whose parents appreciated that classes started later in the fall and let out earlier in the spring than public high schools, thereby allowing them to be home for important seasonal work. The classes were taught by college professors and prepared those who were able, to go on to an agricultural college.

Meanwhile, mom enjoyed living at the Windy Hollow Ranch, helping her father with the cattle. She rode many miles with him and became an excellent horsewoman. She would probably have liked to work in the hayfield too, but in those days women didn't work with the

Mom at Maryland College - about 1919

hired help. Her father always planted a big garden and fortunately her older sister, Florence, liked tending it and shared this interest with her dad. Mom, whose own mother died when she was only four years old, must have inherited her love of horses and riding from her mother, but she hated gardening. Florence and Julia were quite different in other ways too. Mom was the apple of her father's eye and had a sunny disposition. Aunt Florence was a strong-willed child and her father had a hard time dealing with her. In fact, life-changing events involving her sister occurred during Mom's teen years that caused her father to send her out of state for several years to attend school.

The details of my mother's school years were never fully explained to us kids, but she probably went to some of her grade school in Cheyenne and some in a country school at Granite Canyon nearby. We do know that she attended eighth grade in Council Bluffs, Iowa while living with Frank Perry's sister Louise and her husband, Dr. Mathew Tinley. Mom loved Aunt Lu and Uncle Matt and surely enjoyed sharing normal family life with them and her cousin Winifred.

Mom later spent at least part of her high school years at Maryland College for Women at Lutherville, Maryland. The school was founded in 1853 and closed in 1951. Another of Grandpa Williams's sisters, Isabel Hammond-Knowlton, lived in nearby Storrs, Connecticut and had made arrangements for mom to attend this exclusive school. Aunt Isabel was married to C.A. Hammond-Knowlton who, among other things, owned a silk mill in Connecticut. I will add more on the Hammond-Knowlton's in another chapter.

Mom now had to suffer even longer train rides back east than when she visited Aunt Lu in Council Bluffs, and though still homesick, she adapted well to the new environment and made lots of friends. Many of these were wealthy girls from the south who were probably amazed to find a fellow student from the Wild, Wild West in their midst. She equally lacked any understanding of their lives and culture. Mom loved to tell the story about innocently asking one girl from North Carolina why she talked like the Negroes. The young lady looked at her in disbelief and somewhat haughtily said, "Julia, we don't talk like the Nigras, the Nigras talk like us."

One of the highlights of Mom's time at school back East was attending a dance at the Naval Academy in Annapolis, Maryland with her handsome first cousin, Storrs Hammond-Knowlton, who was in his Junior year there. Storrs was following a long tradition of naval service by the Perrys. He was a direct descendant on his mother's side to Commodore Mathew C. Perry, who led the expedition into Yokohama harbor in 1853, opening that country to commerce with the United States.

Evidently Mom and Dad didn't start college the first year they were out of high school. I believe mom taught for a year at a little grade school near a small town called Hecla on the Union Pacific line between Laramie and Cheyenne. In the days of the steam engines there were many such small towns spaced to furnish water and coal to the steam engines. Dad must have worked on the Table Mountain Ranch that year with his father and courted Mom when he could. It was probably no accident that they both showed up for college in Fort Collins the next year

Dad joined the Sigma Phi Epsilon fraternity, the Sig Eps, and Mom joined the Delta Delta Delta sorority, the Tri Delts. Dad loved sports and while not very big, he was fast and athletic, so he went out for the football team. Longtime coach Harry Hughes liked both his linemen and backfield big, subscribing quite successfully to the three-yards-and-a-cloud-of-dust philosophy. Dad didn't see much time on the playing field!

Boxing was another matter. In those days, the Aggies belonged

Charlie Jr. on sled by front porch

to a conference that had boxing as one of the recognized sports. I believe the other teams in what then was called the Rocky Mountain Conference included Colorado University, Denver University, Colorado College, Colorado School of Mines, Wyoming University and three Utah schools, Utah University, BYU and Utah State. Dad's weight bracket was just under 130 pounds. Even though he could beat everyone on the team below 145 pounds, they needed someone in the lower bracket, and he had a competitive advantage at that weight. Dad said training with bigger guys helped him learn to take a punch. He was tall for his weight, had an upright stance and a hard, fast left jab. I know all this because when my brothers were in high school, dad bought us a set of fourteen-ounce boxing gloves. He taught us all to box and shared his experiences on the college boxing team, including the fact he won the Rocky Mountain championship as a Freshman, his only year in college. Being the youngest in the family, I also learned to take a punch, but didn't like it much.

Harry Lilley on Rex

The Lilley boys - Roy, Frank, and Charlie - 1932

2

Kate and Harry

After their first year in college, Mom and Dad were in love and wanted to get married. Two people weren't crazy about this idea: Mom's Dad and Dad's Mom. Kate Lilley didn't particularly like Perry Williams, and Perry didn't think Dad was good enough for Mom. He had hoped she would marry a prominent rancher. They were told in no uncertain terms that if they wanted to get married, they would have to quit school and go to work at one or the other family's ranch. Mom and Dad called their bluffs and were married on May 29, 1923, shortly after their twenty-first birthdays. The wedding was at the home of Luke and Florence Voorhees in Cheyenne, the same beautiful Victorian home in which Perry Williams had married Edith Jenks.

No one ever explained to me why the decision was made for Dad to work for his father-in-law, but Dad and Perry Williams didn't hit it off. Dad was used to working with his father, and Perry wasn't Harry Lilley. An anecdote helps explain the problem. Dad says they were putting up hay at the Windy Hollow Ranch the summer of 1923 and dad was sweeping hay. He needed to cross the small creek in the meadow to get the next sweep load and asked Perry where to cross. "What the hell do I care where you cross?" shouted Perry, and Dad said he headed the team straight at the closest point to the creek, hoping to break the sweep to pieces. As luck would have it, he hit a place without very deep banks and they continued haying.

Before the year was up, Mom and Dad realized something had to be done, so they moved to the Table Mountain Ranch where Dad could work with his father as he had in the summers during his high school and college years.

Unfortunately, Mom then had to live with Grandma Lilley, who made her feel insecure and whose Irish sense of humor she could not understand. Having been raised without a mother, Mom had learned very few domestic skills and she felt completely inadequate as a homemaker. Still, she made the best of things and learned to be a very good cook from Grandma. Her sewing skills remained pretty much limited to darning socks and patching britches. Grandma crocheted beautifully, an art Mom couldn't master or probably didn't much wish to. Dad was always able to joke about his time working for Perry Williams, and Mom always gave Grandma Lilley full credit for acquiring such domestic skills as she felt she had.

It soon became apparent that Mom was not doing well in this new situation and Mom and Dad were encouraged, and probably financed by one of Dad's siblings, to take a belated honeymoon trip. They traveled east by train to visit Mother's Aunt Lu in Council Bluffs, and from there to Dad's eldest sister, Essie, in Lebanon, Indiana. When they came back to the ranch after several weeks, one of the neighbors commented how radiant mom looked since her return, and they soon learned she was pregnant with her first child. Soon after, Harry and Kate bought a small house in Fort Collins and Harry spent weekends in town and commuted to the ranch weekdays.

Grandma Lilley had an active social life in Fort Collins, playing the piano at club meetings and social gatherings, often accompanying the owner of Murphy's Clothing Store when he did his energetic rendition of 'On the Road to Mandalay.' She could play anything from classical to popular hits of the day. Prior to moving to the ranch from Littleton, she had played for dances there. She was a great storyteller and liked the idea of owning a ranch, but enjoyed living in town.

Harry cared deeply about the ranch, his son and his daughter-in-law, and looked forward to becoming a grandfather. He was a hard worker, perfectly able to do the physical labor required on a ranch in those days, but was probably aware that his heart was not the best and was anxious to turn the management of the operation over to his son. He was a great comfort to Julia, reassuring her in her doubts about handling coming motherhood.

Charles Weston Lilley, Jr. was born July 1, 1925 in the new Poudre Valley hospital in Fort Collins and was delivered by Dr. Carey, the family Doctor in Fort Collins. It turned out that mom couldn't nurse the baby, but fortunately 'Little Charlie' was a healthy baby and soon adapted to the milk from the family cow when he got home.

Just seventeen months later on December 20, 1926, Frank Perry Lilley came along. Mom brought him home concerned that she wouldn't be able to nurse him. It turned out she couldn't and cow's milk didn't agree with him. He was a very sickly baby and soon developed the early stages of Rickets (a vitamin D deficiency). After months of Dad and Mom walking the floor with him at night and much worry, he got stronger when he was able to eat the home-prepared equivalent of today's canned baby food.

Harry Lilley had pretty much turned the ranch over to Dad by this time, and while he still spent a good deal of time there, he and Grandma were more often at their home in Fort Collins. They also often visited Harry's best friend, Dr. Frank Rogers, at his beautiful home on Spear Boulevard in Denver. One such visit was during the Denver National Western Stock Show in January, 1928. Dr. Rogers had diagnosed Harry's heart problem as arteriosclerosis and Dr. Rogers often took walks along Cherry Creek with Harry after long days at the Hospital and making house calls, good therapy for Harry and a good chance for these longtime friends to visit.

Late on the night of January 17, 1929, Dr. Rogers, a bachelor, who lived with his mother, was asleep in his downstairs bedroom when Harry evidently got up in the night from his second floor bedroom to go to the bathroom down the hall. Dr. Rogers woke when he heard a thump on the floor above, and fearing he knew what it was, rushed upstairs to find Harry on the floor with a severe heart attack. In the hospital only minutes later, Dr. Rogers had Harry on the operating table where he opened his chest and massaged his heart to no avail. He was pronounced dead early the morning of January 18th.

Dad took his father's sudden death particularly hard and he and Mom often commented how much they wished Harry could have lived long enough for me to know him. Mom often said that I inherited his good disposition, and I know I would have benefited from knowing him if he had lived longer.

Charlie, Sr. was from two generations of big families and would happily have had six or eight kids, but mom was of a different mind. Still, three-and-a-half years after Frank's birth, on May 14, 1930, I was the third Lilley boy born in the Poudre Valley Hospital. Knowing that Dad was hoping for a girl, when Dr. Carey first showed me to him he asked, "What are you going to call him Charlie, Suzie?" Fortunately, I was named after Dad's eldest brother, Roy, with my middle name William, after Uncle Bill, who was just a year older than dad.

    I appeared to be fat and happy, but mom said she wasn't taking me back to the ranch until she found a formula that agreed with me. Fortunately, a new canned product called SMA had just been introduced and I really took to it. Both Mom and Dad often said how sorry they were that SMA wasn't around when Frank was a baby.

This is a picture taken when Dad ran for the
Colorado House of Representatives when he was 32 years old

3

Early Memories

My earliest memories are of the ranch house I lived in the first ten years of my life. It had amenities that were not common for rural homes at that time. It had running water, thanks to the pressure system powered by a one-cylinder gasoline engine pumping out of the cold spring the house had been built over. It had light, from carbide gas generated by a system that metered pellets of carbide into water, which made acetylene gas, which was piped into each room of the house to fixtures with sparkers similar to modern cigarette lighters. And it was hooked up to a community-owned, dry-cell-operated telephone system, which created one big party line for users.

I don't know if all the aforementioned amenities came with the house when Grandpa and Grandma Lilley purchased the ranch or if some were added later. All were appreciated, but it also took a good deal of work to keep them operating correctly. The by-product of creating the acetylene gas was whitewash, which had to be pumped out monthly, a big, messy job. We supplemented the room lights with kerosene reading lamps, some hanging from the wall with a concave mirror behind them. The lamps were prone to smoke if the wicks weren't constantly trimmed.

The best part of the water system was the spring itself. It had been contained in a 3' by 3' square concrete tank about two feet deep. The water bubbled clear and cold out of gravel at the bottom. Dad often floated watermelons in it and they were almost ice-cold by the time we ate them. Neighbors knew they were welcome to help themselves to a drink from the cup that hung by the spring as they drove through the ranch on the road that passed the always-unlocked cellar door on the lower side of the house.

The spring overflowed down a gutter in the concrete floor into a 3' by 3' enclosure with an overflow to the outside designed to keep a level two inches of the cold water flowing through. Into this were placed covered crocks containing our milk, buttermilk, cream and items like leftovers that needed refrigeration.

On one side of a pressure system was the cranky, crank-started gasoline engine. It had one large bore cylinder enclosed by a cast iron water jacket to cool it, and a heavy cast iron flywheel (a necessity on a one-cylinder engine). It had a magneto similar to a model T Ford to provide a spark, since it had no battery and starter. It often backfired when cranked and when it did, it kicked like a mule. One Thanksgiving morning as Dad was cranking it, it kicked and the handle flew off, breaking his front tooth. Needless to say, Dad didn't enjoy his holiday meal much, but he doubled up on the holiday spirits. A more typical injury inflicted by this miserable contraption was a broken or sprained thumb.

I will try to describe the house itself as I fondly remember it. Unfortunately, this historic building was torn down by a subsequent ranch owner. I can't verify the overall dimensions, but it was quite large for a hand-hewn log house of its day. It had a kitchen, living room and three bedrooms, and was heated by three stoves: a kitchen range, a circulating heater and a potbellied stove. The kitchen range had a grate that could be adjusted to burn either wood or coal, a water jacket that circulated the spring water to an un-insulated 20-gallon hot water tank and a set of dampers that could be adjusted to circulate hot smoke around the oven when in use.

In the living room was a fairly new, recently designed, circulating heater, which encouraged air circulation by convection through the space between the fire chamber and a ceramic-coated steel shell. It also had an adjustable coal/wood grate. In the folks' bedroom, the stove was a traditional wood burning potbellied type. We mostly used wood for all the stoves, but kept a small supply of lump coal for exceptionally cold spells when we needed to hold a fire through the night.

Northwest of the kitchen was what we called the light pantry, which had a window above a counter, under which were two tin-lined, tip-out bins, one to hold flour and another, sugar. On the southwest was the dark pantry, whose floor was raised to access the cellar stairs. Adjoining the kitchen to the south was a living room with the circulating heater in the center. The bathroom with tub, sink and toilet, and a small bedroom were entered from the west side of the living room.

The bedroom we three boys slept in was south of the living room, had a double and a single bed and, like most bedrooms of that day, no closet. Out of our bedroom a set of narrow stairs led up to the attic. Mom and Dad's bedroom was south of our bedroom and could be accessed either through this bedroom or through what was a wide hall running the length of both bedrooms and connected to the living room. We called this long narrow room the sitting room. It had a couch and a couple of chairs against the north wall, and a wind-up Victrola (a 78 RPM record player) just inside the living room door. In the attic was an old Victrola, which had a horn for a speaker and played tube-shaped wax records. Later, the older phonograph and a lot of the records, along with other now valuable antiques I would love to have, ended up in the ranch dump in a deep draw not far from the house.

Charlie on Tony

The ceilings throughout the house were just over seven feet high and made, as were the interior walls, of a cardboard-like material popular in those days. All were painted with a water-soluble whitewash-like product called calcimine, which dried to a not very attractive peach color. The kitchen and living room floors were covered with linoleum. A lean-to like porch covered with tar paper had been built off the kitchen to the east, and an attractive front porch built with bark-covered pine pole supports graced the exit to the house from the sitting room, on the south side of the house.

I remember jumping out of bed on cold winter mornings with my clothes in hand and dressing in front of the circulating heater

Mom wrote the following on the back of this photo: *"Mrs. F. Perry Williams riding with Ashley Gleason, Cheyenne Frontier Parade, Aug. 1902. The photo appeared in the Denver Post. Mrs. Williams is the mother of Mrs. Chas. W. Lilley. (Edith) is riding a bay saddle horse named Bunch that was her pride and joy and a top saddle horse of top riding qualities."* Mom was born May 7, 1902!

in the living room. Frank would head for the barn, break the ice on the water tank and milk the family cow, while Charlie did the other morning chores. In the summer during haying, Charlie would ride our registered Arab remount stud, Ibn Zaid, to bring in the work horses (more on Ibn later) and as I got older I would help Frank with the morning chores, looking forward to returning to the kitchen to find my mom pouring my Dad's second cup of coffee hot off the kitchen stove and feeding us all a hearty breakfast. Any memory I have of my early life on the ranch begins with thoughts of the security I enjoyed in that now torn down house.

Among my earliest memories of life on the ranch are of two events that occurred when I was four. The first was of playing in the mud at the side of the road running by the house and being warmly scolded by my mother. She said she had told me several times not to play, roll actually, in the mud, and would have to report this repeated misbehavior to my dad when he came in from work that night. I remember dreading his return, and sure enough, he said he was going to have to spank me for not minding my mother. I had never been spanked before, although my brother Frank, who had a terrible temper, was paddled fairly frequently. Dad told me to take down my pants to prepare myself for the punishment. I remember feeling confident I could talk my way out of the surely well-deserved spanking and was promising faithfully to never repeat the offense as I unfastened and lowered my bib overalls and pulled down my underwear. I realized the worst was going to happen when dad placed me over his knee and lightly slapped me on my naked bottom. I reached back and hit at his arm. This resulted in a real spanking, my first and only one.

My second clear early memory was my first solo horseback ride. I had often ridden with Dad on the front of his saddle, but four was the age that boys learned to ride and this was my time. I wanted to learn to ride, but having a vivid imagination, worried about every possible thing that might happen. Dad put a little hand-me-down child's saddle on Old Charlie, a foolproof kid's horse, who was about eighteen years old. What if he lay down in the creek or tried to run away with me? I had seen horses roll in the shallow water and I had seen my brothers have runaways with their high-spirited ponies. Dad assured me that he was sure Old Charlie wouldn't lie down in the creek when we crossed it and that he surely wasn't interested in running at all. Our one-hour ride went fine and my only problem was kicking my faithful old black horse hard enough to keep up.

The Lilley family took their horses seriously. Mom had ridden many miles with her father when she was growing up on their 18,000-acre ranch and had brought a dowry of three good brood mares over to the Table Mountain Ranch from the Windy Hollow Ranch when she got married. Dad had helped his father work at the family's livery stable in Littleton, Colorado when he was a boy learning the fine art of proper grooming and training horses both to ride and drive. So it was only natural mom and dad gave considerable thought to the kind of horses their kids should ride. A pony was better matched to a four-year-old boy's size, but Shetlands, the most common breed of pony, although among the smallest breeds, were not the handiest for ranch work and had a reputation for cranky dispositions. Many ranchers felt full-sized horses were best for young riders in spite of problems mounting and dismounting. Still, an eight-year-old can learn to shinny up into the saddle on a fifteen or sixteen-hand horse by grabbing saddle strings or a strap hung on the saddle.

Mom and Dad liked the idea of matching the size of the horse to the size of the kid and went looking for Charlie Junior's first mount when he was four years old. They settled on a very small black-and-white three-quarter Shetland, one quarter Arab yearling that they figured would still grow a little bit. Mom loved Arabs and such a cross was quite unusual. They named the colt Tony and turned him out with the rest of the horses for the winter, figuring to castrate him the following spring. Much to their surprise, Tony, obviously a little older than they had thought, somehow managed to get three good ranch mares bred, resulting in what ranchers call 'catch colts.' This turned out to be the most fortunate of accidents.

Tony never grew anymore, so Charlie Junior learned to ride on him while also breaking him, since he was much too small for an adult to ride. By the time Frank was ready to start riding, Charlie moved up to Sally, one of the accidents, and Frank inherited Tony. Tony was high-spirited, and like most kid-broke ponies was hard-mouthed and would run away if he got up a good head of steam. When I was about six years old, I got Tony, and Frank moved up to Oakey, another of Tony's fortunate accidents. As I recall, we sold Sally when Charlie Junior graduated to a full-sized horse.

Tony had three gaits: a slow walk, a hard, fast trot and a runaway gallop. The first gait caused me to fall behind the other riders and be yelled at and the second caused a side ache. The third never ceased to scare the heck out of me and could be stopped only by running him up a hill, if one was handy, and reining him into a tight circle. When we gathered cattle, I very much wanted to be of help, but usually was left holding already-gathered cattle in a fence corner while the other riders were out rounding up more.

I can remember only bits and pieces of a period of time that temporarily affected the daily lives of the Lilley family from 1934-36. Dad was elected to the Colorado State Legislature in 1934. He evidently moved the family to Denver for at least part of his first term and I have vague memories of a house in South Denver. My brothers later told me a few stories about attending school there for a while at least. The legislature was in session for only a part of the year and evidently Dad talked Mom into joining him there the first year of the two-year term. I imagine that he lived with his brother-in-law and sister, Lawrence and Harriett Trueheart, for the second year. Mom joined dad in Denver on special occasions and I do remember that her part-time hired girl, Gyneth, stayed with us when she was gone. I clearly recall talking to Dad many times about his short political career. Those talks very much informed my lifelong view of politics as an essential, but potentially corrupting element of our democratic society.

Virginia Dale School house. Picture taken in 2017.
Notice the WPA out house built in the 1930s in left rear back ground.

Mom and Dad and their three boys in about 1937,
Charlie, Frank and Roy

4

Ranch Life

I started my education in the first grade at the Virginia Dale School. To get there I rode Tony, accompanied by Frank on Oakey and Charlie on Sally. Saddling the horses was quite a chore and our lunches, tied on the back of the saddles, often got squashed, so in the summer between my first and second grade, Dad arranged some new transportation for us. He bought an open, one-horse buggy at a farm sale for ten dollars. When he got home, we hitched it to our gentlest work-horse, Old Lu, and we three boys climbed in and drove it around the yard at a good clip, occasionally getting Lu to break into a trot. The buggy had only one seat and I could barely squeeze into it between my two brothers, so they made me sit on the floorboard between their knees. Just as Dad had hoped, this turned out to be perfect transportation to school. On the coldest days, we put a big horsehide lined with a blanket over our knees and I enjoyed sitting under it on the floorboard. When we got to school, Charlie drove Lu into the horse shed and tied him next to the other horses and ponies there

We had lots of fun at school. At lunch hour and during recess we little boys and the girls played ante-over with a tennis ball around the one room school, and the big boys ranged farther into the nearby hills than the teacher liked. Sometimes they couldn't—or claimed they couldn't—hear her ringing the school bell to announce the start of class.

On one occasion, on the two-and-a-half-mile trip home from school, Charlie took us jolting off cross-country in the buggy in pursuit of some deer that crossed the road in front of us. Fortunately, he gave up the chase before we broke a wheel.

When I started third grade in 1939, I didn't know it would be my last year in country school. Charlie was in the eighth grade and Frank, having entered the first grade when only five, was in the seventh. We continued to use the buggy pulled by old Lu for transportation to school except for the few days our folks took us in the car as they headed to Fort Collins, forty miles south, where they did their shopping. On these days we walked the two and one half miles home. In winter, it would be nearly dark when we got there, and if Mom and Dad weren't home yet, in addition to our normal chores we were expected to start a fire in the kitchen stove, peel some potatoes and start them boiling. At 7,000 feet altitude, it took about forty-five minutes for them to cook.

Our regular chores when we arrived home from school were filling the wood box, and splitting more wood, if necessary, at the huge woodpile about one-hundred-fifty feet from the house. We also had to bring in the milk cow, which was turned out in an eighty-acre meadow near the barn, and milk her before dark, which was when the folks usually got home from town.

On one of these occasions the folks, knowing they were going to be later than usual, called from Fort Collins to tell us they had attended a matinee at the movie theatre and had won the $100.00 weekly drawing, a great attraction during the depression. We assured them we had done all the chores and would have the table set and the potatoes cooked so mom could quickly fix supper when they got home. Unfortunately, we never got to see the $100.00 check because they stopped at Ted's Place, a general store and filling station where they had a charge account, and paid their $105.00 bill.

Summer or winter, Frank and Charlie always found fun things to do, and I usually tagged along trying to join in. They were more patient with me than I probably deserved, though occasionally they yelled at me for being in the way. They often let me get in over my head by allowing me to learn for myself what I could and couldn't do. In winter, we sledded down rough hillsides, belly flopping three deep on our steel-runner sled. In summer, we rode down the same hills in my little red wagon, a cherished gift on my seventh birthday, taking glorious spills in both seasons.

In late June, we usually rode from the ranch to the Virginia Dale rodeo held seven or eight miles due west at the Two Bars Seven Ranch. It was owned by Ted Shaffer, the Larimer County Sheriff at the time. We left in the early morning, stayed all day and got home about dark. Mom and Dad drove over with a picnic lunch later in the day. Our route took us down Mud Creek through the 'eighty meadow' to the Fowlston place on Dale Creek, which was one of the homesteads making up the ranch. We crossed Dale Creek there and headed up another intermittent stream, which I remember as also being called Mud Creek. After going through several wire gates and crossing a neighbor's property, we came to what we called the Craig Cabin on a small acreage just below the State Line filling station.

At the station we crossed Highway 287, the federal highway between Laramie and Fort Collins. We then rode a short way north in the barrow pit and headed west for about five miles, cutting north of the Hosack Ranch house to the Two Bars Seven headquarters located on a native meadow irrigated by Fish Creek. There was a large home, a set of corrals and a big log barn. West of the house was a shop containing a forge for working iron—a pretty typical

Frank on Oakey

set of buildings for a ranch. The rodeo arena was located in a natural amphitheater set in rolling hills and ponderosa pines three miles southwest of the ranch. There were no bleachers and people watched the Rodeo sitting on the hillside north of the arena. The bucking chutes were on the south side and the roping and bulldogging chutes were on either end. The ropers chased their calves down the slope of the arena's length and the doggers pursued their steers uphill. The bucking chutes opened toward the spectators so that the horses bucked uphill for what seemed a short distance where they were confronted by a fence. They then turned and bucked back down the hill toward the chutes. A horse bucking uphill loses power, but when he turns, the situation reverses drastically and it's a long way to the ground if you're bucked off.

Many bulldoggers and calf ropers brought their horses in newfangled horse trailers, but some carried them in their pickup trucks outfitted with stock racks. All they had to do was back up to a gently sloping hill and jump their horse out. Some folks hauled their horses to the rodeo just to ride around during the activities. One well known Fort Collins resident always did so and by the rodeo's end was usually so drunk that he could barely stay on his horse. He would occasionally wander out into the arena and disrupt an event, getting more laughs than the rodeo clown.

We usually departed the rodeo when it was over in late afternoon and got home about dark in time for a late supper, happy and completely worn out.

5

Fort Collins

In the fall of 1940 we moved into Grandma Lilley's house at 418 Magnolia Street in Fort Collins, the home she and Grandpa had bought when they moved to town after turning the management of their Table Mountain Ranch over to Dad in the mid 1920s. Grandma had continued to live there after Grandpa Harry died in 1928. We often stayed overnight there. Grandma had recently suffered a fairly severe stroke and had to go to Denver to what was called a sanitarium in those days, for extended rehabilitation.

Aunt Essie evidently felt her son, Tommy, was ready to take over the management of the ranch. Essie, Dad's eldest sister, and her husband, Tom Shepperd, along with dad's eldest brother, Roy, had purchased it from my Grandpa and Grandma in the mid 1920s. Uncle Roy decided to sell his half of the ranch when Dad left, and Aunt Essie purchased all of it except what we called the southernmost part, which we referred to as the lower place and everyone else called the Chrisman place. Uncle Roy had dad sell the lower ranch for him. Several neighbors were quite interested in it and Dad soon sold it to Bill Logan, whose ranch bordered TMR on the south. I am now married to his daughter.

Dad soon had a job managing Producers Livestock Marketing Association, a cooperative marketing commission firm at the Denver stockyards, and commuted from Fort Collins to Denver.

My brother Charlie had finished the eighth grade in the country school and would have had to go to town for ninth grade anyway. Frank would be in the eighth grade and I in the fourth. We had watched Lincoln Junior High, (seventh, eighth and ninth grades) being built by the WPA across the street from Grandma's house in the late 1930s, and Charlie and Frank just walked across the street to their new school. I walked three blocks northeast on Canyon and two more north on Meldrum to Franklin grade school, long since torn down.

Adjusting to a new school was harder for me than my brothers. They had each other, and two of the three Moen boys from their class in Virginia Dale were classmates in Junior high, while the third was in high school. I didn't know a soul in my fourth-grade class of twenty to twenty-five. I'm sure my new teacher, a beautiful young woman whose name I forget, knew I was from country school and did all she could to make me feel comfortable. I had never before been set down in the middle of strangers and felt like a duck out of water.

Kids that age are not naturally inclined to worry about explaining things to a newcomer, so when we went out to play during our first recess, no one told me anything about the rules of football and I was ashamed to admit I didn't really know any of them. I was used to joining in with anything my brothers did, so when the boys chose sides among the fourth graders for a quick game, I asked if I could play and was naturally picked last for one of the teams. To me, the sport looked like a game of random wrestling while fighting over a ball. I jumped right into the fray and immediately leaped on the back of one of my teammates. I was quickly informed of my stupidity and was greatly embarrassed. I dropped out of the game and simply observed at the next recess or two, but was soon back in the thick of things again.

I quickly adapted to my much-changed life and learned to enjoy the new and different things I could do in town. A new friend down the street let me borrow his mid-sized bicycle, and he, with Frank's help, taught me how to ride it. I can recall clearly how exhilarating it was the first time I was able to glide on my own down the many sidewalks around the Junior high. The few wrecks were worth the thrill. A town kid in the fourth grade who couldn't ride a bike was unheard of!

One of the other special activities that fall was attending Aggie football home games, just about a mile walk from our house. I remember the acrid smell of burning leaves all across town that time of year, a simple pleasure now missing from this town of so many beautiful trees. In those days, every house had an incinerator behind in the alley and the smell of burning garbage sometimes wasn't so pleasant. But on a warm November day, walking to the old football stadium on College Avenue, it seemed the good smell prevailed. At the south side of the arena there was a hole in the fence, and kids small enough to walk through it were let in free to sit in the portable bleachers behind the goal posts or sit on the grass when no seats were available. I don't remember much about any of the games or players, only the feeling of exhilaration brought on by the spectacle of the band, the cheerleaders and, particularly, the firing of the 75mm howitzer by the ROTC after each Aggie touchdown.

One good friend I discovered when I got to town was Teddy Shaffer, who was in the first grade at a different school. He lived across the street from the Court House and next to the Masonic Lodge in a house that was furnished as befitted the family of the Larimer County Sheriff. The Lilleys and Shaffers had lived on neighboring ranches in Virginia Dale and had been good friends for years. Ted had been elected Sheriff a couple of years earlier, but still operated the ranch on the Wyoming-Colorado state line and continued to put on his annual rodeo after moving his family to town.

Ted Shaffer was a colorful figure fully fitting his image as an old-fashioned western Sheriff. He was a genuine cowboy who still wrestled steers at Rodeos, including Cheyenne Frontier Days. He had ridden saddle broncs when he was a bit younger. He had earlier won both the heavyweight amateur wrestling and boxing Rocky Mountain championships sponsored by the Rocky Mountain News in Denver, an unprecedented feat. While Sheriff, he boxed at a couple of smokers sponsored by the local Rotary club, defeating fairly well-known regional semi-pro boxers.

There was a vacant lot between the Sheriff's house and the Lodge, which had a knotted rope hanging from a big elm tree. When I went over to see Teddy, who had been a friend as long as I could remember even though he was three years younger than I, we usually swung on the rope or played a game of marbles that required four holes in corners of a square and one in the middle, the name of which I don't remember. If we got bored swinging or shooting marbles, we played any number of games. This was a favorite weekend destination and there were rarely fewer than three of us there. I often ate lunch with Teddy, and his Mom usually fed us the same sandwiches she had prepared for the prisoners at the county jail, a contract usually left to the Sheriff's wife.

When Christmas approached the family decided to spend it back at the ranch house, which was sitting vacant. Mom packed up enough food for a long weekend and we quickly settled into our old routine. Our first job was to cut a Christmas tree, and we found a beautiful one on the north slope of Table Mountain. Dad built a stand and we decorated it with our heirloom decorations, including clip-on candles. On Christmas Eve, Dad lit the candles and we stood back for a few minutes filled with awe, enjoying a sight no one can expect to see in this day and age. Dad quickly extinguished the candles and we all heaved a sigh of relief that we hadn't burned the house down.

Shortly after we had opened our Christmas presents and enjoyed a hearty breakfast of scrambled eggs and homemade cinnamon rolls, Frank headed out with the new 30-30 Winchester carbine given to him by his grandfather, Perry Williams. Frank had just turned twelve on December 20, 1940 and Grandpa, an avid sportsman, had promised Frank a rifle for his birthday. He didn't dream it would turn out to be this iconic deer rifle. Frank said he was going to hunt coyotes. He departed in a steady but light snowstorm and we didn't see him again till nearly dark, about 4:30 p.m. that time of year.

After school let out, the folks decided to move back for one last summer to the still vacant house, which we referred to as the home place. Dad probably stayed with his sister and brother-in-law when he had to be at the Producers Livestock office at the Denver stockyards, since he had no responsibilities at the ranch. My brothers were not involved in ranch work except occasionally helping cousin Tommy Shepperd and his hired men in the hay field. I was too young to be of any help, but did like killing time along the creek running through the particular meadow where hay was being stacked. Mom usually helped with whatever riding needed to be done.

My bothers had made some good friends during their year at school in Fort Collins and invited three of them to spend a week at the ranch that summer. They spent a lot of that time horseback riding and looking for excitement. I was allowed to tag along as usual. We were able to find a horse and saddle for each visitor and the first order of business was teaching him how to ride, a process that mainly consisted of boosting him on board and letting him learn as he went. I felt quite pumped up realizing this was one skill I could help these otherwise superior older boys learn.

One of the most exciting activities they discovered was riding to the top of a ridge that paralleled the road leading into the ranch from the highway and rolling rocks down. As the day went on they dislodged ever bigger boulders and let gravity do its work. Eventually all five-I was only a nervous spectator-dug up a really big rock perched on the brow of the ridge, which wiped out several good-sized trees on its downward course and wound up within a few feet of the road. Ever logical Frank saw that they couldn't top the last minor avalanche and suggested they had better quit while they were ahead.

Grandma Lilley's house in Fort Collins where we lived when I was in the fourth grade. Grandma is on the Porch.

6

Denver

In the fall of 1941 Dad rented a house in Denver at 707 South Ogden. Grandma Lilley was still recovering from her stroke in the sanitarium and her house in Fort Collins had been sold. We had had a great summer, our last on the ranch, and I don't even recall moving to Denver in the fall. However, I do remember the home we rented. It was a nice two-bedroom brick bungalow with a full basement. It had a coal furnace, as did nearly all the houses on our block, and a garbage pit and one-car garage in the back alley. My brothers and I slept in the basement, leaving a spare bedroom upstairs.

I entered the fifth grade at Lincoln grade school about four blocks south of our home. My brother Frank was in the ninth grade at the local junior high and Charlie began his sophomore year at South High, so all three of us were going to different schools. My brothers and I adapted to our new schools and soon were making new friends. Early on I noticed a good looking red-headed boy named Jerry Weinberger who seemed full of confidence and was easy to approach, and we soon became fast friends. I didn't realize it at the time, but perhaps he needed a friend just as much as I. Jerry and I were inseparable all the time we lived in Denver.

A momentous event occurred that winter that changed all of our lives. The family had driven to the ranch in Virginia Dale for the weekend of December 6 and 7, and on the way to Denver Sunday morning, we had stopped to see our friends the Schaffers who invited us to have dinner with them. Ted was still the sheriff of Larimer County and lived across from the courthouse in Fort Collins. After dinner, my brothers and I invited Ted and Peggy's son, Teddy, to go to the matinee at the American movie theater with us. As soon as we left the theater we could tell something serious had happened. Everyone was standing on the street corners discussing the news that Japan had attacked Pearl Harbor that morning.

When we got back to the Schaffer's house, we all loaded up in the car and Dad drove us back to our home in Denver. I don't remember what we said but I know we were all in a state of shock. We got up Monday morning and went about our routines, Mom fixing breakfast, we kids getting off to school, and Dad heading for work at the stockyards, but none of us could possibly foresee the tremendous changes in our lives this recent event would cause. That night after supper, Dad recalled a conversation with my Aunt Essie's son-in-law over cocktails. Jack, who was a well-educated and successful professional, offered the opinion that if a war should come with Japan our Navy could lick their Navy within six weeks. My Dad had said he allowed that we could probably beat the Japanese Navy, but thought it wouldn't be that easy. That was the summer of 1941, when it looked more and more as if we were headed for war, and at the time we were preparing for it to a greater degree than we realized. Neither dreamed that the war might start in such a manner.

    In the spring of 1942 another unanticipated change occurred in our lives. Mom's father, Perry Williams, sold his ranch to the Warren Livestock Company, which adjoined his property on three sides. He had been having trouble getting and keeping hired men, and with the war and draft he anticipated the problem would only get worse—plus he was then 71 years old. He had decided to give both of his daughters, my mom and aunt Florence, $5000 with which to purchase a home, something neither had ever dreamed of doing any time soon. Aunt Florence and her husband, Spike, both of whom loved roses, purchased a home in North Denver with a yard large enough to have a huge flower garden. Dad knew that Mom missed the opportunity to ride horseback very much, so we needed at least a small acreage if we were going to have a horse or two near town. He managed to find such a property at 1821 Wadsworth in Lakewood, which was then still a semi-rural area. The place had three bedrooms, one bathroom and a full basement. The rooms were small, but it was a very comfortable bungalow with a formal dining room and a small fireplace in the living room. Once again, we boys all slept in the basement. The property had a well in the basement, which furnished hard water that tasted bad but was completely safe to drink. It also had a very small water right; however, the head-gate for obtaining the water was quite a long way away, through several other properties.

We took possession of the new place about six weeks before the end of the school year, so we boys were put in the uncomfortable position of starting in a new school with only six weeks to go. Lakewood had a grade school, junior high and high school adjacent to one another at 10th and Wadsworth just a mile south of our new home; however, we were once again in three separate schools. In my grade school, each grade was large enough to be divided into two classes determined by the first letter of the students last name. I was put in the class in the second half of the alphabet to finish the school year.

I had enjoyed my time at Lincoln school in Denver and very much missed seeing Jerry Weinberger every day. Still I was a gregarious sort and tried to make friends. Evidently, in the process, I offended the class bully, a blond boy named Whitey, who sent one of his henchmen, Murray Williams, to inform me that he was going to meet me after school to knock my block off. I had never had a serious fight in my life and was scared to death. I put on a brave front and acted as if I were preparing for the upcoming battle. After school, I started walking home up Wadsworth looking both right and left expecting to be confronted at any time. Fortunately, Whitey never showed up. As it turned out he soon moved away, and during the next summer Murray Williams became one of my best friends.

There was a fenced playground in front of the Grade school, but serious ballgames during recess had to be out on the dirt football field north of the junior high. During recess that spring, the word spread that there was a fight going on out on the football field between two junior high boys. Naturally all the grade school boys dropped everything and ran out to see what was going on, because watching fights was our favorite form of entertainment. Just as I got to the field I saw my brother Frank running back to class, which was just beginning in junior high, with a look in his eyes that I recognized. Frank had a temper and would not take anything from anyone, even though he was always quite small for his age. He ran right on by me, so I asked someone standing nearby what had happened. He said that a new boy had just whipped somebody a lot bigger than he was. I was a bit embarrassed, but all the same proud to say that was my brother.

7

Lakewood

The first summer in Lakewood was difficult in many ways. I hadn't had time to make many friends with only six weeks of school in the previous spring, so I fell back on what I loved to do, which was to read. I probably read more books that summer than I ever have in a comparable time before or since. I did go swimming a few times with my brothers. I also joined my mother when she went shopping in Denver and occasionally talked her into going to a matinee at one of the downtown theaters. We usually took the streetcar that ran from Golden, Colorado to Denver, boarding it at the stop on Wadsworth just between our home and the grade school on about Twelfth Avenue. Her favorite store was the Denver Dry Goods, at which she had had a charge account since the time we lived on the ranch. If she couldn't make up her mind about something, she often asked my opinion and I talked her into buying a couple of the big floppy hats you saw in the movies those days. Sometimes we would eat at the teahouse on the fourth floor, which was a bit embarrassing to me because there never seemed to be any men there and not all that many children.

My dad had taken a new job with the Department of Agriculture in the War Food Administration. He was blind in one eye and not eligible for the draft, but because of his knowledge of agriculture from ranching, his contacts from serving in the legislature and his experience as president of the Colorado Cattlemen's Association he was able to land the job. I didn't know exactly what it entailed but he had to travel a lot, usually by train, and was often gone overnight. Occasionally Mother and I would meet him late at night at the train station as he was coming back from participating in a ceremony for one of the industry winners of an A award for its contribution to agriculture in the war effort. A local dignitary or perhaps Dad would present a plaque to the president of the company being honored at a special event in the hometown of the company. This was just one of the many efforts to spur food production for the war effort. Agriculture was particularly affected by the shortage of labor because all able-bodied men were being drafted. Dad had a special ration card for gasoline for our car because he had to drive when a rail connection didn't exist to his destination. We were fortunate that we had purchased a 1941 Studebaker Champion automobile in the fall of 1941. It normally got nearly thirty miles to the gallon, and with the 35 mile-an-hour speed limit in force during the war it did even better. Even so, Mom had only enough gasoline to drive to Denver occasionally while Dad was traveling on the train.

Since I had started school so late in the fifth grade when we moved to Lakewood, I hadn't much of an opportunity to make any friends during this summer and was ready for school to start in the fall of 1942. I rode a school bus occasionally, but generally walked the mile to school and sometimes rode the bike Frank had handed down to me. When school opened I was put in the class of students whose last names began with the letters A through L. The previous year I had been placed in the class whose names included the last half of the alphabet, so I was thrown in with an entirely new group of students. The only person in the other class I had known very well was Murray Williams, and of course I could still see him at noon recess or after school. It did allow me to fortuitously have as my teacher possibly the most competent in the grade school, Miss Schaeffer. The Lakewood school system was less modern than that in Denver, but in important ways was more challenging and demanding.

I had always thought of myself as a pretty good student but my confidence had been shaken by the poor grades I received in the last six weeks of the fifth grade. I didn't understand that six weeks in a new school did not give my teachers an opportunity to get any idea of my ability. The fact that Lakewood was a little ahead of Denver schools in the subjects I was taking did put me a bit behind. In any case, I got the only C I ever received in school, in addition to an occasional D in penmanship and art. So, I started the sixth grade with some trepidation.

I need not have worried because the sixth grade turned out to be one of the most enjoyable years of grade school. I had a wonderful teacher, who seemed to like me and really, all her students. Miss Schaeffer was a woman perhaps in her early 30s, whose face had been badly disfigured, probably in a fire. As is often the case in these situations I soon did not even notice the scars. I once again was getting all A's and B's and my confidence returned, perhaps a little too much.

I had begun to notice that girls were interesting in a strange way I could not understand and I wasn't paying as much attention in class as I should have. Probably the rest of the class was going through the same transformation as indicated by a game that seemed to spring out of nowhere that we all participated in. I have always suspected that it was instigated by the girls, but the boys picked up on it quite readily. It was called Winkem or some such thing. It seemed quite risqué at the time, but looking back, I see it was unbelievably innocent. I don't remember the exact rules but it seems that if someone said, "Jinx on you," and you did not have your fingers crossed at the time, he or she could tell you to wink at a person of his or her choice, of course of the opposite sex, and you had to comply. It seemed terribly exciting at the time and I soon learned that the girl I wanted to wink at was a pretty blond named Nancy Jones. It seemed everybody else knew that and sometimes they would be kind enough to instruct me to wink at Nancy. I, of course, was ecstatic when Nancy winked at me. It was a silly game but had all the complexities of any other undecipherable male-female goings-on at that age or any age for that matter. With only brothers and with my mother having been orphaned at four and being pretty much in the dark about them herself, I was on my own.

Of course, Nancy did not occupy all of my thoughts. I very much wanted to participate in the football games we had at recess during the latter part of the lunch hour and sometimes after school. Thanks to Glenn Dyer, Murray's best friend, who often was one of those who seemed to be captain of one of the teams, I wasn't always the last one chosen. These were rather serious games of tackle on the dirt football field. In the sixth grade, I was only slightly smaller than the average boy and quite a bit faster than most. In these games, there was usually only one back, who received a direct snap from center

Murray Williams and me in a picture taken at a photomat at Lakeside Amusement Park in Denver.

and everyone else played on the line. As soon as it was discovered that I was faster than most of the other kids, I either received the snap for an end run or headed down the field in accordance with the directions of the guy throwing the pass. I still didn't know any of the finer points of the game, but did learn it was best to avoid being tackled. I had roughhoused enough with my brothers to pick up on the idea of tackling at which I was reasonably good. The rules were vague and it seemed we spent more time arguing about them than we did playing. But it was a lot of fun.

I have a lot of good memories of what happened in my last year of grade school and my first two in junior high in the building just west of the grade school. I had made another good friend by this time and often walked with him to the pharmacy on the way home from school. It was right on the corner of Colfax and Wadsworth and it had a soda fountain and a few booths. We often met there with several other friends to have a treat. My favorite was a pineapple milkshake made with the pineapple used for ice cream sundaes. They used metal containers to mix the ingredients of the shake and then attached it to the mixer, which seemed to have been used forever. The shakes served in these mental containers cost a dime and would fill two eight-ounce glasses, thus two servings for five cents each, but the drugstore had a strict policy against drinking out of the metal can and would not furnish a second glass. We figured many creative ways to get around this rule, but if we were caught more than once we had a good chance of being evicted from the premises. However, it was worth the risk because nickels and dimes were hard to come by in those days.

The summer after the sixth grade was a lot more fun than the previous one. My friends and I often took long bicycle rides and I got acquainted with quite a bit of the local countryside during those rides. I also recall walking over to Murray's house or him coming over to mine. Glenn lived a good bit further to the north and was usually with Murray when he came to my place. Several times that summer, we walked from my house to the swimming pool at the Lakeside amusement park. We would get there fairly early and spend most of the day in the pool because we couldn't afford to go too often and wanted to get our money's worth. I could barely swim fifteen yards at most and doing that completely exhausted me. Such muscles as I had developed pitching hay, cleaning a ditch with a shovel or similar work required muscles you didn't use for swimming and actually worked in opposition to the ones you did. We came out of the pool looking like prunes and starving. If our moms hadn't fixed us a lunch, we arrived back at my house starved to death, where we always found something to eat.

In bad weather, Glenn and Murray and a couple other friends liked to come over to our house and play Ping-Pong in the basement, where we Lilley boys slept. My brother's friends also seemed to like to come to our home where they played Ping-Pong and often used the boxing gloves Dad had bought for us some years before. When the big boys happened to be there, we younger ones mostly just looked on or went outside, if the weather allowed. My folks never interfered with what was going on in the basement, unless it got too noisy, and then my dad would come to the head of the stairs and yell "BOYS!" at the top of his voice and things would calm down. Years later a friend of mine remarked, "You never had to wonder who was in charge at the Lilley household."

Murray's dad had been in the Marines and had obviously told him about the extreme discipline dispensed in boot camp. For some reason, this idea appealed to Murray, and Glenn particularly, and when they and other friends were at our house we would take turns being recruits while another, most often Glenn, would be our drill sergeant. The drill sergeant would yell at us and insist we say, "No excuse, Sir," when we didn't do exactly what he told us and would hand out punishment, the favorite being pushups. I'm not sure why we enjoyed this so much, but I think it had a lot to do with the war, then well underway. We worried that our brothers would go to war after graduations or about our relatives who were already in the service.

We were all patriotic to a fault and loved the many war movies being made; the more Japs and Huns wiped out the better. This was only the beginning of three years of increasing rationing and well-planned propaganda, which was certainly needed because the war was not going well at the time. I recall that Freddie Patridge and I were selected to have the honor of raising the flag every morning and taking it down again when school let out; I think this honor was passed around every few weeks. We also started class each morning by reciting the Pledge of Allegiance.

When we went to the movies, at the beginning of the show everyone stood up and pledged allegiance to the flag stationed at the corner of the stage. Rationing worked because peer pressure mitigated against cheating, and to not be patriotic was to be ostracized. The internment of the Japanese at the start of the war was an obvious example of the negative side of our shared anxiety, but patriotism was the glue that held us together during the long difficult years ahead

I occasionally rode the school bus, but usually walked because the return trip was circuitous and I usually either wanted to get home early or stop by the drugstore. On the occasions I did ride the bus home, I had an opportunity to get better acquainted with a new friend, Gary Glick, who had moved to Lakewood with his family at the start of the school year. He lived one mile east of me across a vacant area between Wadsworth and Teller Street, just north and west of the Jewish sanitarium or JC RS. His father, Fred, had taken a job as a guard at the new Remington arms plant, which had just been built to manufacture small arms ammunition. I occasionally got off the bus at Gary's house to play in the vacant lot just north of his house with him and his brothers, Ivan, about three years older than Gary, his younger brother, Leon, and Freddie, who was the youngest by several years. They had a backboard and basketball hoop mounted on a couple of posts, and Gary, Ivan, Leon and I often played basketball with perhaps a couple of neighbors, while Freddie looked on. I knew nothing about the game of basketball, still I occasionally tried to join them. I was so bad that I just got in the way, so I mostly watched. Little did I know what fine athletes these Glick boys would grow up to be.

I also made friends with a boy about three years younger than I who lived four houses north of me on Wadsworth on our side of the street. His name was Tom Brown and we loved to play board games after school or perhaps on Saturday. I decided that other than missing Jerry Weinberger, the move to Lakewood had been a good one.

The summer after sixth grade was much more enjoyable than the previous one had been. I had a good many friends to spend time with, so I didn't find nearly as much time to read as I had been doing. In fact, there were so many fun things to do on the weekends that I found myself resenting having to join my dad and brothers doing yard work in our big new homestead. We had fenced off the last two thirds of our acre-and-a-half lot, but the rest of the place was pretty heavily landscaped with shrubs, perennial flowers and a few nice big trees. In the spring, we had to rake all the leaves, trim the shrubs, cultivate the flowers and sack up the debris to be hauled away. There was also quite a lot of lawn, promising a good deal of mowing all summer long. My dad always worked right along with us when he was home and laid out yard work for us when he had to be gone. My brothers made sure that I did my share of the work. When I wasn't upset from being bossed by them, I was trying to make sure I could do everything they did and they were happy to tell me just how to do it. I found it was a lot more fun to work with Dad.

We did get up to the ranch several times that summer to visit my cousin Tommy Sheppard and his mother, my aunt Essie, who usually came out about mid-summer with her black servant, Duane. Servant is now an obsolete term, but that is what he was called at the time. He was a great guy, who did all of the cooking and much of the house cleaning, and served the formal meals at noon and night. He had living quarters of his own above the kitchen, which was accessible by a back stairway called—the servant's stairs.

We had left our eight horses at the ranch when we moved to Denver, but now we had room to keep at least a saddle horse or two behind our new home in Lakewood. Dad arranged to lease some pasture close to Stanley Lake near Arvada for the rest of the horses. Before the summer was over we had moved them all, with mom's favorite saddle horse, Zaida, coming to the new pasture on Wadsworth. The balance of horses were moved to the Stanley Lake pasture.

In September, I made the move from being a big shot sixth-grader to becoming a lowly seventh grader in junior high. The junior high was between the grade school and the new high school but it had the gymnasium and shower room that the high school and junior high athletes and gym classes shared. The high school had the auditorium, which was quite nice. All in all, the physical facilities of the Lakewood school system seemed quite efficiently organized. The junior high had both a football and basketball team, but of course they had to use the football field and gymnasium at the convenience of the high school varsity teams. The gymnasium was quite modern, but the football field was dirt with a few rather primitive bleachers.

I loved sports and had planned to go out for the junior high football and basketball teams, but I quit growing at about that time and was a small seventh grader. By the time I reached the ninth grade I was way behind my peers in weight and height. To my surprise, Coach Hockey told me that I had a heart murmur and couldn't participate in either football or basketball. I protested that I had no idea where this information had come from, but he said that's the way it was and there was no use waiting around for a uniform. I was somewhat relieved because I could see that all of the equipment was too big for me, so I didn't press the matter any further. I did enjoy participating in the version of touch football the seventh-grade boys played during gym class that fall and I set my mind to learn how to play basketball.

Jerry Lincoln occasionally joined me at Gary's house on weekends. He was undersized as I was, but unlike me, not lacking in confidence in any way. He lived at a trailer court a few blocks west of the corner of Colfax and Wadsworth, where there was a basketball backboard and hoop. I started going over to his place as football season wound down, and he and his friends were always shooting hoops. They were patient teaching me how to play the game. I caught on fairly quickly, but couldn't master the art of a two-handed set-shot, which was Jerry's specialty.

As I began to get the fundamentals of basketball down I often walked a couple of blocks up Wadsworth Avenue to see a neighbor named Sonny Sanders and have intense one-on-one games in his back yard. Sonny was one year younger than I and had a younger brother named Gary, who loved to play with us and showed promise of being pretty good in both football and basketball when he grew up, which certainly turned out to be the case in both high school and when he and Gary Glick met up in college.

I liked most of my seventh-grade teachers and settled in and ended up with the usual A and B marks on my report car that year. My mathematics teacher, also the coach of the junior high football team, initially put the fear of God in me with his rough demeanor and tendency to not only chew people out but occasionally grab them and administer a couple of good slaps on the back. Of course, this never happened to any of the girls in the class and I wasn't about to do anything to raise his wrath. Math was not one of my better courses, because it did not come easy and I had to do a little studying, something somewhat foreign to me. Mr. Hockey did scare me into studying math, and the habit seemed to be transferred to my other courses.

    Life for the Lilley family went on fairly smoothly for the rest of the year, but the war was very much on everyone's mind. Boys graduating from high school could expect to be drafted if they didn't' quickly enlist in the service of their choice, which an amazing number did. They were asked to become men at far too young an age. We had the Denver Post delivered to our front yard and every day after school I read the headlines and major news developments even before I read the funnies. Our entire economy was quickly switching to a war footing with the complications of setting up fair systems for rationing food, gasoline, tires, shoes, and probably other items I don't recall. Fortunately, patriotism was the default position of the vast majority of the population and there was an amazing amount of intolerance of hoarding or other actions appearing to not support the war effort. It took some time for the ration books to be printed and the mechanics for using them to be implemented. By the time they were, we seemed to have settled into a new normal of getting along without so much sugar and other items subsequently added to the list of rationed items. We also got used to driving a lot less. The extra gasoline provided by Dad's B ration card was intended only for his work, and because he put more miles on the car, it was nearly impossible to replace worn out tires. Candy bars and chewing gum were hard to get at the store across from the grade school and those you could find came from Mexico, brands we had never seen before and never saw again after the war.

    The next summer both of my brothers got ranch jobs, Charlie, at the Condit Ranch near Encampment, Wyoming, and Frank for our cousin Tommy at the Table Mountain Ranch where we had all grown up. I had been used to following my brothers around a good bit during the previous school year and they were good about letting me do it as long as I stayed quiet and out of the way. I missed them at first, but soon found plenty to do with my new friends. Most of us had chores to do at home and had to schedule most of our playtime during the long summer evenings.

We enjoyed bike rides around the community and I was able to use Frank's old bicycle. Often, Murray and Glenn and perhaps a few other friends and I would meet after supper at a predetermined spot and wander around the unpaved side roads north of Colfax Avenue between Wadsworth and Kipling Street. With that much time on our hands, we were bound to stumble into mischief. On the south side of Colfax where an irrigation ditch passed underneath, there was a farm that raised geese. One night, we were out looking for something to do. After we walked through the underpass for the dry ditch to the other side of Colfax, we found ourselves on the goose farm. We stumbled onto a pile of eggs that turned out to be rotten unfertilized goose eggs awaiting disposal.

We had no business sneaking into this area of the farm in the first place, and to add insult to injury, someone had the bright idea to load our pockets with these rotten eggs and throw them at cars driving by on busy Colfax Avenue. We slipped back under the bridge to the north side of the road and whenever we saw a car coming, we threw rotten eggs at it; we even managed to hit a few. We were down in the ditch and out of sight but still had the good sense to at least be concerned about being caught. When the first driver hit his brakes and jumped out, we took off on a dead run up the ditch. Fortunately, it was a fairly dark night and we were in the shadows and had no trouble escaping. Still, we probably ran at least three blocks without even looking back

Most of our summer night escapades were not as exciting as the rotten egg adventure; however, we were always looking for something exciting to do and sometimes that was nothing more than taking off at a dead run down a country road in the dark. Murray Williams and I were probably the two fastest among the friends that got together at these times. I was more of a sprinter and Murray could run forever. We would start off side-by-side at a dead run, then I would pull ahead and soon he would pass me, and by the time I couldn't run anymore he would always be way ahead of me. We would then gather and sit around in the dark and talk or tell jokes. The F- word hadn't predominated teenage vocabulary yet, but you can rest assured the jokes shared were gross. Fortunately, we did manage to stay out of any kind of serious trouble.

This was also the summer I started taking piano lessons. Mom felt I needed something constructive to do, and being the only Lilley boy with much if any musical inclination, it fell to me to carry on a family tradition. My grandma Lilley had been a wonderful pianist and even after a mild stroke, had recovered enough to start playing again in her early eighties; we knew she would be pleased. We learned of a piano teacher who lived just across the street from the junior high. I can't think of her name anymore, but she had gone to the Blanche Tingley Matthews school of music in Denver and used their books. I had enough talent to get everyone's hopes up, but unfortunately, like many reluctant students of piano, I hated to practice, and worst of all, I hated the recitals that were scheduled from time to time by my long-suffering teacher.

I hung with it for most of my junior high years and got through the third-grade music book and into my fourth before I finally gave up. Mom hated to see me quit and Grandma and a couple of my mother's musical friends were really mad at me. The main excuses I gave were my growing interest in sports and desire to be on the basketball and football teams and that was going to take up most of my time. My unstated hidden reason was that I just couldn't deal with the recitals. One of the worst experiences of my life was my last one. The piece I had been assigned was called Banjo or some such name and had a nice rhythm. It wasn't extremely hard, but in anticipation of the recital I was at the piano practicing hard until a half hour before it began. I did have the piece down fairly pat, but when I sat down to perform at the recital, my mind went blank after the first few bars and I just sat there. I was utterly devastated. My teacher told me to just start over, which I did, and I managed to stumble on through it very badly. No one made fun of me and Mom was certainly supportive, but I thought that everyone there was appalled and the word would surely spread throughout Lakewood about my failure. It was the first, but not the last time I would feel publicly humiliated.

8

Driving a Team

I did get back up to Virginia Dale on numerous occasions during my Lakewood years. The first summer after we moved, Frank worked at the Wooden Shoe Ranch west of Tie Siding, Wyoming, owned by Oscar and Rhoda Marsh, parents of his good friend, France. I joined him there for a few days that summer during haying season and was put to work. I had driven a team of horses a time or two, but had never operated any haying equipment. Early in the morning, Frank took me out to the barn where three teams of horses were tied in separate double stalls. He harnessed the gentlest team for me and then had me drive it out to where three old mowing machines were parked. He showed me how to step my horses across the tongue of the first mower and back them into place in preparation for being hitched up. He picked up the neck yoke on the front of the tongue and snapped a ring on either end of it to the appropriate horse's harness. He then showed me how to hitch the tugs of the harness of each horse to the single tree on the double tree connected to the tongue. He warned me to always reverse the process when unhitching, undoing the tugs first and then unfastening the tongue from the neck yoke. He then showed me how to raise and lower the sickle bar and operate the lever that put the mower in gear and caused the pitman stick to move the sickle, which moved with a reciprocating action back and forth through the guards of the sickle bar. The sickle was made up of three-inch cutting blades, which cut the hay with a slicing action across the sharp edges of the guards. When the mower was pulled through a field, gears from the wheels of the mower powered the pitman stick, which moved the blades. The result was a swath of hay five feet wide.

Frank then showed me how to use an oilcan to lubricate each of about five different moving parts of the mower after cutting three rounds. He pointed out that it was essential to take the mower out of gear every time you stopped to oil and be sure to put it in gear before starting up again. I was nearly overwhelmed trying to remember all these things while keeping the team properly aligned with the last swath I had cut, to say nothing of the chore of making right angle turns, which required stopping the team at just the right time, lifting the sickle bar with a foot lever, which took most of my strength, backing the team slightly as I brought them around and dropping the bar again to continue mowing. While I was laboriously learning to do all this through trial and error, France and Frank were mowing in a circle on the same land of hay. Whenever I had trouble they would just pass around me and continue their work, unless I was in enough of a jam that I was forced to get one of them to help me.

At about 6 PM we three headed back to the barn with our mowers, parked them in a row, proceeded to unhitch and lead our respective teams back to their stalls and un-harness them.

I was almost too tired to eat that night and went to bed early. I spent most of the night tossing and turning, reliving the hectic day I had just put in and dreading the one ahead tomorrow. After a big breakfast at about 5:30 AM we headed out to the barn to catch the six horses and tie them in their stalls. Frank harnessed my team for me again and helped me as I hitched them to my infernal machine. As the three of us headed out to the field to continue the mowing, my confidence was at a low ebb, but I gamely fell in behind them as we started the day. I was amazed to find that I had remembered all I had learned the day before, and in spite of a few bad rounds I did pretty well. About the only problem any of us had was breakdowns with our ancient five-foot sickle bar mowing machines. Sometimes it seemed that only one of us was mowing at any one time, with one of us back at the shop repairing his mower and the third one either going out to the field or coming back to the shop. I had one more day to stay at the ranch, and the third day things went even better. I felt pretty good having learned to drive a team and operate a mowing machine when I was only 12 years old.

Mom and Dad arrived at the ranch the next morning, and after they visited with the Marsh family for awhile, we headed over to see my grandfather, Perry Williams, who had leased a small cabin and acreage from a friend, Lawrence Russell, on the Red Mountain Road. Grandpa had only recently sold his ranch to the Warren Livestock Ranch and evidently felt he needed something to do. There was a small stream running through the property and Grandpa had planted quite a large vegetable garden irrigated from the stream. Mom fixed Sunday dinner for us and after dinner the folks told me I would be staying with Grandpa a few days.

It wasn't that I didn't love my grandfather, it was just that I didn't really know him too well and was rarely away from home. Even over at Marsh's, I was dreadfully homesick even though my brother was with me. I made the best of it and spent the two mornings I was with him hoeing the garden and the afternoons exploring the beautiful country surrounding us.

When Mom and Dad showed up early the third morning, they visited a while with Grandpa and then we headed for the Pearson's. Roy and Olive had been Mom and Dad's friends when we lived at the ranch. They had a son, Roydon, three years younger than I, with whom I was very well acquainted. He had a baby sister named Betty Belle. When we lived on the ranch, we had taken turns visiting each other on either Christmas or Thanksgiving, and had continued the tradition when possible even after we left. The folks had to get back to Lakewood so Dad could go to work the next day, but Roy Pearson said they needed to go to Fort Collins soon to shop and that they would put me on a bus from Fort Collins to Denver. From the bus depot downtown, I could walk a few blocks to catch the inter-urban streetcar that would take me to Lakewood.

Roydon and I had a great time fishing and swimming in Dale Creek, which ran several miles through the Pearsons' Ranch. I use the word swimming loosely, as there are only a few bends in the creek that had pools deep enough to swim more than a few strokes, but that didn't matter as we couldn't swim very well anyway. We mostly just enjoyed getting naked and wandering up and down the creek without regard to how cold the water was or how slippery the rocks were.

Our fishing amounted to digging some fat earthworms out of Olive's large garden, sneaking up to the creek and dropping a worm over an overhanging bank with our simple fishing rods. We usually caught a few 6- to 8-inch brook trout, which we promptly took back to Olive to clean with the promise of fresh trout either for supper or breakfast the next day. These were a few fun and carefree days.

On Monday morning, we drove to Fort Collins in Roy's LaSalle. Roydon and I went to the malt shop while Roy and Olive did their shopping. We then had dinner, which ranch people called the noon meal, and then I was taken over to the station to catch the bus to Denver. I had one serious problem however. I had meant to ask Mom and Dad for a little money when they left me at the Pearsons', but it had slipped my mind and I only had five cents in my pocket. Even though it never bothered me to eat the wonderful meals that Olive cooked on the ranch, I was concerned that Roy had to buy my dinner and I couldn't bring myself to ask for a dime or quarter. I worried all the way to Denver how I was going to get home, as the interurban fare to Lakewood was ten cents.

When I got to the bus depot in Denver I decided to spend my nickel for a call on the payphone to see if my parents could come and get me. They didn't answer and when I got my nickel back I remembered that it only cost five cents to ride the streetcar to the city limits of Denver at Sheridan Avenue, so I got off the interurban there and walked the mile west to Wadsworth and then the three blocks north to get home. It wasn't long before my folks came home. I wanted to tell them about the ordeal I had had getting home with only a nickel, but was ashamed to admit that I was too shy to ask Roy Pearson for the small amount of money it would have taken to solve my problem.

A couple of weeks later my folks were in Virginia Dale again, this time visiting the ranch. Frank was working with Tommy that summer and Aunt Essie and Duane had arrived from Indiana earlier. I really wasn't planning on it, but Frank thought it would be a good idea if I stayed up at the ranch for a few days and worked in the hayfield with him. In those days ranch boys were expected to start pulling their weight with work by the time they were twelve or thirteen years old, and although we had lived in the city for a few years we still considered ourselves ranch people. So the folks decided that I should stay and work with Frank and Tommy in the hayfield. If I were going to stay in Virginia Dale, I would much have preferred to have spent it visiting either the Pearsons or the Schaeffers over at the Two Bar Seven Ranch playing with Roydon or Teddy. I had learned a few weeks before that working in the hayfield was no fun.

It was Sunday and Mom and Dad were planning to head back for Lakewood early the next morning. As usual, before supper Mom, Dad, Tommy and Aunt Essie had cocktails. At about sundown Duane laid out a sumptuous buffet supper on the expansive front porch, which had a view of the Mummy Range, the beautiful snow-capped mountains just west of Fort Collins and south of the Cache La Poudre River. During the next week, I learned that this same layout would appear for each evening meal.

At 5:30 the next morning Tommy, Frank and I went down to the kitchen, shared an early breakfast with Duane and then headed to the hayfield at the Hanna place. This was a homestead bought by my uncle Roy, Dad's oldest brother, from a man named Hanna, who had in turn bought it from the Prosser family. Everyone in the community except us called it the Prosser place. It was about seven miles north and west of the Shepperd house. To get there, we had to pass through the Double X ranch on Dale Creek just north of another homestead called the Foulston place, which was part of the Table Mountain Ranch. We drove over in Tommy's station wagon because it had the necessary clearance to navigate the rocky road.

When we arrived at the ranch the hired men had already tied the three teams of horses in their respective stalls in the barn. Everett Farnham lived at the Hanna place, Doc Macgregor at the Foulston place and Ed Nauta at the Greenacre place, another Table Mountain Ranch (TMR) homestead. Doc and Ed had gotten up early that morning to milk the cows furnished them by the ranch and then driven up to the Hanna Place for their days work. They wouldn't get home until nearly dark because ranch hands worked ten-hour days, six days a week.

The TMR extended approximately 17 miles from south to north and gained nearly 1000 feet in elevation between the homesteads we called the lower place and the Hanna place. Typically, haying started at the Lower ranch shortly after the Fourth of July, then moved to the Foulston place on Dale Creek. Next, it went to the home place where the Lilley family had lived, then to the Greenacre place, which had two meadows on Deadman Creek above the Lower Place. It wound up just before Labor Day at the Hanna place on the Hay Creek meadow. Hay Creek and Deadman Creek were both tributaries of Dale Creek, which in turn ran into the North Fork of the Cache La Poudre river.

That first day, I watched the men hitch up their teams and head out to the hayfield. I spent the rest of the morning messing in and around Hay Creek on the Meadow north of the ranch improvements where the hay had already been put up. Hay Creek was a great little trout stream. In most places it was fairly narrow, about 1 foot deep and 2 feet wide, with the stream undercutting the bank in some places and then spreading out in other places where the flow was slower. Its cold water and natural spawning places made it perfect for native brook trout. Frank and I loved to fish in this little stream, because the trout were more abundant here than in any other streams that flowed through the ranch.

    That afternoon Tommy Sheppard put me to work with a pitchfork. Some of the hay had been cut next to or practically over the stream. I threw it far enough away from the bank so that it could be picked up by the dump rake, which was used to rake the hay into wind rows. The sweep then picked it up and pushed it onto the stacker, which lifted it up onto the haystack. This was not very hard work because the most hay I could get in my pitchfork was not very heavy, but it was boring, and I found it difficult not to lay my fork down and play in the creek every once in a while. I managed to make this job last until the men were coming in from the hayfield at the end of the day, and I walked up to the barn to join them as they unhitched. As we drove home I learned from their conversation that because the men were behind with the mowing, Tommy would leave Everett mowing the next day, while he and Frank and Doc did some cattle work nearby. They said they needed me to rake one field of hay because it was cured enough to windrow.

    Naturally I couldn't sleep that night. I worried because I had never operated a dump rake before, and even though Frank and Tommy assured me that it was much easier than mowing hay, it didn't look too easy to me. Early the next morning we all arrived back at the hayfield and found the horses in their stalls as usual. Frank informed me that it was time for me to learn how to harness a horse. He showed me how to approach the harness hanging on pegs in the wall and first put my arms under the part that went under the horse's tail, then up through the leather straps, grasping the hames in either hand. He had me pull a harness from the wall, approach the left horse on the left side, drape the part I had under my right arm over its rump, reach over the top of the horse—easier said than done as short as I was at the time—throw the right hame over the collar and settle both hames into the grooves built into the collar for them. He had previously shown me how to put on the horse collar. He then showed me how to fasten the many buckles in the proper order. I'm afraid I didn't follow this as well as I should, but I believed I understood what we were doing. We then drove out the team—a pair of fairly well-matched horses called Pete and Lu. Actually, Lu was the Old Lu that we had used to pull our buggy to the country school in Virginia Dale. He was a good deal gentler than Pete, but they were the best team they had for me to learn with. Hooking them up to the rake was similar to hitching a team to the mower I had run earler in the summer. I did everything with a minimum of instruction and was ready to head for the field.

I had often seen my brothers and the hired men raking and knew how to work the mechanism that tripped the steel tines that gathered up the hay. The part that took some experience, however, was knowing just the right time to kick the lever that caused the tines to fly up and dump the gathered hay in a straight windrow. All the while you were worrying about getting this right, you had to keep the team going straight so you wouldn't miss some of the hay or get less than the optimum amount. I thought that I was doing a terrible job and felt sorry for myself, because they had all deserted me while I was doing something I had never done before. Unfortunately, the only way to learn the job was simply to do it, but I didn't realize they would not have given me the responsibility if I didn't already have enough experience driving a team to pull it off.

At noon, we all gathered by the stack we were working on and Aunt Essie and Duane fed us the hot meal they had brought out to the field for us. I still had an afternoon of raking to do so we could start stacking hay on the next field. As I raked, Tommy, Frank and the three hired-men proceeded to move the rather cumbersome wooden stacker from the last field, pull it into place and chain it down so they could begin to put up another ten-ton stack. Having finished the initial job, Tommy put me to doing a much easier job called scatter raking. There was always some hay spilled by the contrivance called a sweep on the way to the stacker, and my job was to "re-rake" this. Since it was so sparse, I did not have to kick the dump lever too often and could even get my team into a trot on occasion, which was fun.

When it got to be six o'clock, we all headed back to the barn and I unhitched my rake, being careful to undo the tugs before I dropped the neck yoke. Then I drove the team back to the barn, unsnapped the lines from the snaffle bits, fastened them through the rings on the collar and looped them over the hames. Next, I led them into their stalls and prepared to un-harness them. I thought I knew how to do this, but obviously I didn't have a clue, because I simply undid all the buckles in the appropriate sequence, grabbed the hames on Lu's harness and pulled it off over his rump, where it landed in a jumbled mess. I could see I was in big trouble and didn't want to repeat the same mistake by pulling the harness off of Pete. I frantically ran after Frank who was then turning his team loose in the corral.

I hated to admit the fix I had gotten myself into and was expecting Frank to really get on me. Fortunately, in addition to having a terrible temper Frank had a great sense of humor and he broke out laughing. He said he was pretty sure this was going to happen and that it was part of the learning process. He then proceeded to lay out the jumbled harness on the barn floor, get it all straightened out and hang it on the appropriate pegs. As he helped me unharness Pete, he said, "You simply take the harness off the horse just as you took it off the peg to keep it untangled." I haven't harnessed a horse in 50 years but I am sure I could still do it if called upon.

Roy Lilley in about the eighth grade

9

Eighth Grade Memories

That fall I entered the eighth grade at Lakewood Junior High School. I had enjoyed my summer but was ready for school to start. I had spent a good deal of time in Virginia Dale working on the ranch and visiting with old friends in the community, but I also read a lot and did many of the things with my friends in Lakewood that I had done the previous summer.

I soon found that I particularly enjoyed three of my classes. Government was one of them and we discussed politics in this class as we studied current events. Lakewood was in Jefferson County, which was strongly controlled by the Republican Party, and one girl and I were the only Democrats in the class. It turned out we were more than able to hold our own with the rest of the class, all of whom seemed to be Republican supporters or completely disinterested in politics. I have an idea this girl was probably the only one in the class who got better grades than I did and had a family that talked around the dinner table like mine.

My two other favorite classes were taught by the same teacher, Miss Kilgore, who was stricter and more demanding than any other teacher. She taught English Literature and a music class that met only three times a week. This was the first music class I had had since the fifth grade in Denver, but I found some of the fundamentals I had learned back then still stood me in good stead. Miss Kilgore was an excellent English teacher but it was obvious she particularly enjoyed music. We responded to her enthusiastic approach to a wide range of music and she eventually developed our entire class into a chorus that participated in several district-wide competitions.

We were into the second year of World War II. Most of the class and faculty had relatives in the service and we were all feeling anxious because the war was not going too well at that time. Captain Eddie Rickenbacker had crashed into the sea toward the beginning of the war and he and his crew spent many days adrift in a life raft before they were rescued. It was a compelling story and there was a best-selling book just out that described the ordeal.

Miss Kilgore found time during each hour of our literature class to read a chapter of that book to us. We were all riveted by the story.

In music class, Miss Kilgore would dictate the lyrics of songs, which included several from the then very popular musical, Oklahoma, as well other hits, and furnish copies of the music and words to pieces we were going to perform as a choir. We would usually warm-up by singing a few popular songs just for fun and then get to work on the Barcarole, Santa Lucia or another choral number.

The third teacher that I really appreciated was Mrs. Zook, who had taught me American history in the seventh grade and was teaching world history in the eighth. She was the one who sparked my lifelong love of history. It was also in her history class in the seventh grade that I had realized how nearsighted I was. When she gave tests she always wrote the questions on the blackboards, which stretched around three sides of the classroom. When she gave her first test that year, I could not read the questions in the back of the room from my front row seat and had to get her permission to move to the back of the room to finish the test. I soon was wearing glasses, which have been a part of my face ever since.

I had started the seventh grade in junior high only slightly under average height and weight for my age group, but during the next several years I found myself falling more and more behind even though I was wiry and reasonably strong from summer work and active participation in after-school activities. I now know that during their junior high years the rate at which kids grow and enter puberty varies greatly, but it's also true that the early maturing kids do have a great advantage during this time in athletics. I loved football and basketball and was developing an interest in baseball, and being undersized was the last thing I needed because my emotional maturity matched my physical size. Still, I didn't really let my stature bother me too much in the informal games played in gym class or before or after school or during lunch hour. I jumped right into the touch football games and did reasonably well. Fortunately, I was realistic enough that the thought of going out for football at my ninety-pound weight and barely five-foot height was probably futile.

I continued to work at getting better at basketball as the season approached, with enough success that I decided to try out for the team. Evidently the concern over my heart murmur had gone away and Mr. Hocking let me get a uniform, which was considerably too large for me. I did get some tough coaching that was very much needed, but I mostly sat on the bench during the few games we had with other nearby junior highs. I did get into one game with Edgewater, which we lost about thirty-four to four. By some miracle, during my few minutes in the game a rebound found me right in front of the basket and I managed to score two points to go with the two free throws we had managed to make. Everyone was too embarrassed by how badly we had played to pay any attention to my minor accomplishment. It did have the effect of giving me some much-needed confidence though.

    The summer after the eighth grade, I decided to get involved in American Legion baseball, so I spent considerably more time at home than I had during recent summers, although I did get up to the ranch with the folks a few times when we visited Aunt Essie. The previous spring, I had played a little baseball after school and on weekends. Gary Glick particularly liked baseball and was a natural catcher. I wasn't natural at anything and had to learn it from scratch, but as usual, I threw myself into the game wholeheartedly. Still I suffered the embarrassment of being picked last or next to last when teams were chosen for sand lot games. Most often before or after school we simply played work-up, and usually by the time I worked up from the outfield to get to bat, school had started, thank goodness.

    It was probably Gary Glick who talked me into going out for the American Legion team for our age group that summer. A neighbor who had a son about my age was our coach and he needed all the boys who signed up to field a team. I started in the outfield spending my time hoping no one would hit the ball my way. Our neighbor was a good coach and I was happy to learn the fundamentals of the game. At first, I used one of my brothers' rather raggedy gloves, and then about midsummer got the folks to buy me an outfielder's glove. We were fortunate to have a good pitcher in Ray Brown, a boy in my class who was also a good basketball player. We also had a couple of pretty good infielders. This gave us the tools to be somewhat competitive in our league. I had pretty good reflexes and managed to get a couple of hits. With a little more experience, I probably would have gotten a little better, but that turned out to be the only time I played baseball during my school years.

10
Basketball and School Politics

I was looking forward to the start of the ninth grade. I had been going to the school grounds quite often the last two weeks before school started that fall, to play touch football with some of my friends in junior high. A new boy named Jack Anderson, who had moved in that summer, showed up and joined in enthusiastically. It was obvious that he was pretty good and after we chose up sides, he was always named quarterback for one team. I was too small to be a lineman so usually lined up on the end to go out for passes and occasionally took the snap from center to make an end run, since I was one of the faster players in spite of my small size. Jack would draw up the plays in the sand and would occasionally throw me the ball, which I often caught.

I still had Miss Kilgore for music and English and Mrs. Zook for history and first-year Spanish, which I had elected to take. We had a new algebra teacher. Math was my least favorite course, mostly because it involved homework and required more studying than I was used to doing. I don't remember the teacher's name and I recall that I wasn't doing very well at first. However, she was the kind of person you could talk to when you got stuck and she was very patient with me. I found out that even though I wasn't good at algebra, with her help the light would turn on every now and again and I would catch up with everyone else. I don't remember if I got an A or a B in algebra that year, but it was a grade that I finally truly earned

I think that was the year Miss Kilgore put on a musical with a cast from the whole junior high. I don't remember too much about it, but I know that a girl named Juanita and I sang a duet. This was the first public singing I had done since Grandma Lilley had arranged for me to sing Home on the Range on the Court House steps in Fort Collins during some kind of town celebration when I was in about the third grade. It was also the last time I ever sang in public, but I continued to enjoy singing. Instead of doing it in the bathtub, my favorite time to let it all out was when I was riding horseback up in the mountains in the summer, sometimes alone, and later, occasionally while I was with dudes during my wrangling days. (In those days, what are now called guest ranches were called dude ranches and the person who took them horseback riding was called a dude wrangler.)

Our junior high had something similar to a Student Council, but rather than having a president we elected a ninth grader to an office called Head Boy. The nominating process for this and other offices was held during an all-student gathering in the auditorium, and our principal, Mrs. Dunston, conducted the affair. When nominations were open for Head Boy, my best friend, Murray Williams, nominated me. Murray was far from one of the fair-haired boys in our class and Murray had no sooner gotten the words out of his mouth when Mrs. Dunston informed him that I couldn't be nominated because I didn't have the grades required for a Student Council office. It was a very embarrassing moment for me because, in the first place, I had no idea I would be nominated for an office, and she had just told the whole school something that I knew was not correct. Fortunately, one of my classmates held up his hand and said that he was quite confident my grades were good enough to qualify. Mrs. Dunston looked at the school records, which she had close by, and allowed my nomination. I would've been too embarrassed to say anything, Murray had used all the nerve he had to nominate me in the first place and he wasn't about to argue with Mrs. Dunston. Interestingly enough, the other person nominated was the new boy in the area, Jack Anderson. Jack was a promising athlete and ran with a more popular crowd than I did, or at least a better behaved one.

After the nomination process was complete, we were divided rather arbitrarily into two parties and the campaign began. All the nominees in the respective parties met after school and with the aid of a faculty advisor drew up plans for the two-week campaign. We were to develop a platform that didn't threaten any school policy and were strictly forbidden to criticize one another in any way. Each candidate chose a campaign manager and a couple of advisors to help with campaign material, which consisted mostly of posters we designed. I picked Gary Glick as my campaign manager and we proceeded as best we knew how.

I don't remember much about the campaign itself, but I do very clearly recall that when the results were announced it seemed I had beaten Jack by one vote. According to the gossip, I had won only because I received the larger portion of the girls' votes. I seriously doubted this because I was completely psyched out by girls. I started my new duties as Head Boy the following Monday and learned that they amounted to little more than joining the new Head Girl, whose name I don't even remember, before school and during lunch hour as glorified hall monitors.

I had grown very little during the past year, but still decided to go out for football. Because I was about five feet tall and weighed about ninety-nine pounds, it was difficult to find a uniform small enough to fit me. I participated in the practices enthusiastically, and on the rare occasions I got in on a scrimmage, I was used as a halfback in our T-formation. When the quarterback called the plays, he would look around to see if there was possibly anyone besides me in the huddle who could carry the ball. I don't remember ever getting more than a yard beyond the line of scrimmage when I did get the ball. I also came out rather badly on one-on-one tackling drills. I don't remember much more from football that fall except that Murray and Glenn were first string guard and tackle respectively and encouraged me to stay out for practice the rest of the season.

When basketball season started, I found that we had a new coach, Mr. Collins. The first few weeks of practice he drilled us on nothing but fundamentals, something that really helped me catch up with some of the more experienced players. We were issued nice red and white uniforms. I managed to get the smallest one and it fit me fairly well. Only 10 players received the newest uniforms and I couldn't believe that I had been among the chosen few. Mr. Collins seemed to see something in me that I surely didn't feel. Even though I wasn't on the starting five, I got to play in the few games the junior high participated in. I don't remember much of anything about those games except trying to use what little I had learned and hoping nobody passed me the ball.

At the end of basketball season, a truly frightening thing happened. All junior high boys were encouraged to participate in a post-season basketball tournament. We were divided into eight teams of eight players and Coach Collins selected each team with an eye to making them as competitive as possible. He then made the best player in each squad the captain of his team. At our last practice coach Collins selected the eight team captains for the tournament and gave them a list of their team members. I was astounded when I was named one of those captains and was terrified at the thought, not so much about coaching the team, but being expected to be the best player on it. I probably wasn't really that bad and, looking back, I think Coach Collins was sincerely trying to help me develop some confidence. Unfortunately it didn't have that effect.

I didn't get a decent night's sleep again until the tournament was over, and whenever I did fall asleep, I had anxiety dreams such as not being able to run or for some reason having my arm stuck inside my jersey. I think we may have won one game, thanks to a couple of the best eighth graders I had been given to balance out the fact I was the eighth ranking team captain in the tournament. I never scored a point, not one. My emotional immaturity had done me in much worse than the fact I was the smallest guy on my own team. My friend and basketball mentor, Jerry Lincoln, who was just as small as I was and played first-team guard that year, bucked me up and we started talking about going out for track that spring. We were both fast runners and I was a fair broad jumper. Naturally there were those in our age group who were better than we, but we were good enough so that we didn't have to apologize for participating. To my regret Jerry moved away that summer and I lost another good friend named Jerry, who had been a friend in need at an important juncture in my life.

Our boys' track team in junior high had to practice early so that the high school varsity could use the track after school, so the junior high track team scheduled their gym class for the last hour of the school day. Both of my brothers were on the varsity track team and I always stayed after our practice to watch them. They both ran the quarter mile and before each track meet their coach held a competition among the quarter milers to see who would be on their mile relay team. It was always fun to watch my 6'3" oldest brother, Charlie, come in first with his long strides, and my 5"6" brother Frank, who was one year behind him in high school, come in second with what could in no way be described as a long stride. They maintained their relative positions on the mile relay team all year, Frank leading off the race and Charlie anchoring it.

Charlie ended the season qualifying for the state track tournament in two events, the high jump and the quarter-mile. Since it was on a Saturday, I got to go along. The tournament was in Fort Collins on a cold, rainy, windy day and the finals of the quarter mile were held when the high jump was scheduled. Charlie had to hurry over between jumps for the race. He stayed with the pack and with his final kick was passing the two ahead of him when he stumbled just at the end and slid across the line on his face, in seventh place. He was scratched up by the cinders, but he jumped right up and went back for his final jump, which he missed. None of this seemed to bother Charlie a bit, but it devastated me to think that he could possibly have won the quarter-mile in the state tournament if he hadn't entered the high jump, for which he barely qualified.

I soon was looking forward to school letting out, hoping to spend more time visiting friends in Virginia Dale and perhaps even working in the hayfield some more.

11

Summer Cabin

I can't recall exactly when I did what during the summers that I was in junior high at Lakewood. Every year, I spent some of my vacation visiting my friends, Roydon Pearson and Teddy Schaeffer, and some time at the Wooden Shoe Ranch. My family also visited the Table Mountain Ranch (TMR) every year to see Aunt Essie and my cousin, Tommy. I have already talked about my first haying experiences at the Wooden Shoe Ranch and when I stayed with Frank at the TMR for several days.

I believe it was the summer after the ninth grade that Mom and I came to the conclusion that we both needed to get out of Lakewood and back into the country. Charlie had graduated from high school and joined the Army Air Force, and Dad was gone much of the time traveling for his job with the Department of Agriculture.

Clara Craig and her husband, Jack, owned the place we called the Craig Cabin, which was on about 150 acres of land near the state line and only one-half mile east of Highway 287. Our families had been friends since the days we lived on the ranch. The Craig girls had grown up and gotten married and Clara had purchased a dude ranch called Brooklyn Lodge in the Snowy Range Mountains west of Laramie. Clara didn't want to leave her cabin vacant and offered to let mom and me spend the summer there. The cabin had one bedroom, a screened porch, a living room, a kitchen and a chemical toilet that had no running water. There was a large storage shed that we could use as a tack room and keep a barrel of oats, and there was plenty of pasture for a couple of horses.

The first or second weekend after school let out, Dad helped Mom and me move the things we needed for the summer up to the cabin. Mom bought a 1932 Pontiac to get around while we were there. She was planning to cook on a kerosene stove she had purchased at a secondhand store and we had to haul water from a spring nearby for all our domestic needs. The place could be referred to as either semi-modern or semi-primitive, but we were looking forward to living there for the whole summer.

After we had unloaded the few things we had moved up to the cabin, Mom tried out our new kerosene stove and fixed supper for us. Early the next morning, Dad headed back to Lakewood, promising to return the next Saturday to help us get two horses moved over from the TMR. During the intervening week, Mom worked to get the cabin comfortable for the two of us and I walked the perimeter fence of the pasture fixing a few places where the barbed wire had come loose from the posts. There was a seasonal stream running through the property with a nice waterhole at the foot of a granite outcropping near the cabin where the horses could drink.

Dad showed up midmorning on Saturday bringing a good supply of groceries. Early the next morning we drove over to the Table Mountain Ranch. Frank was working there that summer and agreed to have Oakie, the pony he had handed down to me a few years previously, and Zaida over at the Fowlston place, from which Mom and I would ride up Mud Creek about two-and-a-half miles to the cabin. We had left several horses at the ranch after we moved away, including the ponies and two one-half Arabian mares that had been born in 1939 to June and Laura, excellent saddle mares, which Mom had brought from the Windy Hollow Ranch as part of her dowry when she and Dad were married. Laura's foal was named Ginger and June's foal was named Zaida. Frank had done a great job of breaking these mares the summer before.

After an early dinner with Aunt Essie, the folks and I drove over to the Fowlston place and Mom and I saddled up for the beautiful ride up to the cabin. After crossing Dale Creek, we headed west up Mud Creek, going through a wire gate after crossing about one mile of Table Mountain Ranch land and then proceeding through another mile or so of land owned by the Moen family before going through another gate that took us into the pastureland that went with the Craig cabin. We unsaddled the horses and turned them out in their new summer home.

Mom and I were soon settled into a comfortable routine. I'm not sure just what all she did to occupy herself, but we both enjoyed having time to do a lot of reading. The cabin was furnished and there were full bookcases to browse through. I particularly enjoyed a set of Shakespeare plays that someone had edited into non-Elizabethan English. They had wonderful plots of course, but I would never have tackled them in their original form. I ended up reading most of them before the summer was over. I also enjoyed listening to records on the Edison phonograph that the Craigs had left among the furnishings. The records were similar to those we played on our Victrola at the ranch, except that the Edisons were much thicker. There were several recordings by Caruso as well as pieces that had been popular in the Twenties and Thirties. I particularly remember one called, On the Banks of the Brandy Wine. I had never heard it before nor have I since, but I still remember the melody and quite a few of the lyrics. When I was bored I would sometimes go out on the screened in porch where the phonograph was located and listen to these records for several hours. Of course, the phonograph had to be wound up every now and again and sometimes I would let it run down just to hear the weird sound of the music as the turntable slowed and then speeded up as I cranked it

    Frank loaned me the neat twenty-two caliber Remington pump rifle, which our uncle Lawrence had given him, for the summer. I had a lot of fun target practicing with it. I was also looking forward to shooting some cottontail rabbits that hung around the cabin and barn. Mom told me that if I shot any she would be willing to skin and dress them as her dad had done, and we could have some fried rabbit for supper. The bunnies were fairly tame but wouldn't sit still for me and I missed my first several shots. I finally slipped up on one that was nibbling on some grass, took aim, and hit him. Unfortunately, I had only wounded him and he was making a terrible squealing sound. I knew I had to finish him off, but really just wanted to turn and run. I gritted my teeth and approached him as he was lying on his side kicking and screaming. I picked it up it up by its hind legs and hit its head against a nearby granite outcropping, killing it. I took the poor thing in to my mother and watched her expertly pull the skin over its head just as her father had taught her, dress it and cut it up for frying. I didn't want to admit my un-manly emotions even to my mother. After all, I was a ranch-raised boy whose grandfather and brother shot about anything that moved and if it was edible, ate it. At suppertime, Mom rolled the bunny in flour, salt and pepper and cooked it in bacon grease. It was delicious!

My next summer adventure came on a weekend when Dad came up again. Evidently Mom and Dad had agreed that we would meet over at the Schaffers' for dinner this particular Saturday. After breakfast, we saddled up Zaida and Ginger, whom we had recently brought over from the Shepperds'. Mom rode Ginger because she was not quite as gentle as Zaida. We headed over to the Schaffers' about mid-morning and the first thing that happened was not a good harbinger for the day to come. When we were about mid-way over to the Schaffers', Ginger whirled and kicked at Zaida. Fortunately, she hit my stirrup rather than my leg. As long as I continued riding that saddle (about two years more) that bent stirrup was a reminder of my near broken leg. Ginger was a good mare and in some ways more pleasant to ride than Zaida but always was a little cranky.

We got to the Schaffers' about mid-day and Dad showed up soon after. Ted and Dad had a drink while Mom helped Peggy finish getting dinner ready. In the meantime, Teddy and I took a walk across the meadow down by Fish Creek. We never seemed to have any trouble entertaining ourselves. We were hoping to do a little fishing after dinner but were concerned the storm that seemed to be brewing might spoil those plans. We were soon called in to dinner and, by the time we had finished, it had started to rain. The folks, worrying about the worsening weather, decided that we needed to get the horses home before it started to rain. For reasons that I can't recall, Mom and Dad didn't leave the Schaffers until later in the afternoon after deciding that I should ride Zaida home and lead Ginger. I wasn't enthusiastic about the idea because I was worried about getting off Zaida to open a couple of wire gates and leading both horses through, but I didn't want to air my misgivings in front of everybody. We headed down to the barn where the horses were tied, saddled up Zaida and put a halter on Ginger.

By the time I left for the Craig cabin, about a two-hour ride away, the skies were getting darker, it was sprinkling a little and I wasn't looking forward to the upcoming ride a bit. After mounting up I was handed the halter rope and took off with more than a few misgivings. Ginger didn't lead too well, lagging behind and making me jerk on the halter rope to get her to catch up. At least once in the first mile, she jerked the halter rope completely out of my hand, but I was able to ride up on her left side and retrieve it. By this time the rain was coming down fairly hard and lightning was starting to strike fairly close. Occasionally I could get Ginger to break into a trot and I was getting along pretty well when I got to the first wire gate. I could have used one more hand, but I was able to get the gate open all right. Leading one horse through a wire gate is hard enough, but getting two through without one getting into the barbed wire takes all your attention. By the time I got the gate closed and was back on my horse with my reins and Ginger's halter rope gathered up, the rain was really coming down with the thunder booming and lightning lighting up the sky. I think that by this time the horses had figured out they wanted to get home just as badly as I did and we were able to move on at a good brisk trot. I was not looking forward to the next gate about a mile farther on.

By this time, I was getting angrier at my folks for putting me into this mess. After all, they had taught me to stay away from wire fences during a lightning storm and they knew I had quite a few gates to go through. Oh the self-pity! I was also aware that I should stay out from under trees and away from the tops of hills, so I took a little longer route that took me into a valley and across a small stream that was a tributary of Fish Creek. When we got to the stream I found that it had cut a fairly deep channel, but was quite narrow. As I looked the situation over, Ginger had come up beside me, and all of a sudden Zaida decided to jump the creek. I had a good grip on the halter rope when the slack came out of it about midstream and my arm straightened out and I was nearly jerked off the back of the saddle. Fortunately, just before I sailed off over Zaida's rear end, Ginger also jumped. I lunged forward, grabbed the saddle horn and we all proceeded on our way at a trot. If I had been pulled off of Zaida, I would've ended up on foot with two horses to catch in the middle of a raging lightning and thunder storm, but I hadn't for which I was very grateful. By the time I got to the next gate the rain had let up and the lightning was moving away. I got through that gate and the next one, which led to Highway 287, then across the road and down the barrow pit until I got to the gate leading into the pasture around the Craig cabin. Now that I was home I felt rather pleased with myself and was almost glad that my folks had enough confidence in me to require me to take such a trip.

A week or so later I decided that I would like to ride Oakey over to the Pearsons' ranch and stay a few days with Roydon. Mom and I got our fresh milk from the Bishops a few miles south where Dale Creek crossed Highway 287 and Mom borrowed their telephone to call the Pearsons and arrange for my visit. On the appointed day, I saddled Oakey and tied some snacks and a few necessary items wrapped inside my Levi jacket on the back of my saddle. I headed down Mud Creek the three miles to Dale Creek and crossed it at the Foulston place. From there I took the dirt road that led out to the highway, taking a shortcut down what we called the sand draw to the homestead we referred to as the lower place. This was within a quarter mile of the little white church I had attended when we lived at the ranch. I crossed Highway 287 again back to the West and headed down to Deadman Creek, which I followed through the meadow till I reached a gate leading into the Pearson property located close to where Deadman Creek ran into Dale Creek. Roydon had been waiting for me to show up and helped me unsaddle Oakey and turn him into their corral. I had arrived at about 11:30 in the morning and the first thing Roydon and I did was head for the house, about 200 yards north of the barn, for dinner.

I always had a good time when I visited Roydon, and one of the fringe benefits was enjoying Olive's wonderful cooking. Since the Lilley and Pearson families had been going to one another's homes for Christmas and Thanksgiving dinners for years, I knew what to expect. My mom was an excellent cook, but never felt she could match Olive when it came to holiday meals. I was always homesick when away overnight, but I felt less so at the Pearsons' than at any other neighbor's place where I spent the night.

After dinner, Roydon and I grabbed a couple of his fishing poles and an empty tobacco can and headed for Olive's extensive garden, where we knew we could dig up a lot of fat juicy worms. When we dug up a particularly big one we always felt it was destined to catch us a big trout. When we had filled the can with a mixture of worms and moist black dirt we headed straight south to Dale Creek to our favored fishing hole, which was less than a quarter mile from the house and garden. Dale Creek carried nearly twice as much water through the Pearson ranch as it did further north at the Table Mountain Ranch because Fish Creek flowed into it halfway between the two places.

We crept up to the creek bank on our bellies the last fifteen or twenty yards so as to not frighten the fish, and dropped our baited hooks over the bank at a place where the creek made a sweeping turn and undercut the bank. We soon caught six or eight nice trout that ranged in size from about six to nine inches long. Most of the fish we caught in Dale Creek were brook trout, but it had been stocked with rainbow. We occasionally caught a good sized German brown that had found its way this far upstream from Halligan Dam four miles downstream where Dale Creek ran into the north fork of the Cache La Poudre River. After fishing for about 45 minutes we grew bored and headed a short distance upstream to a place where the creek flowed around a large granite boulder. The current flowing around either side of the big rock dredged out enough sand and gravel to make the stream considerably deeper than elsewhere, although it was only about four feet deep.

Roydon and I laid aside our poles and our string of fish, shed all our clothes and waded into our swimming hole with teeth chattering. Dale Creek was a stream fed by very cold springs and belly flopping into the shallow water really took your breath away. The stream was deep enough to swim a few strokes before your toes and hands hit the bottom, after a stretch of only about ten yards, and this is where we learned to swim, though not very well. When we got tired of playing in the water we sat on the bank on the nice clean meadow grass in our birthday suits until we were dry enough to dress. It was an unusual but mutually fulfilling friendship. Roydon had only a younger sister and I had only older brothers. I enjoyed having someone like a younger brother over whom I had at least some influence, and he seemed to enjoy looking up to an older brother figure. And there wasn't the complication of any sibling rivalry. Of course, at the time neither of us analyzed our relationship, we simply enjoyed it.

It being midsummer, Roy Pearson was in the middle of his haying season and two high school boys from Fort Collins had been hired to work in the hayfield for the summer. The next morning Roydon and I walked down to the lower meadow where they were stacking hay. I told Roy I had driven a team the last two summers, both raking and mowing, and offered my services. Roydon really wasn't old enough to drive a team yet, and I have an idea his dad figured that if he let me drive, Roydon would feel he should also be allowed to. He said I could clean up around the stack and do any other odd chores that might come up, so I busied myself with the pitchfork, picking up loose hay that had fallen off the stack and putting it on the stacker head to be thrown up on the stack along with the next sweep load of hay.

Soon the ten to twelve-ton stack was completed and the only job left was to put weights on it to help it settle so it would shed rain. The weights consisted of old fence posts tied together with a length of barbed wire thrown over either end of the stack. The stacker threw the posts and a roll of wire up on the stack and then I climbed up to the top of the haystack to help. We wired the posts together with just the right amount of wire so that it hung well over the edge of the stack but didn't reach the ground. In my overzealous desire to be of help, as soon as one of the boys threw the first post over one end, I grabbed the other post and threw it over the other. The only problem was that I threw myself over the stack with the post and went topsy-turvy over the edge. It felt to me that I was going headfirst with my hands held out to catch my fall, and I thought the bump I felt was my head hitting the ground.

I was naturally a little groggy, and as I got to my feet I felt a pain in my right index finger; my fingernail had been torn half off. Of course, everyone had run around to see what had happened and somebody said that my head was bleeding. I replied that I didn't think so but had probably just put my bleeding finger up on my head. They insisted my head was also bleeding and sure enough I had a one-and-a-half-inch gash on top of it. I had no idea how this could have happened if I went down headfirst and the post was hanging off the stack just as it was supposed to. We finally figured out that I had flipped over in midair and landed with my hands up in the air. Thus, the post had torn my fingernail and as it came to the end of the wire, flipped around and hit me on top of the head.

I was more embarrassed than hurt but they insisted on taking me immediately to the house, and when Olive saw me, her motherly instinct kicked in and she immediately thought they should take me to the doctor. Since I didn't show any signs of a concussion and was not bleeding too badly, they decided to call their doctor in Fort Collins. When Olive explained to Dr. Beebe that my wound wasn't that much more than skin deep and not bleeding a great deal, he said we could treat it ourselves. He instructed Olive to use a pair of sterilized scissors to cut the hair from around the wound and after swabbing it with iodine use the hair on either side to tie three or so knots across the wound to close it. Thus, I didn't need any stitches and fortunately didn't get an infection, and if there was a scar it would be completely hidden by the hair on my head. By this time, I wasn't feeling so good and lay down and rested for the balance of the afternoon.

I stayed a couple more days, but the hayfield incident had put a damper on our outdoor fun and provided an excuse to stay in the house and play games. When I headed back for the Craig cabin after dinner a couple of days later, I was ready to get home and see Mom.

12

Sophomore Basketball

In the fall of 1945 I started my sophomore year at Lakewood High School. The enjoyable summer up at the Craig Cabin had left Mom and me with the desire to do more riding when we got home. Instead of taking them back to the Table Mountain Ranch, we brought Zaida and Ginger to Lakewood. In addition, the folks brought a mare that was a half-sister to both and the same age. She was a result of breeding our Arabian stallion to a half-Belgian mare owned by Al Vonvihl, a neighbor who lived east of us on the Red Mountain Road. Al had brought a couple of his half-draft saddle mares to the ranch in 1938 to breed to our remount stud, Ibn Zaid, which dad had obtained to breed to our ranch mares. One of the colts he ended up with was a roan, which he kept, and the other was a buckskin mare we bought, which we imaginatively called Buck. On several occasions when the weather was good, either Mom and Dad or Mom and I or all three of us took long rides, and Mom often rode with a friend who kept her horse at a nearby stable.

I decided not to go out for football my first year of high school because I was still smaller than the smallest member of the team. I still could play sandlot football at noon and after school and hold my own with the other non-varsity boys. As I recall, the solid subjects I took that year were geometry, second year Spanish, history and English. I found I enjoyed school and managed to get mostly As. I got involved in some after school academic activities and as a result, broadened my circle of friends. My best friends still were Glenn Dyer, Murray Williams and Gary Glick, along with the two younger neighbor boys who lived close by.

Even though my experiences in ninth-grade basketball had shaken my confidence some, Mr. Collins had helped me learn the fundamentals that I was lacking, and when I played basketball in gym class my sophomore year, I realized I had improved quite a bit. With some misgivings, I went out for the basketball team and again felt a little overwhelmed. The nice thing about high school basketball was that there was an A squad and a B squad and very few sophomores in Lakewood ever made the A squad. So, the sheep were soon separated from the goats and I found I could complete with some success for the B squad. The head coach got us started and sorted out who was going to play where, and then he turned the B squad over to our geometry teacher, Mr. James, his assistant coach. James was a really nice guy and since we had a really good group of tenth graders and an equally good group of juniors who did not qualify for the varsity team, he divided the B squad into two teams, one with five sophomores and one with five juniors, each of which played one half of the B squad games that preceded the varsity game.

    I managed to make the starting five of the sophomore B squad, but was fully aware that Jack Anderson, who had broken his leg that fall playing football, was probably one of the most talented athletes in the sophomore class and that as soon as his leg healed he was going to push someone off the tenth-grade team. As it turned out, Jack's leg didn't heal enough for him to play basketball until quite late in the season and he never pushed me off the squad. I was still only 5'4" tall and weighed 110 pounds, a little smaller than a fellow member of the sophomore squad, Freddy Patridge. Both of us wore glasses, which we taped on during games. I was faster and a little more aggressive than Freddy but he was a considerably better shooter than I. We sophomores took our basketball quite seriously and met most weekends over in Freddy's backyard, which had a nice basketball court. We had a good season and won most of our B squad games in the suburban league, which included Golden, Littleton, Castle Rock, Arvada and Lakewood.

    The competition between the sophomores and juniors on the B squad was a healthy one, and when we scrimmaged, we sophomores won more than our share of times and often scored more points during our half of a game than the juniors. I was far from the star of our team but managed to play good defense and usually scored some points. I was even highpoint man in a game with Littleton with eight points, including a couple of lay-ups as a result of steals, which helped us win by one point in the last minute. I felt pretty good about this, but the next Monday the varsity coach took over from our geometry teacher/coach for part of the practice and ran us ragged, often yelling at the team and me in particular, inferring that I had let the game the week before go to my head. After feeling abused for a while, the fact that he saw enough in me to even notice pleased and motivated me. Toward the end of the season Jack Anderson was able to join the basketball team, but didn't have time to really get into shape and saw only limited action.

I don't remember too much about the rest of my sophomore year except that girls started interesting me more while I remained completely clueless in dealing with them. I had no problem talking to them in class or even after school at academic activities; but when it came to social settings I was at a loss. In junior high we had mixers in the gymnasium after school, where we had the opportunity to learn to dance to the recorded music of the big bands popular at the time. We were arbitrarily paired up with girls in our class and pretty much forced out onto the dance floor. What I didn't realize was how few of us really knew how to dance. I thought everybody else did and I was the only klutz on the floor. I was used to country dances where nearly everyone fox trotted, which involves a catch step instead of the simple two-step to the left and two steps back, which the other kids did. At the country dances, some of the married ladies whose kids I had gone to grade school with in Virginia Dale used to drag me out on the floor, which is probably where I picked up the fox trot fixation. In any case the socials, which were intended to improve our social graces, were completely counterproductive for me.

Another problem I had dealing with the boy-girl thing was that I was a hopeless romantic. I fell in love with all the popular leading ladies in the movies and tended to daydream about the prettiest girls in class, much as Charlie Brown thought of the little redheaded girl. I knew there were girls in my class that liked me, but I perversely ignored them, because I didn't have a clue about what to do. I didn't realize that my feelings were much like everyone else's. The thing I did know was that daydreaming about the opposite sex was much safer than having to deal with them. The winking game in the sixth grade is where my skill with the girls had topped out.

Then fate intervened. You will recall that the girl I am most enjoyed winking at in the sixth grade, Nancy Jones, had moved away. But in the spring of my sophomore year, she entered my life again very briefly. Evidently Nancy and her older sister, I think her name was Jane, were visiting Lakewood during spring vacation and the quarterback on the football team, Eddie Steinshouer, whom I knew only slightly, approached me, much to my surprise, and asked if I would like to go out on a double date with him and Nancy's sister. Wonder of wonders, Nancy had remembered me and I'm fairly sure her older sister talked her old boyfriend into inviting Nancy and me along on the date. I don't remember whether we went to a movie or what, but I do know that Nancy and I found ourselves in the backseat of Eddie's car on the way home. Eddie pulled up to a deserted spot on the road and he and Nancy's sister got out for a walk. There was an awkward silence as I was getting up my nerve to move over to the middle of the seat where Nancy was sitting. I awkwardly put my arm around her. She didn't seem to mind and looked up to me, so I had no choice but to initiate my first kiss. I knew it couldn't be just a little peck like the one I gave Mom and Dad before I went to bed as a child, so I did my best to imitate the kisses I had seen in the movies so many times, wondering how long I must hold it. I certainly wasn't completely satisfied with my technique but Nancy seemed not to mind. Fortunately, Eddie and Jane came back at about that time and I didn't have to worry about what to do next. Nancy and her sister left for home the next day and I never heard from her again. I had made a major step in my love life even though I didn't have nerve enough to follow up on it for quite a while.

I turned sixteen just before I graduated from the tenth grade and most kids at that age can't wait to get their drivers licenses. This certainly would include Frank, who could drive from the time he was 14 and was saving up to buy a car when he got his license. I seemed to be immune to this urge and might not have had any driving experience if it were not for my friend Roydon Pearson and the young man who was working for his dad on their ranch. My folks left me to stay with Roydon on a Saturday night as they often did when they went up to visit with Aunt Essie and my cousin Tommy Shepperd at the Table Mountain Ranch. Roydon, although three years younger, was already anxious to start driving his dad's 1941 Ford pickup. The hired man, Jack, Roydon and I were doing some chores in the pickup that weekend and, when we were out in the middle of the hay meadow, they decided it was time for me to learn to drive.

I got out and went around to the driver's side and they showed me how to start the pickup, put in the clutch and shift into first gear. I had watched Frank shift gears for my dad when he was about eight and I was five, but I still didn't know where the gears were. Roydon said that wasn't a problem because we could just drive around slowly in first for a while. Of course, the first time I let out the clutch, I killed the motor. They patiently explained that I had to carefully press on the gas pedal as I slowly let out the clutch. After killing the engine a couple more times, I managed to get going forward, but far too fast, and I didn't ease up on the gas pedal and we bounced across an irrigation ditch. They then explained just where which gear was and I spent some hair-raising moments learning to shift gears without killing the motor or running into another ditch. After about twenty or thirty minutes I could drive the pickup around in a circle over the flat, open meadow.

The next morning after breakfast, Roydon, Jack and I took the pickup to the Virginia Dale store to pick up the Sunday Denver Post. On the way home, when Jack reached the turnoff of Highway 287 into the Pearson ranch he pulled over after crossing the cattle guard and suggested I drive the rest of the way back to the ranch. I went around to the driver's seat, got behind the wheel, put the pickup in low gear, got off to a bumpy start down the road and managed to get the four-speed transmission finally shifted up to high gear. With all my concentration on manipulating the clutch and shifting gears, I was wandering all over the narrow gravel road. The last half of the road into the headquarters was down a long hill leading into the valley that Dale Creek ran through. I had never needed to apply the brake while driving on the level meadow. As gravity started to increase my speed against the fairly low compression the engine provided in fourth gear, Roydon and Jack yelled in unison that I needed to use the brakes. That thought had occurred to me, but my reflexes had not developed enough yet that my right foot knew where to find the brake pedal. By the time I did hit the brake I jammed it too hard and nearly ran off the road. Having almost stopped by that time, I had sense enough to ride the brake the rest of way down the hill and pulled up by the barn, which was some distance from the house, with the brakes smoking. Knowing that I had no business driving in the first place, we all agreed that Jack should drive the final distance to the house. When we came into the house we hoped we had not been noticed as we careened down the hill, which was visible from the kitchen window, but after Roydon's mother, Olive, offered us some lemonade, she observed that it wasn't necessary to drive so fast down the hill into the ranch. We didn't deserve to be let off so easy and I lost interest in driving once again.

Some of the improvements on the new farm from left: chicken house, rental house and farm home we all lived in. Parked out front are the folks little 1941 Studebaker and brother Charlie's 1934 Pontiac.

13

First Summer Job

I had been looking forward to a carefree summer in 1946, but I soon learned it was my turn to have a full-time summer job. Bill and Marie Brunel and their children had stayed with us in Lakewood when she and Bill were in Denver attending the stock show in the winter of 1945. During the several days they were there, we learned that they needed a cabin boy for their dude ranch and fishing lodge called French Creek Ranch and wondered if I might be interested. I had enjoyed working part-time for Aunt Essie at the old home place and at the Wooden Shoe Ranch, places Mom and Dad often visited in the summer. French Creek was much farther away and it was likely I would not see any of my family all summer if I worked there. Both of my brothers had worked full-time in the summers when they were 16 years old and I think my folks thought it would be good for me to do the same. We told Bill and Marie that we would think it over and let them know our decision well before their season started in the spring.

I thought it would be good for me to take the job, but I was sure I would be terribly homesick. Even the few days I stayed away from home previous summers, with people I knew much better than the Brunels, always brought on homesickness every night in bed. Neither of my brothers seemed to suffer from this problem and I considered it a personal weakness. Looking back, I know I certainly wasn't the only person to have this problem, but I surely had it worse than most. It is something that you can outgrow eventually but is agonizing to suffer through night after night, and I almost dreaded going to bed. Thankfully, each morning after I shut off the alarm and crawled out of bed at five o'clock to milk the cow and face another day, the previous night's loneliness quickly faded away, whether it was sunny or raining, and my usual optimistic outlook resurfaced.

I enthusiastically waded into my work. The previous year there had been two cabin boys, but only one of them returned, creating an opening for me. My partner was a boy named Pete

Peters whose folks owned a confectionery store in Greeley, Colorado called Peter's Popcorn. He was a husky, nice looking young man who had been a starting end on the Greeley football team. This really impressed me. We quickly became good friends as he showed me my new duties. We shared a room close to the resort's main lodge in a building that also had a one-room sleeping quarter for a man who was cutting poles for Bill in the national forest which surrounded us, and a room that housed the engine and generator that furnished electricity to Bill and Marie's house, the lodge and the washhouse.

There were about 10 three-room cabins and a couple with four rooms. They all had a small wood stove, an old-fashioned icebox and an outhouse in the rear. The only buildings with running water were the lodge, the owners' home where Bill and Marie lived and the laundry/bath house, which had an old-fashioned washing machine. It contained a stove with a water jacket for hot water and a bathtub along one wall with no partitions for privacy. Pete and I took a bath every Saturday night and gave Marie our dirty clothes Monday morning, which she and the hired girl washed along with the accumulation of sheets from the cabins and rooms in the lodge.

Pete and I were responsible for seeing that each cabin had a supply of firewood and a block of ice from the ice house, which had been filled with blocks cut by hand from a nearby lake the previous winter. The icehouse has been built into the side of a hill, with a double wall insulated with sawdust. The blocks of ice were packed in sawdust when they were stored. This is something I was well acquainted with because most ranchers put up ice in similar semi-caves every winter. Dad had put up ice in an old potato cellar on the ranch until we purchased our kerosene-operated Kelvinator refrigerator. It was amazing how long the blocks lasted, and even though there had been some melting by the end of the summer, they were still close to their average fifty-pound weight.

It took a lot of firewood for the fourteen or so cabins, the washhouse, Bill and Marie's home and the lodge. Most of the guests cooked their meals on the stove and found that the nights were cold enough at this altitude to need a fire. Pete and I kept busy most days just hauling wood and ice. Our high-tech mode of transport for these items was a wheelbarrow. One load was about the right amount for four of the fifty-pound blocks of ice or filling the wood box next to each stove. The distance from the woodpile and icehouse to the most remote cabin was several hundred yards. Between hauling the ice and splitting and hauling the wood we got a great deal of exercise every day and developed hearty appetites.

Using wood for cooking and heating is very labor intensive. About three times during the summer Bill took Pete and me out into the nearby national forest to cut dry, downed timber into eight-foot lengths with a two-man cross cut saw. Some of these logs were quite big and it took all three of us to carry them and lift them onto Bill's old one-and-a-half-ton truck. I was by far the smallest of the three of us but always did my share of the work. Sometimes my knees would buckle as we lifted the larger logs into the truck, but Bill and Pete picked up the slack for me. Bill was more than a little irritated that I had not learned how to drive yet because he wanted me to drive the truck occasionally.

I made up for my lack of a driver's license because Pete had no experience with ranch work. I did most of the irrigating on the meadows, which were both upstream and downstream from the lodge, and was responsible for maintaining the ditches that furnished the water. The water right that went with the ranch came out of French Creek, which ran through the property. One of the head gates from the stream was north of the ranch on Forest Service land, but the South Meadow had its gate right on French Creek just south of the buildings. Without a ditch cleaner, a common item on most irrigated ranches, I had to clean all the ditches by hand. By the end of a few days of shoveling I had a handful of blisters. When the summer was over these blisters had turned into some pretty hard calluses.

I actually had had very little experience irrigating and the meadows were far from level. Prior to the start of irrigating season Bill dragged a walking plow out to the meadow with the old John Deere and we did our best to create some small ditches to spread the water more evenly. Bill showed me how to operate a walking plow as he drove the tractor. I'll try to describe the process, but you have to be able to visualize what such a plow looks like to follow. When you drag the plow, you turn it over its right side, the part that throws up the furrow. When you want to start plowing you roll the plow upright and push down the handles so that the point won't go into the ground. When you want to start a furrow, you lift up on the handles to cause the point to dig in, then hold them level when it is at the depth you want. When you want to stop digging the furrow you throw it back over to the right and it comes out of the ground and drags along until you pick up the handles again. Obviously, this is a process that requires some experience and I was getting my experience on the job. After making a few unsightly unwanted furrows we hadn't planned, we finished the ones we had laid out and some even carried water to the desired spots. Unfortunately, a few of them ran uphill defying gravity. Even a good irrigator would've had his hands full on these meadows, but fortunately we had a wet spring and early summer and managed to grow a pretty good hay crop.

Bill had a #5 John Deere hay mower, which he pulled with his tractor when he started haying shortly after the Fourth of July. After he got the first meadow mowed, he said he would need me to rake it while he mowed the second meadow. He apologized profusely for the old dump rake that he had obtained when he bought the ranch, saying the dump mechanism did not function and as a result, I would have to operate it manually with the long handle situated on my right side as I sat on the rake. It took all my strength to operate the handle manually, making it very difficult to create straight windrows. Fortunately, by that time I could drive a team pretty well, but still found it hard to keep the horses going straight as I took the lines in one hand to reach back, grab the handle and pull it down past my knees to dump a load of hay. We then had to load the hay into an old hayrack and haul it back to the corral near the tack room. Pete helped with this job and I got a break as I drove the team after I showed him how to pitch the hay up on the hayrack.

Pete had a reputation for eating prodigious amounts of food. Marie joked that the previous summer there never were any leftovers, because when everyone else was through eating, Pete would clean out the serving dishes. With this good example, I ate heartily all summer. We ate in the kitchen at the lodge, getting the same food that was furnished to the guests in the dining room. The lodge itself had five or six bedrooms, which were more often fuller than the cabins, thus contributing to the need for a full-time cook. Bill and Marie raised their own beef and our diet was heavy on meat, potatoes and gravy, often followed by a good rich dessert, hopefully pie. A fringe benefit of our job was that Pete and I got to help the cook wash the dishes at night after a long hard day's work! The fact that Marie raised a garden that furnished fresh vegetables to our diet, adding balance to an otherwise high-calorie diet, likely contributed to my growing several inches taller and gaining at least twenty pounds that summer.

The summer had one rather sour note for Pete and me. After dinner in late summer Bill sat us down in our bunkhouse and let us know he wasn't happy with our work. He said we were too slow getting the wood and ice delivered and properly keeping up with chopping adequate amounts of wood. He said he was going to have to cut our salaries. I believe we were getting ninety dollars a month and he dropped it back to seventy-five. Pete and I were flabbergasted and visited late into the night about what to do. Our feelings were badly hurt and our first inclination was for both of us to just quit. He decided he couldn't do that because his girlfriend and her parents were coming up at the end of the summer for a week's vacation as they had done the year before, and he didn't want to jeopardize that. I certainly didn't want to call my folks to come up and get me. When I did call them later (collect) on the telephone in the lodge to tell them what had happened, they assured me I had done the right thing swallowing my pride and continuing to work.

Mom and Dad came up over the Labor Day weekend and stayed a couple of nights before we headed for the Fort Collins area to the farm that was to be my new home. Before we left, Marie counted out my full summer wages in cash and cashier's checks. There was no withholding in those days and I had received enough tips delivering ice and wood to the cabins to take care of my cash needs for the summer (about fifteen dollars). Marie never mentioned my reduction in salary but did comment that they had not made very much profit that summer. I had survived my first summer away from home and had what seemed to me a considerable amount of money in my pocket. I kept out enough to buy a pair of boots and gave the rest to my mom to put in their bank account, anticipating another major change in my life as I enrolled in a new school.

14

New School - Old Friend

While I was working up at French Creek I wrote my folks a letter about once a week and called them a couple times from the phone in the lodge. Mom was good about answering my letters and occasionally Dad added a note to one, so they had kept me posted on an impending change in Dad's office location. I did not know exactly what dad's new job with the USDA entailed, but I think it had to do with the distribution of surplus commodities collected by the USDA in connection with its price support programs, which involved among other things the school lunch program in Colorado. He had been notified in July that he would be transferred to Fort Collins, so the folks had decided to put the house in Lakewood on the market, move to Fort Collins and buy a small farm. The market was beginning to heat up in the Denver area and the house was soon sold for $15,000 which was $10,000 more than they had paid five years previously in 1941.

Dad managed to buy a forty-acre irrigated farm on a lane one-half mile west of Taft Hill Road near the Cache La Poudre River, for $14,000. The deal had been completed and the furniture moved to the house on the property by the time they brought me home from my summer job, just before school started. Mom and Dad gave me the option of attending either Cache La Poudre High in La Porte or Fort Collins High School. We were in the La Porte School District, but they said they would pay my tuition if I wished to attend Fort Collins High School. They thought Fort Collins had the better school system, but knew I would be more comfortable in the smaller school. I must admit the prospect of participating in athletics in a smaller school with a good prospect of making the varsity teams weighed on my decision. I was also aware that a couple of my friends, Raymond Nauta and Shirley MacGregor, from grade school days in Virginia Dale attended La Porte High School. Both had gone eight years to the little Virginia Dale log schoolhouse, but Robert Boyd and Billy Logan were also in my Virginia Dale class and they had opted to go to Fort Collins.

I have never regretted choosing La Porte because I had been right about the athletics and I was fortunate to have several very good teachers there.

After registering, I entered my first class and happily greeted my old friends, Ray and Shirley, whom I had seen from time to time when I visited Virginia Dale during the summers. Then as I looked around the room, whom should I see but my good friend from Lakewood, Gary Glick. We both did a double take and simultaneously said, "Where did you come from?" I told him about my dad being transferred to Fort Collins and our purchase of the farm on Taft Hill. It turned out that his father had leased or bought a farm on Shields Street about a mile north of Highway 287 and one mile east of Taft Hill Road. It was probably the happiest coincidence of my life, and knowing both Ray and Shirley, I was able to help him get acquainted.

The first person Ray introduced us to was a sandy-haired bundle of personality named Bozo Simianer. His real name was Harry but only his mother ever called him that. At noon, Ray drove Gary and me over to a nearby restaurant called Vern's place for lunch, where we ran into Bozo and his two step-brothers, Kent and Boyd Goodrich. Gary and I, while far from being goody two shoes, were amazed to see that both Ray and Bozo smoked, and we soon learned they had been doing so for years.

Gary and I were anxious to learn all we could about the football team and our prospects for making it. Both of our brothers, Ivan and Frank, had played for the state championship team in Lakewood, and La Porte had been the second team they met in the playoffs before Lakewood went on to win the championship, so we were aware that they must have some good athletes. Kent and Boyd joined us for lunch and we were amazed to learn that my brother, Frank, and Gary's brother, Ivan, had broken Kent's leg tackling him after he caught a pass during that game. Frank, a halfback, had hit Kent high and Ivan, a linebacker, hit him low. Frank of course wasn't too big, and not being on the first team, was in the game only because they were well ahead, but Ivan was a hard-hitting linebacker who later played on the varsity at CSU. It seems that Kent had played as a freshman on that conference champion team and was now a senior. Those were two amazing coincidences on my first day of school at La Porte. I was to have many more experiences, both good and bad, during my last two years of high school there.

After school that first day, Gary and I reported to the locker room in the basement of the three-story school building, which housed all 12 grades, to join the football team. I say joined rather than go out for football, because the school being so small, the team needed everybody it could get. The coach had just been hired along with his wife, who taught grade school. He was from Oklahoma and had the accent to prove it. I remember primarily being very nervous, because even though I had grown quite a bit the previous summer, I still wasn't all that big. I recall that I did not have an extremely good impression of the coach or the facilities compared to Lakewood's.

The boys' locker room was generally referred to as the boys' basement because it was the boys' toilet for the entire school. We did have decent lockers and good showers. It had an outdoor entrance at ground level. As I recall, that first afternoon the coach gave us a little talk, got the name and grade of the boys going out for football and some other vital statistics. He said we would get our uniforms and have our first practice the next afternoon.

Gary and I soon found that even though La Porte had most of the same required subjects as Lakewood, it didn't have enough teachers to provide some subjects except every other year. For example, I had to take physics with this senior class and biology with the sophomore class. Even then, we still couldn't get all the hours we needed or wanted and found ourselves having to take shorthand, which we hated. Mrs. Maxfield, whom everybody referred to as Georgie, took pity on us and agreed to teach us an English course we would eventually need, in her study hall. We were able to drop shorthand and make the switch, and I was forever grateful to Mrs. Maxfield for getting me out of that hated class. I believe half of the year was actually literature and the other half was advanced English. Gary wasn't t crazy about either and I very much liked both.

The necessity to take physics with the seniors and biology with the sophomores gave me an opportunity to get acquainted with both some of the older and younger students. I remember with particular fondness my physics teacher, Mr. Norton, because he was a teacher who could make a difficult subject like physics come alive. He was charismatic and also had a great singing voice.

La Porte had a unique tradition of jamming all twelve grades into the auditorium on the third floor on Monday morning for a short sing-along and sort of pep rally led by Mr. Norton. It turns out he was the pastor at one of the local churches and I only wish that I had had sense enough to attend it. Looking back, I realize it was nearly a miracle that such a fine teacher would be found at such a small school. Unfortunately, he was gone the next year and I never learned much if anything about his personal history.

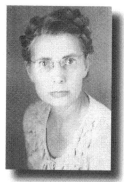

Mrs. Oberto

The class I took with the sophomores was taught by Mrs. Oberto who also taught history and chemistry and became another of my favorite teachers. Her teaching style was old school. She always told you exactly what she expected you to know, which included a lot of memorizing. Her tests were difficult but fair and I always felt that the foundation she laid prepared me for the more sophisticated lectures one receives from the professors in college. I remember sitting in the back of the room in biology class next to a sophomore named Robert Martin, who would later become a close friend. I had a pocket watch with a sweep second hand and I would hold it down between us and we would surreptitiously take turns holding our breath. I have no idea what got us started doing that and it was certainly disrespectful to a teacher we both liked. We never got caught and within a few days were both holding our breaths for nearly a minute.

Mrs. Maxfield

When Gary and I reported for football practice the second day of school, after a brief speech the new coach passed out uniforms. A small school like La Porte couldn't afford new uniforms often, and when they did get them they purchased only enough for the starters and a few top substitutes. The coach probably knew who the top players were from the previous year and had a pretty good idea who his best players might be. After he gave the new uniforms to these returning players, Gary, who used to be almost as small as I was but had zoomed past me in stature the past couple of years, was among those getting the rest. Although I had grown a good bit the previous summer, my skinny body and glasses, along with a demeanor that didn't shout confidence guaranteed me one of the old uniforms.

We had a lot of rain that fall and our dirt football field was a muddy mess a good bit of the early season. Our coach was of the opinion that the best way to deal with this adversity was to run us all out on the field and immediately slide on our bellies while going full speed. He said we might as well get used to the dampness and cold right away. I'm not saying he was wrong, but we got our uniforms washed only just before games, and it made for a lot of dirty lockers when we hung them up after practice.

Neither Gary nor I had played football as sophomores in Lakewood. Wrestling had been added as a varsity sport for the first time that year and Gary chose that; I had been on the junior varsity basketball team. So we didn't have a lot of experience working with a football coach. I knew enough to be flabbergasted to learn that the quarterback drew up the plays in the huddle as if we were playing sandlot football and the linemen worked out who blocked whom between themselves each play. We did have some good athletes and they had played together a lot, so we started the season with high expectations

At the first practice, the coach asked the returning players what positions they had played last year and the freshman and few new players what positions they would like to play. Figuring I didn't have a chance in the backfield I suggested I might play guard. Since we had barely enough people to field twenty-two players to scrimmage, I got to practice every day. I was quick enough to occasionally run a player down from behind on defense, but I didn't have a clue how to block on offense. Gary quickly earned a spot as starting fullback in the T-formation that coach Welsh installed. I was really too small for any position on the line and probably should have gone out for end rather than guard because I might have been able to beat out a senior who started. I was much faster than he was and could catch passes better.

It soon became apparent that I would be more useful as a reserve halfback than a reserve lineman, but I did get to play one down at guard when we kicked an extra point in our first game, which was against Lafayette. We won by one point and the margin of victory came from a pass on the old sleeper play where a player went to the sideline just inbounds between downs, and if everything worked, was all by himself for a pass play. I remember that the pass went to Harold Gardner, who was not only the best player on the team but probably the best athlete in the school. Jim Ackleson, the quarterback, threw him a perfect pass and no one had a chance to catch Harold as he scored. The fans at Lafayette, which was the home team, went wild, but in accordance with the rules, our coach had informed the referees that we might use that play and the score stood.

I don't remember any of our other games that year but I enjoyed scrimmaging everyday against the varsity. I recall at one practice the varsity called a trick play called Goofus or some such thing, which had been carried over from the previous year. They came up to the line of scrimmage with the center, my friend Bozo, lined up at the end, making him an eligible receiver. The deception worked and as Bozo raced by the defensive backs Jim threw him a perfect pass. Bozo had told me about this play, which was his only opportunity as a center to make a touchdown. When I saw Jim dropping back to pass I immediately turned around and took after Bozo. I dove at him, barely catching one of his toes as I fell on my face and he went down. It might have been the only time Bozo ever got mad at me.

The only other things I remember clearly from that football season are three painful but not very serious injuries. Somehow, I sprained my wrist badly enough that the coach taped it every day for a couple of weeks. It was bad enough that I had it x-rayed and the doctor said that I had caused a couple of bones in my wrist to separate, bones that were in the process of fusing at my age. I also sprained my thumb trying to make a tackle and it needed taping for a couple of weeks. My third injury was a badly sprained ankle caused by trying to change direction quickly when a runner I was trying to tackle juked me. Oddly enough, by the time the season ended I had decided I really liked football.

Robert, Harold's brother Maynard and I became great friends during my junior year and I remained close to both of them through my sophomore year of college at CSU in Fort Collins. I came to fully appreciate Robert's tremendous grit only in hindsight years later. I'm afraid we all took for granted the fact that he had Type I Diabetes and had to give himself a blood test and insulin shot every day. I stopped by his house quite often and many times watched him very matter-of-factly draw his blood with a syringe, test it and then inject himself with the appropriate amount of insulin. He never asked for any special treatment, nor did I ever hear him complain.

Robert and his brother Willard, who was a senior, were both very intelligent and well-mannered. I learned that their father, Fred, and Mother were both full-blooded Germans, which surprised me because they both had quite dark complexions. Their farm was leased on shares from Clarence Curry, who also had a large ranch up in Livermore. My brothers and I often provided day labor to Fred for things like shoveling manure out of his corrals. On those days, Mrs. Martin fed us dinner, the noon meal. She was a wonderful cook and always had meat and potatoes, gravy, two or three vegetables, several side dishes including homemade pickles, and pie or something equally good for dessert.

Some of the improvements on the new farm from left: chicken house, rental house, and farm home we all lived in. Parked out in front are the folks' little 1941 Studebaker and brother Charlie's 1934 Pontiac.

15

Questionable Behavior

I was anxious for basketball practice to start after the football season ended. I felt I would have a much better chance to make the varsity team in this sport, but I didn't go to the first practice the least bit overconfident. I had been told that Harold Gardner was probably the best player on last year's team and that Jim Ackelson and the Maxwell twins had also been starters. I was quite confident that Gary Glick would be a starter so I would have to work hard to make the starting five. Our old school house didn't have a gymnasium, so our school district leased a gym in a building that housed the Sunday school classes for the Methodist church about two blocks east of school on Highway 287. When Gary and I walked over after school to report for our first basketball practice, we were far from impressed with what we saw. The gym was a good deal smaller than the smallest at any school in the suburban conference I had played in while in Lakewood. The center jump ring was not too many feet from the keyhole on either end of the court. There was a line from side to side about ten feet on either side of what should have been a centerline to delineate the area the offensive team had to work with without getting a backcourt violation. There was just enough room on either side for the person inbounding the ball to stand and the backboards were fastened to the walls at either end. There was a wrestling mat attached to the wall under the basket to crash into on fast breaks. I soon learned to shoot a layup with my off leg extended to further protect myself. There were no bleachers, only a narrow balcony all the way around the gym with about two rows of seats. It was a good gymnasium for a zone defense.

Our first game was against Wellington and the starters on the varsity team were expected to be Gary at center, Jim Ackelson and Bozo at guard, and Harold Gardner as one of the forwards. We didn't know who the last starter would be until after the end of the junior varsity game, in which I played two quarters. Much to my surprise Coach Welsh started me as the second forward with

Harold. We were ahead at the half, and as we lined up for the jump ball at the beginning of the third quarter, the Wellington coach stopped the game and pointed out that anyone playing in the junior varsity two quarters could play only another two quarters in the varsity game. I believe that if I hadn't done so well in the junior varsity game, Welsh wouldn't have considered starting me as he had not paid much attention to me during practice. It was all rather embarrassing to me at least and should have been for Coach Welsh.

The left-handed Maxwell twin started the second half of the varsity game in my position, the left forward, and I think we went on to win. I never played in another junior varsity game and started all the rest of the varsity games that year except for a couple when I was sick. I was quite sick with what we thought was the flu during part of the Christmas vacation and at least two more weeks after school started again. As I recall, we won one and lost one of those games that I missed, but we still ended the season tied with Estes Park for our conference championship. My first game back from my illness was the playoff game with Estes Park at the nice, big—at least to us--Longmont school gymnasium. I didn't start the game because I had missed so much practice and was really out of shape. We were behind at halftime, but had been holding our own with them pretty well.

Coach Welsh put me in the game at the beginning of the second half. I had a burst of energy from adrenaline and it seemed that my enthusiasm and the half-court pressure applied by Harold Gardner and me got us back in the game. I stole the ball a couple of times and passed to Harold for easy lay-ups. A bit later I intercepted a pass at half-court and drove toward the basket at full-speed in preparation for a lay-up that I ordinarily made quite easily. As I took that last hard step toward the basket my left leg buckled; the defender running down the floor behind me ran over me and I was awarded two free throws. I was probably the only one in the gym who realized I really had not been fouled, including the guy who ran over me. I had no idea what caused my knee to give way.

I may have made one of my free throws, but probably not, because I was a terrible free throw shooter. I was completely out of breath and the coach took me out of the game for a few minutes.

I lay on the floor panting. By this time, we had gotten a few points ahead of them and as the lead changed again the coach put me back in. I don't know if I scored any more points, but the game went down to the last play. We lost the game and the opportunity to go to the district playoffs. I had never been so tired in my life and looking back I had no business playing after such a long illness. The good news is that I seemed to have no ill effects and finished the school year in pretty good health.

My parents never liked the idea that we had to practice basketball at night after supper instead of after school. This was required because the gym at the church was only available at that time. It was drafty and hard to heat and the locker room itself was heated with a coal stove with a water jacket heating our shower water. There were small wooden lockers, and although the janitor usually started the fire before practice or games, we had to keep the fire going ourselves. The crowded facility was usually quite dirty from the coal dust. We each had to take our towels and gym clothes home when they needed to be laundered, which most of us didn't do often enough. After practice, we showered and stuffed everything into our small lockers. The next night we would find not only our towels but our gym clothes damp and wrinkled. This seems to be something that the school had taken for granted for years, but I was amazed that at least the coach didn't complain to the school board. It seems everyone simply accepted that this was the way things were. We made our shower available to visiting teams, but I don't remember any of them taking us up on the offer.

None of the rest of the schools in our conference had regulation gyms either, so we took our facilities in stride and made the best of them. We played a 2-3 zone defense and Gary, who was a great rebounder, really covered the middle under the basket. Often after he had cleared the board, I would take off on a dead run and he would simply lob the ball toward the other basket so I could run under it, take one dribble, make a lay-up or pass off to Harold in the right corner for an easy shot. I learned to shoot fast break lay-ups on a dead run and come to a screeching halt as I hit the mat on the wall.

Unfortunately, coach Welsh had only a rudimentary knowledge of the fundamentals of basketball, let alone the fine points. He always said that where he came from in Oklahoma they played a very slow game and he insisted that we stall whenever we got the lead. Our natural tendency was to run and we ignored him as much as we could get away with. Still, he was the coach and when we had just a few points lead and slowed down our game, we lost our momentum and gave hope to our opponents. Our main competition in the conference were Wellington, Waverley, and Estes Park, and all played aggressive man-to-man defense and a deliberate half-court offense on our part just played into their hands. Still, as I've already indicated, we managed to tie for first place in our conference and nearly won the playoff game to qualify for district.

All of my good friends were on the basketball team, and I'm afraid our bad relationship with, and lack of respect for, our coach helped all of us to develop bad attitudes, which were reflected in a serious lack of respect for authority. I had never had this problem in the past, but then I had never had a teacher or coach who seemed to know less than I did about the things he was supposed to be teaching. He was certainly no inspiration for building character. Once, when we were playing Waverley, their best player was giving us fits and the coach instructed Bozo to throw the ball right into his face when in-bounding the ball. Unfortunately, Bozo followed his instructions and when the ball hit the other player's nose, snot flew in all directions and Bozo was kicked out of the game. I think we still managed to win but probably didn't deserve to. I didn't know until after the game that coach Welsh had so instructed Bozo and I don't think the coach realized Bozo would comply with such enthusiasm.

I was very fortunate that, when we moved to La Porte, I was already well acquainted with some of the students and had a longtime good friend in Gary there. I seemed to be well accepted by all my classmates so I didn't really need a Jerry Weinberger or Jerry Lincoln. Still, I found myself fascinated by Harold Gardner, who appeared to me to be the coolest guy I had ever seen. Looking back, a darker "Fonz" could have been modeled after Harold. He was about the same size and was better looking and better built. He was the best football player, the best basketball player and the fastest runner in school. The girls were all crazy about him, as far as I knew, and the teachers cut him more slack than he probably deserved, even to the extent of one loaning her car to him from time to time.

Harold was cool, not in the modern sense of the word, but in the literal sense. Everyone admired him and sought his attention, but he never really got close to anyone. One of the first days at school my junior year I suffered a tradition of initiation, common in those days for boys like me who tried too hard to please. While I was waiting for school to start with a large group of students in front of the school, several boys led by Harold surrounded me and pulled my pants down around my knees. The observers were all shouting, "Pants him, pants him." Seeing that I was so badly outnumbered, I put up a rather feeble resistance, thanking the Lord that my underwear didn't come down with my pants. I was afraid they would pull my pants clear off and run and hide with them, but when they stopped at my knees and backed off and everyone started clapping, I realized I had passed some sort of initiation ritual. My sense of dignity was offended, but my desire to be accepted caused me to grin and bear it. I quickly learned that this wasn't Lakewood, where such an activity would never have been tolerated in the schoolyard.

I certainly can't blame Harold for my bad behavior during much of my junior year; however, I had reached a point in my life where, for the first time, I was in a position to test the values that I had always honored. For a period, I quite readily rationalized behaviors that had the potential to seriously change the trajectory of my life, although many of the things we did were little different from any group of rowdy boys at that age might have done. We experimented with drinking, and Gary and I both tried to start smoking—unsuccessfully—although all of our friends already did.

One of the more popular beer joints in town, Sol's and Dick's, had a pool hall in the back with an entrance on the alley. Fort Collins served only 3.2 beer and the drinking age was eighteen. We juniors were mostly sixteen and many of the seniors were still seventeen, but they didn't check IDs in the pool hall when they took beer orders. I'm pretty sure I had my first glass or two of dime beer there while I was trying to learn to shoot pool. Bozo and Harold took their pool quite seriously and most often played snooker. When all the snooker tables were filled, they played eight-ball or rotation and I occasionally joined them. Robert Martin and Maynard Gardner, both sophomores, often went to town with us on rainy Saturdays when they didn't have farm work to do at home and I enjoyed playing eight-ball with them. I got to be a mediocre pool player quite fast and managed to stay at that level the rest of my life.

We also spent a lot of time driving up and down College Avenue and usually checked out the drive-in to see if there were some unattached girls there that somebody knew. We often saw some of the Fort Collins town toughs hanging around and Harold was always trying to instigate some trouble with them because he considered himself quite a fighter. I rather think I was not the only one of our group who hoped he didn't succeed because it was generally understood that if one of us got into a fight, the rest of us had to be ready to participate if need be. Fortunately, this never came to pass when I was around.

Occasionally when one of the cars or farm pickups we were driving got low on gas, we would siphon some from a car parked in the middle of a dark street in a residential district. One time someone mentioned that he needed a towel to shower with after basketball practice so we slipped into a backyard and got a couple off of a clothesline. I now realize that what probably motivated us to do these silly things was the adrenaline rush created by the fear of getting caught. Fortunately, adrenaline was the only drug available because we had all become addicted.

With the enthusiasm we had for life, alcohol would have seemed to be the last thing we needed, but obtaining and consuming it was another way to defy authority, and unfortunately there were often older guys who seemed to enjoy purchasing it for us. We did have the good sense to have an understanding that the person furnishing the car when we were out drinking would not indulge. Among our group, Gary and I were the only ones who had really never had any experience with alcohol and our first one ended up very badly for each of us. One night I drank far too much and got sick, and another night Gary did the same and got even sicker.

I have a suspicion that about this time my older brothers, who were never angels themselves, decided my behavior was getting out of hand and told Dad what they knew about what was going on. He immediately gave me a midnight curfew for Saturday night and said that on other nights I had to be in by ten, basketball practice or not. I was already suffering a certain amount of shame at breaking the faith my parents had always shown in me. I had always done what my dad told me to do even though I probably tried to manipulate my more trusting mother from time to time. I didn't know the relationship my friends had with their parents, but I do recall how strange it seemed to me when they exchanged ideas about what lies they could tell to them when we came home after midnight. About a week after Dad laid down the law, I rode into town with my friends about 11:30, when we usually headed home. They decided to sneak into the Lyric theater for the midnight show. I protested that I had to be home by midnight and they said something equivalent to "tough luck." I walked all the way home, about three miles or so, getting there well after midnight. Dad probably thought we had driven in with the lights off, but when I told him I had walked all the way he told me it was a good thing that I had and perhaps I should give some thought to choosing better friends.

Sometime in January I mentioned to my friends that I had enjoyed going to the Denver National Western Livestock show when I lived in Lakewood. Harold said that the previous year several of them had gone to the event and spent the night sleeping with the cattle in the stockyards. For some reason, this seemed like a good idea to me. On one weekend during the stock show when we had no basketball game, Harold, Maynard, Robert, Gary and I headed for Denver when school let out Friday afternoon. I had enough money for a bus ticket, but we decided to hitchhike. We got to Denver just before dark, having had good luck getting a ride from a party who was willing to drop us off at the stockyards. Harold said we could sneak into the grounds and find a fairly warm place to sleep with the livestock. This turned out to be a pipe dream because after we walked all the way around the facility twice, we found no way to get in. By this time, it was dark and getting cold and we needed to find shelter. The best we could do was slip into a vacant boxcar at a siding that ran along the fence on the west side of the showground. We had nothing with us except the clothes on our backs and spent a long sleepless night listening to the trains go by while we shivered in the cold.

At first light the next morning, we walked over to a 24-hour restaurant on Washington Avenue a few blocks away from our boxcar. While we warmed up and ate a hearty breakfast, we planned our next move. Having lost interest in the stock show, I suggested we walk downtown and check out the excellent western store on the sixth floor of the Denver Dry Goods Company at 16th and California in downtown Denver. We arrived at the store shortly after it had opened and took the elevator up to the sixth floor. I had been on this floor many times with my mother or brothers. They had an excellent saddle maker; in fact, they had made Dad's saddle. There was a complete stock of western and work clothes and boots, as well as any tack a rancher might need. We browsed around for about an hour and left without purchasing anything. When we got back on the street I noticed that Harold was wearing a brand-new pair of engineer's boots in place of the moccasins he had on when we entered the store. I was flabbergasted and embarrassed. I'm sure I was not the only one of us who noticed this but no one said anything. We walked around the city for another couple of hours before walking to the edge of town and hitchhiking back home. I finally realized that Harold had a serious problem, the extent of which I was to learn only a few years later.

My teachers had taken note of my lack of effort and I think had gotten word of some of our more egregious activities after basketball practice. I had continued to get straight A's in the fall of my junior year, but on my six-weeks report card just before Christmas vacation, I found two A's had been erased and replaced with B's. Mrs. Oberto who taught chemistry and Mrs. Maxfield who taught English had evidently gotten their heads together and agreed to the changes. This resulted in my having to take the final exams at the end of the year. It was probably one of the best things that ever happened to me, but I surely didn't appreciate it at the time

Each year the La Porte high school juniors and seniors put on a play. The juniors produced theirs between football and basketball season and the seniors put on theirs between basketball and track season. Mrs. Oberto was the junior class sponsor and as such was responsible for directing our junior play. The play she had chosen was called, "The Absent-Minded Professor," popular with school productions around the country. Gary and I decided to try out for it and I ended up getting the part of the professor. I don't remember too much about the play, but we enjoyed getting acquainted with a new group of students during after-school practice. I would never have gotten my lines memorized without my mom's usual good help. The play was held on the stage in the auditorium on the third floor of the high school and was well attended. La Porte was very good at turning out for events like this, as well as football and basketball games.

In the spring, I reluctantly went out for track. Ever since my knee had buckled during the basketball playoffs with Estes Park, my left leg had continued to be somewhat weak. At the first track practice, this became evident when, as I tried to broad jump as I always had, taking off on my left foot, and found I just couldn't anymore. During football season, I had been one of the fastest runners on the team with the exception of Harold Gardner, and now quite a few people could outrun me in the dashes. I decided to try the quarter-mile, which my two brothers had successfully run in high school, but found out that the Maxwell twins and at least two others could outrun me, making any chance at the mile relay remote. So, I decided to try the half-mile, and in the first tryout I was bound and determined to win. I led after the first lap and managed to stay in the lead. I was running out of gas toward the end, but somehow managed to put on a kick and barely beat one of the sophomores. I was gasping for air and my lungs were burning. We ran laps every day but I couldn't seem to get into shape and soon the sophomore, one of the Drigger twins, was outrunning me regularly in practice.

Spring was in the air and I was sick of track, so I decided to quit, much to the disappointment of both the coach and my friends on the track team. I still watched them practice and went to all of the track meets. For some reason, I never told my folks about the lack of strength in my left leg and I never wondered why it had come on so suddenly. It occurred to me only a good many years later that I might have had a mild case of polio instead of the flu during my long sick spell that winter. The polio epidemic was at its height at this time. I had plenty of opportunities to be exposed at a time when my resistance was probably low thanks to our night practice, filthy shower room and lack of sleep.

16

Trail Creek Dude Ranch

When school let out, I decided to stay home and work on the farm, get up to Virginia Dale from time to time to help Frank work with Tommy at the ranch and possibly visit with some of my friends occasionally.

In early June, I suggested to my neighbors to the north and south, Robert and Maynard, that we take a ride up to the foothills west of the farm. Horsetooth Reservoir was being built at that time and, in a year or two, the area we would travel to get to our destination would be covered with water. Harold decided to come along too and rode his own horse. I was able to furnish a horse and saddle for Robert and Maynard. Since we had brought all of our horses to the farm, including our three half Arab mares, Robert and Maynard rode Buck and Ginger and I rode Zaida.

Mom fixed lunches for us and we headed out about mid-morning. We rode west on Vine Drive to Overland Trail, both dirt roads, and proceeded on west across pasture-land through one of the natural cuts in the uplift that would be the eastern shore of Horsetooth. This cut had not been filled yet and after we rode through it we could see Caterpillar tractors and Euclid earth movers at work on the roads surrounding the proposed reservoir, using a lot of dirt from what would become its bottom. I have been told that this was one of the first major projects in the nation that had used these big Euclid earth movers, often pushed with D-8 Cats. They looked huge to us, but by today's standards would seem quite small. We crossed the soon-to-be-flooded valley and rode up the steep foothills on the west side into some beautiful ponderosa pine country. We tied up our horses, enjoyed our lunch and then rode around the mountains exploring country that resembled the Table Mountain Ranch. We headed back in time to make it home for supper.

A while later Bob Swan, a rancher from Livermore, whom my folks knew quite well and I knew vaguely from a visit to the ranch when I was quite young, showed up at the farm. It was a weekend and Dad was home helping us get started with our first alfalfa cutting. We stopped work and invited Bob into the house for some lemonade. It turned out that in addition to managing Trail Creek Ranch at the confluence of Trail Creek and the North Fork of the Cache La Poudre River, he leased the facilities where he and his wife, Ruby, operated a dude ranch. He explained that he needed a combination ranch hand and dude wrangler and wondered if any of the Lilley boys were available. Frank was planning to work at the Table Mountain Ranch again and Charlie was going to stay home, work on our small farm and compete in local rodeos riding saddle broncs. That left me as the only prospect, and frankly, Bob had one of my older brothers in mind when he came to see us. The folks said we would all talk about it and get back in touch with him. I knew I didn't want to be a cabin boy as I had been the previous year at French Creek, and the fact that Trail Creek was a working ranch as well as a dude ranch made the prospect more appealing.

I soon contacted Bob and told him I would be interested in the job and gave him some background on my previous working experience. He offered me the job on the spot and said he would like me to come to work a week or two before the Fourth of July when their guest season picked up. I said I would take the job and when he said the salary would be $115 per month, I was delighted, because it seemed like a lot of money after getting a dollar a day working up at the ranch with Frank in the hay field and $75 a month at French Creek. Bob said he would pick me up when he came to town shopping in about two weeks

On the appointed day, Bob picked me up in a nearly new 1946 black half-ton Ford pick-up owned by the ranch. It was the first new model that Ford had made since the war ended and it was a lot fancier than the last models they had made in 1941, the one I had learned to drive at the Pearson ranch. Bob had loaded the bed of the pickup with ranch supplies and tied it down with a tarp, so I threw my suitcase into the front seat beside us. We drove north on Highway 287 to the Cherokee Park Road, which was a graded, narrow, but well-maintained dirt road. We continued northwest on it for about twenty miles, crossing the North Fork of the Cache La Poudre River, gaining about 1000 feet of elevation going up Calloway Hill and another 1000 feet as we wound our way through the foothills. We passed several ranch buildings and crossed a couple of small streams as Bob gave me a running commentary on who lived where and the names of the creeks and landmarks. The last ranch house we passed was close to a pile of granite rocks which the locals called Chimney Rock. Bob said this was the lower ranch of the holdings of Dick Brackenberry, for whom he worked, and that the dude ranch referred to as Trail Creek Ranch was actually Dick's upper place. In the days to come I would learn a great deal more about this beautiful 17,000-acre combination sheep, cattle and dude ranch and the agreement Bob had with Dick to work as a ranch manager and lessor of the improvements at Trail Creek.

When we arrived at the ranch in late afternoon, Bob took me into the house and introduced me to his wife, Ruby, and seven-year-old daughter, Iris Anne. I had met Bob and Ruby on the visit I made with my parents about the time Iris was a baby. She had grown into a somewhat shy and very pretty little girl. I felt right away that I would be comfortable living with this family. I also met Ann Harper, who was Ruby's hired girl. I learned that she was majoring in music at what is now the University of Northern Colorado in Greeley and working to pay her way through college. Ann was the person who taught me to appreciate classical music.

After Bob and I had carried the groceries into the house and the 100-pound sacks of oats into the barn, Ruby told me to get my suitcase and she would show me where I would be sleeping. I followed her down some stairs from the kitchen and found a narrow bed pushed against the wall in the corner of the basement. There was a little table by the bed to set my things on and a small dresser for my clothes. The basement smelled a little musty as basements will, but it was quite clean. I had told Bob I could milk a cow and he said I would have the opportunity to do so. I noticed a cream separator in a corner of the basement and saw some stairs leading through the south wall to a sloping outside door much like one might find in a storm cellar in tornado country.

Bob joined Ruby and me by means of the outside cellar door and said we had better get the cow milked before supper. He grabbed a shiny three-gallon milk pail from its peg on the wall and led me across a footbridge over the river leading to the shed that covered the stanchion where I would be milking the cow. He took the lid off of a fifty-gallon barrel and measured out about a gallon of oats, which he placed in the feeder in the stanchion. He yelled, "Come boss," and a good-sized red-roan cow appropriately named Roanie walked up, put her head into the stanchion and started munching contentedly. I closed the stanchion, grabbed a three-legged stool setting nearby, sat down and soon the bucket was half-full of frothy milk.

We carried the milk back to the cellar and Bob showed me how to strain it into the stainless-steel bowl mounted on top of the separator. I had no problem with this because it was something I had done for years on the farm. After separating the cream, Bob took it to the kitchen and told me to throw the skim milk into the creek. He said they kept the morning milk for drinking, and since they had no calves or pigs to give the skim milk to, they fed it to the fish. The milk cow was left in the corral at night because the weeds caused a bad flavor in the milk during the summer, but it did not show up in the morning milk, nor ever in the cream.

As there were no guests at the ranch, Bob kept me busy either helping him put in a new shower in the upstairs bathroom or doing routine ranch work. I learned later he had an agreement with the ranch owner to pay me for working with the cattle, building fence or helping with haying, and he would pay me for the dude ranch work. Bob was a true Jack-of-all-trades and I learned a lot from him. I enjoyed the wide range of work I did and had only two jobs that were truly boring, one for Bob and one for Ruby. On rainy days, I would don a yellow slicker and either hoe Ruby's large vegetable garden or peel corral poles for Bob. The latter job involved selecting a sixteen-foot-long by three- to five-inch diameter lodge pine pole out of a pile on a nearby hillside, placing it across two sawhorses, sitting astride it and peeling off the bark with a draw-knife. This was a sharp blade with handles placed at a 90° angle at both ends, which you pulled toward yourself to shave the bark off the poles. This job was best done when the poles were wet. I spent many a dreary day peeling poles, but it was better than hoeing the garden.

I particularly enjoyed looking after the cattle. The ranch had a permit from the Forest Service to graze 100 head from May through late September on about 3600 acres of beautiful, rugged land just across the road north of the headquarters. It was bordered on the south by the north fork of the Cache La Poudre River and on the east by a small tributary called Mill Creek, which joined the river right at a granite outcropping called Turkey Roost.

One of the first things that Bob and I did after I started work was put out salt for the cattle. We put packsaddles on three small mules and hung panyards, somewhat similar to saddle bags, on either side of the pack saddles. We put two fifty-pound blocks of salt in each panyard, a load of 200 pounds for each mule. Bob tied down the panyards with a length of rope using what he called a squaw hitch. We mounted our horses and Bob tied one of his mules to another's tail and led the other. I led the third.

The salt served two purposes. First, it was a necessary part of the cattle's diet and second, by placing it in strategic areas well separated from each other in the grazing permit, it helped keep the cattle spread out. The salt licks, as these locations were called, were placed at least a half mile away from any water, thus keeping the cattle scattered to result in the desired uniform use of grass. This project took most of a day, gave me an opportunity to get acquainted with the topography and learn the trails that led into this very beautiful but steep, rocky country with some scattered and some heavy timber. Often when there were no dudes to take riding, Bob sent me out to check on the cattle and fences. At these times, since I wasn't chattering with the dudes, I had the best opportunity to see the mule deer that frequented the area. These beautiful animals are my favorite among all the wild creatures that God created.

In the summer cattle are greatly bothered by flies of several species and they expend a lot of energy trying to find relief from them. There were several products on the market that had been developed to control flies but they were not very long-lasting nor were they easy to apply. During World War II, DDT was developed and it proved to be very effective in controlling the mosquitoes that carry malaria. Soon after the war it was demonstrated to be extremely effective and long-lasting as an insect spray. Ranchers were quick to take advantage of this new product and twice during the summer we brought the cattle down to the ranch and used a small engine-driven power unit to spray the cattle with it in small pens in the corral. Usually we did this when we had several guests at the ranch because they loved participating in real ranch work.

After we gathered the cattle and had them in the corral across the bridge from the ranch house, we sorted about 15 cows and calves at a time into a smaller corral where we soaked them thoroughly with the spray composed of powdered DDT that had been thoroughly mixed with water in the proper proportions. In those days, we had very little idea of the possible dangers to human health posed by DDT and I recall getting quite damp with the spray before the day was over, as did several other people helping.

Brackenbury ran two bands of sheep on the Ranch in addition to the 100 cows. A band is approximately 1000 head of ewes, and usually a sheepherder can handle two bands by himself with the help of a good dog. The sheep were wintered at the lower ranch and lambed out in April and May in an area just north of the lower ranch headquarters. This consisted of rolling hills and scattered timber with lots of good protection from the elements and excellent winter grass, which had been saved from the previous summer for that purpose. I knew little if anything about the sheep operation, but over the time I worked at the ranch I learned that the two bands of sheep grazed between early July and mid-September on a U.S. Forest grazing permit fairly high on the mummy range just south of the South Fork of the Poudre River. During the rest of the year the sheep ranged over most of the ranch except the large area north of the upper ranch where the cows summered. The cows also wintered and were calved out at the lower ranch on meadows not far from where the sheep were at lambing time. The cows and sheep never ran on the same land at the same time because sheep prefer weeds and browse and cattle much prefer grass. Contrary to Western lore, sheep and cattle are quite compatible on the same ranch and the combination of both uses the range most efficiently.

Much of the ranch had lots of mountain mahogany, also referred to as buck brush, and other shrubs growing primarily on the south slopes of the steeper hills and it was ideal country for both sheep and deer. The north slopes of the rougher foothills had dense stands of ponderosa pine, spruce, and conifer as well as lodge pole pine at the highest elevations. The timbered slopes and areas with large outcroppings of granite provided little if any forage, but good shelter.

I did have one very unusual experience with the sheep. I can't remember just what year it was but it was before the sheep left the ranch for the summer range. The herder had them up on

Prairie Divide at the far southwestern part of the ranch on the road to Red Feather Lakes. Bob had sent me up to that area to fix some fence. As I was riding up a steep narrow canyon that was the shortcut to Prairie Divide, I found a saddle horse standing on the other side of the gate that led into the ranch pasture. I recognized the mare as a horse that had been furnished to the sheepherder. I left the mare at the gate and hurried on up the canyon to where the country opened up to the broad expanse that gave Prairie Divide its name and found the sheep scattered all over the place and no sheepherder in sight.

I rode around until I found the sheep wagon and then spent about forty-five more minutes looking for the herder with no success. I decided I had better get back to the ranch and get some help, so I trotted back down to the gate where I had left the mare and led her back. It was getting late in the afternoon by this time and Bob was home. He immediately picked up a neighbor or two and drove up to the divide to search for the missing sheepherder.

When I got up the next morning I learned that after looking for a couple of hours with the pickup lights, Bob had given up the search but was heading back up there immediately after breakfast. He instructed me to ride up and start helping to round up the sheep, which were now badly scattered. After about an hour's ride, when I topped out at the divide, I started finding small bunches of sheep all over the place. Sheep have a natural herding instinct but are not used to being handled by someone on horseback. I did manage to get the little groups together because they were quite insecure and as soon as one bunch sighted another they would quite readily come together. By day's end, we had most of the herd back together but still didn't know what had happened to the missing sheepherder. A new one had arrived to look after the sheep.

When I got back to the ranch late that afternoon I learned that the sheepherder had been found and was told the whole amazing story. It seems that as they were searching in a rocky area in the middle of the pasture they found an unnatural line drawn in the sand. They followed it a short distance and located the sheepherder sitting against a big rock. He had a badly broken leg, which he had laid over his good leg as he dragged himself backwards, thus leaving the strange trail. The trail in the dirt back from the spot where the herder was found led to an old barbed wire fence with the wires hanging to the ground in places. Evidently the sheepherder had come to the downed fence on horseback and after dismounting, had hooked his elbow through the single rein of the bridle and tried to lead his horse over the downed wire. Horses hate barbed wire and as soon as the mare saw it she reared back, pulling the herder over sideways. As luck would have it his foot was in a crack between the rocks and as he fell sideways his leg broke. In the process, the mare took off in the direction of home, stopping when it arrived at the gate where I found her the day before.

I never had any more experiences with the sheep, but I did help Bob load and then haul the huge sacks of wool that were stored in the shed at the ranch to Fort Collins. I learned from Bob that the ranch received about the same amount of income from the wool as it did from the sale of its calves, and when you added the sale of the fat lambs when they came off the pasture in the high country, it was obvious that it made more gross income from sheep than it did cattle.

On the Sunday before school started in early September, Mom and Dad came up to the ranch to pick me up and Bob wrote two checks for my entire summer's work, one from the Brackenberry Ranch and one from his dude ranch business totaling slightly less than $300.

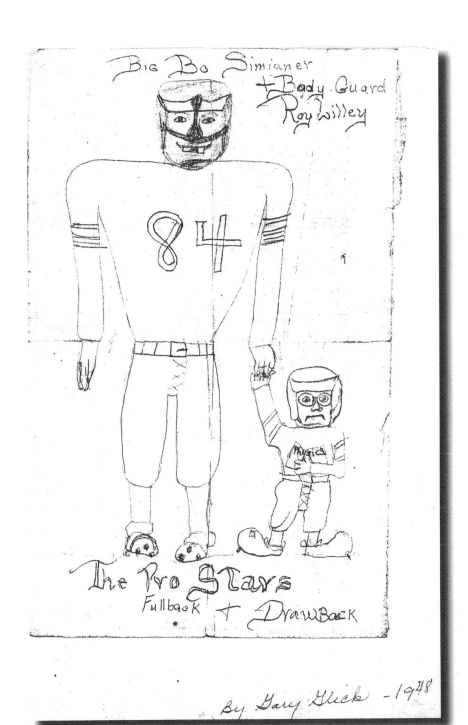

Gary's cartoon depicting Bozo and me in our senior football season.
Bozo actually played center and I was the tailback on our single wing formation.

17
State Basketball Finals

    I started my senior year in high school the day after I got back from the ranch, and football practice began that afternoon. We had a new football coach, Paul Thuelin, a Colorado A&M graduate. He was very short and stocky, had been the starting guard on the football team and a member of the traditionally strong Aggie wrestling squad. Of course, we didn't even have a wrestling team and his knowledge of basketball was limited to what he had learned as a physical education major in college. He turned out to be a nice guy and he coached football as I had learned it was supposed to be coached when I lived in Lakewood. He worked us hard as we got into shape and produced a mimeographed booklet of his offensive plays and defensive schemes, which he expected us to memorize.

    I didn't have high expectations of making the first team. It was taken for granted that Gary Glick would be the best player on our team and that Bozo Simianer would once again be the starting center, but a lot of our best players had graduated, so there was pretty open competition for most positions. At the beginning of the season, we practiced both the T-formation and single wing. My good friend, Robert Martin, who was left-handed and a junior, played quarterback in the T-formation and I played left halfback. Gary played fullback and Maynard Gardner played right halfback. Bozo once again was the center and Edgar Seaworth was his back up. Raymond Nauta, who had never participated in any high school sports before, and Art Roberts, the freshman son

LaPorte Coach Paul Thuelin, Edgar Seaworth, Robert Martin, Roy Lilley, Maynard Gardner, Harry Simainer, Gary Glick, Alvin Schieldt, Allan Miller, Bill Chambers, Gardine Brandt

Laporte Wins 6th Straight

LAPORTE (Special) — Guard Harry Simianer swished the net with a long goal attempt with eight seconds of play remaining to give Laporte High school its sixth consecutive North Central conference basketball victory.

The goal climaxed a torrid battle right down to the wire in the small Laporte gymnasium, in which Timnath held the upper hand all through the first half. The Pirates finally took over command late in the third quarter, but didn't keep it all the way. The score was tied at 33-all and an overtime period seemed a certainty when Simianer let fly with his long one.

Laporte (35) Player—	G	F	P	Timnath (33) Player—	G	F	P
Lilley	4	1	3	Pitcher	3	3	5
Martin	0	0	0	Anderson	0	0	0
Gardner	0	0	0	Cash	0	0	0
Schieldt	5	0	1	Beebe	4	3	1
Glick	3	4	2	Kautz	4	0	1
Brant	0	0	0	Reid	0	0	0
Simianer	2	0	2	Blehm	0	0	0
Seaworth	0	2	2	Horst	1	0	2
				Smylie	1	1	2
Totals	14	7	10	Fritzler	0	0	0
				Solomon	0	0	0
				Totals	13	7	11

Score at quarters:
Laporte 9 13 29 35
Timnath 10 17 28 33
Free throws missed; Laporte—Lilley 3, Schieldt 2, Glick, Simianer. Laporte—Pitcher, Kautz 3, Smylie.
Officials: Blevins and Lynch.

of the manager of a large ranch in Livermore, played the two guard positions. Harvey Jensen played one end and Bob Stacy, Bill Chambers, Gardine Brandt and Alvin (Curly) Sheildt rounded out the rest of the line. Before our first game we had shifted to using the single wing formation almost exclusively, where I lined up as tailback, Gary as fullback, Edgar as blocking back and Maynard as wingback. On passing plays Gary would line up as tailback, Maynard as fullback, and I as wingback. In this formation Harvey Jensen and I were the primary receivers and we would occasionally call a reverse or other trick play. We had a fairly limited number of offensive plays and the change of lineup soon signaled to the opposing team when we were going to throw a pass or run a trick play. To minimize this problem, Gary often ran the ball from the tailback position. Gary and Edgar shared the punting responsibilities. I returned punts and kickoffs.

We won our first game, a non-conference affair with Ault, which is just 14 miles east of Fort Collins. Our first conference game was with Timnath, a suburb south-west of Fort Collins. It ended in a nothing to nothing tie. I particularly remember two things about that game. The first was that on our first offensive play, Gary called a pass in which I slipped through the line of scrimmage into the secondary. After I caught the football, I looked up and recognized an old classmate from my days at country school in Virginia Dale, Don Smiley, who laid a good hard tackle on me. He was their center and a linebacker on defense. The other thing I recall was trying to push their big fullback out of bounds from my defensive halfback position as he was racing down the sidelines for a touchdown. I thought he had scored, but fortunately I had barely gotten him out of bounds. After the game, Frank reminded me that gutsy Maynard Gardner had brought him down several times by hitting him right in the knees. I got the point.

The fullback in question, whose name was Don Pitcher, was also Timnath's best basketball player. In addition to throwing the discus and shot put in track, he also ran in the sprints and pole-vaulted. He went on to Colorado A&M and turned out to be a very good football player there.

Unfortunately, we never won another football game that year. Timnath beat us fairly handily in our second game and the first time we played Estes Park, on a cold drizzly day, they beat us 36 to 0. It was the worst whipping I ever took in a high school athletic event and I was never more physically punished. Early in the game when I was trying to push off a typically crisp downfield block from an Estes Park player leading a sweep on my side of the field, I jammed my middle finger so badly that it felt as if it had bent back to my wrist. The runner, who was also a sprinter on their track team, raced on downfield for a touchdown. In about the middle of the game, when we were already pretty far behind and were backed up nearly to our own goal line, Gary called a trick play where he took a direct snap from center, faked an off-tackle run as tailback—I was lined up as wingback—and when he got to the line of scrimmage simply swung his arm backward and I took it out of his hand and turned up field. A huge hole had opened up and I saw nothing but open space in front of me all the way to the goal line. At about the fifty-yard line, I heard someone coming up behind me. Two steps later someone hit me right in the middle of the back, lifted me up and drove me into the ground on top of the football, knocking the wind completely out of me. It was their center, who had run me down from the rear, something I don't think he could have done the year before.

Three downs later we had to punt, and soon Estes Park was only a few yards away from our goal line with a first down. We held them on first down, as all our defensive backs came up on the line of scrimmage. On second down they again called a run up the middle, no one blocked me and I saw their runner coming through a big hole. I had overrun the play and when I turned and threw myself back in front of him, he hit me right in the ribs with a knee and once again I had all the wind knocked out of me. This is certainly not a life-threatening injury, but at the time it happens you think you're going to die until you can start breathing again. I was back on my feet and in position by the time they ran their third-down play. Of course they scored and my bruised ribs were suffered for naught.

The last big lick I took in that game was a reasonably good play on my part. Estes Park had their second team in by this time, but their reserve halfback was pretty fast. I played left halfback (now called cornerback) on the defense and as this kid was running around their left end on the way to a touchdown, I got the angle on him and caught him from behind on the sideline. I reached out and caught him by his shoulder pads and pulled with all my might. My legs flew forward as I jerked him over backwards and I landed on my back like a ton of bricks. A few plays later they scored again.

Late in the fourth quarter the coach put in the entire second team and they ran student body left and then student body right formations one after the other. The tailback on the second team was my roommate, Teddy Schaefer, who was only a freshman. They made several first downs on this play and managed to keep the second and third team of Estes Park from scoring again while our first team sat on the sidelines, shivered and licked their wounds.

*****

The only thing I enjoyed at that point in my life as much as sports was hunting deer, and buck season started the morning after our Estes Park game. Plans had already been made for us to join Frank's best friend, Boyd Brown, who was living with his wife in the little rental home on our farm while he was going to college at Colorado A&M. Frank rolled me out of bed at 4 AM so we could get the chores done and be up at the Table Mountain Ranch at dawn to start hunting at first light. My left hand was badly swollen, I had a sprained ankle and my ribs were sore. At dawn, it was quite cold and since I couldn't get a glove on my left hand, I put a heavy wool sock on it so I could hold my rifle up to shoot even if I couldn't grip it. I was bound and determined not to let the whipping of the day before make me miss the opening day of deer season.

Boyd's brother Rex, who lived in Lakewood, joined us at the farm in time to ride up to the ranch with us. When we got there, we had to wait in the car about thirty minutes for it to get light enough to hunt. Then we walked the quarter mile east to the north side of Table Mountain. At Frank's suggestion, Rex headed for the timber on the North Slope of the mountain, going straight east toward the Greenacre place. Boyd and I circled around Table Mountain's west slope just above the ranch buildings on the home place. Just before we got to the southwest slope, we saw a nice big buck running just out of gunshot range between us and the mountain at the edge of a big rock fall that distinguished that slope.

The sight of the buck whetted Boyd's and my appetite for the hunt and focused our minds. Just as we started circling East on the south side of the mountain something moving caught our attention; we knew it wasn't a deer. At first I thought it was a bobcat, but upon closer inspection I saw the flicking of a tail and knew that a bobcat had a short tail. Even before the animal slipped out of sight as it continued up the mountain, we both realized we had seen a mountain lion... This was the only time I ever saw one on the ranch. After thinking about it for a while, we realized we probably would have had time to take a shot at it. (In those days, it was legal to shoot mountain lions any time) We both laughed when we realized that we were so stuck on our desire to kill a buck that neither of us wanted to shoot our rifles for fear of frightening any deer in the area. By then we were about halfway up the mountain and continued to slowly and quietly head east until we reached the neighbor's fence. We didn't jump any more deer but did see several moving in the foothills to the south, well out of range. We didn't have time to head that way because we had all agreed to meet back at the ranch headquarters for lunch.

When we arrived at our old ranch house, Frank had already finished hunting the north side, had walked back to get the car and was waiting for us. A short time later, Rex came walking in from the North Slope of the mountain dragging a little two-point buck behind him that he had stumbled upon in the heavy timber. While we ate lunch, we decided to hunt that afternoon in the foothills south of Table Mountain where Boyd and I had seen so many deer off in the distance. Frank said that was great buck country and a little easier to hunt in than where we had spent the morning.

After lunch, we drove about a mile south on the ranch road and then across some open country for about another quarter of a mile to the east and parked the car on the west slope of the hills where we were going to be hunting. As usual, Frank decided who would go where after we reached the top of the broad valley sloping southward from Table Mountain and we split up again. Boyd and I saw a couple of nice bucks out of shooting range, and after a great afternoon of hunting, but no shooting by anyone, we had to call it a day.

We met back at the car at a prearranged time. Rex had to get back to Lakewood that night and fortunately he already had his deer. Boyd's wife had plans for him the next day, but Frank and I had already decided to head back to the ranch the next (Sunday) morning early if we had not gotten our deer. We had made arrangements to meet our cousin, Tommy Sheppard, at the big house shortly after dawn. When we got there, we loaded ourselves and our gear into Tommy's jeep and took off across country, heading south toward the state line. We parked the Jeep and Frank said he would hunt to the east by circling a large grass- and brush-covered mountain surrounded by rough hills about one mile east of Table Mountain which looks like a great big hill, and is nearly as wide as it is tall. We called it Bald Mountain, but it is now called Round Mountain.

Tommy and I headed straight south toward Table Mountain near where we had hunted the morning before. When we were about a quarter of a mile from the mountain, walking along a north-south ridge, we heard the sound of beating hooves just over a low hill ahead of us. Suddenly a shot rang out not far behind and above us. Almost immediately a young buck and a doe topped the low hill, and seeing us, changed direction and were quickly out of sight again. Tommy and I were both startled enough by the shot fired so close to us that neither of us got a shot off at the two-point buck before it disappeared. We looked back over our shoulders and saw Fred Tolliver, the owner of Tolliver and Kinney's hardware store in Fort Collins. Tommy did a lot of business with him and had given him permission to hunt on the ranch. I immediately recognized him because he was known by about everyone in town. He was a rather cross, very successful businessman about sixty-five years old. What really frightened us, in addition to the fact that he just fired a high-powered rifle over our heads, was that he had very noticeable palsy in one arm. Since no harm had been done, we simply waved at him and his hunting companion and we all went on with our business.

It seemed unlikely we would see any more deer in that area because Mr. Tolliver had been coming from the direction we were heading, so we headed back to the Jeep and drove around until we found Frank. He hadn't had any luck either and we decided to go back to the house for lunch, after which Frank and I headed back home to the farm in time to haul a load of hay into the corral for our milk cows before chore time.

We had one more weekend to hunt before deer season ended, so Frank and I made our way back up to the ranch the next Sunday. This day, we hunted in section 21 north and west of our old ranch house, also right up next to the Wyoming state line. This area was considerably less rough than the country north of Table Mountain, composed of rolling hills, scattered timber and good deer browse made up of mountain mahogany, which we referred to as buck brush, and waxy current bushes. On the west, it sloped down towards Dale Creek where the deer watered. We split up as we moved from east to west with the prevailing breeze in our face. As I topped a small rise, I suddenly realized I was looking right at a nice little buck that was walking directly away from me looking back over his shoulder. I already had a bullet in the chamber of the 25/35 Winchester rifle I was carrying and pulled back the hammer as I raised the stock to my shoulder. I tried to be sure to get only a very small part of the front sight in the Buckhorn open sight because I knew this rifle tended to shoot a bit high. I squeezed the trigger slowly as Frank had taught me. Fortunately, the buck was only about 60 yards ahead of me and moving slowly, so I could get my act together before I fired. His rear legs immediately went out from under him but he was struggling to pull himself along with his front legs as I approached him. I shot him again just behind the ear to put him out of his misery and immediately started yelling for Frank to come and help me as I had "got one."

He was within hearing range and shortly came up to where I was standing proudly over my little three-point buck. All he said was, "Well aren't you going to dress it out?" I had watched him field dress several deer, so I took my hunting knife out of the scabbard and tackled the job as he patiently talked me through the process. As I proceeded, we found out why the deer had not been able to get up on its hind legs but had seemed fine otherwise. When I tackled one of the most difficult tasks in this process, splitting the pelvis after opening the belly, it just fell open where you have split it to perform the delicate job of skinning out the anus to remove the rectum and large intestine and in turn the rest of the entrails. It seems my bullet had hit him almost directly in the center of his anus and penetrated far enough into his pubic bone to split it open. We found the expended bullet embedded in the shattered bone.

By the time we got the buck field dressed and tied to the front fender of the car it was getting to be late afternoon and we headed home. At the deer check-in station at Ted's Place, just north of Fort Collins, we got a hamburger and malt and visited with Ted and Nellie Herring, the establishment's owners and old friends of my parents.

With deer season over, I could get my mind back on school and football. School was going better than the previous year, since I had decided to settle down and study more and try to improve my attitude. The football season had turned out pretty disappointing when we ended our conference play. Somehow coach Theilin managed to schedule a non-conference post-season game with Eaton, Colorado. They had done well in their conference and had a great player in Kenney Wilhelm, who was later a starting halfback at Colorado A&M. Fortunately they didn't take us very seriously and we really needed a win to salvage our season. Even though they moved the ball pretty well, we managed to keep them out of the end zone all but one time, and toward the end of the game we were down only seven to nothing.

Late in the last quarter, we managed to get down on about their 5-yard line. After Gary had been able to gain only about one yard on the first and second downs, I told him in the huddle that they didn't have anybody covering wide on the strong side of our single wing formation. Bozo snapped the ball directly to Gary and he took one step forward and raised up to loft a pass to me. I had slipped out in the right flat from my tailback position behind the rest of the backfield. The line had blocked as if it were another line plunge by

Gary and, seeing that there was no one even close to covering me, I probably eased up on my route. Gary threw the ball my way and I kicked into high gear as it sailed well over my head. If I had caught it, I could've walked into the end zone.

I felt stupid for slowing down and I'm sure Gary felt bad about throwing it too far, although neither of us said anything when we came back to the huddle. Gary kicked a field goal on fourth down and we lost the game seven to three. We were able to salvage some pride knowing we had just played our best game of the year. I doubt if the Eaton players got any compliments from their coach after the game, but they went on to do quite well during the postseason.

Laporte Trims Eagles in District Playoff Battle

Cache la Poudre High school's Pirates nipped the Wellington Eagles 31 to 30 during an overtime period here Monday night in a "sudden death" North Central conference basketball playoff game that sent the winner into the district class C eliminations.

Nearly 1,300 persons — more than the combined population of the two towns, and 100 more than capacity of the Fort Collins High school gymnasium— jammed the neutral arena and actually lapped over onto the playing court for a game in which heartbreak rode on every shot.

It was an airtight ball game from the middle of the second period onward, although the Pirates kept the scoring lead until early in the fourth quarter, when the score began seesawing as play surged back and forth on the court. The teeter board was level, however, when regulation playing time expired, the score tied at 29-all.

Only an average of a point a minute was scored in the three-minute overtime, but that was enough to give the Pirates their thirteenth win in 14 starts and send them against Mead, the Weld county winner, in a district playoff game here Friday night.

Second Loss

The loss Monday night was Wellington's second in 18 games. Edgar Seaworth, a cool, imperturbable guard, was the hero for the Pirates. It was Seaworth who twice kept the score even with shots in the dying minutes of the fourth quarter. But it was his one-handed push shot that swished the nets in the third minute of the overtime that the spectators remembered.

That goal came a minute after Roy Lilley had fouled Lee Armijo and the Wellington player had calmly sunk the free throw to put the Eagles temporarily ahead, 30 to 29. There was time after the goal for play to change direction four times and for Laporte's Gary Glick to miss a free throw, but none of it mattered.

Get Early Lead

The one-point outcome fails to reveal that the game started as a one-sided Laporte show. The Pirates stormed ahead in the early moments to lead by 10 points at one time in the first period. But the prospects were too rich for them. They lost all their poise in the second quarter, scoring only a free throw, and were protecting a 14 to 12 lead at intermission.

Center Russel Wood, who led scoring with 11 points, put Wellington ahead for the first time, 25 to 24, with a shot from the corner in the first two minutes of the final period. A photo finish was in prospect from that time onward.

Glick, Laporte's center, followed Wood in the scoring column with 9 points and did a good job of clearing the backboards. Maynard Gardner scored eight points, while a slick job of guarding by Wellington's Alvin DeGabain held Roy Lilley, Laporte's ace forward, to three points.

Wellington (30)				Laporte (31)			
Player—	G	F	P	Player—	G	F	P
McC'ley f	0	1	2	Lilley f	1	1	0
Seder f	2	0	2	Gardner f	2	4	4
Rob'son f	0	0	1	Schieldt f	0	0	0
Wood c	5	1	1	Glick c	4	1	3
Armijo g	3	1	4	Seaw'th g	3	1	2
Bryant g	1	1	1	Simi'er g	2	0	3
DeGab'n g	2	0	1				
Totals	13	4	12	Totals	12	7	12

Score by quarters:
Laporte 13 14 24 29 (31)
Wellington 7 12 22 29 (30)

Free throws missed: Wellington — Bryant 2, Armijo, Wood 2, McCauley 2, DeGabain, Seder 2. Laporte— Glick 2, Gardner 2, Simianer. Officials: Compton and Blevins.

The seniors always held a play each year just as the juniors did. Our class sponsor, Mrs. Maxfield, chose our play, directed it and selected the cast.

She chose an old favorite, "Bashful Bertie." Mrs. Maxfield strongly recommended that all of the twenty-eight students in our senior class try out. I don't remember too much about the plot, but I got the part of Bertie. Neither do I remember who else in my class had roles; however, it evidently was quite a success and we ended up performing it Saturday and Sunday nights to sellout crowds in our little third-floor auditorium at the high school. The junior and senior class plays traditionally had dress rehearsals on Friday night and one performance on Saturday night. I never had found it easy to memorize lines, but thanks to my long-suffering mother, I managed to memorize them well enough to get through both performances with a minimum of stumbles.

My favorite memories of the year are of our basketball season, which proved to be quite successful. Although Coach Theulin had never played basketball, he had a full understanding of the fundamentals, something that we needed to improve. We had learned some bad habits the previous year under coach Welch, who knew little or nothing about the game and for whom we had no respect. We probably had slightly better personnel the previous year, but under Theulin we came together as a team.

Within a couple of weeks, the starters had been determined. Gary was at center, Bozo at guard, I at one forward, Edgar Seaworth the other guard and Maynard Gardner replacing brother Harold, who had graduated, as the other forward. In spite of our very small gym, Coach turned us loose to fast-break whenever possible, which made a lot of sense with Gary being such an exceptional rebounder. Our first game was at home with Wellington and they were even better than they had been the previous year. Their good discipline and tenacious man-to-man defense shut down our fast-break. We had improved our zone defense so we were also hard to score on. It ended up being a low-scoring game with us eking out a twenty-six to twenty-four win. Our first game certainly headed off any inclination for us to get overconfident.

We managed to get through the first half of the double round robin our conference played without any defeats. Estes Park was tough again and Waverley played us one close game. Once again Timnath, Lyons and Berthoud were less difficult, but Timnath did give us one close call. As luck would have it, just before our second round of conference games started, I came down with the chickenpox. I was quite sick and missed several weeks of school, the first when we had our second game with Wellington. It was at their gym and they beat us in a blowout of forty-two to twenty-four. They were good, but I'm afraid our guys had gotten a little cocky after the ease with which we had won our last five games, even beating Estes Park by a fair margin.

Shortly after I caught the chickenpox, Frank came down with them too and he was really sick. About the time I was getting better, Frank was at his worst and my brother Chuck joined the sick list. He was the sickest of us all. Going to country school, none of us had been exposed to chickenpox as kids and we proved the fact that the older you are when you get a childhood disease, the sicker you get. Mom patiently nursed us all back to health and somehow at least one of us was always able to drag himself out to the barn to do the chores in the morning and evening. Of course, Dad was home on the weekends and took a few days vacation to help us through this ordeal.

Fortunately, we had a couple of our easier games after the Wellington loss before I returned. Curly Sheildt had stepped up and played very well in my forward position. We managed to finish the rest of the year without another defeat and were faced with a playoff game for the second year in a row to qualify for district playoffs, since Wellington and La Porte had both lost only one game, each to the other.

The play-off game to determine the conference title was played in the Fort Collins high school gymnasium about three days after our last conference game. I hoped that Wellington might be overconfident, because we had barely beaten them the first time and they had handled us easily in the second game.

Any over-confidence we might have had early in the season was certainly gone as we approached this important game. Gary and I reminded our teammates how close we had come to winning in the big Longmont gym last year in our playoff with Estes Park, and Coach Theulin gave us a good pep talk before the game started. We managed to score early and were ahead of them at half-time in what was turning out to be another low-scoring game. Coach Eyestone of Wellington had put Alvin Degabin, a sophomore, on me and he hounded me the whole game. Howard, Alvin's older brother, told me later that Eyestone had told his little brother to not worry about offense but to stick to me like glue. Did he ever! And he managed to score four points to my three.

Although we were ahead at halftime, Wellington had taken a lead briefly in the middle of the second quarter. Gary and the Wellington center, Russell Wood, who was taller but considerably lighter, battled for rebounds at both ends of the gym. Gary and I were not able to combine on any fast-breaks and Degabin made sure I didn't drive the lane or baseline for any easy layups. Fortunately, Bozo and Edgar stepped up with some long shots and Maynard made some very crucial free throws. The game ended in a twenty-nine-to-twenty-nine tie and it looked as if neither team would be able to score a basket during the three minutes overtime. Then I fouled their guard, Lee Armijo, and he made one of two free throws giving them a one-point lead with less than a minute to go. We got the ball back and could not work it in to Gary. Just as the clock wound down to zero, Edgar banked in a desperation two-handed set shot from near mid-court, his third of the game, clinching a thirty-one to thirty hard fought victory. It took a while for it to sink in that we had won the right to advance to Class B district playoffs and for me to realize that what I considered my worst game of the year was our team's best.

A few days later we met Meade, the Weld County conference winner in our district, for the Class D district championship, which would determine whether we advanced to the state finals. I don't recall too much about the game, but we managed to win it by a fairly close margin and qualified to play Sedgwick a few days later at West High where the first round of class D was being held.

The morning we were to drive to Denver was bitterly cold. We couldn't get our Studebaker started with the temperature hovering near 30° below zero. Dad had planned to pick up our neighbors, Edgar Seaworth, Robert Martin and Maynard Gardner, and drive us to our hotel. We called the Seaworths and Edgar's father managed to get their Dodge started and hauled us to the tournament. We met the coach and other members of the team at the Baker Hotel in downtown Denver, were assigned our rooms and went out to supper with the coach. Many of us had never stayed in a hotel before, let alone play in a state high school tournament.

The gym in West High School was similar to the ones we played in during the qualifying games and, after our warm-ups, we felt reasonably comfortable. We managed to play Sedgwick a close game and were ahead at the half. We found ourselves falling behind in the second and never could catch up, losing by over ten points. As the losing team, we were to play in the consolation bracket at the City Auditorium early the next morning.

The City Auditorium in Denver was a large old multipurpose building. When we left the dressing room and came out on the floor, we were amazed that the basketball court seemed to be set in the middle of a huge cavern with seats and balconies on all sides. I had attended AAU basketball games there when we lived in Lakewood and always sat in the topmost balcony in the cheap seats where you could barely see the gym floor. While we were

Estes, Laporte, Wellingon Win NCAA Contests

NCAA STANDINGS

Team—	W	L	Pct.	Pts.	Op.
Wellington	9	1	.900	543	241
Laporte	8	1	.889	371	224
Estes Park	7	2	.778	422	207
Timnath	5	5	.500	378	334
Waverly	3	6	.333	280	347
Berthoud	1	8	.111	224	462
Lyons	0	10	.000	163	566

Estes Park was the only one of the North Central conference's three top basketball quintets to get an argument Saturday night while the other leaders, Wellington and Laporte were cakewalking to easy victories.

The Bobcats got past Timnath 40 to 28 at Timnath in a game that was reasonably close all the way. Meanwhile at Wellington the Eagles were shellacking a demoralized Berthoud team 75 to 10, and at Laporte the Pirates were whaling Lyons 58 to 13.

Schieldt Makes 20

Coach Milo Sabin's Timnath quintet led Estes Park 8 to 6 at the end of the first quarter and was still a threat to the Bobcats at the half, even though the victors had pulled ahead 15 to 12 by then. After that it was Estes Park all the way, although the Bobcat margin was never wide until the final period.

Forward Alvin Schieldt poured in 20 points in leading Laporte over Lyons. The Pirates stormed ahead 15 to 2 in the first quarter and had everything their own way.

Russel Wood and Rex McCaulley played little more than half the contest but got 21 and 19 points, respectively, for Wellington. The Eagles started slowly, considering their final total, but led 10 to 2 at the end of the first quarter and had a 25 to 7 halftime advantage.

Timnath (28) Player—	G	F	P	Estes Park (40) Player—	G	F	P
Cash f	4	0	2	Swift f	1	0	2
Beebe f	2	2	3	Reed f	2	0	0
Kautz f	0	0	1	Smith c	6	2	1
Pitcher c	2	0	3	Jes'son g	7	1	2
Horst g	0	3	3	Parker g	1	1	5
Smylie g	3	1	0	Ka'ahn g	1	0	5
Fritzler g	0	0	0				
Totals	11	6	12	Totals	18	4	17

Score by quarters:
Timnath 8 12 20 28
Estes Park 6 15 27 40
Free throws missed: Pitcher 2, Cash 2, Beebe 2, Horst 3, Fritzler 2. Estes Park—Swift, Smith 2, Parker 2, Kassahn 2.
Officials: Day and Tavener.

Laporte (58) Player—	G	F	P	Lyons (13) Player—	G	F	P
Martin f	2	0	1	Gapter f	0	0	0
Gardner f	6	2	0	Sch'd'er f	0	0	0
Schieldt f	9	2	1	McC'dy f	0	0	0
Glick c	6	1	4	Johnson c	1	0	4
Brant c	0	0	0	Pantigo g	4	1	5
Simi'er g	2	0	3	Boone g	1	0	2
S'worth g	1	1	0	Mundt g	0	0	0
Ch'bers g	0	0	0	Phipps g	0	0	0
Miller g	0	0	0				
Totals	26	6	9	Totals	6	1	11

Score by quarters:
Laporte 15 28 42 58
Lyons 2   5 13 13
Free throws missed: Laporte—Gardner 2, Schieldt 4, Glick 3, Simianer 3, Seaworth 1. Lyons—Pantigo 27, Johnson 2, Boone.
Officials: Olander and Lynch.

Wellington (75) Player—	G	F	P	Berthoud (10) Player—	G	F	P
Bryant f	3	1	3	Berglin f	0	1	0
McC'ley f	9	1	2	Buech'r f	1	1	1
Seder f	1	0	1	Desch'r f	0	0	0
Poulter f	1	0	1	Garner c	0	0	1
Robison f	2	0	2	Kiehn c	0	1	1
Steiben c	2	1	0	Adler g	0	2	3
Wood c	10	1	1	Engle't g	0	1	4
Armijo g	3	0	3	McC't'y g	1	0	2
DeG'in g	1	1	3				
Blehm g	3	0	0	Totals	2	6	12
Totals	35	5	16				

Score by quarters:
Wellington 10 25 48 75
Berthoud 2   7   9 10
Free throws missed: Wellington—Seder 3, Wood 2, Poulter, Armijo, Bryant, McCaulley. Berthoud—Berglin.

warming up, I realized that I could barely see the balcony from the gym floor. The backboards were the new glass kind and were suspended over either end of the floor.

Our competition was Springfield, Colorado, a small town in the far southeast corner of the state, which was a powerhouse in all sports in their conference. They had lost their first game by a close margin and were looking for redemption. Their center was a good bit larger than Gary and they competed hard for rebounds the entire game. We once again came out and played well in the first half and partway into the third quarter, but couldn't sustain our pace and fell behind.

In an effort to get back into the game, the coach had Maynard and me meet the guards before they crossed the centerline to put some pressure on them. I managed to deflect a pass at midcourt, pick it up and dribble full speed toward the basket, which was a lot farther away than I was used to. When I was near the basket and realized there was no wall in sight to slow me down, I laid up the basketball going full speed. It bounced off the backboard and sailed all the way out to the centerline where Springfield retrieved it. My big moment had turned into an embarrassment in the biggest game I had ever played in. We went on to lose the game by a fair margin and lined up to congratulate our opponents, several of whom I would see again in the fall and one of whom would become a lifelong friend.

Basketball season was now in the past and I was not looking forward to the start of our last athletic activity of the year, my least favorite sport, track. I had managed to compensate for my lack of strength in my left leg when playing basketball by learning to use my left hand for lay ups, which was about the only kind of shot where you have to really drive hard off of just one leg. I had never given much thought to this problem and strangely enough neither my coach nor family nor fellow teammates seemed to notice it, or at least did not say much about it if they did. But track was a different matter. You need two good legs to run or jump.

I decided to quit the track team after the first meet, even though I won the half mile, a race I hated, so I could enjoy my last few months in high school. As it turned out, I probably lost my chance for a straight-A average for a second year in a row, the previous year for goofing off and this year for letting my coach down. When we got our last report card coach Theulin had given me a B in the class that he was teaching that semester. It was a fairly easy elective, hygiene, I think, and I had gotten an A in it the two previous six-weeks periods. He never said anything to me about it and I never asked. I had felt guilty about quitting track because I probably could have been at least some help to my teammates. Gary was a very good high hurdler and Bozo a good pole-vaulter, and I wasn't at all sure that I could even earn a letter in track.

We had a combined senior prom and banquet shortly before graduation and I, of course, didn't have a date for it. I did enjoy dancing with everybody else's girl and went to town afterwards to play pool with Robert and Maynard, who didn't have dates either.

Our graduation ceremony was a fairly simple one and I don't recall that we even rented caps and gowns. I can't even remember who our speakers were other than our valedictorian, Eugene Davis, who had all A's for four years and Jackie Kilburn, who had only one B, our salutatorian. I had gotten three Bs during my two years at La Porte, had transferred a few Bs from Lakewood and was third in our class of twenty-eight. We had only one scholarship to give and that presentation was made by our principal, H. D. Pratt. He carefully explained that the procedure for selecting the scholarship this year was new with the recipient picked strictly by a new state mandated "Joint Honor Scholarship" test given to all seniors and juniors across the state. He said that the school board had previously picked the scholarship winner, but had no control over it this year and the winner was…Roy Lilley.

My folks, who would have been proud of me whether I received a scholarship or not, were surprised at the manner in which it had been announced and I was embarrassed as I walked up to receive it.

I couldn't wait to get up to the ranch and talked the folks into driving me up there on the day after graduation and missed the baccalaureate on Sunday night.

My senior class picture.

Cache La Poudre High School
La Porte, Colorado

Report of

Roy Lilley

For 194**7** - 194**8**, **12th** Grade

To Parents and Guardians:

Report cards are sent home at the end of each six weeks period. Please examine the card carefully, sign and return it.

Your co-operation is earnestly desired for the benefit of the student. We urge that you visit school and confer with teachers as often as possible.

REMARKS

SIGNATURE OF PARENT OR GUARDIAN

Chaser Lilley
Chaser Lilley
Julia F. Lilley
Julia F. Lilley
Julia F. Lilley

Period	1	2	3	4	5	6
Days Absent	2	1	1	7	½	½
Times Tardy	1	0	0	0	1	0

Report card from my senior year. The seven day absence from the fourth six-week period was when I had chicken pox. Notice the B in Health!

SUBJECT	SIX WEEKS PERIOD								CITIZENSHIP	SIX WEEKS PERIOD					
	1	2	3	S	1	2	3	S		1	2	3	4	5	6
English IV	A	A	A	A	A	A	A	A	Industry	S	S	S	S	S	S
									Cooperation	S	S	S	S	S	S
									Courtesy	S	S	S	S	S	S
									Attendance	S	S	S	S	S	S
Health	A	A	A	A	A	A	B	A	Industry	S	S	S	S	S	S
									Cooperation	S	S	S	S	S	S
									Courtesy	S	S	S	S	S	S
									Attendance	S	S	S	S	S	S
Economics	A	A	A	A	A	A	A	A	Industry	S	S	S	S	S	S
									Cooperation	S	S	S	S	S	S
									Courtesy	S	S	S	S	S	S
									Attendance	S	S	S	S	S	S
Chemistry	A	A	A	A	A	A	A	A	Industry	S	S	S	S	S	S
									Cooperation	S	S	S	S	S	S
									Courtesy	S	S	S	S	S	S
									Attendance	S	S	S	S	S	S

GRADING SYSTEM
A—Superior　　D—Below average but passing
B—Above average　　F—Failure
C—Average　　I—Incomplete

CITIZENSHIP MARKS
E—Excellent
S—Satisfactory
U—Unsatisfactory

18
Taking Responsibility

Things at the ranch were about the same as I had left them the previous fall. Ann Harper was Ruby's helper again, having arrived at the ranch just a week ahead of me. There were no guests yet nor were any expected for a few weeks, and then in no great number until July 4th, which was the beginning of their busy season.

Bob had quite a few projects planned for the main house where he was adding a shower to the upstairs bathroom and Ann and Ruby were painting the bedrooms. I stayed busy stirring paint, mixing plaster and hauling it up and down the stairs from the front porch for them. The stairs ended right in front of the entrance to the bathroom. Once, as I was running up them two at a time as I had many times before, as I topped them I saw Anne. She was sitting on the toilet with her dress demurely spread across her knees. I gasped and turned around and raced down the stairs and never showed up in the house again until supper, and then I was too embarrassed to look anyone in the eye.

As soon as I had finished eating, I hurried out to the barn to do what I always did when Bob had not lined me out on another job: clean out the barn. From my first day, he impressed upon me that it was important to keep the barn and tack room as clean as a barn can be, and it was a good place to hide out. I slipped into the basement through the cellar door at about dark and went to bed.

As usual, the next morning I brought all the horses in from the pasture just northwest of the ranch before breakfast. I would then catch those we needed that day, anywhere from two to five head, tie them in individual stalls in the barn and feed them a number ten can of oats before I went to breakfast.

As soon as I came through the door for breakfast, Ann intercepted me and apologized for not having shut the bathroom door the day before. She said it was usually just Ruby and her upstairs and they had gotten in the habit of the leaving the door open so they could visit. This didn't wipe away my embarrassment, but made it possible for me to go on with my day.

The rest of the summer went very well with a good balance of working cattle, which included bringing them in twice to be sprayed, taking dudes out for morning and afternoon rides (we never let them go out alone) and working in the hayfield with the other hired help at the lower ranch. I always enjoyed joining the guests in the ranch house living room after supper singing around the piano from the "Songs America Loves" book as Ruby accompanied us on the piano, or playing canasta, a fairly new card game that was sweeping the country; and sometimes we just talked.

The last week of August, Bob and Ruby took a week off and left Ann and me to manage the ranch. We had only a few guests and Ann was to handle the cooking and housekeeping chores while I put up hay at the upper ranch. Bob said I was to bale the hay on the meadow northwest of the ranch on Trail Creek, but should put the hay on the meadow south of the ranch house across the river in the hayloft.

I protested that my only experience with the haying was at the lower ranch where I had just been hauling in bales. I said I had mowed and raked with a team of horses and mowed with our little John Deere tractor on the farm, but had never operated a baler. He pointed out I had helped him with the baler on numerous occasions and he was confident I was perfectly capable of handling everything. He said I could use the horse-drawn mower on part of the upper meadow because there were some wet spots where the tractor might get stuck, and I could borrow a team of horses from the neighboring Trails End Ranch, which they would leave in their corral for me. I would also need the team for raking and pulling the hay rack.

The Sunday after Bob and Ruby left, I caught a couple of fryers, cut off their heads, plucked their feathers and singed them for Ann to fry for our customary Sunday dinner. While she was preparing the meal, I got a block of ice from the icehouse, washed and chipped it, added salt, put the ice cream mixture that Ann had prepared into the wooden freezer and cranked it for about an hour till it was hard enough. I then packed the whole thing with newspapers to keep it frozen. This was a Sunday routine we both were anxious to carry on. We did this often in the summer when I was growing up. I remember how proud I was when I was able to turn the crank.

The guests certainly seemed to enjoy the fine chicken dinner and homemade ice cream. After finishing my meal, I pushed back from the table and exclaimed, in an effort to act the part of the man of the house, that it was certainly a good meal but perhaps the ice cream was not quite as good as usual. I then excused myself and went on about my business doing a few more Sunday chores. That night, as I was helping her in the kitchen after supper, I asked Ann why she hadn't spoken to me since dinner. She gave me a withering look and asked me how in the world I could possibly say that the ice cream wasn't as good as usual. I tried to explain myself by saying I hadn't a clue that I had said anything hurtful.

Monday morning Ann seemed to be her usual cheerful self and I put our little tiff out of my mind and tackled the job of putting up the hay. Bob had left the Ford tractor parked in the meadow across the river. It was full of gasoline and already had the mower attached to it ready to go. It was late in the season and the hay was quite high and starting to ripen. After I had made a few rounds over the hay field, I learned why this particular model Ford mower was not very popular. It was mounted right under the tractor ahead of the rear wheels. The pitman stick that moves the sickle back and forth, which cuts the hay, was operated by a belt that transferred the power to it. As I mowed a new round of hay I had to drive over the previously cut hay, and if some of it was sticking up too far it would catch in the belt powering the pitman causing a terrible mess. I would then have to turn off the tractor, climb under it and use my pocketknife to cut loose all the hay that had wrapped around the belt. It took me all day to finish mowing the meadow south of the river.

The next morning, I got up about an hour earlier than usual so I could get the cow milked and the tractor gassed up and ready for another day's mowing. Right after breakfast I drove the tractor upstream on a rut road along Trail Creek from its confluence with the Poudre River near the barn, and mowed some of the meadow that lay north of the creek. Just this one portion of the meadow was over twice as large as the one I had mowed the day before and it took me about two days to finish it.

By this time the meadow south of the river was ready to be raked, so I rode horseback over to Trails End to get the team of horses they had left in the corral for me. They were a fine pair of matched Sorrel Belgian workhorses and probably weighed around 1450 pounds apiece. I then went into the house and ate dinner.

After eating, I led the team out to the rake nearby, hooked them up, drove them across the shallow ford near the house and raked all afternoon and all the next day. In a few days, the hay in the first meadow had cured enough to be hauled into the barn. I hitched the team to the hayrack, which was parked near the corrals, forded the river and pulled up in the middle of several bunches of hay. I climbed down off the rack and began throwing the sweet-smelling timothy and clover up onto it with my pitchfork. Pitching hay was a job I was well acquainted with, because we had to haul hay from the stacks in the field to the corral every weekend at the farm for our milk cows and horses. Dad had taught me how to use my left leg as a lever under the fork handle to lift a big load of hay far up over my head and onto a hayrack or into the outside door of a hayloft.

Since I was working by myself, I had to throw several bunches of hay up onto the hay rack, go around to the back, climb up on top, evenly distribute the hay around the rack and then move the team ahead to the next handiest bunches of hay. I then tied the lines to the front of the rack, jumped off and pitched on some more hay. As the hayrack got fuller I had further to throw it and to climb on top. Obviously, this was a job for at least two people, but I did the best I could and got a pretty good load on the rack and headed for the house just about dinner time. I pulled up beside the barn beneath the door leading into the hayloft, unhitched the team and led them into their stalls in the barn. I gave them a good feed of oats and threw some hay that was left over from the previous year down into their manger. I then went into the house, washed my hands and enjoyed dinner.

While we were eating, I told Ann that I sure could sure use some help dragging the hay back away from the door as I unloaded the hayrack. She said she had no idea what I was talking about. I explained that when you pitch hay into the barn you need someone to drag it back from the door to make room for more. She readily agreed to help me but said she would have to clean up the kitchen first. I said I would go ahead and get started. By the time Ann got there, I had pitched a good bit of hay through the window and climbed into the loft a couple of times to drag the hay back into the far corners of the loft. When Ann arrived, I helped her up the ladder and gave her a pitchfork. I showed her how to stick the fork into the hay and drag it along the slick wooden floor of the hayloft out from in front of the door. I suggested it was not necessary to get it clear back to the corner, but to just keep an opening at the window so I would have room to throw in more hay.

As soon as I had unloaded the hayrack, I picked up the lines, clicked to the horses and headed back out to the hay field. It took about half an hour to get another load and when I arrived back to the barn I found a very angry Ann waiting for me in the hayloft. I didn't have the good sense to tell her when I was going for another load and she had been waiting for me to pitch some more hay through the window all that time. She reminded me that she had much better things to do than to sit up in the hayloft waiting for me between loads of hay. My excuse, that I had assumed she would realize when no more hay was coming to the window that I had headed out for another load, sounded pretty lame. I felt terrible that I had again treated Ann so thoughtlessly and once again begged her forgiveness. The proof of Ann's good disposition was the fact that she helped me unload hay the rest of the afternoon. She was the closest thing I ever had to a sister and was much more tolerant of my shortcomings than my brothers ever were.

By the time we got all the hay in the barn, the hay I had mowed in the northwest meadow was ready to rake. I hooked the team up to the rake and did my best to create straight windrows that could be easily picked up by the baler. It was a tractor-pulled John Deere wire tie. It had a mounted Wisconsin air-cooled engine to operate the flywheel and plunger that forced the hay through a chute fed into it by the pickup reel. The weight of the bale was determined by the moisture content of the hay and amount of tension or friction in the chute by the plunger as it was pushed through. It was a rather complex yet crude piece of machinery, which jolted every time the plunger made a revolution. It made a clearly distinctive noise heard above all the other clatter each time the wires were tied at either end of the bale and then kicked out onto the ground by the next bale in line. The 9N Ford was just barely powerful and heavy enough to pull it, and every time the plunger made a revolution, the tractor nearly jumped off the ground

I hooked the tractor to the baler after taking off the mower, loaded two fifty-pound rolls of baling wire in a compartment on one side of it, threaded it through appropriate holes and channels and jammed the ends into the knotting mechanism, which was activated by cams that worked in ways as yet mysterious to me. I fortunately had the manual that came with the baler to help me find my way through the whole process. I pumped grease into all the appropriate zerts with the grease gun and headed for the field. After some trial and error, I got the tension properly adjusted and started producing some fairly decent looking bales. Somehow over the next few days I baled all the hay that I had mowed and raked.

When Bob and Ruby came home from their trip, they seemed well-pleased with the way Ann and I had taken care of things in their absence. Bob was happy to see that I had gotten most of the haying done and was particularly pleased that the hayloft in the barn was now full of fresh hay. I had never been given that kind of responsibility before and Bob had assumed I understood a lot more about the operation of the baler than I really did. Several times, I had nearly given up when the Wisconsin engine wouldn't start and despaired of ever getting the baling wire properly threaded into the knotting machine. But I couldn't face the prospect of having to tell Bob that I hadn't been able to handle the job. His faith that I could figure things out on my own reinforced a growing feeling of self-confidence

In early September, Bob paid me my entire summer wages and I said good-by to Ann and Ruby. He dropped me off at the farm on his way to town the next day. I hadn't been home all summer and seemed to have outgrown the ache of homesickness, at least when I was up at Trail Creek. I was anticipating starting college soon with equal parts of eager anticipation and anxiety.

Mom won a halter class at a horse show in Cheyenne in the summer of 1948 with our yearling filly, Bobbie Sox. This was the first colt we raised in our registered Quarter Horse breeding program.

19

College Freshman

If I remember correctly, the only prerequisite for any Colorado resident to register at Colorado A & M was to show up on registration day. Evidently the Cache La Poudre School Board had sent a letter to the registrar that I had qualified for the Joint Honor Scholarship for Cache La Poudre High School, so when I registered in the fall of 1948 my $35.00 tuition for the first quarter was already paid and all it cost me to register was a $10 fee for an activity card for free admission to all of the football and basketball games and other sports events.

My brothers had gone to school on the G.I. Bill the previous two years and since prerequisites for the first two years of many majors were the same, I was able to use many of their books, especially Frank's, since he had the same major as I chose. By living at home, I didn't have to live in a dormitory as required for all out-of-town freshmen, thus I was able go to to college for practically nothing. Charlie, Frank and I went to class together in the Diamond T pickup. We had succeeded in getting mostly morning classes, so we left every morning at 7:30 a.m. and were usually home by about three o'clock in the afternoon. This created an opportunity to spend quite a lot of time at the library between classes, although I'm afraid all three of us wasted a lot of it drinking coffee in the student union. The union had a good cafeteria and also a coffee shop where we could buy sandwiches and chili if we wished. I often joined my brothers and their friends in the coffee shop and enjoyed listening to their conversations. I did have a couple of friends that I had known when I lived in Lakewood. They were required to live in the freshman dormitory, Braden Hall, and I often went to one of their rooms between classes to visit and occasionally ate at the cafeteria with them.

Freshmen were allowed to take no more than seventeen-and-a-half hours per week, and this included three hours each of military and physical education. You got only half credit for the PE and military so you had fourteen-and-a-half hours left for other prerequisites which included English/literature, chemistry, algebra, history, economics, geology and introductory courses required by your major, which in my case was animal husbandry, now called animal science. You were not allowed to take any electives during your freshman and sophomore years. I took the maximum seventeen-and-a-half hours per quarter allowed.

Military was required only for your first two years, but if you wished to get an ROTC commission you had to take an additional two years plus two weeks of summer camp between your junior and senior years. You were required to declare your intention to take advanced military when you finished your sophomore year. You could receive a commission in either the Army (Field Artillery) or Air Force Administration. I opted for Air Force when I registered. We were all given a uniform but were only required to wear it on Tuesdays, when we spent an hour on the large grass oval that was then close to the center of campus learning to do close order drill and the manual of arms.

Fraternities and sororities were still influential on campus in those days and, during the first week of school, they had what was called "rush week," a period when many members of the freshman class were invited to activities at the various fraternity and sorority houses to become involved in a rather strange ritual. The top athletes and the well-connected were usually rushed by some, and often all of them. I was rushed by the Sigma Phi Epsilon "frat" because both of my brothers already belonged and my father had been a member when he was in college in the early 1920s.

I wasn't really too keen to join a fraternity because I was aware of the hazing you received between the time you pledged, their term for accepting the invitation, and when you became an active member. As part of the hazing during their last week as a pledge, called hell week, they had to get every active member of their fraternity to sign a paddle, which was about three feet long, three inches wide and one-half-inch thick. Each active member had the option of giving you a whack on the rear end with your paddle before signing it and most of them availed themselves of the opportunity. When my brothers went active, both of them were veterans of World War II. By the time hell week was over and they received all their signatures, their butts were completely black and blue and I certainly wasn't anxious to go through that ordeal. Nevertheless, I was the second freshman to be invited to pledge that fall with the Sig Eps and I accepted with the encouragement of Frank and Charlie.

Looking back, it seems that the whole fraternity concept was incongruous. One of the first activities in rush week was inviting potential pledges on "beer busts" where eighteen-year-old freshman were encouraged to drink way too much beer and sit around a campfire with their potential new fraternity brothers singing ribald songs. Later that same week they were invited to the fraternity house and introduced to the housemother, whose job was to instruct everyone on proper table manners and etiquette, and look the other way while the members did outrageous things.

Most of the members lived at the fraternity house, but those of us who lived in town had to go in only on Monday nights to sit down for supper (part of my being civilized was to learn to call it dinner) and take part in various other social activities. The best of those were joint parties with the sororities. The only two I recall were the ones with the "Thetas" and "Tri Delts." Thirty years earlier, Mom, a Tri Delt, and Dad, a Sig Ep, had participated in such events, which were largely held so members could meet the "right" kind of girl. Ironically, Mom and Dad already knew each other before they started college, and both her father and his mother would have preferred they marry someone else.

As the first quarter of college progressed, I was enjoying it and managing to heed my brothers' advice that I had better study in college more than I had in high school. But I was enjoying my fraternity life less and less. There were "actives," who were assigned to the pledges to help us do silly pranks, like putting syrup on toilet seats, for which we could be caught and then punished. My punishment for one transgression was to be held down by several actives while another shaved the hair from around my genitals. They were fully aware that freshman had to use the pool in the field house during gym class where only nude swimming was allowed. How being humiliated was supposed to build character was beyond me.

I soon got a foretaste of what hell week would be like when one of the actives, who was also the starting quarterback on the Aggie's football team, caught me in some minor transgression and told me to bend over, grab my ankle with one hand and use one hand to "protect the family jewels." Then this six foot-three athlete, who could throw a football sixty yards, proceeded to lift me off the ground with a mighty swing. This bit of character building hurt like hell, but I was supposed to be grateful that he'd allowed one of us select few, who were soon to become Sig Eps, to protect myself so that I would not be rendered infertile and unable to pass on my superior genes.

Near the end of the quarter, I had a wreck on a Friday night on the way home from town with Teddy, who was still living with us, and Robert and Maynard, my good friends who were still in high school. We had been shooting pool at Sol's and Dick's and all of us except Teddy had consumed several glasses of 3.2 beer. At about 11:30 p.m. when we were heading home, I forgot that Maynard, who lived on a driveway that turned east just before you crossed a bridge at the top of Taft Hill, was in the back seat. I always increased my speed just before topping this hill, for which Taft Hill road was named, going over it like I was in a roller coaster. Just as I was cresting the hill, I remembered that Maynard and Robert were in the back seat, glanced over my shoulder at them and hit the brakes. They grabbed unevenly and the car swerved to the left. I overcompensated to the right and crashed through the wooden guardrail. Just before we hit the rail, Teddy, who was in the front seat with me said, "Jesus Roy," and the next thing I knew I was sitting in the wrecked car spitting dust out of my mouth. We had flipped off the road and landed right side up about halfway down the hill. The seat had come loose and all the dirt that had accumulated under it was floating in the air. I had fallen over on top of Teddy on the passenger side of the seat and a broken wooden beam from the guardrail had gone through the windshield, over the steering wheel and gouged the roof of the car, which in turn was separated from the broken windshield.

I jumped out of the right-hand car door behind Teddy and started running up and down yelling, "How could I have done this? My life is ruined!" I'm not proud of the fact that I was thinking only of myself at this moment, but I was brought back to my senses when I heard Maynard yelling that Robert was unconscious. I jerked open the back door and Maynard and I helped Robert, who seemed to be regaining consciousness, out of the car.

Miraculously, the only visible injuries were Robert's bumped head and a cut on my left hand—evidently made by the splintered plank—that wasn't bleeding badly, which I hadn't even noticed. Robert asked us what had happened and we explained that we had rolled the car down Taft Hill.

We were only about a quarter of a mile from Maynard's house and it was about a half-mile north on Taft Hill Road to Robert's. We decided that it would probably be best if Maynard walked home while Teddy and I walked Robert home. We put his arms around our necks and proceeded slowly down the road more or less dragging Robert along with us. Every few minutes, he asked us to tell him again what had happened. He obviously had suffered a concussion, but it never occurred to any of us that we should call an ambulance. I think Robert's dad, Fred, drove Teddy and me home. I still remember the accident as if it were a bad dream in slow motion.

I also remember the next morning all too clearly. Mom and Dad had driven to Denver Friday afternoon in the recently acquired two-year-old Dodge that Dad had purchased. They were expected back Sunday afternoon, at which time I would have to tell them what happened. I told both my brothers everything when they asked me why the car was not parked in the yard. Surprisingly, about all they said was how stupid it had been to put on the brakes so violently. Chuck reminded me that any accident of this magnitude had to be reported to the Sheriff. We drove over to take a look at the car and as we pulled up we could see that it was in bad shape, even though it had eventually landed on its wheels. The front wheels were both splayed out from the impact, the roof looked like a metal tent, there were big dents on both sides of the doors and the trunk was damaged.

Then we realized the most frightening thing of all. The plank that had come through the windshield over the steering wheel would have probably taken off my head if I hadn't been thrown over on Teddy. It's almost certain that if seat belts had been in use, I would have been killed. We extracted the plank from the car and I put the front seat, which was lying on the ground where I had thrown it in the back, climbed in and found that the car would still start. Even more surprising was that I could still drive it. Although the front axle was badly bent on both ends, when I put it in gear it still moved forward even though the front wheels rubbed badly on the fenders. Frank and Charlie let down the fence we had flown over and I drove the car back out onto the road. Driving without the front seat, I could barely see over the dashboard, but I managed to slowly make my way to our lane and on the additional half-mile to our house, where I parked the wrecked vehicle right by the front gate to the yard.

I went into the house, called the Sheriff's office and told the dispatcher that I had driven my car off Taft Hill into the barrow pit the previous night, but no one was injured and I was able to get it back onto the road and had driven home. The dispatcher, after asking a few more questions, said that since there were no injuries I could simply bring in the completed accident report form that they would send me, which was quite a relief. However, I still had the rest of the day to dread explaining what had happened to the folks.

Mom and Dad pulled into the yard late Sunday afternoon and parked beside the wrecked car. Of course, they immediately asked what in the world had happened. I told them that I had an accident the night before coming home from town. Mom immediately started grilling me, but Frank interrupted her by simply saying, "Mom, Roy could have been killed." Nothing more was said of the matter and Mom went into the house to cook supper, while Dad changed his clothes and went out to do the chores with us three boys.

Dad drove back to work in Denver as usual the next morning, and later in the week Charlie and Frank helped me get the car into a body shop. The foreman there was surprised to see us drive up in such a terribly torn up car. He thought they probably would not be able to repair it, but suggested we leave it there and he would see what they could do. Next day he called to say they could repair it for $750, not much less than it was worth before the wreck. We said we would let them know when Dad got home on the weekend. Dad decided that we couldn't replace the car with anything better for that amount of money, so we had them go ahead with the body work.

The first quarter of school was to end a few weeks after I'd had my accident and I was scheduled to "go active" soon as a Sig Ep. The fee was going to be fifty dollars for a pin. I had already cost the family $750 that fall and not only didn't have any money to help with that expense, but didn't have the fifty dollars for the pin.

I had been dreading the hell week that preceded going active and had begun to feel that I wasn't cut out for fraternity life anyway, so decided to drop my pledge and save the $50. When I told this to Dad he said he would respect my decision, but they would pay the $50 if I still wanted to go active. The more I had thought about it the more I was relieved at my decision, and I told my brothers and parents that this was definitely what I wanted to do. The whole matter of the wreck and quitting the fraternity left me feeling disgusted with myself. I buckled down for the rest of the school year, got good grades and did my share of the work on the farm with an improved attitude. Some of the friends I made while I was a pledge at the fraternity continued to be friends all the way through college.

When I was a freshman in 1948, Colorado A&M was still adjusting to the big surge of veterans using the G.I. Bill. They were several years older than I and many of them were married and anxious to graduate and settle down. They didn't take all of the fraternity hoo-ha as seriously as the kids just coming out of high school, but did appreciate some of the benefits that having fraternity membership on a resume still provided at that time; however, I never felt my decision affected either my college experience or my career after graduation.

I never had any illusions that I could hope to make the varsity football team, and my chances for the basketball team were nearly as remote. I still decided to try out for the basketball team just for the experience of competing at this level. However, when the season opened toward the end of the first quarter of school, I learned that those trying out for the freshman team would be practicing at night. I wasn't interested in any more night basketball practices and not going out probably saved me the embarrassment of being one of the first people cut from the freshman squad.

I enjoyed my classes and found them not quite as difficult as I had feared. Chemistry and biology covered things that had been taught in high school. My most challenging class was in one of my best subjects, English. My entrance examination score had placed me in advanced English, taught by the head of the department, who was a very good but demanding professor. An elderly professor, who had been department head earlier in his career, taught beginning chemistry. He had a wonderful personality and, on the first day of class reminded us that since we were in college now we should not be treated as we were in high school, so he would not be taking roll. Biology 101 was taught by the head of the department, Dr. Durell, one of the most revered members of the entire faculty. So many freshmen had to take at least one quarter of biology that it was taught in the auditorium of Old Main, the oldest building on campus. There were several hundred people in the class. My introductory course to animal husbandry was also taught by the head of the department. I later learned that these introductory classes were about the only courses taught by department heads, which appeared to be a great idea to me.

Frank was a junior my freshman year and we managed to go mule deer hunting together two weekends of the late October Colorado season. The first weekend we hunted with our grandfather, Perry Williams, in an area known as the "Hole," a rugged area in the southern part of the ranch he had sold to the Warren Livestock Company in 1941 and had retained permission to hunt there. The best hunting was on the steep slopes of a north-south valley that was fairly flat, just before it formed a deep canyon sloping towards Buckeye, Colorado. We worked our way around the east wall of the canyon, walking about a quarter-mile apart and we ran into a few does running at full speed. There were evidently some other hunters moving towards us from the other direction, so we gave up on this location.

Grandpa said that the big bucks sometimes hid in tall brush during the season and we eased down the valley to a fairly flat area at its head that had some scattered brush tall enough to conceal even a good-sized deer lying down. We put some distance between ourselves creeping through this brushy area and suddenly a huge buck, which couldn't have been lying more than eighty yards in front of us, jumped up and bounded away from us with the beautiful gate that only mule deer have. Before I, with a bad case of buck fever, could get my old 25/35 to my shoulder, both Frank and Grandpa got off a shot. Grandpa shot over the buck with his high-powered 30/06 and Frank dropped him with his 30/30 with a shot to the neck that broke his spine just ahead of his shoulders.

The buck was already dead when we got to him. He was a beautiful specimen, probably just past his prime, with an evenly balanced set of antlers with four points and a brush hook on either side. The base of each horn was at least two-and-a-half inches in diameter, which is quite heavy for a mule deer. Frank and Grandpa immediately field dressed him and we were able to maneuver Grandpa's pickup to within fifteen or twenty yards of the buck. It was all the three of us could do to get the animal loaded. We decided to call it a day, drove back to Grandpa's house in Cheyenne, transferred the buck to the fender of our car and headed back toward home. At the game and fish department check station at Ted's place about twelve miles north of Fort Collins we had to stop and let the game wardens inspect the deer and check Frank's license. They recorded its sex and general description and asked where it had been killed. A lot of deer went through this station each year and they indicated it was one of the largest bucks they had checked.

When we got home just before dark, we hung the buck by its antlers from a large apple tree and propped the ribs apart with pieces of firewood to let it cool out for a few days. We then took it down from the tree, cut its head off and took it into the locker plant to be skinned, cut up and wrapped in packages for a family of five, frozen and put into our food locker along with what was left of the pig and steer we had raised had slaughtered earlier. It never occurred to us to go to the expense of having the head of this beautiful buck mounted. We simply threw the impressive rack into a wagon box that we kept by the chicken house for our firewood and coal.

The governing body of Colorado A & M, the State Board of Agriculture. Dad is third from left, president Roy Green is fifth and Board Secretary Jim Miller is sixth. Dad went off the Board about a year before I started college.

20

Round Corral Rodeos

The only extracurricular activity I participated in my freshman year, other than my short-lived fling with the fraternity, was to join the livestock club. The majority of its members were Ag majors, many in animal husbandry. Some were students in other fields who just wanted to participate in the projects of this very active club, the two most important of which were a fall livestock show called the "Little National Western," named after the big event held every January in Denver, and a spring celebration called "College Days." The former event was held on the indoor track at the field house and the latter was a three-day event that included a street dance, parade, a two-day rodeo and a western dance in the ballroom of the Student Union as the grand finale.

The livestock show was put on in cooperation with the Animal Husbandry Department involving its relatively new horse activities and its livestock judging team. The event ran for two days and was well-attended by the students and citizens of Fort Collins.

During College Days, people lined up three-deep to watch the parade, held on the morning after the street dance, travel down College Avenue, the city's main street. All the fraternities and sororities spent days decorating the floats that they entered in the competition for prizes in several categories. The business community, fire department, police department and local dignitaries, who rode in convertibles loaned by local auto dealers, also participated. People from miles away hauled their horses to Fort Collins to ride at the end of the parade led by the college band and its high-stepping leader.

The main attraction of the three-day event was the rodeo. When I was a freshman, it was held in an arena that had just been built entirely by the livestock club with voluntary labor and material donated by local businesses. My oldest brother Chuck, a senior, was manager of the rodeo that year and most of his responsibilities evolved around coordinating the many committees appointed by the president of the livestock club to pull off the rodeo. They included one committee to handle the entries in the rodeo, whose contestants came from about eight different colleges, one to obtain a sponsor for the silver belt-buckles given to event winners and other prizes for second, third, and fourth in each event, and probably most important this particular year, the construction of the arena.

There were several important committees necessary to coordinate other activities during the three-day celebration and they had begun work months in advance of the events. They included the street dance committee, a parade committee and the cowboy ball committee. The rodeo grounds were located in the center of a fairly large field, which was fenced around the perimeter. People bought tickets for the rodeo as they walked or drove their car in, while another group of volunteers saw to the parking. There were no permanent seats at the arena so the livestock club had to rent bleachers. They were obtained in Laramie Wyoming about sixty-five miles north of Fort Collins, and to save money on the per-day charge, they were picked up early the morning of the first rodeo performance and taken back in the late afternoon of the second. It was no easy job putting up and taking down these cumbersome things.

Planning and coordinating College Days was a big responsibility for a campus club that had to be self-financed, and it had become a cherished tradition at Colorado A&M as it evolved over the years. The manager of the rodeo and the managers and committee chairmen of all these activities had either assistants or vice chairmen. These had been appointed with full knowledge that they would be in charge of that responsibility the following year so they would be fully prepared when the time came for them to take on their job. This annual activity was probably the favorite celebration of the year for the entire student body all four years I was in college.

The cowboy ball that was held Saturday night after the rodeo at the Student Union ballroom featured the music of Hank Thompson, a nationally popular western band with several top hits playing on juke boxes everywhere. At an intermission, the winner of each rodeo event was presented a gold-inlaid silver trophy buckle. The rodeo queen, who had been elected from among members of the livestock club, and her date, led off the dance. It was probably a good thing that Fort Collins sold only 3.2 beer because a lot of it was consumed over College Days weekend.

With such a successful rodeo, Colorado A&M naturally had a rodeo club, which I didn't even join until midwinter of my freshman year. I think the fact I wasn't good enough to participate in varsity athletics and had not joined a fraternity, which would have made it possible to participate in intramural sports, encouraged me to join the rodeo club. I was not good enough in any event to be selected as a member of the team for any rodeos that year, but I decided to enter the bareback riding at the College Days Rodeo to get my feet wet. I made a qualified ride but didn't place in the event.

Chuck won second in the saddle bronc riding, but had bad luck in the bull riding. He was making a good ride when, just before the whistle blew, he bucked off, ended up under the bull, and got stepped on. I was scared to death when he just lay there and the ambulance crew pushed a gurney out into the middle of the arena to carry him out. By the time they got him to the chutes he was regaining consciousness and when he opened his eyes the right one was cocked way off center and was quite bloodshot. He managed to recover enough by that evening to attend the dance, present the belt buckles and introduce the rodeo queen at the dance

The College Days Rodeo in Fort Collins was not the first one I had ever entered. Early the previous summer, before I started work at Trail Creek, I had traveled to a one-day rodeo at a place called Table Mountain near Golden, Colorado, with my friends Bozo and his cousin Donnie Simianer. Bozo and I entered the bareback bronc riding and Donnie entered the bull riding. Before that time, I had ridden only a couple of bareback horses at a ranch in Masonville, Colorado, which was owned by a man who had an arena and some horses we could practice on. I managed to win a sixth at Table Mountain, which netted me about $36.00 after deducting the $10.00 entry fee. When I got home, I proudly told my dad I had won some money on my first bareback ride. His only comment was that he was afraid this early success would just encourage me to go to more rodeos. He was right. The next week Bozo, Donnie and I went to Deer Trail, Colorado and rode in their annual rodeo, another one-day affair. I drew a big, stout bay horse that bucked me off about the third jump out of the chute and drove my head into the ground—so much for getting overconfident.

The next bareback horse I rode was the one at the College Days Rodeo, and I was nervous, but not afraid, having decided that the price of riding bucking horses was going to be taking the chance of enduring a hard fall. Frank set my bareback rigging for me and gave me some last-minute advice. I managed to start my horse (have my spurs over the points of his shoulders as he came out of the chute) and ride him the full eight seconds to make a qualifying ride. I didn't spur him particularly well but it did confirm I had some talent for this event. It was the beginning of an eight-year addiction to the sport of rodeo.

Donnie Simianer and I attended several rodeos together the first few weeks prior to going up to Trail Creek Ranch for the rest of the next summer. I don't have many specific recollections of this particular summer, but do recall the log bunkhouse having been completed. I lived in it all summer and didn't miss my bed in the cellar of the main house. Most Saturday nights, Bob and Ruby took Ann and me to a dance at either Red Feather or Livermore.

Three or four times that summer one of my friends came by the ranch and picked me up to go visit a neighboring ranch and have what we called a round corral rodeo by putting either a bareback rigging or bronc saddle on one of the work horses to practice our skills. Often these horses would not buck at all or very little; however, one big, fairly gentle dark brown work horse let me saddle him and get on. When I reached my spurs up over his shoulders and turned out my toes he jumped straight up and then bucked in a tight circle. Knowing I was in big trouble, I grabbed for the saddle horn with my free hand, which was a mistake, because the next jump he bucked me off anyway and I landed on my back gasping for air. I must admit that when they asked me if I wanted to get back on him, I allowed as how I would just as soon not. Earlier in the week, I had cut my right thumb nearly to the bone while sharpening an axe with a file and the wound had barely started to heal. Of course, when I frantically grabbed for the saddle horn, I opened up the wound and it started bleeding. The lesson I took away from this unsuccessful effort at riding a saddle bronc is that if I wanted to be a rodeo cowboy, I would have to toughen up.

I continued to enjoy the variety in my work at the ranch. As usual there were quite a few guests over the July 4th holiday and I was busy taking people riding most of the time. The opportunity to meet a lot of different people appealed to me, but I did not have enough time to really get to know most of them. The guests who came for a week's vacation were a different matter. The combination of chatting while out riding horseback, eating together three times a day, often joining them for cocktails before supper and playing canasta or singing around the piano, or both, was enough time for all of us to feel we really knew each other, and when they left, our goodbyes were as if we were parting with dear friends.

Between the Fourth of July rush and August holiday season I worked in the hay field quite a lot. I often hauled bales into the stack yard all by myself using the ranch pick up. I would put the truck in first gear and as it rolled slowly I would jump out and throw bales into the bed, handling them by their twine or wire, depending on what kind of baler was being used. I could get only twenty-four bales on the truck so it took a lot of trips to make a very big stack. When the pile started getting more than five bales high I had to throw them up on top of the pile and then crawl up and drag them across it and carefully put them in place. There was a particular way you had to lay the outside bales of a layer to tie the corners to keep the stack from falling apart.

The upper end of one meadow was boggy and underwater in some places. This was the kind of bog that was created over the ages when moss on a small pond was created where a stream leveled out, forming a pond of still water, while dropping the gravel it was bearing downstream. When the moss was dense enough to allow dust blowing over it to accumulate, the cover eventually became dense enough for meadow grass to grow from seed deposited on it by the wind. As it gathered more dust and the grass rooted down, parts of what had previously been a pond became a floating meadow.

A tractor could not be used to mow or rake the hay on this kind of meadow, so of course the baler could not be pulled over it either. Bob's hired man who lived at the lower ranch mowed and raked the hay in this area with a team of horses, a difficult, touchy job that could be done only by someone who was well acquainted with this particular meadow. When it came time to bale this hay Bob had me hitch the team to the sweep and push it up to the baler. Then, another hired man pitched it in front of the pickup on the baler, while a third carried the bales away as they were pushed out of the chute. As I drove the team out onto the boggy part of the meadow, I could see the ground out ahead of the team roll as if it were a gentle ocean wave.

When driving a team on such a meadow, it was important to fully understand the kind of bog the hay was growing on, because it was possible for a horse to break through the shallow soil and root system into the saturated gravel beneath. Horses seem to have a sense of when this might happen and will usually balk before going too far. If all four legs should break through, they become trapped (bogged down!) and it can be extremely difficult to pull them free. Bob had put up the hay on this meadow many times over the years and knew how far he could venture out on the wet parts. Once again, Bob's confidence in me greatly exceeded that which I had in myself. A couple of times we nearly ventured too far into the wetter areas, but by leaving some of the hay lying in the swaths rather than risk retrieving it, we managed to get all that part of the meadow finished without any catastrophe. I was glad to go back to hauling bales again, and then to my even less stressful dude wrangling job the rest of the summer.

University of Wyoming Rodeo in 1949.
Amazing simultaneous pictures taken from both sides of the arena
of Frank bucking off bareback horse.

21

First National College Rodeo Finals

Soon after Labor Day, I came home from the ranch with a check for my full summer's wages as usual and an additional few dollars in my pocket from the few tips I'd accepted with a certain amount of embarrassment. About three weeks later, I registered for my sophomore year at Colorado A&M. Charlie had graduated and Frank and I continued driving to college together every morning when our schedules allowed, but some days he drove his car and I drove Mom's car or the pickup. I was glad to see some of my classmates who were also animal husbandry majors and took the same courses that I did. Robert Martin had received the La Porte Joint Honor Scholarship that I had gotten the previous year and I saw I him on campus from time to time. Gary Glick had joined the Navy shortly after we graduated from high school, but I did get to see him when he came home to marry his high school sweetheart, Colleen Mitchell, at the church that housed the gymnasium where we had played our high school basketball. Occasionally, I went to the La Porte basketball games when I was a college freshman, but rarely went to any of their activities my sophomore year.

Frank and I usually went to the rodeo club meeting on Tuesday nights and to the livestock club meetings on Wednesday nights. I tried to get up to Virginia Dale or Livermore whenever they had a Saturday night dance, and I met friends at one of the downtown beer joints most Friday nights and occasionally went out to a beer hall that had a jukebox and dance floor a little west of town. It was referred to as Smitty's, even though no person by that name had owned it for years. I tried to study in the library when I had to wait for Frank for a ride home and did some homework most weeknights. We always had quite a lot of work to do on the farm on the weekends, when Dad was home, hauling hay, fixing fence or some other typical farm tasks, in addition to milking five cows morning and night every day.

I probably studied as much as my friends who lived in dorms and worked as many hours at home as several did who were working their way through school. I kept my grades well above the B average required to maintain my scholarship and in fact received only one B in the second quarter. Then everything fell apart Spring quarter. I don't recall call exactly how we first met, but Tom Knight and I became best friends shortly after spring break and, with spring in the air, our fancy turned toward anything but studying. He had attended Fort Collins High and was a starting guard on their football team and a conference champion wrestler. He had been active in extracurricular activities including singing bass in the school's double quartet and, most important to me, seemed to have a way with the girls. As often happens after high school, his steady girlfriend, who was also very popular, had split up with him even though she was also going to Colorado A&M. He professed to be heartbroken, but didn't let that take him out of circulation.

Tom took it upon himself to find me a date, something I had despaired of doing for myself. We looked through his high school annual trying to pick out girls he knew who were now seniors and tried to think of others who were now freshmen at A&M whom I might pursue. When that didn't work, he remembered two girls who were high school sophomores whom he had dated since he broke up with his steady girlfriend. We looked at their pictures in his annual and I found them more than acceptable. He called and got a date with one, and I called the other, suggesting that she and I double up with Tom and his date. I borrowed the folks' car the next Friday night and Tom and Margaret Ann joined Helen and me for a movie. Helen was a very pretty, quiet girl, and while I thought Tom's date was less pretty, she was quite vivacious. Since Tom knew both of them and he and I were such good friends, we had no problem finding things to talk about.

After the movie, we went to the local drive-in and then parked a while in the moonlight in City Park and listened to the radio. I got Helen home before her midnight curfew and when I walked her to the door, she did not make it difficult for me to give her a goodnight kiss. I was instantly smitten and literally kicked my heels in the air as I walked off the porch to my car. When Tom asked me what I thought of Helen, I told him I thought she was wonderful.

Me bucking off Sweet Nellie.... I was to meet up with her a couple more times.

The next weekend, Tom suggested that we swap dates so I could see what I thought of Margaret Ann. I said I wasn't interested, and anyway I wasn't sure that Margaret would be amenable to the plan either. Never the less, Tom said he would try to set the whole thing up and shortly reported that he had a date with Helen, but that Margaret Ann already had a date. Like an idiot, the next Friday night I dropped myself off at a movie and loaned Tom the car. I waited for him nearly an hour in the lobby after the movie before he picked me up. Tom and Helen immediately started going steady and they were eventually married.

Prior to the foregoing episode, we had tried several other harebrained schemes including one in which I tried to get him a date with a girl in La Porte whom I had dated once—my average number of dates with a girl. She had a very sexy, low voice and beautiful long brunette hair. I rather suspect that she would have been willing to go out with me again, but I was not able to fix her up with Tom.

Several times we borrowed an old 1924 open roadster jitney of some make that his fraternity, Sigma Nu, owned and drove it around town on warm spring nights fantasizing about girls we were going to pick up with it and just enjoying feeling alive. We finally wore out the old vehicle. Driving up the hill out of the oval onto Laurel Street it stalled and we had to call someone to tow it back to the Sigma Nu house. This did not put Tom in very good graces with his fraternity brothers.

While we were having all this fun, we were doing very little studying and even cutting classes, including our late afternoon three-hour lab in advanced inorganic chemistry. This course had turned out to be far more difficult than the first year of chemistry, which had been a rerun of what I had already learned in high school. Also, we had had no laboratory for chemistry at La Porte, so I was completely unused to doing experiments and had the dubious honor of being the first person in our class to set the rubber on the holder for our test tubes on fire with a Bunsen burner.

Quarterly finals were coming up and Tom and I were completely unprepared. The chemistry professor based about one-third of our grade on the final, one third on our lab grade and one third on the grades on our other tests. Tom and I knew we were in grave danger of flunking the chemistry final. One of the less savory services fraternities furnished for their members was keeping stolen tests on file, and as Sigma Nu's was among the best, we hoped they might have one that would help us. We were dismayed when our prof, who was no fool, announced that he would be giving a brand-new test this year. Much to my amazement, the day before the chemistry final Tom told me he had slipped into the prof's office the day before and found a mimeographed pile of the tests on his desk. Of course, he had taken two, one for us and one for his fraternity's files. I unsuccessfully tried to memorize the answers to the test in the short time left. I did manage to get a B on it, but my low grade in lab dragged my grade down to a C. I was sick with myself over the whole episode and knew that I deserved to flunk.

I also got a C, which was also better than I deserved, in a very boring class called the history of geography. It was the only history course I ever took that I didn't like. I got a D on the final on general knowledge, because the test was exclusively from the textbook, which I not only had never read, I had never purchased. These were the first and only two C's I received in four years of college.

After attending several rodeo club meetings and getting acquainted with other students who shared my enthusiasm for the sport, I began to realize that I might have a chance of being selected to be on the team for some of the fall rodeos Colorado A&M would participate in. The previous summer I had ridden some saddle broncs and bulls at local weekend rodeos and found I was about equally good, or bad, in these events as I was in bareback riding. Not many of the club members participated in all three events and the reputation my two brothers had established before me were points in my favor.

The method of selecting teams for the rodeos was fairly simple and democratic. The president of the club simply called for nominations from the floor for members of the six-man team. From time to time, one of the more experienced members from previous teams would not be able to make a trip for some reason or not be able to qualify as the result of not maintaining the required two-point grade average that quarter of school. This opened up a spot for me on the team for a couple of rodeos scheduled that fall.

All the college rodeos charged entry fees, which were put into a jackpot and divided among the winners after the rodeo, the same way that points were awarded to determine individual event winners and team winners at the end of the year. If there were a lot of contestants in an event at a rodeo, the contestants performed only once and the points and money were divided into six places. If there were fewer participants, they would participate twice or more. In this case the points were awarded according to winnings in each go-round, plus the average of all go-rounds. In this situation, each go-round and the average were divided evenly.

I don't recall which rodeos I went to that fall. I had managed to place a time or two in each of my events, however. The National Intercollegiate Rodeo finals were scheduled to be held that year at the Cow Palace in San Francisco during their Grand National Livestock Show for the second year in a row. Frank had gone the year before but couldn't this year, and much to my surprise I was elected to the team with five other very much more experienced members.

This year, only the second year the NIRA had held national finals, they were asking members of each team to dress with their particular school colors, but we were given a lot of latitude in deciding how to do it. We came up with the idea of a green western shirt with a gold neckerchief. We had my friend Donnie Simianer's mother make the shirts for us. She picked out a material made out of cotton called "strutters cloth." They were finished just the day before we left for San Francisco!

A tall, well-built pre-vet student named L. T. Walker, who was a bulldogger and saddle bronc rider, and I rode to San Francisco with our team advisor, a member of the staff at the vet school, Dr. Scott Jackson and his wife. L. T. was a veteran and about six years older than I. The other members of the team all piled into Adrian Weaver's car and met us there. We stayed in San Francisco in a big downtown hotel that was about five miles north of the huge Cow Palace arena, which had been built by the WPA during the depression. We checked into the hotel and then went down to the arena to check in and look at the bulletin board by the chutes to see what stock we had drawn and what performance we would be up in. I saw that I had drawn a horse called Scene Shifter, which had been one of stock contractor Harry Rowell's most famous horses over the years. I looked around the imposing arena contemplating the bronc I had drawn and had the horrible feeling that I was in way over my head.

When we got back to the hotel, the rest of the team went out on the town, but I went down to the coffee shop, had supper and went up to my room early to get a good night's sleep. What a joke! I tossed and turned all night thinking about Scene Shifter. L. T. told me that he was not a very big or stout horse but bucked most people off with his extremely quick moves rather than power. As it turned out, I managed to ride him even though I did not spur him very well or place. As luck would have it, L.T. drew him in the second go-round. After about five seconds Scene Shifter jumped right out from under him, dropping his big frame on the ground hard. We got only one bareback horse and I managed to ride him but didn't place on him either. In the second go-round of saddle bronc riding, I drew the horse that Billy Whitney of the Wyoming University Rodeo Team had won the first go-round on. He was a big powerful horse, but was considered to be a good draw.

I got him started out of the chute in good shape, but about the third jump he stood me up in my stirrups and then the cantle of the saddle hit me in the rear at the full height of his jump and drove my face onto the tan bark when he came down. I was able to struggle to my feet, but my face was a little bloody. As it healed it left the dark brown stain of the bark that took several months to go away. All in all, I had a pretty good showing at my first national finals, even though I never won a thing.

College Days arrived that year about the time Tom and I were in the middle of our spring fling. I had entered all three riding events, having added bull riding to my repertoire. Tom and I wholeheartedly participated in all the fun activities. At the street dance the night before the first performance of the rodeo, we got the bright idea to buy some fortified Tokay wine since it tasted so good and went down so easily. I didn't really drink a great deal that night, but by the time the dance was over I'd had enough of the sweet wine, which, combined with my anxiety over the rodeo the next day, caused me to get sick to my stomach. I was able to drive home fine and slept reasonably well for the rest of the night. Frank and I had to get up early the next morning to do the chores, and Mom, as usual, provided us with a good hearty breakfast, which I wasn't able to enjoy much.

I was up in both the saddle bronc and bull riding that afternoon. I had drawn a little gray mare called Sweet Nellie, which had a reputation for being one of the hardest horses to ride in the string of our stock contractor, Pomeroy and Hawkins. She didn't jump and kick very well so was hard to spur, and she was inclined to duck and dive. A good bronc rider, who was in vet school, Kip Smiley, had drawn her and won the saddle bronc riding the year before at College Days by pretty much just spurring her ahead of the cinch.

I had ridden Scene Shifter in the Cow Palace mainly by spurring from the cinch to the cantle, and surviving his sudden changes of direction by locking myself in with the pressure between my legs under the swell of the saddle with my spurs locked into the cantle or the skirts of the saddle. This style of riding does not impress the judges but it let me at least qualify. This did not work with Sweet Nellie however. After about the fourth jump out of the chute, as I spurred back toward the cantle, she ducked to the left and left me sitting in midair with the hack rein in my hand. I have a picture in the scrapbook Mom kept showing me suspended in time and space as this happened. Unfortunately, a split second later, I hit the ground hard on my back.

The bull riding was a different situation entirely. I had drawn a bull that bucked straight but jumped really high. About halfway through my ride I realized that I was stout enough to ride him if I really concentrated. After the whistle blew, I was even able to throw my leg over his head and land on my feet, a happy ending for any bull ride. On Saturday, I watched the College Days Parade with Mom and Dad, came home for lunch and then put my duffel bag holding my rodeo gear in the trunk of the car and went to the rodeo with them. I was up in the bareback riding, the first event, and had not drawn a very good horse nor did I make a good ride.

I hung around the chutes with my friends for the rest of the rodeo and went back home with the folks, helped with the chores, had supper and got ready for the rodeo dance. After Frank and I got there, I waited in hopeful anticipation for Hank Thompson (again!) to take a break, at which time the buckles were to be awarded to the event winners. The last one awarded was for the bull riding and I learned that I had tied for first with a good-looking, wiry cowboy from Kansas State University. We both agreed rather reluctantly to flip a coin for the buckle and split the first and second money. While this was going on, I learned from him that he had drawn the same bull the second day that I had ridden the first. I won the toss!

It was a beautiful sterling silver buckle with a gold representation of a bull rider in the middle and gold rosettes in the corners. It was engraved with fern designs and had a place at the bottom for a jeweler to imprint my name. I had never dreamed of winning a buckle by the time I was just a sophomore and I must admit I was very proud of it. A week later a good friend of mine in the rodeo club, Jack Lawrence, gave me a Western belt he had hand tooled with my name on the back to wear with the buckle.

Shortly after College Days, I noticed a note on the bulletin board in the hall of the Ag building. It said that Painter Hereford Company was looking for a student to work there for the summer and directed anyone interested to talk to the head of the animal science department, Sherman Wheeler. I decided it couldn't hurt to see what it was all about and dropped by his office later that afternoon. He said that George Williams—someone I vaguely knew as one of three brothers raised in Livermore—who was the foreman for the commercial cattle operation at Painter's, was looking for someone to ride pastures. If I was interested, I was to write to George.

Dan Doody, Bozo and I with three pretty girls at the 1952 Colorado A & M Rodeo Club dance. I won the loud shirt for winning fourth at a Rodeo..

22

Gintsie

I had been assuming I would go back up to Trail Creek at least from July fourth through Labor Day, something I had enjoyed the previous three summers. I told myself it would be good experience to have a job with more cattle work; actually, I was trying to avoid admitting to myself that Stafford Painter, one of the owners of the ranch, had a daughter who had made quite a splash in the Animal Science Department as a freshman during the current year. I had noticed her at the livestock club, and she was very pretty, had a great smile, a nice figure and an outgoing personality.

I decided to apply and wrote George a note indicating that a good part of my summer work experience had been on a cattle ranch and I was not unacquainted with using a pitchfork or shovel. My parents knew his parents and his two brothers and I was sure I had seen him. I soon got a letter telling me that I could have the job, I would be living in the bunkhouse with the hay crew down at the main headquarters where Stafford Painter lived, my pay would be $115 a month, the same as I made at Trail Creek, and that I would get Sundays and every other Saturday off. My ulterior motive for applying had consequences in my life far beyond what I could have imagined.

Dr. Frank Rogers, our longtime family doctor in Denver, had recently retired, and not needing his little 1936 Dodge coupe anymore, gave it to dad. The folks agreed to let me use it for the summer, and shortly after school let out in mid-June I threw my rodeo duffel bag, a suitcase and a bronc saddle I had borrowed from Smokey Krieger, in the trunk and headed for Roggan, about forty-five miles northeast of Denver where the ranch was located. I got there late Sunday afternoon, where George met me and showed me the bunkhouse and bed I would be sleeping in. All bunkhouses I had seen before had woodstoves, a porcelain basin and a bucket of water for washing, an outhouse and the smell of dirty socks. This was a fairly new dormitory-style building with about ten cots, a bathroom with toilet stalls, several washbasins with hot and cold running water and a shower room with three showerheads.

George then took me down to a corral, shed, and tack room, which were halfway between the bunkhouse and the big house where the Painters lived. There was a several-hundred-acre pasture adjoining these improvements, where the horses were kept. George said that the overall ranch manager, Larry Miller, who lived in Denver, didn't like the idea of having to bring horses in every morning, so he had purchased feedbags to feed oats to all the horses every morning so they would come in on their own accord. I had seen oat bags before but had never actually used them. George said that breakfast was served in the dining area next to the bunkhouse at six each morning and I was to get up early enough to go down and feed a gallon of oats to all ten horses before I ate

The first morning I had no problem putting the bags with oats over the horses' ears; in fact, they nearly knocked me over trying to get me to do it. I then went to breakfast and then came back to take the bags off. A few of them wouldn't let me catch them and ran around the corral with the bags flopping. Most eventually came off by themselves, but I had to rope one horse to remove the bag. The corral had obviously been designed by someone who had never tried to catch one horse out of a group. The hay feeder had been placed in the center of the corral and it was impossible to get any of the horses in a corner because they could simply run around and around the feeder. I found a big long rope in the tack room and shortly figured out why it was there. I had to tie one end of the rope to one side of the corral and the other end to the feeder to stop them from playing ring-around-the-rosie with me. Even with the rope, it wasn't the greatest place to catch a horse that really didn't want to be caught, but I was always able to manage eventually. I had my pick of all but three of them on my daily rides. One of those belonged to Larry Miller and the others to Stafford and his adopted daughter, Virginia, who went by the name of Gintsie.

As George had directed, I had a horse caught and ready to go by seven a.m. on my first day of work. He pulled up with his trailer, unloaded his horse and we took off together on a ride that was typical of the kind I would take nearly every day from then on, most often by myself. The 65,000-acre ranch was divided into many pastures of from anywhere between one section—a square mile or 640 acres—to the largest consisting of four sections. Most ranches of this size are not divided into so many pastures, but in the past they had run only registered cattle and therefore, their land had been divided into many small pastures designed to run just the number of cows one bull could breed. The larger pastures could be used for the yearling bulls, yearling heifers or the cows that could be grouped together after the breeding season when the bulls were removed from the herd. In the winter, the cows were run on the meadows that were also fenced off separately, where it would be convenient to feed them hay.

Within the previous two years, a two-thirds interest in the ranch had been sold to a wealthy grocer in Denver and it had been incorporated with Stafford maintaining a one-third interest. They had hired Larry Miller as the overall ranch manager while Stafford remained on the ranch, living at the headquarters with the title of secretary-treasurer. One-third of the ranch and enough registered cows to stock it continued in the registered Hereford business, which was Stafford's main interest.

George explained to me that I would be working purely with two-thirds of the ranch not involved in raising registered cattle. He said that Larry Miller, who frankly didn't know too much about cattle production, had been hired for his marketing skills. He had decided that the best use of the rest of the ranch would be renting it for summer grazing. The large number of pastures lent itself perfectly for such a program because a good number of different customers could run cattle separately. This worked out very well and was the main reason for my job. George and I would be riding every day from pasture to pasture with a map and tally book in hand to see, among other things, that the right cattle remained in the correct owner's pasture.

George and I spent the morning going through several pastures doing just what I soon would be doing on my own. Since there were two of us, we split up and circled each pasture in opposite directions, working our way to the windmill, one of which was in every pasture except for a couple that shared a water tank at the fence line. We were to make sure that each animal that we saw carried the appropriate brand for that pasture, and if we saw any discrepancy to write it down. When we joined at the water tank, we compared notes and added the number each had seen. It is very difficult to count cattle as you ride through pasture in country like the Sandhills in this area, however we felt the number was close enough. We both had made note of a few cattle with brands indicating they were from adjoining pastures. We then sorted these out and herded them to the closest gate to the appropriate pasture and put them back where they belonged. It was obvious we had two other important things to do on each ride. That was to make sure there was water in each pasture's tank and note any fence that need to be repaired. We both carried a fencing tool and hammer tied to our saddle strings and a small bag made out of a boot top with staples tied to the saddle. If the problem with the fence could be fixed simply it was our job to do so. If not, we were to report it to the farm manager, who would have one of his crew take care of the job. If one of the tanks was empty, we immediately notified a man named Phil living in Roggan, whose full-time job was taking care of the many windmills pumping water from the shallow wells scattered all over the ranch. He drove a Dodge Power Wagon, a newly developed four-wheel-drive ranch utility vehicle, because there were many places on the ranch, particularly near gates or water tanks, where cattle congregated and stirred up the sand that would cause any other vehicle to get stuck.

When George and I had finished working the first two pastures the morning of my first day on my new job, we rode back to his house for dinner. George lived with his wife and two children in a nice, older three-bedroom house that was part of the ranch and located about five miles north of the headquarters. When we arrived, we tied our horses in a couple of stalls in the old-fashioned horse barn. George took me into the house and introduced me to his wife and two young children, then we washed up and sat down to a good home-cooked dinner. I felt right at home with George and his family, since he had been raised in the same ranch community I had and he knew my family and its history.

After dinner, we rode east to check two or three more pastures. By the time we had finished the third pasture, it was time to get me back to the bunkhouse for supper. On the way, we reviewed everything we had done that day and I had a pretty good feeling that I would be able to handle the job. George gave me a map showing the layout of the pastures and also a tally book indicating whose cattle were in each pasture and what brands they carried.

When we got back to the headquarters corral late that afternoon, George loaded his horse into his trailer and headed home. I unsaddled my horse and turned him out, and by then it was time to eat a big supper up at the cookhouse. They served plain, simple but nourishing food and always some kind of dessert. I had also had a big meal and some great homemade pie up at George's house where we had stopped at noon. A long day of riding does wonders for your appetite.

After supper, I got in my little coupe and drove in to Roggan to check out their one beer joint. I found one of my bunkhouse mates in the bar and joined him for a bottle of beer. We visited and he told me about the work he and the other hired men did and about their farm foreman, who lived in Roggan. As far as he knew, all the men in the bunkhouse were involved in putting up the hay on the sub-irrigated meadows adjacent to the shallow lakes scattered around the Sandhills that made up nearly all the ranch. After an hour or so and another beer, I headed back to the bunk house and turned in so I could roll out at 5:30 the next morning to do my pre-breakfast chores.

When George had left the evening before, he had lined me out on the pastures he wanted me to check the rest of the week, letting me decide the order in which to check them on each day's ride. The Painter Hereford Ranch was about twenty-five miles wide from East to West and about ten miles deep from north to south. The headquarters was in the south-central part and George's house was almost right in the middle. The manager of the purebred operation lived in a home about three miles north and west of the headquarters, and the ten or more sections dedicated to that operation were the only part of the ranch I didn't have to cover. If I started out heading east, I might go twelve to fifteen miles, and if I rode pastures to the north and west I could also end up twelve to fifteen miles from the headquarters. Consequently, on days I worked on either extreme end of the ranch I rode from twenty-five to thirty miles, not counting the random miles traveled checking the pastures. When I made my longer rides, the ranch cook put up a lunch for me, which I tied on the back of my saddle in my Levi jacket. On my shorter rides, I'd either come back to the cookhouse or drop into George's for lunch. Some days I would run into problems and end up going without lunch. I never carried any water, since there was a windmill in every pasture. When the wind wasn't blowing, I would simply tie my horse to the mill tower, stuff my glove in the pipe flowing into the tank, climb up the tower, turn the blades by hand a few times, climb down off the mill, pull out the glove and drink the water that had accumulated in the pipe. This was a little trick George showed me the first day.

By Thursday night, I had finally gotten up enough nerve to drop by the ranch house after supper at the bunkhouse. I knocked on the back door and Gintsie answered it. It seemed that she usually did the supper dishes and was in the middle of that chore. I said if she wanted to hand me a dishtowel I would be happy to dry them. She accepted my offer and it turned out to be a pretty comfortable way to get acquainted. I had already met Stafford, his wife and Gintsie's younger half-brother, Jimmy. I'm sure her folks were used to having young men knock on their door and they didn't intrude. After we finished the dishes, she invited me into the living room and I immediately noticed a piano. I asked her if she played and when she said yes, I naturally asked if she would play something for me. The stand on the piano was covered with sheet music of both currently popular and standard hits. As she proceeded to play, it was obvious that she had had lots of lessons. I asked her if she had any favorite pieces memorized and was impressed as she proceeded to play Clair de Lune by Debussy. When she finished the piece and came over and sat down beside me on the couch, I suddenly couldn't think of a thing to say, so I told her how much I had enjoyed the evening and made my exit. I walked the 300 yards to the bunkhouse in the twilight with my emotions churning. I was twenty and knew what puppy love felt like, and this seemed like something different. I suspected I could be setting myself up for a fall much more painful than getting bucked off a horse.

The next ten days, I settled into a routine of riding pastures all day and making my way down to the Painters' house to dry dishes and lose my heart to someone I wouldn't have had the nerve to ask for a date a month ago. The first reality check came the next weekend when I asked Gintsie what she was going to be doing

Saturday night and she said she had a date. I had already decided to hang around the ranch that weekend rather than go home and I couldn't keep from watching a nice car pull up after supper and see someone walk up to the house and be invited in. Shortly she came out with her date, and they probably headed for Denver. I knew Gintsie was not going steady with anybody and this might have been just a date that she had already scheduled before school was out—or not. I told myself that it was no big deal because we had really known each other for only a short while, but I realized I was jealous and didn't like the feeling.

On Monday, I resumed my normal work routine, but instead of going down to dry the dishes after supper, I went to town and had a few beers. Riding pastures and working cattle by yourself all day left a lot of time to think. I convinced myself that I had no excuse for wallowing in self-pity, but instead should go ahead and continue enjoying the company of a girl who obviously didn't at all mind the attention I was giving her. So the next night, I was back drying dishes and no mention was made of the Saturday night date.

The Fourth of July rodeo held in nearby Greeley, then called "The Spud Rodeo," was coming up the next weekend and I very much wanted to ride there. I asked George for permission to take that Saturday off and, when he agreed, I called in my entries. I decided to enter the bareback and saddle bronc riding. This was the biggest rodeo in the area and one of the professional rodeos that gave out first place belt buckles for each event. It would be the largest and most competitive rodeo I had entered thus far in my short rodeo career.

Greeley was a three-day rodeo and Gintsie had agreed to go with me the first day. We drove over in my little Dodge coupe, leaving in plenty of time to enjoy a picnic lunch on the park-like grounds surrounding the rodeo arena. It was a romantic setting and when I sat on the grass and leaned back against a tree, Gintsie, caught up in it, sat beside me and laid her head on my lap, a rare display of public affection on her part. Needless to say, I melted into a happy puddle.

Before the rodeo started that afternoon, we made our way to the contestants' stand beside the bucking chutes and I parked Gintsie there. The bareback riding was the first event and my horse was in the chute. I had drawn one that didn't buck very well, and although I spurred him well, I knew I didn't have a chance to place when the pickup man pulled me off at the end of the ride. Even though I had won the bull riding at our College Days rodeo, I still didn't have a lot of confidence in my ability in that event. The stock contractor at the Greeley rodeo had several bulls that were far better than any at the rodeo in Fort Collins, and I guess I wasn't ready to take a chance of drawing any of them yet.

I wasn't up in the Saddle Bronc riding till the next day, so I probably should have gone back to the contestants' stand and sat with Gintsie, but I had a yen to hang around the chutes and visit with some of the contestants I knew and talk shop. About thirty minutes after the saddle bronc riding was over, I went over to the contestants' stand and sat down by Gintsie. She didn't greet me with her usual big smile and wanted to know where I had gone after I had ridden my bareback horse. I said something to the effect that I felt sure she couldn't mind my spending a little time out in the arena. I was far from sophisticated about the art of wooing a girl, especially one who was used to receiving her date's undivided attention. When she indicated she needed to get home, whereas I had expected we would find something to do in town for the rest of the day and then go to the Rodeo dance, I pouted a little, not furthering my cause any.

I knew my parents were driving to Greeley the next day to attend the rodeo and I had hoped I might be able to introduce them to Gintsie. Although we seemed to be getting along fine, by the time we got back to the ranch in the late afternoon, Gintsie said she didn't think she would go to the rodeo the next day. The next morning being Sunday, I slept in a little and then headed for Greeley and got breakfast there. I met my folks at the ticket office below the grandstand and then had to go to the chutes and get ready to ride my saddle bronc. I got him started out of the chute okay and was spurring him pretty well as he bucked straight towards the grandstand across from the arena. Just as we were getting close to the fence I spurred over the cantle of my saddle with my left foot and he bucked me off over his right shoulder. A split second later I hit the ground on my head and rolled. I knew Mom and Dad were watching, so I jumped up as fast as I could, letting them know I was okay. We had supper in town before they drove home and I headed back to the ranch. When I got there just before dark, I went to bed early and tossed and turned as I pondered a Fourth of July holiday that didn't end nearly as well as it started.

I picked up on my job of solitary pasture checking the next morning and didn't see Gintsie again until Thursday when I was coming in from a morning ride for lunch at the cook house. She was working her horse on his reining in the corral as I rode up. We visited cordially as I loosened my cinch, took off the bridle, put on a halter and tied him in the shed. I truthfully don't recall whether she invited me or I invited myself down to the house to help with the dishes after supper that night. In any case, when I got through with my afternoon ride and had supper, I walked on over to the house and we resumed our romantic, to me at least, routine.

August is county fair season and all of the ones in Eastern Colorado have a rodeo on the weekend of their fairs. I managed to get off from my Saturday morning duty to ride in ones at Fort Morgan, Yuma and Wray. I worked all three riding events at some of them and only two at others and managed to place third or fourth in one or two of the events at a couple of them. This earned me enough money to barely cover my expenses and a warning from my boss, George, that I had used up all the Saturdays I had coming.

Out of the horses that I was feeding, I had the choice of seven that I could ride. The other three included Gintsie's good looking pinto, a gray horse named Cozad reserved for Stafford and a cold-blooded big pinto that was reserved for the ranch manager, Larry Miller, when he occasionally showed up to do some cattle work. Of the other seven, there were only three that were very well broke cow horses and two were four-year-olds that were barely broke. When I had demanding cattle work to do, I rode a horse that looked like he was mostly thoroughbred, had a good rein and possessed a lot of cow sense. His only problem was he turned on his front feet, making him extremely rough to ride when cutting cattle. A couple of the others were so bad I tried to avoid riding them entirely. The biggest of the two four-year-olds I was breaking tried to buck every time I got on him. When I mounted I took a short hold on my inside rein, stood by his shoulder and swung up in the saddle as he started to buck. As soon as I was settled into the saddle, he usually stopped and gave me no more trouble the rest of the day.

The other green broke four-year-old was a little less than fifteen hands tall. He seldom bucked with me but was pretty goosy. I never knew when I left the ranch just what problems I might run into. One day when I was riding him while checking one of the bigger pastures at the far eastern side of the ranch, I found eight steers that belonged in the adjoining pasture. By taking my time and being patient we were able to get them cut out and bunched up. I realized that I didn't know just where the gate into the neighbor's pasture was, so I stopped my horse and reached into my front pocket for the map that marked its location. Without thinking, I unfolded the map too quickly while I was sitting there with my reins loose. My horse jumped sideways about four feet, or so it seemed. I reached out for the horn, and barely caught it as I was heading for the ground and managed to pull myself back up into the saddle. I'm not sure I would have stayed on without the adrenaline surge triggered by the knowledge of how far I would have had to walk home. After I calmed my horse, I realized that I was still clenching the saddle horn with all my might with a badly wrinkled map under it.

After Gintsie and I resumed the routine we had before the Greeley rodeo, she had a couple more Saturday night dates that we never discussed. I did enter a few more rodeos, one of which was the Douglas County Fair in Castle Rock in mid-August. Gintsie's family had friends named Sorrell who owned a ranch just south of Castle Rock near Larkspur. When I mentioned that I was planning to enter the rodeo there, she suggested we drive down together and stay at the ranch with the Sorrells, who had quite a large herd of Black Angus cattle.

The day before the rodeo started, we drove to Larkspur by way of back roads, cutting south from Roggan through Kiowa. As I recall, the Sorrels had a son about Gintsie's age named Bill and a younger daughter. When we arrived just before dark they showed us to our bedrooms and we then joined them in their spacious living room and visited until bedtime. We were treated in the morning to a hearty ranch breakfast and were then shown around the ranch for a couple of hours before we left for the rodeo about fifteen miles up the road in Castle Rock.

I very well remember what I drew in the bull riding that afternoon. He was a fairly small black bull that was seldom ridden to the whistle. I got out of the chute on him in good shape and after about two jumps he went into a fairly flat spin to the left as he usually did. I got into the spin with him in complete control and was making a good ride when I felt myself succumbing to centrifugal force. He bucked me off just as the whistle blew and I landed on my back and rolled well away from him. I was, of course, disappointed, but several other bull riders congratulated me on how close I had come to conquering him. I surely would have won the bull riding if I had made it to the whistle, and I believed that with a little more determination I could have.

After the rodeo, Gintsie and I drove back to the ranch for supper with the family. Along about eight p.m. we decided to go back to Castle Rock for the rodeo dance held outdoors at the fairgrounds. They had a good Western band and we enjoyed dancing for several hours before we headed back to the ranch about midnight. I pulled off to the side of the country road leading from the highway into the ranch and we smooched for a while, then went on to the ranch and slipped into the house to our respective bedrooms.

The next morning, we had breakfast with the family again and spent some more time looking at their ranch and cattle. We bade them goodbye and thanked them for the wonderful hospitality because we were going to go back to Roggan after the rodeo that afternoon. I drew a horse called Dewey in the bareback riding, that had bucked me off of at a rodeo in Sterling two years earlier. He was a horse that you could surely place on if you made a qualified ride. He had a tendency to jump and kick for about five seconds out of the chute and then duck sharply to the left.

In those days, we used to tape the handhold of our rigging so the sticky side was out. When your hand was taped like this, it wasn't as likely to slip out. When my name was called I slipped my gloved hand into my properly taped rigging and eased down on Dewey. He was difficult to get out on because he tended to jump to the head of the chute if he heard you call out to open the gate. When I settled down on him and was ready to go, I nodded down at the man pulling the gate and got out on him in good shape. I was making one of my better rides, vaguely aware that he was about due for his little trick, when I heard a strange pop at the same time he ducked to the left. My hand popped out of the rigging and he threw me about five feet to the right as he ducked an equal amount to the left. When I got my rigging back, I noticed that the tape had broken just where I had turned it at the front of the handhold to wrap it sticky side out. This is what had made the pop when Dewey dived to the left. I might have been bucked off anyway, but I've often thought the distraction of that pop as the horse ducked got in my head just enough to make me unconsciously loosen my grip a little. I rode at Castle Rock several times more over the years but never drew Dewey again.

Several times during the summer, I had driven home over the weekend to see the folks and pick up my mail. On one of my trips, I found a letter from the administrative office of Colorado A&M telling me that due to the Korean War, which had started earlier in the year, there was a need for officers, and those of us between our sophomore and junior years who had declined the opportunity to take advanced ROTC would be given a chance to reverse that decision at the start of the fall quarter. I decided, probably not too wisely, I would stick to my previous decision in spite of the war.

A major factor weighing on that decision was the fact that if you received a commission in the field artillery or the Air Force, you would be committed to at least four years active duty. If you were drafted into the Army you had to serve only two years of active service. Enlistment in the Army resulted in a three-year commitment and if you enlisted in the Navy there was a four-year commitment. I was perfectly willing and fully expecting to serve my country, but had no interest in a career in the service. Anyone in college at that time was granted a deferral from the draft until graduation, if they kept a B average, something I had had no problem doing so far. Staying out of this brutal war for a couple of years longer than my draft-age peers turned out to be most fortunate, because the first two years of it were far worse than when I would be there.

Meanwhile back at the ranch, I continued with my long days riding and pleasant distractions in the evenings. I entered one more rodeo, which was held in Pierce, Colorado about fifteen miles north of Greeley on the Sunday and Monday of Labor Day weekend. It was my last and most successful rodeo of the summer. Gintsie went to the rodeo with me. We each had a hotdog for lunch the first day and then I had to prepare for the bareback riding, which is always the first event. I had drawn a good little gray horse that bucked hard and jumped and kicked in a way that almost made you spur him. After the whistle blew, I knew that I had made a very good ride. I also was up in the saddle bronc riding, on what I think was the same horse I had bucked off of in Greeley. He wasn't easy to ride, but I marked pretty high on him. We got a bareback horse and saddle bronc on both Sunday and Monday, but only one bull, which I also had the first day. He was pretty tough and tested my arm but I rode him fine. Just after the whistle, as I was getting ready to jump off, he turned toward the fence and threw me into it. The ensuing wreck tore my shirt up pretty badly and bloodied my back up a bit, but didn't really hurt too much. I thought I had a good chance to place in the bull riding, so was feeling pretty good about how the rodeo had gone when the day was over.

That happy feeling faded fast when I asked Gintsie what she wanted to do after the rodeo. She informed me that she had to get home right away so she could get ready for a date who was coming by to pick her up at the ranch. I had promised myself I wouldn't do any more pouting and managed to pretty well cover up the fact I was mad as hell. When we got into my little Dodge coupe, I just sat behind the wheel for a few seconds hating myself for wanting to punish Gintsie in some way. As I looked down, I remembered that this model still had a pull-out choke on the dashboard. At the same time that I hit the starter on the floor board I pulled out the choke, and a moment after the car started, it of course flooded and then quit running. I kept grinding the starter and finally said it looked as if it just wasn't going to run.

Gintsie nearly cried as she said that she didn't know what would happen if she couldn't get home. With that, my better nature overcame my short bout of vindictiveness and I pushed in the choke, mashed the throttle to the floor to kill the flooding and held it as I ground the starter for a while, until the car started. She gave me a look that indicated she thought I had probably done something to make the car act up, but I didn't feel inclined to explain myself. It took only thirty or forty minutes to get back to the ranch, during which time not a word was spoken. I dropped her off in front of her house and drove on in to Roggan for a cheeseburger and a few beers, torn shirt and all.

I drove back to Pierce on Labor Day by myself and managed to make pretty good rides on both my saddle bronc and bareback horses. I hadn't placed in the bull riding, but managed to place in both go-rounds and the average in the other two events. I got six checks for a total of less than $200.00!

College started for both of us in about two weeks and we continued to run into each other; I probably dried a few dishes. I was putting in even longer hours than usual because this was the time of year when we had to bring the yearlings to the corral to load them on trucks for shipment to market for their respective owners. Since this process would continue into October, George had hired a young man for me to show the ropes of my job before I left. I cried on his shoulder a few times about my love life during our long rides together, and while he was to some degree sympathetic, he suggested I be prepared for much worse to come when I got back to school. He didn't know the half of it.

Aggie Rodeo Team Second

7 Nov. 1952

HUNTSVILLE, Texas (Special — Colorado A&M college's touring rodeo team placed second to Sul Ross college in the Sam Houston Junior college rodeo here last week-end. The winning Sul Ross team had 305 points. The Aggies scored 300 points.

Top A&M riders were Roy Lilley, who won the bareback championship and was second in saddle bronc competition; Gene Brownell, runner-up in bull riding; and Rod Frary, who tied for fourth in bull riding and placed fourth in the bareback event.

The Aggie team will enter the Baylor university rodeo at Waco, Texas, Friday and Saturday, before returning to Fort Collins. Both the Sam Houston and the Baylor contests are sponsored by the National Intercollegiate Rodeo association.

23

Second Rodeo Finals

I started my junior year in college with a problem I never had before—girl trouble. I had stewed in high school and my first two years of college about getting dates, but never before worried about having to hold on to someone I thought, or at least hoped, was my girl. Since Gintsie didn't want to go steady, I was back to having to ask for dates again, and getting one was much less simple than asking, after I had walked a few hundred yards to dry the dishes.

Now I had to call the "Theta" sorority house and ask for Gintsie, with no assurance that she would be able to talk on the phone. If you did get a date, you had to park in front of the sorority house, ring the doorbell, and then stand in the living room and visit with their housemother, while waiting for your date to come downstairs. She then had to sign the checkout book, which meant you had to have her back before their curfew, which as I recall, was ten p.m. on weeknights, midnight on Friday and Saturday nights and ten p.m. again on Sunday night. Looking back, it seems that the sorority girls were kept on an extremely short leash while fraternity boys, supposedly learning to be gentlemen, were encouraged by their "brothers" to behave as if they were on a testosterone diet.

As a junior, I started taking more required courses specific to my animal husbandry major and also could choose electives of particular interest to me. As a result, I ended up taking a lot of history. I really enjoyed the prof in my first quarter of world history and was able to keep him for the next two quarters of the three-quarter survey course, accumulating a total of fifteen hours by the time I graduated. We were also allowed to take as many hours as we could get our advisor to allow. I decided to take as many hours as possible in fall and winter quarters in order to carry a lighter load in spring quarter, when there were a lot of college rodeos I wanted to compete in. I managed to take nineteen hours fall quarter and twenty-one hours winter quarter. I knew

I would have to settle down and start studying harder with this load. I went to the library when I had free hours during the day, instead of drinking coffee with friends in the student union and I got by with a minimum of studying at home.

In those early days of college rodeo, it was difficult to find a stock contractor who would sponsor our national finals rodeo. The previous two years it had been held in conjunction with the livestock show at the Cow Palace in San Francisco. Somehow someone talked a Texas stock contractor into producing the 1951 finals rodeo at the same coliseum where the Fort Worth professional rodeo was held during their livestock and horse show, which followed shortly after the National Western Livestock Show in Denver.

The points calculated toward winning individual and team national championships were accumulated between the end of the previous year's finals at the Cow Palace and the last college rodeo before the finals scheduled in Fort Worth. In my case, I had placed enough in all three of my riding events the previous spring and at the few fall rodeos I had attended, that I was among those high in the standings by the finals. I learned this when I received a letter from James Cathey, the official photographer for several major professional rodeos, asking me to come by an office he had set up in the Fort Worth Coliseum to have my picture taken before the start of the rodeo.

This was to be a three-day rodeo with performances in the afternoon and at night. Our rodeo club sponsor was able to obtain excused absences for the six members of our rodeo team for the full week of school we would miss. The six of us packed all our gear into the trunk of a new 1951 Chevrolet sedan owned by Fred Brown, who rode bareback horses and bulls. Other members of the rodeo team that I can remember well were Gene Brownell, who also worked all three riding events, and Bill Mundell, who rode bulls and bareback horses and was in the two roping events. Bill was at a disadvantage because we could not afford to haul his nice little bay rope horse, Raisin, clear to Fort Worth, so he had to borrow a strange horse to rope with. I borrowed a bronc saddle from Arlo Curtis, an old Hamley saddle made in Oregon. Hamley probably made more bronc saddles at that time than any firm except possibly the Denver Dry Goods company, which had made the original "association" bronc saddle called a "Turtle," after the original name of the Cowboys' union that preceded the Rodeo Cowboys Association.

Arlo had helped me improve my saddle bronc riding considerably, especially by showing me how best to start my horse as it came out of the chute. To make a qualified ride you had to have your spurs over the points of the horse's shoulders as he came out of the gate and ride him for ten seconds, not grabbing the saddle horn—pulling leather—or losing a stirrup. Getting down properly on a saddle bronc in the chute took some finesse. You first straddled the chute above the horse, taking your hack rein in your riding hand where you had already marked it with a bit of hair pulled from his mane, just where you wanted to hold it. You then eased down onto the saddle and worked your feet into the stirrups on either side. If the horse was jumping around a lot, it was helpful to have a big strong friend holding onto your belt in order to pull you out of harm's way if the horse should come over backwards. The traditional way to spur your horse out of the chute was to lean way back and put your spurs up just ahead of the horse's shoulders without touching them, and then turning your toes out just as you called for him to be let out. This was awkward and tricky, for if you spurred him in the shoulders while still in the chute, he might throw a fit. To avoid this problem, some of the more successful bronc riders had learned to sit straight up in the chute with their stirrups at the side of the saddle until the gate opened. They then leaned back and planted their spurs over the points of the horse's shoulders just as he was taking his first jump out of the gate. Arlo taught me this technique.

My first bareback horse didn't buck very well, but my bulls bucked extremely well and I bucked off both just before the whistle. I knew I wouldn't place in the first go-round in the bareback riding, but I still had a chance in the average, if I made a good ride on the second. I drew three average horses in the saddle bronc riding but managed to spur all of them pretty well. I figured I would surely place in at least one go-round and well in the average.

I drew my second bareback horse for the last performance, the same one that Cotton Rosser had won the first go-round on. I got started on him out of the chute in good shape and was making a good ride when, about six seconds out, he tried to duck out from under me much as Dewey had the previous summer in Castle Rock. This time I didn't lose my grip, but I did get off balance to the left, and as he continued to fade in that direction, he dropped me hard on my head and shoulder, straining my neck.

I didn't have any more events to get ready for so I shook off the pain and walked out to the display area in the concourse surrounding the arena to get a snack. I ran into one of the judges of the riding events who was taking a break during the calf roping and got up the nerve to ask him how I had marked on my saddle broncs. I had been told he was an old-time saddle bronc rider from that part of the country, but I had never heard of him. He said, "Young man, you missed them all out," That meant I had not received a score on any of the three. I protested that I seldom had any trouble marking my saddle broncs out of the chute and couldn't believe I had "goose egged" on all of them. His explanation made it clear to me that he thought the only way you could start a saddle bronc was the old-fashioned way he had done it when he was contesting, and even though I had my spurs well over the shoulders of each of my horses as they passed the chute gate, he didn't approve. I just walked away shaking my head as I realized I had been skunked for the whole rodeo. I've never had my expectations raised so high before a rodeo, nor had I ever had them so completely dashed.

We needed to get back to school as soon as possible, so right after that night's performance we loaded up our gear and started the long drive home. I'm pretty sure that Brown or Brownell had placed in the bull riding and perhaps one of our other team members had placed in one of the roping events, but the team as a whole was pretty let down. We drove all night by taking turns at the wheel and arrived in Springfield, where Bill Mundell lived, and stopped by to see his mother, who worked at the courthouse. I had a very stiff neck from bucking off my last bareback horse and Bill insisted on taking me to his chiropractor in town. I explained to him that our family doctor had never recommended chiropractors and tried to get out of it, but he insisted. Later Bill would say I had entered the chiropractor's office with my stiff neck tilting my head to one side and came out with it tilting the other way. We ate our noon meal in Springfield and pulled into Fort Collins late that afternoon broke, tired and not looking forward the least bit to school the next day.

Nation's Top College Cowboys, Ags Included, Go After Rodeo Crowns

FORT WORTH, Texas (Special) — Competing for trophies and prizes instead of cash, but riding and roping some of the toughest professional stock in the nation, the cowboys and cowgirls of two score universities and colleges begin the first go around of the National Intercollegiate Rodeo championships tonight.

The first performance of the five-day rodeo is scheduled for 8 p.m. tonight.

Six-man teams of Sul Ross college, the defending champion, and the nine other top ranked schools in the country will compete for team honors. The other schools entered are Colorado A & M, Texas A & M, West Texas State, California Polytechnic, Oklahoma A & M, Arizona university, New Mexico university, New Mexico A & M and Wyoming university.

Defending his all-around champion crown will be Harley May of Deming, N. M., and Sul Ross college. He twice won the national title when the NIRA finals were held in San Francisco's Cow palace.

His nearest rival is Roy Lilley, Colorado A & M's all-around star, whose home is in Fort Collins.

Maxie Overstreet of Texas A & M is the rodeo's third ranking entrant, followed by Cotton Rosser of California Polytechnic.

Seven events for men and two for girls are on the program. The Cowboys will compete in calf roping, bareback bronc riding, saddle bronc riding, steer wrestling, bull riding, wild cow milking and in a wild horse race.

The cowgirls will seek championships in clover leaf and flag racing.

RODEO TEAM—Five of these six members of the Colorado A & M college rodeo team are in Fort Worth, Texas, competing in the championship finals of the National Intercollegiate Rodeo association. Shown left to right on the top rail are Roy Lilley, Joe Chase and Billy Mandell. Standing are Rod Frary, Bob Wallower and Joe Flores. Wallower suffered fractures of transverse processes in his back in a recent rodeo. His place in the lineup has been taken by Fred Brown of Kremmling.

Clipping of Rodeo Team going to NIRA finals in Fort Worth.

I was fortunate to have two good friends who shared most of my classes and they would always give their notes to me when I came back from rodeo trips. They actually took better notes than I did and I don't know how I could've gotten by without their cooperation. One of these friends was Bob Wheeler, and the other was his best friend, Bob Runner. They got more than a little irritated when, after borrowing their notes, I often ended up getting better grades than they did. I had never been properly initiated when I first joined the livestock club, a somewhat silly, embarrassing ceremony that I very much deserved to endure. Bob Wheeler reminded me on graduation day that I had somehow managed to slip out of it. He and Bob Runner had a right to harass me about this because they had both helped to get me elected as president of the livestock club when I was a senior.

Picture of me on first bareback horse in Fort Worth.

By coincidence, I was also elected president of the rodeo club my senior year. As I mentioned earlier, the livestock club was much more active than the rodeo club and actually put on the rodeo. As president of both during the period of my most active college rodeoing, I encouraged rodeo club members to join the livestock club and several livestock club members joined the rodeo club. The rodeo club met on Tuesday nights and the livestock club on Wednesday night, and afterwards I often went to one of the beer joints in town for an hour or two with my friends.

I nearly always saw Gintsie at the livestock club meetings and occasionally picked her up at her sorority house to take her to a rodeo club meeting. When she checked out to go to club meetings, she was given a little slack as to when she had to check back in, and we would usually spend some time after the meeting parked on a little hill overlooking City Park. This was much more enjoyable than taking her to a beer joint with my rowdy friends. These romantic interludes were enough to keep me in the velvet trap I was caught in. My friends thought that I was an idiot, which I readily admitted to being. Even though I dated her fairly often, if I happened to run into her when she was out with somebody else, I would drive home and sit in the living room for an hour enjoying feeling sorry for myself. My frustrations with Gintsie didn't seem to affect my performance in school or at the rodeos I competed in, and I occasionally dated someone else, but they always knew I was carrying a torch for Gintsie and our conversation generally ended up on that pathetic subject. I still can't believe that I spent over five years wallowing in this self-inflicted misery.

I traveled to several college rodeos with the team in the spring of my junior year and continued placing fairly often in my three events. I won the bareback riding at New Mexico A&M in Las Cruces, placed in one go-round and the average of the saddle bronc riding and was tied for the all-around with Harley May of Sul Ross in Alpine, Texas. Harley was a senior who worked five events and won the NIRA all-around in his junior and senior years. I had bucked off of a good bull the first day and he had him drawn for the last performance. Harley managed to get to the whistle on him and won the hand-carved trophy saddle. He had already won a room full of such saddles and this would have been my first. I did win a beautiful silver and gold buckle for my bareback ride. I had drawn a horse that one of the top professional bareback riders, Jim R. White, had won a go-round on at the RCA Rodeo in El Paso earlier that year. I also won over $250 in the jackpot created by the $20.00 entry fees from the fifty-six entries in the event, plus another $85 in the saddle bronc riding. This was the most money I had ever won at a college rodeo.

At the College Days rodeo that spring, I drew Sweet Nellie in the saddle bronc riding again and managed to get her ridden this time. One judge, Hugh Bennett, a quarter horse breeder from Colorado Springs and past professional rodeo champion, had me marked in first place and the other judge, a calf roper, had me marked so low that I split second and third place when the scores were averaged. I don't think I placed in either the bull riding or the bareback riding. The next week at the rodeo at Wyoming University I bucked off my bareback horse and placed third or fourth in the saddle bronc riding. I can't remember if they had any bull riding. Since the national finals had been held earlier that year, the next finals would not be held until the spring of 1952, and the points earned since the Fort Worth finals would be added to those earned all the next year.

The summer after my junior year, I decided to enter all the rodeos I could, without neglecting the farm too badly, before going up to Trail Creek after the Fourth of July. I had to get the first alfalfa cutting mowed and raked just as soon as spring quarter was over. We had hired someone to bale our hay since Frank had graduated and left home. I put the bales in the fenced stack yards, hauling them in with our one-ton Diamond-T pickup that we had traded the little Studebaker for.

I can't remember the rodeos I went to; however, they were all RCA approved shows, which allowed National Intercollegiate Rodeo Association members to enter as long as they stayed in college. I was beginning to place in at least one of my events at many of these smaller nearby rodeos. I started work up at Trail Creek about the middle of July and entered the amateur bronc riding at Cheyenne the last week in July. I won third in the first go-round and managed to get in the finals, but bucked off my horse in the short go-round. I remember going to the Larimer County Fair in Loveland. I believe I won a fourth in the bull riding, but didn't place in either of the other events. Donnie Simianer won second in the bull riding with the best ride I ever saw him make.

I fell into my usual routine at the ranch, enjoying the mix of wrangling dudes, working in the hay field and cattle work. Ann had graduated from college the previous year while I was working in Roggan and Ruby had hired a girl named Betty Meyers to take her place. She was quieter than Ann, nice looking and for some reason liked to hear my philosophizing when we sat in the living room at the ranch in the evenings talking. Of course, I had entered the summer still carrying the torch for Gintsie, and I blew the chance for another summer romance. Instead, I anxiously looked forward to the occasional letters that arrived from Roggan and fantasized that we would start going steady when school started in the fall. I'm sure I had given Betty the impression that such was the case already.

Winning second go round of saddle bronc riding at New Mexico A & M.

24

Senior Year

In spite of my ongoing fantasy relationship with Gintsie, I had a great senior year, being invited to join the honorary fraternity, Alpha Zeta, for students in Agriculture nationally and appointed to the Ag Council, a group of leaders selected from the various majors offered in the school of agriculture at Colorado A&M. It was difficult to get on the Ag Council without being active in any social fraternity, including the Farm House, a non-Greek fraternity many ag students belonged to, or a member of the Independent Students Association. In those days, it was conventional wisdom that without affiliation with a fraternity or the ISA, it was nearly impossible to attain a leadership position on campus. The fact that I did reflected my independent nature, which often conflicted with my underlying desire to please everyone.

Our rodeo team participated in more rodeos during the fall of 1951 and spring of 1952 than they had during any comparable period of time since the formation of the National Intercollegiate Rodeo Association in 1949. In at least two instances, two college rodeos were held in different parts of the country on the same weekend and the club decided to send a team to each. The first six people elected chose the rodeo they wanted to attend and the second six traveled to the other. I had the good fortune to be elected to the team for every rodeo that year. The other two who were chosen every time were Bill Mundell and Gene Brownell. By the time the year was over, all three of us had become fast friends and usually partied together every weekend we were home. On one of the weekends when the club sent teams to two rodeos, the group that had been selected second came home with the most points, an indication of our depth of talent.

The only rodeos I have a clear recollection of that year were those I won an event in with one exception. Shortly before the end of the first quarter, just before Christmas, the team traveled to a rodeo at Kingsville, Texas that was then called Texas A & I. Knowing that it was in the far southern part of Texas we dressed for warm weather. When we arrived in the late afternoon before the rodeo and checked in at the entry office, we were invited to a barbecue put on by the rodeo club. We were amazed at the green grass and palm trees and greatly enjoyed the party out in the soft, warm night air. In about the middle of the rodeo the next afternoon, it got colder, and by nightfall we all were freezing. The locals said that a "blue norther," which blew in perhaps once or twice during the winter, had hit us. It was cold all night and during the entire rodeo the next afternoon. We packed up right after the last event and started our long drive home just before dark. I knew that I had placed in all three of my riding events, but was pretty sure I had won no more than third or fourth in any of them.

Before the last performance, we had stopped by the rodeo office and asked them to mail us a check for anything we might have won and any of the prizes furnished by local merchants. A few days after we returned to school, those of us who had placed received our checks and a few items like a pair of Levi's, a Western shirt or a gift certificate for a pair of spurs. About a week later, I received the following letter from the Dean of Agriculture:

It seemed that I had accumulated enough points, by placing in three events, to win the all-around and a colt furnished by the top breeder of quarter horses in the United States, the King Ranch. That very night, I composed a letter to Dick Kleburg, who was managing the ranch at that time and was a nephew of Robert Kleburg, who had bred the winner of the Kentucky Derby in 1949. I thanked Mr. Kleburg for the colt and explained that it would be extremely difficult to get down to pick him up before spring, and that in any case I was concerned that he would nearly freeze in our country without any winter hair. Within the week, I received a letter saying that because the colt they were going to give away at the rodeo had gotten sick, they would have to select another one, so it was no problem whatsoever if we came down in the spring or early summer to get it.

Because of my mother's deep interest in quarter horses, thoroughbreds and Arabians, she was well aware of the King Ranch's reputation for breeding horses and was equally well acquainted with the foundation sires used in their program. In one of my animal breeding textbooks, the King Ranch's foundation

Last bareback in Fort Worth, just before he bucked me off on my head!

> **Texas College of Arts and Industries**
> Kingsville, Texas
>
> DIVISION OF AGRICULTURE
>
> November 11, 1950
>
> Mr. Richard M. Kleberg, Jr.
> King Ranch
> Kingsville, Texas
>
> Dear Mr. Kleberg:
>
> This is to certify that the Quarter Horse kindly donated by the King Ranch to the Champion All Round Cowboy has been won by Roy Lilley of Colorado A. & M.
>
> I have asked Mr. Lilley to get in touch with you concerning the horse.
>
> Thanking you, I am,
>
> Sincerely yours,
>
> J. W. Howe, Director
> Division of Agriculture
> and Sponsor, A & I Rodeo Club
>
> JWH;gr

Letter confirming my having won the all around at the Texas A & I Rodeo in the fall of 1951.

quarter horse sire, "Old Sorrell," was used as an example of a stud famous as the progenitor of their line-bred quarter horses. Needless to say, the whole family was excited about the prospect of me getting a King Ranch horse, even if it was a gelding.

Dad suggested that perhaps he and Mom could drive down sometime in April and pick up the colt for me, so I wouldn't have to miss school. Mom readily agreed because the opportunity to visit the King Ranch was something she hadn't even dreamed of. I had told them that since the Texas A & I rodeo was at night, our rodeo team had been able to drive to the nearby King Ranch to attend their first ever public sale of Santa Gertrudis females at the ranch during the second day. This was a breed that had been developed on this huge ranch over many years through the crossing of registered Short Horn bulls with Brahman cows. Before the sale, we watched a demonstration of the work of some of their top cutting horses, most of which were sired by another foundation stud named Peppy.

Come April, Mom and Dad borrowed a single-horse trailer from Ted Schaefer, hooked it to their car and headed for Kingsville nearly 1500 miles away. After three days of driving, they arrived at their motel in Kingsville in the late afternoon. When they called Kleberg, he graciously invited them to join his family at the big King Ranch home for dinner that night. Dad said that Dick's father, Richard, brother to Robert, joined them for dinner and regaled them with stories about his experience breeding fighting cocks, implying that the genetic selection techniques he had worked out with his chickens had been used by his brother in his horse breeding programs. So, there were Mom and Dad, sitting in this huge dining room at the table with Dick Kleberg, his wife and children as they ate and listened to the eccentric, but brilliant family patriarch expound. I told them it reminded me of a scene from the movie, "Giant."

After their meal, the folks said they retired to the sitting room for after-dinner cocktails and a bit more conversation, during which Dad reminisced about the Table Mountain Ranch in Colorado, which he had managed for so many years for his family. The comparison of Dad managing a 17,000-acre family ranch and young Dick Kleburg running the million-acre King ranch for his family is a bit of a stretch, but the hosts seemed genuinely interested. Upon learning of my parents' ranching background, Dick invited Dad and Mom to come back the next morning and he would have their range management manager take them for a tour of the ranch. The folks naturally jumped at the chance. Dad said the young Mexican who had this responsible job had a college degree and came from a family that had lived and worked for generations on this huge ranch.

After the tour, which took a good deal of the day, Dad told his guide they would be back right after breakfast the next morning to pick up the colt they had come for. After an early breakfast, they drove back to the ranch and hooked up the horse trailer they had left there. A groom then led out a sorrel yearling gelding. He had a wonderful conformation but a slightly droopy lower lip and a Roman nose. Always the diplomat, my mother said that she thought he was beautiful and asked the horse manager how he was bred. You could have knocked her over with a feather when he said he was by Peppy, out of Muchacha, Colorado. Mother had of course heard a lot about Peppy, but knew of Muchacha, Colorado only because she was the dam of the last two grand champion quarter horse stallions at the Denver National Western Stock Show and Rodeo, Peppy's Pokey and Colorado Sorrel, probably the only time two full brothers had won such an honor.

The fact the colt had such an ugly head was my good fortune, for without it he would never have been gelded and given away. When the folks arrived home, I couldn't wait for them to get my prize colt out of the trailer. The first thing I noticed was his lower lip. Old Lu, the workhorse that had pulled the buggy we boys drove to school in Virginia Dale, had such a lip. I then noticed the Roman nose and said something to the effect that I couldn't believe that the King Ranch could've raised a horse with such a head. Mom waited a moment or two and then told me about his breeding and his famous brothers. We all knew enough about saddle horses to understand that there was really no correlation between the looks of a horse's head and his performance. It was just that people who paid a lot of money for horses expected them to be good-looking. I named him Dick in gratitude for the wonderful treatment of Mom and Dad by the King Ranch heir and manager, and immediately wrote him a thank you letter. I soon quit telling people about the breeding of my King Ranch horse, since no one would believe me.

The stock show in Denver was held in the third week of January, and as a member of the Livestock Club I could apply to be a volunteer in the press room there. I got the job, and since I would have an excused absence for being in Denver, I decided to enter the bareback riding at the stock show's major rodeo. Since I would be driving back and forth to Denver, Bill Mundell, who was living at the farm with us that year, decided to enter the bareback riding also. The city of Denver had just completed its new Coliseum to be the site of the rodeo and it turned out that Bill was the first bareback rider out in the bareback riding, making him the first person to perform in this fine new facility.

It was a seven-day rodeo, but we got only two bareback horses. I managed to make a qualified ride on my first one. He didn't buck well and because he was running to the other end of the arena after the whistle blew, he got close to the right-hand wall and I made the bad decision to reach out and pull myself off on it. I jammed the middle finger of my right hand into the wall and tore the fingernail half off. I don't know why I didn't let the pickup man get me as I had many times before. I rode my second horse and Bill rode both of his with neither of us coming close to placing. This was the least of our worries because it was worth the $50 entry fee just to be a part of the RCA's first rodeo of the season and one of the biggest.

I enjoyed my work in the pressroom. My job was to go down to the arena and get the judges' results from the various classes of the livestock judging. I brought them back to the pressroom to be incorporated into that day's news release on the judging results. I knew several of the other people working in the pressroom and one of them was Gintsie. She had been the first female to show the grand champion steer in Denver, so naturally she was well known by lots of people and attracted a good deal of attention. The fact that I was one of the rodeo contestants gave me a little notoriety in the pressroom also, but still I turned into a blithering idiot whenever Gintsie was around.

I took her to one school dance that winter and we went to a few movies together, but although we were fond of each other we were growing apart. I took some consolation in the fact that she was dating quite a few other guys, so obviously wasn't going steady with anyone. I promised myself I would try to start dating other girls and actually took one of her sorority sisters, Ann Watt, to a nightclub in east Denver with a bunch of other rodeo club members after a night performance of the rodeo at the stock show. I had a few more dates with Ann that spring and we hit it off pretty well. She knew I was still on Gintsie's string and I knew she had a fairly serious boyfriend—whom she later married—who lived on a neighboring ranch on the Western slope of Colorado.

There were no more college rodeos during winter quarter in 1952, but the rodeo team did make a trip during spring break to two rodeos. The first was at Baylor University in Waco and the second was at Sam Houston State College, now Huntsville State University, which was held at the Huntsville prison rodeo grounds. I won the bull riding at Baylor by making one of the few qualified rides on a rank set of young bulls seemingly being tried out on us by one of the major stock contractors in Texas, Tommy Steiner. He was a fairly small bull that bucked hard in a big circle, and just after the whistle blew he threw me off hard on the ground right in front of one of the chutes and came down on me. He stepped right on my groin and looked as if he was heading back to pin me to the chute. I drew my knees right up against my chest and tried to escape by pulling myself to the top of the chute hand over hand. He just missed my rear end with his horns.

That night in a bar in town (we were never too banged up to miss a party) a cowboy recognized me and said he was sitting up on the chute when I climbed hand over hand toward him, looked up and said "that bull stepped on my nuts fiercely." I don't remember having said it, but after I got to bed that night my left testicle swelled up and hurt "fiercely" all night. It is one of several rodeo injuries that have continued to bother me all my life.

The next morning, we had time to drive to Huntsville, get checked into a motel and go to the arena before the rodeo started. The college used the facilities and rodeo stock owned by the Texas state prison, which was famous for having an annual prison rodeo put on by the inmates. An interesting feature was that the grandstand was separated from the arena by a wire barrier much like a screen to catch foul balls at a baseball park, only much more substantial. It was interesting to look up at the prisoners looking down on us while confined behind the barrier.

I was fortunate to draw one of the best bareback horses I was ever on. He jumped high and kicked, but was not that hard to ride if you kept your hand closed. He almost made you spur him. I won the bareback riding and placed in the saddle bronc riding, but didn't draw a good bull. The entire team had done quite well on this trip and we came home with a lot of points toward winning the team championship for the year. I won two more belt buckles and more than enough jackpot money to pay all my expenses. Counting the two rodeos during Easter break, our home rodeo during College Days and Wyoming, I went to eight rodeos during spring quarter my senior year. I had taken a heavy load the previous year-and-a-half so I had to take only thirteen-and-a-half credit hours, compared to the seventeen-and-a-half average needed to graduate. Thanks to my access to Bob Wheeler and Bob Runner's good notes, I got only one B on my final report card.

The last two rodeos of the spring season were on a Friday and Saturday in early May at the Colorado A & M, and the following weekend on Saturday and Sunday at the University of Wyoming. There was a huge spring blizzard and we had to postpone our rodeo a week, creating a real problem for A & M cowboys wanting to compete in Wyoming. Fortunately, the rodeo teams at both schools managed to work it out so that both schools' team members could get their stock scheduled to compete in each rodeo. At the A & M, Bill Mundell won first in bareback riding and second in bull riding, I won second in the saddle bronc riding and fifth in the bull riding, Gintsie won the girls barrel race and Joyce Zeek won second.

We both also did well at Wyoming. I won the bareback riding, placed second in the saddle bronc riding and fourth or fifth in the bull riding. Bill won the bull riding and was second in the ribbon roping. Gene Brownell added to the points our team accumulated that weekend by winning the saddle bronc riding in Wyoming. Our strong showing at Fort Collins and Laramie put our team in first place in the standings going

I was best man when Frank Married Shirley Wright in Laramie in March, 1952

into the national championship rodeo scheduled for mid-June in conjunction with the Rose Festival in Portland, Oregon about a week after graduation.

    I can't remember a thing about my college graduation ceremony. I was much more interested in the upcoming rodeo finals than the fact I had just received a Bachelor of Science degree in animal husbandry. It was also very much on my mind that I could receive a draft notice at any time.

Winning second in a go round of saddle bronc riding on this fairly tough horse at Colorado A & M. Bill Mundell talked me into wearing his big clown hat.

25

Last and Best Rodeo Finals

Two weeks before graduation, I was busy devising a scheme for traveling to the National Intercollegiate Rodeo finals in Portland, Oregon. Part of it was helping Bill Mundell get his great little roping horse, Raisin, to the rodeo. Another part of my plan was more devious. Bill's girlfriend, Joyce Zeek, and Gintsie both had competed in girls' barrel racing at the Colorado A&M and Wyoming University college rodeos. Even though at that time the girls' events were not recognized in the national standings, there was a girls' barrel race scheduled at the finals in Portland. I ran the idea by Bill. If we could borrow a trailer, we might be able to haul Raisin to Portland, and he certainly liked the idea of having his own horse to rope on. I then suggested that we might as well take two horses as one, and maybe we could haul Gintsie's pinto barrel horse as well and take the girls with us. Bill ran the idea by Joyce, who in turn talked to Gintsie, who was a friend of hers.

Gintsie discussed the idea with her father, who evidently liked the thought of his daughter participating in the national finals rodeo. I got a call from him and he said he had lined up a two-horse trailer we could borrow, and if my mother went along as a chaperone, we could all travel out there together. Bill and Joyce were certainly agreeable and I talked Mom into coming along with us. Stafford Painter made arrangements for us to spend the first night at the Lichtensteins', good friends of the Painter family, who lived near the west entrance to Yellowstone National Park. He also called a friend who owned Baker Hereford Ranch at Baker City in eastern Oregon, who agreed to accommodate us all there the second night.

On Tuesday of the week of the rodeo, I drove over to Roggan to get the trailer, Gintsie and her horse, and drove back to the farm. Bill had been keeping Raisin there that winter and spring. Early Wednesday morning we packed all our suitcases into the trunk of the folks' 1949 Nash, the model that looked like an inverted bathtub. It was quite roomy and had the big six-cylinder engine that furnished enough power to pull a loaded two-horse trailer. The morning of our departure, Bill went into town to get Joyce, while I hooked up the trailer and put the saddles and other gear in the jockey box in the front of the trailer. When Bill got back, we all had breakfast and the girls helped Mom do the dishes.

We headed north on Highway 287. We had to go through Yellowstone to get to the Lichtensteins', so we planned to make a few stops to see the sights as we passed through. We made a quick stop in Jackson to fill up with gas and arrived at the south gate to Yellowstone in midafternoon. A couple of times we parked where there were things to be seen within walking distance of the main road. None of us had been to Yellowstone before and just driving through was quite a treat for us. We were glad we didn't come across any bears on the road, because horses have a natural fear of them and we were afraid they might act up in the trailer and hurt themselves.

It was getting dark when we arrived at the Lichtenstiens' ranch just beyond the west entrance in Montana. They had waited supper for us and we ate as soon as we got the horses unloaded. I had met their daughter, Debbie, a good friend of Gintsie's, at school and she and the rest of the family made us feel at home, then sent us off to bed after a short visit so we could get an early start the next morning.

It was another twelve-hour drive to Baker City, Oregon. We drove south from West Yellowstone to Idaho Falls and then cut west to Boise. It was an extremely hot day and the car heated up once when we went over a mountain pass, but fortunately it cooled off as we dropped down into the valley below and headed northwest into Oregon. It was nearly dark as we pulled into the Baker Hereford Ranch and again we were again welcomed cordially and fed supper. As I recall, the girls stayed in the main house and Bill and I were put up in the bunkhouse where the hired help slept. We had brought oats with us for the horses and we fed them in the barn and then let them loose in the corral so they could get some exercise. Bill and I got up early the next morning, caught the horses and fed them some more grain so they would be ready to load-up right after breakfast. We still had to drive most of the way across Oregon and needed to get to Portland in time to get checked-in at the stable, several miles from the rodeo grounds, where contestants were to keep their horses.

Bill was driving when we reached the outskirts of Portland, and because the traffic started getting heavier, he pulled over and informed me that I would be driving the rest of the way. I had a map of the city and knew where we had to go, but I wasn't prepared for all the bridges and overpasses and the drive through downtown Portland pulling a trailer. I managed to find the fancy riding stable where we would be keeping our horses. A groom led us to the box stalls we would be using and we fed the horses their grain and made arrangements to buy some hay. We unhitched the trailer and as soon as the horses were settled, headed for the hotel in downtown Portland where the contestants in the college rodeo finals were to stay.

We pulled up in front of the hotel and a bellboy carried our luggage into the lobby. I went to the front desk and told them we wanted three of the rooms that had been set aside for the rodeo participants. The clerk said that this was the right hotel but we didn't have reservations. My heart sank. In all my preparations for the trip I had never called the headquarters hotel and made specific reservations for us. This country boy thought that there would just be a block of rooms set aside, which they would assign to us when we arrived. She said she was sorry but the hotel was filled up with the exception of the honeymoon suite, which had two bedrooms, two baths and a living area. I immediately said that sounded wonderful and we would take it. Crisis averted!

We followed the bellboy up to our elegantly furnished suite. It had a bedroom with a double bed on either side of the sitting room. We decided that Bill and I would sleep in one, Gintsie and Joyce would sleep in the other, and we would have a rollaway bed put in the living area for Mom. After we had settled into our respective sleeping quarters, we went down to the coffee shop for supper. When we finished eating, Mom went up to the room and the rest of us walked around sightseeing for a while. All of us were tired from the long drive and came back to the hotel at about ten p.m. Mom, who was sharing the girls' bathroom, was already in bed and the girls retired to their bedroom and Bill and I to ours.

The first performance of the rodeo started at seven p.m. so we had the whole day to kill. Right after breakfast, we drove out to the stables to feed and exercise the horses. I spent my time wandering around the stable and visiting with the hired help there. I learned that most of the horses kept there were owned by people that either played polo or performed in what we in the West called "high-tailed horse shows" with English riding saddles. These kinds of horses, mostly American Saddle Bred or Thoroughbreds, are quite expensive. At this time, some of their owners were also exercising their horses and we four cowboys and cowgirls with our ranch-type horses and saddles made quite a contrast.

When we had taken care of the horses, we drove out to the rodeo grounds in the middle of the area where the annual Portland Rose Festival was held. A large arena and all the necessary pens and chutes had been constructed on a closely cropped field of bluegrass. I cannot remember whether it was the middle of a racetrack or was actually a soccer field. In any case, it was well constructed and bleachers had been set up on either side. Neither Bill nor I could remember ever performing on grass. Most rodeo arenas are covered with fairly soft, loose dirt and it wouldn't be fun to buck off on this field. Besides, it looked as if it would be slick if it rained. Surrounding the arena were acres of beautifully landscaped parkland covered with perfectly maintained rose gardens.

A trailer was set up by the chutes, which served as a rodeo office. We found that our entries were in order and learned that the girls would perform in the barrel race that night and again at the second performance the next afternoon, Saturday. We learned that the saddle bronc riders would get two head of stock and the bareback and bull riders one. When I checked the bulletin board I saw that I was to ride my bareback horse and first saddle bronc and Bill was to ride his bull that night, and both had our barebacks the next day. He was also entered in the calf roping, and both of us were entered in the wild cow milking, an event offered in lieu of ribbon roping at some college rodeos.

We went back to the hotel for dinner (lunch) and found ourselves with several hours to kill before we needed to pick up the horses and go back to the rodeo grounds. Almost all rodeos start with a grand entry, which ends with the playing of the national anthem. The bareback riding is almost always the first event and the horses are loaded into the bucking chutes during the opening activities. My horse was one of the first to enter the chutes and Bill helped me set my bareback rigging, cinch it up and get down on my horse. The National Anthem ended and I heard the announcer say that Roy Lilley of Colorado A&M would be the first bareback rider. I nodded my head, got my horse well started out of the gate and felt I had made a pretty good ride when the pickup man helped me off my horse and dropped me to the grass on my feet.

    I joined Mom in the contestants' stand to watch Bill compete in the roping. Raisin gave him a good run but he missed his calf, a rare thing for Bill. The next event was the girls' barrel racing and while Bill changed the stirrups on his saddle so Joyce could ride Raisin, I went behind the chutes to get ready for the saddle bronc riding. I put my bareback rigging back in my duffel bag, pulled out my chaps and a bag of rosin, laid my bronc saddle on the ground, sat down on it and put my feet in the stirrups. I then reared back and checked to make sure they were properly adjusted so my legs fit snuggly under the swells. I then dusted the rosin, much like the kind violin players use, between my chaps and swells and worked the rosin in till the friction made it warm. I then leaned over to my left and swung my right leg back until my right spur hit the back of the cantle, making sure my leg remained snug against the swell. I then repeated the process with my left leg. Out of habit, I always followed this procedure before riding a saddle bronc.

    I had drawn a horse named Big Three and had heard that he was one of Harley Tucker's rankest horses. The only time I had ever ridden Tucker stock was at the rodeo that Idaho and Washington State had put on jointly in April. I had drawn another one of his best horses there, Coke High, and he had bucked me off just before the whistle as I spurred over the cantle. I knew I had my work cut out for me. When he came into the chute, I attached my hack rein to the halter, measured it to the end of his mane, pulled a piece of it to mark the spot so I could find it when I climbed down on him. As usual, Bill was up on the chute helping me get my saddle set and cinched. I grasped the hack rein in my left hand at the spot where I had tied the hair, eased myself down on him and put my feet firmly in the stirrups. After rattling around for a while, Big Three settled down and I nodded my head to the gate man.

    Big Three blew out of the chute and landed hard. I was confident I had spurred him over the shoulders as he passed the chute gate, and when he hit the ground the first time he jerked my spurs out of his shoulders. When he then jumped straight up, both spurs raked back and caught the cantle as my well-rosined chaps squeaked on the swells but kept me in the saddle. The next jump he kicked high over his head and dropped one of his shoulders. I seemed to have gotten high enough in the saddle to get above his power and still was able to throw my feet forward again and continue catching the cantle with my spurs at the top of his jump. In those days, they called this cantle boarding. Much of the ride is a blur now, but I knew the only way I could finish was to continue spurring him. I was beginning to feel mighty insecure and when the whistle blew I reached down and grabbed the saddle horn immediately. This was a big mistake because it pulled me down in the saddle and, when the cantle hit my rear end, I nearly bucked off between my horse and the pickup man. He yelled at me to drop the horn and hold the hack rein in both hands. I took his advice and shortened my spurring stroke as I handed my rein to him and grabbed him by the waist. He took a dally around the horn with my hack rein and was able to drop me safely on my feet. I felt I had probably just made one of the best bronc rides of my life while appreciating the fact that without such a professional pickup man I would likely have ended up being seriously injured.

Bill still had his bull to ride and he had drawn a good one. I pulled his rope for him and jumped down into the arena as he came out of the chute. The bull went into a slow spin and Bill looked as if he was going to get him ridden; however, at the last second before the whistle, he bucked off. I am sure that if he had finished the ride he would have been in the money.

As soon as the rodeo was over, we loaded Raisin and Paint in the trailer, took them back to the stable and fed and watered them. By the time we got back to the hotel, we were all tired and ready for bed. The second and last rodeo performance was not until early afternoon, so we could sleep in the next morning. Bill and I got up first and slipped out to take care of the horses and let Mom and the girls sleep in. We returned to the hotel in time for all of us to eat an early lunch and go back to the stable in time to haul the horses to the rodeo before it started.

We got only one head of stock in the wild cow milking and I was up that afternoon. I didn't enter the roping events very often, but I did occasionally, hoping that I might luck out and win a few points for the team. I never roped when I couldn't use Raisin, who always put me in a good position. Raisin got a good jump out

The 1952 winners at the Coeur D'Alene Intercollegiate Rodeo. Howard Harris, bareback; Jerry Kardis, saddle bronc; Bob Kennedy, calf roping and all-around; Roy Lilley, bull riding; and Art Fulkerson, bulldogging. Al Munson Photo

Clipping from Coeur D'Alene Rodeo

of the barrier and I quickly found myself in perfect position. My big loop floated out and sailed perfectly over the cow's head, but I missed catching my slack cleanly as Raisin slid to a stop. The cow hit the end of the rope and spun around as my fellow rodeo team member, George Puls, who served as my mugger, raced up and grabbed her head. Between George and Raisin, they held her reasonably still as I jumped off my horse, pulled out the pop bottle that I had in my pocket, raced over to her flank, reached down and grabbed a teat and milked a couple of squirts into the bottle and raced back afoot across the line in front of the chute where a judge would drop a flag to mark my time.

Just as I got to the line, I saw the judge waving his flag to indicate a "no time." By missing my slack, my loop had dropped down too far and picked up one of the cow's front legs; to qualify one needed a clean head catch. If I had made a legal run I would have placed in a roping event for the first time in my life, and at the national finals no less!

I was up in the bull riding, the last event of the rodeo, and had drawn one of Harley Tucker's best bulls, Red Eight. I had won the bull riding at the rodeo in Idaho the previous April on him, but he had fallen down with me as he caught my left knee on the chute on coming out. I had been able to get up with him and make a qualified ride as he went into a spin after the fall, but I wasn't at all sure that I could ride him again. I'm not sure anyone else at the finals thought I could either, but a rather interesting thing happened while Bill was helping me put on my bull rope. The judge of the riding events, a bull rider whose name I think was Roy Beane, came up and offered some advice. He suggested how we should set the rope and how much slack I might want to take in the loop I put around my hand after I put it in the handhold. I don't think it was unethical, but it was highly unusual. Bill and I had never run into this judge at other rodeos, even though he was fairly well known as a top competitor. He even told me Red Eight usually spun to the left and then reversed his spin before the whistle.

I didn't have time to digest everything Beane told me, but I kept his advice in mind as Bill pulled my rope for me. After it was tight I left nearly two inches of slack when I took my rap around my hand. Most of Harley Tucker's bulls were relatively gentle, but Red Eight was inclined to try to hook you after you were on the ground and he was hard to get on out of the chute. Bill and I were as quiet as possible while we got ready and I managed to get him settled down just before I nodded. I had made the mistake of calling out when I wanted the chute gate opened when I had ridden him in Idaho, and the moment he heard me he hit the front of the chute just as a gate was opening and then backed out, catching my leg on the gate, which caused him to fall down. I learned later I had chipped a half-moon shaped piece of bone about the size of my little fingernail off my femur when my knee hit the chute. This time I just nodded and he blew out of the chute and went into a left-hand spin after about two big jumps. I was trying to watch his head and stay in the middle, but about six seconds out I could feel myself being gradually pulled by centrifugal force to the outside of his spin. Just at the crucial moment I saw out of the corner of my eye that he was ducking his head back to the right and he reversed his spin just in time for me to shift my balance and get a new hold with my spurs. To the judges, reversing his spin made my ride look much more difficult, but I knew it had been just in time.

When the whistle blew, my adrenaline gave out, my hand popped out of the rope and I fell right down on his head between the horns. He threw his head and I landed about ten feet away from him on my hands and knees and crawled away as the rodeo clown diverted his attention. Mom told me later that she had been sitting in the stands watching my ride next to a roper named Art Fulkerson, who had kept his horse at the farm during the rodeo at Colorado A&M. When she asked him how he thought I had done, he said, "Don't worry Mrs. Lilley, he just win the bull riding." And that turned out to be the case.

Earlier in the afternoon, I had ridden my second saddle bronc. He didn't buck extremely well and I'm afraid I spurred him rather conservatively, knowing I had already won the first go-round. I didn't place in the second go-round and ended up splitting third and fourth with Cotton Rosser in the average.

We hung around after the rodeo long enough to find out how everyone had done and pick up our jackpot checks. Mine added up to well over $200.00, which in those days paid for my part of the trip. Unfortunately, none of the other team members had managed to place and Sul Ross had won enough more points than we had to move us back to second place behind them in the year-end standings.

We were told that the prizes that had been donated to the event winners would be available back at the headquarters hotel. I found six Hamley saddles scattered on a hotel room floor with the event winners picking them over. By the time I got there, four had already been selected and all that were left were two slick, forked, high-cantled saddles, popular with cowboys called "buckaroos" in the northwest but no longer used much by cowboys in our part of the country. They were extremely well made, as Hamley was one of the nation's best saddle makers, but they had nothing engraved on them to show they were trophy saddles. I dragged one up to the suite and no one was too thrilled with my adding a bulky saddle to our already overloaded car on the trip home. Unfortunately, it turned out those in the back seat had to take turns sitting with it on the floor between their legs.

When we got back from feeding the horses after the rodeo, we parked the car in front of the hotel and carried our luggage out to it, including my little appreciated new saddle. We got up early the next morning and after an early breakfast went out to the stable, bid adieu to some the nice folks we had met there, loaded the horses and started on the long trip home. We decided to take a shorter route by going straight east of Portland up the Columbia River. About an hour out of Portland, we ran into major construction in the canyon and twice had to wait anywhere from thirty minutes to an hour for the highway to be cleared ahead of us.

I didn't think that Bill had his usual energy during the last day of the rodeo and sure enough the first morning on our trip home he started running a fever. I was still pretty pumped up about my success at the rodeo, but since no one else had won anything I tried to keep my enthusiasm tamped down. We fed Bill chicken soup when we stopped to eat, and awhile before dark when we neared a town, we watched for farms that had a barn that looked like it might be able to house our horses for the night. We were getting pretty nervous as it got toward dusk and the map indicated that if we didn't find someplace near the next town it would be hours before we got to another. We weren't looking forward to sleeping in the car or driving all night and possibly running out of gas. Fortunately, at dusk, a mile past town we found a little farm just off the road that had a promising barn. We pulled in, I got out and told the farmer that answered the door our situation. He said we were welcome to check out his barn and if it was suitable they would be glad to have us keep the horses there. It was nowhere near as fancy as the stable in Portland, but it looked mighty good to us as we led the horses from the trailer into it in the gathering dark.

We went back to the town and got three rooms at an old downtown hotel, had a quick meal at the café next door and got to bed about ten pm. I slept like a log, but Bill said he had tossed and turned all night and it was now obvious that he had a fever. We had all put in calls for six am and had finished our breakfast and arrived out at the place where we had kept the horses a little after seven. It was obvious that Bill didn't feel up to driving the car so I stayed behind the wheel till just before dark, stopping only for gasoline and meals. I don't remember just where we stopped that night, but I think we put the horses in a pretty primitive shed and were glad to have found it.

Due to all the traffic delays, the first day it was well after dark when we pulled into the Lilley farm the third night. I unloaded the horses, turned them loose and pushed hay up in the feeder for them. Mom was already in bed when I got into the house and Bill and I weren't far behind. The girls took a little longer to get ready for bed, as usual. Mom had a big breakfast ready for us at eight the next morning. I don't remember her complaining about anything at any time during the trip, which I couldn't say about the rest of us. With the exception of the near disaster with hotel reservations, everything had worked out better than we could have hoped. Bill seemed to be recovering from what seemed like a light case of flu and we were all still on speaking terms; in fact, we later learned that Bill had proposed marriage to Joyce sometime during the trip.

After breakfast, Bill jumped Raisin into the back of his pickup, which he had left at the farm, and he and Joyce headed for his home in Springfield. I loaded Paint in the trailer and took Gintsie to Roggan. Our relationship during the trip had varied from warm to semi-cool and we didn't seem to find much to talk about during the drive or at lunch in Greeley. When we got to the ranch, we unloaded her horse at the corral and parked the trailer there. I drove her up to the house and spoke to her folks and then bid her a rather formal goodbye, with each of us saying we would write to each other during the summer.

I spent a couple of days at home and then drove up to Trail Creek to visit Bob Swan. I was torn between my desire to work at the ranch and to participate in rodeos as much as possible while I waited to be drafted into the Army. I worked out a deal with Bob that he would pay me a daily salary working at the ranch so I would feel free to travel to the rodeos I chose to enter. It was late June and I decided to enter the Greeley Spud Rodeo again. It was the largest and best paying rodeo over the Fourth of July in the area. I entered all three riding events and as I recall I received only one head of stock in each. I didn't draw very well in the bareback or saddle bronc riding, but drew extremely well in the bull riding.

Earl Anderson's Number Two didn't buck in a consistent way, but he was one you could usually place on if you rode him. Both first and second place had been won on him the previous year in Loveland. I was feeling fairly confident after my good ride in Portland and managed to get out of the chute on him just right. The second jump he seemed to explode into the air and turned back jerking my spurs loose. I managed to maintain my grip on the rope and jump back into position while taking a new hold on him with my spurs. He took a mighty jump back in the other direction and jerked my hand out of the bull rope and threw me to the ground hard. All of this had happened in about three seconds. As I picked myself up and walked away I realized I had done everything right and still didn't stand a chance to get him ridden. Once again, I had been skunked at Greeley, and this time I couldn't blame it on the fact that I had drawn poorly, but only too well.

The day after the Greeley rodeo, I went back to the ranch where they still had several of their Fourth of July guests and quite a few more scheduled for the rest of the month. The next week there was a one-day Sunday rodeo in Walden, Colorado that I wanted to go to. I decided to get up early and make the two-hour drive in the morning since their entries didn't close until noon. One of their guests had a fourteen-year-old-year-old boy named Tom March with them who wanted to go to a rodeo, so I took him along. I got there in plenty of time to enter since the rodeo didn't start until two p.m. After I paid my entry fees, we drove to the town's only restaurant for cheeseburgers and fries. We ran into several of my rodeo buddies and my young friend enjoyed listening to us talk shop. After we ate we walked around town for a while and visited a couple of bars where I ran into other people I knew. Walden was a picturesque Western town of about 800 people, most of whom were retired ranchers or local businessmen who depended upon local—within a 75-mile radius—ranchers for their year-round business.

They had learned to exploit their cowboy culture for summer tourist business. I never drank even a beer before a rodeo, but in Walden liquor was the commodity most in demand by both the locals and tourists, and people of all ages visited the bars to soak up the local culture.

Buck Yarborough, who furnished the stock for the rodeo, didn't have any bulls, but his bucking horses were among the rankest among stock contractors in an area of several states. I drew a bareback horse that kicked so high the bareback rigging slipped up over his shoulders and he fell with me. The judges determined that the fall qualified me for a re-ride after the rodeo. I drew a very good saddle bronc that bucked in a fairly tight circle right in front of the chutes. This was a ride that would have won some other rodeos I had attended that summer, but not this little rodeo. One of the local cowboys who didn't travel much but was known as a really good hand, made a better ride on an even better horse.

I got my bareback horse re-ride right after the rodeo. He bucked well again and I managed to spur him about as well as I ever had, which was pretty good with my right leg and not so good with my left. They paid in cash right after the rodeo and I had won second in both events for a total of maybe $220. We got back to the ranch a couple of hours after dark and my young friend slept all the way. He had had a really great time and was impressed with how many cowboys I knew and how well I had done at the rodeo. Everyone needs a fan, even a naive fourteen-year-old boy.

In early July, we had a couple of interesting guests at the ranch. One was Dick Peters, the chief editorial writer for the Cleveland Press, and the other a feature writer for Time magazine. The latter had his wife and fourteen year-year-old son with him and the former was a 40-year-old bachelor. Dick had just come from the Democratic National Convention, which had nominated Adlai Stevenson for President, and had reservations to stay at the ranch for three weeks. The other family was there for a full week plus an additional weekend. They lived in Shaker Heights, Ohio, a middle-class neighborhood that was just then being integrated. The husband, whose name I cannot remember, did not cover this subject for Time Magazine, but had it very much on his mind, vociferously opposing the idea of blacks moving into their neighborhood. His son had picked up on his opinions and expressed them in crude predictions of what n-----s would do to their neighborhood. For myself I had never really thought about black people one way or the other because I had never known any other than my Aunt Essie's servant, Duane. He seemed to be a really nice guy and I knew lots of rich people had servants, black and white. Even though the Time writer and Dick were good friends, Dick was considerably less conservative in his views even though he worked for a Scripps Howard owned newspaper that had certainly never been considered liberal.

Dick was interested in learning to ride so we went out most days for a two or three-hour ride before dinner and another in the afternoon. Part of the time I had another guest or two along but often it was just the two of us. Being a big ranch we were able to ride somewhere different each time in beautiful country, part of which was quite mountainous. Dick wasn't extremely adventurous and liked to keep on fairly good trails, preferably at a walk. After we had ridden for a day or two, he was confident enough to break his horse into a trot and occasionally a slow canter. During these rides, we used to have long talks, often about politics. Even though his newspaper was endorsing Eisenhower he had been quite impressed with Adelai Stevenson. I of course told him that I had been raised Democrat and would surely be voting for Stevenson, and I went on to express my objections to Eisenhower. He responded by saying, "Well Roy, Eisenhower speaks highly of you." He used that put-down several times in the next few weeks when I made less than well-informed criticisms of public figures. It was a real conversation stopper and I often use it to quiet an overbearing know-it-all. By the time Dick departed, we had become good friends and he was calling me coach.

The Cheyenne Frontier Days Rodeo was in the middle of Dick Peters' stay at the ranch and I had often mentioned my love of the sport to him. I had already told Bob that entering the amateur saddle bronc riding was one of my highest priorities and I mailed my entry fee of $50.00, a hefty amount, from the ranch. We got only two horses over the course of the rodeo because there were more than the usual number of entries. I knew in advance which days I would be riding, so I commuted to Cheyenne, about a two-hour drive each way, from the ranch. Bob and Ruby always took whatever guests we had during Frontier Days to at least one performance of the rodeo and this year was no exception, but they weren't there on the day that I rode.

My first horse in Cheyenne was a good-sized gray gelding named Snowball. I was making a good ride as he jumped high and kicked into the middle of the arena and then bucked in a fairly tight circle, almost a spin, but I was able to continue spurring him without missing a jump. I felt I had probably marked pretty high, but in those days the two judges' scores were not immediately added together and announced, so I had no idea where I might be in

NATIONAL INTERCOLLEGIATE RODEO ASS'N
Hardin-Simmons University
BOX 60
ABILENE, TEXAS

NATIONAL CHAMPIONSHIP N.I.R.A. RODEO
Portland, Oregon
June 1952

POINTS FOR YEAR WINNERS

Bareback:
1. Dick Barrett, Okla. A.& M. — 951
2. Roy Lilley, Colo. A.& M. — 368
3. Tex Martin, Sul Ross — 345.5
4. Jim Carrig, Mont. S.C. — 305
5. Don Tabb, Texas A.& M. — 270.5

Dogging:
1. Don Driggers, N.M. A.& M. — 725
2. Eldon Dudley, H-S.U. — 658
3. Dick Barrett, Okla. A.& M. — 587
4. Bill Guest, H-S.U. — 346

Calf Roping:
1. F. C. Stover, N. M. A.& M. — 710
2. Dick Barrett, Okla. A.& M. — 581
3. Art Fulkerson, Wash. S.C. — 497
4. Bill Teague, Odessa — 495
5. Eldon Dudley, H-S.U. — 419

Cow Milking: (Ribbon Roping)
1. Dick Barrett, Okla. A.& M. — 406
2. Art Fulkerson, Wash.S.C. — 377
3. Roy Reynolds, West Tex. S. — 346.5
4. Bill Teague, Odessa — 299.5
5. Sonny Sikes, Sam H.S.C. — 294.5

Saddle Bronc:
1. Joe Chase, Colo A&M — 1148
2. Roy Lilley, Colo. A.& M. — 717.5
3. Dutch Taylor, Ranger — 524.5
4. Cotton Rosser, Cal Poly — 440
5. Tex Martin, Sul Ross — 365

Bull Riding:
1. Johnny Ackel, Sul Ross — 415
2. Roy Lilley, Colo. A. & M. — 411
3. Charles Herod, Sam H.S.C. — 328.5
4. Gene Brownell, Colo. A.& M — 231

****

ALL-ROUND COWBOY
1. Dick Barrett, Okla. A.&M. — 2515
2. Roy Lilley, Colo. A.&M. — 1501.5
3. Joe Chase, Colo A&M — 1315
4. Eldon Dudley, Hardin-Simmons — 1206.8
5. Cotton Rosser, Cal Poly — 1194
6. Art Fulkerson, Wash. S.C. — 1151
7. Don Driggers, N.M.A.& M. — 1056.5
8. Bill Teague - Odessa JC — 1009.5
9. F.C. Stover - NM A&M - 989
10. Ross May - Sul Ross - 862

HIGH TEAM
1. Sul Ross College, Alpine, Tex — 3203.5
2. Colorado A.& M., Ft.Collins — 2976.5
3. Cal Poly, San Luis Obispo — 2290 2253
4. Univ. of Wyoming, Laramie — 2086
5. Washington State College — 2031
6. Oklahoma A.& M., Stillwater — 1971.5
7. Montana State College — 1873
8. Hardin-Simmons — 1667
9. New Mexico A&M — 1645.7
10. Pierce Jr. College — 1592.5

Final 1951/52 standing including Portland finals.

the standings. A few days later, Holabird, my second horse, was one that I had won third place on in the amateur bronc riding in 1951, so I figured I knew how he would buck. It turned out that he was more than pretty good this time because he turned back in front of the chutes and nearly bucked me off. I missed a couple of spurring strokes as I managed to survive with my spurs jammed under the saddle skirts just below the cantle, which let me regain my rhythm and finish the ride in good style. It had been a much more difficult ride than my first one, but I knew I would be marked down some on my spurring score. In the riding events, one-half of the score was for how well you spurred the horse, or your riding style, and one-half was for how hard it bucked. No one really spurred a bull so the scoring on them was figured differently.

In both amateur and professional saddle bronc riding, the contestants with the top ten combined scores on their two horses were brought back for another horse the last day for what was called the short go-round. I was one of the ten selected in the amateur bronc riding and drew a horse that didn't buck as well as either of my two previous ones. I knew I was in a good position to place in the average and probably didn't spur the horse as well as I might have. In professional bronc riding, the short go-round paid just the same as the previous two, but in the amateur the score was added into your average, but no go-round money was paid.

Since bull riding was the first event in Cheyenne, the rodeo ended shortly after I had ridden in the finals. By the time I got to the office, most of the standings had been figured and the checks were being written. I approached the desk where they were being passed out and asked if I had won anything. When I gave my name, the clerk said I certainly had and handed me a couple of checks. I started to walk away and she called me back, saying to wait a minute because there was one more just being prepared. I was pretty sure I was going to win something but nearly fainted when I saw that I had been first in the first go-round, second in the second go-round and first in the average. The checks totaled well over $600, the most money I had ever won at one rodeo by far.

Just as I was leaving, somebody told me photographs would be taken of the winners of each event with their trophy saddles at a downtown hotel at seven p.m. When I showed up at the Plains Hotel there was a row of hand-tooled Denver Dry Goods saddles

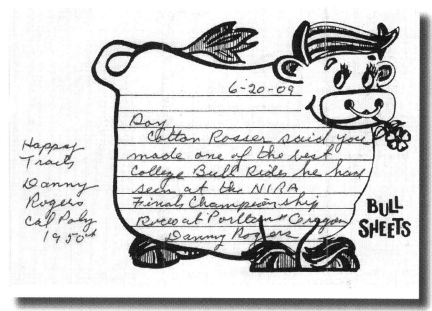

Note sent to me after the NIRA Alumni gathering that I missed while I was having by-pass surgery.

on individual stands lined up in the middle of a meeting room. A Denver Post photographer asked each event winner to stand behind his saddle for a group picture while a reporter got our names and a little information on each of us. I don't remember all of the other event winners, but I do know that Billy Weeks, a short, wiry all-around hand from Eastern Oklahoma, had won one event and the all-around. The saddles for all the other events had the name of that event carved on the fenders of the saddle; however, mine simply had C, B and Q carved on it in recognition of the Chicago, Burlington and Quincy, which had sponsored the amateur bronc riding. I had a lot of fun in later years explaining what the initials meant and was usually met with skepticism when I said how I got it.

There were quite a few people in the room lined up to congratulate all of us and I was fortunate to have a few friends among them. In the middle of all this pleasant activity, who should walk up to shake hands with me but Gintsie Painter. She was with Monte Belle, a classmate whom I knew fairly well. Needless to say this took some of the wind out of my sails. I learned later that Monte had given Gintsie his fraternity pin shortly before school let out that spring, just before we had taken our trip to the national NIRA finals. To give a girl your fraternity pin was much like giving her your class ring in high school, an indication of going steady but not being engaged.

After the rodeo ended, I had decided to get a room at the hotel and drive back to the ranch early the next morning. As I recall, I had more than a few drinks that night at the Plains hotel bar and celebrated with several of my old friends who were there, plus a few new ones I had met at the rodeo, including Duane Howard, an eighteen-year-old from North Dakota, who I think had won third in the amateur bronc riding. He went on to an outstanding professional career.

I arrived at the ranch the next day about midmorning, drove into the yard, opened the car trunk and pulled out my nice new saddle. The folks at the ranch were aware that I had done pretty well on the two horses I had already ridden, but had no idea I had won the whole thing. Needless to say, they were much impressed and I was busting with pride.

26

Dick Peters

When I came back from Cheyenne, Dick Peters was still at the ranch, and he stayed another week or so. We continued to ride daily, talking endlessly about a variety of subjects. I expressed my interest in the various places Dick had worked before he became chief editorial writer for the Cleveland Press. He said he had begun his journalism career with the Washington Daily News and had many friends still living there whom he would like to introduce me to. I also asked him about his military service during World War II. He told me several funny anecdotes, but I learned only later that he had served as a press officer on General MacArthur's staff.

A few days before Dick left to go home, he invited me to visit him in Cleveland. He said he would use the last few days of his vacation to take me to a ball game in Cleveland and drive to Washington D. C. to visit his mother, who was married to a man who played in the Washington Symphony Orchestra. This was her second marriage; her first husband, Dick's father, was the longtime headmaster of University School in Cleveland. By this time, I had received my notice and had to report to the draft board in Fort Collins on October 1, 1952. A week after he left the ranch, I received a letter from Dick enclosing a coach ticket on the overnight Union Pacific streamliner from Denver to Chicago with a transfer to the Northern Pacific, which would take me on to Cleveland. I don't remember the exact dates, but the return ticket got me back to Denver a few days before I reported for the draft.

I had three more rodeos I wanted to compete in before I made my visit to Cleveland and reported to the draft board. I drew my meager summer wages and headed for the Wyoming State Fair in Douglas, Wyoming. It was a big RCA rodeo with many of the top hands competing. I had tried to call in my entry to the Estes Park rodeo the day after Cheyenne Frontier Days, but the secretary of the rodeo committee told me that I could no longer use my

National Intercollegiate Rodeo Association membership card to compete in RCA rodeos. Perhaps someone had reported I had graduated from college, or maybe it was because I had won the amateur bronc riding. Anyway, I mailed in my dues to the Denver office but gave up on the Estes Park rodeo.

I entered only the saddle bronc riding at the Wyoming State Fair. When I arrived in Douglas the morning of the rodeo, there was not a room to be found in town and the Chamber of Commerce directed me to one of the private homes it lined up annually for the overflow crowds during the fair. They sent me to a nice small home not far from the fairgrounds. A middle-aged lady answered the door and led me to my bedroom where I deposited my small suitcase. It was close to noon and she invited me to have lunch with her and her two grown daughters, who were dressed like eight-year-old girls. When we sat down to eat she asked me if I would like to say grace. We had seldom said grace at home or at the ranch and she had caught me by surprise. I couldn't come up with a gracious way to get out of it and stumbled through a rather clumsy prayer. She said, "Thank you, young man, but you really should memorize a proper blessing." We had a nice home-cooked meal and I hurried out to the fairgrounds.

The rodeo was just getting underway when I arrived. I checked the bulletin board and found I had drawn a horse called Boomerang. I asked Adrian Weaver, who was riding bulls at the rodeo, if he knew anything about the horse. He said he had heard that he did not get ridden very often. It was good news because, if I got him rode, I had a good chance to place. The bad news was that I was probably going to get bucked off. When he came into the chute I could see that he was a fairly good-size buckskin gelding with a white saddle mark on his back. This meant he was probably a spoiled saddle horse. Adrian helped me measure my hack rein, set my saddle and get down on him. I marked him out of the chute and immediately knew I was in for a rough ride. He went into a fairly tight spin about the third jump out and then fell down with me. I was able to kick my feet out of the stirrups and get away from him as he got up, and the judges signaled that I would get a re-ride. When I got back on him after the rodeo and was toughing out a decent ride, he dropped a shoulder and I spurred back over the cantle and hit the ground.

I drew a good horse again the next day and ended up losing a stirrup about two thirds of the way through the ride, something that happened to me only two or three times during my career. I managed to get to the whistle without pulling leather in the vain hope that the judge did not see what had happened. Of course he did, and I was disqualified.

I had already entered the rodeo in Kemmerer, Wyoming, a long drive across the state, nearly to Utah. I left before the Douglas rodeo was over and arrived in Kemmerer late that evening. I rode both horses in Kemmerer well, but didn't place with either. My string of good luck seemed to be running out, I was a long way from home and I couldn't wait to get back to the comfort of my own bed at the farm.

I was driving a Ford V/8 coupe, which mom and I bought before I went up to the ranch. It was a nice little car but had what was called a South Wind heater that burned gasoline. It was installed in a few Fords after World War II. I had never seen such a heater, but got to test it out that night. I found myself getting sleepy and needed to stop at the side of the road for a nap at about midnight. I fell asleep right away and woke up about two hours later shivering. I managed to ignite the gasoline heater and slept for another hour before I woke up, worrying about running out of gas out in the middle of nowhere and possibly getting carbon monoxide poisoning from the heater. I turned off the heater, started up the car and managed to make it to Rawlins about dawn with about a quart of gas left in the tank and chilled to the bone.

I got home shortly after noon and called in my entries for the three riding events at the Douglas County Fair in Castle Rock. The next day I put on some clean clothes, put my dirty clothes in the laundry basket for Mom to wash and headed for the two-day rodeo in Castle Rock. Like many rodeo cowboys of the day, I was not very fastidious about my grooming and carried only my shaving kit, a change of underwear and perhaps a clean shirt if I was going to be gone overnight. At about noon, I checked into the rodeo office and then found a cheap hotel room in town.

I didn't place in any of the events and this may have been the rodeo at which I pulled leather before the whistle blew, one of the few times in my career I did so. My saddle bronc was bucking straight toward the arena fence and when he hit it, rather than fly over the fence, I reached down between my legs and grabbed the saddle horn. Somehow, he peeled himself off the fence and continued bucking, but I had already disqualified.

I knew that the bull I had drawn was not a very good one. Sure enough, he didn't buck very hard but lost his flank rope before the whistle blew, so I was awarded a re-ride. Mine was the last of several re-rides after the rodeo. My bull didn't buck any better the second time even with the flank rope. By the time the whistle blew, he was halfway to the end of the arena and the rodeo clown who was evidently tired of chasing us just yelled at me to jump off. I turned my head and looked back at him just as I threw my left leg up and rolled off to the right, something I had done many times before. Right at that moment, the bull threw up his head and I caught my leg on his horn, and instead of jumping off I rolled under him. He stepped in the middle of my back and knocked the wind out of me. Fortunately, the bull had run on down the arena by the time the clown caught up to me. I staggered to my feet and limped over to the fence. He never said a word to me as I walked by him on my way back to the chutes, hunched over and obviously in pain. Nearly everyone was gone and the few people still around pretty much ignored me.

Feeling sorry for myself, I gathered up my bag of gear and bronc saddle from behind the chutes and loaded them in the trunk of my car. I drove on into town and pulled up in front of the bar, which was close to my hotel room, went in, sat down on a barstool and ordered a whiskey sour. As I was sitting there, Jim Like, a good all-around hand, from Kim, Colorado, came in, took one look at me and said, "Lilley, you need to go clean up." I turned half way round on the bar stool and could see in the mirror behind the bar that my shirt was badly torn. I finished my drink and walked to my hotel room. When I took off my shirt I could see that it was not only torn, but covered with dried blood.

I walked to the restaurant downtown and had a light supper and then went back to my hotel and lay down on the bed for a nap. I woke up at about eight o'clock feeling better and decided to drive over to the rodeo dance being held at a local hall, so I took a shower and put on my clean shirt. There were several unattached girls there and I danced a time or two. By then my back was starting to really ache. I told a friend of mine from college, Larry

Kirk, who was there that I feared I had been hurt worse than I thought. His father was the county agent in Douglas County and they had a home in Castle Rock. He took me to his house and when his mother saw me and heard what had happened, she led me to their spare bedroom, laid out a pair of Larry's pajamas for me and told me to get into bed. By that time, my back was really throbbing, and I was ready for some motherly care.

The pain kept getting worse during the night and I woke up Larry and suggested that maybe we needed to call a doctor. He said there wasn't one in town, but he knew someone who could at least clean my wound and dress it. This person turned out to be the father of a girl Larry was dating, who was the town's undertaker. Larry called him and he agreed to meet us down at the mortuary. He looked at my back and said that the wound was not too deep, but certainly did need to be cleaned and dressed. The whole idea of going to the mortuary was a little spooky, but the mortician was a very normal-looking, friendly person. I had evidently worked up enough adrenaline to help with the pain somewhat and to ease the tension, I said I appreciated his help but asked him not to come near me with a needle. He ignored me and had me lie on my stomach as he cleaned and disinfected the wound and put a light gauze bandage over it. It seems I had a six- to ten-inch furrow down my back where the bull's dew claw had gouged me as his foot slid off my back.

I felt guilty that I had kept everybody up half the night and tried to get back to sleep when I crawled back into bed. The throbbing pain seemed to get only worse and I tossed and turned until morning. Larry's mother came in and checked on me about daylight and I told her I was still in a lot of pain. She said there was a doctor in Sedalia, which was only about twenty miles north of Castle Rock. She called him and he agreed to meet us at his office in about thirty minutes. He looked at my back and said the undertaker had done a very good job of dressing it. He gave me a few codeine pills and a prescription for a few more. He said I might want to consider an x-ray, but he thought my pain was simply due to spasms in my back muscles due to a delayed reaction from the severe trauma they had suffered.

I had never taken codeine before and it knocked me out. I slept all morning and then called my mom, who in turn called

Dad, who was at work in Denver. He called me at Kirk's and after I explained what happened he suggested I drive to the home of our longtime family doctor in Denver, Frank Rogers. Dr. Rogers confirmed that my pain was caused by the severe spasms triggered by the damage to the muscles in my back. He said that my aching, well-toned back muscles had very likely prevented any injury to my spine.

    I had planned to enter the rodeo at the Colorado State Fair in Pueblo, which was scheduled a few days after Castle Rock. Dr. Rogers strongly recommended that I not do this and suggested I spend a few days at his home to recuperate. We had often stayed at the Rogers' over the years, and even though I had very much wanted to ride at the state fair, I decided to accept the invitation. Dr. Rogers' wife, Emma Brady Rogers, a concert pianist and composer who was the music critic for the Rocky Mountain News, had always wished I had continued my piano lessons and had never understood why I wanted to be a "rodeo cowboy." I never expected to be a reasonably successful professional bronc rider but thought that was more likely than my being a pianist.

    The rodeo at the Colorado State Fair would have been my last rodeo before taking my scheduled trip to see Dick Peters and was before reporting for the draft on October first. After a couple of days lying around at the Rogers' home, being pampered by Mrs. Rogers, and getting better acquainted with Dr. Rogers, a man our entire family idealized, I drove home and enjoyed a weekend helping Dad around the farm and eating Mom's home cooking before leaving for Cleveland.

    I had to buy a few clothes before I started on the adventure that Dick Peters had planned for me "back east." I bought a couple of sport shirts, a white dress shirt and two pairs of dress slacks to go with my favorite sport jacket. I had a pair of dress shoes I seldom wore and I borrowed a couple of neckties and a dress belt from Dad along with his well-worn two-suiter suitcase. On the appointed day, Mom and Dad drove me to the Union Station in Denver and put me on the overnight streamliner to Chicago.

    I had heard that eating in the dining car was very special and I was not disappointed. Even walking back from my coach seat to the diner at the end of the train, through six swaying rail cars traveling at nearly one hundred miles an hour was quite an experience. I slept pretty well in my reclining seat until dawn, when the conductor said we were about one hour from Chicago. The men's rest room had a couple of small sinks with mirrors above them and I soon learned that it was easy to cut yourself shaving on a fast-moving train. I was back in my seat when it slowed while going through the outskirts of the city and I got a good look at part of the industrial district and slums of Chicago. With the patient directions of the conductor, I was able to make my connection at the Union Station. The track from Chicago to Cleveland through Detroit followed the Great Lakes in many places and I found myself glued to the window the rest of the trip.

When I arrived in Cleveland late that afternoon, Dick met me at the station in his convertible. He drove me straight to his one-bedroom apartment, where he had made up a daybed for me in his living room where I was to sleep. We had only one day in Cleveland before heading to Washington. In the morning, he showed me his office at the Cleveland Press building and introduced me to his staff. After lunch, we went to see the Cleveland Indians play the Detroit Tigers. We had seats in the private box of Louis B. Selzer, the editor of the Cleveland Press, right behind home plate. Bob Feller was playing for Cleveland at that time but did not pitch that day. I had naturally heard of Feller, but since there was no major league team anywhere near Colorado, I didn't follow baseball and never dreamed I'd ever see a game. We had hot dogs and beer and enjoyed watching Cleveland's second-best pitcher beat Detroit.

The next morning, we departed for Washington on the Pennsylvania Turnpike and pulled off on the first rest stop for breakfast. At that time, Howard Johnson had a monopoly on the rest stops and eating at one was an important part of the mystique of driving on what was the nation's first major turnpike. Speeding down the highway at seventy-five miles an hour in Dick's convertible with the top down was exhilarating. I had never been on a non-access four-lane highway before and driving on it was almost as big a treat as the ride on the train. When we arrived in Washington, we checked into the Willard, one of the better known old downtown hotels.

The next day, Dick showed me so many sites around the Capital that I don't remember most of them very well. It was just getting dark when we arrived at the Lincoln Memorial. Dick found a place to park the car and we approached it from the rear. I walked around in front just under the statue, looked up and gasped. It was one of the most moving experiences I have ever had. Suddenly Lincoln materialized out of the dark, far bigger than life, gazing down at me. I had read all three volumes of Bruce Catton's history of the Civil War and when I read the inscription on the pedestal, I felt as if Lincoln was speaking to me personally.

The next morning, Dick dropped me off at the capital. I looked at the various memorials along the mall and ended up spending most of my time at the Smithsonian Institute. Dick picked me up near the Lincoln Memorial at about 11:30 and we had lunch with his mother and stepfather at their apartment not far away. They had a nice buffet laid out and offered us a cocktail before we ate. Dick suggested that I try a Manhattan. I had seen people order them in the movies but had no idea how they were made. My idea of a cocktail was bourbon and ginger ale, and this mixture of Bourbon and a bit of sweet vermouth went down about like a drink of whiskey straight out of the bottle at a Saturday night country-dance. My hosts explained to me diplomatically that cocktails were meant to be sipped.

Early that afternoon, we returned to the hotel for a short rest and then departed for a cocktail party at the apartment of one of Dick's best friends from the days he had worked in Washington as a reporter. When we arrived, there were about a dozen couples, all of whom were Dick's age or younger. I had been at many family gatherings where we had highballs before supper, and we nearly always had a few drinks with the guests for the evening meal at the ranch, but I had never attended anything quite like this. It was obvious that all the people there liked and respected Dick, and they enjoyed the opportunity to exchange tales about their experiences when they worked together in the nation's capital getting started as cub reporters before the war. The life they had led was far different from anything I had ever experienced, but their work sounded exciting.

Dick introduced me to everyone as we circulated around the room with drinks in our hands. As they all knew where he had met me, they were interested in hearing about the Wild West. They seemed genuinely interested as I talked about my rodeo experiences and told them how quickly and well Dick had learned to ride a horse. I caught on to the art of making small talk fairly readily, and possibly due to the low altitude, seemed to handle my martinis as if I were used to them. Actually, I had had one before while I was trying to impress a date in college. At that time, I thought the combination of dry vermouth and gin tasted like Mennen's shaving lotion. After three or four, I decided they weren't too bad and certainly better than Manhattans. I'm sure I was not nearly as sophisticated as I thought I was, but Dick was kind enough to say that his friends had enjoyed visiting with me and had been pleased at how I had fit in. We met Dick's mother and stepfather at a fancy downtown Washington restaurant for a late dinner after the cocktail party to celebrate our last night there.

The return drive to Cleveland on the turnpike and the train ride back to Denver were very much an anti-climax to a memorable trip. My folks met me at the depot when I arrived in Denver and we drove back to the farm. I had only a few days left before reporting for the draft on October 1, 1952. I had decided not to take advanced ROTC at Colorado A&M (recently changed to Colorado State University), when I had the opportunity, so the die had been cast. The war had reached a stalemate in Korea, but we were still suffering casualties there. Mom didn't say too much when she dropped me off at the bus station for the trip to Denver for my physical; however, I knew she had hoped her youngest boy would not have to go to war.

There were only eight people in my Supply School class and I got a cigarette lighter for getting the best grade from the commanding General of the 10th Infantry Division that our basic training unit was a part of. This is the only picture I could find from my time in the service

27

Reflections of a Korean War Draftee

The Korean War started in 1950, when I was a sophomore at Colorado State University in Fort Collins. Being a land grant university, it had ROTC and I was in the second year of my mandatory two years. I had never considered the military for a career and had chosen the Air Force option over the Field Artillery for no particular reason. All the cadets drilled together on the oval once a week and you were required to wear your uniform that day. I don't remember anything from the classes, but I did enjoy the close order drill. I had already opted not to take the second two years necessary to get a commission. I knew I would be drafted eventually like everyone else, and since the fighting was going badly in Korea I wasn't looking forward to the prospect.

Both my older brothers had served in WWII, one in the Army Air Force and one in the Navy, and I was very close to them. They had often let me tag along with them when they were with their friends in high school. I kept track of them as they graduated from high school and enlisted in the various branches of the service. After graduation, my oldest brother went immediately with some friends to enlist in the Marines, but he failed the physical. He was later accepted by the Army. One of those buddies was killed on one of the Pacific islands and another was wounded twice on Iwo Jima. Charlie was disappointed, but the rest of the family will be eternally grateful he was turned down by the Marines and ended up in what was then the Army Air Force.

My brother Frank was only seventeen when he got out of high school and immediately enlisted in the Navy. When he got out of boot camp he was assigned to a destroyer working in the engine room. When he was on his shakedown cruise the war ended, so they were called back to port and proceeded to decommission the ship. One of his jobs was scraping asbestos off of pipes and the result was mesothelioma forty years later and an early death.

The reason for this side trip to WWII is that my feelings about war were developed then. We were all extremely patriotic and consumed by the war. My junior high classmates and I loved to go to the war movies and usually managed to hide our fears for our loved ones. After the war, I was left with the feeling we all owe something to our country, not the other way around.

The summer after my sophomore year, I received a form letter from CSU announcing that anyone who wanted to take advanced military, but had already opted out, would have the opportunity to reconsider. They needed more second lieutenants I guess. In any case, before the war started I had decided I didn't want to be an officer, so I naively thought I still didn't. Also, the minimum tour an Air Force ROTC officer could serve was four years while a draftee served only two. I was quite successful riding bulls, bareback horses and saddle broncs in college rodeo competion and wanted to continue participating in rodeos as long as possible after graduation

I kept my grade average up to the level required by the Draft Board and got to finish college with an animal science degree the spring of 1952. I had done very well at the Intercollegiate Rodeo Finals that spring in Portland, Oregon and had won a fair amount of money that summer. I was drafted October 1, 1952, later than expected, and took my basic training at Fort Riley, Kansas after processing at Camp Crowder, Missouri.

My first exposure to the supply rooms at both Camp Crowder and Fort Riley left me with a loathing for Supply Sergeants, whom I blamed for many of the indignities bestowed on us recruits at what was basically our first exposure to Army life. But the army evidently had all the meat inspectors they needed so they sent me to supply school at Fort Riley for eight weeks after my mandatory eight weeks of infantry training.

After graduation at the top of my eight-man class in supply school and receiving an engraved cigarette lighter for the honor, I was immediately ordered to go to Korea. After a delay en route through Denver, I left by troop ship from Fort Lewis, Washington for assignment to what unit I knew not in Korea. After two weeks at sea, the first three days of which we were in a violent North Pacific storm, which caused two thirds of the troops on board to be violently seasick, we arrived in Yokohama harbor. We spent a couple of days picking up our rifles, two wool blankets each and field equipment at what was said to have been a Japanese officers training school during WWII.

We re-boarded the same ship and headed for Inchon, where we disembarked over the side on rope ladders into some kind of large landing craft. We immediately boarded a train headed somewhere straight east along the 38th Parallel. We arrived at the replacement depot for the Second Infantry Division, the first clue we had as to where we would be assigned. We heard rumors that we had either just taken or lost "Baldy" again and there had been a lot of casualties, and that most of us were going to end up in a foxhole to replace them. I wasn't too thrilled at that likelihood since, if I had to be a rifleman, every draftee's primary MOS, I sure wished the Army had given me more than eight weeks of infantry training!

After a few days I was assigned to Baker Battery, 38th Field Artillery Battalion, 2nd Infantry Division and we headed north in a jeep. Soon we saw a sign on the road saying tops down and helmets on. A bit later we could hear what must have been 50 caliber machine guns in the distance and I knew we were going to be close to the front lines, which had pretty well stabilized close to the 38th Parallel by March 1953.

When we got to the battery area, I was turned over to Sergeant First Class Duke Zakowski, a stereotype of just what you would expect a supply sergeant to be. I was given a canvas cot and told to bunk in the supply tent. Everyone else still had their down-filled sleeping bags but I had to make do with my blankets and nearly froze for a few weeks. We had a fire mission that night and the sound kept me wide awake. I was told we were a fully mobile l05 mm howitzer battalion. After a few days, I hardly heard the roar of the firing.

I was trained by Zakowski's assistant, a corporal who forgot to show me the 2nd Divisions SOPs, so I proceeded to set up the records as I had learned in supply school. I soon found out half of what I was doing was unnecessary. This greatly amused Zakowski and his assistant, neither of whom had been burdened by any supply school training.

Duke Zak, as he was called, soon rotated home and I learned what I could from the corporal whose name I can't recall. Soon he rotated and I was left in charge of Baker supply. I was given a duce-and-a-half 6X6 truck to drive back to service battery to leave off boots for half soling, field kitchen burners for repair and various other stuff for replacement or repair. I was supposed to have a three-quarter-ton truck, but I was given the bigger truck and learned to drive it quickly because we moved eight times in eight weeks during one stretch.

When I first arrived, our battery was on the forward slope of a hill facing the Chorwon Valley. Able and Charlie Batteries were on the other side of the hill south of us. We all got a few rounds in from time to time, but our biggest bombardment came as a result of a careless accident. Our dump blew sky high, probably from powder sacks left from fire missions. A few days later, we got one white phosphorous shell in a few hundred yards out in the valley to the north. The day after that we got creamed. The shells were coming from about twelve miles across the valley from caves dug into the forward slope of Whitehorse Mountain They were the Chinese equivalent of our 155s. Fortunately, we shortly got effective counter battery fire from behind us by 155s, eight-inch guns and a new gun that I think was a 240-mm monster. My supply truck got a little piece of shrapnel and one covered gun emplacement was hit. Able Battery's mess tent was burned and one of their officers was wounded. To my knowledge there were no other casualties.

When the 2nd went in reserve, we supported either the Marines or a ROK (Republic of Korea) division. We felt more comfortable having the 2nd or Marines in front of us, but the ROK units held their own. Our only real scare came when a self-propelled 155 battery bugged out on our flank when there was a push. Fortunately, the infantry plugged the gap and our untested perimeter of defense remained untested.

The night the truce was to go into effect, a lot of rounds came in and we returned heavy counter battery fire. We were to stop firing at 10:00 p.m. Both sides stopped at 9:40 and there was an eerie silence for a few minutes. I don't remember any celebrating, just a general feeling of relief and some skepticism.

We immediately moved back just behind the newly established demilitarized zone on what was called bulldozer drive, one of many amazing roads built in Korea by the engineers. We also appreciated their bunkers, which we sometimes had to use. We stayed in this location until I rotated home in early June of 1954.

Boring would best describe our lives after the war ended. The gun crews did go out on what I think was called RSOP every few weeks. These were training exercises. We continued to live in the same squad tents we had occupied during the war for the next ten months, and other than getting a Quonset hut for a mess hall it was like being on bivouac back in Fort Riley.

Being a supply sergeant during the war was much different than after the truce. My first job was helping our battery commander, a captain whom we all admired and respected, be rotated back to the states. He was replaced by a first lieutenant already in our battery, and the Captain had to conduct a joint inventory of all the equipment and supplies in Baker Battery. I was accountable for everything, but the commanding officer was financially responsible. This wasn't a problem except for a fifty-caliber machine gun that had disappeared just before the war ended. We had picked up an extra BC scope somewhere along the way and I was able to trade it to a Greek unit nearby for the needed machine gun; our Captain got his well-earned trip home. Before I went home, I had to rotate two more company commanders and had to learn most of the tricks of the hated supply sergeant trade to get it done because the joint inventories got more and more detailed.

Of course, after the cease fire, we got to brush up on some military etiquette, such as saluting officers and shining our boots. I advanced from PFC at war's end to SFC, the proper rank for unit supply, by the time I rotated home.

Thanks to the various episodes of incoming rounds I had enough combat points to rotate home early, and I ended my two-year tour in twenty-one months and twenty days. Two days later, I was entered in a rodeo and rode both my saddle bronc and bareback horse, not well, but I made the whistle on both. The next two months of the summer rodeo circuit I bucked off more stock than I had in the two years I had contested before going into the Army. I was so bad I had to continue riding for two more years to get good enough to quit the profession with some pride.

*As previously mentioned I had no artillery training whatsoever. I did run into a college classmate attached to FTC back at Headquarters Company and visited him a couple of weekends, when I got to see how fire direction control worked. I also caught a ride to visit our forward observers a couple of times during the war and got to look over the bunker through a BC scope across Chorwan Valley at Chinese soldiers doing much the same as we did during a lull in firing. Another time, I was down by the howitzers delivering a pair of resoled combat boots to a gunner when they were firing H and I (harassing and indirect) in the general direction of the enemy to let them know we hadn't forgotten them. My customer suggested I pull the lanyard on the next round, which I did: my only round fired at the enemy was from a 105-mm howitzer that I never had a moment's training on.

28

Adjusting After Korea

I took a bus to Fort Collins after mustering out in Colorado Springs. I was pretty nervous carrying over $1,200.00 with me, more cash than I had ever seen before. I was discharged with just the summer uniform I was wearing, which included my combat boots. I don't think I ever wore the khakis again, but I loved the boots, which I wore for work and hunting until they fell apart. Mom met me at the bus station and I immediately went to the Poudre Valley National Bank to open a checking and savings account.

When I went to the army, Dad and Mom rented a small apartment in Denver within walking distance of his office, and drove to the farm most weekends. Dad had arranged to have our neighbor to the north, Fred Martin, do the farming on the place, and a college student named Doc Munson took care of the horses and looked after the main house, keeping it warm enough that the pipes didn't freeze when the folks weren't there. When I got home, I moved back into the house, took over the chores, the irrigating, and haying. The folks continued to come home on the weekends and Dad and I enjoyed working together on the farm again.

During my fourteen months in Korea, I had looked forward to getting home and resuming my rodeo career. It never dawned on me that spending that length of time in what was basically a sedentary job, never even seeing a saddle horse and gaining nearly twenty pounds would diminish my skills. I did manage to ride both the bareback and saddle bronc that I drew at the Woodland Park Rodeo only two days after I was discharged, but I was in a fog with little awareness of what I was doing. I entered two small local rodeos before I entered the professional saddle bronc riding in Cheyenne and bucked off of both my horses there. Over the next two months, I was thrown off more horses than in the two years before I went to the Army. I did get a few ridden, but I was bucked off of ones that I would have surely placed on before. I thought I had lost my balance, my reactions were too slow and I seemed to be thinking too much.

I particularly remember a couple of things about readjusting to civilian life that I would never have expected. I had driven either a two-and-a-half or three-quarter ton truck a lot in Korea, sometimes on muddy roads, but usually on the excellent gravel roads that the engineers had constructed along the 38th Parallel. There was a strictly enforced thirty-five-mile-an-hour speed limit and I found it difficult to start driving down the road sixty or sixty-five miles an hour again. I hadn't seen much combat, but I had been caught in an artillery barrage once when I was driving back to my unit from the service battery. I stopped my truck, jumped out and ran to a nearby bunker. I hit the ground flat on my stomach when an artillery shell whistled in and landed within fifty or so feet and shrapnel flew over my head. Over the Fourth of July just two weeks after I was discharged, a loud firecracker went off nearby and I nearly hit the ground the second I heard it.

Sometime during the summer, I decided to spend the money I had saved while in the Army on a new car. I fell in love with a red and white 1955 Chevy two-door with the new high compression V/8 engine. It was a demonstrator with a few thousand miles on it and cost me about $2000. It was a stick shift, three-speed with a Borge-Warner overdrive. If you pressed down the accelerator just after you had gone into overdrive in second gear to make it shift back to standard, you could burn rubber. I also learned that shifting into overdrive when you were in second gear when you were driving on mountain roads worked great. I quickly got over worrying about not driving over thirty-five miles an hour and soon added driving too fast to a growing list of bad habits.

I continued living on the farm between rodeos and drove over to Roggan for a few dates with Gintsie. I had written to her at least once a week while I was in Korea and received about half that many letters in return. I had prevailed upon her to send me a picture and when I received a nice 8 x 10 portrait, I fastened it to the tent wall over my canvas cot. I had no reason to think she wasn't dating during that time, but I very much looked forward to her letters. Anyway, on about our second date after I got home she asked me if I had seen John Beckstead lately. I told her I had seen him at a rodeo or two when I first came home, but to my knowledge he had gone to the upper Midwest to work that rodeo circuit with a couple of mutual friends. I wasn't aware that she even knew John, but I later learned that he had been dating her quite a bit since he had been discharged from the army a couple of months before I came home. Evidently, when I returned and he learned I was still carrying a torch for her, he took off for a while without even telling Gintsie. John was a good friend of long-standing and unfortunately this incident was just a continuation of what I had gone through my last couple of years in college; I should have been the one who cut and ran.

I went up to the ranch at Trail Creek every week or so between rodeos. Their dude wrangler was a young man who had been a guest a couple of summers before I went to the Army. He once told me he couldn't understand how I could expect to be paid for such an interesting job, and I suspect he did a lot less work than I did for his board and room. Bob and Ruby made me feel at home when I visited and stayed in the bunk house. I was trying to get my rodeo career restarted and had no interest in getting my old job back.

I spent the summer going to rodeos on the weekends, trying to get the irrigation done and putting up the hay. I was going into town every night, drinking too much beer, sleeping late when I didn't have a rodeo to go to and hoping for letters from Gintsie that didn't come very often. After the euphoria of being home from Korea wore off, I seemed to lose my usual enthusiasm. I had never learned to irrigate very well because that job had seemed to fall to Frank and Dad, who both had a knack for it. Our farm was quite hilly and the ditches were on contours, making distributing the flow of water evenly from them more of an art than a science that required vigilant oversight. Rather than enjoying the challenge, I found that I grew bored while irrigating and never gave it the attention it needed. Consequently, there were areas of the meadow that got too much water, and others under the brow of high spots that got none at all and turned brown as the growing season progressed.

I found myself sleeping late in the mornings, hurrying out to do my few chores and then going back to the house to escape into the pages of a book or magazine. Instead of working myself back into shape and losing some weight, I remained nearly as unprepared for the physical demands of bronc riding as I was when I first got out of the Army. I had made a conscious decision while in Korea to quit riding bulls when I came home, realizing that all of my serious rodeo injuries had been inflicted by bulls I had made qualified rides on. In fact, two out of the three injuries I considered serious were on winning bull rides.

Getting bucked off so much was eroding the confidence I had gained during the summer before I was drafted. Even when I had first started, I hadn't bucked off very often and the possibility of giving up the sport entered my mind. I had made somewhat of a reputation in the area and I decided that I at least needed to keep rodeoing until I got good enough again to quit with my pride intact. So, I persevered for a few more months and finally started, in cowboy lingo, to get my lick back. I placed in the saddle bronc riding a couple of times in the late summer and early fall. I still went into town nearly every night I was home, sat at the bar and drank 3.2 beer and tried to feel sorry for myself. Fortunately, I nearly always knew somebody from either College Days or rodeoing or both who showed up. When they invited me to join them, I always returned to my usual talkative self. I usually stayed until the place closed, continued to sleep late and then lay around the house reading most of the day. On Friday afternoons, I would rush outside to start some of the jobs that Dad and I had laid out for the week before he and Mom came home from Denver.

I think the folks understood better than I did that readjusting to being home would take some time, but I'm sure they were pleased when I decided to use my GI Bill benefits and enroll at Colorado State University to work towards a master's degree when school started in September. My most logical choice was in Animal Breeding and Genetics, but I did talk to the professor of Sociology from whom I had taken several courses, who was now head of the Sociology Department. He said he would very much like to have me as a graduate student but he thought that pursuing an advanced degree in the field of agriculture would be much better as far as job prospects were concerned, even though the courses I would have to take would be much more difficult. I knew he was right in both instances

I made an appointment to visit Dr. H. H. Stonaker, who had taught my most difficult—but favorite—animal husbandry course called simply, animal breeding. The textbook for that course had been written by Dr. Lush, the leading geneticist at Iowa State University where Stoney, as he was called by his friends and peers but certainly not by his students, had received his master's and doctor's degrees. He said he would be pleased to have me join the group of students who were working for master's degrees in animal breeding and reminded me in no uncertain terms that getting an advanced degree required a complete commitment and lots of hard work. I told him I would like to accept the challenge. We reviewed the courses I would be taking and they were indeed challenging.

The first quarter, I signed up for advanced algebra, veterinary physiology and cytogenetics. I wasn't very fond of math and had forgotten a lot of my first-year algebra, so I had to study hard to catch up to my classmates, many of whom actually enjoyed math! Cytogenetics was the study of genetics at the cellular level. This was not too long before the code for DNA had been broken and the field was advancing rapidly. This course required a lot of study, but I found it very enjoyable. The physiology courses required for my advanced degree were the same ones taken by sophomore veterinary medicine students. The first quarter was only lecture with no lab and was fairly rudimentary, but the next two quarters included hands-on lab classes as well. I found I could get by largely on general knowledge the first quarter and managed to get a C with very little studying. I had to study algebra II and cytogenetics and managed to get Bs in both, mostly by cramming hard the night before tests.

At the end of the first quarter, I found myself on academic probation. A graduate student was required to maintain a B average! I had earned my two Bs and probably didn't deserve my C considering how little I had studied. My pride was wounded, but not badly enough to make me change my ways when the second quarter started shortly after the first of the year. The three hours of lecture in physiology was considerably more difficult than the previous quarter and I was completely unprepared to handle the lab work. I took statistics, a very necessary branch of mathematics for the study of genetics, and found it no more difficult than algebra but much more interesting. Regression equations are used to measure the degree of heritability of traits in animals that are to be bred to increase the gene frequency of desired traits. I also had a two-hour seminar with Stony each quarter specific to my major. This quarter we were all required to write a seminar paper, on the subject of our choice, that related to genetics. I chose to review the genetic basis of the inheritance of color in horses. Since we always had a small group of brood mares, I had some understanding of the subject, but I knew that most conventional wisdom about it on the part of horse breeders was far from accurate.

During the winter quarter, I struggled with my lab work in veterinary physiology and got another C, but managed to get Bs in the other subjects. I also went to the library enough to get my seminar paper that was due at the end of the spring quarter well underway. When spring quarter started we had a spell of beautiful weather and I lost all my enthusiasm for attending classes and got a yen to get started with the spring farming. I had only one class that I really enjoyed, logic, taught by a wonderful professor from the English department. I decided to quit college about a third of the way through the quarter and withdraw passing, which meant that if I wanted to pick up my studies again I could repeat the quarter. Stony gave me an incomplete on my seminar paper. I know he was disappointed in me, but not more than I was in myself.

I had talked to Dad about dropping out of school so I could replant some of the hay ground that was no longer producing well. I know he regretted my dropping out, but as always didn't pass judgment. We made a budget for what additional farm equipment we would need and set up a drawing account at the bank that I could use. (Personal banking was really personal in those days). We were going to need a bigger tractor, a plow and a disc. Over the next several weeks I went to a number of farm sales and managed to buy a 1935 John Deere D tractor, a sixteen-inch two-way plow and a fourteen-foot tandem disc that turned out to have one broken bearing, all for about $600.00. As soon as the frost went out of the ground, I started farming like mad. I not only plowed some of the fields that we had discussed, but also part of the farm that was very hard to get irrigation water to, which I should have left as it was. The old John Deere tractor was really meant to be a dry land farm tractor and had plenty of power to pull the one bottom plow, the disc or a three-section harrow. The only problem was that it would go only about 2 or 3 miles an hour while plowing and 4 or 5 miles an hour with the disc or harrow.

Regaining some enthusiasm and energy, I got up early and worked till dark. Dad and I had decided to use oats for a nurse crop and re-seed everything to alfalfa. We were lucky to have a wet spring and managed to get everything planted between the timely rains. Dad worked just as hard as I did when he was home and we managed very well with our old farm equipment. We used the little John Deere H to pull our eight-foot grain drill to plant the oats and sow the alfalfa seed.

After we got the spring farming done, I entered several rodeos. Instead of entering the College Day Rodeo in mid-May as a graduate student I drove to Strong City, Kansas that weekend for a rodeo produced by the Roberts Brothers in their home-town. I had become acquainted with a Kansas State Rodeo Team member, Jim Louder, during college rodeo days and had visited his family's ranch just a few miles south of Fort Riley in the Flint Hills a couple of times on weekends while I was in supply school. Since his ranch was near Strong City, I took advantage of his hospitality again and stayed with him during the rodeo. I found that the state highway in Kansas just east of the Colorado state line went miles and miles without any curves and practically no traffic. I decided to find out just how fast my little Chevy would go and opened it up on a piece of road where I could see that no one was coming for miles ahead of me. In short order, I was up to the 110-miles-an-hour maximum on my speedometer and I kept it there for a couple of miles. I was all by myself and I guess I figured that if I had a blowout I would be the only one killed in the wreck. I opened it up that fast only a couple more times while I had it, but rarely drove under eighty miles an hour on the open road. Amazingly, I was never caught for speeding in that car.

I didn't place on either of my saddle broncs at Strong City but made credible rides on both. I greatly enjoyed seeing Jim and his parents again and went to the rodeo dance with him and some of his friends. On the way home after the rodeo, I drove by Cottonwood Falls, Kansas and said hello to the parents of my good friend Bob Dent, with whom I rodeoed in Colorado a lot. They were the kind of down-to-earth ranch folks I expected them to be. I then slipped a little north and worked two rodeos in southwestern Nebraska, one in Benkelman and one in McCook. I qualified on all my saddle broncs but failed to properly spur my bareback horses out of the chute at both rodeos. While I was in the Army, they changed the rules for starting a bareback ride slightly and I just couldn't seem to get a handle on it. After Benkelman, I decided to give up riding bareback horses and concentrate on improving my saddle bronc riding.

I felt that I was getting close to riding saddle broncs as well as I had before going into the Army, so I entered the professional saddle bronc riding in Cheyenne. I decided that if I did reasonably well there, I would go ahead and rodeo full-time for the rest of the summer. Because of the wet spring, I hadn't had to irrigate the alfalfa much and had just enough time to get it mowed and raked before the Cheyenne rodeo started. I seemed to have snapped out of my blue funk and was enjoying life again. I had already called in my entry fees in Cheyenne and was able to learn from the rodeo secretary's office when I had my stock. I don't remember just what days I rode but I showed up in Cheyenne only on those two days and continued putting up hay between times. I drew two fairly good horses and spurred them about as well as I ever did, and I thought there was an outside chance that I would make the finals in professional bronc riding. It was wishful thinking, but I had to be there the last day of the rodeo in order to find out if I would be in the short go-round for the finals. As I feared, I hadn't won a thing in Cheyenne but had done well enough to decide to go on with my plan to rodeo full-time for the month of August.

The rodeo in Boulder, Colorado immediately followed Cheyenne, and I drew Buck Yarbough's horse, Black Powder. I had won second on him at the Wyoming University rodeo in 1952. I took too short a rein on him and he came out of the chute bucking straight up and down without kicking. Everyone was yelling at me to slip some rein, but for some reason I couldn't. He had bucked well enough that I couldn't get a re-ride and I felt bad that I had wasted the best horse I had drawn in quite a while.

I went on from Boulder to Monte Vista, Colorado, the next major show and drew fairly average horses once again, so didn't place. I then went on to Durango, Colorado in the southwestern corner of the state. Just as I pulled into town the oil pressure gauge on my dashboard started dropping. I pulled over to the shoulder and looked under the hood. To my dismay, I discovered I had broken an oil line. I limped on into town and made it to a garage before the car heated up and learned that the line could be

This horse at Belle Fourche was a lot better than he looks.
I lost a stirrup and disqualified.

easily fixed. The problem was that I was nearly out of money, and after paying the garage, I had just enough left to get a very cheap hotel room in downtown Durango that had no windows in it nor a bath. I needed very badly to win some money but I drew one of the same mediocre horses I had had in Monte Vista, and another on which I couldn't place in the second go-round.

I realized that I didn't have enough money to buy gasoline for the drive home. There wasn't anyone entered in the rodeo whom I knew very well, but I had to face up to the prospect of borrowing some money. I saw Jim Like standing behind the chutes and explained to him I had had to get an oil line fixed in my car and didn't have enough money to make it home to Fort Collins. He had made all the rodeos I had attended since Cheyenne and probably knew I hadn't won anything. He handed me a $20 bill and said to pay him back when I could. I had already paid for my cheap room and checked out early the next morning and drove back to Fort Collins. Fortunately, gas was cheap in those days. I paid Jim's $20 back when I saw him at the rodeo in Loveland a week or so later.

I had had my fling with the big rodeos that followed Cheyenne and had learned that the farther I got from home, the broker I got. At Loveland, I started the first in a series of rodeos at county fairs across Eastern Colorado in August. I had contested in many of these affairs off and on since I first started rodeoing in 1948 and began placing often enough again to pay my expenses and a little more. The biggest of these Rodeos was Longmont. In the first go-round, I drew one of the saddle broncs that had been listed among the top ten horses performing at RCA-approved shows the previous year. I managed to win second on him in the first go-round and drew a horse in the second that I felt confident would allow me to place high in the average if I made a good ride.

I had traveled to this rodeo with Bob Dent and Bobby Beckstead, who was John's first cousin, and they helped me saddle and get down on my second horse just as they had with the first. Longmont had terrible, long, deep and narrow chutes, which made it difficult to get your feet in the stirrups as you got down on your saddle. Just as I was about to nod to the gate man to let me out I realized that my left foot was not completely in my stirrup and I tried to reach down to reposition it. He evidently thought I was nodding to open the gate and did so. When my horse blew out of the chute, I was leaning off to the left. Of course, I missed spurring him out of the gate and bucked off after the second jump. I felt I might be awarded a re-ride, but I wasn't. Bob Dent always said about that rodeo, "If Lilley had of gotten out of the chute right on that horse he would have won it all at Longmont". We will never know, but at least I was riding a lot better by then. I once again finished up the fall county fair circuit in Castle Rock and again drew good old Sweet Nellie. I managed to get her ridden for the second time out of three tries. I won either a third or fourth on her this time.

Between rodeos during the second two years after getting out of the army, I made a little money breaking colts for local ranchers and helping Bob Swan with a couple of new enterprises that he had taken on to supplement his income from the dude ranch. He had won a few contracts let by the National Forest Service to plow sagebrush and fence off areas that were reseeded to grass. He leased a D-7 Caterpillar for one job and a D-8 for another to pull the specially designed one-way disc-plow the USDA had developed, which could be used in areas that had some exposed outcroppings of granite that a regular dryland one-way plow couldn't navigate. Instead of having an axle that went through all fourteen discs, it had seven separate pairs that were spring-mounted so they could rise over individual rocks. One of these jobs was located in the Roosevelt National Forest in Northern Colorado and the other in the Medicine Bow National Forest immediately north of the state line in Wyoming. The best grazing on these grazing permits was in the valleys and on plateaus scattered throughout the forest, where they had fairly dense stands of sagebrush. In the mid-fifties, the range management experts decided to plow this sagebrush under and plant non-native cool-season grasses, such as intermediate and/ or crested wheat grass, orchard grass and fescue, in an effort to increase forage production. After about ten or fifteen years, the Forest Service discontinued this practice and decided that it had been counterproductive; in fact, they would like to forget these projects were ever undertaken.

Bob asked me to work with him on several of these jobs and we soon were hard at work spending long hours pulling this unique plow with the leased Caterpillar tractor. We were able to finish up most of the jobs in a few weeks. The first one was just north of the Wyoming border and west of the Laramie river in the Medicine Bow Forest. Bob had located a small used house trailer to park on the site. The first couple of days we spelled each other on about eight hour shifts of plowing. At that time of year, the sun came up about 5 AM and didn't go down until 8 PM. We got up while it was still dark, cooked breakfast on a little portable bottle-gas-fueled stove and one of us was at work soon after.

After a couple of days, Bob went to town to get supplies and spend a couple of days at the ranch. While he was gone, I plowed steadily until nearly dark with a thirty- to forty-five-minutes break for lunch. When Bob returned in the afternoon of the third day, he relieved me on the Cat until dark, at which time I had supper prepared. It took us about four more days to complete the job, during which we again spelled each other throughout the day, usually on four to six-hour-shifts. When we finished the job, I went back to the farm to put up hay and continue rodeoing.

Our next sagebrush plowing job was in the Roosevelt National Forest about twenty miles to the north and west of Trail Creek Ranch on Sheep Creek. The site was within sight of the Eaton reservoir and Bob had obtained permission from its caretaker for us to camp in a log cabin on their property about hundred yards up the hill from Sheep Creek. This job was also within about a half mile from the property of Lyle Van Waning, who was the main character in the book, "The Meadow," celebrating the very area we were in the middle of. The routine for this job was much like that of the one that preceded it, however Bob found less and less time to help with the plowing as he dedicated more to another project, that of building telephone lines for some of the more remote areas in that part of the country. We began the job in the early fall and were at an altitude where the first freeze comes early. Since we had no antifreeze in the Caterpillar I had to drain it every night and then refill it every morning with water carried from Sheep Creek.

I had two memorable experiences in the middle of this job, one pleasant and one quite tragic. First the pleasant one: The first Saturday after I started work on this job Colorado State University was playing Wyoming University in Laramie. On Thursday night, I drove about 12 miles north into Wyoming to the ranch that my brother, Frank was managing and called Polly Schaffer, Teddy's little sister, who was going to the University of Wyoming, and asked her for a date to the game. She was agreeable and we decided to meet in the middle of the field as soon as the game was over because I planned to work all morning and wouldn't arrive until after game started. I got up early as usual and plowed til about 10:30, then drained the Cat, went back to the cabin, washed and shaved using water carried in a bucket from Sheep Creek. I don't remember who won the game but Polly and I did meet after the game, had supper and partied with mutual friends till about midnight. It was good to see her and she brought me up to date on what her brother and my good friend Teddy were up to. I got back to the cabin at about 1:30 AM and slept in until 7 and then plowed until dark on Sunday.

The tragic incident happened the middle of the next week. I was in the middle of a round with the Cat when a forest service employee drove up beside me in a pick-up. He asked me if I had seen the man driving the tractor pulling the grain drill. I said I saw him about 30 minutes ago. The driver said he was supposed to relieve this man and couldn't find him.

I shut off the Caterpillar, jumped in the pickup and we drove around for about fifteen minutes looking for the tractor and driver. There was a fairly steep draw down the middle of the area where he had been working and as we drove closer to the edge of it we spotted the orange tractor lying upside down about sixty yards below. When the pickup stopped, I jumped out and galloped down the hill. I reached the bottom of the gulley and found the driver face down under the overturned tractor. He was lying with his head and one arm sticking out from under the tractor. One glove was halfway off of his hand and his gold rimmed glasses were askew on his face, which was blue. I thought of trying to push the tractor off of him but decided it was too heavy and I might just make the situation worse. I was confident that he was dead. I ran back to the pickup and the other employee was in shock. We contacted the Roosevelt National Forest headquarters in Fort Collins somehow, and were told to do nothing until they arrived. About an hour and a half later the assistant supervisor of the Roosevelt National Forest and the Larimer County coroner arrived with a couple of people from the sheriff's office.

I showed them where the accident had occurred and after about ten minutes studying the scene they backed a pickup to the brow of the hill, tied a heavy rope to its trailer hitch, tied the other end around the tractor and drove the pickup forward slowly. To our amazement, after no more than a gentle pull, the tractor rolled off of the dead man. I realized then that I would have had enough strength to roll the tractor off the body by myself.

    I gave a statement to the officials present and they drove me back to my Cat, which I cranked up, and continued my round to the spot closest to the cabin. It was getting dark by this time and Bob had arrived. The coroner loaded the body into the hearse and he and the rest of a now fairly large group of people headed down Sheep Creek towards Fort Collins. I finally got to sleep a few hours later, but when I woke up in the morning, the previous day's events popped into my mind and remained with me all day. With each round, I passed close to the place where the tractor had hit one bump too many at too high a speed, careened straight down the hill with a very frightened driver, come unhitched from the grain drill and made a last-minute turn before it flipped over.

    After a few more long days, we finally finished the plowing and hauled the Caterpillar back to Fort Collins. This was the last plowing job I helped Bob with, but he had gotten contracts to do the fencing around this one and the one in Wyoming. This was to keep the cattle that were allowed to graze on forest land out of the newly planted areas until the new grass was established, probably at least two years. He asked me to help him with both. We commuted to the job from the ranch to fence the Sheep Creek permit near the Eaton reservoir and completed that job later that summer. We had a portable Johnson posthole digger with two handles about two-and-a-half-feet long attached to either side of the fairly powerful two-cycle gasoline engine. It had both an eight-inch and a twelve-inch auger that could be attached to the drive shaft extending from the bottom of the engine. With the auger attached, the handles would be about waist high when the digger started spinning. One operator controlled the trigger-accelerator and the weight of the engine was sufficient to start the hole. If the digging became difficult, the operators could add their weight to the handles, and if a rock or a root was encountered and slowed the auger, they could be thrown off their feet. The posthole digger was a great labor-saving device, but using it was about as hard on your body as operating a jackhammer.

We then made a couple of day trips to get started on the Wyoming fencing job. I helped Bob chain (measure) and mark locations for the posts on the fence line the forest service had already surveyed. We would build several miles of four-strand barbed wire fence through some fairly heavily timbered, often rough country. We were allowed to attach the wires to the ponderosa pine trees when necessary, but couldn't staple the wires directly to a tree because in a year or two it would grow around both the staple and the wire. Instead, we cut down nearby quaking aspen trees three to four inches in diameter, cut them into four-and a-half foot lengths, trimmed two sides with an axe and nailed them with twenty-penny nails to the trees being used in lieu of posts. We would then staple the four strands of wire to the Aspen stays. This was necessarily slow work because it was difficult to stretch wire more than a few rods (a rod is sixteen feet, the required distance between posts) at a time through the timber. On level ground, it was possible to stretch an entire fifty-rod (quarter mile) roll.

We had set and braced just a few corner posts when an early fall snow forced us to postpone any further work until the next spring. We had a dry, mild winter, so we were able to resume the job in early April. Bob asked me if I would be willing to set up an on-site camp and live there until the job was completed. He had some other jobs lined up and said he thought I could finish the job with the help of a couple of men. I readily agreed and negotiated a split on the profit. I was able to find a young man from Fort Collins, who had been drafted the same day I was, who said that he and his brother would be glad to work on the fence until the job was completed. They seemed to like the prospect of living in a tent for a few weeks in the beautiful country I had described.

We arrived at the proposed campsite in the early afternoon, pitched our tent, dug a slit trench for a toilet and unpacked all our gear. We had a couple of five-gallon propane tanks to fuel the three-burner gas hotplate, our only modern convenience. Having helped us set up camp, Bob headed back to the ranch in the pickup, promising to be back in three or four days with some more supplies, leaving us the Jeep. For supper, I fried some round steak and potatoes in our big iron skillet, made some milk gravy by browning a handful of flour in the grease and opened up a can of green beans. After supper, we washed the dishes in the cold water hauled up from the nearby mountain stream in a three-gallon milk bucket. The snow was still melting only a few miles upstream from us, but fortunately the water was running clear. As the sun was going down, we each found a relatively smooth spot in the tent, rolled out our bedrolls, and were sound asleep by the time it was completely dark.

I woke up at daylight the next morning and cooked a breakfast of bacon, eggs and pancakes. I used Bisquick for the pancakes, adding a tablespoon of the hot bacon grease and an egg to the batter. Bobby laid out our plates and utensils on our folding table and his brother made the coffee. After breakfast, we placed the breakfast dishes in a wash pan and covered them with water to soak. We loaded the Jeep with our posthole digger, shovels, digging bars, hammers, staples and fencing pliers and took the road across the creek. It was two miles through the timber to where Bob and I had already put in the corner and brace posts for the first section of fence, and almost three miles as the crow flies to our camp where the fence would end.

After a few days, we got better and better working as a team and we found we could build a quarter-mile or more of fence in a day. When we got into the timber we were slowed down considerably, however. Where we could set posts, we had to fight roots with our posthole digger, and stretching wire adequately through the timber was not easy. We also had several drainages to cross and it took some improvising to stretch wire across them. If you tied wire to a steel post in a low spot, it tended to pull out of the ground, and by the time you had fastened all four stretched wires to it, it was impossible to hold it in the ground without wiring a rock of 100 or more pounds to it.

The weather had turned out to be better than we could have hoped for. We had expected to get some snow, but instead, one afternoon we were caught in a very unseasonable thunderstorm with lightning crashing all around us. The last thing you want to be near when lighting is striking the ground is a wire fence with steel posts. When this storm came up we were on the north slope of a fairly good-sized hill in fairly heavy timber. As the strikes got closer, we moved about a hundred yards away from the fence and spent about thirty minutes wishing we were anywhere else.

Being caught in a lightning storm in an area that has both trees and a wire fence to attract it reminded me of being in an artillery barrage. In both cases the sound can't hurt you, and if you are hit directly you won't know what happened.

By the end of our second week in camp, we were getting mighty tired of ham and bacon and Bob hadn't come back for a while with supplies. I had learned that hunting parties in those days nearly always killed what they called some camp meat the day before the start of deer season. Dad told me this when he came back from his only hunting trip when we lived on the ranch. He had joined several other members of the State Board of Agriculture at Colorado State University in a remote area near Craig, Colorado. He said their guide shot a yearling deer and brought it back to camp the night before season started. The game wardens surely didn't approve of this practice, but didn't go out of their way to stop it. We needed some fresh meat far worse than they had, so I called off work early one afternoon hoping to get us some venison for supper with Frank's 30/30. After walking about a quarter of a mile north of camp, we came into some scattered timber and I had Bobby and his brother get about forty yards on either side of me as we moved forward. Soon I saw what I thought was probably a dry doe in an opening about sixty yards from us and dropped her with a shot to the heart. I ran up and began field dressing her quickly. We were all nervous about getting caught even though we hadn't seen another soul except Bob since we arrived. When I opened her up the first thing I saw was a nearly fully formed fawn. I felt like hell, but there was no undoing what had just happened so I finished dressing her and removed her hindquarters. We dragged the rest of her carcass and the offal into some heavy timber and headed back to camp with the thought of fresh meat for supper overwhelming our guilt. I sliced three good-sized steaks off of one quarter and wrapped the rest of the meat in a raincoat, which my two partners carried into some nearby heavy timber and tied about six feet off the ground. I fried the venison with some potatoes and plenty of salt and pepper, opened up a can of pork and beans and another of peas and made my usual milk gravy. I'm not the world's greatest cook, but we all ate as if it was our last meal and topped it off with a can of pears in heavy syrup.

We wound up the job in about four more days and spent the last afternoon getting ready to leave early the next morning. I left out a box of dry cereal and a can of milk for breakfast so all we had to do was bury our garbage, roll up our beds and take down the tent in the morning. When we woke up the ground was covered with a light skift of snow.

Our luck with the weather had finally run out! The first few mornings we had been in camp there was ice on the creek, but the rest of the time we hadn't even had frost at night. An indication of the unseasonably warm weather was the fact that on the third day, after we had hung our venison in a tree, we found maggots all over the meat. We didn't eat any that night, although up to that time it had been tender and tasted fine. I was tempted to brush off the maggots and make one more meal out of it before throwing out what little was left. My partners overruled me, saying they would be quite willing to go back to ham for a few more meals.

We managed to get everything loaded into the Jeep and squeezed the three of us into the two seats in front. The snow was starting to fall harder and by the time we had crossed the Laramie River at the Honholtz Ranch and headed east on the dirt road north of Red Mountain near the Wyoming state line, it was beginning to pile up. Even after bundling up in the winter clothes we hadn't needed thus far, we were about to freeze in the open Jeep. I was driving along at about twenty-five miles an hour when suddenly the Jeep started missing and slowly ground to a halt. Bob had told us before he left that if we had carburetor trouble we should blow into the gas tank. I dismounted from the Jeep, removed the gas cap and firmly pressed my mouth over it and started to blow without too much hope of success. In the meantime, Bobby's brother ground the starter till we were in danger of draining the battery. I removed my mouth and took a deep breath for about the fifth time and just when I thought I might blow out my eardrums from the pressure, the motor caught. I jumped behind the wheel and managed to keep the motor running by pumping the gas pedal. With our hearts in our mouths we continued down the road. It was at least forty miles between the Honholtz Ranch and the next habitation at Tie Siding, and we hadn't met a vehicle. The Jeep started to die several more times, but by pumping the gas pedal furiously I managed to keep it going until whatever was wrong with the carburetor managed to cure itself. We finally got to Highway 287 close to the little store, filling station and post office at Tie Siding, Wyoming, nearly out of gasoline. After filling the Jeep and the two five-gallon cans attached to the side of the Jeep with gas, we bought a couple of candy bars, piled back in the Jeep and drove the fifty miles to Fort Collins without further incident.

    I dropped my partners off at their parents' house in Fort Collins and made it home to the farm in late afternoon. During the entire two weeks of having camped in the high country in a tent, we had never been so cold and miserable as we were on the 100-mile drive home. The next day I drove up to Trail Creek in the Jeep and got Bob to write checks for my two helpers. I couldn't have asked for harder workers or better companions. I think it turned out to be quite a bit more primitive than they had expected, but they never once complained. I can't remember exactly how much they each made, but it was a good deal more than they could have earned in such a short period elsewhere. Nor were they likely to ever have another job where they got to work so hard for ten hours a day, seven days a week with such great board and room! I wasn't paid my $300 until a month later when Bob was paid for the contract.

29
Great Job Opportunity

One night shortly after I got home from the fencing job, Mom called from their apartment in Denver. Dad was in the hospital! She said Dad's asthma had been flaring up worse in the last few weeks, and after supper he had an attack that became so severe he lost consciousness. She said getting him to the hospital had been an ordeal she would never forget. She had called an ambulance, and when the attendants arrived, they had an empty oxygen bottle and had to go back down the old elevator to the ambulance to get another. They finally got him into the ambulance and allowed Mother to ride to the hospital with them. On the way, they barely avoided a serious collision. When they arrived, Dad was immediately sent to intensive care

Early the next morning, I drove to St. Joseph's Hospital near downtown Denver. When I arrived, I found Dad in an oxygen tent in the urgent care unit. He was pale and extremely frail looking, but alert and able to visit with me. Even though he had never enjoyed very good health, I had never really thought about it and was suddenly confronted with the possibility that we could lose him.

Mom told me that Dad's health had been failing badly all summer and Doctor Duman was at a loss as to what was causing his asthma to get so much worse. It had been stabilized with medication for years and that, plus mother carefully watching his diet to avoid any of the various items that he was allergic to, had kept it in check. While he was in the hospital, Dr. Duman discovered that Dad had tuberculosis in his kidneys, which was quite unusual. He was finally able to find an antibiotic that worked and Dad began to slowly regain his health. Duman wasn't sure he could completely cure the TB, but felt it could be possible to keep it under control. Dad later said that Dr. Duman came to the conclusion that he had developed TB in the testicle that had been removed in 1929 and the TB had migrated to his kidneys and remained dormant there for 45 years. When the infection became active, it reduced his general resistance, causing the asthma to flare up more often and with greater intensity.

Seeing my father, whom I loved dearly and had always taken for granted, laying in the hospital looking vulnerable had a dramatic effect on me. I quickly decided that I needed to start looking for a decent job, greatly reduce my trips to town to drink beer and take my responsibilities at the farm more seriously. Surely I had higher expectations for myself than to become a fair-to-middling part-time rodeo hand, while doing odd day jobs and letting my parents pay all my expenses for doing a mediocre job of managing the farm. I had met the only goal I had set for myself when I got home from Korea, becoming nearly as good a saddle bronc rider as I was before being drafted, but I had given up riding bareback horses and bulls in the process.

I immediately started looking for a job in the field of agriculture.

Several of the animal husbandry graduates I went to school with had taken jobs as livestock buyers for one of the large packing plants in Denver, a job I was not particularly keen on. My degree also qualified me for an entry-level job with the Extension Service as an Assistant County Agent or as an Assistant County Supervisor with the Farmers Home Administration, which made direct government loans to producers that couldn't qualify for commercial loans with banks or insurance companies. Both of these agencies had offices in Fort Collins and I made a call on each. Neither had an opening at the time, but suggested I place an application on file with their state office. I then went to the local office of the Production Credit Association, which was a quasi-government agency that also made loans to farmers and ranchers based on a federal law that created this producer owned organization. They had nothing available either and the officer I talked to in Fort Collins was not very encouraging. I had no interest in working directly for a commercial bank, and jobs with the big insurance companies that made agricultural loans were difficult to land without prior experience.

I forwarded the application form I received at the Fort Collins office to the state office of the FHA, previously called the Farm Security Administration. I heard back within a couple of weeks that I had been accepted for a job as Assistant County Supervisor in Prowers County with headquarters in Lamar. It was gratifying to know that I could get a job, but I wasn't ready to move that far away from Fort Collins or Denver without searching some more. If this same job had been available in Larimer County, I probably would have accepted it. Dad had actually worked for the Farm Security Administration briefly during the Second World War in an administrative capacity and it was a field I was quite interested in. It is possible that if I had taken the job in Lamar my career would have been spent in agricultural lending, but Dad soon turned up an opportunity that offered a chance to pursue an entirely different career with a much broader horizon.

In the meantime, I continued riding in the rodeos at the county fairs in Northeastern Colorado and Southeastern Wyoming. I started drawing better horses and placing regularly. The excitement of looking for a job and the prospect of changing my life renewed my enthusiasm for everything I did. I kept Dad and Mom posted on my job hunting efforts and Dad said he would see what he could find around Denver. For many years he had belonged to an organization in Denver called the Ag Club. It was a group that met for lunch once a week, made up of people like him with roots in agriculture but not directly related to production. Most were either owners or managers of agribusiness corporations, CEOs of nonprofits, public relation representatives for large agricultural enterprises or senior employees in agricultural-related government jobs, like Dad. He was well acquainted with most of these people and had put the word out that his son was looking for a job.

One of these men was Radford S. Hall, who had recently been elevated to the job of Executive Vice President of the American National Cattlemen's Association (ANCA), whose headquarters were in Denver. Before joining ANCA's staff as assistant to recently retired Ferd Molin, their long time Executive Officer, Rad had worked at the Record Stockman, a livestock publication serving the Western United States, under Editor Willard Simms, who would go on to manage the National Western livestock show in Denver. Rad had said that he would be happy to give me an interview for his old job. Dad called me with the news and I called and set up an interview in early September.

I had recently placed either second or third in the bronc riding at three rodeos in a row: second at the Douglas County Fair in Castle Rock, Colorado; third at the Goshen County Fair in Torrington, Wyoming; and third at the Platte County Fair in Wheatland, Wyoming. I was already entered in the Grand County Fair at Kremling, Colorado on the weekend before the ANCA job interview. I did not place at Kremling, but came away with a chunk of hide off the knuckle of the ring finger of my left hand. I had scraped it across the saddle horn when my horse took his head. This is something that happens quite regularly to saddle bronc riders who take too short a rein when using an older saddle like mine, which still had a saddle horn.

I showed up for the interview in a sports jacket and necktie, more than a little nervous. They didn't ask about the Band-Aid on my finger nor did I bring it up as ranchers didn't think very highly of rodeo cowboys in those days.

Joining Rad for the interview was Don Collins, who was the president of the ANCA at that time. Don owned a large ranch in the Kit Carson area of Southeastern Colorado, the Kit Carson Bank and the Franklin Serum Company, a large agricultural pharmaceutical company. Don's father, Charlie Collins, had been president of the ANCA when Dad was president of the Colorado Cattlemen's Association in the mid-thirties. Dad had also known Don's wife and her mother when he went to college in Fort Collins. None of these things really helped my cause, because Dad was a Democrat among a sea of Republican cattlemen and used to lock horns with Charlie Collins at cattlemen's meetings over policy matters. Charlie was and still is a legend in the cattle industry for his strongly held conservative views, much admired by most ranchers, while Dad, then only in his early thirties, was one of the rare men to stand up and debate him at meetings.

My single strong point was the fact that Rad had no ranch background and I did. My college degree helped, but wasn't necessary in those days for such a job. Rad went out of his way to make me feel comfortable during the interview and I could tell he liked me. That I looked even younger than my twenty-six years surely wasn't any help, and I got the impression Don thought I needed more experience. When we reached the point of talking salary, they asked me how much I expected to make. I told them I had been accepted for a job with the Farmers Home Administration, which had a $350 a month starting salary. I indicated that I would much prefer this job and would be willing to start for that amount. When the interview was over Rad said he and Don would make their recommendation to the Board of Directors, which was meeting soon. He called me two weeks later and said I had the job and could start work on October 1, 1956.

A few weeks into my job I had lunch with Hugo Stuckenschneider, the current editor of the Record Stockman and student body president when I was a junior at Colorado A&M. While visiting, after he had interviewed me for an article, he surprised me by saying that he had also applied for my new job. He said I had blown him and all the other applicants out of the water by agreeing to work for so little. He thought the job was worth at least $150 or $200 more a month than I had asked. Later in my career I often made the possibly overblown statement that I could have afforded to work for nothing in order to get such an interesting and challenging job.

By this time, we had rented the big house at the farm to Gerald, one of the seven or eight sons of the Hoff family, from whom we had purchased our little John Deere tractor soon after we bought the farm. I was living in the small house. When I went to work in Denver, Dad arranged for Gerald to take care of the farm in lieu of the rent.

When I mentioned looking for an apartment in Denver, Dad and Mom said they could see no reason I shouldn't move into theirs with them. It was only about a six- or seven-block walk from the apartment just west of the State Capital to the ANCA office at 17th and Clarkson. One would think that at twenty-six years of age I would be anxious to get a place of my own, but I had inherited my father's frugal ways and we all enjoyed each other's company. I paid $30 a month toward the rent, with Mom's good home cooking thrown in. We put a daybed in the living room and I used a few drawers of a buffet as a dresser. It was difficult to find parking near the apartment, so I usually left my car at the good-sized parking lot at the ANCA office and walked back and forth to work.

About two years before I took the job, the ANCA had moved their headquarters from an office building in downtown Denver after building a modest, by today's standards, but very functional new building less than a mile from downtown Denver. The entire staff of this organization, which had represented the interests of the nation's entire cattle industry since 1898, consisted of the Executive Secretary, the Assistant Executive Secretary (now yours truly), the Director of Public Relations, the editor of its official monthly publication called the American Cattle Producer, a bookkeeper and three secretaries. We also had a janitor who came in a couple of hours every day. Rad had a big office, and mine, also quite large, joined his with a door between us. There were also offices for the magazine editor and the public relations director and a fairly large room at the rear, which was used for addressing and mailing our biweekly newsletter and served as the break room for our morning coffee. The bookkeeper had a semi-enclosed area in the middle of the large open space that also accommodated the three secretaries. There was also a small fifth office used by Mr. Molin, who had been retained part-time as the association's treasurer for one year as part of his retirement agreement. I learned later from the minutes that he had also been paid a $25,000 lump sum upon retirement plus the modest monthly salary for his year as treasurer. The idea of a formal retirement program was foreign to ranchers in those days.

    The building had a modern heating and air conditioning system and a full basement for storage. We worked from 8 a.m. to 5 p.m. five days a week with a one-hour break for lunch, and from eight to noon Saturdays. Lyle Liggett, who was our public relations director, a position created only a few years before, said that Ferd Molin had paid new-hires a one-month salary bonus after one year on the job, as long as we were within our annual budget and he thought Rad would continue the policy.

    Lyle had previously worked as a writer in the news department of a local Denver TV station and had occasionally filled in as a news reporter. Rad had influenced the association's Board of Directors to create the new position, Director of Public Relations, and hiring Lyle. He had proven effective in his job of promoting the interests of the cattle industry to the general public. In the first month or two of my employment Rad was busy getting settled in his new job and didn't have a lot of time to work with me, so I spent quite a bit of time with Lyle. In addition to writing the monthly newsletter, he put out at least one news release each week, which were well received by the media, especially the many weekly newspapers throughout the country's small towns. A lot of the things that I learned from Lyle during the first six months of my new job stood me in good stead for the rest of my career in cattle association work.

    I liked the team spirit that pervaded the staff, which was never more needed than on Friday afternoons, when we put our newsletter in the mail to our 12,000 members. One of the secretaries put the addresses on them with an old-fashioned Address-o-graph machine, which semi-automatically imprinted the individual addresses with what were called Addresso-graph plates. These plates had to be individually embossed for new members and discarded and replaced when a member had a change of address. As the machine spit out the addressed newsletters an assembly line team sorted them into mailing zone groupings, tied them in bundles within states and between states and threw them into canvas mail sacks furnished by the Denver Post Office, which picked them up late Friday afternoons.

Rad had played an essential role behind the scenes throughout his career as Molin's right-hand man, but unfortunately was often not fully appreciated, especially by some allied industry executives and PR types. One of these, the rather blustery PR man for the big packing plant, Armour and Company, let anyone who would listen know he didn't think Rad was up to replacing Molin. Rad, who had a soft, but well-modulated speaking voice, and a quiet demeanor was aware of his detractors, but carried himself with confidence as he moved into the big office. Resentment by some members of the ANCA ruling Executive Committee for this interference in their internal business may have helped Rad's cause.

I took it upon myself to learn as much about the organization's history and current and past leadership as I could while Rad showed me the ropes. Not being as good at remembering names as a guy with my new job needed to be, I memorized the names of our living past presidents, who also served on the Executive Committee, the president and executive officers of our affiliated state cattle associations and our committee chairmen. I also acquainted myself with the organization's by-laws. Leaving my car parked at the office and walking to and from work replaced at least some of the exercise I was used to at the farm. Mom said it was just as easy to cook for three people as for two and I know the folks enjoyed having me stay with them. I always had a high ball with Dad, usually bourbon and ginger ale, when I got home from work as we sat watching the MacNeil/Lehrer news hour, while Mom fixed supper.

A girl who had dated my good friend, Jack Mitchell, during my rodeo days lived nearby and I often took her out dancing on Friday night at a bar that featured a western band. We were usually joined by a friend, Solly Sollenberger and his wife. I had graduated from college with Solly, who was working for Cudhay Packing Company as a hog buyer. Solly had married a girl who had two children and this was their one night out. We usually closed the place up after drinking a lot of beer. I hate that I can't remember my date's name, but she was a great dancer and good company.

Gintsie had graduated from college just before I got home from Korea and had continued playing the field. It had never occurred to me that she might be interested in getting married and it was the furthest thing from my mind. I knew that she had added Bob McNey to the list of men she was dating, but was taken by complete surprise when I heard that they were engaged. Bob and his older brother, John, had been raised on a ranch in Livermore, just north of Fort Collins, and I had been slightly acquainted with them all my life. I had run into Bob a few times when we were both going to Colorado A&M. I had been told that he had suffered with rheumatic fever in his teen years and was thought to have been left with a damaged heart. His older brother, John, was the cowboy of the family and had rodeoed in college. I had been falling farther and farther behind in the Gintsie competition and Bob did me a big favor taking her out of circulation. After my nearly five-year fruitless pursuit of her, I began to think that I might very well become a lifetime bachelor.

I often drove to Fort Collins on weekends and stayed with Doc Munson, who was now living in the little house at the farm. If there was a dance at either Livermore or Virginia Dale I went to it, otherwise I hung around Fort Collins and met old friends at the various 3.2 beer parlors. By this time Sol's and Dick's had fallen out of favor with the college crowd and the Dew Drop Inn a few buildings down Linden Street was the favorite hangout.

Although I really enjoyed my new job and appreciated the practical side of living with Mom and Dad, it didn't take long for me to get tired of city life. We had no interest in giving up our horses, but I thought perhaps we could sell the farm in Fort Collins and find another within commuting distance of Denver. Mom jumped right on the idea, but Dad was doubtful that we could find anything within our budget very close to Denver. I started checking the want ads and Dad suggested Mom and I go ahead and look at some places, but said he didn't want to be involved until we found something promising. We decided to just consider the area north of Denver and checked out five or six places over the next few weeks. Northern Colorado had been suffering from a drought for about three years and we were having a warm open winter. The only places in our price range either had no improvements or very little irrigated land. We did find one sixty-acre, mostly irrigated parcel not far from the small town of Arvada that we liked, but it had no house. It was owned by Andy Anderson, the man that currently owned Trails End Ranch about a mile from Trail Creek Ranch. He wanted to sell it soon to raise money for another investment and we got Dad to take a look at it. We figured we could fence it on weekends, then bring the horses down from the farm and build a house later. Dad recognized that the location close to Arvada would make it a good investment, but Anderson wanted cash and wouldn't wait till we sold our farm.

By late February, Mom and I were about to give up when we stumbled onto a place about seventeen miles north of downtown Denver, a mile west of what was then called the Washington Highway and later became I-25. It was an irrigated eighty acres that was about to be foreclosed on by Prudential Life Insurance Company. The owners had not been able to harvest a crop for two years due to the drought, and their water right came out of the Marshall Reservoir not far from Nederland. During the mid-fifties, the snow pack in the Rockies, which fed the reservoir, had gotten so low that the reservoir had nearly dried up and hadn't furnished enough water to deliver more than about twenty-five percent of its shareholders' normal supply the previous two years. This was not enough to harvest a corn crop and their wheat yields had been far below average. The farm's owners said the same thing had happened during the drought in the thirties and one year, instead of planting any crops, they had spent the summer digging the small reservoir in the southwest corner of the farm at its highest point where the Marshall irrigation ditch entered the property. This allowed them to store a full two-day run of irrigation water when the head gate that metered their allotment was opened a quarter mile west of the property.

The dry west wind had blown so much topsoil off the farm during seedbed preparation the last two springs that dirt had blown into drifts in the barrow pits along the north-south road in front of the farm on Huron Street. The Marshall reservoir was nearly empty again this spring and the prospects for water were dim. The place had a pretty good set of corrals, a dairy barn for about a dozen milk cows and a loafing shed west of the house, as well as a separate corral and shed north of the house. The house itself was a very small frame structure with a fair-sized kitchen and living room. There were two bedrooms on the second floor, reached by a steep dark stairway. There was also a screened porch on the west side off the kitchen. The farm had a fairly shallow well, about eighty feet deep, which the owner said had been dependable during the dry weather. It turned out that the water was quite hard and didn't taste very good, but was safe to drink. All in all, it was a pretty sorry looking outfit.

When we got back to the apartment at about 7:30 p.m., Mom fixed supper while we told Dad about the place we had stumbled onto late that afternoon. We said that it didn't look like much but we might be able to fix it up. I said they were asking $25,000 and probably needed to sell it very badly. The next day was Saturday and Dad said he would go look at the place with us. We arrived there at about eight o'clock and spent until noon looking it over. Dad asked the owners what their terms were. They said they had an overdue mortgage with Prudential Insurance Company for $10,000 at 4% interest and would like the balance in cash. Dad said we would go eat lunch, talk things over and then come back and let them know if we wanted to make an offer.

We drove to Broomfield, about eight miles to the southwest, which had the closest restaurant. We all agreed that everything about the place was rundown and the house needed some repairs before we could even consider moving in. Dad said he was pretty sure we could assume the $10,000 mortgage and since they wanted a cash offer they might take considerably less than $25,000. We all thought it would be ideal for our horses, and even though it was not a very desirable farm for cash crops even in a season with a full allotment of irrigation water, it seemed to be priced right. Dad said he thought he could borrow the $10,000 from the Poudre Valley National Bank in Fort Collins. After some soul-searching to assure ourselves that we were committed to spending our weekends and quite a few hours in late spring evenings after work doing a lot of hard work, Dad decided to make them an offer. When we got back to the farm, Dad told them all we could come up with would be $10,000 in cash if we could assume the Prudential loan. They replied they wanted considerably more than that, but after Dad held tight, they said they would talk it over, check with the insurance company and get back in touch with us.

In the meanwhile, Dad checked with the Van Schock Real Estate Company, which was handling the sale for Prudential, and they were confident we could assume the loan. Within a few days we heard back from Van Schock that our offer had been accepted. Dad said he was pretty sure that Prudential had leaned on the owners because they were far behind on their mortgage payment. We needed to get the deal closed as soon as possible and Dad was able to borrow the $10,000 from his older brother, Bill. Dad put the Fort Collins farm on the market as soon as we closed and we made immediate plans to get the spring farming under way. Our tenant in Fort Collins, Gerald Hoff, agreed to haul our two tractors and other farm equipment from the Taft Hill Farm to the new place and we started spending every spare moment out at the new Lilley poor farm.

At the same time we were fixing up the farmhouse, Dad and I worked the ground into shape to plant as much of the farm as we thought we could irrigate. We decided to plant a mixture of cool-season grasses along with one pound of alfalfa to add to the protein content of the hay. The grass seed included Lincoln Brome, Orchard Grass, Intermediate Wheat Grass and Fescue, the latter two being a bit more drought resistant than the first two. By planting such a mixture, we were hedging our bets against a possible continuation of the drought.

We leased and filled an elevated 300-gallon gasoline tank, filled up the John Deere D, hooked it to the disc and started preparing the seedbed on a twenty-acre field that had been planted to corn the previous year. The corn crop had not been worth harvesting for lack of water and if we didn't get some rain this spring, our newly seeded crop might not germinate. Dad called the Marshall ditch company and they indicated the snow pack on the watershed feeding their reservoir was much improved over the last two years; however, it would be mid-June before any water would be delivered to the farm. While I was finishing up the seedbed preparation for the first twenty acres with the big tractor, Dad started drilling the grass. By the time we had finished drilling about one half of the first field, just before dark on a weeknight, it started to rain.

Our routine had become for Dad and I to leave the office just as soon as we could in the afternoon on weekdays and immediately get started with the farming. We would work til dark and then go to the farmhouse for a late supper laid out by Mom, who had been busy cleaning out the house. By the time we headed back to the apartment, it would be after nine o'clock and we would all fall into bed. The gentle rain that fell all night and much of the next day made it impossible to continue the farming for a few days, which was great with us because we had been praying for moisture and there was plenty of work to do in the farmhouse.

There had been some water damage in the kitchen from frozen pipes, but the wood floor had not been badly affected. Mom had linoleum laid in the entire kitchen and we were able to use our nice old Persian carpet in the living room. There was a gas heater in the living room that looked as if it would serve to keep the entire house warm. As soon as the work in the kitchen was finished, Mom found a used combination gas and wood-burning kitchen stove similar to the one we had in Fort Collins and we got a new medium-sized refrigerator. Dad gave up the lease on the small apartment in Denver, we moved the furniture and took up residence at the new farm.

Since Dad's office was only about a mile from mine, we drove my car to work most of the time. Fortunately, our office hours were the same and he would be standing out on the street corner waiting for me after work. To get to our offices, we went three miles south on Huron to 120th and then 1 mile east to Washington Avenue. From there it was only another 13 miles to my office. Thornton, which was at about 84th Avenue, was the northern-most Denver suburb at that time and the point at which we ran into our first serious traffic. Dad wasn't above doing a little backseat driving. The most irritating part of that was the fact he was quite often right. With my hot little Chevy, I could weave in and out of traffic with the best of them with a lot of accelerating and slowing down. My frugal father pointed out that kind of driving was bad for your gas mileage and possibly a little dangerous. He always felt comfortable offering advice and I felt just as comfortable ignoring it.

It took us quite a while to get the Fort Collins property sold. The same drought and the Eisenhower recession, which had made it possible for us to buy the place on Huron Street so cheap, made it difficult to find a buyer. Dad listed the place for a few months with Frank Monroe, from whom we had purchased our stallion, little Nick. He had a little place not far from our farm and specialized in acreages and tracts. Dad then listed it with John McNey, by then Gintsie's father in law. Dad had known John for years and he had been quite successful in the real estate business since he had sold their Livermore ranch and moved to town. It was not too long before he had an offer from a rancher from Walden, Colorado, who had sold his place and wanted acreage near Denver.

John called Dad and they set up a meeting at the Elks club in Laramie, Wyoming on the weekend of their annual Jubilee Days celebration in mid-summer. The Jubilee featured a carnival, street dances and steer roping with pari-mutual betting. Dad and I headed for the Elk's about 10:00 a.m. and found John McNey and his client, a grizzled looking North Park rancher, in the bar. I passed as the three of them ordered bourbon and water and began their haggling. Here we were in the middle of a noisy bar trying to negotiate a real estate deal between three men, two of whom couldn't hear very well. Dad wanted $22,000 for our farm and the Walden rancher wasn't willing to pay more than $20,000 cash. Both John and his client, the two who were a little deaf, and Dad had to raise their voices and repeat about everything said to be heard over all the noise. John finally offered to give one half of his $1,000 commission to the buyer if he would meet Dad's offer. After a little more dickering and a couple more drinks, they agreed to John's suggestion and shook hands. As John was filling out the paperwork, Dad and the rancher had their last drink, the papers were signed, a closing date was determined and I drove my father, who was feeling no pain, back home in the early afternoon. It was a productive morning for us and I'm sure an entertaining one for the bar patrons at the Elks in Laramie. Dad could pay his brother back and have over $10,000 left. The monthly payment on the $10,000, thirty-year loan at 4% interest was not much more than the apartment and utilities had cost. In effect, Mom and Dad had just traded an eighty-acre irrigated farm eighteen miles from downtown Denver for the $5000 home they had bought in Lakewood in 1941 with Grandpa William's gift.

A clipping about Gary from the Oct. 18, 1955 issue of the Springfield Union sports page

Gary Glick when he was with the Baltimore Colts.

30

Learning the Ropes

The ANCA's convention was always held the last week of January, so most of our time after the first of the year was spent preparing for that big annual event. I was amazed about how much detail was involved. When he was the assistant executive secretary, Rad had done nearly all the pre-convention planning, and since I was green I wasn't much help to him, but he involved me in each step of the way. He sent Lyle and me to the convention headquarters in Phoenix a couple of days early with all the convention supplies packed in Lyle's little Studebaker Lark. We spent the first night in Albuquerque, arriving there in a driving rain. We arrived at the convention headquarters, the Westward Ho Motor Hotel and Convention Center in Phoenix, by late afternoon. It was a fairly new facility and was big enough to accommodate all of our meetings and social activities and house most of our convention attendees. Lyle and I got a couple of bellhops to help carry all the supplies into the meeting room that was to serve as our office during the convention. We unpacked the boxes of paper and set up the mimeograph machine we had brought to make copies of committee agendas and policy resolutions that would be adopted at the end of the convention.

The next morning, I got up early and looked in all of the meeting rooms and the large banquet hall, which in turn could be divided into smaller rooms. As soon as the convention coordinator got to work, I sat down with him, went over all the assignments for committee meetings and double-checked the times scheduled for the various activities. Then I walked through the extensive grounds surrounding the motor hotel complex, which were scattered over a large area, with amenities such as an outdoor swimming pool, tennis courts, horseshoe pit and a place to play shuffleboard, a game that I had only seen played on cruise ships in newsreels. It was beautifully landscaped with palm trees and flowerbeds, all surrounded by well-manicured lawns. I had left home in the middle of winter and two days later arrived in what appeared to me to be Shangri-La.

Rad and his wife, Florence, flew in later that day and, as soon as they had gotten settled, I went up to their room and we reviewed the things he had asked me to check out when I arrived. He said he would depend on me to check that each meeting room was set up appropriately with the proper number of chairs and a head table for the chairman, vice chairman and secretary. He said he would be busy with the officers and committee chairmen, but I should be sure to find him and ask if I had any questions.

Association policy was established by resolutions that primarily originated in committees at the convention. They were worded in formal language beginning with several "whereas" introductory clauses and concluding with one or more therefore "let it be resolved" conclusions. These were taken very seriously and it was the committee chairman's responsibility to see that the office staff received their resolutions in time to get them typed and mimeographed for consideration by the entire membership at the end of the convention.

At noon on the day of the committee meetings, the women attended a traditional style show put on by the leading women's apparel stores in Phoenix. The luncheon scheduled for the men indicated the influence that the major meat packer of its day, Swift and Company, had with the organization. Most cattle industry leaders were in attendance at the convention and many of them, at one time or another, had gone on what was referred to as "The Swift Trip," a three-day expedition by about thirty influential livestock industry leaders. It followed a pen of fat cattle that were marketed in Chicago, slaughtered at the Swift plant there, sent to their distribution center in New York and then peddled by their salesmen to retail grocers. It was a masterful public relations program whereby the least glamorous segment of the beef industry, cattle slaughterers, could influence the policy makers of the most glamorous segment, the ranchers and cowmen. Anyone who had ever gone on the Swift Trip was invited to a sumptuous meal featuring Swift Premium beef. The event was listed on the convention program, but was attended by invitation only. It was a prestigious thing to be invited, and of course I was not. Rad had told me a good bit about the Swift Trip when we were planning the convention and said that he planned to see that I was invited in a year or two. One of the highlights of the luncheon, he said, was when Tom Glaze, the director of industry relations, introduced every one of the 150-200 persons in attendance without any notes—and he never made a mistake. Tom also arranged the trips and mothered the attendees throughout the trip.

The committee chairmen introduced their respective resolutions at the business meeting at the end of the last session of the convention, and the presiding officer asked for discussion from the floor. Most of the resolutions sailed right through, but a few were quite controversial, and the ability of some of these ranchers, often association past presidents, to express their opinions extemporaneously on the convention floor was something to see.

For years the ANCA had adopted a resolution calling for a constitutional amendment to do away with the income tax. One of the main proponents was a past president from California named Hub Russell. When it was time to discuss it Hub stood up and gave his usual brilliant oration. Then a considerably younger rancher, Cliff Hansen of Wyoming, spoke with equal eloquence to the effect that even though nearly every rancher present could agree with the resolution, it had no chance of ever passing and the inclusion of it in our policy statements made us look out of touch with the times. Both men received applause and several other members joined the fray. Finally, a motion was made calling for the question and the resolution was once again adopted and made a part of official ANCA policy. By that time, it was getting late and the rest of the resolutions passed quickly. Those loyal members who had stayed through it all rushed back to their rooms to join their wives getting ready for the social hour and banquet that was the grand finale of the convention.

When we got back from the convention, we were all worn out, but we had a lot of work to get done. Lyle had phoned in news to the wire services every day during the convention, but he needed to quickly get a wrap-up story and summary of the policy statements and biographical information on newly elected officers out to his media mailing list. Most of the weekly livestock publications sent staff to cover our convention, but the many small-town dailies, which couldn't, faithfully printed our news releases and provided a great way to get feedback to our membership in rural areas. Rad had me work with my secretary typing the minutes of each committee meeting and getting them mailed back to the respective members, and he did the same with the board minutes, which were also mimeographed. Their mailing was made somewhat simpler by the fact that we had addressograph plates for each of these categories. All of this was very labor intensive and everyone pitched in on it except the boss.

Rad soon started to delegate to me more and more jobs that he had handled for Mr. Molin. The first time I represented the ANCA at a meeting was in the spring of 1957 when Rad sent me to the Gunnison County Cattlemen's Association in the Colorado Rockies, about a hundred and fifty miles southwest of Denver. I wasn't scheduled to be a speaker, but I was expected to attend their committee meetings and update them on our policies and efforts on their behalf. I felt pretty well abreast of most of our activities, but I knew they would be particularly interested in the latest efforts of the organization's fact-finding committee, actually a task force, which was delving into the causes of the precipitous decline in the cattle market in the mid-1950s. I was quite sure I would be asked to address this subject in the marketing committee and decided to write and then memorize a summary of its progress.

I arrived at the hotel in downtown Gunnison fairly late the night before the meeting, got up early the next morning and after breakfast made my way to the registration desk before the meeting. The secretary of the county association, who was also a prominent businessman in town, introduced me to the officers and committee chairmen. He said the committees were scheduled to meet that morning followed by a board luncheon and an afternoon membership meeting with a banquet and dance to wind up the day's activities. I made brief stops at each of the committee meetings and found that fortunately they needed very little input from me, with the exception of the marketing committee, which I had saved for last. Just as the meeting was almost over and I thought I had escaped having to do any talking, the committee chairman introduced me as Rad Hall's new assistant and said I would tell them all they needed to know about the new fact-finding committee that everyone was talking about.

I took a deep breath and rather than going to the head table by the chairman, I stood in the middle of the room surrounded by committee members and waded into the talk I had memorized.

I was getting along fairly well when someone interrupted me with a question. I had no problem answering the question, but when I tried to resume my talk, my mind went completely blank. I babbled a few words and then admitted that I had lost my train of thought and simply sat down. The committee chairman covered for me as best he could, the meeting ended and he adjourned us for lunch. I'm sure what I did was no big deal to most of the ranchers there, but to me it was devastating. I was, of course, invited to the luncheon and introduced there. I then sat through the whole afternoon membership meeting thinking everyone was looking at me. I covered up my embarrassment as best I could and continued to mingle and visit with the members after the meeting.

Fortunately I didn't have to sit at the head table at the banquet, and during a cocktail hour that preceded it, I ran into a girl named Helen Brown, whom I had dated a few times when I was working on my master's degree at CSU. I remembered that she was raised on a ranch near Gunnison and had hoped I might see her at the dance. We had a drink or two during the cocktail hour before the banquet and I began to feel that I might live down my horrible flub earlier in the day. I asked her if she would like to sit with me at the banquet and she said yes, and invited her two brothers to join us. It turned out they were two husky, good-looking guys about my age, and as soon as I met them I was sure that they had been told all about my horrible performance earlier in the day. The meager self-confidence I had mustered during the cocktail party melted away. After the banquet was over and during a short break as the band set up for the dance, Helen disappeared for about twenty minutes. When she returned, I asked her why. She diplomatically pointed out that she knew a lot of people at the meeting and went to spend some time with them. I danced with Helen a few times when the music started and of course a lot of other guys also asked her to dance. I abandoned the race and sat down in a corner of the hall trying to stay out of sight. A little while before the band stopped playing, she headed back to the ranch with her brothers. I felt that I had completely flopped in my first assignment outside the office and had demonstrated once again my complete ineptness with the ladies.

The day after I got back from the meeting in Gunnison, I told Rad about my memory lapse in the marketing committee meeting. He told me not to worry about it and said it is best never to memorize any kind of presentation word for word. He promised me that I would get over my nervousness as I had more experience.

Later that year, Rad sent me to another meeting to represent the organization. He had been invited to speak at the annual meeting of the Nevada Cattlemen's Association in Elko, but had an important ANCA committee meeting on that date and he told them he would like to send his assistant in his place. I knew they would rather have had my boss on the program but they graciously said they would accept me in his place. Nevada was not a large state affiliate in terms of members. The ranches in that semi-desert state were few and far between and so ranked low in total cow numbers. It had, however, produced a disproportionate number of key industry leaders over the years.

I made reservations to fly into Reno, and after Rad made a couple of phone calls, arrangements were made for me to share a rental car with Bill McMillan, Tom Glaze's assistant at Swift and Company, and the executive officer of the Western States Meat Packers Association, who were also on the program, to drive from the airport in Reno to Elko. I had met both of these men at our convention in Phoenix and appreciated the opportunity to save some travel expense. I had also met the president and executive officer and several active members of the Nevada Cattlemen's Association in Phoenix. Not wanting to risk a replay of my first effort at public speaking, I put a lot of effort into writing a fairly short speech for myself and ran it by Rad, who said it sounded fine. I figured I would be standing at a podium in front of a microphone this time and had every intention of reading my talk verbatim. Rad did tell me that it was important that I have some opening comments in mind apart from my speech. When my turn at the podium arrived, I acknowledged the master of ceremonies and a few people I knew in the audience, made a couple of comments about how much I was enjoying my new job and passed on Rad's regrets for not being able to attend the convention. I then read my prepared speech, which included a couple of lame jokes, and sat down to moderate applause. A week or so later, Bill McMillan called Rad and said that I had done a good job of representing the association at the convention, which I greatly appreciated.

One of the first jobs that Rad handed me was soliciting advertising for our monthly magazine, "American Cattle Producer." I quickly learned it was difficult to sell advertising for a small-circulation magazine representing a nationwide organization. Our best pitch was the fact that we represented the leaders of this multi-billion-dollar industry, but advertising executives uniformly were interested in our circulation as listed in the bible of the industry, called Standard Rates and Data; ours was small, about 12,000. When Rad was the assistant, he had started a project aimed at ad executives for the larger corporations advertising agencies that sold products and services to cattlemen. The association had a large file of beautiful black and white photographs depicting haying operations in scenic mountain valleys, cattle grazing in picturesque settings, great old photos of cattle roundups and cowboys sitting around a chuck wagon. Once a month, he would make about thirty prints of one of these pictures and send them to a select list of people responsible for placing ads for major farm machinery and implement manufacturers, auto manufacturers, Ag pharmaceutical companies, major railroads and, of course, the four big packing companies. I gladly continued the practice. The Union Pacific Railroad and Franklin Serum Company were our only two regular big advertisers. The fact that the UP had a monopoly on large portions of the cattle hauling business across the west and Franklin had the patent on the black leg vaccine used by nearly every cattleman at branding may have had something to do with it.

ANCA worked closely with and provided several board members to the biggest and most successful non-profit organization serving the livestock industry: The National Livestock and Meat Board, headquartered in Chicago. This group was funded primarily by the meat packing industry, particularly the big four, Swift, Armour, Cudahay and Hormel, plus the American Meat Institute, which represented the entire industry. It also received strong support from the big central livestock markets and livestock commission firms associated with them, and also the general farm organizations such as the huge and politically powerful American Farm Bureau Federation. In the fall of 1957, Rad decided to send me to the National Livestock and Meat Board annual convention and let me try to sell some national advertising while I was there. This was a huge three-day, very professionally produced, convention and trade show. They had a large staff, which included meat scientists, nutritionists, home economists that worked with the women's groups and the best public and press relations professionals in the industry. They worked closely with all segments of food production, processing and marketing. They made every effort to stay out of politics and were a highly respected voice in an industry, which at the beginning of the century had been pilloried by Upton Sinclair's exposé of the meatpacking industry. It was founded by some very forward-looking ranchers who represented the segment of the industry still largely admired by the American public at that time.

When I began making my plans for the Chicago trip, it dawned on me what a big deal this would be. I would fly to Chicago on the recently introduced Boeing 707 jet into Midway Airport and stay for three nights at the Chicago Hilton, a huge hotel. While reviewing my list of potential national advertisers, I saw that most had offices on Market Street in Chicago, and I wrote a letter to the advertising manager of each of them requesting a meeting. I identified myself as the person who had been sending them the nice glossy photographs of the livestock industry monthly and I believe that helped open the door to several of them who agreed to see me.

I had been looking forward to my first flight on the 707. After the pilot cranked up the engines and released the brakes for take-off, I found myself breathless when I was pressed back against my seat, as we roared down the runway. It was nothing like taking off in a DC 7, the largest airplane I had flown up to that time. In about an hour, we were stacked up waiting to land at Midway Airport, which looked from the air as if it were in downtown Chicago. I took a cab to the Hilton and checked into a very small, relatively inexpensive, room.

The next morning after I had breakfast at the coffee shop, I went outside and took a walk through a few blocks of downtown Chicago. Although overwhelmed by it all, I was exhilarated by the sudden appreciation for the adventure I was having, the traffic noise and the elevated train roaring by overhead. I was pre-registered for the NLS&MB meeting, so when I got back to the hotel, all I had to do was go by the registration desk and pick up my nametag and program. There was a large crowd already milling around the convention hall and I didn't see a soul I knew. I sought out some members of the staff and introduced myself to them so they would know there was a representative of the ANCA in attendance. A good deal of the program consisted of presentations by staff specialists with, so it seemed to me, the professionalism of a movie actor. I was keeping a low profile while I took everything in, happy to know that I would not have to take part in any of this well-oiled production.

I had scheduled my visits with the ad executives for the third day of the convention during the NLS&MB's business meetings. As I recall, I had appointments to make my pitch at John Deere, International Harvester and Ford Motor Company's Implement and Tractor division. All of their offices were in huge buildings on Market Street and were within walking distance of the hotel. I made my way to each appointment, found the proper office by taking an elevator halfway up a tall building, announced myself to a secretary and then waiting for an audience with the advertising manager. Each visit was much like the other. I was allowed to present my case and was treated cordially by middle-aged executives who were in charge of massive advertising programs. They said they would pass my information on to one of their underlings, but not to get my hopes up because our circulation was far too small for them to consider for advertising their equipment. One said he might consider recommending running what he called an institutional ad in a special convention issue.

I was finished with my very educational mission shortly before noon and stopped at a downtown café for lunch before going back to the hotel. I went into the large ballroom where the business meeting was being held and sat in the back, reviewing the last few days' activities. It was obvious that I had landed a job with an organization whose leaders had built an association that was greatly respected and surprisingly effective given the small staff—at least compared to the Meat Board—and very modest budget. I had stumbled onto the perfect job.

31

Farm and Horses

Meanwhile, back at the farm, continued timely rains promised a good hay crop from our newly seeded mixture of oats, alfalfa and grass. It looked as if we wouldn't have to irrigate at all before the hay was ready to cut. It was a rare spring that this happened, but it appeared that the drought had broken and we had gone from several record dry years in a row to above average rainfall in June. As a result, after the seeding was done we were able to turn our attention to getting the house, corrals and fencing in shape without having to spend time irrigating. I had moved from the small upstairs bedroom under the eaves to the porch off the kitchen. There was just enough room there for the double bed I had used in Fort Collins and a chest of drawers, while leaving enough room for me to get in and out of bed and get dressed.

A narrow strip of land on the south side of the farm extending from the corrals west to the reservoir could not be irrigated. Dad and I spent one weekend fencing off this area using an electric fence on the north side of a lane and the existing fence on the south and west sides of the farm. This allowed us to let the horses out of the corral and keep them off of the newly planted crop, while letting them water either at the tank in the corral or in the reservoir nearly a half-mile to the west. We also had to do considerable repairs on the perimeter fence that already existed around the entire farm.

We knew we would have to start irrigating immediately after the first cutting of hay in early July, so we needed to get the ditches in shape. The hardest job would be digging out the head gate about 200 yards west of our property line, where our water was diverted from the feeder ditch to our property. The diversion had a simple wooden device called a weir, where the one-acre foot-per-second of water we were allowed could be transferred to our ditch. The ditch company was responsible for getting the water to our head gate and we were responsible for getting it from there to our own property. Unfortunately, there was from one to three feet of blown dirt covering the weir and our access ditch all the way to the reservoir. This would have to be removed by hand.

I knew from experience that cleaning the ditch with a shovel would be hard, hot work. I decided to tackle the job just after daylight in the morning before work and again right after supper in the evenings. The two hours of daylight available at each of these times was as long as I could work, considering the shape I was in. It took an entire morning to uncover the weir, and by the time I reached it, I had begun to think it might not even be there. It turned out to be a simple wooden diversion one foot wide by one foot deep and about two feet long. All that remained to do was shovel off a foot of dirt out of the remaining several hundred yards of ditch!

Mom had supper ready when we got home after work and immediately after eating I put on my work clothes, grabbed my shovel and walked the half-mile to my ditch-digging job. It was about seven p.m. by that time and it wouldn't be dark until nine. I managed to get my tired body to do another two hours shoveling, traipsed home and fell into bed. I wasn't able to talk myself into getting up at 4:30 the next morning, but after a day at the office, I recuperated enough to put in another two hours digging after supper. My hands were getting blistered, but my muscles were adapting to the work and I completed the job over the weekend.

While I was digging out the ditch, Dad had been patching up the corral, sharpening sickles in preparation for mowing hay soon and fixing up a small outbuilding just west of the house into a workshop. Mom continued to make our little farmhouse more livable and do all the other things that Dad and I simply took for granted. We were beginning to see the end of the tunnel as far as getting settled in our new home was concerned, and were looking forward to harvesting our first crop of hay.

In a few days, the alfalfa had reached the one-quarter bloom stage and was ready to be mowed. When I got home from work I cranked up the little John Deere H tractor, hooked it up to our number five John Deere mower, and slid one of the sickles Dad had sharpened into the sickle bar. At 4:30 the next morning I was cutting the back swath of the largest of the several fields, which were delineated by the location of the irrigation ditches. I had finished mowing about half of the field by the time I had to go in for breakfast in order to head for the office by 7:30. I jumped on the tractor again as soon as I got home from work that afternoon and was able to finish mowing the area I had laid out in the morning. I repeated the whole process again the next day and quit mowing for a couple of days. By Saturday, the hay I had mowed was ready to rake. Not wanting to unhook the mower from the little John Deere and then put it back on when it was time to mow again, I hitched the side delivery rake to the big old John Deere D. It had a large turning radius, but I managed to rake all the hay that was down by Sunday night.

By the middle of the next week, the hay was ready to bale. The man whom we had hired for the job was able to do it in one day, but it took another two weeks to get the rest of the hay put up. During one rain delay, Dad and I managed to get all the irrigation ditches cleaned. Dad drove the John Deere D as I walked behind the big, old, heavy ditcher, which was much like a big walking plow and was pulled by the tractor with a short length of log chain. Dad did his best to straddle the ditches following the contours on fairly steep slopes with the four-wheeled dry land tractor, while I wrestled the ditcher. Because it cut to the grass at the bottom of the ditch and threw the sod out on either side, I yelled at Dad to speed up or slow down or perhaps stop. I was having a terrible time holding onto the bouncing ditcher and it was difficult for him to keep a wheel from falling into the ditch. It was fortunate we could yell at each other as we muddled through jobs like that and never get mad beyond the moment at hand. And it was far better than cleaning the ditch with a shovel.

By the time we got our bales hauled to either the stack yard or the feeder by the corral, the ground was getting quite dry and it was time to get our irrigation water running. Dad called the ditch rider, who saw to the distribution of water to the farmers in the area who owned shares of the Marshall Reservoir. We met him at our head gate, as he adjusted it to start our one-cubic-foot-of water-per-second (cfs) down our ditch. One cfs is a volume of water one foot wide and one foot deep flowing at a velocity of one foot-per-second. This flow of water would completely fill our reservoir, which had a capacity of two acre-feet in twenty-four hours. We had the option to either run the ditch water down the ditch that followed the highest elevation on the farm above the reservoir or divert it into the reservoir, depending on which land we wanted to irrigate. When the head gate at the lower end of the reservoir was open, it fed a ditch that divided into other ditches, all of which covered over half our farm. We kept the reservoir half-full at all times so we would have at least one half-day's irrigation water left when the main head gate was shut off.

We had made a couple of canvas dams using a piece of canvas that was about six feet by six feet attached to an eight-foot pole. We would back up the water with one of these in the ditch and open up small cuts on the downhill side every two or three feet to let the water spread over the part of the meadow we wished to irrigate. The trick was to let just enough water out of the ditch to give the area you wanted to cover a two-inch drink in twelve hours. We usually started a "set" running at seven a.m. before we left for work in the morning, and after work saw if it had covered the desired ground, making little ditches with the shovel to cover spots that had been missed. While I was finishing this, Dad put the second canvas dam in the ditch below the first and made the cuts he thought would work best for the next run. After supper around seven p.m., I would pull out the upper dam and as the ditch filled up behind the lower one, check to see if the cuts Dad had made were doing the job. It was amazing how Dad could anticipate how the water would run just from eyeballing the slope. Of course we could have done a better job if we could check the water several times during the day, but our jobs in town came first and we knew we could do better the second time we irrigated the entire meadow later in the summer.

The primary reason we bought the farm was to have a place for our horses, and we had had them hauled from the farm in Fort Collins just as soon as we got the fences in good enough shape to turn them out. We fixed a place for our stud, Little Nick, in the corral and shed just north of the house, which was well away from the other corrals. Most of our foals came in May and June, and after we got the hay put up and the first round of irrigation done, Dad and I started halter breaking them. Dad lead a mare into the barn and got the colt into a corner behind its dam. I reached around the mare and slipped a halter on it. As Dad led the mare out of the barn, I followed with my right hand around the rump of the colt and a short hold on the halter with my left hand. We then walked around the corral with the colt beside me, jumping around in a loose embrace. When we stopped, I petted and rubbed him or her all over. We were soon walking or trotting beside the mare.

Dad had learned as a boy working at his father's livery stable in Littleton, Colorado that just a little handling of a baby colt made it much easier to halter break as a yearling.

We hadn't been able to handle our colts the same way the year before, so that year's yearlings were more difficult to halter break. We separated them from the other horses and kept them in the corral so we could feed them grain twice a day and handle them from time to time as we grew them out. We had sold a few yearlings the year before, but still had three two-year-olds that needed to be broken. I tried to work with them as least once every weekend. I started them by throwing a saddle blanket over their backs a few times until they got used to it, and then putting a light saddle on them and letting them run around the corral with it for a while. After one or two such lessons, I put a hackamore or a bridle with a snaffle bit on them and led them around in a circle for a while before I got on them the first time. All of our horses showed the gentle disposition of their sires, either Little Nick or the Arabian remount stud we had used on the ranch, Ibn Zaid, and I never had one buck with me, at least not while I was breaking it.

I never claimed to be an expert at shoeing horses or a professional horse trainer, but I had been taught well the fundamentals of both skills. I never had a horse whose feet I had trimmed or shod go lame, and the colts I started, or "green broke" rarely had any bad habits and developed into good ranch horses. Several were sold to breeders who further trained them and entered them in horse shows where they did very well in performance events, such as barrel racing and cutting. A good many of the registered fillies we sold to other quarter horse breeders turned out to be among their best brood mares.

My Mom, who had purchased our first registered quarter horses in 1946 and was the brains behind our breeding program, nearly always chose the colts' names. She realized that a small operation like ours found it difficult to gain recognition for its horses, so she always put the prefix Lilley's on all our colts' names when we registered them, as in Lilley's Meg. We also had a Beth, Jo and Amy because Mom had loved the book, "Little Women," growing up.

Between the challenge of my new job and the total involvement in the never-ending farm work, I had turned my life around, and the hard work had also been good for Dad because his health was better than it had been for a good many years. Mom was thrilled at the opportunity to expand our horse operation. She had discovered an old friend who could ride horseback with her from time to time, Helen Michaels, with whom she had ridden to Trail Creek when we had our farm in Fort Collins.

We still had our three half-Arabian saddle mares, Zaida, Ginger and Buck, who were now about sixteen years old and showing no signs of aging. Mom still preferred to ride Zaida. We had bred each of these mares about every other year to Little Nick and had produced several outstanding saddle horses, but we all agreed Zaida's were the best. Among them were Hungry and Thirsty, whom Frank had broken, later named and used on the ranch he managed in Wyoming. Her youngest was named Rex and I broke him and later took him up to Trail Creek while I was working there. We also had four or five brood mares we had raised that were well-broken saddle horses. In addition to selling a few yearlings each year, we occasionally sold one of our mature horses to make room for the new colt crop.

Dad and I had to learn to make the farm work fit into the demand of our office schedules. I traveled a lot; he had a cook's workshop to manage at Colorado State University every summer and was occasionally called to Washington DC in his role as Legislative Committee Chairman of the National School Food Service Association. This was the nonprofit association representing school lunch programs nationwide. Sometimes we had to leave hay in the field un-baled for an extra few days, turn the irrigation water off when we didn't want to irrigate or put off needed repairs to the place. On the rare occasion when we both had to be gone at the same time, we had to leave things so Mom could do the chores, which she did gladly and capably. We had been well aware of what we were taking on and had no regrets.

AMERICAN NATIONAL CATTLEMEN'S ASSOCIATION
801 EAST 17TH AVENUE ... DENVER 18, COLO.

OFFICERS
DON C. COLLINS, PRESIDENT
 KIT CARSON, COLO.
G. R. MILBURN, FIRST VICE-PRES.
 GRASSRANGE, MONT.
RADFORD HALL, EXEC. SECRETARY
 DENVER, COLO.
F. E. MOLLIN, TREASURER
 DENVER, COLO.
LYLE LIGGETT, DIR. OF INFORMATION
 DENVER, COLO.
CHARLES E. BLAINE, TRAFFIC MGR.
 PHOENIX, ARIZ.
CALVIN L. BLAINE,
 ASST. TRAFFIC MANAGER
 PHOENIX, ARIZ.
RUSSELL THORP
 FIELD REPRESENTATIVE
 DENVER, COLO.

SECOND VICE-PRESIDENTS
A. R. BABCOCK
 MOORE, IDAHO
N. H. DEKLE
 PLAQUEMINE, LA.
O. W. LYMAN
 BURDETT, KANS.
HAYES MITCHELL
 MARFA, TEXAS
DON L. SHORT
 MEDORA, N. D.

PAST PRESIDENTS
HENRY G. BOICE
 TUCSON, ARIZ.
ALBERT K. MITCHELL
 ALBERT, N. M.
HUBBARD RUSSELL
 MARICOPA, CALIF.
A. D. BROWNFIELD
 DEMING, N. M.
WILLIAM B. WRIGHT
 DEETH, NEV.
ARTHUR A. SMITH
 STERLING, COLO.
LOREN C. BAMERT
 IONE, CALIF.
SAM C. HYATT
 HYATTVILLE, WYO.
JAY TAYLOR
 AMARILLO, TEX.

GENERAL COUNCIL
CARL B. THOMAS
 HUNTSVILLE, ALA.
ERNEST CHILSON
 WINSLOW, ARIZ.
CLYDE E. BYRD
 LITTLE ROCK, ARK.
HARVEY McDOUGAL
 RIO VISTA, CALIF.
TOM FIELD
 GUNNISON, COLO.
B. J. ALDERMAN
 OBANDIN, FLA.
C. E. WILLIAMS
 GRIFFIN, GA.
MILFORD B. VAUGHT
 BRUNEAU, IDAHO
FRED WINZELER
 LAMONT, KANS.
WATKINS GREENE
 YOUNGSVILLE, LA.
IRVIN O. WOLF
 WESTMINSTER, MD.
MORRIS BALLEW
 NATCHEZ, MISS.
JACK S. BRENNER
 GRANT, MONT.
DON B. REYNOLDS
 NORTH PLATTE, NEBR.
ROY G. BANKOFIER
 FERNLEY, NEV.
RICHARD SNYDER
 CLAYTON, N. M.
ROBERT WATSON
 CLYDE, N. Y.
JOE MILTON
 McLEOD, N. D.
J. K. HALEY
 MOUNTAIN VIEW, OKLA.
GARLAND MEADOR
 PRAIRIE CITY, ORE.
WALTER TAYLOR
 RAPID CITY, S. D.
JAMES B. NANCE
 ALAMO, TENN.
JOHN BIGGS
 VERNON, TEX.
T. RAY THEURER
 PROVIDENCE, UTAH
GEORGE C. PALMER
 CHARLOTTESVILLE, VA.
JOHN McMINIMEE
 OUTLOOK, WASH.
NORMAN W. BARLOW
 CORA, WYO.

June 21, 1957

W. D. Farr, Acting Chairman
Beef Grading Committee
1914 14th Avenue
Greeley, Colorado

Dear Mr. Farr:

Enclosed are the minutes of the Beef Grading Committee meeting for your inspection. I would appreciate your returning them with any additions or corrections as soon as possible.

If I don't hear from you by the 28th I will assume that the minutes as written meet your approval and will send them to the rest of the gentleman present at the meeting.

Sincerely yours,

ROY W. LILLEY
Ass't. Executive Secretary

RWL:vla

Encl: 1

Same letter sent to:
Van Vranken
Lyman
Armstrong
Scobel
T. Armstrong
J. Armstrong
George Tucker
Mr. Pierce, USDA

Letter to Bill Farr on ANCA letterhead showing
current officers and state affiliate presidents.

...My first meeting with ANCA state affiliate executives. *"Fred Harris, Nevada; Jim Orton, Editor Kansas Stockman; Clair Michels, North Dakota; Dave Foster, Washington, Roy Lilley, Assistant ANCA Secretary; Horace Hening, New Mexico"*

32

Learning Job

Colorado, Wyoming, Nebraska and South Dakota all held their annual cattlemen's conventions in June and their dates overlapped to varying degrees. It was traditional for ANCA to try to have a speaker, usually our president, vice president or chief executive officer, at each of their affiliates' conventions at least once every other year, so in June it was not unusual for three representatives of the national office to be on the road. Occasionally, they would send Lyle Liggett or even me, as in my first outing to Nevada. In June 1957, Rad went to the Wyoming Stock Growers convention in Cheyenne, and since it was close enough to drive, he took me along. They had a tradition of having one keynote speaker at their opening session, while for the rest of the program the president called on allied industry people to come up to the podium for short, informal presentations. Everyone at the convention knew the drill and the representative of the Denver stockyards, Safeway, Swift, Armour, the U. P. Railroad and other allied industry representatives would get up and try to outdo each other.

Since Rad was at the convention, I was sure they wouldn't expect me to talk. This was a relief because my skill at extemporaneous speaking was a work in progress. Some of the old-time Wyoming ranchers there remembered my dad or had heard of him, and were aware of my Wyoming roots on my mother's side. When I was talking to one of the Wyoming ANCA members that I had met at our annual convention in Phoenix, I thanked him for his ANCA membership and veered off into the subject of our travel budget. I said something to the effect that just getting me up to the WSGA convention had probably cost nearly $40.00. His only response was, "You mean just getting you up here cost my entire annual dues?"

As Rad progressed in his new job he was very good at taking the time to train me to assume more of the chores that he had handled as an assistant. He handed me some of the more routine correspondence that he felt needed a personal answer, had me take the minutes at our Board of Directors meetings and occasional special committee meetings, and told me to be prepared to handle most of the details of our next convention, which was scheduled for Oklahoma City. He also had me arrange the occasional meetings we hosted in Denver that were too large to handle in the office. These were generally in the Cosmopolitan Hotel in downtown Denver, only a few blocks south of the office.

My first experience planning such a meeting kicked off with a lunch with the events manager at Cosmopolitan Hotel. We ate at Trader Vic's, a popular Polynesian restaurant, located in the hotel. I had never eaten there before and was impressed with the atmosphere. It specialized in seafood, something I told my host I knew little about, trout being about the only kind of fish I had ever eaten. He suggested the Maui-Maui and it was delicious. I told him the time and date of the upcoming meeting and the approximate number expected. I said some of the attendees would come in the day before and leave right after the meeting, and others could arrive in the morning ahead of the meeting and leave the next day. We couldn't pay volunteers travel expenses but, always furnished them either a great midday or evening meal, or both. After lunch, we finished discussing the upcoming event, he showed me the meeting rooms and we discussed menu options and prices. He then referred me to the reservation manager to work out arrangements for reserving rooms for those attending the event.

I was soon working on the preliminary plans for our next annual convention in Oklahoma City in late January, 1958. The host organization, the Oklahoma Cattlemen's Association, in accordance with tradition, had appointed a committee to coordinate the convention with ANCA. The chairman of that committee, Roy Turner, was a wealthy cattleman and oilman and a past governor of Oklahoma who lived in the Skirvin Towers, a high-rise apartment building across the street from the Skirvin Hotel, which was to be the headquarters for the convention. When I made my first trip to Oklahoma City to meet the host committee about the upcoming convention, I took the milk run on a Frontier Airlines DC 3 that stopped in Colorado Springs, Liberal, Kansas and Guyman and Enid Oklahoma. Our magazine had an agreement with Frontier Airlines called a "due bill," trading an advertisement for airline tickets that could be used only for multi-stop flights--- and this one certainly qualified.

It took all day to get from Denver to Oklahoma City, but as the junior member of the staff, my time was not worth much. When I arrived in Oklahoma City I took a cab to the Skirvin and checked into my single room. This was an old hotel and catered to traveling salesmen, so it had quite a few inexpensive rooms. A single room like mine had a single bed, a sink and a hall tree to put your clothes on rather than a closet. It was really small! The bath was down the hall. The Skirvin was selected as the headquarters hotel because it had a lot of rooms and was within easy walking distance of the City Auditorium, the only facility in the city at the time that could accommodate our general sessions and banquet. The Skirvin's own convention facilities were more than adequate for all our other activities.

I had an appointment for a breakfast meeting with Governor Turner at nine a.m. so had time to go downstairs, get a morning paper, and read it before meeting him in the coffee shop. He was a distinguished looking man with gray hair and a pleasant, but authoritative manner, fitting all my preconceived notions of what a governor should look like. He immediately put me at ease by saying that he would be depending on my guidance as we proceeded to lay out plans for the convention. I had prepared a tentative schedule based on our traditional annual convention activities, a list of all the committees that would be meeting before the convention and an estimate of attendance for each. I told him that our pre-convention registration numbers would be the best guide in determining how many meals to order for the board breakfast and men's luncheon, but it was difficult to anticipate the turnout for the banquet the last night because we sold tickets for that event throughout the convention.

He had a meeting scheduled later in the day for the entire Convention Planning Committee at the Oklahoma Cattlemen's Association office not far from downtown. It was made up of the association's past presidents, current officers and their executive officer. Most of these people always attended the ANCA's annual convention and had a good idea of what was expected. The first day of the convention was dedicated to standing and a few special committee meetings, and that night was kept open for a reception sponsored by the local affiliate. A good bit of the meeting was taken up discussing that event. At the conclusion of the meeting, we decided we had things well enough in hand that it would not be necessary to hold another full committee meeting; however, Chairman Turner, the local executive officer and myself were to keep in touch with each other and inform the committee if any problems came up that might necessitate a meeting. Governor Turner kindly invited me to have dinner with him that night at the hotel and I left early the next morning for my return home. At an approximate speed of 200 miles an hour and with four intermediate stops, I had time to read an entire science fiction magazine before arriving back in Denver—two days of travel and one of meetings.

One of the most boring jobs Rad passed on to me early on was reading the Federal Register that came in the mail every day. This was the journal that kept track of all the rules and regulations relating to the many agencies of the Federal Government. I was supposed to ferret out from this catalog sized publication, rendered in small print, anything that might pertain to the cattle industry. Frankly, over a period of four years I found only a dozen or so things that we didn't already know and I'm sure I must've missed at least that many. When the mail came in, I bravely thumbed through this document and passed on the few things I found to Rad.

Rad kept for himself the much more important job of keeping track of what was going on in Congress. He scanned the Congressional Review and sorted out bills introduced in Congress concerning our industry. An equally big task was following legislation that had already been introduced and was making its way through congressional committee hearings. Bills that had to do with association policy needed to be forwarded to appropriate committee chairmen. This involved a lot of mailings and phone calls to the leadership. When hearings on extremely important pieces of legislation came up in Washington, we tried to send one of our elected leaders to testify. Occasionally this was not possible and Rad would handle the job. We were fortunate to have some extremely capable members step up to this job and they were well received. Ours was probably the country's largest industry that did not yet have paid lobbyists in Washington and our volunteers who paid their own expenses found their testimony was taken seriously.

33

Sprinkler System

By the fall of 1957, the staff started working on next year's ANCA budget and preparing for the January convention. In addition to the two secretaries who worked for Rad and me, we had two young women whose main job was sending out membership renewals, mailing billings for magazine advertising and getting out solicitations for new members. I spent a lot of time in the back room helping them put out these mailings, particularly at the first of the year when we sent out our first dues statements. I was also responsible for preparing the cover letters that went out with these billings and with our new member solicitations. We had a solicitation list that had been developed over the years and we did our best to keep it up to date. Some of the states sent us their membership list for us to contact directly, but most of them refused to release theirs.

Dues and advertising revenue were our only sources of income, and membership in the association was strictly voluntary. Although I'm confident the vast majority of cattlemen recognized that the ANCA accomplished many things they could not do on their own, a surprisingly small percentage of them belonged. Many of our state affiliates had county organizations and some ranchers believed that support at that level was adequate, although a good many more belonged to both their county and state associations. It was widely thought that the ANCA was primarily an organization for just the larger cattle producers, and it was true that most of the biggest operators did belong, but we needed revenue from a much broader base. The membership solicitations stressed the fact that our most important service was influencing legislation in Washington to their advantage, and to be effective we needed to be able to say that we had a broad base of members behind us. The problem was they received these benefits whether or not they belonged to the ANCA, or even a state or county cattlemen's association.

Often when our volunteers were testifying on a bill before a legislative committee in Washington, the committee chairman would ask how many members we had. Since this came up so often, they had been primed to reply that county associations were affiliated with the states, which in turn were affiliated with ANCA, which added up to a large number. What we didn't tell them was that we got very little financial support from those sources. A couple of huge local organizations, like Kerr County in California, did send us a nice dues payment directly, but such revenue didn't total more than a few thousand dollars. The staff was reimbursed for its travel, but the organization was not able to pay officers and committee chairmen's expenses when they represented us in Washington legislative hearings or meetings with federal agencies.

It is ironic that these early leaders, most of whom had put together large successful ranches, readily donated their time and money traveling to Washington or meeting with allied industry groups across the country, but as board members, they were very hesitant to increase our minimum dues. We did request a small per-head fee above a certain minimum amount of cattle owned, but all but our most loyal members ignored it. We managed to stay within each year's budget and present the board with one the next year that they would approve. Somehow, we managed to get enough new members to more than offset the numbers who had dropped during the year, and our magazine editor, Dave Appleton, made the magazine break even.

Dad, Mom and I continued to work hard at the farm and Mom fed us like the hay hands we often were. We put up our high-quality crop of hay and harvested an oat crop from ten acres we could not irrigate. There was enough rain in the spring so that the oats ripened and we could combine it. We sold several loads of the oats to a commercial granary in East Lake, a small farming community about six miles north and east of us, our first cash crop! I hauled the rest of it out of the field in our old Diamond T pickup and unloaded it with a scoop shovel into an old metal granary, which Dad and I had been able to repair enough so it would shed water. We now had not only enough hay for the horses for the coming year but enough oats to grow out our yearling colts.

When we irrigated our hilly farm, a good bit of water always ended up running to a low spot by the fence that ran along the east boundary of our farm. Sprinkler irrigation was just being perfected and Dad and I got the idea early on that we could irrigate another ten or fifteen acres by pumping that potential waste water back on the currently dry land with a sprinkler irrigation system, provided we could find one that we could afford. Sometime in March, we found an ad in the Denver Post for a system that sounded about right. It was at a farm about halfway between Denver and Ft. Collins. Dad and Mom drove out and looked at it, negotiated what they thought was a fair price, purchased it and said we would be by to get it soon. Dad called Gerald Hoff, who still lived near Ft. Collins to see if he could go get it for us. Gerald allowed as how he could and would try to bring it the next weekend. Late the next Saturday afternoon Gerald drove up the road in front of the farm pulling a stripped-down hay rack loaded down with about thirty 16-foot long aluminum pipes behind his one-and-a-half-ton truck. The truck was loaded with the pump and power unit for the system and all of the casings, sprinkler heads and other hardware, all of which rattled. He looked like an old-fashioned tinker on steroids. I don't know what Dad paid Gerald to deliver all this but, whatever it was it was, he more than earned it.

    Now that we had this fine new irrigation system, we worked up the dry land and planted it to grass and alfalfa with a nurse crop of oats. We then parked the new pump by the fence and positioned the intake hose in the low spot where the surplus irrigation water would collect. It now appeared that my lack of talent for irrigating could be mitigated by saving the water that had been wasted the year before. This turned out to be true, but I had no idea just how hard moving the pipe to irrigate this new field would be.

    This spring turned out to be considerably drier than the previous one, but there was enough snow in the mountains to fill the Marshall Reservoir, which furnished our water. We filled our little reservoir and began irrigating our established hay fields in late May. By early June our newly planted field needed water. We set up the irrigation system one Saturday, started the motor, let it run all night and all the sprinkler heads worked just as they should.

    The first thing I did early the next morning was to fill the engine with gasoline again and set the switch so it would begin pumping when I started it again. I then crawled through the fence and approached the portion of the field that we estimated should have received two inches of water by way of our fancy new irrigation system. When I got close and my irrigation boots sank into mud up to my ankles I knew the sprinkle had done its job. I then had to disconnect all of the pipes that had been sprinkling from their casings and carry them approximately six strides down the hill to line them up for their next setting. I then walked back to the pump and cranked up the power unit hoping everything was connected right so my next ten hours of sprinkling could begin. It took six days or twelve setting changes to get our newly planted field properly irrigated.

    Our new irrigation system worked even better than we had hoped, and by early summer our newly planted oats and irrigated pasture mix was over a foot high and needed to be irrigated again. We had left the pipes in place just where we had finished the last watering and I was able to simply reverse the order in which I had made my settings the first time. We actually set the pump to deliver three inches of rain equivalent this time in the hopes that we wouldn't have to irrigate again. We got just enough timely rains to make this work, and shortly before we put up our second cutting of hay on the previously planted meadow, we were able to cut and bale our new crop. We were extremely pleased to see what a good crop of grass had grown under the oats with just enough alfalfa to improve the hay's protein content.

    We had now achieved our goal of having the entire farm planted to grass and alfalfa and should not have had to do any more dirt farming for the foreseeable future. We put up only a third cutting of hay on the fields that had the thickest stand of alfalfa and saved the rest for winter pasture for our horses. We finally had more time to work with the horses and even hired some part-time help to irrigate, giving us more time for what we really enjoyed. We didn't have, or particularly want, much social life because Dad and I found that need fulfilled in our work, and Mom was in seventh heaven with our increasing breeding herd of quarter horses.

34

Deer Hunt and Convention Chores

In the summer of 1957, with so much work to do at the farm, I actually had not thought very much about deer hunting. However, when October rolled around and the weather started getting cooler, I found myself getting buck fever. I had earned a week's vacation by that time and was able to take off for the first week of deer season in Northern Colorado. Dad said he and Mom could handle the chores before and after work and they told me to go and spend a week up with Frank and Shirley.

There were a lot more big bucks up at Frank's than at Trail Creek. A buck deer needs to be at least four years old before he has a full set of antlers and they keep getting bigger and bigger for another four years. Even though Trail Creek had a good population of deer, there were a lot of people hunting in a fairly small area and not too many bucks lived long enough to be trophy size. The Chimney Rock Ranch had over 100 sections of land and was not nearly as heavily hunted so there were some monsters around; the trick was to get a shot at one. Although October was a busy month at the ranch, Frank had arranged things so that he could spend most of the first weekend hunting with me. I arrived at the ranch fairly late Friday night and Frank and I were up at daylight fixing breakfast so we could be out hunting by the time the sun came up. We had to drive about two miles south of the ranch to get into Colorado because Frank's home was in Wyoming. About half of the ranch was in either state, much like the layout of the Table Mountain Ranch where we had hunted so much in the past.

The first morning Frank drove in the pick-up down some rough trails that he knew went through good deer country. Deer are on the move in the early morning and again just before dark, the best times of day to see them out in the open. We saw several does from a distance but didn't jump any bucks. By the time the sun was well above the horizon, Frank drove to some canyon country and we got out and walked the slopes for a couple of hours, hoping to jump a buck that had bedded down, but without success. We got back to the ranch a little after noon.

After lunch, we both took a short nap and then went out to the shop where I helped Frank work on some machinery for a few hours. We then took the pickup out for the evening hunt on a different part of the ranch. We spotted some more does in the distance, so Frank parked and we worked our way around a hill to get closer. We slipped up to within about 200 yards of the does without them seeing us. Frank whispered to me that there were probably some bucks in the vicinity scoping out the does because breeding season was only a month away. He scanned a brushy hillside almost a half-mile away with his binoculars and spotted a nice buck. We were too far away to get a decent shot and when we tried to slip around the hill to get closer he spotted us and took off. We ran around the hill and spotted him just before he dropped out of sight again. We went back to the pickup, knowing we wouldn't see him again, and made our way back to the ranch just as it was getting dark.

The next morning it was windy and we knew hunting would be difficult. We decided to skip the early hunt and enjoy the nice big breakfast Shirley prepared for us. Frank thought our best bet would be to walk some rough ridges with the wind in our face hoping to stumble onto a nice buck lying down in the buck brush. We drove up Running Water Creek which empties into Sand Creek right at the ranch headquarters, until we got to the improvements where Frank and Shirley had spent their honeymoon on the old homestead called the "Running Water." To the north and west of the buildings the grass-covered hills slope fairy steeply upwards for about a half-mile and then break into a deep ravine southwest down toward where Sand Creek flows north on the west side of a big sandstone outcropping called Chimney Rock The main ravine was cut by a series of smaller ones flowing south. My plan was to walk up and down the small ridges trying to maintain a distance about one-third from the top of the main ridge. Walking slowly and carefully with the wind in my face, I could peek carefully over one rise after another through the small draws.

After I eased over the fourth rise, a huge buck, which had obviously been lying down facing my direction but couldn't get my scent because of the high wind blowing away from him, jumped up about sixty yards in front of me. This was just what I had been hoping for and I had my rifle cocked and at the ready. At the same moment, he jumped to his feet, I raised my rifle and shot. As often happens at such a short range, I fired over him. Fortunately, the sound of the shot froze him just long enough for me to lever another shell into the chamber and get off a second shot as he jumped forward just enough for me to hit him in the gut. He went down immediately and stayed down long enough for me to run up and finish off with a shot to the spine just ahead of the shoulder. Frank and I had hunted in this area a few times and had gotten glimpses of these humongous bucks, but always just as they were going on a dead run over the hill at least a quarter of a mile away. Once when we were out checking fences at the top of this draw, we had seen about eight bucks in one bunch at the bottom about a mile away, and at least four of them were huge.

Frank heard my shots from the top of the ridge and made his way down through the buck brush by the time I started dressing out the deer. I was still in somewhat of a state of shock and was happy to turn the job over to Frank, who was much better at it than I. He wasn't much for gushing, so when he said it looked like one of the biggest bucks he had ever seen killed on the ranch, I knew I had something special. We were about sixty yards below the ridge where the pickup was parked and it took all our strength to drag him up to it.

It was late afternoon when we got back to the ranch and instead of driving up to the barn door to unload the buck where we planned to hang it, Frank took it to his livestock scale. We found that he weighted 210 pounds hog dressed. Frank said that very few mule deer bucks ever dress over 200 pounds, and this one had very little fat on him. We then loaded him in the pickup, took him into the barn and hung him by his antlers from the rafters with a block and tackle. By that time, it was nearly dark and I had to be at work in Denver the next morning, so I decided to leave the buck with Frank, who would skin it and cut up the venison for his freezer.

When I drove by the game and fish checkpoint at Ted's Place north of Ft. Collins at about 8:30 that night, I wished I had my trophy buck with me to register there. I would have liked to listen to the oohs and ahhhs of the game wardens and hunters who happened to be there as they caught sight of my buck. His antlers, which had only a respectable thirty-inch spread, were higher than any buck I have ever seen. I arrived at the farm a little before midnight and went to bed without waking up the folks.

The next morning, I drove to Denver as usual, dropped Dad at his office and arrived at eight a.m. ready to resume my life in the city. I could hardly wait for the ten a.m. coffee break so I could tell the staff about my successful hunt. The idea of a coffee break was new to me, but we took turns bringing doughnuts, which I enjoyed more than the coffee and I readily adapted to it. Rad was the only member of the staff who did not gather for this morning ritual, but I figured I could tell him over lunch about the tremendous buck I had killed. Everyone listened politely, at least for a few minutes, as I explained how I had cleverly stalked, found and shot a buck that was far bigger than anything I had killed before. I soon realized that none of them were interested in hunting in general, and only slightly more interested in my particular hunting adventure.

I gradually understood that I had much more in common with the ranchers which we all worked for than with the staff. Lyle couldn't understand my desire to rush home after work only to spend several more hours working on the farm. In fact there were times when he intimated that living so far from work and being so deeply involved in the farm was a conflict of interest. Dave Appleton, who was one of the most thoughtful and tolerant people I had ever worked with, was just pleased that I enjoyed it. Rad, who had wanted to hire me in the first place because of my ranch background, and whose opinion was the only one that really counted, made it his business to see that my involvement in the family farm never conflicted with my responsibility to the association.

That fall a great deal of our time was spent getting ready for the annual convention in Oklahoma City in January of 1958. Rad prepared the agendas for our standing committees in cooperation with the respective chairmen, invited the convention speakers with input from the host committees and officers and coordinated a myriad of additional chores he assigned to our staff.

The staff was encouraged to attend social activities at the convention whenever possible and mingle with the members. This was no problem for me because I enjoyed getting acquainted with ranchers from all parts of the country and learning about their operations. I found that there are usually cattle grazing wherever there is grass. Whereas there might be two or three cattle per acre during the summer in the Midwest or Southeast, in Arizona and New Mexico carrying capacity was measured by the number of head per section, with the average in New Mexico being ten or eleven head per section on a year-round basis, or sixty-four acres per head. I found that the members loved to talk about their own operations and appreciated that I was interested.

A good many of the resolutions that passed on first reading were ones carried over from year to year, such as the one calling for legislation to greatly increase the tariffs on beef from Australia and New Zealand, which were wildly popular with the membership, but couldn't garner enough national support to be passed by Congress. Others, like the infamous resolution to do away with income tax, always received considerable opposition from some of the younger or more practical members but continued to pass every year because a majority of the members followed their hearts and not their minds

The resolutions that called for changes in regulations by the Federal Government, most often the United States Department of Agriculture or the Bureau of Land Management within the Department of Interior, required specific action by the staff and officers and generated a lot of work for all of us throughout the year. Two of these went to the beef grading committee and the brucellosis committee respectively. Another issue that was relatively new caused our president to direct Rad to get actively involved in a national coalition of organizations concerned over the growing interest in setting aside large sections of public land as wilderness areas. Most of the support for this effort was by organizations such as the Sierra Club.

I was deeply involved in all of these activities because Rad had me take the minutes at almost all committee meetings. Since he had been elected chairman of the coalition involved in defeating or at least greatly amending the proposed "Wilderness Act," I also took the minutes at its meetings. I never got involved in any of the discussions, but had to pay close attention to everything that was said. I took fairly copious notes by hand and then had to condense them into minutes that would accurately summarize not only the actions taken, but much of the discussion that went into them. I, of course, reviewed these with Rad before having them mimeographed and mailed out to the respective committees. I was keenly interested in the subjects covered in these meetings at which the best minds of our organization and the allied groups we worked with wrestled with problems of serious consequence. I was learning the fundamentals of managing a nonprofit organization and getting the equivalent of a Master's Degree in the issues of greatest concern to the cattle industry.

Buck killed near Chimney Rock, which Frank had mounted and sent to cousin David williams in Texas

35

Swift Trip

I took a flight with a layover in Oklahoma City on my way to the 1958 "Swift Trip." Rad had recommended me for the representative for ANCA. I got into Oklahoma City late the afternoon before I needed to arrive in Chicago for the indoctrination, and checked into one of the small rooms in the Skirvin Hotel. I got to bed a little after midnight. My flight the next morning out of Oklahoma City to Chicago was at seven a.m. and would have gotten me to the hotel in plenty of time for our indoctrination. I could usually wake up any hour in the morning I chose, but I overslept and missed my flight. I was able to catch another and still get to Chicago before the indoctrination was over, but I could tell that Tom Glaze who ran a tight ship was furious with me when I slipped into the room. I'm sure he told Rad of my malfeasance, but fortunately Rad was not a big fan of Tom, for reasons I'll explain later, and he never mentioned it to me.

In 1958, Swift and Company was the largest of the big four beef packing companies: Swift, Armour, Cudahay and Hormel. It was big, aggressive, and very well managed. There had been rumblings again within Congress about the growing power of the large packing plants and major railroads that shipped most of the feeder cattle to the large central livestock markets along the Mississippi River; these were referred to collectively as the River Markets. Swift had signed a consent decree in 1920 not to enter into the retailing of beef, among other things, to head off further anti-trust action. In recent sessions of Congress, bills had been introduced to either break up or limit the power of these institutions that held so much sway over the livestock industry. The railroads were regulated by the Interstate Commerce Commission, whose rules were so complicated there was a full-time expert who contracted with ANCA to negotiate claims with them. The central markets' demise was still well down the road.

Swift and Company did not spend a chunk of their so-called agricultural research budget wining and dining cattle industry leaders as an altruistic gesture during a three-day tour. The indoctrination, part of which I missed, was only the beginning. Every event was carefully orchestrated with Tom Glaze conducting. Before each activity, usually during a meal, we would be told exactly what we were going to see and then we would subsequently go over what we had just done.

After an early breakfast the first morning we were bussed out to the Chicago stockyards to watch as the Swift head cattle buyer purchased a pen of long-fed Hereford steers that were to go into the kosher trade. After we watched him negotiate with the farmer who owned the cattle, the Swift's buyer, who had roots in the West and was known by a good many of our tour members, explained to us that these cattle would grade USDA Prime, a requirement for the kosher trade. Most prime cattle were provided by Midwestern farmer feeders who marketed their corn through their cattle and liked to get their animals as fat as possible. He also said, as Rad had already told me, that Swift did not have USDA trained professionals grade all their cattle, but sold many under their own house brands. He said that their very best carcasses were graded Swift Premium, which he claimed was more uniform than USDA Prime graded beef carcasses. I was well aware that USDA provided beef grading, the use of which was optional for packers; this was one of the few government programs the ANCA strongly supported.

When the cattle buyer asked for questions, I raised my hand and asked if they ever ran out of Swift Premium, because it was well known that during certain seasons there are fewer fully fattened beef cattle than others. He knew exactly what I was driving at and replied that there were such times, and buyers like him had to pay more to fill the demand for Swift Premium grade during these periods of shortage, but most customers felt it was worth it. The question was only one of many from our well-informed and truly interested group. Still the suspicion that Swift Premium might not be as consistent in quality as USDA Prime was not put to rest, and I noticed Tom Glaze, who was standing nearby, give me a dirty look.

We were told that Orthodox Jews could eat only the front beef quarters and they wanted that to be very fat. This left the rear quarters with the most expensive cuts for the hotel and restaurant trade, which also wanted cattle with a high degree of "finish," (very fat). Without the white table cloth and Kosher trade, Prime would have had little demand because most consumers preferred to buy Choice beef with less waste fat.

After a great lunch, we went to the Swift packing plant in the Chicago stockyards and watched the cattle we had seen purchased in the morning being slaughtered. In order to be sold into the Kosher trade, they had to be slaughtered according to Jewish ritual by a shochet who, after the animal was hoisted into the air by its rear legs by a chain while living, cut its throat with a long sharp knife. The blood simply poured from the animal and it died instantly. The shochet then inspected the knife to see there were no nicks or blemishes in it, that the cut was as proscribed and that the animal immediately and fully bled out. The carcass was then carried by conveyer to an adjoining area where it was skinned, its head and lower limbs removed and the carcass split. The hanging carcasses were then railed into a huge cooler, washed and covered by a shroud.

We were then led to a series of large walk-in coolers where hundreds of carcasses were hanging on railings and working their way through the facility so they would arrive at the cutting floor when they were completely chilled. Some of these had been slaughtered according to Jewish ritual the previous week. Those chilled, split carcasses were cut in half again, into quarters, and many of the rear quarters were shipped in either refrigerated trucks or boxcars to white linen restaurants who featured high priced steaks from the loins and barons of beef from the rump and round. If there were more of the high-quality front quarters available than could be sold into the kosher trade, a good portion of that part of the carcass could be sold to the hotel and restaurant trade as prime ribs. Most of the swinging carcasses, so called because they were shipped in refrigerated containers hung on rails by hooks, thus left to swing freely, were shipped to distribution centers owned by Swift and Company all across the United States. From these warehouses, they were wholesaled to retailers of all sizes and to the bigger grocery stores, mostly as swinging carcasses, and the rest were divided into sub-wholesale cuts for the smaller grocery stores or restaurants.

The next day we were flown to New York and bussed to one of the main downtown hotels. Our rooms were all on about the thirty-fourth floor, and a hotel employee herded us to one of the many elevators like sheep into a corral. My roommate was the president of the North Dakota Cattlemen's Association, a big dark-haired, good-looking man about forty-five-years-old named Jim Connelly. We were given the afternoon off to do some sightseeing around New York and had an open night to sample one of New York's restaurants.

At breakfast the next morning, the Swift staff explained the working of their distribution system which featured salesmen assigned to various parts of the city who called on restaurants and small grocery stores, taking orders for their next several days' supply of fresh meat. This order was shipped to them the next day out of a huge refrigerated warehouse in New York, which was similar to many others situated throughout the United States. My roommate and I were assigned to one such salesman and we spent the day with him as he went from customer to customer, occasionally getting no order, sometimes selling quite a few different cuts and quite often selling only just one popular item, which they referred to as a knuckle, a cut of meat I had never heard of before nor have I since. At our dinner meeting that night, someone asked how many individual salesmen like the ones we traveled with that day Swift employed. I do not remember the answer but it was a lot.

After an early breakfast, we checked out of the hotel, boarded a bus and made our way down the East Coast headed for Baltimore. At noon, we stopped at a well-known seafood restaurant for a great lunch of clam chowder and crab cakes, our first meal other than breakfasts that had not featured beef or lamb. By the time we got to Baltimore and checked into our hotel, it was fairly late in the afternoon, which gave us about an hour to do a little sightseeing before dinner, where we got a preview of what we would be doing the next day. We were told that the area we would be visiting, the Del-Mar-Va Peninsula, was a major producer of poultry and that Swift had its largest poultry processing facility there. There was a bit of a groan from the audience when they announced that we would not just be seeing how the chickens are slaughtered and processed, but also would have a fried chicken meal right at the facility. The Swift staff acknowledge our reaction by pointing out that our biggest competitor had become poultry rather than pork, and it was important for us to learn just how sophisticated poultry production had become because it was quickly changing from many small farms to vertically integrated mega producers.

We loaded onto our bus again the next morning and continued south of Baltimore for about an hour and a half until we reached the poultry processing plant. I can't remember if Swift got any of their fryers from contract producers or if they got their supply from the large number of independent producers in the area or both, but in any case, it was an extremely large facility and we got a whiff of it about ten minutes before we arrived. The majority of our group were raised in the country and had probably helped cut the head off of a chicken, scalded it and plucked off its feathers, so we had some idea of what a wet chicken smells like. We weren't prepared for an assembly line of hundreds of decapitated chickens being dragged through hot chlorinated water, mechanically plucked and even mechanically disemboweled. A beef slaughtering facility is not a very pleasant place to visit, but this was far worse in the way it assaulted your senses.

After we had watched the chickens being processed, we had about an hour's presentation from the staff about how Swift marketed their poultry and a bit more on the economic position poultry now held in the nation's consumption of protein, because it was quickly increasing its per capita market share in relation to beef and pork. We were then served a great meal of fried chicken in another part of the building. The dining room was air-conditioned and there was no hint of the odor that hovered over the plant, but the unappetizing odor of wet feathers and chicken offal remained in our nasal passages to the degree that we all agreed afterwards that the meal would've been much more enjoyable at some other time and place.

We left the poultry plant in the middle of the afternoon and after stopping for supper en-route, arrived back at our hotel in Baltimore sometime after dark. We were tired after the long day and were happy to hear that breakfast would not be served until eight a.m. the next morning, so we could sleep in a bit longer than usual. The tour was basically over and our last formal get-together would be at breakfast. Most of us would be catching planes back to our various destinations later in the day, but before any of us left, we were advised by Tom Glaze at breakfast that each of us would have a private meeting with him before we departed. We were all given an appointment at fifteen-minute intervals with Tom in his room. No one was told exactly what the meeting was about. We asked the other staff members what we would be talking to Tom about and they said it would be a private meeting and we were requested not discuss it with one another afterward. It all seemed a little weird to me.

When my appointed time came, I knocked on the door to Tom's room and when he invited me in, he had me sit down in a chair across the coffee table from where he was sitting. It had the feeling of being sent to the principal's office in high school. Tom asked me rather formally how I had enjoyed the trip and I truthfully told him that it had been a wonderful experience. I was rather uncomfortable and mumbled something inane and then waited for him to pick up the conversation. He asked me if I had incurred any expenses getting to the airport on the trip and would I have any on the way home. I had no idea where he was coming from and simply said that my father had brought me to the airport and would be picking me up again, so I had had none. He then asked if I had had any other out-of-the-way expenses related to the trip because they didn't want us to have any financial burden as result of it. It suddenly became obvious to me that he was expecting me to suggest some amount, and I said that since we lived seventeen miles from town there had been some gasoline used. He said it was up to each of us to name a figure and he would cover it. I said $10 would be fine. He handed me a $10 bill and dismissed me.

The first day I was home from the Swift trip, Rad invited me into his office to tell him all about it. He of course had taken it several years before and as I outlined the trip he said it was almost exactly the same as his. Dad had taken one of the first Swift trips when he was president of the Colorado Cattlemen's Association almost twenty years before. Dad and Rad both commented that one of the greatest benefits of the trip was the lasting friendships they made with other industry leaders. I specifically asked Rad about the uncomfortable meeting with Tom Glaze. We both agreed that he probably thought I was a fool for not taking more than $10.00, and those who may have taken the bait became the Swift and Company sycophants that they sought.

Rad then told me a story that he said he had not wanted to share with me until after the trip. Evidently Ferd Molin's son had worked for ANCA as his assistant for a while and had once accompanied his father on the train that the association's legislative committee took on their annual trek to Washington DC for some serious lobbying. Evidently the son had a drinking problem and Tom Glaze, who had recently come to work for Swift and Company, was also on the train and talked the son into furnishing him the association's mailing list, a firing offence. When this was discovered he had to be let go, greatly embarrassing the highly respected Molin. None of this was ever made public, but was of course known by the Executive Committee members who had the unpleasant duty of punishing him. He admitted and explained his folly, but ANCA didn't want the problems that pursuing it with Swift would cause both organizations. Swift subsequently made Tom their Public Relations Director.

36

Cattle Industry Issues

By the Fall of 1958, we had finished the work we needed to do on the house and were feeling pretty good about having gotten all the irrigated land established in hay and pasture. Mom and I occasionally talked about either trying to expand the little farmhouse or possibly building a new one, but Dad had no interest in doing so. I was perfectly comfortable living with the folks, but really didn't want to be a bachelor the rest my life and had begun to think maybe I should consider having a place of my own.

There was a small new subdivision being developed just across the interstate, west of Thornton, that was about halfway between the farm and my office. One weekend early that fall Mom and I stopped to look at their open houses. It was not a pricey development and they had a nice two-bedroom home with one bath and a one-car garage that would work fine as a starter for me. I figured I could drive the ten minutes back to the farm in the morning and pick up Dad most days or he could drive to my place to meet me. Dad wasn't wild about the idea but Mom encouraged me to look into buying one of the little houses.

My growing desire to have a home and family of my own was what motivated me to want to buy a house; however, I had never even broached the subject of marriage to any of the girls I had dated. In my typical cart-before-the-horse fashion I decided to see if I could buy one of the houses on the G.I. Bill.

About a week later, I heard from the builders about my offer to buy the two-bedroom house with a GI thirty-year loan. I don't recall whether it was the VA or the developer, but in any case, my offer was turned down. When I asked for details they said they would not make a loan with no down payment to an unmarried man. It wasn't a very expensive house or a fancy subdivision and I made an average starting salary for the time. I didn't try to contest the decision because I had jumped into making a serious commitment without too much thought and was, in fact, somewhat relieved.

Beginning to think I probably was going to be a lifelong bachelor, I threw myself back into my great new job and picked up life on the farm again without quite the enthusiasm I had felt during the previous summer of hard work. The folks probably recognized my desire to buy a house as an effort to start building something permanent for myself. Dad broached the subject of me taking a part interest in the farm. He said he and Mom were sure they never could have begun to accomplish what was done during the past summer without me. After kicking around ways to get me more deeply involved, we came up with a plan wherein I would earn a third interest in the farm by continuing the work I had already started the last six months. We drew up a document giving me one-third interest in the farm and committing me to pay one-third of the operating expenses. This rather unusual document was not filed at the courthouse, but was signed by all three of us and placed in the folks' safety deposit box at the Poudre Valley Bank in Fort Collins. I realized I was getting a good deal financially, even though it was somewhat of a velvet trap.

At the office, the subjects of wilderness legislation, beef grading and brucellosis occupied a lot of our time in the summer of 1958. Our efforts to forestall the passage of legislation to close excessively broad swaths of the national forests to multiple use required working with other commercial users of public lands. We were pretty much on our own with the grading problem. The brucellosis eradication regulations being proposed by the USDA created a unique situation, wherein we had to play a positive role in solving a public health problem while protecting cattle producers from having unworkable management practices thrust upon them.

The goal of eradicating brucellosis, the bacteria that also causes undulant fever in humans, was one in which the cattle industry had a big stake because it caused abortions in cows as well as sickness in humans, including many ranchers and dairy workers. The problem was that the means initially recommended for the eradication were a one-size-fits-all approach recommended by the dairy industry. They called for testing every breeding age bovine female and immediately slaughtering her if she tested positive for the organism. The problem was that whereas dairy cows are brought into a barn every day for milking and are easily tested, large numbers of the U.S. beef cow herd ran on the open range and were seldom readily available for testing. Also, research had already shown that the prevalence of the disease was much greater in dairy cattle than beef cattle in all but the gulf states.

The ANCA took a leading role in organizing a broad coalition of organizations to address this problem. The initial rules promulgated by the USDA, which delegated to the various state departments of agriculture the responsibility for enforcement of a program that called for a test and slaughter process needed to be modified. Our organization had a good working relationship with the state veterinarians in most states and they were in turn very influential in an organization called the United States Animal Health Association. That group and several general farm organizations that had large numbers of cattlemen among their membership were invited to join with the ANCA to make the rules more workable. One of our members, Tom Arnold from Arnold, Nebraska, had already been quite active working with the dairy industry to bring the human health aspect of the problem to the attention of the country and was instrumental in adding some common sense to the proposed rules and regulations for testing range cattle. Fortunately, he was made chairman of the new national coalition.

A third issue receiving a lot of attention by ANCA that year was the voluntary beef grading system used by the packing industry, which was widely supported by beef producers, that endeavored to rank beef carcasses based on their eating quality. Objective factors were the weight of the carcass and age of the animal that produced it. Elements such as color, texture and marbling (the amount of intra-muscular fat) were more subjective. All these and other factors were checked by paid government graders. They looked at a cross-section of the loin when it was cut between the twelfth and thirteenth ribs of the hanging carcass to measure the area of the rib eye and estimate the amount of marbling of the loin eye. Marbling was considered to be the primary factor effecting flavor, juiciness and tenderness.

The grades at that time were called prime, choice, good and commercial. The names have been changed from time to time over the years, but in general the higher the grade the higher the price, so the grade assigned by an inspector had a great bearing on the value of the carcass. Thus, the feeder in turn paid more for cattle entering their feedlots that were perceived to have the genetic ability to produce the highest percentage of such carcasses. One of the greatest concerns within all segments of the production chain was the perception that beef graders did not apply their own standards uniformly. Graders on the West Coast were thought to apply a higher grade to the same cattle than might be applied in the Midwest.

Owners of the two major breeds at that time, Hereford and Black Angus, had a vested interest in how the grading standards were applied. Angus, which were more prevalent in the Midwest, had a genetic propensity to marble at an earlier age than Herefords, which were the dominant breed in the Western range states. There was also the perception that younger cattle were more tender, which was at cross purposes with the fact that marbling tended to increase with age

The three issues just discussed were at the forefront and vigorously debated during my four-year tenure at ANCA and for years after. I took the minutes at most of the meetings, and after checking my notes with Rad, I mailed them to all participants. I couldn't help but be well posted on these major issues that impacted the cattle industry in the late 1950s.

Sometime during the summer of 1958, Lyle was authorized to hire someone to help him with his public relations work. This turned out to be an attractive twenty-year-old girl who had a lot on the ball. Her name was Karen Voss and she had a very noticeable V shaped scar down her cheek below what I think was her right eye. I can't even remember which one it was because after you knew her a while you simply didn't notice it. She was self-conscious about it and was quite shy in public, something that I think would not have otherwise been her nature. She told me she had had a bicycle accident in her teens and was thrown through a plate glass window.

After she had worked at the office for two or three weeks I learned that she liked to dance and asked her for a date. Elitch Gardens, one of the two amusement parks in Northwest Denver, had a beautiful, large dance pavilion that featured some of the top big-name bands of the day and she agreed to accompany me there. It turned out to be a beautiful late summer night with the fragrance of the many flowers the park was noted for in the air. I believe this was the night that Les Paul and Mary Ford were performing. She turned out to be a great dancer, or at least she made me think I was. When the band played one of their pieces currently on the hit parade, we joined other dancers standing in front of the band stand, swaying to the rhythm while we watched Paul work his magic on the electric guitar and listened to Mary sing. We had a great time and agreed that we would have to go out dancing again soon.

We started dating nearly every Saturday night and I learned that she had gone to high school in Southern California. It turned out that she had been a classmate of Johnny Mathis, who had been, along with his other talent, a very good athlete in high school. His songs were just beginning to hit the charts and we were both great fans. We found it easy to talk to each other. When we were discussing the difficulty some parents had in those days with their daughters listening to records by black artists, she related the anecdote of a father in California who destroyed all of his daughter's Harry Belafonte records. This resulted in the father and daughter being completely estranged from each other and her eventually marrying a black man.

I brought Karen out to the farm to meet the folks on a Saturday, after I had spent the morning at the office. I had learned that she liked horses and knew how to ride, so after lunch we saddled up a couple of our young mares. As we were riding from the corral up towards the reservoir, a pheasant flew up out of a ditch and spooked her horse. As it shied, she was thrown off and landed awkwardly on her ankle. I jumped off my horse and as I helped her up could tell her ankle hurt badly and I figured she had sprained her ankle. I helped her back on her horse, we rode back to the barn and I helped her into the house to take a look at the ankle. We managed to get her boot off and could see it was hurt badly enough that we needed to get her to a doctor. I took her to the emergency room where they x-rayed her ankle and discovered a bone was broken. They put a cast on it right there and I took her to the home of one of the secretaries who worked with her at the office, Sue Wittstruck, who was a good friend of Karen's. By this time, it was nearly midnight and Sue said she would look after Karen for a few days.

Cow Pony Corral

By Roy Lilley

ONE OF THE MOST encouraging things I have noticed over the past few years in activities involving horses is the increase in shows and rodeos for the junior set—boys and girls 18 and under. Kids just naturally take to riding, and there is nothing they like better than a chance to utilize their ability in competition.

During the summer that has just whizzed by I had the opportunity to judge several of the "kids" shows—and I take my hat off to those young folks. In many cases the youngsters who came out on top in the performance classes were riding colts they broke themselves —generally not a pedigreed animal trained at great expense but some handy and sensible little horse that responded nicely to a lot of time and effort on the part of its young owner.

Another thing I must rather reluctantly point out is that the girls do better than hold their own in all the events, with the possible exception of roping. When it comes to horsemanship, reining and the various timed events, I'm afraid the boys are sometimes a little outclassed. And I don't think I'm prejudiced, either. At least the effect of a winsome smile from a young lady can be balanced by the judge's natural desire to see the young men uphold the honor of their gender.

Still another interesting and surprising observation is how well the city cousins compare with the ranch kids in these affairs. And these town-raised youngsters take their riding seriously, too. Getting out to the edge of town every day to the pasture, vacant lot, or what have you, to feed and groom their mount and work at their favorite hobby leaves little time for getting into trouble in the city.

A friend of mine in a medium-sized town in northern Colorado puts in a lot of time with such a group of young riders. He tells me it is a real pleasure to work with this conscientious, sincere and well-mannered bunch of kids, especially in this day and age when you keep hearing about how teen-agers are going to the dogs. The town thinks so much of these youngsters that a group of civic leaders is going to help them finance building an arena for their gymkhanas and drills. I think these men are making a fine investment in the future of their town.

AMERICAN CATTLE PRODUCER

Cow Pony Corral article in October 1957 "American Cattle Producer"

37

Rad

In addition to the important coalitions, the ANCA had a major role working on problems like brucellosis or wilderness legislation, we were also members of a couple of nonprofit organizations that shared some of our interests. Two of these were the National Highway Users Conference and Livestock Conservation, Inc. Rad had me represent ANCA in those two organizations. The NHUC had a field man who visited several times a year and always took me out to lunch or dinner. We got to be good friends over the years on his nickel, and I faithfully read their monthly newsletter and attended their annual convention. We were interested in maintaining the farm-to-market roads, as the state and county highways were referred to, in the interstate highway system then under construction. These highways had become more and more important to our members, because they depended more on cattle trucks and less on railroads to get their cattle to market.

We strongly supported their policy of opposing any diversion of gasoline taxes from the highway trust fund, which was to be spent only for the construction and repairs on the interstate highway system. Congress didn't seriously start raiding this fund until the highways were old enough to really need the repairs; now they are in terrible shape.

Livestock Conservation, Inc. was an organization that had two loosely affiliated offices, one in Chicago and one in Kansas City. They had a broad base of membership among organizations representing all species of meat animals. They had a rather modest dues structure and simple offices with few staff members, but because of their broad representation in the livestock industry they were quite influential in some areas. When I first became involved, I was appointed to the livestock handling committee, which worked with the first and, at the time, was the only USDA employee who studied the handling of cattle at livestock markets and slaughter facilities. The main concern at the time was less with humane handling of animals and more with economic losses caused by bumps and bruises during handling. This man was a mentor to the autistic professor at Colorado State University, Temple Grandin, who took his study on injuries to cattle as they moved through gates and down alleys and livestock pens and refined it. He simply sat on a fence by the facility where the cattle were held awaiting slaughter, and counted the number of times animals bumped their ribs, hips or shoulders as they were herded toward the kill floor. He then inspected the carcasses and correlated them with the bumps he had observed in the pens before slaughter. Many of the bruises were severe enough to require being cut out of the carcass and used as dog food. The balance of the carcass was then discounted. This seems like a no-brainier now but at the time, some packers objected to extra effort involved in tracing the carcasses back to the live animal just driven to slaughter. Now all the major packers have much improved, more humane facilities designed by Grandin.

We were invited to furnish a speaker for the 1958 LCI convention in Omaha, Nebraska and Rad sent me. I was asked to be on a panel on the subject of animal handling and to keep my opening remarks to about fifteen minutes. My dad's older brother, Bill, and his wife Virginia lived in Omaha and I arranged to stay with them while I was there. The convention lasted two days and I stayed at Uncle Bill and Aunt Virginia's apartment both nights. Uncle Bill was kind enough to take some time off from his work with the Alcohol Tax Division of the Treasury Department (he had been a revenuer during prohibition) to listen to my little talk. During my ten-minute presentation, I pointed out that as the youngest brother, I had been relegated to pushing our cattle through the chutes when we handled them on the ranch. I said I didn't remember ever being told to be careful, but was yelled at a lot to hurry up. Uncle Bill kindly said that I had done fine. The Omaha World Herald covered the event and the next morning my name was mentioned in the paper with the other speakers.

Uncle Bill and Aunt Virginia had no children and lived simply in a pleasant two-bedroom apartment near downtown Omaha. Aunt Virginia had prepared a special prime rib dinner the night after the convention. Like all the Lilleys, Uncle Bill enjoyed his before dinner cocktail—martini in his case—so we had a leisurely drink as we caught up on family matters before eating. My brother Charlie had been having chronic health problems for several years and we had just learned that he had finally been diagnosed with multiple sclerosis. All of the family had been afraid this might be his problem, but we didn't want to tell anyone until we knew for sure. In the middle of telling Uncle Bill and Aunt Virginia about Charlie, I suddenly broke down and just bawled and couldn't quit sobbing. My aunt and uncle were very understanding, but initially their comforting words simply made me worse. I soon got myself under control and we had dinner. Nothing more was said of my episode.

By early fall Rad, Lyle and I were working out our 1959 convention schedule and contacting speakers. I made a trip to Omaha to meet with the host committee and get everything coordinated with the convention manager at the headquarters hotel. I don't remember anything in particular about this convention except that Herrell DeGraff, the Cornell University economist who had been hired to study the cattle cycle for us, had completed his report and presented it to the membership.

The low cattle prices and labor shortages that existed during World War II had caused cattle numbers to stay fairly constant, and with price controls on nearly all their inputs, cattlemen had been able to get through the war in fairly decent economic shape. When the ranchers in the service returned home, they started keeping back replacement heifers and building up the nation's cowherd in anticipation of better times ahead. With meat rationing gone, beef consumption increased greatly and cattle prices started rising, sending an economic signal to increase numbers even more. By 1950, there had been enough consecutive profitable years in the cattle business that even people who were not in the business started renting any pasture they could find and stocking it with yearlings, or buying old cows that would normally go to slaughter and raising another calf or two out of them. By this time, heifers kept back for replacements were having calves and the artificial stimulus of having been kept out of the normal slaughter mix was reversed. Within a year, the bubble burst because the nation's cowherd had grown to a record number, which hasn't been exceeded to this day. There was a huge drop in prices in the mid-1950s and as nontraditional producers got out of the business, ranchers started selling off their older cows. The greatly increased cow slaughter further depressed the price of beef. This sudden and continuing loss of profitability motivated the leaders of the cattle industry to consider investing some serious money to find out what had gone wrong and see that it never happened again. In an unprecedented move, we sent out a letter from the ANCA office in 1956 requesting a special one-time donation to fund the hiring of one of the nation's top agricultural economists. He would work under the direction of a special task force that had the rather straightforward, if simplistic name, "The Fact-Finding Committee." The chairman was John Marble, who had ranching operations in both California and Nevada.

With the benefit of hindsight and a lot of number crunching, Dr. DeGraff drew a graphic picture of the wreck the cattle industry had just gone through and suggested ways to dig our way out. He said historical numbers show that we have always had cattle cycles and probably always will, but by better understanding them, cattlemen can plan their operations in ways to better deal with them.

The governor of Nebraska spoke during the convention, and after his presentation he called Dr. DeGraff and me forward to receive certificates designating us as "Admirals in the Great Navy of Nebraska." This was a tongue-in-cheek way to honor people who had provided some kind of service to the state. DeGraff's presentation was widely covered by not only the livestock press, but in the big city dailies as well. Since he presented his findings in Nebraska, one of the most important cattle states in the nation, he was a natural for the award. I had worked closely with the Chamber of Commerce preparing for and conducting the convention and they evidently thought that qualified me for the recognition. The chairman of the local host committee, Glen Le Doyt, a prominent businessman active in the Omaha and Nebraska business communities for years and also the owner of a large ranch in the Sandhills was already an Admiral and joined the Governor in making the presentation.

Later that spring Rad was to lead the ANCA legislative committee, composed of officers and committee chairmen, on their annual trip to Washington D. C. to lobby Congress and Federal agencies on behalf of our policy positions. Each affiliate state also sent a similar group to lobby its own state delegation and visit agencies involved in policies specific to their areas of interest. This annual influx of cowboys to Washington DC was amazingly well received. Rather than depending on high-powered lobbyists, ANCA brought a group of well-informed, focused cattle producers to plead their case as they testified before legislative committees and met with department heads in the executive branch.

Rad had accompanied Ferd Molin on the Washington trip the previous several years before he had retired. He had the meetings lined up and appropriate background information prepared for the meetings scheduled with the congressional committee chairmen and, usually, the Secretary of Agriculture and Secretary of Interior. Some years the President would briefly address the whole delegation for a few minutes. As we were putting all the material together, Rad told me he would try to take me to Washington next year.

About a week before the Washington trip, Rad made a strenuous trip to Washington, New York, Tennessee and Texas. He came home on a late flight and his wife Florence met him at the airport as usual. When the office opened the next morning, she called to say that Rad had suffered a stroke and was in the hospital. Evidently, on the way home from the airport they had stopped by the office and dropped off his briefcase, because I found it lying on his desk that morning. I went to see him that afternoon and found him in an oxygen tent in a coma. Florence said that the prognosis was not good, because his brain hemorrhage was still seeping.

When I got back to the office, I opened the briefcase and found that Rad had already written a complete report on the Washington part of his trip on a yellow tablet. I couldn't believe it. Obviously, he had taken time after a long day trekking through Washington to record that day's activities. Although everyone in the office was in a state of shock, work went on as usual while we reassured each other that he would surely recover soon.

Rad never regained consciousness and died three days after he was stricken. I had already started preparing a full report from Rad's notes, working several nights in a row at the office, hoping and praying that he would be able to check them over for me. Instead, I found myself attending his funeral a few days later.

Nearly all of the officers and living past presidents came to the funeral, but I have no clear memory of the funeral itself or the interment. I do recall one thing though. Dad and I had ridden in one of the mortuary's stretch limousines along with Russell Thorpe, the retired Executive Director of the Wyoming Stock Growers. He had been married at one time to Grandpa William's youngest sister, Anna, so Dad and Russell had known each other for a long time and were visiting on the way to the cemetery. I had not attended many funerals and thought that one was supposed to act quite somber throughout. I was sitting between Dad and Russell, not saying a word or even paying too much attention to what they were saying. Suddenly my dad turned to me and said, "What do you think, sweetheart." My dad often referred to not only Mom but all us boys that way from time to time. I was embarrassed and probably said something like, "Oh Dad!" in reply. I had been so busy dealing with the work created by Rad's death I had not yet assessed my own feelings about his departure. I suddenly went from being embarrassed by what Dad said to being upset with myself for thinking only about my own feelings at a time like that.

After the funeral, the ANCA president, Jack Milburn, met with other directors to decide how to proceed until the board could meet and work out a procedure for selecting a replacement for Rad. Milburn appointed Dave Appleton, the senior member of the remaining staff, as Acting Executive Secretary, until a permanent replacement could be hired and instructed him to make the annual Washington trip. In the meanwhile, I confirmed the plans Rad had already made, got the information mailed to the appropriate people and took care of the routine things that had piled up on Rad's desk. I answered his mail and, in most cases, was able to deal with the matters at hand.

At a specially called board meeting, Lyle Liggette was instructed to get out a general news release announcing that applications to fill the vacancy left by Rad's death should be received at the office within the next month. As I recall, the officers were authorized to act as a committee to interview applicants and present their recommendations at another board meeting to be held later in the year. I was instructed to receive the applications, acknowledge them, copy them and forward them to the committee for review.

In fairly short order, we received an application from the current executive secretary of the Texas Hereford Association and the current executive secretary of the Montana Stock growers. In the meantime, some of the officers were seeking individuals they thought would be good candidates. Among those that the staff knew had been approached were an Assistant Secretary of Agriculture and Tom Glaze's assistant with Swift and Company. The first two showed a great deal of interest and had a good many letters of recommendation attached to their job applications. I also got phone calls from each of them to let me know they would look forward to working with me if they got the job. Little did they know how little pull I had.

I don't believe the Assistant Secretary of Agriculture ever made a formal application, but a good many board members had met him on Washington trips and liked his rural background and knowledge of the regulations pertaining to grazing on the National Forest. I was aware that Albert K. Mitchell, one of our past presidents from New Mexico, was quite interested in Glaze's assistant, Bill McMillan, whom I had met several times. At the convention in Omaha, Glaze had given the job of introducing all previous attendees at the luncheon for trippers to Bill, and he did an impressive job, stumbling over only one name, with many, like my dad, going back to trips taken years ago. Having attended the trip, I was in attendance and marveled at his talent for something I was so terrible at.

It soon became apparent that Albert Mitchell was pushing pretty hard to hire Bill McMillan, and Bill was playing hard to get. When the board met to make a final selection, Lyle, Dave and I were asked to leave the room when the final selection was being determined. The board voted to hire Bill, who informed them he could not start until he had fulfilled several obligations to Swift and Company. As I recall, his salary was set at $13,000 a year, several thousand more than Rad had been making when he died. I had secretly dreamed of being offered the job, but it never occurred to me to apply for it, because I thought I was far too young. I had prepared myself to accept whomever they hired and I felt that Bill was surely qualified, but I had had visions of working for Rad until he retired at sixty-five and stepping into his job when I was about forty-three. I knew Bill was older than I was, but I was surprised to learn he was thirty-three, only three years older than I!

I loved my job and had no interest in trying to find another, but I knew my relationship with Bill could never be anywhere near as close as it had been with Rad. He had been a mentor and good friend, and looking back I like to think that perhaps I helped him as he grew into his new job. One of the leaders of an allied industry group, with whom we both had worked, said he felt Rad was just hitting his stride when he died at the woefully young age of fifty-two.

38

Major Issues

I believed it was my responsibility to continue the organization's routine activities, as well as the projects Rad was working on when he died. Membership renewal billings and acknowledgements continued to be routinely handled by our bookkeeper and secretaries, and new member solicitations were already my responsibility. Thanks to his having left such a good record of Washington affairs in his brief case, I was able to get off to a good start picking up on one of ANCA's most important activities. This gave me the confidence to tackle other projects Rad had been handling. Lyle continued to edit the newsletter and do an outstanding job of handling the association's public relations, and Dave found that his new title of Acting Executive Secretary added very little to his daily work load editing the American Beef Producer Magazine. I continued to write my monthly column, "Cowpony Corral" in addition to helping prepare and mail solicitations for ads.

My main concern was to see that we followed through on projects that were already underway. I contacted the appropriate people in allied industries with whom we had been working, indicating it was our intent to continue to be actively involved. Rad had been chairman of the group leading the effort to make the legislation creating wilderness areas more workable for agriculture. I sent a letter to the committee, reporting Rad's death and suggesting the first order of business at the next meeting needed to be the election of a new chairman.

We had also been actively involved since our 1954 convention in Colorado Springs with the development of the rules and regulations that USDA was writing, while the cattle industry wrestled with the challenge of eradicating brucellosis. As mentioned earlier, Tom Arnold from Nebraska, a member of ANCA's executive committee, was the first chairman of the brucellosis committee, which represented a broad range of private and public groups interested in the subject. A meeting in

Denver had already been scheduled before Rad's death. The group consisted of state veterinarians, dairy interests, a representative of the land grant universities, central markets, livestock auctions and other organizations concerned with animal health and interstate movement of cattle. ANCA continued to furnish the chairman for this committee for years, as the rules continued to get more stringent the closer we came to eradicating the disease.

The third, but no less important current issue the association was dealing with involved conflicting suggestions for changing the manner in which beef carcasses were graded, and the ANCA's president had appointed a special committee to deal with this issue. Most leaders of the association raised Hereford cattle, by far the most predominant breed in the industry at the time. The leadership of the breed's registry, the American Hereford Association, thought that the marbling, or intra-muscular fat, requirement for the top grades, choice and prime, were too high. A meeting of that committee was also held in the Denver office that year.

It was generally acknowledged at the time that the manner in which cattle deposited fat throughout their body when they were put on a ration of grain varied between breeds. It took from 140 to 210 days in a feedlot for steers or heifers to reach the degree of fatness desired by the consuming public, depending on the age and weight of the animal when it was put on feed. All the major English breeds, Hereford, Angus and Shorthorn, tended to require approximately the same amount of time to reach the desired weight and amount of finish, but the manner in which they deposited fat varied. Both Herefords and Angus seemed to deposit outside fat over their loin in about the same manner, but the Angus breed tended to start depositing intra-muscular fat within the loin at an earlier age and more abundantly. The Shorthorn breed was known to deposit fat over the loin in an uneven manner, causing the fat on the carcass to appear patchy, which was undesirable.

Degree of maturity as determined by the density of a particular bone in the carcass also was an important factor in quality grading. Everything else being equal, carcasses from younger animals required less marbling than those that were older.

This controversy within the cattle industry over grading played into the hands of the major meatpackers, because they preferred that grading by government inspectors be done away with. Further muddying up the water, particularly among consumers, was confusion about the fact that grading by government inspectors was voluntary, whereas inspection for wholesomeness and purity was mandatory. Still, it appeared that consumers liked the grading system and were willing to pay a substantial premium for the choice grade.

Legislation to do away with the beef grading system was introduced in Congress. This bill was supported by the American Meat Institute, the packers trade organization, as well as many individual cattle producers who believed the system penalized their particular breed of cattle, so ANCA's beef grading committee was forced into the fray. They needed to make a recommendation to the membership to either oppose the bill outright, make recommendations for changing the grading system or support it.

As I took the minutes during the beef grading committee meeting in Denver, I realized that this was an issue that had the potential to split our organization wide open, or at least further jeopardize our opportunity to obtain members in the Midwest, where the Angus breed was most popular. Some proposed changes in the grading system would likely take away the advantage that the Angus cattle held because of their genetic ability to deposit fat in muscle at a young age.

The American Hereford Association, which had successfully created breed loyalty among the thousands of commercial Hereford operations across the West, took the position that beef grading must be substantially changed or done away with. This point of view was strongly represented at our meeting and found an ally in Tobin Armstrong, a King Ranch heir, who was on the committee. The King Ranch was the founder of the Santa Gertrudis breed of cattle, which was developed by crossing Shorthorns with Brahmans. These large, rather slow-to-mature cattle were perfectly adapted for the semi-desert country they had been developed in. Not too many Santa Gertrudis cattle were found outside the Southwest and little was known about how they performed in Midwestern feedlots, where most slaughter cattle were produced at that time. During lunch, Tobin told me their steers were shipped to holdings they had in Pennsylvania, where they were fed, slaughtered and readily marketed through private contracts.

When the meeting reconvened after lunch, a consensus began to develop in the committee as to what should be recommended to the ANCA membership at the next convention. Even though the organization had long supported the concept of beef grading, a majority of the committee believed that there was enough concern about the rules governing the system that unless serious changes were made, the volunteer grading program should be discontinued. The committee voted to meet again at the convention and develop a resolution for the membership to consider. The staff was instructed to invite the chief of the inspection service in the USDA to the convention to meet with the grading committee the day before the convention.

At the annual meeting in Omaha, the membership had voted to hold their 1960 convention in Dallas and we started getting ready for the convention about midsummer. A host committee had already been formed by the Dallas Chamber of Commerce and it was chaired by Ben Carpenter, President of Southland Life Insurance company, who was also the current president of the Texas and Southwest Cattle Growers Association, by far our largest affiliate. I scheduled a meeting with Mr. Carpenter and he met me at the airport.

With Rad gone and his replacement not yet hired, I found myself working most Saturdays and going back into the office a couple of nights a week to keep up with my work. Other than a couple of trips to Dallas for convention planning, I didn't do much traveling. Our president or Lyle filled in any speaking engagements that Rad had committed to and I assumed nearly all of his other duties. It was fortunate that Rad, having been an assistant himself, involved me in all his duties, including having me read all of his correspondence. This gave me a lot of insight into to what was going on or coming down the road.

When Bill McMillan reported for duty, he immediately imposed his more corporate management style on the office. He informed the officers and me that since I had made most of the arrangements for the upcoming annual convention, I would continue to be in charge of planning it, with one exception. He thought it was foolish that we handled hotel reservations through the office. It was a lot of work, and I agreed that we caught some flack for some problems, but many of the smaller members appreciated it and the biggest advantage was having complete knowledge of the attendance. He said he knew of no other similar organization that handled convention reservations for their members and we were going to stop doing so! This new policy freed up some time for me, but I still had to deal with the inevitable complaints.

By the time Bill came on board, Lyle, Dave and I had the next year's budget pretty well laid out. Because of the date of our convention, our fiscal year started on March 1. We had pretty much followed the previous year's budget and had penciled in a modest increase in travel, a few other expenses and a two or three-percent wage increase across the board for the staff. The tradition of giving a month's salary bonus to staff members was not included in the budget, but had always been approved by the executive committee during the convention, since Molin had initiated it. When we mentioned the bonus to Bill he would have none of it. He said the total salary budget was to be a single line item, the individual amounts were to be known only to himself and the president, and no one was to know any other staff member's salary. Knowing that when Bill was hired he received a considerably larger salary than Rad's, the staff gritted their teeth over what they believed was an eight-and-a-third-percent cut in their salary.

J. Edgar Dick, who was the Executive Vice President of the California Cattlemen's Association, probably the most active affiliate of ANCA after the two Texas associations, was approaching retirement age, and with his encouragement his board had authorized the hiring of an assistant to train for his job. I was unaware of this until just before our Dallas convention; however, I had watched Ed Dick operate over the previous several years and he was one-of-a-kind. California always came to the national convention knowing just what policy positions they wanted to push on behalf of their state's cattle industry, and Ed would stay in his room orchestrating things as he sent his officers and committee chairmen down to the various meetings to lobby for the support of other states. There was some resentment about his tactics, but more admiration for their success. At any rate, Ed had talked to Bill McMillan and requested permission to interview me for the job during our Dallas convention. Bill gave his permission and probably encouragement.

AMERICAN NATIONAL CATTLEMEN'S ASSOCIATION
801 East 17th Avenue, Denver 18, Colorado

February 21, 1959

TO: EXECUTIVE COMMITTEE:

We know that all of you were as shocked as we were here at the office when we learned of the death of Rad Hall. He had just got back from a trip to Washington, New York, Tennessee and Texas on association work, and during that trip had prepared the following "Report to the Executive Committee."

President Milburn, First Vice-President Fred Dressler and Past President Don Collins have been in the office to confer on association work, which of course will be disrupted because of the death of Mr. Hall. However, President Milburn, through his appointment of Dave Appleton, Producer editor, as acting secretary and Myrtle Black, office manager, as acting treasurer, both long-time members of the staff, has shown confidence in the office force, and, with the cooperation of Lyle Liggett and the young ladies in the office, I feel confident that things will run along smoothly. I can assure you that all of these individuals will do their utmost to try to make up for at least a part of the great loss of your secretary.

Sincerely yours,

ROY N. LILLEY
Ass't. Executive Secretary

Mr. Hall's report follows:

Because of last fall's election, there are more new faces in this Congress than usual. Some of our best friends and most faithful spokesmen for the industry in committees and on the floor retired or were replaced. It would be impractical to name them all, but, so far as your secretary is concerned, those who will be missed most are Frank Barrett (Wyo.) from the Senate and William Hill (Colo.) from the House. Both could always be depended upon for wise and authentic counsel and genuine helpful action on all matters of interest to the beef cattle industry.

During my few days in Washington it was not possible to become acquainted with all the new members from American National territory, but I did have highly pleasing visits with two freshmen congressmen who, I am certain, will be real champions of our cause: Representative Don Short (R.,N.D.) already is taking an active part in the affairs of the important committee on Agriculture, and Don McGinley (D.,Neb.) brother of our genial host at the Omaha convention (G. J. McGinley) obtained appointment to the equally important committee on Interior and Insular Affairs.

BEEF PROMOTION: The fact that a number of bills have been spontaneously introduced in both houses of Congress gives ample evidence of considerable support for the legislation to permit voluntary, but automatic deductions for beef promotion and research. However, it is also readily apparent that failure of the legislation during the past two sessions has left its mark on the proposal.

Congressmen dislike championing what they think might be a losing cause, and even our most effective exponents in the last session are reluctant to go into high gear again without assurances that we have cleared away some of the stumbling blocks of last year, most important of which was disunity within our industry.

It appears to me that our next move should be a series of personal interviews with the members of Senate Committee on Agriculture to obtain if possible the endorsement of a majority of that group. Without such endorsement there is little to be gained by going through

A few days before Lyle and I left for Dallas in his car, I got a letter from Dick inviting me to breakfast at 6:30 AM the first morning of convention, to interview for the job as his assistant. I went into the next office and told Bill about the letter. He said he had already talked to Ed and that he thought it would be a good opportunity for me, but he would like some time to replace me if I took the job. I said I would talk to my folks about it that night and make a decision whether or not to apply before leaving for the convention. The unexpected offer caused me to take a realistic look at my situation. Initially I had hoped to work for Rad until he retired and step into his job, as he had done with Molin. When we started receiving applications for Rad's job, my first reaction was to wonder what kind of a boss each would make, still thinking of making a career working for ANCA. As the process of reviewing applicants dragged out and I found I could not only do Rad's work but was greatly enjoying it, I found myself hoping (daydreaming?) that the job might be offered to me. When Bill was given the job, I couldn't imagine myself remaining his assistant until I was at least in my early sixties. I already knew him fairly well, having seen him at conventions and having spent some time around him on the Swift trip, but I had no idea what he thought of me. I knew that I could never be as close to him as I had been to Rad.

I didn't know how to break the news to my folks that I might be applying for a job that would take me all the way to California. I had greatly enjoyed the challenge of buying and getting the farm established with Mom and Dad and sincerely appreciated their willingness to let me become a one-third owner. They were somewhat shocked, but their first response was that we should talk it over and then do what was best for me. I really needed someone to talk to by that time and I simply poured out everything I had been thinking, dreaming and worrying about ever since Rad died. I told them I had been getting restless the last year or so and the challenge of keeping things going when Rad died had rekindled my enthusiasm. When I referred to Bill's youth and the dashed prospect of getting the top job in the foreseeable future, both Dad and Mom stated their biased opinion that they thought I could do a better job than Bill and that he might consider me a threat, something that had never occurred to me. We were all in a bit of an emotional state and decided to discuss my decision at breakfast. I tossed and

NEWS RELEASE

Lyle Liggett, Director of Information

For Release AM's of July 13, 1959

Denver, Colo., July 13----Appointment of C. W. "Bill" McMillan, widely known representative of Swift and Company, Chicago, as executive secretary of the American National Cattlemen's Association was announced today by G. R. "Jack" Milburn, the organization's president.

McMillan will fill the position left vacant last February with the death of Radford S. Hall. David O. Appleton, editor of the association's magazine, "The American Cattle Producer", has been acting secretary. McMillan will assume his new duties in August. His appointment is subject to formal confirmation by the association's 235-man executive committee, representing the 29 affiliated state cattle organizations.

McMillan, a native of Fort Collins, Colo., has been with Swift's Agricultural Research Department since 1954. Previously he had served with the Colorado Extension Service as county agent in Sedgwick and Conejos counties and as assistant 4-H leader in Denver county. He is a 1948 graduate of Colorado State University. He also served on the CSU resident staff before joining Swift. He was a Navy lieutenant in the Pacific theater during World War II.

Milburn said that McMillan has gained wide acquaintance among livestockmen of the nation and "is familiar with the problems confronting livestock producers and feeders."

McMillan is married to the former Jardell Hollier of Lake Charles, La., and they have one son, Brett, 3. They now live at Clarendon Hills, Ill. He is the son of the late Mr. and Mrs. Charles McMillan of Fort Collins. A brother, Lawrence, is assistant state 4-H club leader for Colorado. Another brother, Chester, is in the abstract business in Raton, N. Mex.

#

Portion of news release announcing the hiring of Bill McMillan as Executive Secretary of American National Cattlemen's Association.

turned all night and by morning had decided I should quit planning on working for ANCA the rest of my life. I should put my mind to thinking about what the California job would entail and consider what working for one Mr. J Edgar Dick would be like. At breakfast, we quickly decided that I had nothing to lose by being interviewed for the job.

When I got to work, I immediately talked to Bill and told him that I had decided to interview for the job. I called Ed to say I'd talk to him, then tried to get my mind back on packing up for the convention. On the way to Dallas, Lyle told me a few interesting stories about Ed and suggested that he might not be the easiest guy to work for. He did think California was one of the best among the state affiliates and was a great opportunity, provided Ed didn't wait too long to retire.

Lyle then told me about what he thought was then a more important cattle organization in California than the CCA. It was the California Beef Council, managed by a mutual acquaintance named Walt Rodman. This semi-independent organization had been formed in 1954 and was funded by legislation passed by the California legislature. The law required the livestock auctions in the state to collect ten-cents on each head of cattle they sold and remit it to the beef council to be used for the promotion of beef in the state. This council was governed by a board of directors appointed by the governor. The organization's budget was secure because the number of cattle sold annually was fairly constant and large enough to generate a lot of money. The concept had been kicked around in quite a few states, but California was the first one to pass enabling legislation. The whole idea of beef councils was divisive within ANCA affiliates, because some states felt it was a threat to the National Livestock and Meat Board, which operated on voluntary funding from all segments of the industry, was well established and had a policy of not using any of its funds for direct advertising. Beef councils, however, believed strongly in advertising generic beef directly to consumers through the popular media.

The California Cattlemen's Association and the South Dakota Stock Growers Association were probably the strongest proponents of a national beef council. The affiliates in Texas, Oklahoma, Kansas and New Mexico were the ones that most

THE UNIVERSITY OF WISCONSIN
COLLEGE OF AGRICULTURE

Madison 6

DEPARTMENT OF VETERINARY SCIENCE

May 5, 1959

Mr. Roy W. Lilley
Assistant Executive Secretary
American National Cattlemen's Assoc.
801 East 17th Avenue
Denver, Colorado

Dear Mr. Lilley:

 Enclosed is a list of delegates who make up the representation of the National Brucellosis Committee---those who attended the Denver meeting are not included. If and when the minutes of the Denver meeting are mailed, it is my hope that these men who's names appear on the list can receive a copy of such minutes or proceedings.

 I want you to know that it was a real pleasure to work with you on the Denver meeting. It is my hope that things will not get out of hand entirely.

Sincerely,

Sam McNutt

S. H. McNutt
Professor of Veterinary Science

SHM:dmh

A letter concerning a Brucellosis committee meeting while I was holding down the Fort after Rad died.

strongly felt that beef councils competed with and even threatened the National Livestock and Meat Board. This issue was just gaining steam about the time Bill McMillan came to work for ANCA, but like beef grading and brucellosis, it was an issue that triggered much discussion within the industry for years to come.

When I got to my room after Lyle and I had finished getting the staff office set up and had dinner at the coffee shop, I found a message on my phone from Ed Dick asking me to give him call. He confirmed that he had set up our breakfast meeting in one of the hotel's small meeting rooms for 6:30 the next morning. I told him I would be there, hung up the telephone and wondered what I was getting myself into. On the one hand, I enjoyed everything about my current job, but on the other I faced the reality that my future there was not what it had once been. I finally decided to just enjoy the interview, went to bed and slept surprisingly well.

I was impressed by the fact that Ed had ordered the most expensive breakfast entrée on the menu, Eggs Benedict, something I had never tasted. He introduced me to his president and first vice president and proceeded to tell me what a progressive and effective organization the California Cattlemen's Association was. Since I had heard from several sources that the CCA was highly respected in California, and I already knew it was one of the two or three most influential state affiliates, I felt confident that he wasn't selling me a bill of goods. He said that they had not approached anyone else for the job, and if the interview went well they were quite interested in hiring me based on the reputation I had already established, particularly since Rad had died.

I asked several questions about their office, which I knew was located in downtown San Francisco, and his staff. He said it was an unpretentious office and that he had only two people working for him currently, a bookkeeper and a secretary. He said he lived down the peninsula from San Francisco in Menlo Park and generally rode the commuter train to work. He said he planned to immediately hand me the job of editing their monthly magazine, "The California Cattleman," and would involve me in every aspect of his work because he planned to retire in two or three years. The prospect of having full responsibility for the magazine caused me some misgivings, but the reassurance that he planned to retire before too long was what I wanted to hear. When I brought up the subject of salary they didn't make me any offer, so I said I would need at least $100 per month more than I was now receiving, which was about $450 as I recall. Ed responded that they probably couldn't pay me that much, but said he got a one-month salary bonus at year's end and I could probably expect one my second year. This appealed to me even though I had just learned that bonuses were not a sure thing. By 8:00 a.m. I needed to get to work and we agreed in principle that I would take the job. We agreed to meet with Bill right after the convention to work out a transition. I obviously didn't have Bill's negotiating skills.

I called my folks that night and told them I had tentatively accepted the job and planned to try to negotiate a starting date no sooner than midsummer so we could get things squared away on the farm. I felt guilty about leaving since there was all the work Dad and I could both handle waiting for us every day, but as always Mom and Dad supported me. Later that day, I had a few minutes to visit with Bill and he agreed that it would be best if we put off the time of my departure to some time in the summer.

The Executive Committee always met ahead of the convention and, among other things, approved a budget for the following year. I had hoped for a raise, because I knew my handling of affairs since Rad's death had been appreciated. I ended up getting a $50 a month raise and learned later that Bill had recommended no raise whatsoever for me since I was going to be leaving the Association in six months. The person who told me this said that Sam Hyatte, an ANCA past president from Wyoming, had gone to bat for me and pushed through the $50 raise. I ended up making my resignation official as of August 1, and I agreed to start work in California on August 15. I can't remember whether I got any vacation pay.

39

Ingrid

Bill made a great first impression at the Dallas convention with his rousing initial report as Executive Vice President. He had a wonderful smile and engaging personality and was an exceptional speaker. He already knew most of our leadership and quickly won over the general membership. One matter caused some internal stress. Our newly elected president, Jack Milburn of Grass Range, Montana, had supported the executive secretary of the Montana Stock Growers Association for Bill's job and they had gotten off on the wrong foot with each other. Under our bylaws, the elected president was the titular head of the association and appointed all the committee members and their chairman. As Jack began this process, some tensions arose. I think Bill didn't think Jack gave him enough input and Jack thought Bill didn't have enough experience to be as involved as Rad might have been.

Over the years, Rad had put together an extensive list of members in the respective states whom he thought had the qualifications needed to be the committee chairman. The previous year, we had gone over that list thoroughly before committee chairmen were picked, and then Rad let me sit in as he and the president made the selections. When Jack arrived at the office for their meeting, Bill took him into his office and shut the door that led into my office, so I knew that me being involved in my boss's activities had come to an abrupt end.

It didn't take long for Bill to stamp his own management style on the office. He didn't concern himself much with the nuts and bolts of routine activities like dues solicitation, membership recruitment and the manner in which we handled mailings, but insisted that any mail leaving the office on such matters would go out over his signature. Also, Rad's habit of letting me read all of his mail was reversed as I prepared routine letters for Bill to sign. I soon learned to occasionally drop in his favorite phrases such as "relative to."

Cow Pony Corral

By Roy Lilley

Roy Lilley

Because it's October — and that means hunting season — I've got to figure out some way to tie this column to my favorite hobby.

In the first place, it is obvious that hunting deer or elk would be a lot less fun without the services of a horse to pack you in and your game out. Also, a mountain horse is better at spotting game than the average hunter (especially a nearsighted one like yours truly).

There are a few problems that occasionally occur when you're hunting on horseback, however. I once owned a gelding that was the most lonesome thing you ever saw. If you weren't with another horse or two, Rex was liable to get homesick and start whinnying at any moment, preferably just before you came over a ridge that brought the next likely hillside into view.

However, not all horses are uncooperative. I remember one time when I got a fairly big buck a long way from any help. My joy over such luck was short-lived when I thought about getting the thing on my horse. The buck was lying on a steep side-hill and I finally maneuvered old Zephyr under a ledge in a gully, dragged the buck downhill to this ledge and right over onto my patient and understanding horse.

Still another horse pulled the goofiest trick yet. I had been hunting on foot and shot a little buck a couple of miles from the ranch. I dressed him out late in the afternoon and walked back home. The next morning I saddled a young gelding and rode back to the deer. The colt didn't see the carcass until I was right up on it, and then when he did he snorted and started to buck. After finally getting his head pulled up I led him up to the deer, hoisted it up on his back and tied it on with the stirrups and saddle strings. I led the colt (with the deer perched precariously on the saddle) back to the ranch, and he never so much as looked back at it.

Bill and I went to lunch together on occasion, but we didn't have too much in common to talk about. I finally realized that I was spilling my guts about myself and wasn't learning anything about him in return. He had no interest in philosophical conversations or discussing how he came to conclusions about things. As one might expect, the staff was having problems adjusting to Bill's style. We found ourselves rolling our eyes when he prefaced a change in procedures by saying, "This is the way it's done at Swift." I found myself losing enthusiasm for my work, and even though I never argued with him, I found myself using passive resistance when following through on some of his ideas that I didn't particularly like.

Fairly soon after the convention, Lyle, Bill, and Ed Dick collaborated on a news release announcing my departure for the California Cattlemen's Association and the opening at ANCA for my job. I don't remember much about the applications that came in, but I'm certain that Bill knew just the kind of replacement he wanted and the choice had been entirely left up to him. He winnowed the applications down to three and then interviewed and hired a well-qualified man about my age from Texas named Dudley Campbell. Dudley and I became good friends during the several weeks that our tenure at ANCA overlapped and he was well received by all the staff.

Sometime in early spring, we had received an invitation from the Boy Scouts of America to participate in the jamboree they held every four years, with an educational display about the cattle industry. The jamboree is a huge event attracting thousands of Boy Scouts from all over the nation. This year it was to be held in a rolling grass pasture about one-quarter square mile just east of the Air Force Academy, north of Colorado Springs. The land was owned by Rex Bennett. Rex and his bother, Hugh, best known as a quarter horse breeder and ex-champion (P)RCA Rodeo champion bulldogger, were both prominent ranchers in the area. Lyle thought it was a great opportunity to reach a large number of boys who often became leaders in their respective communities, with a positive message about the importance of the cattle industry to the US economy. He asked me to support him in talking Bill into taking part. Bill wasn't particularly enthusiastic about the idea at first, but when I mentioned who the person furnishing the ground for the Jubilee was, he decided to have us look into it. He had me call Rex and I set up an appointment to meet him for lunch in Colorado Springs. It turned out that Rex liked the idea and we kicked around a few ideas about what we might do. It seemed that the various educational displays would be set up on the perimeter of the pasture, while the pup tents the Boy Scouts would sleep in, along with several big tents for a dining hall, administrative area and latrine, would be set up in the middle. We came up with the idea of a couple of corrals with a modern Hereford steer and a Texas Longhorn steer placed side by side as a live, visual demonstration of the progress the industry had made since the trail drive days. Rex said he could probably put together a local committee of ranchers to build the corrals and perhaps furnish the material. I mentioned that the dude ranch I used to work at had an old-fashioned chuck wagon that might look appropriate parked next to the corral. I took these ideas back to Bill and he told Lyle and me to go ahead and handle the whole project. I called Bob Swan at Trail Creek Ranch that night and asked him if I could borrow their chuck wagon. He said it was fine with him, if I could figure a way to get it down to the jamboree and back to the ranch safely.

The next weekend, I drove up to the ranch. Bob and I thought we could load the chuck wagon on the trailer we used to haul bales and chain it down securely enough to make the trip. As it was getting close to noon, their new wrangler came riding in with a couple of dudes in tow. I couldn't believe my eyes. The wrangler was a beautiful blonde girl who looked completely at home in the saddle. When they rode up to the barn and dismounted, Bob introduced me to Ingrid, and I made some inane statement about being replaced by someone so much better looking. The dudes walked to the house with Bob and I helped Ingrid unsaddle the horses and lead them into their stalls for their noon feed of grain. I had the feeling that Bob and Ruby had purposely not told me anything about their new wrangler, so they could enjoy my reaction when I saw her the first time.

Since it was Saturday, Ingrid had the afternoon off and I was suddenly in no hurry to get home after dinner. As we visited in the living room I learned that Ingrid Arko had come from Germany to La Junta, Colorado with her mother and stepfather when she was eight years old. She graduated from high school there and attended the junior college in Lamar for one year. Her interest in horses had developed when she got acquainted with a man who owned a fairly large ranch not far from La Junta, and she worked for him several summers. She said she had run barrels for the junior college rodeo team and then worked for the telephone company in Denver. She had a very outgoing personality, perfect for the job she had, and as I realized when I thought about it later, loved to be the center of attention.

Bob and Ruby invited me to stay for supper and offered to let me stay in the bunkhouse, if I wanted to spend the night. Even though I knew there was work to be done at the farm, I took them up on their offer and called the folks and told them I wouldn't be getting home till about noon on Sunday. We had a leisurely breakfast Sunday morning and I brought Bob and Ruby up to date on my plans to take a job in California. After breakfast, I continued the fascinating process of getting acquainted with

Ingrid. She told me she had some Gypsy blood and was good at reading people's fortunes with a deck of cards. She asked me if I would like for her to read mine and, of course I did, even though I wasn't the least bit inclined to believe in such things. Later that morning, she took me out to a cage she had built by the barn to feed a lame magpie she had rescued and was nursing back to health. I was impressed with her gift for gently handling and feeding the bird. I don't know if it was a case of love at first sight, but there is no doubt that I was smitten.

About 10:00 a.m., I headed back to the farm after telling Bob I would call and let him know when I would be coming up for the chuck wagon and trailer. I got home in time to have Sunday dinner with the folks, and Dad and I spent the afternoon catching up on farm work.

The next morning at work, I told Lyle I had made arrangements to get the chuck wagon. In the meanwhile, Lyle had been working on a script for the presentation we would be making to each group of Boy Scouts as they came by our display. A few weeks later, I went back to the jamboree and met Rex, who had already unloaded the poles and fence posts for the corral. He had rounded up several ranchers to help with the construction of the corral, one of whom was Bob Norris, who owned a ranch just to the north in the Black Forest area. He was a tall, dark and handsome cowboy who later became one of the Marlborough Men. We all pitched in and had the corral built by suppertime. We then drove to a restaurant at an intersection just north of Colorado Springs and Rex bought the crew supper.

A few days before the jamboree started, I had to get back up to the ranch to get the chuck wagon. Upon arriving I hooked the trailer to the folks' mid-sized Studebaker and backed it up to the chuck wagon so Bob and I could load it with a little help from the Ford tractor. We chained it down securely and I started for Colorado Springs. The Studebaker wasn't really adequate for pulling this kind of load and I had a nerve-racking trip. If I wasn't careful going down hills, the trailer would start swerving. I wasn't prepared for this and the first time it happened when I decelerated, the trailer nearly overturned. I managed to finally get to the jamboree site, park the trailer by the corral and get back home after dark, a nervous wreck.

Lyle got the idea that it would be more authentic if we were sitting on a horse by the display while we were giving our little spiel. One of the ranchers furnished us a nice gentle old horse and I hauled some hay and grain down for him along with a saddle, blanket and bridle. We were able to turn the horse loose at night with the Hereford and keep him tied up all the time we were using him during the day. Lyle hadn't figured on the fact that we had to clean up the messes the horse made several times a day. He commuted back and forth from home every day, but I slept in a bedroll by the corral at night, ate three meals a day with the Boy Scouts in their big mess tent and used their shower facility that was set up much like a shower point in Korea.

The second day, we were told just a few hours in advance that President Eisenhower was going to visit the facility and to be prepared for his arrival at any time. Shortly after noon, he showed up in a convertible and drove around the entire group of displays waving, so Lyle and I got a fairly close up look at him. After the jamboree ended we had to get everything back in the shape that it had been, and Bob Norris took possession of all the poles and posts after we had dismantled the corral.

I wasn't looking forward to pulling the chuck wagon back to the ranch and I made sure I got an early start the next morning. I managed to avoid swerving but had trouble getting up the hills with my under-powered vehicle as I gained the 2000 feet in altitude from Fort Collins to the ranch. When I arrived in an overheated car, Bob helped me unload the chuck wagon and unhitch the trailer. I thanked him for the generous gesture but didn't tell him that it had not been as easy getting it back unharmed as I had hoped. I spent the night with them again and enjoyed another evening with Ingrid.

I had gone to the ranch every weekend I could get away ever since I had met Ingrid. I would usually head out from home after work on Friday, without any supper, stop at Ted's Place for a hamburger, malt and a couple of six-packs of beer and be at the ranch before dark. On Saturday mornings, I usually went out for a ride with Ingrid and the dudes or helped Ingrid clean the barn. In the afternoon, Rob Flullerton, whe son-in-law of Dick Brackenbery who managed the lower ranch, often dropped by and drank beer with Ingrid and me. After supper, we would visit with the dudes and continue to get acquainted; very well acquainted.

The Estes Park rodeo was held the weekend following Frontier Days and I got it into my head to enter the saddle bronc riding, obviously to try to impress you know who. I wired in my entry fee and dropped by the office of the Rodeo Cowboys Association during my lunch hour on Monday to pay my dues. I didn't tell my folks about entering the rodeo. I drove up to the ranch as usual on Friday evening and the next morning Ingrid and I drove to Estes Park, where I found I had drawn one of Earl Anderson's best horses, a stocking legged sorrel called Pretty Socks. He wasn't the hardest horse to ride, but was considered a very good draw because he jumped and kicked just right. I managed to get him started out of the chute and eked out a qualified ride. If I had drawn him in 1956, I probably would have won a go-round, but I didn't spur him nearly as well as I would have then. Earl's son, Jackie, picked me up after the ride and commented that he hadn't seen me for a long time as he dropped me off on the ground. Of course that was because I hadn't been on a bucking horse in four years. The next day I drew my old nemesis, Pinto Pete, whom I had drawn when I just started rodeoing, and he bucked me off hard again. The fact that I was in good shape from working on the farm was the only reason I didn't make a complete fool of myself. Of course all my old rodeo friends were quite impressed with Ingrid and I enjoyed a good bit of kidding. We stayed for the rodeo dance that night and got back to the ranch about two in the morning on Monday.

Ingrid and I had gotten more serious and the date for my departure to California approached, so we had to give some serious thought to our future. We decided that it was best that I go ahead to California, get settled into my new job and let her finish her season working at the ranch. I could send for her if our feelings for each other hadn't changed. We promised to write each other regularly.

In the meanwhile, the folks and I had been making plans for dealing with my departure as it related to the farm. We tore up the agreement we had made concerning my buying an interest in it and Dad assured me he could handle the normal chores and would get the hay put up on shares so he didn't have to deal with the mowing, raking and bale hauling. We managed to get the second cutting put up and in the stack before my departure date.

I had long felt that Mom and Dad deserved to have a better place to live than the patched up little farm house we now occupied. It took some doing with help from Mom, but I talked Dad into applying for a Farmers Home Administration loan on the farm to build a new house just north of the one we lived in. The request was approved and the interest rate for the expanded loan remained at 4%. They picked a plan for a simple frame, two-bedroom, one bath, house with a fireplace, an over-sized attached one-car garage, and a full basement with one finished bedroom and second bath. They ended up with a livable house for about $14,000 and Mom lived in it with Dad until he died in 1978, and then was able to enjoy it for another thirteen years until her death.

September, 1960

ROY LILLEY VISITING WITH BOY SCOUTS

Roy Lilley Joins CCA Staff

Roy W. Lilley, Secretary of the American National Cattlemen's Association, joined the staff of the CCA last month as Assistant Secretary. Lilley, northern Colorado ranch and farm native, began his duties with the American National in November, 1956.

An outstanding 1952 graduate of the Colorado A and M College, Lilley majored in animal husbandry, served as president of the school's Livestock Club and of the Rodeo Club.

Lilley, 30, is the son of Mr. and Mrs. Charles W. Lilley of Broomfield. His father is a past president of the Colorado Cattlemen's Association. His greater grandfather, John G. Lilley, was a founder and early president of the Colorado Cattlemen's Association.

A top collegiate and amateur rodeo performer, Lilley won the amateur bronc riding title at Cheyenne Frontier Days in 1952 and ranked second in all three riding events and the "all-around" of the National Intercollegiate Rodeo Association.

Several weeks prior to coming to California, Roy was in charge of a unique exhibit of beef cattle production for the 50th Aniversary Boy Scout Jamboree near Colorado Springs.

Nearly all of the 56,000 participants had a chance to compare modern beef production methods with the "movie-TV concept" and to ask thousands of questions about livestock. Many of the Scouts had never seen—let alone petted a cow or a horse before.

The picture shows Roy on the white horse and a Scout feeding the animal.

Article in September California Cattleman magazine announcing my joining the CCA staff.

40

J. Edgar Dick

    In early August, I loaded my little Rambler American with my clothes and a few other belongings and started my journey west with a mixture of excitement over the new job, guilt for leaving my folks to look after the farm and regret that I didn't know how soon I would see Ingrid again. Before I left I called the president of the Western States Meat Packers Association, whom I had met at several meetings, and asked where might be a good place to stay in that area until I got an apartment. He suggested I stay in a hotel in downtown San Mateo. I got to San Francisco in the afternoon of my second day of driving, stayed on the freeway, crossed the Oakland Bridge, went south on the Del Camino Highway down the peninsula to San Mateo and checked into the hotel.
    I stayed there for several days looking for an apartment. On my second day there I had an experience that I wasn't prepared for. After an afternoon of looking at furnished apartments, I returned to San Mateo and stopped by the bar next door to the hotel for a before dinner drink. I sat down at the bar and ordered a martini. As I was sitting there sipping my drink and reviewing the apartments I had looked at in my mind, my knee brushed up against the person sitting next to me. I looked up, apologized to an ordinary looking guy about my age and turned back to my drink. In short order my knee touched his again and I didn't recall having moved my leg. I looked up and he gave me the kind of come-hither look I never had the good fortune to get from girls. Suddenly a light bulb went on in my head, and I gulped down my drink and bolted out of the place. It was my first and only, to my knowledge, contact with a gay person until years later.
    A couple of days before I had to start work, I found a one-bedroom furnished apartment I thought I could afford. It was in a slightly rundown part of Burlingame just north of San Mateo on the Del Camino Highway. It was not very far from the commuter train that ran up and down the peninsula from San Jose to San Francisco. I made a one-month deposit on it and moved

in. The first day at work I drove my car to the office. I took the elevator up to the office on the sixth floor and found two young women already at work. Ed's secretary and office manager, Peg, introduced herself and a pretty young Chinese woman, Mary, who was the bookkeeper. The office was one large room with a big desk in the middle that was used by Ed, and two smaller ones on either side used by Peg and Mary. They had evidently moved some furniture around and pushed a small desk against an inside wall for me. It was a far cry from my big office in Denver with a door out to the main office.

Ed, who lived south of San Mateo in Menlo Park, came in about 9:00 a.m. He said he nearly always rode the commuter train and arrived either about 7:30 a.m. or 9:00 a.m. I had already learned that I could catch a train from San Mateo that would get me to the office by 8 a.m. after a twenty-minute walk from the downtown train station. I continued to drive for a few days before I got up my nerve to ride the train. Within a couple of weeks I was joining hundreds of other commuters on the trip to San Francisco, squeezed into a narrow seat with the San Francisco Chronicle on my lap in what was called a commuter fold.

Ed seemed just as anxious as Rad had been to involve me in all of his duties, but was not nearly as patient a teacher. He and the young women were involved in putting the California Cattlemen Magazine together the first week I got there, and it was obvious that he didn't understand the job very well and probably hated it. He said he expected me to take it over right away! I had watched Dave Appleton edit the American Cattle Producer and had written a regular column for it, as well as a few feature articles, but he had never involved me in making it printer ready.

I soon learned to continue putting out just as bad a magazine as we already had when I got there, but I hated it also. Ed immediately put my name on the masthead as editor. Soon after we mailed my first issue to all the state affiliates and ANCA, in addition to our members, I received a marked up copy back from Lyle Liggette with more constructive criticism than I could hardly deal with. One of the many things he suggested, using more white space around the copy and ads, was something Ed would not stand for. He insisted on squeezing every word possible on each page with small headlines. Pictures, which members loved, were kept to a minimum because we had to pay by the square inch to have plates made. Most frustrating of all, he wanted it put out on time, but didn't want to catch me working on it. As soon as I came to realize that Ed really didn't care what the magazine looked like, I gritted my teeth, got it out as best I could and proceeded to take the opportunity to learn all I could from him about managing a state cattle association.

The California Cattlemen's Association was governed by a board of directors elected from each of its county affiliates, which were semi-autonomous, but worked closely with the parent organization. In order to keep tabs on specific issues of concern in each county and in turn keep local members apprised of the many issues the cattle industry was dealing with at the state and national level, the CCA had developed a tradition of meeting with them annually. These meetings took the form of a tour of each county association, meeting on consecutive days so that a similar educational program could be held at each meeting over a minimal length of time. The affiliates of the ANCA were an independent bunch and I admired Ed's organizational skills getting these local groups to work with him coordinating their meetings. As I got to know members individually, I found that they liked to joke about Ed's obvious idiosyncrasies, but greatly respected him.

Most issues discussed at the panels were similar to ones I had been involved with at ANCA, but one burning issue was unique to California and it divided this state right across the middle, north and south, into competing camps. The state legislature was just beginning to thrash out the complex issues involved in diverting water from northern California where there was usually a surplus, to the south where it certainly was not, but where the larger number of people lived. Most of the cattle were in the northern half of the state and a large majority of the CCA members were opposed to the diversion. My knowledge of Colorado politics surrounding the diversion of water from the under-populated western half of the state to the eastern slope made me think we were fighting a losing battle over this issue

As soon as the tour was over, I found myself with nothing to do on Saturdays and Sundays. Since I had rejoined the Rodeo Cowboys Association, I decided to enter the saddle bronc riding in some of the rodeos close to San Francisco. I found that there were relatively few saddle bronc riders on the West Coast, so I thought that I had a chance to make some money. I managed to ride my first two horses, but was goose egged out of the chute on both of them at Willows. After it happened the second time, I asked the judge how he could have "egged" me when I had my spurs well over the points of the horses' shoulders when I passed the chute gate. He said, "Yeah, but your toes weren't pointed down." That was a new one for me. Not enough people had made qualified rides to fill the four slots that were paid, so the balance was paid to the remaining entrants as "ground money," the first I had received since I started competing twelve years before. I qualified on both of my horses at Salinas, but it was a much more competitive rodeo and I was well out of the money. At Plymouth, I drew the stock contractor's best saddle bronc and was dumped unceremoniously on my head about the fourth jump out of the chute.

I soon started to get claustrophobia in the office with three people looking over my shoulder and found living by myself in a small apartment not much fun. I was also getting lonesome. Then Ingrid called one night crying and mumbling that she didn't know what she was going to do. Being better at seeking solutions than I am at comforting, I said that whatever the problem is we would deal with it. She finally blurted out, "I'm pregnant"! Strangely enough I took that as good news. I said that I would talk to my boss the next morning and try to get a few days off from my not-yet-earned one week vacation. We decided to meet in Denver just as soon as I could get there. The next few days are a blur in my memory; Ingrid was living at home by that time and took a bus from La Junta to Denver. I had reserved her a room at the Shirley Savoy Hotel in downtown Denver for the night. I flew to Denver and joined her there at about 8:00 p.m.

I don't remember how we got to the farm the next day, but after we explained the situation to my surprised parents, my pragmatic Dad and I worked out a plan. We decided we would borrow the Studebaker, drive to La Junta to talk to Ingrid's folks, and if it was agreeable with them, rent a U-Haul trailer for Ingrid's things and drive back to San Francisco. This left Mom and Dad with just one car, but they did have a pickup at the farm for a second vehicle if needed. We agreed that Ingrid and I would get married in Nevada as we drove back to California.

When we got to La Junta, Ingrid's folks took the news with surprising calm. When we went into the house I confirmed what Ingrid had told me: her mother, Ruth, was an excellent artist and had been trained in classical painting in Berlin before the war. Both her parents spoke with a marked accent and talked to each other in German most of the time. I took an immediate liking to Ingrid's stepfather. He was tall, extremely thin, had poor posture and appeared to be at least fifteen years older than Ruth. One painting showed Ingrid in a wedding dress holding a bouquet of flowers. It was just one of so many that I simply didn't pay much attention to it at the time. When I asked Ruth about it later it she explained that Ingrid had gotten married right out of high school to the son of a car dealer in La Junta, and they had succeeded in getting the marriage annulled after a couple of weeks, for reasons I didn't completely understand. I told her that Ingrid had never bothered to tell me and the subject was dropped.

One of the most interesting things about Ingrid was the story of how she had come to this country from Germany with Ruth and Ciro (Ciril's nick name) when she was eight years old, shortly after the war ended. She told me Ruth was a war widow trying to look after the two of them the best she could in war torn-Berlin when she met Ciro, who was a displaced person who had fought with the underground in Yugoslavia. Because of his status he was able to qualify for a passport to emigrate to either Australia or the United States and could bring Ruth and Ingrid with him after he married Ruth. I always suspected it was a marriage of convenience that grew into one in which they coexisted quite happily. They had originally thought they wanted to go to Australia but ended up on the quota to the United States. I learned later that acquaintances who were shipped to Australia wrote to them and said they were lucky to have come to America where upward mobility for immigrants was much more possible. The Catholic Church, which had sponsored the Arkos in La Junta, helped them find a small apartment and located a janitor's job for Ciro. Well-educated before the war, he was able to apply for and obtain a job as a math teacher at the high school a few years later. time and took a bus from La Junta to Denver. I had reserved her a room at the Shirley Savoy Hotel in downtown Denver for the night. I flew to Denver and joined her there at about 8:00 p.m.

I don't remember how we got to the farm the next day, but after we explained the situation to my surprised parents, my pragmatic Dad and I worked out a plan. We decided we would borrow the Studebaker, drive to La Junta to talk to Ingrid's folks, and if it was agreeable with them, rent a U-Haul trailer for Ingrid's things and drive back to San Francisco. This left Mom and Dad with just one car, but they did have a pickup at the farm for a second vehicle if needed. We agreed that Ingrid and I would get married in Nevada as we drove back to California.

When we got to La Junta, Ingrid's folks took the news with surprising calm. When we went into the house I confirmed what Ingrid had told me: her mother, Ruth, was an excellent artist and had been trained in classical painting in Berlin before the war. Both her parents spoke with a marked accent and talked to each other in German most of the time. I took an immediate liking to Ingrid's stepfather. He was tall, extremely thin, had poor posture and appeared to be at least fifteen years older than Ruth. One painting showed Ingrid in a wedding dress holding a bouquet of flowers. It was just one of so many that I simply didn't pay much attention to it at the time. When I asked Ruth about it later it she explained that Ingrid had gotten married right out of high school to the son of a car dealer in La Junta, and they had succeeded in getting the marriage annulled after a couple of weeks, for reasons I didn't completely understand. I told her that Ingrid had never bothered to tell me and the subject was dropped.

One of the most interesting things about Ingrid was the story of how she had come to this country from Germany with Ruth and Ciro (Ciril's nick name) when she was eight years old, shortly after the war ended. She told me Ruth was a war widow trying to look after the two of them the best she could in war torn-Berlin when she met Ciro, who was a displaced person who had fought with the underground in Yugoslavia. Because of his status he was able to qualify for a passport to emigrate to either Australia or the United States and could bring Ruth and Ingrid with him after he married Ruth. I always suspected it was a marriage of convenience that grew into one in which they coexisted quite happily. They had originally thought they wanted to go to Australia but ended up on the quota to the United States. I learned later that acquaintances who were shipped to Australia wrote to them and said they were lucky to have come to America where upward mobility for immigrants was much more possible. The Catholic Church, which had sponsored the Arko's in La Junta, helped them find a small apartment and located a janitor's job for Ciro. Well-educated before the war, he was able to apply for and obtain a job as a math teacher at the high school a few years later.

The next morning, I rented a U-Haul trailer and we stuffed all of Ingrid's things into it, the last of which was her Italian motor scooter. We made it all the way to Ely, Nevada on US Highway 50 by about 9 PM after a long hard drive. The next morning, we went to the courthouse and got our marriage license. We then went back to our room and I put on my suit while she changed into a nice dress. I bought a corsage and we headed for the justice of the peace and were married.

I needed to get back to the office as soon as possible, so we drove hard the next day and made it to our apartment by dark. We unloaded the trailer the next morning and while Ingrid unpacked, I returned it to the local U-Haul dealer and went to the office for the rest of the day. It was a stressful beginning for what probably was the happiest six months of our marriage.

Ingrid soon turned my bachelor's quarters into a cozy home. She quickly assumed the role of what she called a house frau. I often picked up a bouquet of cut flowers, which were readily available from street vendors, to give to Ingrid when I got home. She made an appointment with an obstetrician in Burlingame and we prepared for the changes in our life that would arrive with the baby. She had an easy pregnancy with no morning sickness, however was in labor for nearly twenty-four hours. Fortunately, the delivery went off without a hitch and she had what I was told was a beautiful baby girl. She was the first baby I had ever seen immediately after its birth and she certainly didn't look beautiful to me. We enjoyed picking a name for her and settled on Elizabeth Ruth.

New grandma Ruth made arrangements to fly out as soon as she heard the baby had arrived in spite of Ingrid's objections, and we put her up on the couch. About the third day she and Ingrid got into a squabble over what seemed to me a minor issue and Ruth headed back to La Junta in a huff. We had attended a class together on caring for a new baby, which covered all the new chores, including formula preparation, feeding. bottle washing, changing diapers and bathing the newborn, and we felt prepared for the many new challenges that arrived with Elizabeth.

I thought Ingrid might hit it off well with Ed and she did. She charmed him by not taking him too seriously and appealing to his dry sense of humor. After the tour Ed had involved me in his current big project, which was writing what he called a "white paper" outlining the CCA's position on beef grading because he knew I had worked extensively with the beef grading committee at ANCA. He believed that his having served as a meat inspector for the USDA gave him a perfect background for taking the lead in recommending specific changes in the current system. The main thrust of our recommendations was to require less marbling for the carcasses of younger cattle. He had me present our proposal at the Western States Meat Packers Association convention in San Francisco where it was well received. We then sent it to the ANCA and its affiliates and released it to the media. The changes we proposed became the basis for the discussion that continued for several years with the cooperation of the USDA's Director of Grading Service. I knew that Ed was going to take our beef inspection proposal to the 1961 national convention and try to push through a resolution supporting it. I hoped he would take me along, however he said we didn't have enough money in the travel budget, so I missed my first ANCA convention in four years.

I was adapting to my new office environment, but Ingrid and I felt cramped in our little apartment, which was right on a main highway with the noise that entails. We immediately started looking up and down the peninsula for a little house to renovate. We soon stumbled on a new subdivision of modest homes between the Del Camino highway and San Francisco Bay on the east side of San Mateo. It was built on land that had been reclaimed from a marshy area. We were able to rent a two-bedroom, one-bath house that had a fireplace and a modest sized yard for only about $25 more a month than we were paying for our apartment, but even that stretched our budget. It was close to the San Mateo station and I rode the commuter train nearly every day, joining the parade of briefcase toting, well-dressed office workers walking the mile from the station to downtown San Francisco through skid row. The drug culture was already well-established in the city, but the hippies were just beginning to move in.

Shortly after starting to work, I asked Ed if he had any children. Peg had already told me that he had been divorced some time ago and had a new wife. Ed replied that he had one son and that he was crippled. He didn't say anything further and immediately changed the subject. For some reason, I had a vision of a man with an amputated leg. I learned years later that the son was no other than Philip K. Dick, the well-known science fiction writer, who had been a part of the drug scene in San Francisco. I learned from the internet that he had damaged his health with LSD and other drugs and had died quite young. I had been a science fiction fan since my brother Charlie brought his first copy of a science fiction pulp magazine when I was in the fourth grade. Even though I had read a good many of Philip Dick's articles, the possible connection to Ed had never entered my mind until years later when I looked him up on Wikipedia.

Ingrid and I were amazed by the wonderful winter climate in San Francisco and often drove to the beach to watch the sea lions or took the beautiful drive up to the Crystal Lakes in the mountains just south of San Francisco. I was not enjoying my work nearly as much as I had in Denver, but it seemed obvious that Ed was grooming me for his job, and I had the prospect of being able to be the executive officer of one of ANCA's leading affiliates in a few years. Out of the blue, in mid-March, I received a telephone call at the office from the president of the New Mexico Cattle Growers Association, John Stark. He said that their executive secretary, Horace Henning, had unexpectedly resigned and they needed to replace him in short order. I told him I certainly wasn't looking for a new job, but was flattered by the offer and would talk to my wife about it and call him that night. I had the good sense not to say anything to Ed about the call; however, no calls in that small office could be private.

As soon as I got home I told Ingrid about the call and the more we discussed it the more we realized that San Francisco was just too big a city for us. I told her the New Mexico Cattle Growers Association was a much smaller organization than the California Cattlemen's Association, but that cattle were a major part of the economy in New Mexico. To my knowledge Henning had run a good office, the headquarters was in Albuquerque and I had a good friend from my rodeo days in college named Gene Brownell living in the area. Ingrid seemed enthusiastic about the prospect and we were soon talking ourselves into going for the job. I realized that it would never pay as much as Ed was making, but I had not taken into account the high cost of living in San Francisco when I moved there, and we hoped that we might be able to get an acreage in the suburbs of Albuquerque where we could keep a couple of horses.

After supper, I called John Stark and said I would be interested if we could afford to make the move. He said he was authorized to go ahead and hire me and offered me about $50 a month more than I was currently making. I figured there was at least a $75 a month difference in cost of living, accepted the job and said we would be there in two weeks. After I hung up, I wondered if I had been a bit too hasty but Ingrid said even though she enjoyed our little house, she had figured that I had not been very happy in my work and agreed that she too was ready for a change. I told her that I would give Ed my two-week's notice first thing in the morning.

Ed came in on the later train the next morning and I immediately told him about the phone call I had received the previous day. When I said I had accepted the new job and was giving my two-week's notice, the only thing he said was that he didn't need two weeks and told me that I should be able to wind my work up by the end of the week. I knew that Ed took it as a personal affront that I wasn't taking the opportunity to step into his job after only eight months on the payroll, and I couldn't really expect any severance pay.

I spent the rest of the week doing my least favorite job, getting the April issue of the California Cattleman Magazine to the printer. I had done us both a big favor during the past month when I got his permission to look into farming the magazine out to a newly formed company that was already publishing the magazine for the Colorado Cattlemen's Association and a couple of other state affiliate's house organs. I was sure none of those magazines were making money either, and when I learned that we could negotiate for a percentage of our gross advertising receipts, I quickly realized that a guaranteed income of any amount without any costs whatsoever was a good deal for the association. Ed had not shown too much interest when I explained it, but I was not surprised to learn that he had made a deal with them shortly after I left.

WIKIPEDIA

Philip K. Dick

Philip Kindred Dick (December 16, 1928 – March 2, 1982) was an American science fiction writer. Dick explored philosophical, social, and political themes in his novels with plots dominated by monopolistic corporations, alternative universes, authoritarian governments, and altered states of consciousness. His work reflected his personal interest in metaphysics and theology, and often drew upon his life experiences in addressing the nature of reality, identity, drug abuse, schizophrenia, and transcendental experiences.

Born in Illinois before moving to California, Dick began publishing science fiction stories in the 1950s, initially finding little commercial success.[1] His 1962 alternative history novel *The Man in the High Castle* earned Dick early acclaim, including a Hugo Award for Best Novel.[2] He followed with science fiction novels such as *Do Androids Dream of Electric Sheep?* (1968) and *Ubik* (1969). His 1974 novel *Flow My Tears, the Policeman Said* won the John W. Campbell Memorial Award for best novel.[3] Following a series of religious experiences in February–March 1974, Dick's work engaged more explicitly with issues of theology, philosophy, and the nature of reality, as in such novels as *A Scanner Darkly* (1977) and *VALIS* (1981).[4] A collection of his non-fiction writing on these themes was published posthumously as *The Exegesis of Philip K. Dick* (2011). He died in 1982, at age 53, due to complications from a stroke.

In addition to 44 published novels, Dick wrote approximately 121 short stories, most of which appeared in science fiction magazines during his lifetime.[5] A variety of popular films based on his works have been produced, including *Blade Runner* (1982), *Total Recall* (adapted twice: in 1990 and in 2012), *Minority Report* (2002), *A Scanner Darkly* (2006), and *The Adjustment Bureau* (2011). In 2005, *Time* magazine named *Ubik* one of the hundred greatest English-language novels published since 1923.[6] In 2007, Dick became the first science fiction writer to be included in The Library of America series.[7][8][9][10]

Philip K. Dick

Born	Philip Kindred Dick December 16, 1928 Chicago, Illinois, United States
Died	March 2, 1982 (aged 53) Santa Ana, California, United States
Pen name	Richard Phillipps Jack Dowland
Occupation	Novelist, short story writer, essayist
Nationality	American
Period	1952–1982
Genre	Science fiction, paranoid

Top: Wikipedia article on Edgar Dick's son, Philip.
Bottom: A fairly young picture of J. Edgar Dick.

41

New Mexico

The first thing I did after accepting the job with the New Mexico Cattle Growers Association (NMCGA) was to call my old college rodeo friend, Gene Brownell, whose office was in Albuquerque. Gene worked for the Farmers Home Administration for several years as an Assistant County Supervisor in South Dakota after he graduated from Colorado A&M in 1953. After several years of that good experience, he landed a job with Travelers Insurance Company in their farm and ranch loan division, and I had heard that he had arranged the financing for several large ranch purchases in New Mexico in recent years. I was also well acquainted with his wife, Bobby Jo, and had traveled with them when we went to a rodeo in Belle Fourche, South Dakota shortly after their first child was born. When they heard we were moving to Albuquerque, they insisted that we stay with them until we found a home there.

I gladly accepted the invitation and told them we would be seeing them in a few days. We still had the folks' Studebaker and once again loaded our few belongings in a U-Haul trailer, then hitched it behind our little Rambler and headed for New Mexico. Little Elizabeth turned out to be a good traveler and we made it to Gene and Bobby Jo's home in east Albuquerque in two days. We parked the trailer in front of their house, carried our suitcases into their spare bedroom and enjoyed the nice supper Bobby Jo had prepared for us. They had a daughter who was just a baby when I traveled with them to the rodeo about five years earlier and had since added a son to the family.

We left the furniture on the trailer while we looked for a house to rent. I didn't have to report for work for about four days and it took us three of those to find a place to live: a pleasant three-bedroom, one-bath house in a fairly new subdivision in northeast Albuquerque, one of the nicer parts of town. The rent was a little more than we were paying in San Francisco, but the house was a lot bigger and was only about a mile from my office downtown.

Our friends made us feel right at home and introduced us to some other couples our age who also had rural backgrounds. The second night in town, Bobby Jo got tickets for the four of us to a Jim Reeves concert at the new City Auditorium. We left Elizabeth with their kids in the care of Bobby's mother, who lived in town. Reeves was just reaching the height of his popularity and getting to see him was a pretty big deal. We were feeling pretty good about our change in scenery.

    I reported to my new office on Monday morning. It was on the mezzanine of the Hilton Hotel—long since torn down—in downtown Albuquerque next to the office of the Executive Director of the New Mexico Liquor Dealers Association, Frank Padilla. It had two rooms, an office and big desk for me in front of a window overlooking the street, and a large outer office for the secretary and bookkeeper, with room left over for a big automatic typewriter that they used to prepare mass membership solicitations. I had been fairly well acquainted with the association's previous executive officer, Horace Henning, and certainly was well acquainted with the general duties associated with my new job. I introduced myself to the two young women in the office and they briefly explained their respective responsibilities to me. It was obvious that the one who had been Horace's secretary had pretty much run the office, and I quickly figured out that it would take some diplomacy to develop a good working relationship with her while I got my feet on the ground.

    I was well aware of the unfortunate circumstances that had led to my new job becoming available. Horace was known among his peers to be the kind of alcoholic who was able to drink nearly a fifth of whiskey a day and still effectively do his job. The problem was that recently, on occasion, he had gone on weekend binges that left him out of commission for days. He was well liked by the officers and his family had a deep connection to the association. His father had started the New Mexico Stockman Magazine, which was technically owned by the NMCGA, and it had grown to be very successful. As a fairly young man, Horace had taken over as not only as magazine editor but also as executive secretary of the association. I soon learned that I had landed in a situation exactly the opposite of what I had with the California cattlemen. The magazine had become the tail wagging the dog. I learned that five dollars from each member's dues went for a magazine subscription and the minimum dues, which most people paid, was only $10. As long as Horace was managing the association he could draw a salary from both the magazine and the association. When Horace was finally let go, his assistant editor, Parley Jensen, had applied for the job I had just filled hoping to continue in the same manner. President John Stark had explained when he first called me that the organization needed someone with professional association management experience and didn't mention the magazine. Parley was not left without a job because he assumed the editorship of the magazine. I didn't learn the rest of the story for a couple of years.

The board of directors of the New Mexico Cattle Growers Association met quarterly, and their spring meeting was held in Raton, in the north central part of the state, a few weeks after I started work. Ingrid and Elizabeth accompanied me to the meeting and they were both well received. We pinned a nametag on Elizabeth's fanny so it would be clearly visible when her mother hauled her around. Even though New Mexico had no women's auxiliary—Cow Belles—as many other states did, most wives accompanied their husbands to the meeting and Elizabeth, who at six weeks was definitely a beautiful baby, was a big hit.

The board of directors was made up of the association's past presidents, current officers, the president of the Wool Growers Association and, as I recall, members appointed by the president from each quadrant of the state. I was aware that the boards of the ANCA state affiliates were selected in a number of different ways, but New Mexico's was among the most conservative, because it would seem that an organization governed largely by its past presidents would not be the most forward looking. Still this group included some outstanding individuals who were well respected statewide, several of whom were also past presidents of the ANCA. President John Stark and his wife, Goldie, had flown in his private plane to Albuquerque from their ranch near Silver City in the far southwest corner of the state the day before the meeting and helped me prepare the agenda. When we drove home late in the afternoon following the meeting, Ingrid and I decided that I had probably gotten off to a good start in my new job.

After a couple of weeks at the office studying the organization's bylaws, trying to memorize the names of our board members and committee chairmen and looking at Horace's correspondence files, I learned that the office routine was pretty much set on automatic under the able direction of Horace's old and my new secretary. I believed that, unlike Bill McMillan, it was best to learn everything possible about a new job before making changes. Since it appeared that everything was running smoothly, I fell into the trap of letting the staff do things as they had always done, coasting on the status quo. It took a while to realize that an unsupervised office will be run at the convenience of the staff, and making things easy for the boss was an essential part of maintaining that process. I was embarrassed when our immediate past president, Buster Driggers, from Santa Rosa stopped by the office to see how I was getting along. He mentioned that he hadn't been reading anything about our organization in the Albuquerque Journal or the two livestock publications he subscribed to as much as he had in the past. As soon as he left, I called my friend, Lyle Liggette, at ANCA and asked him to send me a sample news release and the publications in New Mexico on his mailing list. He said he would be happy to do the former and that all I had to do was call the New Mexico Press Association to get a list of all the daily and weekly newspapers in the state.

I soon was putting out regular news releases to most of the media in the state as well as the Associated Press. I used the same format as Lyle and addressed myself to learning how to write a decent release. As I presented my first one to my secretary to be typed, mimeographed and mailed to selected members of the press, she wasn't too pleased. She said that Horace had always just called his news items in to the AP by phone or hired a commercial PR firm to do it. I sometimes did call my story to the AP from a pay phone on the way home from meetings, knowing they would accept the basic facts and write the item up themselves. We got our best results from the small town weekly newspapers and the livestock press, who seemed willing to pick up about anything we sent.

When I brought up the subject of soliciting new members, my secretary said that about twice a year she used the automatic typewriter to send a personal letter to everyone in the state who had a registered brand. This was a list about twelve times bigger than our membership list and included all people who owned at least some cattle because branding was compulsory under New Mexico law. She said we generally got a two or three percent return on each mailing. Since the office records showed that we had a one to four percent attrition rate each year, something like these mailings was essential just to stay even.

While talking about new members, I asked her about the shipment of pre-addressed and stamped solicitation letters from the ANCA that Horace had agreed to mail to NMCGA members that didn't already belong to the ANCA. This mailing had been prepared by our ANCA staff, when I was working for them around 1959, in exactly the same way that Horace prepared his solicitations with a personal letter signed by their president. This had worked very well for us with the strange exception of usually supportive New Mexico. She said she didn't know what I was talking about. A few weeks later I stumbled onto the answer as I was sorting through things in the rather messy storage room off my office. Back in the corner, I found box after box of the stamped letters we had sent to Horace that had never been put in the mail. The letter enclosed was now out of date and I couldn't think of a way to salvage the stamps. I ground my teeth a little.

Ingrid and I enjoyed living in Albuquerque, which at that time was probably about one-third the size of Denver and a lot smaller than San Francisco. We often got a babysitter, ate out and took in a movie. We particularly enjoyed eating at one of the long-established Mexican restaurants in the old part of Albuquerque, which were well known for their authentic Mexican food and their unique decor. Before long we started thinking about an acreage where we could keep a couple of horses like the Brownells, who had moved to Bosque Acres about a month after we rented our home. It was about twenty miles south of Albuquerque on the river, just north of the Sandia Indian reservation. Whenever we visited them on weekends, they encouraged us to think about buying one of the acreages near them that were for sale on contract. When we looked into the idea it was obvious the land was beyond our budget, and anyway I had learned from my dad that purchase contracts, or contract for deed, were not a good way to buy real estate and were, in fact, illegal in many states.

We decided there surely must be something just outside the city limits of Albuquerque that we could afford. The Rio Grande River Valley to the north and south of the city had quite a few improved acreages for sale that would have suited us, but I quickly learned there was no way we could finance them. We eventually found a nice new brick home on one acre, a couple of miles south of the city limits. It was for sale by the owner, who had built it himself only recently. We liked it and the zoning allowed us to keep horses. It also allowed septic tanks, even though there was a water table of only about four feet and a well on every acre. I asked the owner about this potential problem. He said that we were sitting so close to the Rio Grande River that the underground flow through the sandy soil was sufficient to dilute the groundwater enough to head off any health problems. We did get the well water tested and it was fine. When we started talking seriously about price and financing I mentioned I was a veteran. The owner suggested that since the house was newly built, I might be able to get a G.I. loan on it. I checked with the VA and was happily surprised to find that I might be able to do just that. I made formal application, was approved and the owner accepted an offer on the appraised value. It was a four percent, nothing down, thirty-year loan.

It was early fall before we were able to close on the house and move in. The first job I tackled was putting a woven wire fence around the house, so I could then fence the rest of the acreage for horses. There were several sawmills in the area that cut the pine timber they got from the nearby Sandia Mountains. It turned out that rough lumber would be the cheapest material I could use for the fence. I bought eight-foot four by fours for posts and eight-foot two by twos for the line fence. The ground on our acre was almost pure sand with about two inches of topsoil, so the post holes were easy to dig. By working most evenings after work till dark and on weekends, it wasn't too long before I completed the fence.

The folks were anxious to see Elizabeth, so we made arrangements to meet them one weekend at a motel in Raton about halfway between Denver and Albuquerque. By this time, Elizabeth was seven months old and a beautiful child with a wonderful disposition. The folks were delighted with her and Ingrid was amazed at how good Dad was with the baby. While we were together, we talked about the possibility of bringing a couple of horses down to our new place from the farm. We decided to drive up fairly early in the spring with the Studebaker and borrow the folks two-horse trailer to bring Janet, the three-quarter Arab palomino mare I had used up at Trail Creek, and Dory, a registered Quarter Horse mare that I had taken up to Trail Creek for a while, for Ingrid to train for barrel racing.

That winter, our first in Albuquerque, was one of the coldest on record. Several copper pipes broke, which caused some drywall damage before I could get the water shut off. The pipes had been laid in the attic, something that would never have been done in Colorado. I had to put an electric heater in the attic and keep it running for several nights to keep the water from freezing again. In the meantime, the pump, which was in the garage, froze. Fortunately, no damage was done and I was able hang a one-hundred-watt lightbulb beside it to keep it from freezing again. Closing the barn door after the horses got out, I went to the hardware store and was able to find split, insulated tubes to put around the pipes in the attic to insulate them enough to keep them from freezing again. The man we had bought the house from had bought another acre nearby and had built another home, so I confronted him with my problems. He was sympathetic while pleading that this was an unnaturally cold winter. He turned out to be right and we were not the only people to have such problems that winter.

We took a long weekend in April and drove to La Junta to see Ingrid's folks, where we spent the night, and then drove on to the farm in Fort Collins. We spent Saturday night with the folks and, right after Sunday dinner, loaded Janet and Dory into the trailer and arrived home at about dark. We now had one of the folks' cars and their trailer!

The next weekend I ordered and had delivered enough rough lumber to build a small corral, tack room and shed in the far corner of our pasture. I have basically no talent as a carpenter, but managed to get everything cobbled together over the next few months. Meanwhile, our one-acre pasture had sprouted a great crop of tumble weeds, which, unfortunately, horses will not eat except when they first come up. We put a water tank across the fence closest to our house, connected one end of the hose to our outside water hydrant and the other to an automatic shut off on the tank. We moved our saddles and other tack from the garage out to our new tack room, put 100 pounds of oats in a garbage can and ordered a ton of hay, which I stacked next to the corral.

Just across the highway to the west stretched miles of open country rising gradually toward the horizon. There was one set of buildings and corrals about a half mile north of our subdivision on that side of the road. Access to this vacant land went through these improvements, and one afternoon after work, Ingrid and I pulled up to the house there to seek permission to ride horseback in the land to the west. A rather formidable looking lady, who could best be described as looking very much like Maude in the sit-com, greeted us at the door. We told her we were neighbors across the road and asked if she would mind if we rode horses through her yard and out into the open country where we saw some Hereford cows from time to time.

She invited us in for a cup of coffee and we had a good visit. She was interested to learn that Ingrid had come from Germany and told us that she was originally from Austria and had been on their equestrian team. She spoke with a fairly marked accent and told us her name was Anita Hazik. When she spoke to Ingrid in German, Ingrid could understand most of what she said, but she no longer felt comfortable speaking the language. Anita said she had come to this country some years before, had purchased this small ranch and now ran about thirty cows on the open country to the west of her. She said the area had once been subdivided, but the project had gone bankrupt and the land had been more or less deserted since. She said there were no fences for miles; however, her cows had to come back to the corral for water, so they would travel no more than a few miles away. Of course the highway had an excellent fence and she had a cattle guard entering her property from it. New Mexico had what was called a fence out law, which meant that if you did not want livestock on your property you had to build your own fence to keep them out. When we got ready to leave, she told us we were welcome to ride in the area where her cows were running anytime we wanted and invited us to come over for dinner the next Sunday.

We soon became fast friends with Anita and ate over there at least once a week. She was a great cook and loved to put some kind of liquor in nearly all of her dishes. I felt the need for her usual strong after dinner coffee before driving home after dinner. She still had her jumping horse but said she had quit jumping when she retired him about five years previous. He was twenty-seven years old. When the horse died about two years later, she talked me into burying him on a sand hill just to the west of her house. I saddled up Janet and drug the dead horse with my rope dallied on my saddle horn to the top of the hill, dug a hole six feet deep by six feet wide and about seven feet long, rolled him into it and covered him up. It was the most digging I had done since I cleaned out the head gate on the farm in Fort Collins.

We rode horseback at Anita's place nearly every weekend. I helped her brand her calves and do any other cowboying she needed. We had another neighbor, Bill, who rode with us from time to time. He was a homebuilder specializing in quickly constructing small, inexpensive, stucco houses in the area. On weekends, he often entered the bull dogging event at the local rodeos and occasionally rode horseback with us on Anita's range. We also had dinner a couple of times with him and his pretty brunette wife.

I was amazed at how far Anita's cattle could graze away from water. Anita had figured out how many cows she could run on this unusual operation, and during a dry spell cattle would sometimes get three or four miles from their water in the corral searching for grass in the semi-desert terrain. They stayed quite thin but managed to raise surprisingly good calves.

I had to travel a good deal but rarely had to be gone more than one night. Albuquerque was pretty much in the center of the state and nearly everywhere I went seemed to be about 200 miles away, with the exception of the Capitol, Santa Fe. The ANCA annual convention lasted three days and nights and I occasionally traveled out of state for other purposes. One of these times, Ingrid drove me to the airport to catch my plane. I gave her my schedule and phone number at the hotel where I would be staying and told her I would look forward to meeting her at the airport the day after next. When I arrived back in Albuquerque in the afternoon Ingrid was not there to meet me; however, I didn't worry too much as punctuality was not one of her long suits. I tried to call her at home and she didn't answer. After I waited about three hours and made several more phone calls from a phone booth, she finally showed up without a word of explanation and couldn't understand why I was upset. She said she had been shopping and just lost track of the time.

I can't remember just when it happened, but about a year and a half after we moved into our new home in the South Valley I received a letter by certified mail from a law office. It turned out to be from the lawyer of our friend Bill's wife and contained a subpoena from his wife, who was filing for divorce. I had no idea what the lawyer had in mind, but I had noticed that Bill's wife had been pretty stand-offish with Ingrid the last time we had dinner with them. I felt no need to get a lawyer for myself. The only other persons in the room were the lawyer, Bill's wife and a clerk. I nodded to Bill's wife and sat down. The lawyer explained that he just wanted to show me some pictures and ask some questions concerning what I saw. The first picture was one of Ingrid sitting on her horse out in Anita's pasture and he asked me if I recognize where she was. I answered that it was the pasture where Ingrid and I often rode together. He then asked if we ever went riding with anyone else. I said that Bill occasionally rode out there with us. This answer seemed to please him and then he asked if Ingrid ever rode out there by herself. I said no, because she would have to get a baby sitter to do that. The lawyer then dramatically reached across the table with another picture, which was nothing more than another photograph of Ingrid sitting on her horse, this time under a power line in the pasture. It dawned on me that he was on a fishing expedition and I got a little huffy. He said to just answer the questions, because he had a good many more pictures. There was no sign of Bill in them and my righteous indignation had stood me in good stead. It was obvious he was hoping I would express some concern, on the record, that something might be going on. I was confident that nothing had been, and although Bill and his wife were soon divorced, we heard nothing more from her lawyer.

In late January 1963, Ingrid was able to accompany me to the ANCA convention, which was held in Las Vegas, Nevada. We were able to get someone to stay in the house with Elizabeth while we were gone. We drove down interstate Highway 25 to La Cruces and then across southern Arizona to Las Vegas, and were able to make it in one long day. The first day of the convention I was tied up in committee meetings all day and Ingrid spent a good bit of the day resting up from our previous day's drive. That night we got tickets for the dinner show at the Riviera where we were staying. One of the acts was an acrobatic group from Austria and the grand finale was a man balancing with only one finger in a coke bottle, an amazing feat we had seen on the Ed Sullivan show.

After the dinner show, we took a cab from casino to casino taking in the bar shows that we could see for just the price of a drink. As we were wandering through one of the casinos watching the people gamble, we spotted the man who had balanced on his finger talking to some of his troupe. We walked over to where they were visiting and Ingrid spoke to him in German. He was a wiry guy with rugged good looks much like Steve McQueen. He responded in German and then looked me over and said something further to Ingrid. She laughed and shook her head and we walked on through the casino. I asked her what he had said and she replied he suggested she ditch that guy she was with and meet him in the bar. She was flattered and I guess I was too, in a left-handed sort of way. We continued our bar hopping, recognizing other performers mingling with the gamblers. By the time we made all the casinos on the strip it was 5:30 in the morning and I realized we had to be back at the hotel for our New Mexico breakfast at seven a.m.

We took a cab back to the Riviera and showered. I quickly shaved, got back into my suit and went to check on the room in which our breakfast would be served, while Ingrid put on her makup. We were the first to get to breakfast and were probably among the most wide-awake at the gathering. President Orndorff and I briefly reviewed the upcoming ANCA agenda and outlined the policy issues we were interested in that would be coming up at the business meting. There was a consensus as to which resolutions we would support and the few we would oppose. Albert Mitchell, who had been NMCGA's president many years before, wos our most effective spokesman.

When all the resolutions had been dealt with at the end of the closing session, it was nearly time for the annual banquet and I was pretty well out of gas. When I got to the room, Ingrid was ready to go in the new dress we had gotten her for the occasion, and she sported a beehive hairdo! Not everyone can wear this style, but it looked great on her. It did take me awhile to get used to it though. I took another shower, changed suits and we got to the banquet just as everyone was being seated. We had the usual cattleman's banquet meal choice of either prime rib or steak. Our old friend from ANCA, Dave Appleton, had gotten us tickets for the late show at the Sands that night featuring Frank Sinatra, Dean Martin and Sammy Davis Junior. This was the show in Las Vegas we really wanted to see and it more than lived up to our expectations. As entertaining as the show was, by the time it was half over, I was dozing off in my seat. When we got back to the hotel and got ready for bed, Ingrid wrapped toilet paper around her new beehive hairdo and laid the back of her head carefully on the pillow, hoping she would be able to get it to hold its shape til we got home.

We were so exhausted that we slept until ten the next morning and didn't get away from Las Vegas until about noon. I drove until about an hour after dark and stopped at a motel somewhere on I-10. We were anxious to get home, so I got up fairly early the next morning and took a shower. Ingrid finally got up by the time I was ready to leave and when she turned on the faucet in the tub to draw herself a bath, I heard her scream. I rushed into the bathroom to see what was the matter. She looked up at me with her behive hairdo melted down around her face. When she had turned on the water, the shower had come on and before she could turn it off, her beehive hairdo was ruined. I had forgotten to switch off the valve that diverted the water from the bathtub faucet to the shower. I very likely had been admonished for this before, but never with such serious consequences. Ingrid didn't speak to me all the way home and for two days after.

Roy and Ingird - 1960

42

Domestic Problems

I enjoyed not being involved in any way in the production of the association's magazine. Even though it was owned by the NMCGA, the only direct contribution we made to it every month was a letter from the president inside the front cover. This was the leadership's vehicle for communicating directly with our members on vital current issues affecting them, and the current president and I always gave a lot of thought to its contents. My first president, John Stark, decided to let me write the letter, which he would edit; my second, Will Orndorff, wrote the letter and had me edit it for him; my third, Les Davis, didn't need any help from me whatsoever. I was equally comfortable with all three approaches.

It just so happened that a consequential political debate affecting New Mexico's cattlemen was going on during John Stark's tenure. A new state land commissioner named Johnny Walker had been elected the year I arrived on the scene, and he had run on a platform of greatly increasing the fees livestock producers in New Mexico paid for grazing on state land. When New Mexico had entered the Union, it was able to reserve a great deal of its unsettled land to the state. Most of this land had a very low carrying—grazing—capacity and a good deal of it was so barren of grass cover that a section, one square mile, was needed to maintain three cows. On less than three head per section, a cow and her calf would basically starve to death. Because it took so many acres to run a cow, the state land office measured carrying capacity in cow units per section rather than acres per cow unit, a cow unit being a cow and a calf. I was told that the average carrying capacity across the state was only eleven head per section. In some areas of the Midwest on land suitable for growing corn, the carrying capacity is more than one cow per acre! This explains why an average ranch in New Mexico with 6,400 acres could run only a few more than 100 head.

The livestock industry in New Mexico had almost unanimously opposed Walker, and afterwards he made very public his resolve to see that the lease rates were increased significantly. The legislature was responsible for setting these fees and the land commissioner led the charge in support of a bill to more than double state land grazing fees. The NMSGA and the New Mexico Wool Growers Association geared up for the battle. Floyd Lee owned the huge Fernandez Ranch, an old Spanish land grant and the largest sheep operation in the state that also ran cattle. It had a lot of state land spread across it. He was an eccentric but brilliant character and president of the New Mexico Wool Growers Association, as well as being an outspoken member of NMSGA's Board of Directors. He was to the sheep industry in New Mexico what Albert K. Mitchell was to the cattle industry. The two titans often clashed on NMSGA policy matters as well as in state politics. On this issue, however, they and their respective organizations, were firmly united. Both had passed resolutions at their conventions opposing any increase in state land grazing fees whatsoever.

One reason raising grazing fees on state land was so controversial was hardly mentioned during the debate. The amount of state land varied considerably from ranch to ranch and the degree to which grazing leases on state land were less than that for private land had been capitalized into the sales price of New Mexico ranches over the years. If a ranch had a lot of state land and had been only recently purchased, its resale value would immediately decrease if the rates were raised substantially. The established ranchers mainly opposed these raises on the traditional grounds of protecting the status quo, but this said, the issue really got the attention of the big insurance companies, which made most of the loans on sales of the largest New Mexico ranches. My friend, Gene Brownell, worked for one of them and had arranged the financing for several of the biggest deals. The fact that most state land was not fenced off from private land also muddied the water.

Although the livestock industry in New Mexico had always had a lot of clout in the state legislature, there was concern within the NMSGA Board of Directors that it would be impossible to hold off any increase whatsoever in the grazing fees for state land. Floyd Lee spoke strongly for not giving an inch, but the board saw fit to give the officers and staff some time to see if there was any possible compromise that might satisfy our membership. It occurred to me that we needed to start preparing them for an inevitable raise in grazing fees. Not every member had state land or at least not any appreciable amount, and there was some antagonism toward the landholders who had a lot. Being fairly new to the state, I needed to review the political history and learn the reasoning behind the unique way that these fees were charged. It turned out that the carrying capacity was well grounded in the science of range management, but fees were potential political dynamite.

John Stark and I decided to use his monthly letter in the magazine to discuss the ramifications of this important issue. We agreed on the issues, but he insisted that I ghost write the letters for him. The first one simply laid out the issues, and in subsequent issues we went deeper into the political weeds. Since John's letters were really editorials, the press and the state legislators, all of whom were on our mailing list, started looking for them. They turned out to be more effective than news releases in laying the groundwork for our policy, which was still in a state of flux.

Finally legislation was passed that substantially raised the grazing fees on state land, but left them still far less than that on privately owned land of comparable carrying capacity. We got some blowback from our members, but they were well enough prepared for the inevitable that we lost very few. Most important, the issue of grazing fees on state land did not come up again for many years.

Ingrid and I had an active social life with the Brownells and several other couples our age who shared our interest in horses. On either Friday or Saturday night most weekends we had a party at one of our homes, and once a month the men in our group would get together for a poker party while the gals had a hen party. When the party was at our house, we would put Elizabeth to bed around 8:30 or 9:00 p.m., and when it was at a friend's house we would take her along and bed her down in one of their bedrooms until we left the party at 1:30 or 2:00 a.m. Elizabeth was a joy to both of us and Ingrid was an excellent mother, but our relationship was gradually deteriorating and I wasn't sure why.

Between the payments on the considerably more expensive home than we had initially planned on and the payment on the adjoining acre we had financed separately, we were living slightly beyond our means. I thought that this financial stress was contributing significantly to our domestic problems and suggested to Ingrid that perhaps we should consider selling our house and finding something we could better afford. She was agreeable and we put the house on the market; however we didn't think through just what we would do next. We were able to sell the house at a considerable profit, but by the time we had to give possession we had not found anything suitable to rent that would accommodate our horses. I was interested in holding on to as much money as we could; however, Ingrid was adamant that one-half of the profit we had made was hers, and she wanted to use the money to do some horse-trading, a business I had learned long ago was not for amateurs.

I was able to find a rather rundown house to rent just south of the city limits that had a large fenced-in lot and no zoning to prohibit keeping our horses there. We could certainly afford it, but it was not a place we wanted to live in for any length of time. Just before we moved, we purchased a fourteen-foot, tandem axle trailer, which would barely haul four horses. Ingrid put her share of the profit on the house that was left into a separate bank account and headed out on her horse-trading excursion. I managed to find someone to look after Elizabeth while I was at work. Ingrid's plan was to buy broke saddle horses at various auction sales and resell them quickly at a profit. Word got back to me that while she was enjoying this endeavor, the experienced horse traders were enjoying doing business with this extremely pretty young woman who had joined their ranks, even as they took her to the cleaners. When she came home with the trailer and pickup truck, which we had traded with the folks for the Studebaker, from this strange sojourn, with her bank account empty, she expected me to welcome her back as if nothing had happened. I was glad to have her home, but our marriage was now on thin ice.

I checked the want ads every day looking for a better place to live and came upon an ad for someone to care for a stable in exchange for a portion of the rent on a second home on the facility. I immediately called to see what they were offering. It turned out to be just what we were looking for. The couple that owned the place had a few of their own horses at the stable and traveled a lot, so they needed someone to feed them when they were gone. Ingrid and I stopped by to check the place out immediately after work and we all hit it off very well. The tenant house was a very nice two-bedroom affair with a third bedroom and bath that had been tacked on. The stable consisted of several corrals and a series of box stalls. We worked out a deal with them to keep our horses in one of the box stalls, and the living quarters were more than satisfactory. The owner's wife and Elizabeth immediately took to each other. Earning part of the rent, we paid less to live there than at the first rental we had when we moved to Albuquerque. We became good friends with our landlords and lived there for about a year. We got our finances back in shape and it looked as if we might salvage our marriage.

I had found it strange that although the association officially owned the New Mexico Stockman, our board of directors had no oversight. Since I could not draw any of my salary from the magazine as my predecessor had, our budget was quite tight. I couldn't imagine why our conservative directors had signed a contract with Horace Henning's father guaranteeing such a large portion of the dues to it. With some difficulty, I managed to get a copy of the contract, and after reading it I told my new president, Will Orndorf, that I thought we should recommend to the board that we renegotiate it. Although the association had a complete audit each year, it did not include the magazine, and I found out it owed approximately $15,000 to the company that printed it. I could tell that Will did not really want to open that can of worms, but neither did he look forward to raising our dues to balance our budget. I said my biggest concern was actually the money owed to the printer, because if they called it in, we as the magazine's owner would be liable for it.

I had a good relationship with their editor, Parley Jensen and his new partner Bill Hunt, but I could tell they weren't happy with me getting into what they considered none of my business when I asked them about the unpaid bill. They said there wasn't any danger of NMCGA ever having to pay it off and saw no reason to change something that had served the association so well over the years. I talked Will into putting the magazine contract on the next board meeting agenda and it became apparent that very few of the board members knew anything about the unpaid bill or understood the relationship between the magazine and the association. I explained my concern over the potential liability. I pointed out that other state publications and the American Cattle Producer Magazine, owned by ANCA, sent members their magazines as part of their membership, and, at the most, transferred something in the order of $2.50 to the magazine if they were audited separately. No action was taken, but Will and I were instructed to come back to the next board meeting with more information and a specific proposal if we thought it was appropriate.

We were not able to find much guidance in the minutes of board meetings over the years in which the debt had been accumulated. There were no indications of any malfeasance and it appeared that the lack of oversight was due to NMSGA's auditor not ever reviewing the magazine contract. The debt probably accrued during an extremely tragic period of Horace Henning's life, during which his wife and a son both committed suicide and he slipped into acute alcoholism. Less than a year after I went to work for the NMCGA, Horace also committed suicide, and I was a pallbearer at his funeral along with several past presidents. All of the problems I have just discussed were carefully kept out of the public eye and I don't remember for sure how we settled the matter. I believe Will and I recommended that we negotiate with the printer to write down the amount owed and change the contract so that the magazine received only $2.50 per year.

During Will Orndorf's term of office, he and I traveled to Mission, Texas to participate in a meeting of the Southwest Anima Health Research Foundation. We flew down in the private airplane of the new president of the New Mexico Wool Growers Association, who represented that organization at the meeting. SWAHRF was a nonprofit organization formed to help the USDA fund and built support from livestock producers for the massive effort to eradicate screwworms in the United States. Screwworms are the larvae of flies that produce maggots that feed on live tissue rather than dead. The flies that lay the eggs that grow into screwworm larvae cannot survive in temperatures below freezing, so they were most severe along the Mexican border in Texas, southern New Mexico, Arizona and California. The eggs are laid in any open wound, such as those left from the practice of dehorning or castrating cattle and in some cases, from branding. The only effective treatment for infested animals was to swab or spray rather toxic medicine deep into the wound to kill all the larvae. Individual producers in the affected areas incurred great costs in labor and lost production, and the cost to the U.S.livestock industry was millions of dollars annually. Wild game and even pets were also at risk from infestation.

At the meeting, we heard from USDA researcher, E. F. Knippling, who through dogged determination had been instrumental in pushing to implement an amazing and unprecedented remedy to combat the screwworm scourge. He demonstrated that enough sterilized male screwworm flies released in a limited area could overwhelm the native male population and reduce reproduction rates enough to eradicate the flies in the treated area. A plant was built near Mission, Texas, to raise and sterilize, through radiation, enough male flies to protect large areas bordering Mexico from infestation. We were invited to the meeting by the SWAHRF chairman, Texas Governor Dolph Briscoe, to try to get our association behind the effort and sell the eradication effort to our state's livestock industry. We recognized the great benefit, but since only about one-fourth of our state was far enough south to be affected by screwworms, we knew we had our work cut out for us. At our next board meeting we voted to endorse the program and send a mailing to our members asking for voluntary contributions for SWAHRF; we raised significant money from our members in the affected areas. The program had its ups and downs and succeeded in its mission only after it managed to get Mexico and the Central American countries to participate. Thus, the battle line could be drawn at the Isthmus of Panama after slowly being moved south through Mexico.

Tragedy struck the association again at the end of our 1963 convention. It was the last general session and all of the business had been concluded except the election of officers for the coming year. According to tradition, one of the recent past presidents of the organization served as chairman of the nominating committee and it was the turn of Buster Driggers of Santa Rosa. Buster had just accepted Les Davis's nomination for president, along with the other officers, and someone moved that they all be elected by acclamation. Just as Buster was accepting the motion he grabbed his chest with his right hand and fell backwards. I was sitting nearby taping the activities and rushed forward to try to catch him as he fell. I was too late and his head hit the riser as a loud thump. He was obviously unconscious, but continued to laboriously breathe for a short period of time. An ambulance arrived within ten minutes and took him to the hospital, where he was declared dead on arrival. Linda Lambert, a board member, was concerned for the health of some of the elderly past presidents sitting on the front row and was seen dispensing nitroglycerin tablets to several of them in the midst of the confusion. Floyd Lee had the presence of mind to step to the microphone and pronounced the meeting adjourned. The coroner recorded a massive heart attack as the cause of death. Buster, a tall, rugged, lifelong rancher, was only 52 years old.

Our new president, Les Davis, managed the 130,000-acre CS Ranch for its owner, his uncle, Ed Springer. In the spring of 1941 after finishing his senior year as a premed student at Dartmouth, Les had written to his Uncle Ed that he would like to come west and learn the ranching business. Ed invited him to join him and Les took over management of the ranch in 1947. The ranch was founded by Frank and Charles Springer in 1873 and was part of the 1.7 million acre Maxwell Land Grant. In 1953 Les married Linda Mitchell, daughter of Albert K Mitchell who owned the 180,000-acre Tequesquite Ranch.

Shortly after Les took office, he and Linda invited Ingrid, Elizabeth and me to come up to the ranch for a couple of days. We were put up in their nice guesthouse and were made to feel right at home. When we went to breakfast the first morning Les was helping Linda in the kitchen as she prepared bacon, eggs and hotcakes and the children joined us for breakfast. I knew that Linda had graduated from Cornell, which is New York's Land-Grant College, with a degree in animal science in 1952, the same year I graduated from Colorado A&M with the same degree. I had run into Les and Linda at several ANCA conventions along with her younger brother, Albert K., Jr., and was looking forward to Les's term in office.

NMCGA had always been a strong advocate for increasing tariffs on beef imported from Australia, and a meeting of ANCA state affiliates on the subject was scheduled for November 21st and 22nd in 1963 in Oklahoma City. Les was not able to attend, so I flew to Oklahoma City to represent our organization. As I recall, at the morning session the first day ANCA affiliates were divided by regions to discuss the issue and then report their findings at the general session. Our group came up with a unanimous report, and for some reason they made me spokesman. Several well-known economists spoke at the morning session the second day, and at the afternoon session, presided over by Oklahoma Governor Boren, each regional group presented its position. A broad consensus agreed to recommend that ANCA work for a contra-cyclical quota system that would limit beef imports from Australia and New Zealand during years of high U.S. domestic production and increase imports when our domestic production decreased.

Just as Governor Boren was addressing the group towards the end of the meeting, an aid walked out on the stage and whispered in his ear. Boren looked startled, then composed himself and announced that the President of the United States had just been shot and that there was no further news at that time. The meeting immediately adjourned and we all went our respective ways in a state of shock.

When I got to the airport and boarded my aircraft, rain was beginning to fall. When the plane reached cruising altitude the pilot came on the speaker to announce that the president was at a hospital receiving surgery and he would update us if he learned anything more. In the meantime, we were experiencing some of the worst turbulence I had ever suffered through. The pilot said he could not get high enough to fly over the many thunderstorms in the area nor could he go around them. Shortly before we reached Albuquerque, the pilot announced that the president had died. It was raining in Albuquerque, a rare event there, and I walked through the rain, got in my pickup and drove home in a daze.

Our December annual convention was coming up and the memory of the death of one of our most respected past presidents the previous year and the recent assassination of John F Kennedy may have been factors in a disappointing attendance. When I had worked on the budget for the coming year with finance committee chairman Will Orndorf, it had become apparent it would be impossible to give any of the staff a significant raise. He said I deserved a bigger salary but was afraid NMCGA would never be able to pay me what I likely could earn elsewhere. I knew he was right, but I hated the thought of looking for other work. Soon after the convention, Gene Brownell left Travelers Insurance Company, and he suggested I call his regional sales manager and apply for his job making ranch loans. I called his boss without doing much homework and neither of us made much of an impression on the other, so I decided to put job hunting out of my mind.

My relationship with Ingrid had continued to deteriorate and, not long after the convention, I suggested that we see a marriage counselor. She wasn't excited about the idea, but said to go ahead and check one out. I went to see a pastor recommended by a mutual friend and he thought it would be best to interview us separately and then perhaps come in for a joint session. I went ahead and met with him right away and a couple of weeks later I talked Ingrid into talking to him. I called the counselor the day after her visit to schedule a joint meeting and he said he thought one probably would not do any good. I pressed him for reasons and came away with the conclusion that Ingrid just wasn't interested in saving the marriage. I moved into the spare bedroom and we agreed to be as civil to each other as possible for the sake of Elizabeth.

In early March, I received a telephone call from a man who introduced himself as Hap Canning. He said he owned the Adobe Ranch, which I recognized as one of our members. He told me that in addition to running commercial Brangus cows, they had a fairly large herd of registered Brangus Cattle. I had heard of the breed and knew there were quite a few in New Mexico, but little else. He said the executive secretary of their breed registry, the International Brangus Breeders Association, had resigned and they were looking for someone to replace him. He said their office was in Kansas City, Missouri and they would like to start interviewing applicants there within the month. I said that he had caught me by surprise and I would like to do some research on the cattle and organization and talk to my wife. He said that was understandable, but he would like to hear back from me within a week.

I told Ingrid about the call and she said she had no interest in moving to Kansas City. I said I thought a change would be good for us and my chances for advancement in New Mexico were limited. My first phone call was to Dr. Stonaker, who was by this time head of the Animal Science Department at Colorado State University. He told me that there was considerable ongoing research on Brangus at Louisiana State University's research station in Jeanerette and it had found the cattle to be very well suited to the Gulf Coast climate. He knew nothing about the International Brangus Breeders Association, but thought the cattle had a good future in the southern states. I had heard that New Mexico State University had a research project going on to compare production of Hereford and Brangus cows in the semiarid country found in New Mexico. I called Bobby Rankin, who had been on the New Mexico A&M rodeo team when I was in college and was now an Extension Beef Specialist there. He told me a bit about their research project and said that one of his co-workers, whom I also knew, Bill Ljungdall, had applied for the job and probably had a good chance of getting it. I called Bill and it turned out that he was a good friend of the departing executive, Jesse Dowdy, who had talked him into applying for the job, but he had withdrawn his application. After hearing that I called Hap from the office and said I would like to apply for the job. I called Les and told him about the job I had been invited to apply for. I said if I planned to pursue it I would need to take a couple of days off to fly to Kansas City with Canning for an interview, and then I should know within a few days if I had been accepted. He said he would hate to see me leave, but encouraged me to pursue what could be a promising job. He did ask that I try to delay my departure until after our trip to Washington DC later in the year to testify on the countercyclical beef import bill, which I said I would try to do.

Hap picked me up at the Albuquerque airport the next Thursday in his four-passenger Beach Bonanza and we flew to Clovis, New Mexico. We picked up another Brangus breeder there, who was also on their Board of Directors, and flew on to the Kansas City airport, arriving in time for my afternoon job interview. There was only one other applicant and he was interviewed just before me. There were about fifteen men in the room. I was welcomed by the president of the IBBA, Al Face, and introduced to Jesse Dowdy and the rest of the group, who were all members of their Board of Directors.

Most of the Directors participated in the interview and asked a variety of questions; they seemed pleased about my previous experience. Then the president took over the interview, asking specifically about my knowledge of Brangus cattle and if I felt qualified to make judgments on which animals were suitable to be registered. He explained they had a requirement, unique among breed associations, that all animals be inspected as yearlings before being issued registration papers.

I replied that I knew nothing about the Brangus breed, but had taken livestock judging in college and spent the last ten years working for commercial cattlemen. I said I felt confident I could quickly learn to be an inspector. Al then asked me to wait until the board meeting was over because they thought they would reach a decision by then. About forty-five minutes later, they invited me back into the room and indicated they would like to hire me if we could agree upon terms. I asked for a salary of about $100 a month less than I knew they had offered Bill Ljungdahl, and said I would like a contract that stated if they found my work unsatisfactory

Ingrid entered Elizabeth in a beauty contest in Albuquerque in about 1962 which she won.

they were to give me six months notice to improve it before they could discharge me. There was a brief discussion that primarily involved the rather unusual contract. I was asked to leave the room while they voted on the applicants and a few minutes later was told I had been selected on the terms I suggested.

Immediately after the meeting, Al Face, Jesse Dowdy and I got together to discuss the timing of the transition. I had mentioned during the interview that I had quite a few loose ends to tie up at my current job and would like to wait several months before I reported for work. They suggested I visit with my president and then call Jesse and work out a schedule. Al said he would like me to spend a few days with him at the Bruce Church operation in Yuma, Arizona, which he managed, so I could look over their sizable Brangus herd and get some training toward qualifying me as an inspector. I told them I was anxious to get on the job and would be in touch with Jesse early the next week.

Hap flew me home the next morning and I was apprehensive about what Ingrid was going to say when she heard I had accepted the job.

43

Washington D. C. Trip

When I got home from Kansas City I immediately told Ingrid that I had accepted the job. She replied that was fine because she had decided to leave me anyway. I didn't have a reply to that, so I went into the bedroom to see Elizabeth, whom Ingrid had just put in bed. I picked her up, gave her a hug and kiss and then handed her a package containing the pajamas I had picked up for her at the airport. She opened them and seemed to really like them. I put her back in bed and was standing looking at her when she said, "Thank you for the plessent, Daddy." I turned, walked out of the bedroom swiftly and broke into tears. Since I rarely cried but couldn't do it just a little bit, I was soon sobbing. I finally had to face the reality of leaving Elizabeth.

    I walked into the living room where Ingrid was sitting and asked her just what her plans were. She said that she and Elizabeth were planning to move in with Anita Hazek, who had plenty of room for them. I had no desire to discuss the matter with her further and went to bed in the back bedroom where I had been sleeping for several weeks. I had not been sleeping well, so I had moved a lamp by my bed and escaped into a book, probably science fiction, until I fell asleep.

    I got up early the next morning, fed the horses and left Ingrid a note indicating I had done so, drove the pickup to the office and had breakfast in the coffee shop at the Hilton. When the young women arrived at the office I told them I had taken the job in Kansas City and would be making plans

Elizabeth and Daddy

with Les about my departure date. When I called Les, he said he would be in Albuquerque in a day or two and we could make some decisions. In the meantime, I called Jesse Dowdy and had a good visit with him. I knew that he was on the IBBA's board of directors as well as on their staff, which was rather unusual. He told me that he was the one vote against my getting the job, but wanted me to know he was honor bound to vote for the other candidate because he was a friend, whom he had talked into applying. He said he had been impressed by my credentials and was looking forward to working with me as we made the transition. Evidently his board had authorized him to work out a mutually agreeable arrangement. He said he wanted me come to Kansas City for a couple of weeks to get acquainted with his staff and the general operation of the office, after which I could come back to Albuquerque and take whatever time I needed for us to hire my replacement. I told him Al Face had suggested I visit him at the Bruce Church operation and Jesse agreed that would be a better idea and he could show me the ropes after I came to work. When Les got to the office, we agreed to the suggestions made by Dowdy. We had a board meeting coming up within the month and we thought that would give us an opportunity to discuss a job description for my replacement and work out a timeline for hiring him.

The main items on the Board of Directors meeting agenda were my departure and a hearing in Washington DC on the 1964 Meat Import Act in the Senate. The ANCA wanted to get as many representatives of state affiliates as possible to oppose this bill. It would increase what the industry believed was too high a quota of beef from Australia in the face of currently increasing domestic supplies. The board voted to send both Les and me to testify because defeating this legislation was the number one priority of our organization, as well as ANCA's. I don't recall the date of the hearing, but it was shortly after I was to get back from my trip to Arizona.

I was instructed to get out a news release announcing my departure and indicating the organization would be receiving applications for my position. A committee was appointed to review the applications and hire someone in time for him to be on board before the December annual convention. Shortly thereafter, I drove to Yuma, Arizona and spent a few days there. The IBBA reimbursed NMCGA for my expenses and salary during this period.

It was a long drive from Albuquerque to Yuma, Arizona and I arrived at Al's home just in time for supper; I stayed with them two nights. Everything about Yuma was new to me. The Bruce Church Company was primarily a producer of lettuce and cantaloupe on their extensive, irrigated land. The cattle were run on irrigated pasture and the corrals and improvements were located on the less valuable non-irrigated land. There was an upright, airtight silo called a Harvestore located by a small feedlot. Al said that on the rare occasion when they had damaged crops, they could put either the cantaloupe or the lettuce into the silo and feed the resulting silage to their cattle. Brangus cattle were noted for their ability to thrive in dry country, and this certainly qualified as dry. However, their cattle were either fed in dry lots or allowed to run on lush, irrigated pasture. Al said they had a very long growing season and preferred that it didn't rain because that would delay their harvesting or planting.

The second morning Al took me out to the corrals and showed me a dozen of their yearling replacement heifers and an equal number of yearling bulls. He explained a few of the specific things to look for when inspecting Brangus so they could be issued registration papers. Since these cattle were three-eighths Brahman and five-eighths Angus, they didn't always breed true as to color, and there were a couple with some degree of brindle—reddish stripes—over their shoulders. Al said this was a disqualification. He said there was also not supposed to be any white ahead of the navel on their underline. Many Brangus cows had some white on their udders, but for some reason or other they discriminated against those with too much, possibly because it could be an indication of Holstein blood, and arbitrarily chose the navel as the stopping point. The tendency to show brindle came from the Brahman side. Some Brahman cattle have horns and others, scurs (hornlike growth on the poll attached only to the hide). He said horns are a disqualification, but animals with scurs could be registered provided their presence was noted on their papers. Following the lead of the American Angus Association, the IBBA would not register red cattle, the result of a recessive gene in Angus.

I noted that none of the things we had discussed thus far actually had any bearing on the productive value of cattle. He agreed that I might be right, but said those were the rules of the breed association and they must be followed. I allowed as

New Mexico State Land Office Grazing Fees

19-7-29 NMSA states, in part, that the Commissioner shall determine the annual rental to be charged for grazing lands belonging to the state and may take into consideration other determinations made by other state and federal agencies regarding this subject.

The current fee formula, which was established and implemented following various feasibility studies in 1988 by the then Commissioner of Public Lands, takes into account various factors from multiple sources, such as current private grazing land lease rates by western livestock ranchers, beef cattle prices, and the cost of livestock production. For instance, if cattle prices decline and the costs associated with the livestock business increases, the grazing fee would decrease in response to the market conditions. Conversely, if forage is more abundant than normal, or more in demand by ranchers, it would tend to increase the numbers in the indices used in the formula(s) resulting in an increase, for example, of the carrying capacity (cc). Therefore, certain factors adjust state trust land grazing fees up or down depending on value of forage and economic conditions in the livestock industry.

The Current Grazing Lease Annual Rental Fee Formula is:

Base Value x Carrying Capacity x Acreage x Economical Variable Index =Rental Fee

- The Base Rate was established at 0.0474 after evaluating the study results and holding a public hearing.
- Carrying Capacity (cc) = the number of cattle each section (640 acres) of land will sustain based on the quantity and quality of forage as determined by an appraisal performed by a Land Office District Resource Specialist of the subject area.
- The Economic Variable Index (EVI) is calculated based on the three following indices compiled by the National Agricultural Statistics Service (NASS) of the USDA:
    o BCPI-the Beef Cattle Prices Index, an index of USDA annually reported prices of beef cattle over 500 pounds;
    o PPI-the Prices Paid Index, an index of prices that producers of livestock pay for selected production items; and
    o FVI-the 11 Western States Forage Value Index - an index of annually surveyed private grazing land lease rates.

Application of this formula is illustrated in the following example.

SEC	TWN	RNG	Base Value	Carrying Capacity	Acres	EVI	Rent
15	24N	26E	$ 0.0474	14	160	1.90	$ 201.73
17	24N	26E	$ 0.0474	14	640	1.90	$ 806.94
16	25N	27E	$ 0.0474	14	640	1.90	$ 806.94
17	25N	27E	$ 0.0474	14	360	1.90	$ 453.90
20	25N	27E	$ 0.0474	16	320	1.90	$ 461.11
21	25N	27E	$ 0.0474	14	480	1.90	$ 605.20
					TOTAL RENTAL FEE		$ 3,335.82

Formula for determining grazing fees for cattle on New Mexico state-owned land as outlined in feasibility studies done in 1988. This was a refinement and update to the changes made in the early 1960s.

how it was certainly not my place to disagree. He said the rest of the inspection procedure was much as I had learned in beef judging class in college. He said to look for soundness of feet and legs, good muscle development with adequate bone to carry it and above average size and weight for age. He said the animals should also show adequate breed characteristics, which were intermediate between their Angus and Brahman forebears. Since Bruce Church had such a well-established breeding program, all except the few head exhibiting some brindling across the shoulders were acceptable for registration. Al said it appeared I would qualify as an inspector with a little more experience. I was frankly a little confused by the whole process, and the inspection program was one of our most controversial policies over the years. I drove back to Albuquerque the next day and didn't see Al again until the Brangus association's annual convention in Houston in mid-February.

 I had a few weeks back in the office before Les and I had to fly to Washington for the Congressional hearing on the Meat Import Act. We arrived at Washington National Airport in the late afternoon and took a shuttle to the Willard Hotel, where all the visiting cattlemen were staying. When we got to the reservation desk, they had only one single room left. We said we had reserved a room with two beds and told them they surely must have something else. The desk clerk did some more checking and said that the only vacant room in the hotel was the bridal suite, which had a king-size bed. Les responded that we could probably make that do and the Bell Hop led us up to a beautiful big room with a canopy-covered king-sized bed and two bathrooms. For years when we saw each other at cattlemen's meetings we enjoyed telling our friends we shared the bridal suite at the Willard Hotel in Washington.

 The next morning, we found ourselves in a Senate hearing room filled with what seemed to be mostly cattlemen. We both signed a roster listing those wishing to testify. After about an hour Les was called. He said that we had long supported quotas and tariffs for imported Australian beef to compensate American producers for the Australians' lower cost of production, which put us at a competitive disadvantage. He pointed out that the timing of this bill could not be worse because our current production was in a cyclical upturn. I spoke briefly after him, seconding the things he had said and endeavoring to get a little deeper into the details of our cattle cycle. I was amazed to learn that the transcript of the hearing would be available shortly after the close of the hearing "for corrections and additions" by Senators and those who had testified. While waiting to look at our testimony, Les and I visited with Senator Eugene McCarthy, whose state greatly depended on the steel industry and shared the cattlemen's protectionist views. We thought he might be one of the few Democrats whose vote we could swing our way. As I recall, we were unsuccessful. When my turn came to review my hearing testimony, it looked terrible. I started making corrections and gave up, thinking that I might just be making it worse. Fortunately Les had done quite well and, even more fortunately, he didn't ask to look at my remarks.

I spent the rest of my allotted time at the NMCGA making preparations for the year-end convention and forwarding applications for my job to the membership committee. There were surprisingly few of them and I can't remember any other than one brand inspector and one applicant with experience in the journalism field. After Buster Driggers had gotten my attention, I had become pretty proficient in working with the print media and was interviewed from time to time on the Albuquerque TV station. The board seemed to want to continue this trend and wound up hiring the one with media experience. I met him at his interview and we had one week together in the office before I was due to report to Kansas City, about three weeks before the convention.

The day before I was to leave for my new job, I got a call from Ingrid. She asked me what I thought about her and Elizabeth going to Kansas City with me. Without blinking an eye, I said that would be great, but we would have to get busy packing. I had planned to take only my suitcase, clothes and personal items, and we didn't have much in the way of furniture, but we did have two horses and quite a lot of stuff. When I got home, I asked what had changed her mind. She simply said that Anita had advised her not to burn her bridges behind her. I'm sure Anita said more, but if so, Ingrid didn't share it with me. The obvious winner in this sudden change of plans was Elizabeth, and of course she didn't know how close we had come to splitting up.

I called Jesse about the change in plans and he said we could keep our horses on a farm that he leased. He had also suggested I rent a two-bedroom, fairly new, furnished house on that farm. He and his wife were delighted to hear that Ingrid and I had reconciled and said we could go ahead and stay in the house he had mentioned earlier for the time being. I told him it would be well after dark before we arrived so he gave me directions to both the barn and the house and said that there would be a key under the door. Ingrid and I had been estranged for nearly a year and I had been operating on autopilot for that entire time. I had managed to get my work done, which had become pretty routine, and somehow was able to get a new job, even though I had to tell my new employers that I was leaving my wife behind because I thought our marriage was breaking up. All of a sudden, I could look forward to an exciting new job with a whole new lease on life.

Elizabeth's first birthday

44

Jesse Dowdy

When we arrived at the farm where we were staying, it was well after dark. I managed to find my way down the county road off the highway and found the buildings Jesse had described. We immediately unloaded the horses and led them into the barn, lighting our way with a flashlight. When I shined the light around the inside I saw what looked like big rat curled up in the corner. It was a possum doing what possums do, playing dead. We had never seen one before, but Ingrid wasn't the least bit frightened and would have liked to make a pet of it. We gave it a couple of nudges without a response, so we tied up the horse, fetched some water in a bucket from a nearby water hydrant, got some hay out of the jockey box on the trailer and shut the horse and possum in the stall. We then made our way to the house a few hundred feet away, found the key and were happy to find it ready for us to move in.

The next morning I got up early, found the corral in good shape and turned the horse loose in it. There was a water tank by the hydrant and hay in a nearby feeder. We had been invited to breakfast by Jesse's wife, Ione, and found her to be a wonderful cook. In addition to the usual bacon, eggs and biscuits, she served us delicious fried apples, which, we soon learned, she was famous for. After breakfast Ione helped Ingrid and Elizabeth get settled in the house and Jesse took me to the office in the Kansas City Stock Yards. It was considerably bigger than the similar building at the Denver Stock Yards and somewhat smaller than the one in Omaha. As we walked through the lobby I saw a cafeteria, and Jesse said its food came from the kitchen it shared with the famous Golden Ox Steak House, also off the lobby. He said there was also a barber shop and a bank in the building. So far I was pretty impressed.

We got on a rather old-fashioned elevator and exited on the sixth floor. The office consisted of three rooms: a large office with three desks, a smaller one on one side that was Jesse's and one of the same size on the other side used as a storage and work room. Both the main office and the one I would occupy had doors to the hall across from a men's room that served the entire floor. All the desks were the big heavy oak type, going out of style but not yet collector's items. I've never had a desk I liked more. My office had an old-fashioned leather couch against one wall, a matching chair and a single light fixture and fan combination with a pull string in the middle of the ceiling. Jesse introduced me to his office manager, Emma Matney, without whom, he said, he could not possibly get things done. I soon found that I could not either. She had two clerks who worked under her. Mrs. Matney had grey hair tied in a bun, looked to be middle-aged and left a first impression that this was a no-nonsense lady. When Jesse introduced us, she welcomed me with a pleasant, warm voice and when I asked her what I should call her she said, "I choose to be called Mrs. Matney." She then introduced me to the other two young women and they proceeded to show me how they handled the applications for registration, checked pedigrees by searching through files by hand and prepared registration certificates, each of which Jesse said he signed by hand.

The official publication of the International Brangus Breeders Association was the *Brangus Journal*, a publication that Jesse said averaged about twenty-four pages and was printed in Kansas City. He said the man who set the type also laid out and pasted up the magazine, which was good news to me. Jesse said that he wrote a monthly column called "Riding the Range," which covered all of his activities. Most of the rest of the copy was from press releases that we received about agriculture in general and reports on cattle shows and sales from the regional IBBA affiliates. It seemed that the association was divided into area groups consisting of the West Coast Brangus breeders, Heart of America Brangus breeders, Southeast Brangus breeders, Northwest Brangus breeders, Canadian Brangus breeders and the Texas Brangus breeders. I soon learned that the latter group made up over half of the memberships and almost two-thirds of the registrations.

The most recent *Brangus Journal* had just come from the printers and I could see that the percentage of advertising compared to editorial material was too little to cover the magazine's expenses at the current advertising rates. It was obviously being subsidized from registrations and annual membership dues. I didn't yet know how important a good magazine was for a breed association and Jesse left me with the impression that it practically printed itself. I should have known better. I soon got the full story on Jesse's version of his problems with Texas and quickly decided that there must be a great deal more to it than he was telling me. When we got back to the office, Mrs. Matney gave me a copy of their previous year's audit and the financial report, as well as a copy of the organizations bylaws for me to review.

I spent most of the week I had left, while Jesse was still on the payroll, traveling around the Heart of America area (Missouri, Kansas, South Dakota and Iowa) meeting breeders and looking at cattle. Jesse was a substantial Brangus breeder himself and his cattle carried important foundation bloodlines. He was extremely proud of the fact he was a charter board member. He obviously knew a great deal about the breed and was an effective spokesman for the organization and its cattle. I had an opportunity to pick his brains about office procedures, which didn't concern him much, and learn about the board of directors and the governance of the association. It soon became obvious that there had been an ongoing feud for years pitting the Texas association against Jesse and all the other affiliates. It was probably just as well I didn't fully understand the extent of it.

Ingrid and I soon figured out that the thirty-five mile commute to the office was farther than we wanted to drive each day, and when I told Jesse this I was surprised to learn he paid himself mileage to and from the office. He rationalized this by the fact that he traveled so much it didn't matter were he started from. We spent several hours a couple of days feeding and checking on his cattle, and as we visited his fellow breeders it was obvious that he was had sold most of them their foundation stock and was instrumental in helping them market their cattle afterwards. We were welcomed everywhere with open arms and were fed dinner at each stop. I soon realized that I couldn't hope to replace Jesse in-kind, and since he was on the board his influence was going to continue to be quite substantial. He was easy to like and we became good friends, but I knew I had a lot to learn other than what I could glean from him.

By the time my week working with Jesse was up we had found an apartment that appealed to us very much. It was about a mile north of Kansas City, Missouri, across the Missouri River in Riverside. It was a recently finished, small complex of about thirty

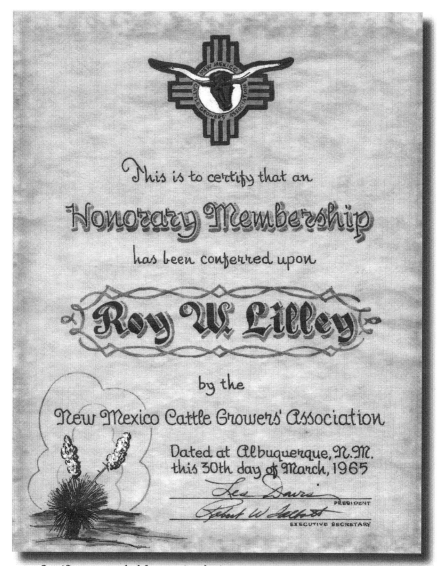

Certificate awarded for service during my tenure as executive officer of the New Mexico Cattle Growers' Association.

one- and two-bedroom apartments with an outdoor swimming pool. It was built on open ground overlooking the river on recently farmed land. There was an old wooden barn standing in the valley north of the apartments on about a quarter section of hilly, wooded land. The first time we approached the apartments we saw several white tail deer trotting on the hill above the barn. It was a beautiful setting and made a great first impression. We found a two-bedroom, one-bath apartment in our price range and quickly signed a one-year lease.

Ione and Jesse were disappointed that we weren't going to stay on the farm, but agreed to let us keep our horse there for a while. I told Jesse how much I enjoyed farming and he was happy to let me do some fall plowing for him a couple of weekends. We enjoyed our new apartment and found that most of our new neighbors were fairly young, married couples with whom we had a lot in common. We immediately made friends and enjoyed warm fall evenings and week ends at the pool while Elizabeth splashed around the shallow end with other small children. Neighbors took turns hosting Saturday night parties and we became particularly close to our next-door neighbors, a paving contractor and the woman about Ingrid's age he was living with. We naively initially assumed they were married. It appeared that our marriage was on the mend. I had to travel a lot, often a week at a time, but Ingrid felt comfortable and safe in our new surroundings.

It took me only a few days in the office to appreciate what a gem I had in Mrs. Matney. At first I found it strange that she, the office manager, answered the phone, but it was immediately apparent that she had a more pleasant voice and telephone personality than anyone I had ever worked with. All our members were used to talking to her and reasonably expected her to solve whatever problem they had. She was completely loyal to Jesse and transferred that loyalty to me, never passing judgment on either of us in some of the difficult days that followed. I felt well prepared to manage the business of this new organization, which had a budget comparable to my previous job's and a similar sized staff. I prepared a news release to the agricultural editors of the large newspapers throughout the country and all the livestock publications, announcing I was replacing Jesse Dowdy. I added information on the organization and the history of the Brangus breed from a professional promotion piece Jesse had printed. This was a no-brainer to me, but new to the office staff. With Mrs. Matney's advice I selected one of the clerks to be my secretary.

I soon found a pile of breed registrations certificates on my desk to be signed. These certificates, carrying our official seal, confirmed that the cattle they individually described met the standards set out in the organization's bylaws as attested to by the breeder on the registration application. In addition to listing the recorded sire, dam and birth date, the application for registration of each animal had to be signed by an inspector approved by the IBBA Board of Directors. Our two main sources of income were a fee we received for first recording individual animals and another whenever a registered animal was transferred to a new owner. About a fifth of our revenue came from an annual membership fee. Only members could record cattle and the fee was doubled when non-members transferred animals, a strong incentive to join.

As previously indicated, all the above work was labor intensive. Parentage had to be confirmed by pulling a copy of the registration papers of the sire and dam on each animal presented for recording; membership had to be confirmed because the applicant had to be the current owner. This information was typed on a pre-numbered registration certificate with a copy for the file. All the paperwork and new copy was then returned to the appropriate file.

When I first applied for the job, I learned that the IBBA was incorporated in 1949 and the first Brangus were recorded that year. Of course, Brahman and Angus cattle had been crossed by commercial cattlemen by that time, but an oil man in Oklahoma named Frank Buttram, who owned Clear Creek Ranch was the first to recognize the superior performance of cattle that were three-eighths Brahman and five-eighths Black Angus. He achieved this percentage in two ways. The first and most common was to cross a one-half Brahman one-half Angus cow back to a Brahman bull, thereby obtaining a three-quarter Brahman bull, which he a mile north of Kansas City, Missouri, across the Missouri River in Riverside. It was a recently finished, small complex of about thirty one- and two-bedroom apartments with an outdoor swimming pool. It was built on open ground overlooking the river on recently farmed land. There was an old wooden barn standing in the valley north of the apartments on about a quarter section of hilly, wooded land. The first time we approached the apartments we saw several white tail deer trotting on the hill above the barn. It was a beautiful setting and made a great first impression. We subsequently bred to a purebred Angus cow, arriving at the desired three-eighths Brahman, five-eighths Angus. The reciprocal cross was also acceptable, but since Angus cows are much more plentiful than Brahmans, it is seldom done. The association always listed the Brahman percentage first when describing foundation

Elizabeth at about the time Ingrid and I were divorced.

stock or Brangus. Really good three-quarters bulls were hard to find and fairly expensive. The association by-laws referred to Angus and Brahman cattle (they had to be registered with their respective breed associations) as enrolled, the intermediate crosses as certified and the final product as registered Brangus.

By 1949, Clear Creek Ranch and a few other breeders were far enough along with their programs to codify their procedures in bylaws and incorporate as the International Brangus Breeders Association. Its first CEO was Raymond Pope, manager of Clear Creek Ranch, and owner of an adjacent ranch, Clear View, which also raised Brangus. Pope's champion Brangus bull, Jumbo, was featured in the movie "Giant," loosely based on the huge King Ranch in Texas, which developed the Santa Gertrudis breed based on a program crossing shorthorn cattle with Brahmans. Jesse had nothing good to say about Pope, who left the Clear Creek Ranch under circumstances that were never fully explained publicly.

Soon after I assumed management of the association, I received a letter addressed to the IBBA about a meeting of an informal group called something like the Beef Records Committee. As I recall, it was made up of a group of breed association executives who wanted to compare notes about the cattle industry's breed registries' early efforts to become involved in performance testing. I asked Jesse, a strong proponent of keeping production records, about it and he said he had attended their organizational meeting and thought it was important that I continue to participate in their activities. I responded to the letter indicating I would be at the meeting and was looking forward to working with the group. This is the organization that evolved into the Beef Improvement Federation, which has done so much to make various breed association programs more uniform. I never missed a meeting of the BIF and served on its board of directors for several of the years that I worked for the Brangus Association.

45

Maxine

While I was preparing for my first annual convention as Executive Vice President, I realized I would be walking on a tightrope dealing with the tension between the discontented Texas Brangus Breeders Association and most of the rest of the IBBA's regional affiliates, who had seemed to support Jesse Dowdy before I was hired. I had heard Jesse's side of the issues, but had little first-hand information about the Texas breeders' concerns except that Jesse had made it clear they very much resented the fact the organization's headquarters was located in Kansas City. Jesse had told me that the host affiliate, Texas, was responsible for all the convention planning. I made the grave error of not checking this out for myself and working in conjunction with the part-time staff person who worked for the active Texas group. Our current vice president, Ed Schock, whose operation was in the Kansas Flint Hills, and Jesse, were crossways over the degree to which Ed had allied himself with the Texas folks. As a result, Ed had fallen out of favor with his own affiliate, The Heart of America Brangus Breeders, the second most active in the IBBA, and Jesse thought there would be opposition to his being elevated to the presidency.

When I headed for the convention in San Antonio, I was less prepared for the convention than I should have been and did not fully realize the degree of animosity between Texas and Jesse's followers. President Al Face and I had corresponded about the agenda for the board meetings held before and after the convention, but had discussed little else before I left for the long drive to San Antonio. When I arrived at the headquarters hotel, I looked up the TBBA staff person, Ann Slyer, who was waiting for me at the registration desk that she had already set up, and we compared notes. She had all the necessary meeting rooms lined up and the meals and social events organized. What she didn't have, and said she had expected me to furnish, were the agendas for the committee meetings and the annual business meeting, which should have been in a printed program she assumed I would be bringing. I apologized profusely. She simply shrugged and blamed our lack of coordination on Jesse. I said I couldn't accept that because I had enough convention planning experience in my career to have done better.

Ann was great to work with and was fully posted on the activities of the various committees. We got busy and typed up a simple program and took it to a local print shop, which said it could have it ready by the next day. I felt as if I had dodged a bullet as I went up to my room to change for the opening convention event, a 6:00 p.m. cocktail party. I was ready for a drink when I got there. I walked into the room full of many strange faces and I was happy to see Al Face and his wife. They took me around the room and introduced me to almost all the couples present. I had briefly met all the directors who were present at the meeting in Kansas City. Every one appeared genuinely glad to meet me and enthusiastically welcomed me on board. I had reviewed the background of all the organization's leaders before I left home and knew this was a considerably different group of people from those for whom I had worked in my previous jobs. Among the board members were three prominent physicians, a lawyer who had been instrumental in settling a highly publicized offshore drilling case, the owner of an extensive rice farm on the Gulf, the oil man who owned the Houston Oilers AFL football team, Bud Adams, a couple of substantial business owners, the independent owner of a printing business, the manager of one unit of a ranch in New Mexico that was one of the country's largest and only a couple of full-time cattlemen/farmers. The common denominator among all of them was an amazing enthusiasm for Brangus cattle and their faith in the breed's future.

I had the feeling I was making a decent first impression on my new employers and only hoped that their enthusiasm would last for the rest of the convention. After the cocktail party, I joined a large group for a late dinner at a private club at the Hotel. It was preceded by more drinks and finished off with after dinner drinks while several couples danced to a great jazz band. I had never been in a private club like this before and was reminded of the nightclubs one saw in the movies. It was obvious that although our organization had a small budget, my hosts did not. I got to bed a little after midnight, a little tight and too full of rich food. This was a group that would veto my habit of scheduling early breakfast meetings.

I joined Al for breakfast the next morning and we went over the coming day's activities. He seemed to think the improvised program was fine and confirmed my feeling that I was off to a good start. I expressed my concern about the obvious tension between regions; he said he recognized the problem but had confidence in my ability to steer the organization through the current difficult situation. I thanked him for the vote of confidence while wondering if I might have gotten in over my head.

The committee meetings were held concurrently during the morning and Al suggested I drop in on each of them. As I walked through the lobby, a good many people came up and introduced themselves and wished me good luck. A couple of them volunteered some pretty hateful things about Jesse and I simply replied that I had enjoyed working with him thus far and would reserve my judgment. It was not the reply they wanted, but I was not about to take sides in a fight that appeared far from settled.

I was not expecting the reception I got at the committee meetings. When I walked in the door things came to a halt; the chairman introduced me, reviewed what they had done so far and asked for my input. Somehow, in each case I had some practical ideas about their respective activities. Their committee structure was not that different from what I was very accustomed to, but in my previous organizations I usually gave my input to committees ahead of the meetings while the chairmen and I were planning the agenda. I managed to get to all the committees, going through the same routine. I was pleased to find that my previous experience was adequate to carry me through the morning with one exception: the show committee. It seemed to be in the hands of the professionals who fed, fitted and hauled many of the members' show cattle to the various livestock shows. Several of the larger breeders had a manager qualified for this rather esoteric part of the registered cattle business. I had sense enough to defer to their experience and said I was looking forward to learning all I could from them. Over the years I proceeded to learn more than I wanted to know about cattle shows. This was the last year the Houston Livestock Show was held at the Port of Houston Stockyard. By the next year the newly completed Astrodome and adjoining facility, the Astroplex, were available for it.

At the business meeting Al Face gave his annual report and Ed Schock was elected president, along with the other officers presented by the nominating committee. Houston was selected as the site of the next convention and the show was to be called the first "International Brangus Show." When I was formally introduced I was pumped with adrenaline and gave the first of what would be an annual extemporaneous report. When the committee chairmen gave their reports, each one asked me to join him at the podium and share some of my ideas. I had never before, nor have I ever since, been carried so high.

At the board meeting following the general session, there were a few items of unfinished business concerning Jesse. They were somewhat contentious because Jesse voiced concerns on behalf of the Heart of America affiliate, the one he continued to represent on the board. The discussion that followed confirmed my fear that the regional antagonisms were far from healed. Fortunately, I managed to avoid antagonizing Jesse's loyal followers, even though I seemed to have made a good impression on the Texas faction, which obviously controlled the board.

As I subsequently tried to deliver on the lofty goals I had encouraged the organization to set for itself, I found I had bitten off as much as I could chew.

Once again, I found that a magazine requires a lot of attention. I didn't have to make it camera ready, as I had in California, but I had far more demands on my time now than I did then. Although a small organization, IBBA covered all but the northeast section of the US. Each of our local affiliates wanted me to attend at least one of their functions a year and I was expected to be on hand for all the approved Brangus shows. These included Fort Worth, San Antonio, Houston, Dallas (the Texas State Fair), Oklahoma City (the Oklahoma State Fair), Muskogee, Oklahoma, Little Rock (the Arkansas State Fair), the Phoenix Livestock Show, Tucson (the Pima County Fair and Rodeo), Kansas City (the American Royal Livestock Show) and the Clay County Fair (a huge county fair at Spencer, Iowa). In addition, there was a Brangus sale somewhere nearly every other week, usually on a weekend, a good many of which I felt I needed to attend. Also, I was expected to inspect cattle for individual breeders before registering them. The latter I endeavored to schedule in conjunction with my other travels.

I soon was driving 50,000 miles a year, and once within one week I flew on three airlines and stayed in five different motels, renting cars at one airport and returning them at another. I enjoyed visiting operations all across the country to inspect cattle and I was always enthusiastically welcomed at the area affiliate meetings, so the work was not in itself a strain, except occasionally at the Brangus shows. At the smaller ones I sometimes had to act as the Ring Steward, lining up classes, passing out ribbons and occasionally announcing the results. I also had to be sure I got home with the results and had made arrangements with the official photographer (when there was one) to mail me pictures of the champions.

As soon as I got home from these trips, I put out a news release to the livestock press and appropriate local papers reporting the event. In the releases about Brangus shows I always sent a picture of the grand champion male and female to the livestock press. I subscribed to a national clipping service and was amazed at how many were being picked up.

Needless to say this frantic schedule didn't contribute to mending a marriage that was already shaky. I came home from trips worn out. I occasionally took Ingrid and Elizabeth to the nearby events, but they were often pretty boring for them, and I was occupied with members a major portion of the time we were there. About this time, Ingrid's stepfather, Ciril Arko, applied for and was accepted for a professorship at Park College, a small liberal arts college at Parkville, Missouri, within a mile of our apartment. Both Ingrid's mother Ruth and Ciril were crazy about Elizabeth, who called Ruth Baba and Ciril Dedek.

Soon problems that harked back to our days in New Mexico resurfaced and Ingrid asked for a divorce. I moved into a dilapidated trailer house nearby and went to see a lawyer. I soon learned that it was just as hard to get a divorce in Missouri as it was easy to get married in Nevada. He said there was a one-year waiting period and about the only legal grounds was adultery. When I conveyed this information to Ingrid she wasn't about to admit to adultery and I certainly knew I hadn't committed it. I talked to the lawyer again and he said it was quite common for a man wanting out of a marriage in Missouri to admit to adultery he hadn't committed. I told him I thought that was atrocious, but went ahead and filed and told him I wanted to come up with terms fair to both of us. I said I expected to pay child support, but indicated I was reluctant to pay alimony, although I would pay tuition so Ingrid could get a BA degree from Park College. Some of her junior college credits from La Junta were transferable. I agreed to the child support he suggested and had him prepare the papers, which Ingrid soon agreed to. We saw no need for another lawyer and shared a sincere desire to spare Elizabeth as much stress as possible. We asked for and got joint possession based on our mutual convenience.

The next year and a half I was married to my work. Ingrid was glad to let me look after Elizabeth on weekends when I was home. I soon moved into a garden level one-bedroom apartment overlooking the Missouri River where it ran by the Kansas City Stockyard. One of my board members, Royal Buckley, lived there during the week. He had a printing business in Kansas City, Kansas and owned a farm near Ottawa, a small town about thirty-five miles south of Kansas City, Kansas. The apartment had a swimming pool was within walking distance of downtown Kansas City, Missouri, just across a viaduct from my office and almost within view of the old Kansas City airport. Whenever I was home, I picked up Elizabeth on Friday night and brought her back to Ingrid, or Baba and Dedek if Ingrid was gone, on Sunday night. When the year's wait was up, the only thing that changed was that I sent Ingrid child support instead of paying all her bills and she enrolled in Park College. She and I and her folks remained on good terms, but I sorely missed some kind of home life.

One day I was having lunch at the Golden Ox with Bill Van Horn, a casual business acquaintance from whom the association purchased all its business insurance, and when I told him my divorce would soon be final he mentioned his next-door neighbor was recently divorced. He said she had two young children and that he and his wife, Georgie, had been good friends with both her and her husband, Jim. He didn't tell me much more, but said he thought she might be just right for me. I had been giving some thought to dating, but didn't have any idea where to start, so I said I'd like to meet her. He said he would set something up, and few days later he called saying he had talked her into meeting us at, of all places the Hereford House, a fancy steak house in Kansas City. We got there a bit early and were seated before she arrived. Pretty soon he pointed to the door and said there she was. I looked up and saw a well-dressed, attractive young woman who radiated class. Bill got up and led her over to our table. I got up and helped her to her seat and Bill introduced us. Her name was Maxine McClanahan, and I immediately sensed that she was someone special. I said something inane hoping to impress her. She seemed quiet and a bit shy, but Bill in his irreverent way made us both reasonably comfortable.

As we were enjoying our after-dinner coffee, Maxine told us she would have to be getting home soon because her mother was looking after her children. When I asked her to tell me about them she said that she had a seven-year-old daughter, Shaun, and a three-year-old son Brendan. I told her about Elizabeth and said she was about the same age as Shaun. After a few more minutes of visiting I walked her to her car and asked if I could call her. She said that would be fine and I could get her phone number from Bill. As she drove away I knew I would be getting her number and calling her, and I hoped she would go out with me. She told me later that she had made up her mind that no matter who showed up with Bill, she was determined not to see him again because she really didn't feel ready to start dating.

Fortunately Maxine did decide to go out with me when I called and we went to a movie on our first date. I knew she

Maxine with Shaun and Brendan taken a few months before we met.

worked near down town, and after our second date, asked if she could meet me for lunch the next day. She agreed and suggested a little Italian restaurant downtown where she ate occasionally. I suggested we split a bottle of Chianti, the kind in a little wicker basket, with our lunch order of Lasagna. We both admitted that we rarely drank at noon, but would make an exception for our first lunch date. Sometime during the meal, we looked across at each other and spontaneously reached across the table and momentarily held hands. I don't remember saying much, but we later agree that was the trigger to a much more serious relationship.

The next time I called, she invited me for dinner in to her little two-bedroom house on the bluff overlooking the Missouri River in North Kansas City. When I came in, I saw Shaun peeking at me around a corner, and soon Brendan marched in, looked up at me with his big brown eyes, with long lashes that girls would kill for, and asked my name. They were beautiful children and their presence completed a domestic atmosphere that completely captivated me. Maxine fixed us a delicious fried chicken dinner. After she put the kids to bed, we sat on the little front porch in an old-fashioned swing. It was a beautiful summer night and we proceeded to talk about the primary thing we had in common, our respective divorces.

I told her my divorce from Ingrid had just been finalized and it turned out hers had been too. She said she had worked while her husband had attended the University of Kansas to help him get a degree in Civil Engineering. She didn't tell me much more then, but it gradually came out they started a small business designing and creating sewer systems for small towns and were quite successful. She had tried to hold their marriage together when he started drinking and picking up women in bars. During this time, he had purchased a small private airplane and he eventually flew to Mexico City with one of these women. She contacted a lawyer and the first thing he had her do was remove her husband from their joint business checking account. She said Jim couldn't understand why she would do such a thing because until then she had been working hard to salvage their marriage. She was granted a divorce with alimony and child support payments. She learned shortly after they were married that he had been married before and had two children. Ironically, Maxine had been making child support payments to Jim's ex-wife the whole time they were married, but subsequently Maxine never received any child support from Jim for Shaun and Brendan!

We were soon spending as much time together as possible. After I picked up Elizabeth on Friday night we usually had supper at Maxine's house. On Saturday I cleaned my apartment while Elizabeth watched TV and then I would do my laundry in the apartment machines and change my bed. In the meantime, Maxine did her chores and took her mother, Ilene and Grandma Frock, Ilene's mother who lived with her, shopping. They both lived a couple of miles away. We often took the kids to a movie or one of Kansas City's beautiful parks. Sometimes after I took Elizabeth home I picked up Maxine and her kids and we went over to Ilene's to watch the Sunday night TV shows.

Soon we were talking about possibly getting married. The problem was that because Maxine had been so badly burned, she thought we should wait. Still, she accepted a formal proposal just before Thanksgiving, only four months after we had met, and we decided to get married right after Christmas. Each of us arranged for a few days off from work in addition to the New Years Holiday for a short honeymoon in California.

Maxine holding Jennifer while riding her favorite mount, Dickie.

While we were dating, I had started attending All Saints Episcopal Church with Maxine. They had a wonderful pastor, Father Hingston, who had been a great help to Maxine, counseling her before and during her divorce. I felt comfortable in this denomination, in which I was baptized and attended in 1940 when we lived in Fort Collins, so I took instructions and was confirmed before our wedding. Nevertheless, since we were both divorced we couldn't be married in the Church, so a Methodist minister performed our simple wedding at Ilene's house, with two of Maxine's friends standing up with us. I spent Christmas Eve with Elizabeth, Ingrid and her parents, went on over to Maxine's early Christmas morning where we opened our presents, then went over to Grandma Ilene's to open more gifts and have Christmas dinner.

The morning of December 27, Maxine took Brendan and Shaun to Ilene's, we met Bill Van Horn back at her house and he took us to the airport for our flight to San Francisco, where I had hotel reservations for that night. The next morning I rented a car and we drove leisurely down the coast to our motel on the ocean near Santa Barbara. We spent three wonderful days walking on the beach and made several trips to San Diego to Sea World, the Naval Station and other sites. We drove back to San Francisco on the Freeway and flew back to Kansas City on New Year's Day, where Bill picked us up and drove us back to Maxine's house.

Since I was thirty-seven and Maxine was thirty-two, we decided that if we were going to add an "ours" and become a yours-and-mine-and-ours family, the sooner the better. Maxine was soon pregnant and although we loved her house, we thought we would need a bigger place to live. We found a three-bedroom town house with three small bedrooms and a bath upstairs, a living room-dining room, kitchen and bath on the main floor, and the washer and dryer in the basement. The complex had an outdoor pool and parking for both our cars and was a short drive to both our offices. Jennifer was born on January 29, 1970, while we were living there.

Considering the number of miles I was driving, the board decided it would be cheaper to rent or buy me a car than continue paying mileage. The first year they rented one from a dealer in Kansas City, but the next year Bud Adams, a board member, who had a Dodge/Plymouth dealership in Houston in addition to his other interests, sold the association a new Plymouth Fury III low-mileage executive vehicle for a good price. It had all the optional features Plymouth offered and the hottest engine of any car I had ever driven since my 1955 Chevy. I was soon driving to Houston on the Kansas Turnpike with my automatic speed control set at the 85-mph speed limit until I had to stop for gas. Of all the cars I have driven in my life, this one was probably my favorite.

I usually had enough show and sale results to furnish most of the copy in the magazine. I modified my news releases and added the pictures of class winners and members at the events. Royal Buckley had convinced the association to buy me a twin lens 4" X 4" reflex camera with a prism. At the smaller shows I took pictures of the class winners, but still hired a professional photographer for the big ones. By the time I added my column, called "Brangus Topics," our problem was not having enough ad revenue to print as many pages as we needed. Fortunately, with the growing number of sales to advertisers, we were able to make the magazine break even most months.

After several years of calm, the clamor to move the office started coming up at board meetings again and Paul Davis, a breeder who owned a large appliance dealership in Oklahoma City and a good-sized Brangus herd at a farm nearby, lobbied for his city as an intermediate choice between Kansas and Texas. Finally, the board appointed a committee to study locations for an office move, making my neighbor, Royal Buckley, the chairman. On weekends Maxine, the kids and I often drove down to the Buckley farm for a Sunday picnic. It was located in beautiful rolling country with a good population of white-tail deer, which we often spotted. Naturally Royal and I talked about the move and he, more than most, appreciated the seriousness of the politics involved with his Heart of America affiliate, which considered it heresy to even talk about it. Royal and I were pretty sure a majority of the board would vote to move, but doubted if the association could afford to build an office, and we realized that we could never get cheaper rent than at our present location.

When Royal reported at the next board meeting he said his committee had looked at all the options and thought that moving the office south, closer to where the great majority of our members lived, was logical, but with our current financial situation an increase in registration and/or membership fees would probably become necessary. After considerable discussion, the board voted to recommend that Royal and I proceed to look for suitable locations in Oklahoma City, San Antonio and the Dallas-Fort Worth area. There were supporters on the board for all three locations and a couple still devoted to keeping it in Kansas City. Royal and I indicated we had no preference and would do our best to find something the association could afford.

Artists rendering of new headquarters of International Brangus Breeders Association new building in San Antonio

46

Moving the Office

One of our most active board members, Dr. Herman Gardner, who owned Willow Springs Ranch in Burton, Texas, stumbled on an angel who gave our dreams of building a new headquarters building new hope. Somehow he had made a friend in Israel, when he was there at a medical convention, who wanted to invest in American real estate, and Dr. Gardner had told him that IBBA needed money to finance a building. He said he would consider financing a building for us on a contract for deed, wherein he would put down $10,000, carry the rest of the financing and charge us interest for only ten years. The board decided it was too good an offer to pass up and told Royal and me to start looking in earnest for a new location. We had been instructed that, if possible, we would buy the land and build specifically to our needs.

The son-in-law of another board member, Owen Womack, who had a ranch near Menard and a home in San Antonio, put us in touch with a large real estate firm in San Antonio, who offered to put a package deal together for us. They showed us several properties, including a small tract of land that seemed like an ideal spot. It was on I-10 just south of I-410 in the northwest quarter of San Antonio. We learned that the zoning would allow us to put up a large sign clearly visible from I-10. It had good access to the freeway.

Royal and I were sure we had found the right spot, but continued to look at other locations as Owen's son-in-law negotiated on behalf of the association for the property we really wanted. We found nothing that looked nearly as suitable, and by the next board meeting we had a tentative proposal ready. The deal called for the real estate company to sell us the approximately six-tenths of an acre and construct a building that our architect had designed, all to be paid for by the Israeli, who would lease it to us in monthly payments based on the annual interest. This turned out to be little more than the rent we paid for the current office in Kansas City.

No one had anticipated that anything might move this quickly with so little upfront cost and such reasonable monthly payments. I pointed out that there would be substantial moving costs and cash flow problems during the move, when we wouldn't be able to process paperwork. A Texas board member moved that we submit the proposal to an attorney, and if the details could be worked out as presented, we proceed with the move. The motion was seconded and fully debated, with several board members picking up on my concerns and wondering if any of the staff was willing to move. The motion passed with a two-thirds majority and I was instructed by the board, provided the lawyers said the proposal was sound, to prepare to move the office within the approximately six months period estimated to prepare the site and build the office.

The likelihood of an office move had been a constant for the six years I had been on the staff, but we hadn't anticipated that it might be thrust upon us so suddenly. Maxine and I had bought a home in southwest Kansas City, Missouri after about a year in our town house. We loved Shaun's and Brendan's school, used the big swimming pool at the Jewish Community Center about a mile away and had recently worked very hard painting the entire house. I knew the two married women who helped Mrs. Matney could not move and I doubted that she would.

As our registrations and transfers increased, I realized that we couldn't keep up with our labor-intensive hand system of checking pedigrees without hiring more staff; plus we were running out of space for more files and it would be hard to find room for more staff, even if we could afford them. Finally, I had to get help with the magazine, so I hired a man with a newspaper background to help with the magazine and public relations. I knew we had to look into automating our registration processing and was aware a couple of the smaller breed associations were farming out their pedigree preparation to Boeing Aircraft Corporation, which was doing custom work for other businesses in order to better utilize its huge mainframe computer. I called those breed association executives and picked their brains about this option. They both said it worked well except for the extra time it took getting their applications to Boeing and the registrations papers returned. It added about two weeks to the turnaround time.

On the bluff across the river from our office sat the biggest breed registry in the country at the time, the American Hereford Association. I had met their business manager, who was in charge of their fully computerized registration system, when he had made a presentation at a United States Beef Breeds Council meeting. I made an appointment to visit him about their operation. He agreed to see me and enthusiastically showed me his computer, which was much smaller than Boeing's, but still had enough excess capacity to easily handle our registrations on a custom basis. He said his software would suffice with minimal modification since they would basically just be printing registration forms from registration or transfer applications we submitted to them. He said he could create the certificates for $1.00 each, which we could cover with a one-dollar increase in the cost of registrations and transfers. Our office would still have to check applications and transfers to prove the applicant was a member and owned the sire and dam on the registration application.

We worked up a contract, which the board approved at the next meeting along with a small increase in fees to cover part of the added expense. The way it worked, we simply carried a week's worth of applications to them each Friday afternoon and picked up the new registration certificates on Monday, because they had data entry staff working on weekends. The only change we made in the registration certificates was to program the AHA printer to automatically affix my signature to them.

The news that the office move was now a sure thing was met by the office staff just as I suspected. The only person who wanted to go was the one I did not want to take, and that was the magazine editor. Maxine loved our new house, we disliked the thought of Shaun changing schools and we hated the prospect of not being able to have Elizabeth every weekend. I even looked into job prospects in the area. Both the Horned and Polled Hereford Associations had offices in Kansas City, but I wasn't fickle enough to consider jumping ship to one of them. I did look into Farmland Industries, a big agricultural co-op that slaughtered and processed mostly hogs. I found they had a tradition of hiring young people and bringing them up within the system. Also even though it involved lots of travel and long hours, I loved my job and felt a responsibility to help carry through on the fairly ambitious course we had set for ourselves. However we felt about the move, there was nothing we could do but get busy preparing for it.

    The logistics of the move and getting up and running at the new location turned out to be formidable. All our records, which were so vital to our operation, were stored in old metal fireproof cabinets with sliding drawers, about ten of them. We would need them up until the day we moved and would have to get into them almost immediately after arriving at our new location if we were going to avoid falling dangerously behind in our work. We hoped to get moved and back in operation in two weeks, and then we had to add a week's turnaround for the paperwork we would now have to mail to the AHA in Kansas City. On top of that, I faced the prospect of training new help to receive applications, check them and box them for shipping. Thank God I was able to talk Mrs. Matney into making the move and staying until she got the office set up. Her husband had died a year earlier, and although she had reached retirement age, she decided she would like to work for another six months to a year. Without her, the move would have been a disaster and was difficult enough as it was. She had recently hired an eighteen-year-old daughter of a member in Iowa, and after some hesitation, she agreed to come along too. She decided she didn't like being so far from home and ended up moving back after a couple of months, but it greatly helped having only one new person to train initially.

    I had to fly to San Antonio every week to meet the builder and architect, and on one trip there I visited a man I had met at Texas Brangus shows who published a magazine called "The American Zebu." I can't remember his name, but everyone called him Slim, which he certainly was. Zebu is the name used to describe the many Bos Indicus types of cattle originating in southeast Asia from which the American Brahman breed was developed by crossing it with Bos Taurus (mostly English breeds) cattle in America in the early 1900s. For a period of years there was a Zebu breed registry that registered cattle under that name in competition with the American Brahman Breeders Association, but it was struggling and Slim's magazine suffered with it. He was an old pro in magazine publishing, which was just what I needed to keep the Brangus Journal viable while I was so busy with all my other duties, and I was fortunate to get him to join our staff.

Before we moved, Maxine and I had to sell our house, find a place in San Antonio and see what her mother and Grandma might want or need to do. Ilene didn't drive, so when Maxine and her sister, Beverly, were growing up they had all learned to get around Kansas City on the street car. Bev left home for college in Iowa right after high school, but Maxine stayed home and worked while she went to night school. She bought a big old Chrysler from a neighbor, learned to drive when she was sixteen and had been driving her mother and Grandma Frock wherever they needed to go ever since. They were both attached to Shaun and Brendan, whom they had looked after most weekdays since they were born and quickly decided to move with us.

I thought Ilene might like a break from looking after Grandma Frock and suggested we consider building a house in Texas with little living quarters in it for her mother, while she could get an apartment. I subscribed to a San Antonio paper, started looking for property and apartments there and listed our house with a realtor. We also looked at acreages listed within driving distance of the office because we agreed we would love an acreage, if we could afford to buy one and build a house.

In mid-summer, Maxine joined me on one of my trips and we spent a weekend looking at property. I had called the owner of a seven-acre lot in a sub-division near Boerne, called Friendly Hills, about a mile and half from town, that looked promising. It was one of about ten acreages there, most of which already had houses on them. It was reached by an asphalt road winding through rolling hills covered with scattered cedar trees, live oak trees and brush, with outcroppings of rock that had been formed by an ancient lava flow. The seven acres were fenced, with a dirt road leading to the center, where there was a good building site. We saw a roadrunner when we drove in and had already seen small white tail deer nearby. We decided the acreage was just what we were looking for and told the owner we would be back the next morning to talk further. We spent the night in Boerne, a picturesque little town of about 2,000. In the morning we visited the office of a local builder, Mack George, who, the acreage owner said, had built several of the attractive rock homes in the sub-division. We told him what we had in mind and showed him a floor plan we had found in "Successful Farming" magazine. They said they had someone who could draw up a set of blue prints for us from it and they would give us an estimate. They were active in the community and gave a glowing report on the small town and its school system. When we looked at the seven acres again that afternoon, we learned that the owner had bought it on time and would be willing to let us make a down payment covering his small equity and take over the payments.

We went back home with a lot to think about, but were enthusiastic about the prospect of building in such a beautiful rural setting; now, if only we could pull it off. We needed to get started soon if we were to build a house and be moved in by the time the office was completed.

We soon had a couple of lookers at our house in Kansas City but no offers. We needed to get close to our asking price to afford a down payment for a new home. We knew that it would be a miracle if the office was completed, our house sold and a new one built all in the same time frame but we barged ahead. We finally sold the house to a Rabbi who needed a place within walking distance to the synagogue. Unfortunately, we had to give possession earlier than we wanted to, but we couldn't take a chance waiting for another buyer.

When the house was sold, we immediately dealt for the acreage. Mack sent us a slightly amended floor plan that looked as if it would be perfect for our family and Grandma Frock. They altered the master bedroom to make a small kitchenette, creating an efficiency apartment. The other three bedrooms were along a hall with a shared bathroom. The house also had a two-car attached garage, a domestic well and a septic tank. We were able to get a thirty-year loan, and the lot had only about six more payments left on it. Mack said he was pretty sure he could have the house ready to occupy by the date we had to give possession on our Kansas City home.

As the time approached when we were going to have to move out of our house, it became apparent that neither the office nor our new home would be completed on schedule. I told Mack George we would have to find a place to rent while he finished our new house. He finally came up with a small two-bedroom house in the country about ten miles from Boerne at just about the time we were loading our furniture on the moving van in Kansas City. We decided to leave our youngest daughter, Jennifer, with the grandmas until we were moved. Our friend, Bill Van Horn, offered to look in on them and get their groceries until our new home was finished.

We had two days en route and arrived at our little house the night before the moving van was due. We found the house to be a delightful little bungalow that obviously wouldn't hold all our furniture. While Maxine and the kids were cleaning the house and deciding who would sleep where, I went to Boerne and picked up a roll of plastic to cover the furniture we would have to store outside for a while. We were expecting our furniture after lunch the next day, so after spending the night at the rustic old hotel in Boerne, we ate breakfast and then went to see our nearly completed house. We had decided to use Mexican brick instead of rock on the exterior and it turned out to be an attractive pinkish earth tone. They were far enough along for us see how the interior looked, except for the floor coverings, interior paint and ash paneling, which was popular at the time.

We got back to our temporary home right after lunch and walked down to a little brook running about 100 yards from the house. We saw a few fish swimming around in a pool under some overhanging rock. We spent the afternoon out in the sun watching hopefully for a moving van that didn't show up until dusk. The driver said he didn't have anyone with him to help unload, so would have to wait until morning to get someone. When I said I'd sure like to get it unloaded right now, he said he would pay me if I helped him. By midnight we had stuffed everything we could in the house and piled the rest outside. The driver thanked me profusely, handed me a well-earned twenty-dollar bill and went on his way. We had somehow managed to get our big dresser and mirror, smaller dresser and queen sized bed in the bigger of the two bedrooms and a bunk bed in the other for Shaun and Brendan. We ended up having to spend about ten days in our little house and got quite attached to it. The kids and I even caught a few little perch in the stream a couple of times, which Maxine cooked for us.

Maxine and I found an apartment for her mother within walking distance of a grocery store close to the Brangus office in northwest San Antonio. The move to Texas took place in stages. Maxine drove her mother, Shaun, Brendan and a U-Haul trailer load of furniture to San Antonio; I accompanied Grandma Frock and two-year-old Jennifer on an airplane from Kansas City to San

Antonio; and finally, I helped Maxine carry Ilene's furniture from the U-Haul up to her second-floor apartment, all in a twenty-four-hour period without a wink of sleep.

Our new office turned out to be quite distinctive, built in an H shape featuring lots of large glass windows. The architect was extremely protective of his plans and got crossways with the construction foreman on several occasions, each resulting in several days' delay. He selected unique and hard-to-get bamboo floor coverings in several rooms instead of carpet and ordered modernistic canvas chairs for the waiting room in the lobby, which I hated. He was sensitive, temperamental and completely oblivious to my concerns about scheduling the shipment of furniture from Kansas City and getting it unloaded in San Antonio in a tight time frame. We nearly had to store our office furniture and supplies when he balked over some minor (to me) thing during the final inspection, just as our moving van was due to arrive. I did get to pick the desk and credenza for my overly large, fancy office and he wasn't impressed with my choice. He told me we needed to keep to the modern décor, so I ordered a red telephone for the reception desk. He walked in the front door and bellowed, "Who ordered that atrocious thing!" I finally lost it and unloaded on him. I can't remember just what I said, but it was something to the effect than I had a lot more important things to worry about and I was sick of his fussy ways. He looked as if he was going to cry and walked out. As is often the case, under stress I blew up about one of the least important issues that had come up.

Actually, most of the members who visited the office were impressed with our new digs and fortunately cut us a lot of slack when we were three weeks behind getting their registration papers returned. Mrs. Matney soon had a new young woman trained, and when our homesick young staff member went back to Iowa we were able to replace her with a highly competent young woman, who showed promise of being able to replace Mrs. Matney on the registration side. My greatest concern was that when Mrs. Matney left I would have to hire a full-time bookkeeper, and sure enough, the one sent to us by the employment agency didn't work out, putting us further behind on our billing. We were able to get Temple University in San Antonio to print our registration certificates, but it still took us about six months to be back on schedule after getting a second bookkeeper up to speed. By that time the membership had gotten pretty upset and the excuse that we had just moved wasn't working any more.

However, our new staff got up to speed and we were soon on schedule and continued to sign up new breeders while our registrations and transfers grew steadily. Unfortunately this growth barely covered the cost of the two staff members I had to hire to replace Mrs. Matney. She deserved better, but since we had no retirement program I had talked the board into buying her a good used car when she agreed to go get the office running in San Antonio. Without her steady, hard work and complete loyalty we could never have made it through the office transition. She remained a close friend to Maxine and me until her death about ten years later.

Shortly before the move, IBBA applied for membership in the U.S.Beef Breeds Council, an organization made up of the executive officers of the associations of all the established breeds of beef cattle in the country. The most prominent members were the AHA, Polled Hereford Association, American Angus Breeders Association, American Shorthorn Breeders Association--these four associations being about the so-called English breeds—and the American International Charolaise Breeders Association, The American Brahman Breeders Association and IBBA. Even though we all competed fiercely with one another, we put our differences aside when we got together for these meetings to promote the value of using pedigreed cattle to improve commercial herds, and we enjoyed talking shop about our mutual problems. When IBBA joined the council, the old heads of this group were the Swaffar brothers: Paul, who headed the AHA and Pete, who ran the American Shorthorn Association, the longest established breed in America. Their deeply conservative, traditional approach to the role of breed registries caused them to lead a rearguard action against the growing practice of performance testing. Oddly enough, the AHA opposed incorporating records, such as weaning and yearling weights, along with pedigree information, although their usefulness were best being demonstrated by one of the breeds most prominent commercial Hereford herds at the Bell Ranch in New Mexico.

After we were all settled in San Antonio, the breed continued growing at a slow but steady pace, and a good many more herds began to fit and show cattle at the stock shows and fairs across the country. Since the Houston Livestock Show had moved next to the Astrodome, it had grown greatly, and our Brangus show was already well established there; consequently, the IBBA board decided to designate it as the International Brangus Show. They instructed the staff and officers to work with the management to schedule a special event right after our show, which was to be designated as the International Brangus Sale. We were able to build a great deal of publicity around this first International Brangus Show and Sale, and managed to draw a record number of cattle to the show. The fact that the grand champion bull was entered in the sale and sold for a record price greatly enhanced the prestige of these two events the first year, and we generally had our annual convention in conjunction with them.

To protect the credibility of the breed as a unique combination of the best of the black Angus and Brahman breeds crossed and back crossed to the exact level of three eighths Brahman and five-eighths Angus, I asked the board to reverse some previous policy decisions that were actually contrary to our by-laws. One was to let a few Brangus that didn't have a registered sire and/or dam into the herd book. In the discussion that ensued I learned that few people knew there were any "certified" Brangus in the herd book, and that previous board action was quickly rescinded.

Jesse had told me the base of his foundation Angus herd had come from the Wye Plantation, one of the largest Angus herds in the nation, and he was a good friend of their manager, Jim Lingle. What I didn't know at that time was that many Wye cows had a considerable amount of white on their udders, and the AAA, like the IBBA, would not record any animals with white on the underline ahead of the navel. These animals were discriminated against because some thought this was an indication of possible Holstein breeding in their backgrounds. In any case, Clear Creek, Jesse and possibly a few other early Brangus breeders were able to buy some of these valuable cows, and no one knew whether they could have been registered or not. There is no doubt that Wye Plantation Angus made a valuable contribution to the Brangus Breed's genetic base, and to my knowledge Lingle's integrity had never been doubted. If the exception could have been limited to this one herd, the issue might have gone away, but with our breed's recent growth in popularity we had recently had an influx of inquiries for Angus with no papers and I had to get the issue cleared up. I was told to require registration papers, but the board reserved the right to consider individual cases where registered parentage could be documented, such as Brangus breeders who might choose to enroll Angus produced from their own enrolled Angus.

My training in animal breeding and genetics in college caused me to question some of the seemingly arbitrary rules in the purebred world. For instance, "breed character" was a visual measure of the intermediate physical appearance of Angus and Brahman cattle, while Herefords have to be red with white faces with or without horns and Angus have to be black. Brangus simply must look as if they are three-eighths Brahman and five-eighths Angus.

I often invited some of the most highly respected young animal science staff members from land grant universities, such as Texas A & M, Penn State, Nebraska, Wisconsin, VPI and Iowa to speak at our conventions. These were men in the forefront of the performance testing movement, and several of them were also invited to judge many of our biggest shows—and this during a time when the tension between using show ring results and performance testing data was growing.

Frank, Dad Chuck, Mom and me at the folks'
fiftieth wedding anniversary party in Denver in 1973.

Left to right: Frank's youngest daughter, Julie, Jennifer and Grandpa Lilley,

Brendan, Jennifer on Grandpa's lap and Mark, Chuck's youngest child.

47

Brink's Brangus

The steady growth in the Brangus breed greatly accelerated after the dispersal sale of the Riverby Ranch, one of its best-known Texas herds. The man who bought the best part of this foundation herd, Lloyd Brinkman, was the catalyst. Brink, as he was often called, brought his brother Glenn in to manage his new registered Brangus operation, "Brink's Brangus," while he expanded his role as the foremost marketer of carpet in the nation, labeled, "Brinkcrest." Lloyd and Glenn leased several properties before they settled on their highly improved ranch at Sisterdale, Texas, not far from Kerrville, where they expanded into breeding quarter horses. By adding several proven Brangus herd sires and hiring one of the best men available to fit and show their cattle, "Brink's Brangus" were soon winning more than their share of Brangus shows and establishing a production sale that was the envy of the breed, as it set new records annually. These sales featured a catered white tablecloth steak dinner the night before the sale. Drinks were delivered to buyers viewing the cattle, before the sale and also in the stands, when it was going on, much like gamblers in a Las Vegas casino. People who knew bloodlines came to realize that, everything else being equal, an animal bought at a Brink's sale had extra value, and this fact was demonstrated by the record prices realized at these carefully orchestrated events.

Timing played a hand in the dual success of Lloyd Brinkman's string of record-breaking sales and the growth of the Brangus breed generally. The prices of registered breeding stock had historically followed the price cycles of the commercial cattle industry, but wealthy folks discovered that some of the quirks of our income tax code made owning breeding stock in a rising market a good tax shelter, or at least tax deferral, which distorted the traditional relationship between registered and commercial cattle. Large herds were being put together by selling limited partnerships to investors who didn't need to own real estate to get into the business. These cattle were managed on large ranches owned or leased by a managing partner who had spread ownership of the herd over many limited partnerships.

These operations, whether they knew it or not, resembled pyramid schemes dependent on a constant supply of new investors. In a stable market, the primary source of income to a registered cattle breeder is range bulls for commercial operations and a few herd sire prospects for other registered producers. The demand for registered heifers was limited to replacements in their own herd and a few going to other breeders and new people in the business, with the tail end sold as feeders or replacements in commercial herds. Because of this, the average price of bulls offered for sale normally considerably exceeded the price of their heifer mates. The growth of limited partnerships added new demand for registered females, and nearly all breeds saw a growth in numbers at advancing prices. The boost in energy that the Brinkmans injected into the IBBA, at the time limited partnerships were growing, greatly increased the number of registered Angus presented for enrollment and built a fire under the demand for good three-quarter blood bulls. This put pressure on our inspection system, which hadn't had to deal with such an influx of Angus before. Changes in show ring standards, fueled by the growth in performance testing, among other things, had established registered Angus breeders competing for the kind of females that were not appreciated in the fifties and early sixties, but had fortunately been sought out by pioneer Brangus breeders.

Suddenly a lot of these registered Angus that had fallen out of favor were presented for enrollment as their owners were looking to tap into the growing demand for Brangus. A lot of these smaller Angus, many of which we had to turn down, were being bred to the newly arrived, large-framed continental breeds in top crossing programs. These programs were being used by their newly formed breed associations to grade up to cattle that would be designated purebreds after the fourth top cross. Few of these organizations had specifications for the females being used. As a result there were tremendous calving problems in many new operations. At an industry meeting, I heard the CEO of one of the continental breeds tell the CEO of the American Angus Association, with his tongue planted firmly in his cheek, "We did your breed a huge favor when you sold thousands of your undersized females into our upgrading program and they died calving." The purebred industry was in the middle of unsustainable growth, a bubble that was pricked with the Reagan 1986 income tax overhaul.

By 1973, it became apparent that I couldn't keep up with the growing demands on my time. We had picked up several more cattle shows, more breeders were having their own production sales and our state affiliates were getting more active and demanding staff attention. We were also faced with the fact that as the interest in performance testing of registered cattle grew, we would soon need to keep production records for our breeders, a service that would almost certainly require a computer. Nearly all software at that time was proprietary and, if you could buy it at all, very expensive. Software for recording and updating performance records was also much more complex than that for just maintaining pedigrees, and these programs were just being written. Good code writers (we called them programmers in those days and computer salesmen joked they were all kept locked up in their attics) were extremely hard to find, very independent and expensive. Still, I was faced with the fact that, when we added performance testing to our services, our service bureau wouldn't be able to handle it for us.

After talking to several smaller breed associations that were using Boeing's computer and one association that had bought its own computer, I decided our best bet would be to go with a computer, a couple of data entry stations and a printer.

As all this was going on, I was authorized to hire someone who could help me with all my current responsibilities and was at least somewhat computer literate. Our news release announcing the job opening didn't attract a lot of applicants, but fortunately one of them, David Whitman, seemed to be just what I had in mind, and I was able to hire him. He was thirty-two years old, raised on a ranch in Sedalia, Colorado and had an animal science degree from Colorado A & M. He had received an ROTC Air Force commission in administration and had just been discharged with the rank of Captain. He had learned the fundamentals of computer programming while in the service and liked the idea that we were contemplating incorporating performance record-keeping into our services. He was married with two young children and I was impressed with his quiet, but confident personality. I knew he would fit in well with the staff and the members would like him as well. My goal was to involve him in all aspects of our work, much as my first boss at the ANCA had done for me, and I was looking forward to splitting my travel with someone.

With Slim as editor, the Brangus Journal had improved in general appearance and advertising revenue had increased, but the job got to be more than he could handle as he passed retirement age. I needed someone who could not only edit the magazine but also travel, sell ads and work as a ring man at our sales, a service we didn't currently offer. I had my eye on a man named Kenneth Archer, who worked for the Denver-based livestock publication, "The Record Stockman." His sales reports were well written and his articles had a little more edge to them than most in the rather conservative field of agricultural journalism. I called his boss at the paper, whom I knew, and asked for and received permission to interview him. I called Ken and made an appointment to meet him at a sale we would both be attending soon. He was about Dave's age and a little brash, at least compared to Dave. He obviously understood the nuts and bolts of preparing and printing a magazine and said he enjoyed traveling to sales, selling advertising and particularly taking bids at sales. He said he was ready for a change and agreed to come to work for IBBA.

When Ken arrived a few weeks later, he hit the ground running. He was an excellent salesman and quickly increased our advertising revenue. His willingness and ability to take bids from monkeys in the rafters made him popular with sales managers, auctioneers and those selling cattle. I was aware that ring men sometimes took phantom bids to run up the price to unsuspecting buyers, but he was an artist at it. When Ken made a big deal about how much money he had "stolen" at a Brangus sale, I reminded him the IBBA had as big an obligation to the buyers as it did the sellers. When he pointed out that what he did was a time-honored tactic in livestock auctions, I hated the fact that he was right, but I checked my righteous indignation and got off my high horse, not wanting to cost the magazine sale advertising when it was finally more than paying its own way. I had never had to wrestle with that kind of problem in my previous jobs.

Soon after we moved into our new house in Boerne, Ingrid called me and rather casually asked if Maxine and I would like to have Elizabeth come and live with us. I put my hand over the phone and asked Maxine if she would like to have Elizabeth join the family. After thinking no more than a few seconds she simply said that would be fine and I told Ingrid we would be happy to have her. I made arrangements to buy Elizabeth a plane ticket that Ingrid could pick up at the Kansas City airport and she flew down by herself. Later, neither Maxine nor I could believe what a major decision we had made on the spur of the moment and wondered what had motivated Ingrid to make such a suggestion. We concluded that she had decided her somewhat bohemian lifestyle would not be good for Elizabeth now that she was approaching her teens, and our "conventional" family life would be better for her. I knew that Baba and Dadik would miss their granddaughter, but suspected they supported Ingrid's decision.

When we lived in Kansas City Elizabeth almost always had spent weekends at our house, even when I wasn't home. Maxine was even-handed with the two girls and I'm sure Elizabeth enjoyed being with us, but we noticed she became a little distant when Sunday afternoon rolled around and I got ready to take her home. We knew she dearly loved Ingrid and her grand parents and we were careful never to criticize Ingrid in front of any of the kids. To my knowledge Ingrid never spoke ill of us. Shaun and Elizabeth had already become close, even though they were different in looks and temperament, and they got along as well as or better than most sisters. They had particularly liked to play with Barbie dolls together and were reasonably good at letting Jennifer join them. Much to Jennifer's chagrin, just about the time she was old enough to really enjoy Barbies, her sisters decided they were too old to play with them any more.

When the kids started school in Boerne, we were glad Shaun had skipped a grade in Kansas City. Shaun and Elizabeth were both beautiful girls, but Maxine thought Shaun was intimidated by Elizabeth's long blond hair and blue eyes and they would probably be more comfortable in separate classes. The one thing we weren't looking forward to was the fact we had two girls only five months apart who were just entering their teen years.

We liked everything about Boerne, whose population had not yet been affected by its proximity to San Antonio. It had a good school system and we felt at home immediately in its little stone

Episcopal church. Before long I found myself elected to the vestry and we both taught Sunday school classes. Maxine always went to church with the kids when I was traveling on weekends, which was not uncommon.

The first summer, Brendan played baseball in the Boerne Little League, and being left-handed and fairly tall he played first base and pitched occasionally in relief. This was about the time when girls first were allowed to play with the boys at the youngest level in Little League and Jennifer started playing just as soon as she was old enough. I watched both of them play whenever possible and was a typical parent, booing the hapless volunteers who umpired if they made any call disadvantageous to my kids. Jennifer wasn't the best player on her team, but she did get on base often. In one close game when she was on third with the bases loaded, one of her teammates got a weak infield hit and Jennifer came storming for home standing straight up as the throw went to the catcher. I yelled at the top of my lungs, "Slide Benny-Boo, slide," as she ran head-on into the catcher. Not only was she out, I had let slip my pet name for her and she took a lot of kidding about it from her team mates.

We quickly learned that Texans were unbelievably proud of their home state and were gracious and welcoming to new residents. One thing that Maxine had a problem dealing with was how to respond when we were told how lucky we were supposed to feel for having moved to the Lone Star State. She couldn't resist telling a few who gushed a little too much that even though we enjoyed Texas, we had been very happy in Missouri and the decision to move had been difficult.

The winters in Boerne, which was in the Hill Country of central Texas, were mild, with only a few days below freezing, unusually carried in by a Blue Norther. We were well-removed from the humidity coming from the Gulf of Mexico and were favored with cooling breezes much of the summer. The first winter we were in Boerne we got several inches of snow, not realizing how rare it was. When we went out with our kids on the sled we had brought with us, we learned it was the only one in the community. The neighborhood kids lined up to ride it down the hills on the paved road connecting the homes in Friendly Hills.

Our acreage was typical of the Hill Country landscape in that it had very shallow but fertile soil scattered around protruding moss-covered volcanic rocks. There was far more brush than grass, making it ideal country for goats, which thrive on browse. In fact, this area was considered the goat capital of the country. Still, such soil as there was was quite fertile and the open bottomlands were often covered with hybrid coastal Bermuda grass, which had to be planted by sprigging in bits of recently dug sod because the seed was sterile. It then spread like crab grass and over the years had to be plowed up and reseeded because it became sod-bound. Our seven acres had a lot of brush and some scattered cedar, but I figured there was enough grass for a couple of horses and I talked the folks into hauling a couple of saddle mares when they came to visit in the spring.

That first winter, I built a fence dividing our pasture in half, a small corral and a small barn with box stalls on either side of a tack and feed room. I ordered several tons of good topsoil to spread over the shallow soil around the house and planted annual rye grass, intending to sprig in St. Augustine grass in the stubble the next spring. This lawn grass was popular in the southern states where Kentucky Bluegrass doesn't do well. Since it was a spreading hybrid grass like coastal Bermuda, I bought one roll of sod and broke it into about two-inch square pieces, which I planted about four to six inches apart. It took about two years for them to spread into a solid lawn. I put a chain link fence around the house and lawn, fenced our lane into the house from the main road and we were ready for some horses again.

The folks brought us two good broke registered mares, Nan and Meg, and later I took a weekend to get Maxine's Arab gelding and Suzie Belle from the farm. Often on Sunday afternoons, I would ride on one of the mares with Jennifer on the front of the saddle. During one such ride we saw a fox, and as we watched it disappear into a culvert under the road I said to Jennifer, "Did you see that fox go into that tunnel?" When we got back I made a batch of fudge and after supper we all watched the Wonderful World of Disney. The next Sunday Jennifer started a new Sunday afternoon ritual when she said, "Daddy lets go riding, look at the fox in the noodle, make some fudge and watch Walt Dizeny."

The second year we had the mares in Texas, we decided to breed them. We had a lot of fun selecting a stud, and after consulting with Mom on pedigrees, we picked one we felt would fit with their blood lines. They got with foal and the next spring Nan had a beautiful filly. A few weeks later Meg—the original Meg's daughter—went into labor on a Saturday morning and we watched her nervously for a couple of hours before she finally lay down and started to deliver. After the front feet showed up, she continued to strain for what seemed like a long time. I was concerned because our experience had been that mares either foaled easily—nearly all the time—or they had really serious trouble. I finally got impatient and sat down behind her, put a foot on either side of her tail and proceeded to pull each time she started to push. The colt finally came, but it wouldn't start breathing. Its heart was beating but it just wouldn't breathe. I gave it a slap and finally picked it up, dropped it and told Maxine to call the vet. I squeezed one nostril shut and started breathing into the other. A horse can't breathe through its mouth. I was able to keep its heart beating until the vet showed up and he took over the respiration for a while. Finally, as a last resort, he gave the colt a shot of adrenalin directly into the heart as I continued to breath through the nostril. Its heartbeat immediately became faster and stronger and then quit.

I told him just what had happened and, as diplomatically as possible, he said I should have left the mare alone for a good bit longer. He said it very well might not have breathed in any case, but it is rarely a good idea to pull a foal as you might a calf. It was a beautiful, fully formed sorrel filly and we were all devastated. We raised several more colts during our stay in Texas, and fortunately Meg had a fine healthy colt the next year.

48

Tight Budget

The next major activity the association took on was the creation of the International Brangus Futurity in Fredericksburg, Texas, a show sponsored by the association featuring the best of the breed from across the United States. Fredericksburg was the seat of Gillespie County in the heart of the Hill Country and quite an art center. Its fair grounds had excellent facilities for a livestock show and sale, and all the animals entered in the show were required to be put up for sale. We went all out getting trophies for show winners and obtained a nationally recognized judge. We had a big banquet the night before the sale and booked cowboy cartoonist and humorist, Ace Reid, as speaker. We also hired Red Steagall to play for a western dance after the banquet. We worked hard to entice members to bring cattle that they would normally have retained in their herd and promised to go all out promoting the event. The first year was a nail biter, but it went well enough that we were able to make it an annual event of nearly equal importance to our international show and sale at the Houston Livestock Show and Rodeo.

At our 1973 board meeting, we decided to budget an unprecedented amount of money to promote the breed's twenty-fifth anniversary the next year. We produced a high quality brochure, which turned out to be by far our best piece of literature. We scheduled our anniversary convention during the Houston Livestock Show and managed to attract the best group of show and sale animals yet for that event. As usual, we stretched our budget to cover all the special activities. Since the board continued to resist increasing fees, they approved the purchase of many attractive gold and silver pieces of jewelry, bearing an excellent reproduction of a Brangus bull's head. Tie clasps and tie tacks were for the men and gold necklaces for the ladies. We ordered hundreds of small stickers showing a Brangus bull's head over the words, "Brangus Booster," which we sold to members for distribution at their local fairs, and we also passed them out to anyone that would take them at the Houston Livestock Show that year. We were amazed to soon see Brangus Booster stickers all around the show grounds. We also ordered several hundred bumper stickers carrying the words, "Brangus Booster," in gold on a black background. We sent a couple to all new members and sold them to current members to pass out at local cattle shows. This had to be paid for upfront and the staff managed to come up with creative ways to get enough sold to get back our front-end money. They were really nice items and within a couple of years we moved the balance of the jewelry and reordered the stickers.

Dr. Herman Garner was elected president at the 1973 convention and was the last to serve two terms. The cattle produced at his Willow Springs Ranch had not only been winners on the show circuit, but cattle sold at their annual production sales made important contributions to the development of the herds of a growing number of new breeders. One day when I was struggling with our budget, I approached him with an idea for increasing our registrations by tweaking our color requirements for registered Brangus. Many animals that were otherwise outstanding had some white just ahead of the navel, and some showed barely discernable traces of brindling, neither of which affected their productivity. I wrote some amendments to the bylaws to implement such a change and he agreed to present them to the board. The show committee had a fit, the amendment failed to be approved by a considerable majority and Dr. Gardner came under considerable criticism for even bringing it up. I felt bad, but he didn't let it bother him and he defended me for being the author of such a thing. In his president's report he said something that was painfully true and meant it as a compliment: "Roy tries awfully hard to be all things to all people."

When we purchased a computer, our goal was to start a performance program sponsored by the association for those who wished to use it, and charge a fee for the additional service. We also wanted to integrate our bookkeeping and billing system into it. The bookkeeping software available at that time was not very user-friendly and journal entries to correct errors were time consuming and difficult. When we printed our annual dues statements, the fee went into the receivables and they were billed automatically the next month, which was a good thing, but at the end of the year at audit time the unpaid members showed up in accounts receivable. In the past, we had not recognized dues income until we received it. Since we had quite a turn-over in members after a few years, unpaid dues receivables loomed quite large. I tried to explain this was the only way our software would let us bill memberships and it actually saved us money.

The problem of excessive receivables unfortunately went much deeper than just the dues. We were probably the only breed association that didn't require payment for registrations and transfers to accompany the applications, but instead billed members for fees. A few took advantage of this policy. We naturally tried hard to collect past due bills, but it had become a serious problem and I was derelict in not having gone to the board and insisted we adopt a policy that all bills be paid before we issued papers. Some of our big new breeders owned cattle that were spread among many limited partners and a couple of them pushed the problem to crisis proportions. They registered all their cattle under one ranch name, but their customers had an undivided interest on theirs, so they often did not have an individual membership. These operations, which were generating a significant portion of our revenue from advertising in the Brangus Journal and were submitting substantial numbers of registrations and transfers, often paid only a portion of their bills each month. When I took it upon myself to say that we must receive full payment with their registrations and transfers, they still often let payment for advertising slide. The managers of these big outfits, the people I dealt with, were very active in the organization and great to work with, but they didn't write the checks!

As the association had grown, my board of directors had given me more and more leeway to direct our affairs. When I said I was uncomfortable with so much authority, they told me that was what they paid me for and if they didn't like what I did they could always fire me, but of course I already knew that. I had always had a large board in my previous jobs and had learned to work with one, but I was relieved when a year or two before we moved to Texas, we changed the bylaws to add an executive committee to approve policy between board meetings, subject to its subsequent approval. As I recall, the new executive committee was made up of the president, immediate past president, president-elect, treasurer and secretary. The two latter offices were largely ceremonial, but the treasurer usually did help me prepare the budget. The executive committee usually met four times a year and the president could call a meeting of the group at any time. They were particularly helpful during the stressful period when the new building was under construction and the office was being moved.

I continued to attend all regional affiliates' annual meetings and went to as many sales and shows as I could, so I became well-acquainted with a broad cross section of our membership. I soon began to hear rumblings of resentment that our organization was being dominated by larger breeders, who were overrepresented on the executive committee. When I passed these concerns on at a meeting, saying I was worried we were developing a clique, I knew exactly what I meant, but they acted as if they didn't know what I was talking about and we continued our meeting after an uncomfortable silence.

My concerns were borne out as the next annual convention approached. Our bylaws stipulated that the office solicit nominations for board members to represent the regional associations, and that the president appoint a nominating committee to review these recommendations. The nominating committee added a couple of members at large and a slate of officers who, of course, were also on the board. The president could serve only one term and the president-elect traditionally was elevated to the presidency. The secretary and treasurer usually served multiple terms. However, there was a rarely used provision for nominations from the floor. When the nominating committee's slate was published in the Brangus Journal, a very active breeder near Houston named Ludwig Brand put together his own slate of nominees and circulated it to the membership. Only a few of them had also been selected by the nominating committee. The fat was in the fire!

I proceeded to prepare for the convention, something I had a lot of experience doing, but I had never faced a situation like this. I told the staff to stay neutral and we bent over backward cooperating with any member who asked questions about nominees or provisions in our bylaws for elections.

The convention went off amazingly well considering the tension in the halls. The chairman of the nominating committee presented his slate and moved it be accepted. He then called for further nominations from the floor and Ludwig nominated those on his list who were not already nominated. When a voice vote for the nominating committee's slate was indecisive, ballots were distributed and members were instructed to vote for the appropriate number of directors, all of whom ran at large.

The meeting was recessed and the ballots counted. Every person on Brand's list was elected! The losers bowed out graciously and we all prepared for the annual banquet that night. I table-hopped as always, and Maxine and I went out for after dinner drinks with past president Charles Cob and his wife, and Owen Womack and his wife. Owen, who was on the executive committee as the reelected secretary of the association, had stayed neutral during the recent squabble and Charles had already dropped off the board. We especially enjoyed these two couples, especially because they rarely talked about association business.

Wayne Pruett, a partner in Pruett-Wray Cattle Company, which had purchased the Bruce Church Brangus herd in Arizona, was the new president, and Billy Harry of Sulfur Springs, Texas, the president elect. As I recall, the other members of the executive committee were Owen Womack and Ed Norton of Dallas, who had been elected Treasurer. Bill McCombs, president of Lincoln County Land and Livestock Company of Roswell, New Mexico, stayed on the board and executive committee as immediate past-president. The old board had reviewed the audit and approved the next year's budget, which had been balanced by amortizing over several years, the anticipated cost of new software purchased from the Red Angus Association, reducing our already small surplus. Dave Whitman had worked with the programmers at Data Point to make it handle our data entry and print our pedigrees, but we were far from our goal of including weaning and yearling weights of newly recorded animals and computing herd averages. This required not only accessing the sires and dams to confirm ownership, but updating entire files with each new registration. Such sophisticated software was expensive to write and few programmers could do it.

I had hoped that the dramatic turnover in the board would calm the waters, and it took me a while to realize that I had lost some of the trust I had enjoyed within the executive committee.

At a sale, a relatively new breeder who was well acquainted with a couple of the new board members told me my job might be in peril. This possibility had never occurred to me before and I pushed back at his suggestion, probably giving him the impression that I thought I was indispensable.

Because our growth had leveled off and buyers at our sales had become more quality conscious, I became concerned that we may have lowered our standards in pursuit of increased numbers. IBBA's unique requirement, that all cattle presented for registration be inspected, had been met by staff and volunteers, who had been trained at training sessions we held several times a year throughout the country. If an inspector's decision was questioned, a breeder often asked for and received a second opinion from a different one. As more and more complaints about inspections arose, the matter became the subject of intense discussion within the board and was finally dealt with by a policy change that really didn't suit anybody. The bylaws were amended to allow anyone who had attended an inspection seminar to inspect his own cattle. Most breeders took our standards seriously, but the policy change effectively wiped out one of the breed's most respected traditions at a time when registered Angus breeders had suddenly done an about-face on the kind of cattle they preferred.

The kind of Angus cattle that had provided Brangus their strong foundation were now in great demand, instead of being readily available to those who had the foresight to appreciate them. Perversely, there was now an oversupply of the wrong kind of registered Angus females. We were put in the position of needing to be more selective than ever about the foundation females we enrolled. A good many of the new limited partnerships were using three-quarters blood semen on newly enrolled Angus to build their Brangus herds more quickly. Good three-quarter blood bulls were hard to find, and the culling level on first generation Brangus due to color problems alone was high and often for other reasons. Tensions grew between older, established breeders and new ones, but the politics involved in the sudden change in board leadership was more about personality conflicts than policy problems, and the latter remained unresolved.

I still enjoyed going to work every day and had a great staff. After he had the magazine built up, Ken Archer needed help, and we got him an assistant, a talented young woman from Arizona named Kathy Gary, who took Ken's place when he left. We then hired a second young woman to help Kathy, and gradually discontinued providing ring service with little loss of magazine revenue. I took bids occasionally and hated it as well as being very bad at it. Still, our overall budget was getting harder to balance each year while our accounts receivable remained excessive.

My habit of drawing up aggressive budgets resulted in our chronic lack of reserves, and was catching up with me. I often pointed out that our fees were lower than competing breed associations and that some of our largest members were our slowest payers, but I failed miserably getting fees raised or collectables down. Somehow I had always managed to rise to the challenge of finding some creative way to muddle through.

I recall Wayne Pruett saying, after we approved my last tight budget, "Well Roy, you pulled another rabbit out of the hat." I liked a challenge, but was beginning to feel as if I was finally between a rock and a hard place, and unfortunately I was no magician.

***

When the arrival of several colts gave us more horses than we could handle in our small pasture, I was able to find some good bottom land pasture a few miles from home. This saved the expense of buying hay and grain and provided open country in which to ride whenever I was home on weekends. Unfortunately we lost our lease after about eight months and had to get out on fairly short notice. I stumbled onto a much larger place than we really needed and was faced with deciding rather quickly whether to take it or not. A prominent Simmental breeder, who had been using an absentee owner's small, rundown ranch to pasture some of his commercial cows used as recipients for his embryo transplant business, had suddenly cancelled his lease. To justify taking it over, I would need to run some cows along with our horses. The place had a set of dilapidated working corrals with a water tank filled by a nearby well, which also furnished water to a hunter's cabin. The grass lease stipulated that the landowner could lease the property for hunting deer and was not responsible for any cattle that were shot during hunting season!

I talked to the president of the Colonial National Bank where we had the association's bank account and he offered to loan me enough money to buy about fifteen commercial cows. After I tied up the lease, we found an ad in the San Antonio paper for thirteen mixed-breed cows and a yearling bull, and Maxine and I went to see them the next Saturday afternoon. They were about as mixed as could be, and most of the cows obviously carried one-quarter to three-quarters Brahman blood. Some were black, a few red and most multi-colored or brindle. One was a crippled red and white dairy cow and one was a Hereford. A very ugly eighteen-month-old Santa Gertrudis bull came with the deal. The owner said he would sell them only as a package deal. Surprisingly, there were several decent looking calves and they were pretty typical of the kind of cows one saw on small operations in the area. I told him the best of his cows were worth his asking price, but I would have to greatly discount the crippled cow and bull. I was not surprised to learn that the calves had been sired by an Angus bull he had used the previous year and then sold. I ended up paying him about $300 per head for all of them and had them delivered to the pasture the following Sunday.

I spent all day the Saturday before the cows were delivered walking the five or six miles of fence that surrounded the 800-acre, hilly, partially brush-covered pasture. A few posts were broken and the barbed wire was old and rusted, but the previous lessee had done a lot of work on it and it was still in reasonably good shape. I set a few posts and spliced a lot of wires and was confident I could keep our new cows in their new home. I had already turned our horses out into the new pasture before the cows got there. After looking over our new herd, Maxine and I agreed the bull had to go. We decided we would try to find a good two-year-old Brahman bull, if we could find one that suited us. I bought a homemade trailer I could pull with my little secondhand Toyota pickup, and after work we went shopping for our bull. We had heard of a nearby registered Brahman breeder who had cattle that were noted for their gentle disposition. We pulled into his place with our rickety trailer and underpowered pick up and told him we were looking for a eighteen to twenty-four-month-old bull. He took us to the pasture where he had about a dozen such animals and we walked out among them. One let us walk right up and scratch his back. I didn't know a lot about Brahman cattle, but he looked good to me and we decided he would be just right for our little cow herd. I dealt for the bull and we squeezed him into the trailer. We got to the pasture just before dark and unloaded him with the cows. From then on, whenever we came out to the pasture to check the cows, he always moseyed up to get his back scratched.

In the winter, I often had to feed our little herd hay and or cotton cake. Because the days were short, I checked the cows during my lunch hour. I'd get a malt at a nearby fast food place and drink it during the five-minute drive to the pasture. When I got there, I put on coveralls and fed either a few bales of hay or a sack of cotton cake to the cattle, and was back in the office before my lunch hour was up. When I had to be gone for a day or two, I put out extra feed and occasionally, when I was traveling for several days, Maxine would have to feed for me. I had never played golf or had any hobbies except deer hunting. I don't think any weekend golfer ever enjoyed his game more than I enjoyed my solitude looking after these few sorry cows.

Picture of Sox as a yearling.... Note my crude home-made hay feeder.

Registration of Sox on my Birthday
using maximum number of letters allowed by AQHA.

49

Foreign Marketing

During my tenure with IBBA, I made several trips to Mexico and Central America, and one to Argentina. My first was to a huge, international cattle show in Mexico City in an effort to promote sales of Brangus into that country. The main thing I remember about this trip was the dangerous cab ride from my hotel to where the show was held. On one trip, while I was sitting on the edge of my seat as my driver maneuvered through three lanes of traffic, leaning on his horn, we passed an accident scene that had several badly injured or dead people laid out on the side of the road. From my limited experience I was ready to think that Mexican cab drivers were the most reckless in the world.

I was ill prepared for the trip, but was fortunate to run into the editor of the Charolais Journal, Norm Jackson, whom I had known when he had edited the official publication of the Oklahoma Cattlemen's Association. He was at the show as the official representative of the American International Charolais Association. He took me under his wing and after we shared our first hair-raising cab ride to the show, we ate most of our meals together. At the show I learned what a great variety of Zebu cattle there were and that the major strains included Gir, Guserat, Nelore, Red Sindhi. Indo-Brazil and American Brahmans, most of which had greater numbers than the English breeds—Herefords, Angus and Shorthorn—and the new continental breeds such as Charolais and Simmental. The American International Charolais Breeders Association was one of the fastest growing breed registries in the States at the time I was in Mexico City with Jackson, and I took the opportunity to pick his brains about some of their more successful programs. He said his organization had a contract with the Foreign Marketing Branch of the Agricultural Marketing Service of USDA for around $40,000, to promote the export of their registered Charolais cattle and, in fact, his expenses to this show were included in their current contract.

Shortly after I returned to the states I called the chief of the Foreign Marketing, Agricultural Marketing Service, USDA. He said that it might be possible for us to get such a contract for the IBBA and he sent me the necessary forms to get the procedure started. After wading through all the paperwork, we put in an application for enough money to have 5,000 copies of our twenty-fifth anniversary brochure printed in Spanish, and $10,000 for the production of a film in Spanish promoting registered Brangus cattle. The request was approved and I was able to put the production of the brochure and film into my next year's budget.

We were able to find a man who agreed to make a 16mm color film for us for the $10,000 we had budgeted. Some of the film was shot during a one-week trip to Mexico, where we took shots at a few places that were using Brangus bulls on both Hereford and Brahman type cross-bred cows. We also used some excellent footage from a ranch in the Nebraska Sandhills country that was using Brangus bulls on Hereford cows. The film was made with both an English and Spanish soundtrack. We were pleased that one of our bi-lingual members thought the Spanish language version was quite acceptable although flawed in a few places. We promoted the film's availability in Latin America through the agricultural attaché in each country. The English version was promoted to cattlemen's groups and schools throughout the states.

Our contract with the Foreign Agricultural Branch of USDA had to be renewed annually, and the second year our budget included a visit to several Central American Countries: Guatemala, Honduras, El Salvador and Panama. These trips were coordinated closely with the State Department, and I was met in each country by the agricultural attaché, who treated me to a dinner at the American Embassy. The attaché took me to visit various leaders in the cattle industry in each country, and I often found Americans managing their most progressive ranches. Going through customs as I traveled from country to country was always a frustrating trip through layers of make-work red tape. At Honduras I found armed soldiers stationed throughout the airport and at every corner because they were at war with Nicaragua. After arriving on Pan American Airlines in Guatemala City, my trips between countries were on aging aircraft flown by local airlines. I particularly remember a meeting in Tegucigalpa, Honduras that consisted of sitting at a big table with about ten prominent ranchers as they took turns talking at great length while taking a drag out of a bottle of whiskey that was being passed around. When my turn came to talk I took a drink, inhaled deeply and proceeded to tell them through an interpreter about the merit of using Brangus bulls on their Zebu type cows, explaining that no matter how long they used Brangus bulls their herd would never have more than 3/8 Angus blood. After about three hours we had made it around the table at least three times. I didn't have much of any idea what any of them said, and though they listened politely and thanked me for joining them, I was not sure that the rancher interpreting for me could speak English much better than I did Spanish.

About a year later, our executive committee was invited to a meeting with the Brangus Association of the Mexican State of Chihuahua. Lloyd Brinkman, then president, flew us there in his Cessna King Air. We arrived in time to attend an evening banquet that featured huge marinated beef steaks from grass-fed cattle grilled over an open fire. The next morning, we presented a program to their membership and distributed the Spanish version of our twenty-fifth anniversary brochure. In the afternoon we visited a large ranch that had been using Brangus bulls on their commercial Hereford cows for a number of years. We were told their calves, weighing about 400 pounds at weaning, were in great demand by ranchers in Arizona and New Mexico. There they grazed until they gained another 400 pounds, when they were sold to a feedlot to put on their last 400 pounds before being slaughtered and sold to the American consumer as choice beef—a great example of adding value to an imported product. Before we departed, we were each given a gift crafted by their talented caballeros. I got a saddle blanket made from a sheepskin stitched to a cotton blanket, which I still haven't worn out.

A rancher from Guatemala, who also owned that nation's largest brewery, showed up at our annual convention during the Houston Livestock Show in the mid-seventies and we invited him to our board of directors' meeting. He gave a brief description of his operation and invited someone representing the IBBA to attend his first Brangus production sale. He said he had bred his registered Angus herd up to Brangus, and held out the possibility he might register them with IBBA and then buy some top bulls from the U.S. to further upgrade his herd.

The board agreed to send me to his sale, which was about a month later. I flew into Guatemala City and took a cab to the Hilton Hotel in downtown Guatemala City. It was quite new and was much like every other Hilton where I had stayed in the U.S. Soon after breakfast the next morning, my host picked me up and flew me in his private plane to his ranch, where I stayed for three days. It was a beautiful operation with meadows irrigated by sprinklers and highly improved pastures.

His sale was a big social event with most of the nation's top ranchers attending. They really enjoyed themselves at the big noon barbecue where they drank lots of beer and a good bit of harder stuff, which it seemed they brought with them. It reminded me a lot of a Brink's Brangus sale. I was introduced before the sale started by my host, who interpreted the few words I said on behalf of the IBBA. The auction itself was conducted much differently than one in the U. S. Afterwards, I visited with some of the successful bidders as best I could with my practically non-existent Spanish (two years in High School).

That night I slept fitfully as I listened to the singing of many tropical birds and thought about my host's promise to fly me in the morning to his two other operations, another cattle ranch and a banana plantation. We first flew near the Pacific coast over the plantation where he raised bananas exclusively for a corporation—Dole, I think, that harvested and merchandised them. We didn't land there, but from the plane I had a rather surrealistic view of a couple of smoking volcano peaks rising out of the mist of the jungle further inland. We then flew another hundred miles or so to his other, larger ranch, what I would call a Central American version of a cow camp. There he ran his commercial, mainly Brahman type, cattle. When I visited with the manager, who spoke some English and lived there with several indigenous native employees, he was quite enthusiastic about using Brangus bulls on their native cattle and thought the breed had a great future in Central America.

We then flew back to my host's home in Guatemala City, where I spent the night. The next morning after a breakfast that featured bacon and eggs, pancakes (pan que-ques) and black bean paste, which I learned was a part of every meal in that country, I was given a tour of the brewery, which was not large by American standards but was modern in every respect. Later that morning, I was put on a commercial flight back to the states. I greatly enjoyed my stay in Guatemala and hoped we might develop a market there, not only for registered bulls, but also registered females as other Guatemalans developed herds.

A year later I flew back to Guatemala after they had had a devastating earthquake. Although the Hilton Hotel showed visible signs of the damage it had suffered, it was open for business. I was visiting the only other Brangus breeder in the country. He met me at the airport and we drove several hours to reach his home on his ranch. The roads got worse and worse as we got further from the city. The owner, who had a German name, had been born in Guatemala and was married to a farmwoman from the states. They both spoke English well. Theirs was not a big ranch and their primary source of income was from sugar cane and coffee, but they loved their Brangus cattle and were anxious to have them inspected to qualify for registration with IBBA. They had purchased their foundation stock from Jesse Dowdy and all but a couple passed inspection with ease. I was quite pleased to see how good they were.

After we looked at the cattle, we drove to what looked like a little village. It turned out to be the area where they processed the coffee beans and sugarcane raised on their modest plantation. I knew nothing about coffee beans, but I had some knowledge of the operation of the sugar beet factory in Fort Collins, Colorado. It processed the beets raised in the irrigated valley where the family farm I lived on for ten years was located. I was surprised at how much the coffee beans had to be processed before being ready for grinding. A fairly large diesel engine powered pulleys, which turned belts, which ran the machinery used to process both their sugar cane and coffee beans. Their foreman had a crew of indigenous Indians who worked at the farm and processing facility, and lived in the village with their families. He explained that plantations that processed their own crops like this one were still using equipment that had been used by the British when they left around the turn of the century. He was extremely proud of the diesel engine. He said the whole operation had originally been powered by steam. I learned that after the coffee beans had been soaked in a solution and dried, they were put in large sacks for shipment. The sugar cane underwent processing somewhat similar to sugar beets. The end product was four-inch by six-inch soft blocks of brownish sugar unlike the brown sugar we are used to. Most of the locals used these blocks, which crumble easily, in their cooking. Producing white sugar like ours in America requires considerably more treatment.

The following day, my host took me back to my hotel in Guatemala City and I met the Brangus breeder I had visited the previous year. I had sent him a letter telling him I was going to be in Guatemala again and told him I would call him before I went back to the states. I had scheduled an extra day before my return so I could go to his ranch and inspect his Angus cattle. This was required to make them eligible for enrollment with IBBA to produce registered Brangus when bred to three-quarter blood bulls. I had suggested that he might want to use artificial insemination from one of the top three-quarter bloods in the U. S. since he had mentioned he used AI in his registered Angus operation.

He met me at noon for lunch and I talked enthusiastically about the growing opportunity for sales in Guatemala of Brangus registered with IBBA. He beat around the bush for a while and finally said he had changed his plans. He wasn't going to enroll his Angus because he wouldn't be registering any of his Brangus with us. I was terribly disappointed because he had shown a lot of enthusiasm for enrolling his entire herd when our board agreed to send me to his sale the previous year. I resigned myself to the fact that I would certainly not cover my travel expenses with the fifteen registrations I had obtained from our only member in Guatemala. This was not my first or last disappointment in our many efforts to market Brangus bulls or develop herds of registered Brangus in Latin America.

My last Latin American trip took me all the way to Argentina. In the summer of 1978, during an all-breed cattle show in Texas, I met an internationally respected registered Angus breeder, the patriarch of the large Firpo family in Argentina. He was visiting the states to judge several major Angus shows and buy a few top Angus bulls to ship to Argentina. He told me he had converted part of his Angus herd in the more tropical part on his ranch to Brangus. His Angus breeding herd was maintained on his family's farm/ranch in the famous Argentine Pampas grassland. He invited me to visit his operations there and take in the annual meeting of the Argentine Brangus Breeders Association, La Asociación Brangus de Argentina. His offer to pay for the expensive round-trip airplane ticket and all my expenses while I was there was too much for the IBBA Board to pass up and they authorized me to make the trip.

Mr. Firpo made a reservation for me at a large hotel in downtown Buenos Aires for the night I was to arrive, and said he would meet me there at about 9:00 a.m. the next morning. It is further to Buenos Aires from Houston, where I departed, than it is to Europe, and the only stop my Pan American Airlines flight made was at Rio de Janeiro in Brazil. We parked on the runway there for about an hour refueling and changing crews just before dawn. I didn't deplane and stood at the door opening onto the ramp for about fifteen minutes and looked out across the city's lights while visiting with one of the stewards. It was the longest flight I ever took and turned out to be my most enjoyable trip during my career at IBBA.

I arrived in Buenos Aires around noon and took a cab to the hotel. I went right to my room on the fourth floor and looked out of my window overlooking a large park. I had evidently arrived on a national holiday and I heard bands playing and observed groups of young people marching into the park from all directions, each under a different banner. I decided to go down and see what was going on. I felt very much as I had the first time I visited San Francisco when I was just nineteen years old and in fact, Buenos Aires reminded me of San Francisco. The difference was that not being able to speak much more Spanish than ¿Como se llama? or Hablo espanol, I felt even more like a fish out of water. At the same time, I enjoyed the surreal feeling I had joining the crowd gathering around the edges of the park to observe what was going on.

I managed to learn from some of the people standing around me who spoke a bit of English that the young people were from surrounding Catholic schools. Each seemed to be led by a young priest exhorting his group to exceed the others in their enthusiastic cheering as they marched in. All the while I found myself caught up in the excitement of the moment. I was aware that Argentina was then governed by an autocratic and ruthless regime that seemed to have the full support of the church. I put that thought out of my mind and decided to enjoy the experience of getting caught up in such an activity, while remembering I had not made the trip to get involved in politics.

The event ended with a speech, or perhaps sermon, from what might have been a bishop or cardinal and I returned to my hotel as the groups of young people marched off again. I enjoyed a good dinner in the fancy dining room and observed patron's manner of the eating was the European style of holding the fork in the left-hand and the knife in the right. I soon learned that Argentina was far more influenced by European culture than by that of the U. S., and in this respect, it was much different from Mexico or Central America.

The next morning I was met by one of Mr. Firpo's nephews, Luis, who said he would be squiring me around their extensive operation during the next couple of days. Luis spoke excellent English and it soon became evident that he was involved in all aspects of the extensive Firpo cattle empire. An hour or so west of Buenos Aires we were well into the grasslands called the Pampas. I had heard of them and they were even more impressive than any one of the three famous grasslands in the United States, the Sandhills of Nebraska, the Flint Hills of Kansas and the Bluestem country of Oklahoma. They had deep fertile soil, rainfall similar to our corn belt and were located in a latitude that had an even longer growing season. The Firpos owned a large acreage of this beautiful country, which in America would be dedicated to the growing of corn, but as the Argentines ate only grass-fed beef there had been no incentive to grow large amounts of it. And even though I prefer corn fed beef, when I ate it I immediately understood why Argentine grass-fed beef had established a worldwide reputation

When Luis showed me their Angus herd, I was impressed by the fact that they were ahead of their counterparts in the U.S. in getting away from watch fob sized cattle. Luis pointed out that the fad for small Angus had never found popularity in Argentina because they didn't fit an industry based on grass fed beef. After a calf was weaned, the year on grass required to reach slaughter weight favored larger, more slowly maturing cattle. In fact, at this time there was more interest in the shipment of Argentine Angus bulls to the U. S. than the reverse. We spent a full afternoon looking at the registered cow herd, their replacement heifers, herd bulls and the bulls they were growing out for sale. They had some land primarily dedicated to growing hay and a little for the production of corn, which they used sparingly in growing out their younger cattle. Luis said they didn't grow much alfalfa, which they called lucerne.

At about six p.m. we drove to the beautiful home of Luis' uncle, who managed this particular operation. I was graciously welcomed and introduced to the extended family that was present, as well as to several guests, some of whom seemed to be there to meet me. They were in the middle of their extended before-dinner cocktail hour. Luis acted as my interpreter when necessary, however many spoke quite good English. Initially most of the talk revolved around comparing cattle production in the states and Argentina; however, before long the conversation drifted to our respective political systems, and as usual the assumption was that I was a Republican. When Luis' uncle learned to his dismay that I was a Democrat, I got an ear full and soon learned that the politics of the landowners in Argentina were far to the right of the typically conservative ranchers and farmers in America. In an effort to change the subject, which backfired, I innocently mentioned that I hadn't seen any Indians thus far in Argentina. I was told that quite a few people from India had settled here and many were very successful in business. I said I really meant the indigenous people who were here when the Spanish arrived. My host laughed and said they had solved that problem long ago by killing them all off as we should have done in the U. S. when we had the opportunity. I learned later that Luis didn't share those views, which gave me hope that the younger generation was perhaps more broad-minded. I managed keep my opinions to myself for the rest of the evening. We had a wonderful, somewhat formal, dinner much later and after a many more cocktails than I was used to. Luis and I excused ourselves shortly after eating, saying we had had a long day and would have another the next. Luis and I had an early breakfast on the patio the next morning and spent the next day inspecting more of the Firpo holdings.

About mid afternoon, we drove back to Buenos Aires and Luis—he was a member of the Board of Directors of the Argentine Brangus Association (ABA)—and I flew on a commercial airline to Resistencia for the annual meeting of the ABA and a field day being held in conjunction with it. He, like many other ranchers in

Argentina, lived in a condominium near the Atlantic Ocean and commuted to his rural holdings. When the plane was airborne, I could see row after row of condos, much as you would see along the coast in Miami.

I met with my counterpart in the Argentine Brangus Association, their executive director, Victor Tonelli, for breakfast the next morning, after which he drove me to the meeting site. The convention was much like one I might have arranged. There were a couple of speakers who had graduated from agricultural schools in America, one of whom I had met at a meeting in the states. He had a PHD from the University of Nebraska. I spoke at the general session that morning, attended a noon luncheon and sat through a long afternoon series of speakers giving learned talks in a language I couldn't understand. I was seated at the head table during their banquet, which was preceded by a great many toasts and introductions and concluded with a heavy meal served at abut 9:00 p.m. By that time I had a severe migraine headache, something I rarely suffered. The next morning my head still ached and I called my host to beg off going to the morning program, which featured four more speakers. He said he was sure everyone would understand my need for a little rest and that he would pick me up at my hotel right after lunch to join him for the field day and tour of the ranch owned by the association's current president, Carlos Dowdall.

Dowdall had one of the top herds of Brangus in Argentina and his gauchos had placed groups of cattle in adjoining pens in his corrals. They represented the best categories of Brangus that were recognized for registration in Argentina, which gave their breeders a wide range of options. Using American terminology, they registered not only three-eighths by five-eighths but also one-half bloods, one-quarter bloods, three-quarters bloods and the reciprocal cross of our Brangus, five-eighths by three-eighths. I had explained that in the U. S. only the three-eighths by five-eighths were registered and the other categories certified for breeding up to registered status. It occurred to me that a couple of the black, polled three-quarter blood bulls would be very valuable in the United States for Angus breeders producing Brangus.

Dowdall also bred top saddle horses and had several of those on display. One of his gauchos asked me if I would like to ride one and I, of course, said I would, and barely managed to keep from completely embarrassing myself as I galloped around in a couple of circles. Their horses don't "neck rein" like our cow ponies, but instead responded to leg pressure. Another gaucho gave me a sip of the mate, which he had been sharing with his fellow workers. It reminded me a bit of the sage or Indian tea mom used to make occasionally from a dwarf variety of sage that grew on the ranch. This drink was made by pouring hot water over mate leaves placed in a dried calabash gourd and drunk through a metal straw.

I flew back to Buenos Aires that night to catch a midnight flight to Houston. Before boarding the plane, I purchased a calabash gourd for mate that had a gold collar around the opening and a stainless-steel straw with a gold mouthpiece. I had been told that gold was cheaper in Argentina than at home and this was a good way to bring some home with you without paying a duty as you went through customs. It is a memento that I still treasure.

Roy in his spacious new IBBA headquarters office.

50

Software Disaster

I arrived home from Argentina in late October of 1978 with considerable concern about things at the office. Wayne Ratliff, the bright young programmer I had contracted to update the software for our computer, was way behind schedule. I had paid him in advance for one-half of the considerable amount of money that he was charging for his service. I had agreed to pay him the other half when the job was completed around the first of November. Dave Whitman told me that Wayne had been in the office for several days while I was gone and then hadn't shown up again. It took a day or two to run him down. When I did, he told me his computer had broken down and he would like to borrow ours along with our printer for the weekend to wind up another job he was working on. I told him I needed him to finish my job on time or my job was in jeopardy, but agreed to let him use our computer so he could finish his other job. I went to the office the next Saturday morning and found Wayne printing out reams of paper on our computer. I had no idea what he was doing, but he assured me he would have his computer up and running soon and would be able to work on our programming at home in the evenings.

In a few days Wayne showed up again and informed me that we would not be able to use the computer for a few days while he finished, downloaded and tested our new software. I said we were way behind in our work and needed to get it back up and operating quickly. He worked several hours and then didn't show up again for a couple of days. He had not finished our job nor would he tell me when he might. I was at my wits end. Registrations that needed to be printed were backing up and such work as we were able to do had to be billed by hand, which put pressure on the bookkeeper because she would have to reenter all of it if and when the computer was operating. I told Wayne I would have to let him go if he couldn't dedicate all his time our project. He said something to the effect that he was in the middle of a major project that he had to finish first. I said that the only thing left was to terminate our agreement. He wasn't the least bit disagreeable; he left the office and I never saw him again.

I called the office of our Data Point computer manufacturer in San Antonio and managed to find somebody who could recommend a programmer to try to bail me out and salvage some of the work already done. The person they recommended listened to my sad story and said the only hope we had was if Ratliff had left his coding in our computer. Thank God, everything was there. He dumped—printed—everything in our processor and was able to sort things out enough to get us back to where we were before we started. He separated the Red Angus performance portion, which he didn't understand, to be integrated another day. All of this cost a good deal of money that we did not have to spare, but we were soon back up and running, wiser but poorer. More about Ratliff later.

While I was in the middle of this computer muddle, I had to get ready for our annual convention, the hardest part of which was preparing a tentative budget. Data entry and printing our registrations and billing had saved us considerable money over the past several years, but our futile effort to add performance testing to our services had been costly. I lined up what I thought was a good group of convention speakers and prepared what I called the "continuity" for the business meeting at the convention. This was a folder I left on the podium during sessions. It included all the introductions for speakers, instructions for handling committee reports, all the formalities to conduct the election of officers, concluding with the call for old and new business at the end. Dave prepared most of the committee agendas and oversaw the preparation for the show and sale that we held in conjunction with our convention, which was being held during the Houston Livestock Show and Rodeo again.

Trying to balance our budget had never been more difficult. We had seldom had much in the way of reserves and there was little doubt that this budget would require an increase in fees. I had shared these problems with the executive committee at a tense, but typically informal meeting in the early fall. They had not been as active recently as in the few years before the big shakeup of the board of directors at the 1977 convention, and I thought there would probably be some more controversy at the coming annual meeting. I was sufficiently concerned to share with Dave my feeling that someone on the staff might be made a scapegoat, naïvely thinking to myself that it might be he. I was partly right and the axe fell nearly a month before the convention.

The Texas Brangus Breeders Association was holding its annual convention in San Antonio in early February, about a month ahead of our convention in Houston. On the opening day of the TBBA convention, I was working with Dave in the office preparing agendas for the convention, when our president elect, Wayne Pruett, who was in town for the TBBA meeting, called. He said he would like to meet me for dinner at about six p. m. I said I would be happy to come down to the meeting and visit with him there if he wished, but he said he would rather talk to me at dinner, so we agreed to meet at the Steak and Ale, a restaurant owned by his partner Peter Wray.

After I called Maxine and said I would be late getting home, I decided to take a rough draft of the board agenda over to Wayne at the TBBA convention hotel so he could check it over before we met later. I drove downtown to the convention hotel, and as I walked in I saw Larry Gardner, the son of past IBBA president Herman Gardner, and asked where I might find Wayne. He told me and I slipped into a meeting, delivered my agenda and headed back to the office with the intention of attending the formal part of the meeting the next day. I found it odd that Larry had seemed a little distant and that no other members came up to speak to me when I came in. In fact, they looked at me and then looked away.

I knew something was going on and was looking forward to finding out from Wayne just what it was. We sat down at our table, exchanged a couple of pleasantries and, after Wayne didn't volunteer anything, I started giving him an update on the coming convention. He didn't respond and after a few seconds said, "Roy, the executive committee has asked me to ask you for your resignation." I had never been fired before and it had never occurred to me that I ever would be. I can't remember exactly what I said, but he assured me there was no issue of misconduct and they simply thought it was time for a change. I told him he had caught me completely off guard, but that I had no desire to resign, was surprised that they had not given me any warning and was sure we could work our way out of our current financial situation, as we always had.

I asked him how this came about and he said that the executive committee had met earlier in the day and come to this decision. He admitted that only three of the five executive committee members were present and I was pretty confident that the two who were not there would have voted against such action. He bluntly told me that as far as the three of them were concerned they would prefer my resignation immediately because their action would have to be confirmed by the board if I didn't resign on the spot. I was in complete shock and he was obviously very uncomfortable. I agreed to call him in the morning to let him know what I planned to do; then I left.

As I drove home in a daze, I realized that I had never given any thought to changing jobs since we had moved to Texas. I dreaded the thought of telling Maxine and tried to get my mind clear enough so that after I broke the news we could immediately start talking about our options. When she met me at the door, I simply told her that there was something we needed to talk about after the rest of the family went to bed, passing it off as something less important than it was. I had my evening drink as usual while she got dinner and tried to concentrate on the evening news. I don't think the kids noticed anything different except that I didn't fall asleep in my recliner immediately after we had eaten as I usually did.

I told Maxine all that I could remember of my conversation with Wayne, which to my surprise turned out to be nearly every bit of it. She knew that things had been difficult at the office the past few months, but was just as shocked as I had been. I told her I felt like a fool for not seeing this coming, at which point I nearly broke down. She kept her composure and provided me the reassurance that I badly needed. She agreed that giving me advance notice was the least I deserved, and the manner in which the decision had been made with only three-fifths of the executive committee present was strange. As we were talking it dawned on me for the first time that I had signed a contract with IBBA when I went to work for them over sixteen years earlier, and I fervently hoped I could find it.

I went into the office early the next morning, looked in the fireproof filing cabinet where I kept our most important papers and finally dug out my contract. I remembered keeping it in my desk at the Livestock Exchange Building in Kansas City and had hurriedly stuck it in the file when we moved. It was not a very impressive looking document because I had composed it and even typed it myself, but it was signed by then president, Al Face, and me and dated. I had never been so happy to see a piece of paper in my life! It simply stated that if the association was not satisfied with my performance at any time they had to tell me what their concerns were and give me six months to rectify them to their satisfaction, at which time, if they still were not satisfied, I could be fired. I called Wayne and told him I was not williing to resign.

I knew that one of the best lawyers in Texas was the one in Kerrville that Lloyd Brinkman used for all his many interests. His office was not more than forty-five miles from where I lived and I was able to schedule an appointment with him within a few days, probably because of my acquaintance with Brinkman. I still had a few things to wind up for the convention and continued to go to the office every day. The staff had been shocked by the news of my being fired and were naturally apprehensive about their own jobs, because they had all always been extremely loyal to me. I told them to keep their heads down and do their work, and we would see how things worked out between now and the board meeting during the convention. We had fortunately gotten the computer and billing system working and were caught up with our paper work and billings.

We were in the middle of our annual audit when I was fired, and I found the man who had handled it for the last several years suddenly very cool and formal, telling me that he would just be working with my bookkeeper. We usually worked closely during the audit because it was at the same time I was finishing up my annual budget for the convention. I had had dozens of audits over my career and for the first time I was in an adversarial relationship. I called the vice president of the large auditing firm we had used since we moved to Texas and told him it was difficult to properly complete my budget without knowing what the auditor was doing. Looking back, I think he wondered why I was still hanging around the office because he glad-handed me somewhat. I finally faced up to the fact that I had completely lost control and all I could do was try to help the staff keep things working as close to normal as possible while I was waiting for the board to act on the executive committee's action.

By the time my appointment with the lawyer arrived I was feeling pretty low. He greeted me in his fancy office and motioned me to sit down in the chair in front of his beautiful big desk. He put me at ease as we exchanged a few pleasantries concerning our mutual acquaintance with the Brinkman brothers. He then asked me to explain just exactly what had happened to cause me to see him. I told him of my meeting with Wayne Pruett and my complete surprise at having been asked to resign. I said I had negotiated a rather informal contract with the president who had hired me sixteen years before, and handed it to him. I was greatly relieved when he said that it looked like a valid contract to him and explained that to be legal, such a document did not have to have all the lawyer talk in it that they liked to make people think is necessary. I heaved a sigh of relief and thought to myself, "I really like this guy."

He said that before offering any advice he would like to hear what I thought I should do. I replied that I had never been fired and hoped to avoid that outcome, so wanted the executive committee to list their complaints and give me the opportunity over the next six months to keep the job. He then asked me what I planned to do if I was not given that opportunity. I said I would, of course, expect them to honor my contract by allowing me six months to find a new job, and in addition would like to keep the company car. Then he asked me what I thought my chances were for getting the board of directors to overturn the executive committee's request that I resign. I told him I thought the odds were pretty good that I could get a majority vote, but that I was not very good at defending myself. I hesitated a bit and suddenly realized that no matter what happened, my job could never be the same. I had learned long before that successful organizations must operate with a strong consensus, and anything less than eighty percent of the board's support would make my job untenable.

After about an hour, we concluded that my options appeared to be limited and he thought I had handled the situation wisely thus far. As I was leaving the office he put his arm over my shoulder and said he was confident I had a bright future ahead of me whatever happened. The only advice he offered was not to do anything stupid based on my injured pride.

I went directly home from the lawyer's office and Maxine was greatly relieved to hear that it appeared my contract protected me from the possibility of having to look for a job while uncompensated. I said I still wanted to see if there was hope for keeping my job, but we agreed that if I could not, we would make every effort to find new employment nearby so we could continue living in our new home and the kids could stay in school in Boerne.

I continued to go the office every day. I did get phone calls from several board members who had heard I had been asked to resign, who said they hoped I would not and that they were prepared to go to bat for me. As the meeting date approached, I got more and more uneasy about where I really stood. I finally drove up to Kerrville to see my good friend, Glenn Brinkman, who had stayed out of the political infighting that caused the dramatic turnover on the board the previous year, and asked him for his reading on my situation. He told me frankly that there was concern that I was too lenient with the staff and had not managed the budget prudently. He said there was no effort to challenge my integrity, but at best it might take a knockdown, drag out fight with the board to keep my job. I told him that was the last thing I wanted and asked if he would represent my interests at the meeting if I decided not to attend. I told him I had visited Lloyd's lawyer and showed him my contract. I said I wanted him to tell the board I wanted to continue working for the IBBA, and if that seemed an impossibility, to negotiate on my behalf to make sure they honored my contract and gave me the car. He said he would do the very best he could.

On the fateful day, I drove to Houston, arriving before the night board meeting, and got a room a block from the convention hotel. I called Glenn and gave him the hotel phone number, and we agreed that if he was able to work out something he would call me so I could come on over to the board meeting. If not, he would let me know what kind of arrangements he had been able to make for me. I had supper sent up to my room and lay on the bed for over three hours waiting for Glenn's call. Somehow, I had been able to convince myself that the executive committee might have a change of heart or, at the very least, would ask me to discuss the problems that caused them to ask me to resign so I could help resolve them over the next six months.

At about 11:30 p.m. Glenn called and said he had done his best for me, but after a long discussion, they decided to confirm the executive committee's action and honor my contract and my request for the car. All I could think to say to Glenn was they must have really wanted to get rid of me to put out six months salary when our budget was so tight. I thanked him and said I would be up to see him in a day or so. I was so wound up that I knew I couldn't get to sleep, so I drove the 200 miles back to San Antonio, got home a couple of hours before dawn and crawled into bed without waking Maxine up.

    It took me several weeks to realize that I had not taken my lawyer's advice in one respect. I had let my pride allow me to make a very serious error. As soon as I had located my contract and assured myself that the family would not likely suffer any financial consequences from my dismissal, I should have pretended to resign. I am sure there would have been no objection, but in fact relief, on the part of the executive committee, if I had put out a news release indicating I was resigning to pursue other opportunities. Unfortunately, I didn't use that highly effective, phony face-saving technique. The news release would have gone out to nearly 100 publications and likely would have resulted in some job offers because I was by then well known within the livestock industry. As it was, no one knew that I was unemployed. A year later I ran into my friend, Hop Dickinson, my counterpart with the American Hereford Association, whom I had invited to speak at the convention I never attended. He said he had no idea I wasn't going to be there and my name was never once mentioned.

51

Paid Vacation

The day after I returned from my vigil at the hotel in Houston, I drove to the office at noon and started cleaning out my desk. Dave was still in Houston for the balance of the convention and the International Brangus Show and Sale. All of the staff soon showed up in my big fancy office. They were curious to know just what had happened and I told them that I knew little more than the fact that I had been fired, but thanks to my contract I would be on the payroll for six more months or until I got another job, whichever came first. I said I didn't plan to come into the office anymore, but that if there was anything I could help them with to feel free to give me a call. They embarrassed me by saying all the right things and I told them how much they all meant to me. I then gathered up my personal items starting with the fancy desk set the staff had given me a few years before engraved with the words, "World's Greatest Boss," and a picture of the family that I kept on top of my desk. I also kept a copy of my partially finished current budget, a copy of the previous year's audit, several of each of the various brochures we had printed over the years, a copy of the bylaws, considerable printed material related to the many allied industry groups I had worked with and our news release list. I then filled a shoebox with the junk I had accumulated in my top drawer over the years.

The first weekend after Dave returned from the convention, I dropped over to his house to get a report. He said that many people, including the speakers, asked where I was, but no mention of my departure even came up at the general session. He said he had not been invited to attend the board meeting where my fate was determined, but I had told him what my strategy was and when I never showed up he knew the outcome. He said he learned upon his return that the association had hired a new staff member with the title of field representative to start work at the office during the convention. All he knew about the man was that he was an ex-Marine.

Dave was surprised to learn when he got back to the office that this person had full authority over all the staff and had fired Susan, who was in charge of overseeing computer operations, such as data-entry and printing and mailing registration certificates and billings. He learned from Susan that the auditor had been asked to write off a large portion of the accounts receivable, as well as several thousand dollars' worth of inventory items we held for re-sale, neither of which changed the previous year's income or expenses, but caused a large decrease in assets in the audit which was laid at my feet.

Dave said that he called Wayne Pruett immediately after the convention to see what was going on and he confirmed that the field man would be in charge of the office. Evidently they were in no hurry to replace me, and the "excessive transparency" of my management style had ended. My first call from the office was to ask about the distribution of refunds of membership dues to the affiliates, which no one seemed to know a thing about. I explained that if they would check the board minutes they would find the most recent policy outlining the amount and procedures for paying these refunds. I never heard from the office again and I suspect that the new field man had shut off any further communications with me.

We decided to take advantage of this unexpected paid vacation by taking the kids to South Padre Island for four or five days during their spring vacation and we had a great time. Though I had made peace with this sudden turn in my life, I felt burned out on cattle association work and decided to make an effort to get involved in the production side of the cattle business if possible. I was actually making more than most ranch managers at that time, but those jobs usually had the fringe benefit of a house with paid utilities. Unfortunately I did not particularly like the show ring emphasis of the purebred cattle business and the best jobs usually were on ranches that were deeply committed to it.

I subscribed to several leading weekly livestock publications that carried want ads and responded to a few that turned out to be not too promising. In the meanwhile I enjoyed doing things I had little time for previously, like changing the oil in my own car and even replacing a leaking radiator on Maxine's car. I went out to see the cattle much more than I really needed to, enjoying the opportunity to spend hours outdoors once again. In an effort to find some part-time work, I visited Glenn Brinkman and asked if I could break some of the colts at their highly improved quarter horse breeding and training facility in Sisterdale, about fifteen miles north of our home. I told him I didn't pretend to be a horse trainer, but I had a lot of experience starting, or green breaking, two-year-olds. I had noticed they had a big round corral with a six-foot-high solid wood fence and several inches of soft sand on the ground. Glenn said they did have a few two-year-olds that had not been started yet, and if I felt up to it he would let me work with a couple. I got along with them just fine because they had been handled a good deal, the same as the colts I broke for the folks at the farm, although as they had been fed a good deal more grain than those and were considerably bigger and fatter for their age than any two-year-olds we raised. I worked each of them in the round corral for a couple of days before I got on them, and although they were skittish, only one bucked when I got on him. I then let them out in the open corral where a couple of moonlighting Texas brand inspectors were busy riding other colts and probably wondering what I was doing there. After about a week, the young assistant manager of the horse operation hailed me down as I was galloping past him and said he didn't need me to work the colts anymore. I stopped by Glenn's office to tell him I had been canned. He apologized as he wrote me a check for the work I had done thus far and said that his horse manager was away on the cutting horse circuit and had left his assistant in charge. I laughed as I said I didn't want to cause him any personnel problems and was getting too old for this business anyway.

 A few days later I saw an ad in one of my livestock publications for a fairly large, well-improved ranch for lease in southern Missouri. Glenn had told me that his brother, Lloyd, was considering moving part of the Brink's Brangus breeding herd to another location, possibly even out of state, since the quarter horse business was expanding and using more and more of the pasture and facilities at Sisterdale. I called the broker handling the Missouri property for more details and it sounded as if it would fit Brinkman's needs. It was highly improved, with a decent house, and was quite large for a Midwestern ranch. I called Glenn about it and he offered to pay my expenses to fly up to Springfield, rent a car and take a look at it for them. I told him there was nothing I would like better.

The ranch turned out to be even better than I had hoped. It was in the area of south central Missouri referred to as the Missouri Ozarks. Most of that country is covered with brush and hardwood timber, but this ranch sat on an open plateau, about half of which was planted to improved pasture, mostly brome grass, and the rest was in native bluestem and lespedeza, an annual legume high in protein. A good bit of the improved pasture could be put up for hay if desired, and the combination of the early season improved pasture and later maturing native pasture lent itself to a long grazing season. The south boundary of the ranch faced a deep canyon of largely hardwood trees that was the north part of the Mark Twain National Forest. When the broker showed me that part of the property, I got out of the car and walked to the fence to look out on the forest's vast sea of mixed hardwood and pine. Just then a wild turkey at the edge of the open plateau flew down into the canyon and disappeared into the forest's misty depths. It was a sight that has lingered in my memory as one of the most beautiful and moving I have ever experienced.

When I returned home, I wrote up a report on the ranch and took it up to Sisterdale to show Glenn. He said he would share the report with Lloyd, talk it over and get back to me. I had told him I would be interested in managing the place for them if they decided to lease it, and he said he was sure I could handle the job. He indicated they would continue fitting their show cattle at the Sisterdale operation, being aware of my aversion to that part of the purebred cattle business. He knew my contacts with members of the American National Cattlemen's Association and the New Mexico Cattle Growers, for whom I had worked, would be useful to them in marketing their range bulls, and my acquaintance with the owners of several of the largest quarter horse breeders in the nation, also a result of those jobs, could be of benefit to their horse enterprise.

About a week later, Glenn called me and said they had decided to delay expanding their operation. I told him I was disappointed but was happy to have had the opportunity to look at that part of the country. I also appreciated the several hundred dollars he paid me for checking it out for them.

I couldn't get the Missouri ranch out of my mind and called Dave to tell him about my trip and ask if he knew anyone who might be interested in the property. He replied that, as a matter of fact, Robert Freeborn, who had a registered Brangus herd in Oregon, and his silent partner were looking to expand their operations and might consider it. I called Freeborn, a fairly new board member with whom I had become well acquainted over the past year. He was a bit of a character who knew he looked a lot like a young Teddy Roosevelt with his bushy mustache. He confirmed that they were looking to expand. He said they had an advisor who evaluated properties for them and asked if I could meet him at the ranch so he could check it out. I readily agreed. I told him I was ready to get back to work and would be interested in managing the property. He knew of my ranch background and said they would give me full consideration for the job.

I spent the better part of a day inspecting the place with Robert's financial advisor, who asked my opinion about the ranch's potential carrying capacity and hay production, but was otherwise quite noncommittal. That evening we drove back to the Springfield airport where he had left his private plane. He dropped me off at my departure gate and headed back to California to report his findings, none of which he had shared with me. Robert called within a week and said they were seriously considering leasing the property. He asked me if I was still interested in managing it. I said that I sure was, but the least I would be able to work for was $25,000 per year with the house and utilities furnished. He was aware I had been making $30,000 with the IBBA. He said he, his partner and financial advisor would be meeting soon and he would be back in touch.

A few days later, Robert called saying they had leased the ranch, but their financial guru, whom they paid well for his services, did not support the idea of my managing the place. He said he had gone to bat for me but his partner and advisor had out-voted him. After telling him how disappointed I was, I said that Dave was no longer comfortable with in his job with IBBA and would be a good choice. He knew and liked Dave and said he would give him a call. Dave called me the next day and asked for some details about the ranch in general and the home in particular. I told him I thought it would be a great place for his family and we both knew Robert would be a good guy to work for. He ended up taking the job and managed the operation for many years.

Maxine supported me in my desire to find a ranch job that would at least come close to my current salary. A few years after we had moved to Boerne, she had taken a job as bookkeeper for the city government, and within six months had organized it to the point that she could get the job done working just half days. We decided that if I could find a job that would allow us to continue living in our home, we could get along for less than I had been making. Within the next several weeks, three more job opportunities presented themselves in Texas, but only one of them was anywhere near driving distance from our home.

The first job I checked out was with Latimer Murfee, who had been on the IBBA board for most of the years I worked there. He was a successful, wealthy lawyer and had been a good board member, if a bit eccentric. He had a beautiful home in Houston where his law firm was located, and also a farm in the country where he raised his registered Brangus cattle and had built another lovely home. He also owned a large ranch in the Panhandle of Texas that ran commercial cattle and used most of the bulls that he raised. He also had a small show herd and had succeeded in raising one outstanding bull, which had been named Grand Champion a couple of times on the show circuit. That had whetted his appetite and he very much wanted to develop one of the top show herds in the breed.

I had heard he was not satisfied with his current manager, so contacted him to see if he was interested in my working for him. I didn't tell him about my distaste for show cattle because I hoped I could be involved in his Panhandle ranch as well as his registered operation not too far from our home. He said he would be very interested and invited Maxine and me to lunch with his wife at their farm home to talk it over. He seemed confident I could help him develop a top herd, using his champion bull as a foundation, and produce the best set of show cattle in the Brangus breed. He reluctantly agreed that he would probably have to buy a few more good females. When he asked me about salary I reminded him that I had been making $30,000 with IBBA and couldn't afford to take less than that. He said that was considerably more than he paid his current manager, but offered to pay me $25,000 and let us use the trailer on the property that his current manager lived in. Maxine and I thanked him for the wonderful meal and kind offer and said we would talk it over and get back to him soon.

It did not take Maxine and me long to decide this was not the job that I wanted. Latimer had complained during our lunch that his current manager had not been taking proper care of their big manicured lawn and landscaping, which included an artificial lake filled by a ditch that was made to seem like a stream of clear water running by their place. The ditch was fed from a small irrigation well. They had asked if Maxine would be willing to keep their house in readiness for their weekend visits. I rather lamely joked Maxine would surely do a better job of taking care of the house than I would caring for the landscaping. I knew the likelihood of my building a show herd that would compete with Willow Springs and other well-established herds was pretty remote, and I was disappointed when Latimer said I wouldn't be involved with the Panhandle ranch. When I called Latimer to tell him I would not be interested in the job, he seemed genuinely disappointed

I had one other interview for a ranch job. I had decided against trying to work for another registered cattle association because my loyalty to Brangus was so deep I wasn't sure I could effectively work for one. However, when I read of an opening at the ranch of one of the largest Beefmaster breeders in the country, Harrell Bothers of Gonzales, Texas, I decided to look into it. Beefmaster cattle had been developed by Tom Lasater, one of the most progressive cattlemen in the Southwest. They had been bred up over many generations as a three-way cross from a Hereford cow base using American Brahman and Shorthorns bulls. They were said to carry approximately three-eighths to one-half Brahman. A couple of breed associations had been established around Lasater's cattle, and I knew Harrell Bother's were among the largest operations.

I found an advertisement for the Harrell Brothers' upcoming production sale in my weekly livestock publication and saw that their manager was someone I had met when the Brangus office was in Kansas City. I called and learned that sure enough he was the same person, but that he was leaving, thus creating the job opening. He said it was a good job and suggested I send a resume and a letter requesting an interview to the elder Harrell brother, Wallace, who managed the purebred operation. I immediately did so, got a telephone call a few days later and was able to schedule an interview with both brothers in their Gonzales office.

When I arrived for the interview, I discovered that Wallace was recovering from a severe stroke and had only recently started coming to the office again. Although his left arm and leg were paralyzed and he had great difficulty speaking, he had arranged a mechanical lift to his second story office so he could get to it and he showed every intention of continuing to run the operation as he convalesced. His brother, who was in charge of their order buying business, was on hand too, but Wallace tried hard to conduct the interview. He was difficult to understand and I could tell he was quite frustrated when I didn't catch everything he said. His brother, who had obviously learned to communicate with him fairly well, diplomatically guided me through the interview. They seemed to like my credentials and I learned that they would want me to handle all of the advertising and promotion for their registered herd. The brother was interested in involving me in his part of the partnership, buying calves with from one-half to three-fourths Brahman blood and shipping them to feedlots in Kansas, Colorado, Nebraska and the Panhandle of Texas. He said he could use me to both help find homes for these calves in the big feedlots as well as acquire them. I didn't think the interview had gone very well, at least with Wallace, when they thanked me for coming and said they would be in touch.

I was both surprised and pleased when they called a day or two later and asked me to come down and visit them again. After a short visit and a tour of their operation, they said they were interested in hiring me if we could arrange a mutually agreeable salary. I told them how much I had been making. They asked me to leave the room for a while and when I came back offered me $25,000 a year. As I recall, they did have a modest house available we could live in. I said I would go home, talk to my wife and get back in touch with them within the week.

I had a lot of time to think during my two-and-one-half hour drive back to Boerne. I rather liked the idea of order buying calves for shipment to northern feedlots, but although I admired him greatly for his determination, I feared Wallace would be hard to work for. In addition, even though I knew public relations was one of my strong suits, it was the part of my work I had least enjoyed and was what I was hoping to get away from. I told Maxine about the interview and she concurred with my concerns about the job. We thought that if Gonzales were a little closer, so I could commute to work it might be worthwhile to try to negotiate a little higher salary, but since we still had three months before my contract ran out we decided it would be best to continue looking. I seriously doubted that Wallace Harrell would have negotiated for more money, but he was obviously upset when I called to tell him I was no longer interested in the job.

While I was looking around for a ranch job, I saw an ad for a position with a recently formed cattle association in Texas that I was well qualified for. In recent years the press had been taking notice of an organization called Independent Cattlemen of Texas, which had been formed in 1974. The founder and president of the new organization, T. A. Cunningham, was a vocal critic of the powerful Texas and Southwestern Cattle Raisers Association and claimed that significant numbers of ranchers were joining his newly formed nonprofit organization. I called the executive vice president of the Texas and Southwestern, whom I knew fairly well and asked him about the new organization and its president. He was rather dismissive of both and said their only policy seemed to be to oppose anything the Texas and Southwestern did. I responded by telling him that from what I had read I would have to agree with him. He, of course, knew I was looking for a job and said if a position opened up in his organization he would let me know. He probably had at least three or four positions paying $30,000 or more and I was sure I could qualify for any of them, except the job of editor of their "Texas Cattlemen" monthly magazine, one of the most successful livestock publications in the country.

I didn't even consider checking into the Independent Cattlemen of Texas job until after half of my six months' paid vacation from IBBA was up and I realized that a decent paying ranch job was going to be hard to find. I decided to call Cunningham and find out just what the new organization was all about. He said they had only recently grown to the point where they could afford a full time executive officer and thus far he and one secretary had been doing all the work. He said he would like me to meet him at his office in Fort Worth. It turned out he was looking for someone with just the kind of experience I had. I thanked him and said I would be back in touch with him shortly.

I told Maxine it looked as if I had a good shot at a job I was well qualified for, but shared my misgivings about working for an organization like the Independent Cattlemen. I told her it was an outspoken, anti-establishment outfit and that although I had an independent streak, all the organizations I had worked for fit firmly in the mainstream, conservative traditions of the cattle industry. We decided that I should go ahead and find out for myself what the Independent Cattlemen organization was all about.

I phoned Cunningham and we scheduled a meeting at his office later in the week. I told him about my background and he was particularly interested in my experience with ANCA and the New Mexico Cattle Growers Association. He said in no uncertain terms that he was very unhappy with the way ANCA and its state affiliates were dealing with a number of issues. He believed they were not taking a tough enough stance against beef imports. He also thought that the rules the industry had worked out for conducting the national brucellosis eradication program were completely unfair to the typical cow calf producer. I told him I had not been as involved with the national cattlemen's organization during my time with the Brangus Association as I had previously been, but we had become an ANCA affiliate during my tenure there. I did not share with him that I had been actively involved in and generally supportive of the formulation of many of the policies he and his organization opposed.

He said he wanted someone capable of helping him communicate the positions of the Independent Cattlemen of Texas to the press and plead their case at the state and federal levels of government. I assured him that I felt qualified in those areas, all the while wondering if I could in good conscience do so. Further discussion confirmed what I already suspected: this would be an organization run from the top down, made up of members whose views coincided with those of T. A. Cunningham. I diplomatically tried to point out that the organizations he was so critical of were ones I had found to be primarily grassroots driven. He strongly disagreed and said he was convinced they were dominated by large operators with axes to grind. He was rather vague about the size of the organization's budget, but said their membership was growing rapidly and he was sure they would be able to meet my $30,000 a year salary requirement. If they hired me, they would want me to start in about three months. I said that would work for me, but I wanted to start work no later than three months. I asked him if there was a chance they might locate the office in San Antonio and he left me with the impression that was a possibility, but that he preferred Fort Worth, which was a much more cattle-oriented city. I strongly suspected that his do-it-all secretary would oppose such a move. I left with the feeling that he had misgivings about me but suspected I might be as well qualified an applicant as he could hope to find, and I had serious misgivings about the job. We agreed that since he didn't need anyone immediately and I was not in a great hurry to start work, I should be back in touch with him in about a month.

I drove home from the interview very much conflicted. I was fairly confident that I could get the job if I really went after it, but knew I would be faced with building an organization that I was not excited about and promised very little security. After telling Maxine about the job interview, I confessed that perhaps I was being a little too high and mighty being so judgmental of the Independent Cattlemen. She assured me that the last thing I should do was accept a job for which I had little enthusiasm.

About a week later, I received a telephone call that gave me new hope. It was from Pat McGinley, who was the current president of the Nebraska Stock Growers Association. He said their executive secretary, Mickey Stewart, had been appointed Secretary of Agriculture for the state of Nebraska and they were looking for someone to replace him. The Nebraska Stock Growers was one of the stronger affiliates of the ANCA. I knew most of their past presidents and was slightly acquainted with Mickey, who had managed the Washington Cattlemen's Association when I was with ANCA. I also knew their magazine's editor, Bob Howard, who had also been their executive officer when I was with ANCA. I told Pat that I was interested in the job and we scheduled a job interview at the association office in Alliance the following week, about mid-May. I had met Pat when I visited his father's ranch with the photographer who had produced our

Brangus film, and I had spent several days there shooting footage of the Brangus cross calves from their Hereford cows. On that trip I had gotten reacquainted with Pat's brother, Mike, whom I had met when we were both in school at Colorado A & M. Mike had talked his father into using Brangus bulls on their large family ranch several years earlier.

About halfway through our telephone conversation, Pat said that the person who got this job might very well soon be managing a much larger operation because the NSGA was negotiating a merger with the Nebraska Livestock Feeders Association. I knew that the NFLA was an affiliate of the Corn Belt Feeders Association, but little else about it. That evening I told the family that I may have finally found a job opportunity that I could be enthusiastic about, and we discussed the fact that we might be moving soon. Shaun had graduated from high school the previous year and had a local boyfriend whom she was seriously considering marrying. Elizabeth was graduating that spring from Boerne and planned to attend San Marcos State College in the fall. Brendan would be a freshman in high school in Boerne in the fall and Jennifer was entering the fourth grade. We dreaded the thought of our two girls being so far away, and our two youngest didn't relish the idea of changing schools, but we were resigned to the fact that we must go wherever my job led us.

The next day, I called Bob Howard and asked him to send me a copy of the NSGA's bylaws, their latest budget and several recent issues of the Nebraska Cattlemen Magazine so I could prepare for my interview in a couple of weeks. I reminded the family that there was no guarantee that I would be offered the job or that they would pay enough to justify the move. I received the packet of information from Bob a few days before I left for Nebraska. I was relieved to see that Mickey Stewart was making exactly $30,000 per year when he resigned, and took comfort in the fact that the budget was no tighter than any other I was used to wrestling with. But I was shocked to learn while reading the four most recent magazines that although the Stock Growers Board of Directors had voted to support the merger and instructed the staff to prepare a program promoting it to present to each of their eighteen area affiliates, there was considerable pushback by many NSGA members. As a result of this grassroots opposition, shortly after all the areas had heard the staff tout the advantages of the merger, the board of directors, which was made up of the presidents of these very area affiliates, reversed a long-standing policy of not printing letters to the editor. The most recent issue Bob sent me had several pages of very strong letters opposing the merger, with some voicing criticism of the leadership for not giving more opportunity for members to hear both sides. I called Pat a couple of days before I drove to Alliance for the job interview to get a little more background on what was going on. He said the NLFA had already approved the merger and NSGA would be voting on it at their annual convention in mid-June. He said he was fairly confident the membership would approve it, but if not, they would fill the position and continue to be the effective organization they had always been.

  I had a lot to think about during the two-day, 1,100-mile drive to Alliance. I didn't share Pat's confidence that the NSGA membership would approve the merger and couldn't be sure that NSGA's executive, whoever it might be, would automatically become the head of the new organization, but I was looking forward to the interview!

52

Nebraska

I arrived in Alliance, Nebraska late in the afternoon the day before my job interview. I checked into a motel just as it started pouring rain, which continued for about two hours. I had planned to drive around town for a while, but by the time the rain let up it was past suppertime, so I had supper at the restaurant adjacent to the motel, after which I went to my room to review some notes I had made for the interview.

The last 120 miles from North Platte to Alliance on state highway 2 took me through the heart of the Nebraska Sandhills, an area I had never seen before. I had often heard about this amazing grassland, but was blown away by its unique beauty. After about an hour of driving, winding around and over huge, gently sloping hills, which I knew were composed of nothing but sand, and suddenly coming upon lakes varying from two acres to a quarter of a section in size, it occurred to me that this is how the Sahara Desert would look if it were covered with grass and had a lot more oases. I could see why ranchers from this part of the U. S. thought theirs was the best cattle country in the world. The only other time I had been in Alliance was in about 1955, when I had traveled from Fort Collins to a rodeo. The road from Scottsbluff crossed just the far western edge of the Sandhills and didn't reveal the true nature of the area. In fact, possibly because I hadn't won a cent at the rodeo and had been bucked off hard by my saddle bronc, I left with a pretty poor impression of Alliance.

When I got up the next morning, the sun was out and the rain had left the air crisp and fresh. Alliance was a town of only about 10,000 people and I had no problem finding the Stockgrower's office on the main east-west street one block from the main intersection. I arrived at my 9:00 a.m. interview fifteen minutes early, introduced myself to the receptionist and asked her if Bob Howard was in. She directed me to the first office on the right down the hall and I had a short visit with him before Pat McGinley arrived. He was one of a three-man committee appointed by the board to interview Mickey's replacement. Pat said the other two members of the committee were his vice president, Jim Gran, from Gordon and Jack Maddux, the immediate past president who lived in Wauneta, Nebraska. He said that Jack had called that he would not be able to make the meeting, but had told Pat that he would be fine with whomever he and Jim selected. I had met Jack when was in college. He was one year behind me, but we had been in several classes together and I remembered that he was on the livestock

Roy

judging team. While we were waiting for Jim, I asked Pat if he had talked to Jack about me. He said he had and Jack had indicated he knew me and his only comment was that, "I was a smart little bastard." I chose to take it as a compliment because I recalled that several of our professors posted test grades in the hall outside their offices and I got quite a few As.

When Jim showed up, he and Pat shook hands rather formally and we went into Mickey's office. Pat explained to Jim that we had met while I was with IBBA and suggested Jim begin the interview. Jim asked me to briefly review my work experience and asked several questions that indicated he had a good understanding of what an association manager should do. Pat was particularly interested in my lobbying experience and seemed satisfied with my answers. When they asked if I had any questions, I asked if NSGA's new executive officer would be managing the new organization if the merger went through. Pat indicated that he was pretty confident that it would be approved and left me with the impression that it had already been agreed that Mickey was to have been the CEO, but that Paul Johnston, executive officer of the NLFA, would be assured of the job as second in command. Jim was noncommittal about the merger's prospects, but they both agreed that NSGA would want an executive who would make the organization the best it could be if it was voted down.

After a few more questions, they asked me to leave the room for a few minutes before we talked salary. I stepped out and surveyed the office. It was very much like a cutdown version of the office building that housed the ANCA in Denver, and looked to have been built at about the same time, probably in the 1950s. After about ten minutes, they called me back and told me the job was mine if we could agree on terms. I had told them about the conditions under which I had left IBBA and said I would like to start work in mid-August for the same salary I made there, $30,000 per year, and requested that they pay my moving expenses. Pat said that if the merger was approved at the convention in Kearny in mid-June the NLFA would then surely vote to merge with the Stockgrowers at their convention in August. After a bit of dickering, during which they mentioned their goal was to hire someone for less than Mickey had been making, and my pointing out that I had at least as much experience as he, they offered me the job on my terms and I accepted. We decided that I would come to Kearney to be introduced to the members and then I would start work in mid-August for either the NSGA or the newly merged organization.

When I got home, I told the family that I had a new job and explained the rather unusual circumstances. The situation left it up in the air as to where we might be living, where Jennifer and Brendan went to school and even whether or not I would be boss of the new organization. Even though Paul Johnston had agreed that Mickey would head the merged group, I couldn't be positive that he would defer to me.

Unfortunately, the housing market in Boerne had greatly slowed down and it appeared the situation was just the opposite in Alliance. Bob Howard had told me the Union Pacific Railroad had just completed a big repair facility in Alliance and greatly increased the number of tracks coming in and out of town. As a result, it was almost impossible to find a place to rent there and housing prices had gone through the roof. We thought we needed to wait until after the convention in Kearney, when my job situation would be clarified, before we put our house on the market, but I immediately put an ad in the San Antonio newspaper advertising our cattle for sale. I also contacted the man handling the land where I ran the cattle to see if I could terminate the lease early. He told me the only way I could get out of it was to find someone to take it over.

Maxine and I talked over our situation with her mother, indicating we would be happy to take her with us wherever we went, if she didn't want to stay in Boerne. Grandma Frock had moved into an apartment next door to Ilene a couple of years earlier and had passed away a year later at the age ninety-three. She died at home and to our knowledge had never spent a day in the hospital. Maxine and I had moved into Grandma Frock's quarters and our bedroom had become the guest bedroom.

The next three weeks were stressful. I hadn't gotten any responses to my ad for the cattle nor had any luck finding someone to take over the lease. I hauled four horses back to the folks' farm in Fort Collins in our trailer and managed to sell the three-year-old black mare we had raised to one of their neighbors. I took the trailer on up to the ranch near Laramie that Frank was managing, talked him into buying it and made the drive back to Boerne in one very long day. This left Susie Belle as the only horse left in the pasture with the cows. Elizabeth was spending the summer with her mother and Shaun was making arrangements to move into the home of the boy she was engaged to. He was a year younger than she and they weren't planning to get married until fall. The boy's mother insisted this rather unusual arrangement would be better than trying to move up the wedding date. Maxine and I liked the young man but thought that both of them were too young to get married and were not very comfortable with the situation, even though Shaun thought it was just fine. Jennifer and Brendan were both in the middle of their little league baseball season and were definitely not looking forward to moving.

I left for Kearney and the NSGA convention with a lot of important questions up in the air. I told Maxine I would call immediately after I knew how the vote on the merger turned out. When I arrived at the convention, I found I already knew a lot of people and was pleased with the warm reception everyone gave me. As I visited with folks in the hall, I could tell that the merger was in big trouble, and I found out to my surprise that Jim Gran was one of its primary opponents. I knew Pat was its most outspoken supporter from having read his "President's Letters" in the Nebraska Cattlemen. The opposition expressed in the letters to the editor that had been allowed in the most recent issues had been a pretty good indication that the merger was not a sure thing. The discussion at the annual business meeting before the vote was pretty hot. Pat and the staff once again presented the program that all the area associations had seen, which touted the benefits of merging with the feeders. Pat called on supporters to speak first and then the opposition presented its case. Their main complaint was that there had not been enough grass roots input on the details of the plan, and many of the members believed that western ranchers and corn belt feeders simply did not have enough in common to be represented by the same organization. As the merger was voted down, it occurred to me that it was probably a good idea that had been oversold and pushed too fast.

The merger vote was something of a repudiation of Pat's leadership, but he took it well and was reelected to his second year of office later in the business meeting. Immediately after the convention adjourned, Bob Howard took a picture of me for the cover of the next issue of the "Nebraska Cattleman." I called Maxine and said that we would be living in Alliance, Nebraska and I would report for work on August 15, 1979 as anticipated. We agreed that I should drive over to Alliance and see about finding a house before I headed home.

I soon confirmed that there was not a decent house for rent in Alliance. There were very few homes for sale, and those that were got snapped up right away. Maxine said she didn't want to make a trip to Alliance and suggested that if I found one that would work for us to go ahead and make an offer. She also asked me to try to find something that would work for her mother. The best house I could find for us was a bi-level with two small bedrooms, a three-fourths bath downstairs and a fairly good-sized bedroom and full bath upstairs. It was certainly a decent house, but quite a step down from what we had built for ourselves in Boerne. I gave up on finding an apartment for Ilene and put a month's rent down on a fairly new trailer in the trailer park on the east side of town.

I can't recall what we paid for the house in Alliance, but the payments were considerably less than for our home in Boerne. The problem was that if we did not sell our Texas place we were going to be making payments on two houses, and we still had to sell our cattle and transfer our land lease. The time left to get these things done was slipping away fast and I was about ready to take the cattle to the auction market, when I got a call in response to our ad. I met the man who had called, along with his son, at the pasture and was not only able to make a deal for all the cattle; he agreed to take over the lease as well. He had a small acreage close by and had initially planned to buy only a few cows. His son saw Susie Belle and asked if she was for sale. I said we had not decided what to do with her yet, however I would consider selling her. I caught her and rode her around bareback for a while and he was amazed to see how handy she was. I ended up selling her to him along with the bridle, a small saddle Mom had given to us and a saddle blanket. The next day I took the checks for the cattle and horse to the Colonial National Bank and paid off my loan.

About a week later, I learned that the man who had purchased our cattle had died suddenly. When I stopped by to visit his son to pay my respects, he said that the cattle had been sent to market and the lease terminated. I noticed Susie Bell tied to a tree nearby and asked him if he would like for us to take her back. He said he wouldn't think of giving her up because his daughter was crazy about her. I was moved by the graciousness of this family in the midst of their tragedy that was intertwined with our good fortune.

By mid-August, we had still not received an offer on our house in Boerne and were faced with two undesirable choices. I could leave Maxine and the kids in Boerne until our home was sold, or we could all move to Alliance and leave the house vacant. After we talked to our realtor and he assured us he would take care of the house and continue to show it, we decided to move and enroll the kids before their new school year started. During the day that the moving company packed our dishes, pictures and clothing, we loaded our two cars with our suitcases and the valuables we needed to carry with us so we would be ready to leave as soon as the furniture was loaded and on the way to Alliance the next day.

By mid-afternoon the moving van that was scheduled to unload at our new home within three days pulled out and we followed with Jennifer, Brendan, the dog and a couple of cats distributed between our two cars.

We made it to a motel in San Angelo, Texas by a little after dark. I left our dog, Honey, and the cats in the car. At about five a.m. I got up and took Honey for a walk, but didn't dare let the cats out of their traveling cage. We got an early start and drove to Springfield, Colorado to spend the night with Bill and Joyce Mundell at their ranch, which was about twenty miles from town. I had not seen Bill and Joyce since our eventful trip to the International Collegiate rodeo finals in Portland, Oregon in June of 1952. We got there just before dark, turned Honey loose to get acquainted with their dogs and carried the cats in their cage into a box stall in the barn, where we turned them loose and carefully shut the door. Joyce and Maxine had a glass of wine and Bill and I downed a couple of stiff drinks of bourbon before we ate a big meal featuring steaks from one of their home-fed Brangus steers. After supper I took some food and water out to the cats and as I opened the barn door they came flying out past me and disappeared into the night. It was too dark to look for them and I was afraid we would never see them again. Bill and Joyce assured us that we would surely find them around the barn next morning. Unfortunately, next morning they were nowhere to be found, after a half hour looking and fruitlessly calling "Kitty, kitty," Maxine and Jennifer were particularly upset. We thanked the Mundells for their hospitality and invited them to come up and see us in Alliance, which was about 300 miles northwest on US Highway 385. They assured us they would look after the cats until we could get them if they turned up.

We arrived in Alliance in the early afternoon and pulled up in front of our unpretentious new home. Maxine asked me to get the vacuum cleaner, mop and other cleaning equipment out of the trunk and we all went to work. The house was not in bad shape, but Maxine was not about to move in the furniture on top of "someone else's dirt." By supper time we had everything but the cupboards clean, a job Maxine planned do the next day before the furniture was unloaded. Just before we left the house to eat supper, Maxine sat down on the floor and burst into tears. As I tried to comfort her, I suspected that it wasn't just that the house left something to be desired, but that she was mourning once again having to leave a place where she had built a cozy nest for her family, and start over.

The furniture arrived the next morning and after it was unloaded we all went over to look at the office and meet the staff. A few days later Maxine enrolled Jennifer and Brendan in their respective schools and I drove back to San Antonio to get Grandma Ilene. When I got there, I rented a U-Haul trailer, loaded her furniture and we took two days to drive back to Alliance, arriving early enough the second day to unload her furniture. I'm not sure that Grandma Ilene was much happier about the trailer than Maxine was about our little bi-level, but I didn't hear a word of complaint.

On the first of September, I reported to work at my new office. In addition to Bob Howard, the staff consisted of a receptionist/secretary, a communications director and a field man/advertising salesman for the magazine, who lived in central Nebraska. This was more staff than I had in my similar job in New Mexico, but NSGA had a bigger membership and Nebraska had far more cattle and thus potential growth. During the six months there had been no executive secretary, Pat McGinley had filled in as best he could by coming to the office several days a week. I knew he enjoyed it and I think he hated giving up Mickey's desk to me. Bob Howard and Troy Smith, our field man, did all the magazine work. The communications director put out a bi-weekly newsletter, "The Fenceline," taped a weekly news show, which she mailed to most of the radio stations in Western Nebraska, and sent out occasional news releases.

The second week I was in the office, I inadvertently crossed wires with the communications director. When she finished writing the "Fenceline," I asked her if I could proofread it. She wanted to know why and I told her there had been a policy in all of my previous jobs to proofread everything that left the office. She gave me her copy, I made a couple of minor corrections, handed it back to her and the next day she mailed it as usual. The following Monday she handed me her resignation, saying it appeared I didn't approve of her work. I told her that, to the contrary, she did a good job and proofreading was just a normal routine of shared responsibility. I said that if I wrote an article, I would expect her to proofread it for me. She was still quite upset and my response did not mollify her, so I accepted her two-weeks' notice.

It just so happened that the Alliance area affiliate had a meeting a few days after I started work and I got a chance to meet many of the ranchers whom I would be seeing around town from time to time. Bob Howard, who went to the event with me, said the activity we were attending would be fairly typical of the meetings of the local affiliates of the associations that I would be attending during the year. The eighteen local affiliates were not circumscribed by clearly delineated boundaries, such as county lines, but were broken up into trade areas throughout the western part of Nebraska. For example, cattlemen in northern Sheridan County belonged to a different affiliate than those in the south. More on this unique feature of NSGA later.

The current area president often hosted a picnic in the summer and most areas had from two to four meetings annually. This particular meeting at the Freiberger Ranch included a short business meeting featuring Pat and me as speakers. Pat and several directors from adjacent areas attended. I had met a couple of the folks years before at ANCA meetings, and among the families in attendance were prominent registered Hereford breeders whom I knew by reputation. One of these was Charles Iodence, an active member whose operation was in the northwest area. Charles and I soon became good friends and have remained so to this day.

I had reviewed the association's bylaws before my interview, however, Pat and Bob explained their unique and effective structure had largely been the brainchild of Merlyn Carlson, who had been the association's president eight years before I came on board. Before that time the board structure had been similar to that of the ANCA in that the past presidents largely controlled the organization. Merlyn appointed a committee to reorganize the board and it came up with the unusual, but effective plan, calling for the area associations' presidents to concurrently serve two-year terms as their local organization's leader and director of NSGA. They were limited to two terms or a maximum of four consecutive years of service. The new bylaws made the past presidents ex officio members of the board without vote, and it soon became obvious to me that they took the opportunity to attend and participate, and their influence remained quite strong while less binding.

My daily routine was amazingly similar to what it had been with the NMCGA. The only new chore was preparing and getting out the weekly radio show. Fortunately, I had watched ANCA's communication director, Lyle Liggette, use his reel-to-reel recorder many times and had even been interviewed by him a time or two. The machine we had was exactly like his and it didn't take me long to learn how to use it. However, I found that preparing a fifteen-minute radio show was different than writing a news release. Mickey had evidently copied the feeders' organization in doing such a weekly program. However, the feeders had retained the services of Rex Messerschmit, a farm news broadcaster at KRVN to do theirs and he was well known and respected within Nebraska agricultural circles. I dictated a fifteen-minute script each week to make a master copy of the program and then made a dozen copies. All I can remember is that I labored harder over that one chore than any other, and usually ended up with a product that I was not overly pleased with. It was usually aired on small town radio farm programs, and always on Saturday morning by KRVN, the 50,000-watt station out of Lexington, Nebraska, which was a co-op owned by the Nebraska agricultural community.

The NSGA had always prided itself on its effectiveness in dealing with legislative affairs in Lincoln. However, Mickey Stewart, Pat McGinley's predecessor as president, Jack Maddux, and several other leaders of the organization had become convinced that we needed a more active presence in state legislative matters on a daily basis when the unicameral legislature was in session. State senators—unicameral members are called Senators—were critical of the fact that on occasion the NSGA and NLFA came out with opposing views on issues. These mainly conservative rural senators, outnumbered by the typically more liberal senators from Omaha and Lincoln, usually supported cattle industry causes and couldn't understand why the two organizations couldn't get their act together. Pat was determined to remedy this situation even though the merger had been defeated.

When the legislature went into session that fall I, like my predecessor, subscribed to a service that mailed us all the bills that were introduced daily, along with information as to when hearings would be held and updated as amendments were made. The first thing I did each morning was review this information. Then I forwarded the bills pertinent to their area of interest to each of our committee chairmen so they could review them and offer their recommendations. A few weeks into the session, we called a special board meeting in Lincoln to review all the bills thus far introduced and stake out our positions. Later in the session, we had another board meeting to discuss the progress of the bills we were following and refine our strategy for meeting our objectives. In the meanwhile, Pat and I would have spent several days each week in Lincoln and, on occasion, called in a committee chairman to testify on a particularly important bill. As I rubbed shoulders with the paid lobbyists in Lincoln and tried to learn a few tricks of their trade, it became obvious to me that Senators looked to these professionals for technical information and financial support from their employers. Still, it was obvious that people who actually worked in these industries and volunteered to testify carried a good deal of weight. The cattle industry's long tradition of using volunteers gave our officers and committee chairmen a great deal of credibility at the hearings.

Partly to sooth the feelings of the NLFA after the defeat of the merger, our board had agreed to pay them $100 a month for a room in their new Lincoln office near the Capitol, which I could use while in town during the legislative session. Paul Johnston set up a desk in a seldom-used storage room and furnished me a manual typewriter. Unfortunately my typing was very bad, and having no secretary or copying machine, I couldn't very well prepare written testimony for committee hearings. I tried to use the office during this first session; however, I found myself using it less and less as time went on. Paul and his wife, Maxine, had been the sole employees of the NLFA for many years and had moved to Lincoln only within the last year, when it looked as if they were going to merge with the NSGA. Paul and I became best friends over the years, but there was a certain amount of tension this first year. He didn't understand some of our procedures and some of his were quite different from ours. He also had affiliates, but they were smaller in size than ours, but equal or greater in number of members each due to the denser rural population in the East. Their county affiliates were responsible for collecting dues and then forwarding the state organization's portion. We, of course, collected all our dues from the state office. Paul and his wife had a finely tuned system that worked perfectly for the small office run out of their basement, before they moved to Lincoln. I couldn't help wonder how far Mickey and Paul had gone working out the nuts and bolts of the operation of the merged organizations.

The first several times I drove to Lincoln after the legislature convened I stopped at Pat's home in Oshkosh to pick him up. During the remainder of the four-and-one-half-hour drive, he had lots of time to fill me in on the history and traditions of NSGA. Early in the session we spent most of our time lobbying individual senators on bills important to us whose hearings came up soon. After the hearings were underway, Pat testified for us, and when hearings on two bills in which we were interested were scheduled at the same time, I would also testify. I had the testimony prepared before I left the office and we left a written copy with the chairman. We always made it a point to meet Paul Johnston, along with any of his officers in town working on legislation, to coordinate our efforts. On particularly important bills, we would often visit the key senators together.

My first year seemed to go by fast, and even though I traveled just as much as with IBBA I was gone overnight fewer times. Working with a board made up of full-time commercial cattlemen was much less stressful than with a heterogeneous group made up of doctors, lawyers and business people, who were involved with their cattle business only on weekends and often with the goal of sheltering taxes. The family had settled into our new home and Jennifer and Brendan enrolled in their new schools. We joined the very active Episcopal Church in Alliance, which had a wonderful priest and had a lot to be thankful for in our new circumstances.

NEBRASKA STOCK GROWERS ASSOCIATION
Alliance, Nebraska

NOTES TO FINANCIAL STATEMENTS
(Unaudited)

Note 1: ASSOCIATION DUES
The billing procedure was changed in December, 1978, effective with the calendar year 1979. Previously dues had been on an annual basis from the date of joining. Now dues are all on a calendar year basis. Thus some members have paid more than 12 months dues in this period while others have paid less than 12 months dues. Based on the current membership the annual dues would be approximately $102,000.00.

Effective January 1, 1978, the minimum dues figure was increased from $20.00 to $30.00 a year. One year ago the membership was approximately 4,000 compared with a current membership of 3,088.

Note on 1979 Nebraska Stock Growers Association annual audit showing the significance of a substantial dues increase to a non-profit organization. Fortunately this was done the year before I was hired and we were able to re-coup most of the members in about three years just before the agricultural financial crisis hit.

53

Feeders

In the mid-1970s, the University of Nebraska had been involved in an effort to establish a veterinary college in the five-state area that also included North and South Dakota, Wyoming and Montana. There were no veterinary schools in any of these important cattle producing states and large animal practitioners were especially in short supply. By 1977 there was a consensus that a vet college should be built on the University of Nebraska Campus in Lincoln, with a goal of welcoming its first class in 1981. Promoting this project was the number one priority during my first two years with NSGA. This project bogged down in 1980 but NSGA and NLFA led the formation of a thirty-four-member statewide committee, representing every segment of Nebraska's livestock industry, to launch a two-million-dollar fundraising drive to revive it. Pat McGinley was named co-chairman of this committee, and a subcommittee, which included Pat, Roland McClymont of NLFA and Glenn LeDoyt representing the state's business community. They chartered a plane and over a period of several weeks met with representatives of four other universities in the five-state region. In spite of the valiant efforts of our two cattle organizations, with wide industry support, the effort stalled again and finally died from lack of funding in 1984.

Preparing for the business meeting of my first NSGA convention was much the same as it had been for all the previous cattle organizations I had worked for, but they all had unique traditions for their social activities. NSGA did not have a separate ladies luncheon and style show, but instead had an active women's auxiliary, the Cow Belles, which met concurrently with the men. It also had a strong junior auxiliary, which produced a skit as the entertainment for the first night of the convention. The communications director traditionally worked with the junior group and I had hired a young graduate of the University of Missouri's journalism school, Mark Russell, to fill the job. He enjoyed the assignment and with his enthusiastic help the juniors put on one of their best skits ever. Mark got so involved in it that he didn't have much time to help me with other convention activities!

Jim Gran was elevated to the presidency and Pat McGinley was presented with the traditional gold watch for his two years' service. The tension that went with the merger discussion the previous year seemed to have dissipated, although I was aware of the resentment some of the leaders of that effort still felt. I was pleasantly surprised when Jim, in his acceptance speech, said that one of his priorities as president would be to continue to work toward an acceptable process that could eventually lead to a merger with the feeders. A by-law change made the year before kicked in at the convention and Jim Gran and subsequent presidents were eligible for only a one-year term. To my knowledge, Jim was the first person elected to the presidency of NSGA who was a ranch manager with no financial interest in his operation. He ran the large Mission Ranch just north of Gordon. It was owned by a Jesuit Catholic Indian school located in South Dakota, just north of the Nebraska line.

Jim and/or I attended all of the area meetings that summer and fall. Jim was active in the Toastmasters Club in Gordon, Nebraska and was an excellent extemporaneous speaker. At the meetings that were held in conjunction with a picnic, he and I usually made up the entire program, however some were supper meetings at a restaurant or American Legion Hall in the major town in the area. The meal at these was often sponsored by a pharmaceutical company, Elanco, which had recently introduced a new growth-enhancing product for cattle called Ralgro. In return for a free meal, one of their field representatives was given the opportunity to make a thirty-minute slide presentation. Non-member ranch families were invited to these events and Jim and I always made a strong membership sales pitch during our presentations. It was a mutually beneficial arrangement and one of our best membership tools.

Jim was much less enthusiastic about traveling to Lincoln during the legislative session than Pat McGinley had been. He thought we should get involved in only the most important legislation and use volunteers to present testimony if possible. Not all the board members agreed with him. I continued the organization's policy of screening all the bills and getting copies in the hands of the appropriate committee chairmen. As usual, our entire board of directors met in Lincoln after most of the bills had been introduced and we identified a lot of bills to be monitored, but earmarked fewer than usual for testimony. When the latter bills came up, I tried to pick up the chairman of the committee responsible for the bill on the way to Lincoln and often helped him prepare his testimony. I usually joined him at the table in the hearing room that faced members of the committee hearing the bill. I was the closest thing to a paid lobbyist that Jim would tolerate.

Not long after the convention, Mark Russell left us after he found a better paying job. I now had so much to do that I didn't want to write the newsletter or record our weekly radio reports. I soon found and hired a young lady with a journalism school background similar to Mark's, and for a while I thought she was going to work out fine. However, she soon began to think she should be allowed to unilaterally make whatever changes she wanted in our procedure. I told her I thought she didn't have enough experience to assume such responsibility. She didn't get angry and quit, but instead came to the next board meeting and tried to have me fired. I can't remember the exact complaints she presented, but the board was just as surprised as I was and suggested she might want to consider working elsewhere.

The next time I spent a little more time interviewing applicants for the communications director's position. Bob Howard was always willing to give me a hand with the newsletter and I had nearly mastered the art of duplicating my radio broadcasts, even though preparing them took much longer than it should have. After a few weeks, another applicant showed up with promising credentials. Her name was Mary Guynan and she had been raised on a livestock farm near Schuyler in Eastern Nebraska. I was impressed with the interview and put her right to work. She proved to be especially good at one of our most frustrating, but necessary, ongoing projects: soliciting new members. The cattle associations I had worked for nearly always suffered the loss of about ten-percent of their members annually, so it was essential to have a successful recruitment program just to stay even. Our most effective tool was a one-day membership drive in each of our area association's territory. All our staff and as many volunteers as we could recruit formed teams and called on ranchers who were non-members.

Mary quickly proved to be particularly effective at getting new members during these drives and it seemed that whichever team

Mary was on obtained the most. Our most effective sales pitch was reminding these non-members that largely through the efforts of our association their taxes had been reduced enough to pay their annual dues several times over. (A few years before my arrival the NSGA, NLFA and the Nebraska Farm Bureau had, after several years of intense effort, managed to get legislation passed exempting cattle from the state ad valorem property tax rolls). Mary had the gift of determining which of the many issues confronting cattlemen was most important to the potential member, and focusing her pitch on that area. I was a reasonably good salesman, but I loved to talk and often continued a philosophical conversation with someone who had already made it quite clear he wasn't going to join. This wasted a lot of time and we had a lot of country to cover trying to visit eight or ten ranches a day in the boonies of Western Nebraska. Mary was hard to say no to, but when she realized the sale wasn't going to be closed, she diplomatically ended the conversation and went to the next place. Unfortunately, I got to travel with her only once or twice because usually only one staff member accompanied each team.

Most considered the Nebraska Stock Growers Association an organization of primarily ranchers who were either cow/calf operators or those who purchased feeder cattle to use their grass. The Nebraska Livestock Feeders Association was thought to be an organization made up of strictly cattle feeders. As a matter of fact, the NSGA represented only commercial cattlemen in the two-thirds of the state west of Kearney, including that part of the Sandhills that continued to the north and east toward O'Neill. The NLFA primarily represented the eastern third of the state where there was also a lot of land suitable mainly for grazing. This area's cow/calf or yearling operators were most often referred to as farmer/stockmen and they made up an important segment of the NFLA's membership. Still, this area was best known as part of the nation's corn belt.

Thousands of acres along the Platte River were almost exclusively dedicated to growing corn and it was one of the earlier areas to install sprinkle irrigation systems, making its farms nearly drought proof. Traditionally many of these farmers had purchased feeder cattle in western range country each fall, fed them their own corn during the winter and sold them for slaughter in the spring at the large central markets along the Missouri river. These folks represented the more typical NFLA member.

The NLFA was a founding member of the Corn Belt Cattle Feeders, later called the National Livestock Feeders Association, which in turn merged with the ANCA in 1976. The National Livestock Feeders Association had evolved after the Second World War to represent the interests of this important segment of the cattle industry. Before long, some of these Nebraska farmer feeders grew into large operations that were purchasing corn from their smaller neighbors, who had discontinued feeding their railcar load or two of cattle for themselves.

In the meantime, pump irrigation out of the Ogallala Aquifer allowing corn to be grown there, led to the development of a whole new era in cattle feeding in the Panhandle of Texas. Many of the pioneers contributing to the explosive growth of this dynamic new industry in the Panhandle had previously been successful cattle feeders in Nebraska, and soon a powerful new voice in the cattle industry, the Texas Cattle Feeders Association, was organized. It represented the interests of these big, progressive new feedlots filled with cattle that were often owned by absentee investors with income they wished to shelter from income tax. Rather than affiliate with the Corn Belt Feeders, this group joined the American National Cattlemen's Association, and before long they and the Texas and Southwestern Cattle Raisers Association had the two most influential organizations in the ANCA.

At about the same time that feedlots with capacities of 50,000 to 100,000 were springing up across the Texas Panhandle, several similar large feedlots were established in Southwest Nebraska using pump irrigation out of the same Ogallala Aquifer. Several of the feedlots in Eastern Nebraska had grown to exceed a capacity of 50,000 head. The NLFA, in an effort to keep their big feedlots in the fold, started a large feeders' council and Paul Johnston told me that he thought it was working well for them.

Shortly before I arrived at NSGA, the organization had been inviting new, large-scale feeders to become members; evidently, they had been quite vocal in favor of the merger. After Jim Gran promised to resume efforts to that end, we again reached out to this significant segment of the nation's cattle industry that wasn't affiliated with either the NSGA or NLFA, even though several belonged to ANCA. We believed they were getting a free ride on the coattails of both organizations, which were dedicated to solving problems that vitally affected them at the state level.

We succeeded in re-enlisting several of the same feedlot owners who had promoted the earlier merger, plus several others. Out of this group, a special committee was appointed to discuss by-law changes addressing their representation on the board of directors and arranging annual dues assessments based on average feedlot capacity. Nearly all the NSGA officers and board members were enthusiastic about the amount of revenue that could flow in from these big operations; however, some were still skeptical as to whether their goals were sufficiently akin to the NSGA's membership. After all, ranchers wanted to sell their calves and yearlings for as high a price as they could, and the feeders wanted to buy them as cheaply as possible. Proponents of the effort pointed out that this was a once-a-year situation; the rest of the time both groups had nearly identical concerns with such things as environmental problems, taxes, transportation issues and animal health matters.

Our family life had certainly improved with the reduction in my travel since our move to Nebraska. I didn't miss the long airplane rides, driving rented cars and lonely motel rooms. Jennifer had little trouble adjusting to her new grade school; however it was more difficult for Brendan, who was beginning his sophomore year in high school. Alliance had a considerably bigger school than Boerne and he was not able to make the basketball team as he had hoped—and might have been able to do so back in Texas. He had made friends with a boy who also hadn't made the team. I hung a backboard and hoop above our garage and enjoyed playing with the two of them and other kids in the neighborhood after work and on weekends. I gained some weight with no horses or cattle to look after and began jogging, an activity that had never appealed to me much. I had looked for places in the country before purchasing our house, but couldn't find anything comparable to what we had in Texas. After we sold the place in Texas, I continued to keep my eyes open for acreage near town. However, the building boom in Alliance had caused all of the smaller acreages within twenty miles of town to be priced at subdivision levels, and we didn't want just a house on a lot. In any case we were certainly not in any hurry to move again.

Jim Gran's desire to do everything possible to lay the groundwork for another merger effort within the next two years included a scheme that had the effect of putting a move right back on the front burner. He believed having our office closer to the middle of the state would increase NSGA's bargaining power to locate the new organization's headquarters west of Lincoln. I certainly shared Jim's view that the long-range interests of the cattle industry would be best served by one organization and that it would not make sense to have its headquarters in the far west of the state when the Capitol was on the opposite side. I reminded him that the NLFA had probably moved their office from Schuyler to Lincoln with the same strategy in mind; however, we agreed that if we could sell our office and buy or build a new one in the middle of the state along I-80 we would be in the far stronger position to keep the headquarters out of Lincoln. Jim presented the idea at the next board meeting and I was instructed to look for appropriate office space in North Platte, Kearney and the towns in between.

About two weeks before our mid-June annual convention held in Kearny in 1981, NSGA and NLFA made their first tangible move toward bringing the two organizations closer together. Jim Gran and Larry Schram, president of the NLFA, signed an agreement whereby the "Nebraska Cattleman" also became the official monthly publication of the Nebraska Livestock Feeders Association, nearly doubling its circulation. A magazine committee made up of members of both organizations and chaired by Henry Krug, Jr. of Benkelman was appointed to oversee the publication and assure balanced coverage of both organizations.

When I passed through North Platte or Kearney, I often scheduled a few hours with realtors to look at office space for sale. I found that there were not many properties available with the number of square feet we were looking for and all would have to be completely remodeled to serve our purpose. I was well acquainted with the director of the University of Nebraska's Agricultural Experiment Station near North Platte and decided to ask him if he knew of any land that we might purchase for a building site close to the city. He was enthusiastic about the prospect of the NSGA office moving to North Platte and said that they might have a piece of land that would work. The experiment station was about ten miles south of North Platte on the road to McCook and most of their land and improvements were located on the north side of the road. The director said they had a few acres on the south side that were of no use to them because they had been isolated from their other property when the highway had been moved a few years before. We drove about a half mile south of the station entrance on the highway to the top of a hill with several scattered pine trees. There appeared to be a good building site among the trees, which would have a great view of the city of North Platte and the river valley below. I told him I thought it would make a wonderful location for our office. He said he would contact the appropriate officials at the university and let me know if they would consider letting us build there. A few weeks later he sent me a letter indicating that there would be no problem making the land available to us and there would be no strings attached other than that we build an attractive building that complemented the landscape.

Jim reported my finding at the next board meeting. The fact that the land would be donated was a major factor in gaining board support for the move. When asked if we had received much opposition to selling the office in Alliance, Jim said it appeared that the local people didn't seem to care that much. As he said that, I looked at the Alliance area president, John Frieberger, and thought his face turned a little red, but he didn't say anything. The board voted to authorize the move if the cost of relocation was covered by proceeds from the sale of the current headquarter's property. Although the bylaws of NSGA authorized the board of directors to determine the location of the headquarters of the association, it chose to present the resolution for a vote at the convention to make sure they were not thought to have gotten out ahead of the membership. The motion passed by a vote of 100-62. Another important resolution that passed at the 1981 convention was a pet idea of mine. It gave the Nebraska Stock Grower's members the option of paying dues to the American National Cattlemen's Association along with their state dues, in an effort to increase our representation on that organization's board of directors. This resolution passed by a vote of 110 to 51.

When the board had approved the move to North Platte the previous fall after the experiment station made its offer, we were faced with another move. I appreciated recommending a membership vote, although it seemed not to be required and I was confident it would pass. This time Maxine reacted more positively to our job-related move because we had never been completely happy with our Alliance house, and we looked forward to another chance to get a house in the country. As I well knew, there are a lot of moving parts involved in moving an office, but I waded in with my usual enthusiasm. I started checking for rural acreages within ten or fifteen miles of North Platte and advertised our house for sale. We really didn't want to live in North Platte, but there was a small town about fifteen miles to the west called Maxwell, and another to the east about the same distance called Hershey. They both had high schools and we hoped to find something near one of them.

It turned out that there were not very many small acreages available anywhere in the area, but I finally managed to find a rather odd-shaped twelve acres on an irrigation ditch with a nice house and a few decent outbuildings about a mile south of I-80 and halfway between Maxwell and North Platte. The property was priced close to what we hoped to get for our current home. Over a weekend, I drove Maxine and the kids to take a look at the place. We liked it reasonably well, but couldn't make an offer until our house sold. We had to hope it stayed on the market that long.

In the next few months, I drew up specifications for our new office building in North Platte and got a contractor in that area to give me a rough estimate on a floor plan to show to the board. It appeared the earliest we could get into our new office was late fall, and we were faced with the possibility of having to move in the middle of the school year. We decided to try to move during the summer if we could get our house sold. Fortunately, or so we thought, a few weeks before the convention we found someone willing to pay the full asking price for our house. The offer included a large down payment on a fifteen-year contract for deed with slightly above the current, quite high, average interest rate. We accepted the offer and arranged for the Guardian State Bank in Alliance to do the billing and receive payments into a special account. The payments included taxes and insurance to come out of a separate escrow account. A contract for deed is a much better instrument for selling a house than purchasing one. If the purchaser misses even one monthly payment the deed holder may file to foreclose and regain possession within an additional thirty days. Our buyer had a good job with the local REA and seemed a good credit risk.

The association was responsible for the expense of our move; however, Maxine immediately proceeded to box up as many things as possible and I headed for North Platte to make an offer on the property we had found there. After a little negotiating, I made a verbal offer on the property and promised to return within two weeks to close. The down payment we had received on our Alliance house was more than enough to get financing for the new home with a North Platte bank or an insurance company. A few days before we were to go to North Platte to close on our new place, I received a letter by registered mail that caused all the plans we had made to fall apart. A group of members in the Alliance area, led by John Freiburger, had filed a petition with the court to stop the sale of the office. They had hired a local lawyer to look into the matter and he had discovered that the Nebraska Stock Growers Association articles of incorporation contained a clause that said a two-thirds majority vote of approval by the membership of the organization was required if a substantial majority of the property was to be sold. The vote in Kearney had been four votes shy of a two-thirds majority! District Judge Robert B. Moran of Alliance had granted them a restraining order prohibiting the sale.

I immediately called the people in North Platte and withdrew my verbal offer on their property, and Jim Gran called an emergency meeting of the board of directors in Alliance for the next week with the only item of business on the agenda, the court order. Jim and several other board members wanted to fight the case, arguing that we could show that the building alone was not a sufficiently substantial portion of our property to require a two-thirds vote. One board member, who was a lawyer, said that the magazine and the membership list, which provided our financial support, should outweigh the value of the building. The board members from the Alliance area, of course, disagreed with this, and others were concerned that a lawsuit, even if won, could result in the loss of a lot members and was not worth the risk. Jim thought that the board should at least hire an attorney to look into the feasibility of defending our position. On a split vote, the board voted to abandon the resolution authorizing the move, which had passed at convention with a simple majority.

54

Farm Crisis

Even though the decision of the board of directors not to move the office to North Platte had the result of leaving the Lilley family in a predicament, it was a relief to a majority of the office staff. Bob Howard had indicated he would probably retire rather than move, and neither my bookkeeper nor secretary would have come along. It didn't affect Troy Smith one way or the other because he worked out of his home just north of North Platte, and I imagine Mary was looking forward to having a job closer to her hometown of Schuyler. Unfortunately, since we had already sold our house and had to give possession in August, we had to start house hunting again

There was a real estate broker across the street from the office who was part owner of a farm about ten miles north of Alliance, which he had been unsuccessfully trying to sell for a couple of years. He had recently remodeled the house on the property, which fortunately had just become available. When Maxine and I looked at it, it seemed to be the kind of place we had been looking for when we moved to Alliance. It was an old, two-story farmhouse sitting on twelve acres amid a group of outbuildings, one of the four such parcels left in the corners when a pivot irrigation system is set in the middle of a quarter section of land. After I tried unsuccessfully to talk him into selling us just the improvements and twelve and a half acres, we agreed to rent it on a month-to-month basis, subject to sale of the whole property. We were out about the same amount as our monthly payments on the house we had just sold. We bought a $15,000 Federal Land Bank bond at fourteen and a half percent interest with the down payment we had received from the sale of our house.

The remodeling of our new place had included wall-to-wall carpeting in nearly every room, new kitchen cabinets and a second bathroom in the largest of four bedrooms on the second floor. There was a very old gas furnace in the basement with unusual round ductwork to all of the rooms. There was a fairly large lawn surrounding the house and an automatic sprinkler system that we appreciated, when it worked. There were a lot of tools and some small farm implements lying around the outbuildings, all covered with about an inch of dust. The three-sided open garage had an old-fashioned oil pit, which you could drive your vehicle over when you changed oil. I built a corral, which I attached to a closed shed that would work as a barn for our horses, when we got around to bringing them back from the farm in Fort Collins.

We decided to let Brendan attend St. Agnes Academy, a Catholic school in Alliance, for his second year of high school, and Jennifer would be going to a K-8 country school about a mile west of the farm. I would drop Jennifer off at her school and then Brendan at St. Agnes on the way to work. When I was away, Maxine would take the kids to school. Jennifer usually walked home and I picked up Brendan after football or basketball practice. We soon helped Brendan buy a little Datsun pickup to drive to school.

Eddie Nichols, a rancher who ran yearlings and had a medium-sized feedlot at Max, Nebraska was our new president. He, like Pat McGinley, was a protégé of past president Jack Maddux. Of all the presidents I worked for over a forty-five-year career, Eddie was probably the most conscientious. Even though he was often different from Jim in his approach to things, I enjoyed working with him and we became good friends over the many long days we worked together. During his tenure, we mailed out a questionnaire with the help of Chadron State College, asking our members to prioritize the issues we normally dealt with, add ones not on the list and suggest ways we could improve our operations. We spent a good bit of time and some money and found out that we were not doing things too badly.

When the legislature went into session, Eddie approached our efforts there much as Pat had. He lived about seventy miles west of McCook, Nebraska, and I usually met him at either Ogallala or North Platte when we drove to Lincoln. It was about a seven-hour drive from Alliance. It was impossible to get to Lincoln early enough to get any work done so we usually spent the night in York. The only time you could be sure of catching a legislator in his office was before the session and/or committee meetings, which started at eight a.m., so we always left the motel early enough to drive the last forty-five miles to Lincoln and arrive at the Capitol about 7:15 a.m. We usually stopped to see Loren Schmit, one of the most of influential members of the legislature, first and Eddie would always hand him a big, expensive cigar when we arrived at his office. This is the closest the Stock Growers ever came to bribing a legislator.

Paul Hoefs, who had a big ranch in the Sandhills east of Valentine was elected president at the 1982 convention. His ranch was located on a country road across the Sandhills, miles from any highway, so Paul was one of the many similarly situated Nebraska ranchers who owned a Piper Cub airplane. When we traveled together in the west, he would usually fly into the Alliance airport. If we had business in Central Nebraska, I would pick him up at small rural airport or whatever country road he landed on. I often met him at the Lincoln airport. Chuck Schroeder, who managed a registered Hereford operation in Palisade with his father, was made president elect. George Chilton, who had married a ranch girl from Gordon and moved from his ranch in Wyoming to take over the management of his new in-law's place, was elected vice president. Chilton had been an ally of Jim Gran as a strong opponent of the merger with the feeders.

When he was elected, Paul pledged to increase the membership of the organization and to establish a checkoff fee deducted from each head of cattle sold within the state to be used toward beef promotion. Increasing membership was a noble goal, but unfortunately was very difficult because the cattle industry, and agriculture in general, were sinking into a disastrous financial crisis. In the mid-1980s, the agricultural economy was in a perfect storm of record low prices, a wide spread drought and the highest interest rates seen since the 1920s, while inflation was pushing up production costs. Faced with such a bleak economic situation, ranchers necessarily reduced their discretionary expenses, which unfortunately included dues to our organization. Paul was disappointed, but without his enthusiasm in the face of such circumstances our budget would have suffered considerably more damage than it did. In the seventies the cattle business had enjoyed a period of relative prosperity, farm and ranch land prices had steadily increased and NSGA had prospered and enjoyed a period of membership growth.

Agriculture has high capital requirements and an average annual return of only three percent on its main asset, land, so it was particularly devastated by this decade's record high interest rates orchestrated by Paul Volcker, the head of the Federal Reserve Bank. Most ranchers hold him and President Carter accountable for bursting the bubble of record land values, but a series of very dry years in the corn belt and most of the cow/calf states during this time certainly exacerbated the problem. Another important, but less well understood contributor to agriculture's financial problems, was the steady easing of agricultural credit in the previous decade, resulting in an unprecedented availability of both short- and long-term low interest loans to farmers and ranchers.

Many thoughtful people had grown concerned as the price of ranch land in Nebraska reached record-breaking levels and continued to climb. Economists, who should have known better, recommended that farmers and ranchers leverage their current holdings and buy more land, spreading their fixed costs over more acres to make their newly expanded operations more efficient. The staffs at the locally owned Federal Land Bank and Production Credit Association offices seemed particularly aggressive in pushing this idea. The farm loan officers at local banks, who were in competition with the FLB and PCAs for short-term credit, were seduced by this questionable concept as they tried to maintain their share of the business. Traditionally conservative life insurance companies, which had always financed a major share of the purchase of large ranches, were caught up in the competition. As some of the weaker borrowers became delinquent in their payments, their loans were put on watch and their interest rate was increased to force them to refinance elsewhere or push them into default. Some new, poorly capitalized lenders got into the game late by refinancing some of these weaker loans, probably at a discount. Most of those went bankrupt when the bubble burst, as did a lot of commercial banks, especially in small rural towns.

The history of the Federal Land Bank tracks the unique problems involved in providing credit to agricultural producers. In 1916 Congress enacted the Federal Farm Loan Act, which established a Federal Land Bank in each of twelve districts across the country, along with many national farm loan associations; to sell and service long term loans to farmers and ranchers. This was the first component of what became known as the Farm Credit System. In 1923 Congress tried to meet agriculture's need for short-term credit by creating intermediate credit banks in the aforementioned twelve districts. By the 1920s, agricultural commodity prices were suffering severe declines as the wartime-induced demand went away, and soon farmers were further devastated by the depression. The Farm Credit Act of 1933 completed the establishment of the farm credit system, but by this time farmers didn't need more loans, they needed income to pay off those they had.

The 1953 Farm Credit Act created a federal farm credit board with thirteen members—one each from the twelve farm credit districts—and one appointed by the Secretary of Agriculture, giving farm and ranch borrowers a voice at the national level. All government capital allocated to the Farm Credit System was repaid by 1968, making it wholly-owned by their rural borrowers. The FCS grew rapidly in the 1970s and early 1980s as its loan volume grew to over $80 million. The end of this boom was hastened in 1979 with the tightening of currency by the Federal Reserve Board to rein in inflation. The rapid growth in farm production, triggered in part by ill-conceived crop subsidies during this period, resulted in massive surpluses by the mid-eighties. In 1985 and 1986, FCS institutions reported net losses of $2.7 billion and $1.9 billion respectively, at that time the largest losses in history for any financial institution. In 1985, Congress stepped in and imposed greater oversight of the Farm Credit Administration, and the 1987 Agricultural Credit Act authorized up to $4 billion in federal assistance, including up to $2.8 billion in treasury-guaranteed fifteen-year bonds. The Farm Credit System Insurance Corporation was created to ensure timely payment of interest and principal on the bonds.

From 1982 to 1988, the NSGA suffered right along with its members from the serious economic crisis in which agriculture was mired. We lost many members, who had simply gone broke, while several of our larger, most loyal members could no longer afford to pay dues at the level they had in the past. Our dues were thirty dollars minimum and an additional ten cents for each head of cattle beyond 250. The free meals furnished by Ralgro at our area membership meetings became more popular than ever and

Notes

The Countercyclical Aspects of the U.S. Meat Import Act of 1979

James R. Simpson

The U.S. Meat Import Act of 1979, the so-called "countercyclical" meat import bill, was signed into law on the last day of that year by President Carter. This law, which reflects a desire to help stabilize the fluctuations that have taken place in cattle inventory numbers and prices, has received wide attention by the U.S. livestock industry and countries exporting to the United States (Reeves 1979, U.S. Congress). There is evidence that the United States is a price maker at the international level as a result of being the world's largest beef importer, producer, and consumer (Simpson). Consequently, a major change in the U.S. meat import law can be expected to have a tangible influence on international trade in beef and the policies set by both beef exporting and importing countries as well as on the U.S. cattle industry.

The purpose of this note is to analyze some potential effects of the new U.S. meat import law under two radically different assumptions about change in cattle inventory to determine if the act really is "countercyclical," i.e., resulting in a higher import quota when U.S. beef production is declining and vice versa, in a lower quota level when U.S. production is increasing.[1] It is not intended as a comparison with the 1964 law, which has been evaluated in the documents prepared by the U.S. Congress. It goes beyond the work of Weeks, whose concern was evaluating the two laws under two different production situations. It also builds on the work of Reeves (1980), Nelson et al., and Conable, who clarify and examine various aspects of the new law. Apart from analyzing the law's potential effect on the domestic beef cattle industry, these results contain implications for further refinements in such stabilizing schemes.

The Meat Import Act of 1979

The new law was designed to permit greater meat imports when domestic supplies are low and consumer prices high, thus supposedly moderating the rise in beef prices. On the other hand, it is supposed to reduce meat imports when domestic supplies are abundant and consumer prices low, thus moderating the decline in prices for producers. The law covers fresh, chilled, or frozen beef, veal, goat, and sheep meat. Lamb and pork are excluded as are cooked, preserved, and prepared meats and "high quality" beef processed into fancy cuts. However, noncooked portion control and prepared meats are included. A major change from the 1964 law is subtracting live cattle imports (other than breeding stock) from the domestic production of quota meats.

The new formula for determining the annual import quota as presented in the law is as follows:

$$\text{Annual quota} = \text{Average annual imports (1968-77)} \times \frac{\text{3-yr. moving average of domestic production}}{\text{10-yr. average of domestic production (1968-77)}} \times \frac{\text{5-yr. moving average of domestic cow beef production}}{\text{2-yr. moving average of domestic cow beef production}}$$

The average annual imports of meat subject to quota for 1968–77 (the base) was officially set at 1,204.6 million pounds on a product weight basis. A floor of 1,250.0 million pounds is included.

The ten-year average of domestic production of quota meats for 1968–77 is 23,184.0 million pounds (carcass weight basis). From this the total carcass weight equivalents of live imports for 1968–77 (220 million lbs.) is subtracted. The moving average of domestic production of quota meats (1978–80) is 22,500.0 million pounds, from which the average total carcass weight of live cattle imports must be subtracted. The five-year moving average of domestic cow beef production, actually calculated on a per capita basis, is 17.4 pounds, while the two-year moving average (1979–80) is 13.4 pounds (the formula's cow beef component provides the countercyclical behavior of the formula). The re-

---

James R. Simpson is an associate professor of livestock marketing at the University of Florida.

Special thanks are due several anonymous reviewers who commented on this note.

[1] A detailed paper with a complete explanation of the method and assumptions, along with all data series, is available from the author.

not only helped us maintain our current membership, but were our best, and nearly only, source of new members.

At the 1982 convention, the association had given the membership another opportunity to vote on moving the office to North Platte. Realizing that we would have to come up with a two-thirds majority vote to avoid further legal problems, Jim Gran persuaded the board to offer proxy voting on the issue. A majority of the total votes were cast by proxy and once again the members voted not to move the office from Alliance. In spite of that vote, a resolution was passed instructing the association to continue working to find common ground to merge with the NLFA.

The association didn't let its tight financial situation stop it from continuing to play a leading role dealing with the unprecedented number of problems the cattle industry was facing, and we managed to avoid cutting back on services. The staff got few, if any, raises in salary for about five years in a row, nor had they expected any. The officers and other volunteers continued to give of their time, with no travel expenses whatsoever, as we muddled through the hard times. At one point I loaned the association $10,000; occasionally we had to charge some of our office expenses to a credit card the organization had originally obtained for me to use for travel expenses. These efforts kept us afloat, but came back to haunt me later.

During Hoef's term there were several staff changes, the most important of which was triggered by the retirement of Nebraska Cattleman editor, Bob Howard, who had served the organization since 1949. Since the organization had no retirement plan, I persuaded the board of directors to name Bob, Editor Emeritus, with a stipend of $100 per month and a desk in the office as long as he chose to use it. Bob continued to come in nearly every day and was a great help as the association went through a complex process replacing him.

Mary Guynan was named managing editor and we were able to enlist the help of Sally Schuff, an experienced newsperson, from North Platte, to help for a few months. When Guynan married later that year, the board named Troy Smith editor of the Nebraska Cattleman, and he and his family moved to Alliance. Just before she left, Mary arranged a retirement dinner for Bob at the American Legion in Alliance, with past president, Chester

Paxton, serving as master of ceremonies. Many of the people Bob had worked with over the years came and paid him tribute. The event was a smashing success. However, in an effort to make it first-class we had insisted the meal be served on China, and learned at the last minute that getting the dishes washed was not in our contract. Since there was another activity at the Legion the next morning, the dishes had to be washed and put away that night. When the event ended, Mary, Charles Iodence and I rounded up a group of volunteers and we had a great time as we washed the huge pile of dishes. As I recall, Bob insisted on staying to help us.

Later that fall, we were able to hire Joyce Koch away from the ANCA in Denver to fill the communication director position vacated by Mary. Joyce was a graduate of Chadron State College with a journalism degree, and had landed a position in the ANCA public relations department in Denver right out of college. Having been raised on a ranch about thirty-five miles east of Alliance, she was willing to take a slight cut in salary to get a job close to home. Her father, Ray, was a past president of the Grant County Area affiliate and her mother was active in the Cow Belles.

Troy Smith had recently been instrumental in getting NSGA to sponsor a sport growing in popularity among ranchers called Team Penning, and after Joyce came on board she often helped Troy with this ranch-related activity. Team Penning did not generate many new member, but it helped us retain a lot who normally didn't get directly involved in policy matters, but depended on the Association to represent their interests. The sport became so popular that I became concerned it was taking too much staff time. However, since Troy and Joyce were willing to dedicate so much of their own time to it, I didn't say anything. Before long the NLFA members took up Team Penning within many of their local affiliates.

Near the end of Paul Hoef's term, President Elect Chuck Schroeder was appointed Secretary of Agriculture by Governor Bob Kerrey, making it necessary to elevate Vice President George Chilton directly to the presidency at the June convention held in Scottsbluff. Everett Anderson was moved up from vice president to president-elect. Schroeder was one of the young men groomed by the leadership development committee, which had been formed shortly before I came to work for NSGA in 1979. He was the first of several to be nominated for president over the years, all schooled by this unique, forward-looking committee formed for the sole purpose of preparing the younger members of the association for leadership roles. The committee's founding chairman, Jack Ostergard, had enlisted the services of a professor of sociology at the University of Nebraska to devise the program. Some people considered Schroeder rather young to be nominated as the heir apparent to the president of the of the association, so they were understandably surprised when Kerrey made him Secretary of Agriculture, the same important position my predecessor was appointed to under the previous administration. Schroeder later went on to become the CEO of the National Cattlemen's Beef Association--previously ANCA and NCA—and then director of the National Cowboy and Western Heritage Museum in Oklahoma City.

In 1983 the Legislature passed legislation fulfilling one of the association's major priorities when they passed LB 19, creating the Nebraska Beef Industry Development Board. Governor Kerrey appointed the current members of the existing voluntary Nebraska Beef Industry Council (NBIC), and one additional cattleman to serve until a permanent board was elected at the November 1984 general election. The NBIC was a nonprofit organization, supported by both the NSGA and NLFA, which was funded by voluntary contributions from ranchers who chose to participate in a ten-cent check-off when they sold their cattle. The new legislation called for the mandatory collection of a check-off fee by the state's brand inspectors at the same time they collected the brand inspection fee at time of sale. In order to get the bill passed, it had been necessary to include a provision allowing for a refund of the check-off by making the appropriate application to the Beef Board. Many ranchers who strongly supported the bill disliked the idea of any branch of government collecting a "mandatory" fee. Funds raised through this program had to be spent only for the promotion of beef. The newly elected board hired a staff, and for the first-time cattlemen had an organization with a truly significant amount of money to spend promoting beef, the end product of the cattle industry.

55

Merger

I learned soon after we were married that Maxine was prone to bouts of depression. She was aware of the problem and could usually tell when an episode was coming on and get on top of it within a day or two. When it did occasionally take full control of her, she would lie on the couch with her face toward the wall whenever she was not engaged in her daily routine. The stress of having to leave our beautiful home in Boerne, the aborted move to North Platte and the resulting quick move to our current rental house brought on one of her most serious bouts. I had never been around anyone suffering from depression before, and my tendency to think that any problem could be dealt with by talking it through logically was counterproductive. She'd soon tell me to knock off my simplistic, Pollyanna talk. I didn't fully appreciate the severity of these spells, until she finally cried out for help by making a halfhearted attempt to take her own life. When Jennifer and I came into the house after a horseback ride on a Sunday afternoon, she looked dreadful and was in tears. After we calmed her down, we learned she had just thrown up the full bottle of aspirin she had recently swallowed.

After this frightening experience, I managed to get Maxine to open up and talk to me, and for once I really listened to what she said. I learned of nagging health issues she had suffered for years, the most serious of which was an embarrassing case of nervous bowel syndrome, something I surely would have picked up on if I had been more attentive. She said her transverse colon sagged nearly on top of her uterus, which caused, or at least exacerbated, the syndrome and the embarrassing side effects that she managed to conceal. She confessed she had finally gotten so afraid of her recurring bouts of depression that she wouldn't let herself get enthusiastic about anything for fear of the downer that might follow. We agreed that the stress of the last year of our marriage had surely helped to bring the problem to a head. I had figured out soon after our marriage that she continued to blame herself for the failure of her marriage to Shaun and Brendan's father, even though she fully understood his actions had made it impossible to remain married to him. She was very much a perfectionist and could not forgive herself for this perceived failure in her life. I pleaded that my thoughtlessness stemmed from the fact I was raised in a family of men, with a mother who had had no mother, who believed that if you got a little down you just kicked yourself in the rear end and got on with your life. I knew I had a lot to learn about depression when I realized that Maxine, a workaholic, who had far more self-discipline than I, couldn't deal with it.

We got a local doctor to make an appointment with a psychiatrist in Denver who he thought could help Maxine. After several sessions, which Maxine described as having been of little benefit, he prescribed a drug being used to treat depression at that time. It helped some, but the side effects caused their own problems, problems that Maxine made every effort to deal with. Not only was she a hard worker, she loved to jog or run on our treadmill and had never had any weight problem. Unfortunately, the depression medicine made her feel lethargic in a way that was completely foreign to her and caused her to be obsessed with the thought she might gain weight.

In the meantime, our new doctor in Alliance treated her lazy bowel syndrome by increasing the roughage in her diet. This was unsuccessful, and on top of everything else she started to develop symptoms of asthma. A chest x-ray indicated some scar tissue on her lungs, which surprised us since she had never smoked. When we were talking about what possibly could have caused the lung damage, Maxine recalled having cleaned a shower stall with Clorox and inhaling a lot of the fumes before she realized what was happening. In any case, in order to deal with the asthma so she could continue her jogging and running on a treadmill in the winter, the doctor prescribed an inhalant that was to be used in modest amounts.

After we had lived eight months in our rental house, our landlord informed us the property had been sold and we had thirty days to move out. We had been anticipating this and had been on the lookout for another place. When I had been on membership drives, I had often noticed a place about eighteen miles due north of Alliance, which was completely surrounded by beautiful, mature trees. It was visible for miles in all directions and I had always been intrigued by it. The quarter-mile lane that led into the place off the oiled highway continued past the house and followed the property line a half mile east to the Chadron highway. The home and many outbuildings were barely visible through the trees in the middle of the farm.

The first Saturday after we learned we must move, I talked Maxine into driving up to this intriguing farm to see if we could talk the owners into selling us an acreage where we could build a house. We found the owner working in his shop near the house and when we told him what we wanted, he said that would not be possible, but if we would come up to the house his wife would pour some lemonade and we might be able to work out something else. Thus we met Frank and Audrey Dee. We learned later that Frank was a bachelor, had lived with his parents on this farm until they passed away, and then many years later, when he was sixty-five years old, had married Audrey. It seemed that the Dees had leased their farm, bought a home in Eastern Nebraska and would consider renting their small farmhouse to us. It was a cozy, two-bedroom, one-bath home with a full basement. The farm had many outbuildings with a particularly beautiful large barn containing several box stalls and a hayloft. Maxine and I immediately fell in love with the place, fully realizing that it would be hard to squeeze our whole family into it. We said we would talk to our kids and get back in touch with them soon.

There were several obvious drawbacks to moving to this farm we liked so much. In addition to the house being small, Jennifer would have to go to a different country school, and the commute to my office and Brendan's high school would be about ten miles farther. Still, we all agreed that we didn't want to move back to town if we could avoid it, and we couldn't find another place in the country before we had to vacate our current home. Shaun had moved back home and said she would be willing to share the small bedroom with Jennifer, and Brendan agreed to sleep on a single bed in the basement. We contacted the Dees and when they agreed we could use all the outbuildings and a small pasture next to the corrals for our horses, that clinched the deal.

It was the most ideal set up we had ever had for the horses. I loved using the large shop and the full set of tools that Frank had left and Maxine managed to make the house cozy and livable. Jennifer attended a good K-8 country school five miles east of our new home, and though it was a couple of miles out of the way, I could still drop her off on my way to work when I wasn't traveling. Maxine's health problems continued, but in the new environment her bouts of depression were much less frequent and less severe.

George Chilton and then Everett Anderson, who became president in 1984, served during extremely trying times when numerous ranches in the Sandhills, ranches that had been in the same family for generations, went bankrupt. Low cattle prices, drought and record high interest rates were devastating agriculture in general and the cattle industry in particular. The theme of the 1985 convention was a hopeful, "Think Positive in Eighty-five," when Rodney Aden, farmer/feeder and registered Simmental breeder from the Gothenburg area, was elected president. While recognizing the need for the cattle industry to unite in seeking a solution to the agricultural financial crisis, the Association strongly opposed a radical proposal for a federally chartered entity to purchase agricultural land from farmers and ranchers. On September 4th, Aden testified in a House-Senate Joint Economic Committee in Huron, South Dakota. He said that institutions created to serve the cattle industry often seemed to be aiding large packers and retailers at the expense of producers.

During this period, a prominent Nebraska rancher was selected to lead a national effort to address the problems of the Farm Credit System. Elvin Adams of Nenzel was made chairman of a special committee that developed a "Nine Points" agenda for the system's leaders' consideration. Later that year Congress did impose greater oversight of the Farm Credit Administration, but it took several years before the agricultural economy started to heal.

A couple of years after I went to work for the NSGA, I hired perhaps the best secretary I ever had. She could type nearly 100 words per minute, and in fact, typed so fast the newfangled IBM Selectric typewriter, which used a new kind of carbon ribbon and a rotating ball containing all of the type faces, would shed bits of carbon on the letter she was writing when she got going full speed; a regular electric typewriter couldn't keep up with her at all. Shortly after I hired her, we purchased an office computer with an MS-DOS operating system and a matrix printer. IBM trained Deb in their use. Our main software was a product called Dbase II, which was sold by a firm called Ashton-Tate. Software was rapidly improving during that period and Ashton-Tate had captured a large share of the small office market. As I recall, it cost seven hundred dollars, far less than custom written software that was still needed for many operations. Deb became very skilled at using it and put it to work for us right away, still keeping up with her work as my secretary/receptionist. Thanks to the computer, we were able to mail personalized membership solicitations to non-members, gleaned from various sources, to complement our membership drives. We usually got a three to five-percent return on our mailings with a breakeven point of just under two-percent. Everyone on the staff stuffed and sealed a lot of envelopes.

I recently learned that Dbase I and II grew out of a program called Vulcan created by Wayne Ratliff in 1978 and purchased by Ashton-Tate from him for a royalty share in 1981. Ratliff was the young man I had hired to write software for the International Brangus Breeders Association in 1977, who left the job half done just before I was fired. He was far from incompetent; he just had much bigger fish to fry.

In the spring of 1986, the beef cattle industry was blind sided by a "Dairy Whole Herd Buyout" proposed by the USDA to buy and slaughter one-and-a-half million dairy cows, hoping to raise the price of milk for the dairy industry. Cattlemen were outraged because this number of culled dairy cows dumped on the market would put tremendous downward pressure on the price of cattle at a time when beef prices were already well below the cost of production. Cattle industry leaders immediately organized to fight the proposal, pointing out that the milk surplus had been caused by the dairy price support program in the first place. In early April, NSGA President-Elect, Richard Lackaff, appealed personally to Secretary of Agriculture, Richard Lyng, to do everything in his power to ease the pressure on beef producers. A coalition including the National Cattlemen's Association, with support from most of its state affiliates, won a stay of the program in court and Secretary Lyng ended up signing an agreement with NCA to proceed with the buyout program in a much more orderly fashion. USDA also agreed to increase purchases of meat for the school lunch program and endeavor to increase foreign sales of meat. The Commodity Credit Corporation, which had oversight of agricultural price support programs, agreed to purchase more than sixteen million pounds of ground and canned beef. The latter action bothered some cattlemen because the industry had always opposed price support programs, but the actions helped make the buyout less disastrous than it could have been. It is hard to imagine a step the USDA could have taken that could have caused more resentment by beef and pork producers and more conflict within commodity groups. Even the dairymen seemed to some degree to be stepping on their own toes since they received a significant portion of their income from cull dairy cows. General farm organizations like the National Farm Bureau Federation, which represented all segments of agriculture, were split internally.

The effort to bring the NSGA and NLFA into a closer working relationship took a new turn in 1986 with the formation of a Feedlot Council closely affiliated with both organizations. An ad hoc committee made up of members of both organizations made several informal contacts, and before the end of the year had outlined a structure for a new council designed to attract new members for both organizations, particularly from among the larger custom feedlots that had grown up across the state in the last decade or so.

The group directing their respective organizations then put together an informal set of bylaws for the council, which included authority to hire a full-time staff member to oversee day-to-day activities, with particular emphasis on selling new memberships. There was a stipulation that the income from the council would be distributed back to one of the parent organizations based on the geographic area from which it came. This was one of the weaknesses of the plan, due to the considerable overlap in territory in which both organizations had current members, and obviously would depend on close cooperation between Paul Johnson, who managed the NLFA, myself and the new staff member. By the end of the year the planning committee, with full participation by Paul and me, were ready to interview applicants for the new position. Only a few people applied for the job and early in 1987 we hired Tom Scott, who we thought was the only one sufficiently qualified. As I recall, he had retired from the

Army, possibly a National Guard unit, as a Major. Scott reported to an executive committee composed of five members from each parent organization. The initial members representing the NLFA were Larry McQuatters, Herb Albers, Jr., John Klosterman, Warren Mitchell and Jim Roberts. NSGA's first members were Dale Kugler, Eddie Nichols, George Chilton, Dar Heggem and DeLayne Loseke. The problem of billing for dues collected by this newly created group was related to the fact that both parent groups had IRS 501(c)(3) certifications, allowing for the deductibility of dues. The new Feedlot Council did not.

Scott recognized the tremendous potential of the new Feedlot Council and hit the road selling memberships. Dues in the Feedlot Council were based on the member feedlot's size and could be paid on either cattle as they were placed on feed or on the feedlot's one-time capacity. This structure was designed to provide a dependable cash flow and was based on the highly successful model of the Texas Cattle Feeders Association; it was also used by the Kansas Livestock Association for its feedlot members. When the Feedlot Council was formed, its founding executive committee made it clear that their goal was to be an intermediate step in the final formation of one strong organization representing the entire Nebraska cattle industry. The last thing they sought was a third independent organization representing cattlemen in the state. In his zeal to sell memberships, Scott often failed to convey this fact and treated it as an autonomous organization. Budgeting for such a three-headed monster became impossible, and Paul and I completely lost control of the Feedlot Council's expenditures as it sent us less and less of its collected dues.

The best solution for the unanticipated problems created by our efforts to get the big feedlots involved was to move quickly toward the merger of all three organizations. The Nebraska cattle industry was still in the middle of unprecedented financial stress, and cow calf/yearling operators, typical NSGA members, were suffering the most due to their plummeting land values. A committee representing respected leaders from all three entities was appointed by their respective governing bodies and given authority to proceed to write a set of bylaws for a single organization representing the interests of all three groups. The Feedlot Council was represented by John Klosterman, Logan

MClelland and Warren Mitchell; the Nebraska Livestock Feeders Association by Larry Hudkins, DeLayne Loseke and Donovan Yoachim; and the Nebraska Stock Growers Association was represented by Ernie Gotschall, Jim Gran and Pat Vinton, our current president.

Each of the groups had a great deal to offer to a newly merged organization. The new Feedlot Council had already demonstrated it would raise a lot of new revenue from the big feedlots across the state that had not been previously affiliated with any state organization, although most belonged to the National Cattlemen's Association. The Nebraska Livestock Feeders Association had a strong base of loyal members and had managed to maintain a reserve of $100,000 through frugal management. The Nebraska Stock Growers had a headquarters building, a computer and a highly respected statewide cattle publication, as well as a valuable separate chartered foundation. Over the years, the "Nebraska Cattleman Magazine" had provided significant income; however, during the current hard times its main source of revenue, advertising for registered bull sales, had greatly fallen off and had actually lost money for the past few years. It probably would have done even worse had it not been for the addition of the members the NLFA added to our circulation. All three had competent executive directors, each of whom probably hoped to run the new organization—I know I did—and Paul and I had long been committed to working to bring the organizations together for the common good.

Tom was certainly committed to growing the Feedlot Council. He and I had gotten off to a rocky start when, shortly after he started to work, he called Deb and got on her for not getting the Feedlot Council's money to him soon enough. When he visited the office a few days later I shut my office door and got in his face, and with my finger pressed against his chest told him if he had problems with my staff to talk to me. This turned out not to be a career-enhancing move.

At the first meeting of our bylaws study committee, John Klosterman distributed a rough draft of bylaws that were a composite of both the NLFA's and NSGA's, along with some necessary legal boiler plate. Paul Johnson and I were treated as ex-officio members of the committee and were fully involved in all of the discussions. Tom Scott thought he could be more effective on the road signing up new feedlots. After reviewing John's draft, we agreed to meet once every two weeks, alternating between Alliance and Lincoln or a town on the interstate halfway between the two current office locations. We set some ground rules and kept working until we had something that we could present to our respective boards. Whenever we arrived at a problem we could not immediately solve, we laid it aside and went on to something else. We ended up having only two really contentious issues, and although we worked around them, they were not settled for many years. These were the headquarters office location and brand inspection. The NSGA members were loathe to give up their office and both the Feedlot Council and NLFA thought the office should be located at the state capital. This problem was finessed by agreeing to keep part of the staff in Alliance, but house the executive officer and most of the staff in Lincoln. The cattlemen in the western part of Nebraska would not consider giving up their traditional brand inspection system, and the cattlemen east of Kearny, where the brand inspection area ended, had always lived without this traditional range cattlemen's program and were not about to have it thrust upon them. The only solution was to leave the somewhat outdated brand laws just as they were and perhaps deal with the issue at a later date, a date that has never arrived as of this writing.

With the exception of the aforementioned issues, most of the time was spent on governance and organizational matters. Both NLFA and NSGA had local associations whose presidents were on their respective boards. It was agreed that the new board needed to recognize these areas. The problem was that using the area presidents from both groups would make the board too large, because it was felt that the different kinds of operation needed to be represented on the board as well. In the end, the latter issue was solved by creating four councils representing cow/calf/yearling operators, purebred operators, cattle feeders and a special category to accommodate the NLFA farmer/feeder. Members would be free to choose their council and would indicate their preference when they paid their dues. Each council was to elect a chairman and vice chairman from within their group who would serve on the board. To ensure regional representation on the board, the new organization would be split into eight regions, half of which would be in old NLFA territory and half in NSGA. Two directors would be elected within each region by members in that region. The president, president-elect and immediate past president would make up the balance of the board. There would also be an executive committee made up of the three elected officers and two more elected from among the board members.

As the bylaws committee continued its work, they realized that in order for these bylaws to be adopted by all three organizations, it was important that all be treated equally. The inclusion of regional representation was much more important to the NLFA, who had long traditions of community involvement and grassroots input to policy, than to the Feedlot Council, which had been in existence for only a year. Although the Feedlot Council was likely to have the fewest members of the four, it was projected to produce the most income. The newly created Purebred Council would probably have the fewest members and produce the least income, but their members comprised a vital element in the continued genetic improvement of the beef industry. The Feedlot Council members on the bylaws committee insisted there be a monetary component to representation on the board, making it necessary to segregate sources of income by council and allocate those board members based on revenue, which would result in something different than two board members from each.

As soon as the bylaws for the merged associations were finalized by the study committee, they were sent to the three founding organizations for review. NSGA's Board asked its area associations to go over them at a specially called meeting of each. They were fairly well received even though, as expected, a certain number of current members indicated they would never support the merger under any circumstances. Within a fairly short period of time, all but one of NSGA's eighteen area associations had voted to support the merger.

Because our next convention, in North Platte, June 8-11, 1988, was to be our 100th anniversary, we had planned several special events. We had engaged Rex Allen Jr. to play for the dance following the banquet the last night of the convention and scheduled a team penning for the day before the convention, which would earn double points towards final standings. Governor Kay Orr and Congresswoman Virginia Smith were among our featured speakers. Bob Howard, "Nebraska Cattleman" editor emeritus, was the banquet speaker and did a wonderful job of reviewing the 100-year history of the Nebraska Stock Growers. The merger vote assured a record convention turnout of our members and we invited the members of NLFA and the Feedlot Council to join the celebration.

I had been given the job of looking into the legalities of bringing the three organizations together and learned from our lawyer and the Secretary of State that it would be quite complicated to merge the three organizations. They suggested that the NSGA go ahead and celebrate its 100th anniversary at the convention, and at its conclusion vote to change its name to the Nebraska Cattlemen, the name the bylaws committee had suggested for the new organization. The other two organizations could vote to merge with the newly named 100-year-old organization under the already existing Articles of Incorporation. The Feedlot Council and NLFA downplayed this aspect of the process, but it was a key factor in gaining a large majority vote in support of the process by the NSGA members in attendance when the vote was held at the final business session. On July 1, 1988, Bob Lute, who was selected president of the newly named Nebraska Cattleman, joined Nebraska Secretary of State, Allen Beerman signing the amendment to the articles of incorporation formalizing the name change, and in August both the NLFA and Feedlot Council voted to merge with the Nebraska Cattleman.

On August 24, 1988, the newly consolidated Nebraska Cattleman Inc. held their first convention in Kearney, Nebraska. John Klosterman of David City was elected president, E. J. (Ernie) Gotschall, Atkinson president-elect and Larry Hudkins, Malcom vice president. Approximately 650 people representing the three predecessor organizations attended the three-day session. Efforts in several other states to bring together the feedlot and cattle producing organizations had failed, and the livestock press covering the convention gave the accomplishment wide coverage. Speakers at the convention included National Cattleman President-Elect Bob Josserand, from Hereford, Texas who had been a classmate of mine at Colorado A&M and Robert Peterson, president of the largest meatpacking company in the nation at the time, IBP. The committee structure remained much as it had been in both the NLFA and NSGA, but the addition of the councils was a new feature and it took a while to sort out just what these groups' function would be. Their formation encouraged the three organizations to get together, and not surprisingly, turned out to be a somewhat divisive element in the new organization.

Tom Scott remained staff officer for the Feedlot Council, Paul Johnson was to staff the farmer Stockman Council, I would remain in Alliance and provide staff services for the Cow/Calf Council and Troy Smith would service the purebred Council. Tom Scott was named acting CEO.

Food for Thought

by Roy W. Lilley, Executive Vice President
Nebraska Stock Growers Association

WATER ISSUE TAKES A NEW TWIST

Water is an emotional issue and recent controversy over water quality, water development and water sales has raised the intensity of discussion.

Cattlemen in Nebraska need to sort through the emotion, a large part of which is triggered by fear of the unknown...we have a lot of water and used to take for granted that the major source of that water, the Ogallala aquifer, is among the purest in the world. Ogallala water in Nebraska lies close to the surface, and since it is available in such volume, there will always be the temptation to use it to develop irrigation and expand production of crops whenever there is any tax and/or economic incentive to do so. Of course, with our sandy soil types, perculation of nitrates and other poluters is a potential threat...and when we start talking about radioactive waste storage sites, our concerns over water quality are raised to the maximum.

How do we sort out our concerns, fears and prejudices in ways that will effectively deal with the real world we live in? First, we don't have to apologize for our seeming paranoia on this subject. The Nebraska Stock Growers Association was a leader among the groups that pointed out the perils of excessive development of center pivot irrigation in the Sandhills. We distinguished between a couple of circles to enhance the feed supply of a ranch unit and what we referred to as "wall to wall pivots."

Another concern of most people who own land over the aquifer relates to the sale of water. Our instincts tell us to be against it; however, the consequences of selling water are less clear cut than the consequences of mindless irrigation development. For one thing we are operating in an environment that is still evolving. Statutory water law in Nebraska is less voluminous here than in some states and there are far fewer court tests on the subject here than in some western states. Our underground and surface water are not clearly linked in our statutes as is the case in Colorado, for example.

Most of the court cases relating to the sale of water relate to surface water which has a long history of appropriated use and is fairly well understood. Even the decision that indicates water is a commodity in interstate commerce more clearly relates to surface than ground water.

So, where do most land owners come down on the prospects of selling ground water. It seems most concerns are based on our understanding of other states' laws, particularly Colorado's. The whole idea of developing water and then putting it to use (supposedly productive use) in order to establish the right to sell it is repugnant to many. In Colorado the whole issue is really academic, because all the readily available water has been claimed and underground water is linked to surface water. (My understanding is that unless you are over a closed basin, any water under your place is considered to be a part of the watershed on the surface which you may be assured is fully allocated.)

In Nebraska we have very little, if any, unappropriated surface water, but the vast store of water in the Ogallala aquifer can become surface water when you drill a well and pump it to a stream that is part of an established irrigation system or could reach the outskirts of a town needing domestic water. The other thing to remember is that the state owns the water, but the owner has the right to use it. Any value ever received by a land owner for underground water would be for the loss of the right to use it.

Considering all the uncertainty in current rights to our water and fears of what may develop, what can we do as the organization representing members who probably own more surface above the Ogallala aquifer than any in the nation?

Maybe we should consider those things we don't want to happen, and then those we do want, and see if we can sort them out. Number one, we don't want further development of irrigation wells to produce crops that aren't needed and which, at best, result in additional land for the conservation reserve at high cost to the federal government. At worst, many systems are dismantled when bankruptcy occurs and the land is ruined for years while leaving the neighbor's land to be damaged from resulting wind deposited sand. We also don't want investors, or opportunists or whatever we name them, to draw large amounts of water out from under our land and sell it to someone wanting it bad enough to pay big bucks for it. The result could be the drying up of our wet meadows and reduced opportunity to develop irrigation at some future date if economics actually dictate it.

And what do we want? Most folks want to retain the right to develop irrigation as needed to compliment their current operation, or as stated above, develop it more intensively if there is legitimate economic justification. We also want the right to continue *not* to

ing the water without the threat of someone pumping it out from under us with no compensation and the probable loss of hay production on wet meadows.

Now comes the hard part, figuring out what can and can not be done right now to design the kind of legislation that will make sure we have an environment to do right when we agree what right is. I'm no water law expert; however the lawyers disagree on where we currently stand on constitutional and statutory law so my impressions couldn't be much worse than those expressed by anyone else.

It appears that our constitution says the state owns the water and legal precedent, and perhaps law (under the current groundwater management act) says anyone owning land above water has the right to use it. However, if there is a shortage that shortage must be shared. At the heart of the controversy over the discussion of selling water as outlined in LB 146 introduced by Loran Schmit is the fact that the courts have said water is an article of commerce and can be bought and sold. If that is true, then our problem becomes not if we will sell it, but how we regulate its sale so the interests of all are best protected.

The worst thing that could happen to ranchers and farmers is that they collectively fought *any* sale of water and then ended up losing not only the philosophical point, but found that the opportunists had designed a body of law that let them obtain the rights to the water at no (or very little) cost, pump it out from under the land owner and sell it to third parties at a nice profit.

It appears that land owners must have a contingency plan moving parallel with their efforts to stop any water sales that recognizes several very serious possibilities. If water is an item that can be sold in interstate commerce and the state can't stop it, then someone will be working on a means of obtaining water and putting it up for sale. To avoid the legal precedents of surface water rights that say you must develop and put water to productive use before you have either any property, or in our case use right, in it, we must establish the point that *potential use* of water, deferred until a time of greater need, is still a value for which a land owner must be compensated if the water under his land is sold to another party without the owners consent or desire.

This little piece raises more questions than it answers, but my only hope is to raise the level of discussion above simply whether we want water to be sold or not. That question may already be out of our hands.

1988 Beef Sire Directory
Call 1-800-ABS-STUD

Here it is! The most complete offering of A.I. beef sires ever presented by a single organization . . . 128 genetically superior bulls representing 25 different breeds. Each is pictured in full color and accompanied by the facts you need to make the right decisions for your beef breeding program. We expect tremendous demand for the brand new, 52-page, high quality catalog of beef breeding opportunity. So don't delay. Get your copy today by calling our toll-free number . . . 1-800-ABS-STUD. Or send the coupon below.

AMERICAN BREEDERS SERVICE
Division of W R Grace & Co
P.O. Box 459, DeForest, Wisconsin 53532

Yes, I'm ready to look at 128 of the best beef bulls in the world today. Send my free copy of the 1988 ABS Beef Sire Directory right away.

Name _____
Address _____
City _____
State ____ Zip ____ Phone ____
I'm primarily interested in _____ and plan to A.I. _____ cows in 1988.
          (breed of bull)   (number)

FREE SEMEN! For a limited time, we'll be giving 10 free straws of semen from the ABS beef bull of your choice to every 100th request for our 1988 Beef Sire Directory. Value limited to $150. Call or write today.

B-1003

Aerial photo of Farm near Hemingford.

56

Our Little Farm

After we finished moving into the house on the Dee farm we had a lot of furniture left over, which we stored in one of the many outbuildings that Frank had let us use. He told me he and his father had moved two barracks, which had been at a training facility for gliders during World War Two, from the Alliance airport to their farm. They had removed two inside walls and set them side by side, built a roof over both of them, and a large entrance to the north and installed a wide sliding door. They had moved a large coal furnace into the center of the building. It came from the basement of their house when they replaced it with a new oil burning forced air furnace. There was a workbench against one wall with cabinets above and below, with about every tool a farmer could need neatly arranged along the wall. He said I could use them, if I always put them back where they belonged.

    The large barn sixty yards east of the shop building was equally impressive. It had sliding doors that opened to an area large enough to park several vehicles. Built around this area in a U-shape were about five or six box stalls of varying sizes, one of which opened to the east into a corral that had a covered shed. Another opened to the south into a corral that was lined with feed bunks on one side, and another had a sliding door that opened onto a chute for loading cattle leading out of the barn. Above all the box stalls was a hayloft accessible by a ladder from the big open area. Frank had covered all of the stalls with four inches of clean straw. In fact, everything about the farm showed the signs of immaculate care. There was a good-sized outbuilding for storing grain, another enclosed storage shed and a relatively modern potato cellar with a large entrance for vehicles and a single door on one side. I don't know how many tons of potatoes it may have held, but we learned the third year we were at the farm that we could store 2,500 bales of hay in it. All of these outbuildings were wired for electricity and well lighted, and the shop and potato cellar were wired for 220 volts. Frank told me he and his dad did all the wiring, including burying lines between the buildings and to the transformer, and like everything else on the place, it was professionally done.

The system for furnishing water to the house and livestock water to the corrals was a complex, well thought out one. It connected access to the domestic well for the house and a small irrigation well on a hill southwest of the house, making it possible to use either the pressure system or to get water by gravity from a cistern filled from the irrigation well. Like most rural water systems developed before World War II, the pressure system was located in a six-foot by six-foot cement lined pit about six feet deep. The water from the well was piped into the bottom of the pit, connected to the pump and pressure tank, and piped into the house. A buried two-inch pipe also entered the pit from the cistern and was piped from there to the various stock tanks around the farm. It was possible to manipulate valves and divert water from the pressure system to the corrals. In an emergency, water could be diverted into the house from the cistern. Frank told me to leave everything as it was to get water to both the corrals and the house through the pressure system, because filling the cistern on the hill from the irrigation well involved a complicated Rube Goldberg like process he explained to me later.

Within a few weeks, we had decided we liked everything about our new location, even though we all had to squeeze into the small house. The Dees visited the farm every weekend, staying with some old friends in Hemingford, and the next time they showed up, we approached them about purchasing a small acreage and the improvements. They said they had never considered such a possibility, but would talk it over that night and we could discuss it more in the morning. That evening Maxine and I had a long, serious talk and decided we could happily live out the rest of our lives on the place and maybe even try to buy the balance of the farm some day. We agreed we would want to expand the house as soon as possible and would need to buy some cattle soon to justify depreciating the many improvements on our income tax return. We didn't relish the thought of borrowing so much money in addition to using up a lot of our considerable savings, but decided to try to negotiate a deal.

The next morning, the Dees dropped by with sweet rolls. Maxine made some coffee and we soon learned that they were willing to try to work something out. They said they wanted interest only the first ten years and would sell twenty-five to thirty acres and the improvements for from $75,000 to $80,000 depending on the number of acres.

Since the association had its checking account with the Guardian State Bank, I had opened our private account with the First National Bank, which was owned by an old established family in Alliance. I had gotten acquainted with the son, who had recently taken over its management, and told him what we had in mind. He said he would consider financing it only if we bought thirty acres, including the improvements, and had it surveyed and platted. Brendan and I staked out boundaries around all the improvements and about fifteen irrigated acres, which included one small fenced pasture and one twelve-acre hayfield with the well that I would need to fence. The outbuildings, which surrounded a large well-graveled lot about the size of a football field, and the house situated in a huge tree-covered yard took up the other half of the acreage. It suddenly dawned on me that Mom had over $100,000 sitting in the bank drawing 4% interest and I would have to pay sixteen to eighteen percent for a bank loan. I called my brother Charlie and suggested that he check with Mom to see if she would loan us money. She agreed to loan us $75,000 on an open note for eleven percent interest, payable to her at $687.50 per month. I said Maxine would prepare a note for both of us to sign, mail it to Charlie and he would put it in Mom's safety deposit box.

When we next met, I told Frank and Audrey that it appeared we could finance the place; however could not justify paying so much for so many improvements on such a small acreage. To my surprise Frank made an offer that enticed us to go ahead and close the deal. He said he would give us full use of the established irrigated pasture, about sixty acres, which was fenced into four pastures, the middle one having a small stream feeding a two-acre pond. I thought the use of this additional land would let us run up to thirty head of cattle in the summer and put up enough hay to winter them. We had our lawyer draw up a contract to purchase the land we had surveyed, with interest-only payments on $75,000 for ten years, at which time entire amount would come due. We sent semi-annual payments to the Dees.

We had the horses we had kept at our previous rental property and planned to visit Mom at the farm in Fort Collins to bring back the gentle Arab gelding that Maxine was so fond of, and perhaps a three-year-old gelding that needed to be broke.

A few years before we left Boerne, we met a Brangus breeder who raised quarter horses and had a stallion with a pedigree we really liked. When we moved to Nebraska, we made a deal with him to take our two older mares, Lilley's Nan and Lilley's Meg, and two three-year-old fillies we had raised, on a share agreement. He was to keep the mares for us, breed them to his stud and give us every third colt. As soon as we closed the deal on the farm, I called him and told him we were ready to bring our horses home. I was disappointed to hear that one of the older mares had died and he had gotten only three colts out of them over two years. He agreed to bring us back the surviving older mare and the two young ones, along with a two-year-old colt for our share of the increase. He soon arrived with the three mares and a good-looking, big blue roan gelding. I did not press him as to why he had had so many problems with our horses, but the fact the two-year-old was not even halter broke led me to believe that the horse operation had been a low priority for him. He unloaded the horses and went on his way. I looked over this skittish sixteen-hand colt that I suddenly had on my hands and wondered if I was up to breaking it. The horses I had broke since I reached my fifties had all been handled since they were baby colts and were relatively gentle. .

So by mid-April, we found ourselves the owners of a piece of the prettiest farm in Box Butte County and saddled with a big debt to Mom. The next half-dozen years were among the happiest of our married lives. Although her chronic irritable bowel syndrome and occasional bouts of asthma still nagged her, Maxine had her depression under control, had obtained a satisfying, well-paying three-day-a week bookkeeping job with one of the larger ranchers in the area and soon enthusiastically joined me putting together our little herd of Angus cows. I was back to working the long hours I had worked when I was living on the farm with the folks over twenty years before and loved it.

That fall we started putting together our cow herd. We were able to purchase a dozen "broken mouthed" bred cows from Bill Jaggers, a classmate at CSU, who owned a good-sized ranch about fifteen miles north of us. Like most Sandhills ranchers, Bill had his veterinarian, in this case his brother Dick, check his cows' teeth each fall at the same time he pregnancy tested them. He would cull the open ones and any that were so old that their teeth were worn down near the gums. These were cows that had been good enough to stay in his herd for eight to ten years, and with the care we could give them on the farm we should get a couple more calves from each of them, which should include some excellent replacement heifers. I was able to borrow enough money from my Northwest Mutual Life Insurance policy at five percent interest, twelve percent below what the bank would have charged me at the time, to pay for them and get them through the winter with hay already on the place, which I bought from Frank Dee.

I bought about a dozen fourteen-foot steel panels, enough to make a round corral to break and train the two-year-old, which I called White Wash, which I had brought from the farm in Fort Collins, and the big blue roan colt from Missouri. After a few days of ground work, I was able to start riding the cream-colored colt, which I had gentled and halter broke when I had visited Mom while on vacation my last year in Texas. I eventually got the blue roan colt, which we had named Blue, to let me walk up to him. Getting him saddled was even more difficult because he threw the saddle off several times before I got it cinched up. I hazed him around the corral on a long lead rope for a while and then left him standing with the saddle on for another hour or so, thinking I would ride him later in the afternoon. He let me walk up to him when I returned and I carefully slipped a hackamore on him, took a short hold on the inside rein, put my foot in the stirrup and stood straight up, hesitating a moment before I swung over into the saddle. Suddenly I thought better of the whole thing stepped back down on the ground, un-saddled him and turned him loose. The next day, I called our local brand inspector, Del Clark, who did a little horse trading, and sold Blue for considerably less than his good looks and pedigree should have warranted. I explained that I felt I was just getting too old to be trying to break such a big stout colt and wished him well.

A few weeks later, I ran into Del and asked him how he got along with my blue roan horse. He said that after he had been bucked off three times he sold him to a rodeo contractor! I knew that Del had ridden bareback horses at the amateur rodeos around Nebraska in his earlier days and was reported to have been pretty good. He didn't hold against me the way Blue turned out because he knew he had bought him plenty cheap and would've made a good profit if he could've broke him. I had the feeling that Blue must have had a traumatic experience in Missouri before I got him, and I thanked the Lord that he had given me the good sense to climb down off of him before I was badly hurt.

When winter came, I always fed the cows hay in the morning before I went to work. The calves started coming in early February and I always checked each of the cows carefully when I fed them and again as soon as I got home from work. Maxine kept her eye on them too and I told her that if any of them had trouble when I was gone to call the vet. When I had to be gone overnight, I left enough bales of hay in the pickup so that she and the kids could feed them.

As I recall, that first year we had eight heifer calves and only four bulls. Each cow had a numbered ear tag and I put a tag with the same number, but a different color, on her new calf within a day or two after it was born. The kids had a lot of fun giving each cow a name. I named one though. Bill's cows were of average size except one. She probably weighed less than 800 pounds and was far from good-looking, so I called her "Little Bitty Ugly." Maxine worked up a spreadsheet that listed all the cows' names and she recorded each new calf's date of birth, sex and tag number. I had managed to register the reversed LIL brand in Nebraska, the same brand Harry Lilley had registered in Colorado in 1913, which the folks had always used on our horses, and had an electric branding iron custom made.

A few weeks after the last calf was born in early May, Bill Jaggers and his wife, Billy, came over on a Sunday morning and helped us with our first branding. I moved some of the panels to the corral and we squeezed the calves into a small pen. Brendan and a friend, who had come over for the occasion, would grab a calf by the leg and drag it into the corner. After a little instruction from Bill and me, the boys were able to throw it and hold it down while I branded it, Maxine gave it a shot of vaccine and Bill castrated the bull calves. I had helped Bill brand his several hundred calves the previous year and he had everything organized just so. I don't think he was too impressed with my set up, because it took us two hours for just our dozen, but he didn't say anything. When we finished, we went to the house to leisurely enjoy a couple of drinks and the great Sunday dinner Maxine had prepared for us.

We summered the cows in the pond pasture and the one to the north of it. I bought a Brangus bull that Bill had raised using three-quarter Brahman and one quarter Angus semen that I had talked him into buying some years before for some of his cows. This bull, crossed on our new cows, would produce calves with three-sixteenth Brahman, about the most tolerated this far north. We put up the hay in the other pastures with half the bales going to the neighbor, whom we got to windrow and bale it for us. Brendan helped me load our share of the sixty-five-pound bales on the pickup and a trailer that we also used to haul irrigation pipes. We unloaded them in the potato cellar east of the other outbuildings and ended up with more than enough hay to winter the horses and cows.

We kept our horses in the pasture where the irrigation well was located after I enclosed the two unfenced sides with an electric fence. I bought a 300-gallon water tank for the pasture and we filled it with a garden hose from a winterized water tap nearby. I had my round corral in this pasture and used it to finish breaking the three-year-old registered quarter horse colt I had gotten from Mom. I also often rode our three-year-old stocking-legged sorrel, Sox On My Birthday, which had been born in Texas, on my birthday of course. I used the maximum number of letters the American Quarter Horse Association allowed in his name. I had broke him the previous summer and fall when we were living at the twelve-acre place we had rented after our aborted move to North Platte.

I went to several farm sales that next winter on the lookout for a side delivery rake, a mower and perhaps a bigger tractor than the 8N Ford we had talked Frank into selling us with the farm. At one of these sales. there was a boat with an outboard motor large enough for water skiing. I knew Maxine had loved to water-ski before I met her and I thought the sport would be great fun for the family on summer weekends at Box Butte reservoir, which was only about ten miles from the farm. I decided to bid on it and bought it for what I thought was a good price. The family was surprised and thrilled when I pulled into the yard with it behind the pickup. At a later sale, I managed to buy a twelve-year old John Deere A tractor and a mower made specifically for that model. At yet another sale, I found a reasonably good used windrower and we were all set up to start mowing and raking our own hay come summer. I would still have to pay someone thirty-five cents a bale to bale it, but I could keep the whole crop.

We had only four steers to sell that first fall, because I kept all the heifers to add to our cow herd. They brought less than $400 each, so our farm income the first year was only about $1500. I kept the heifers in the corral that winter and fed them a few pounds of grain every morning, along with all the good hay they would eat. Then I gave the cows a few bales of hay and checked the water tanks. Frank Dee had placed a small stock water tank with a floating electric heater and turnoff valve in each corral so they would stay open at temperatures down to thirty below zero. Unfortunately, it often got colder than that and I sometimes had to break ice. I had things organized so that Maxine could do the feeding after the kids left for school when I had to be gone overnight.

Waterskiing with the family the next summer turned out to be just as much fun as I had hoped. I drove the boat for Maxine and the kids while they skied and Brendan drove it for me. It took me only two or three tries to get up on my skis, but I never could get the hang of slaloming on one ski as Brendan always did. Jennifer and Maxine would usually ski as doubles except when they wanted to cross the boat's wake, which involved the tricky task of ducking under each other's tow ropes.

When winter came, we decided we were ready to take up snow skiing and took a short vacation to try our hand at it. I was raised within sight of the Rocky Mountains but had skied only once. When I worked for ANCA, Lyle Liggette had taken Karen Voss and me skiing and dumped us out at the bottom of the mountain to wallow around helplessly in the snow. Vowing not to let that happen again, as soon as we got to the ski slope about thirty miles northwest of Denver, we rented our equipment and signed up for lessons. We all learned the fundamentals from a great instructor, and Brendan, Jennifer, Liz, who was home for Christmas, and I took right to it and were soon on the intermediate slopes. Shaun and Maxine enjoyed skiing too, but were happy to stay on the bunny slope. We skied until nearly dark and were back on the slope by nine the next morning. About the time I was getting fairly decent at making my way down the steeper slopes, my left knee started getting sore and I found myself trying to ski on just my right leg. I obviously wasn't good enough to be doing that and started wiping out, which felt very much like getting bucked off a horse, something I had never enjoyed. By afternoon, my knee was swollen and I had to call it off and watch the rest of the family enjoy themselves for the rest of the day.

    I was motivated by the ongoing challenge of keeping the Association afloat during this period of record low cattle prices, high interest rates and falling land values. The merger with the two feeder groups had stayed on track, perhaps partly in response to those problems. The purchase of the farm had turned out to be a wise move for all of us and everything went well for five years.

57

Tom Scott

When Tom Scott was named acting director of the newly named Nebraska Cattlemen, I was pretty confident that none of the three of us heading the respective consolidated organizations would get the top job. We had broached the subject only among ourselves once during the year-long effort to bring the NSGA, NLFA and Feedlot Council together. That was when Paul, Tom and I attended the 1988 NCA convention in January. We all stayed in the same hotel and had dinner together the first night. I barged right into a conversation about who might get the top job and how the other two of us would fit into the organization after the choice had been made. I allowed as how we needed to work together to see that we all kept our jobs and that we would all deserve an increase in salary for our efforts getting the task accomplished. As I recall, Paul added that the association might not be able to afford the three of us if they hired a new, high-priced executive. Paul and I were both making $40,000 a year at that time. Tom had earned a couple of raises in the short time he had been with the Feedlot Council, but was still making somewhat less. We came to a consensus, quite naïve in hindsight, that whoever got the top job should make about $60,000 a year and the other two should get raises to $50,000.

One of the events that Paul and I most enjoyed at national conventions was the meeting of all the state affiliate executive officers. We had both been around long enough to be well acquainted with most of them and we invited Tom to join us when we headed over to their annual gathering. He begged off, saying he a bad headache. Naturally Paul and I both reported at some length on our efforts to merge our organizations in Nebraska and we thought Tom wanted to share his success getting the larger feedlots organized in the state. There was a consensus among our peers that pulling it off would be quite a coup, because such a merger had been tried and had failed over the years in several other states.

Paul and I privately admitted to each other that we were surprised when Tom was made acting executive secretary because we had assumed it would have been one of us. We suspected it was now even more likely someone new would be hired as the new boss before the next convention, and we hoped that the job would attract someone qualified.

A few days following our August convention, I received a call from the newly elected president, John Klosterman, with whom I had worked closely on the new organization's bylaws, saying he was coming out to visit me shortly at our office in Alliance. I had made peace with the way the situation had turned out and was trying to rekindle my enthusiasm for making the new organization work. When John arrived, he wasn't his usual cordial self. He followed me into my office, shut the door, sat down and announced, "We recently had an executive committee meeting and decided to let you keep your job, Roy." All I could say in response was, "What?" He went on to say that since we had a computerized billing system and I was good at recruiting new members, they were going to let me continue to manage the Alliance office. I was a little hot and simply replied, "Thanks a lot John," sarcastically. After I cooled off, I asked him what was going on, but he didn't give me a very satisfactory explanation. I knew that Ernie Gottschall could not have been at the executive committee meeting because his cancer had advanced to the point where he couldn't attend the convention, and the association had probably been faced with the necessity of finding another president-elect. The person who knew me best was not involved in the decision! John said they had heard some things that caused them to doubt my integrity, and without fully explaining just what he meant, he departed. I was left feeling very much as I had after my visit with Wayne Pruitt about ten years before, when he asked me to resign from the IBBA, only this time I didn't have any golden parachute and was asked to stay on in spite of my seeming ineptitude or unreliability. Actually, this was far more painful in many ways than that situation because I had had nothing but good feelings about my work leading up to the merger; whereas, my relationship with my president and executive committee in Texas had been deteriorating for a couple of years. I immediately called Jim Gran at the ranch to see if he knew what was going on and Helen said she would have him call me as soon as he came in.

When Jim Gran called me at home that night he said he had no idea what John had been talking about, but said he would get it straightened out at the board meeting scheduled about three weeks hence. In the meanwhile, I called Paul Johnston and he said he thought that Tom Scott had told the executive committee it appeared I had in some manner misappropriated or at least mishandled a considerable amount of money. I decided not to confront Tom with the matter and instead wait to straighten it out at the monthly board meeting.

Jim and I drove to the meeting together, and when it was called to order he immediately climbed all over President Klosterman, asking him why in the world he had basically threatened to fire me. Jim was not known for his diplomacy and I was a bit embarrassed by the way he raised the subject, but I appreciated the fact he had gotten everyone's attention. John, who had gotten to know Jim well during the process of drawing up the new organization's bylaws, took his outburst in stride, called the board into executive session and asked Tom, Paul and me to leave the room.

Over a third of the board members had been members of NSGA. I was at least acquainted with all of the members who had roots in the NLFA and most representing the new Feedlot Council. But I had not met a couple of the board members who were managers of large commercial feedlots, whom Tom Scott had brought on board. The three of us cooled our heels in a nearby room for about thirty minutes. I naturally asked if they knew what was going on and the degree of discomfort in their reply indicated they had a pretty good idea of what was being discussed. I told them I was in the dark, although it finally dawned on me it probably had something to do with the money I had lent the NSGA a few years previously.

When they reconvened the open board meeting and we were asked to come back into the room, John confirmed my suspicion. He told me that the executive committee had learned that NSGA's final audit showed the association owed me $10,000. He said that Jim and several other board members had explained the matter as best they could and he was personally satisfied that I had done nothing illegal, but he asked me to explain, in my own words, what had happened, and then respond to any questions board members might have.

While I tried to explain myself, I knew I was talking to some good friends who basically didn't remember what I was talking about, another group who trusted me, but couldn't understand why I had done what I did and two or three individuals who, even if they believed me, distrusted my motives. My talent for extemporaneous speaking was sorely tested as I tried to make them understand that during the mid-eighties, when the magazine was losing money, I knew it was a temporary, cyclical problem and that after the merger a bigger and better magazine would evolve. I told them of my desire to maintain it as a highly respected, first class house organization, the only statewide publication devoted strictly to the cattle industry. I made clear that I could not afford to give the organization ten thousand dollars, but was confident that in a few years after the merger they could repay it. I said the loan had been reported at a NSGA board meeting, a promissory note had been placed in our fireproof cabinet and the amount showed on each subsequent annual audit as an account payable. As I struggled with my explanation, I realized that the two groups I had worked so hard to make a part of the new organization, the NLFA and Feedlot Council, had been led to believe that at best I was stupid and at worst some kind of a crook.

When I had finished speaking, a couple of new board members asked me questions reflecting their skepticism about my explanation of the loan. Fortunately, several others immediately rose to speak of my dedication to the NSGA and expressed complete confidence in my integrity. John said that since no formal complaint had been filed, if there was no objection, he would simply consider the matter closed and proceed with the rest of the agenda. I had been confident from the beginning that I was in little danger of being fired, but was left with the feeling that I now stood little chance of any further advancement within the new group I had taken so much pride in helping to create.

Tom Scott took little interest in the management of the association and was happy to let the Alliance office continue to manage much of the nuts and bolts of the operation, as in the past. He spent most of his time traveling and continued to bring in new feedlot members while he let Paul handle the management of the Lincoln office and deal with the legislature. In the meantime, a committee was formed to interview candidates for a permanent Executive Vice President of the organization.

All three of the current staff members were invited to apply. I had no reason to think that any of the three of us would be hired and didn't make much effort to sell myself to the committee, which was chaired by Merlyn Carlson. We didn't attract as many applicants as I had expected; however, I was not made privy to the names of those who applied nor much of anything else that was going on among the organization's leadership. Fortunately, I could, and occasionally did, call Paul Johnston to see what was going on in Lincoln and I knew I could depend on what he told me.

As chairman of the cow/calf council, Jim Gran was anxious to continue providing services to that segment of the industry. He received permission from the board of directors to organize an educational program in Norfolk, Nebraska, which was well into old NLFA territory, and we got the help of the University of Nebraska Extension Service in locating speakers. I made the arrangements for the event in a restaurant in Norfolk, with several speakers scheduled in the morning, a noon meal set up with round tables to encourage socializing and a few more speakers in the afternoon. The program was built around balancing the use of cool season pastures with species like brome grass, which is common in Eastern Nebraska, and the area's less prevalent warm season grasses. Many of our members from Western Nebraska attended, but we were disappointed in the turnout of area Farmer/Stockman Council members, who typically ran a small herd of cows in conjunction with their crop production. The goal really had been to get the Eastern and Western producers acquainted with one another more than it had been to educate them, and in that respect, we were pretty successful.

I organized several membership drives that were successful. I was fully aware that we were going to lose several hundred members who had opposed the merger. I remained confident that we would pick up members in central Nebraska. Cattlemen there had not felt particularly close to either the NSGA or NLFA, but the merger would be our strongest selling point. In their enthusiasm, the new board of directors had convinced themselves we would automatically gain several thousand new members. In fact, we picked up nearly 1,000, but they had not made allowances for the 800 disgruntled NSGA traditionalists that did not renew the first year. As a consequence, our success in attracting a record number of new members the first year after the merger did not result in any pats on the back for me. We were still doing Ralgro meetings for Elanco, but they had changed their policy and now paid only for the meals of the new members who signed up at the meeting, a change that was not fully explained in advance and resulted in a good many disgruntled current members when they were unexpectedly billed.

I found it difficult to maintain my usual enthusiasm for my job, but the necessity to get up early and feed our little cow herd turned out to be the tonic that kept me going. Jim was encouraging and his determination to make the merger a success helped turn something I had been concerned might be a negative, into a positive force for the new organization. With Paul, Tom and me each more or less operating a separate branch of the association, the competition between each council seemed to encourage growth in each rather than detract in any significant amount from cooperation on industry issues.

I had tried to downplay my desire to head the new organization as we worked on the merger, but I had to plan how we might offer specific services to the four councils. I knew that it would be particularly important to provide daily marketing information to our Feedlot Council members, who sold pens of fed cattle every week and then bought replacement feeder cattle. In the months ahead of the merger vote, I had visited the Kansas Livestock Association, managed by Dee Likes, and the Texas Cattle Feeders Association, managed by the highly respected Charlie Ball, to pick their staffs' brains as to how they met this need. The KLA encouraged their members to subscribe to the services of Cattlefax, a subsidiary of the National Cattlemen's Association, and the Texas Cattle Feeders had a fully staffed, sophisticated service of their own. I also made a trip to Denver to meet with Cattlefax Director, Topper Thorpe, to find out how KLA was plugged into their service. There were advantages to both approaches and I wanted to be able to offer the Feedlot Council the information I had been able to glean from these visits. Of course, I never got the chance.

The newly configured Nebraska Cattlemen did not wait too long to hire a permanent executive officer. At a special meeting in North Platte on November 18, 1988 the board hired Chuck Ball. I was not at the meeting but I talked to Jim Gran immediately afterward. When he told me who had been hired I responded that I couldn't believe Charlie Ball was interested in the job. Jim laughed and replied that it wasn't Charlie Ball of the Texas Cattle Feeders but his son. I had met Chuck when I was in Washington, D. C. the previous February at NCA's annual Washington gathering of state affiliates. He had recently become a junior member of their staff. I recalled that he was a neat, personable, somewhat quiet guy and I knew he certainly had a good pedigree, but I knew nothing of his previous work experience. Tom Scott must have learned that he wasn't going to get the job because he almost immediately was hired as Executive Officer of the Nebraska Beef Council, a job which had fortuitously just opened up.

I had hoped the association would hire someone whom I already knew and had worked with in the industry, but I figured, like everyone else, that if Chuck was even close to being as competent as his father at running a cattle association he would be able to handle the job. I had already made up my mind to do everything I could to help whoever got the job be a success, and was resigned to ending my career as a staff person for what would become one of the three most influential affiliates of the National Cattlemen's Association.

58

4-H Fiasco

When we were living in the rented farmhouse north of Alliance, Jennifer went to the District 39 K-8 grade school located about one mile east of the house on the road between Alliance and Hemingford. She became best friends with a farm girl named Nikke Johannes, who was active in the local 4H club. Jennifer joined this club, which was fortunate to have as its 4H leader a young man named Ted Price, whom all the kids adored. He had been an active participant in Box Butte County 4H and had shown sheep and steers at the county fair, as well as participating in the horse show. Each week throughout the summer, he taught his club members the fundamentals of each event. On certain days, everyone rode over to the farm where Ted lived with his folks and younger sister, and practiced the various horse events. On other days, they hauled their cattle or sheep over by trailer and practiced fitting and showing. On Ted's advice, Jennifer decided to show a fat lamb her first year at the fair. She also planned to enter in her age-appropriate horsemanship class with the one-quarter Arab X three-quarter Welsh pony she had gotten from her Grandma Lilley.

We decided to raise our own show lamb, so we purchased a couple of bred ewes from a farmer who was the only person in the area who both bought and sold sheep. The Box Butte County Fair was in mid-August, and by that time we had weaned three lambs from our two ewes; Jennifer selected one of the females to show at the Fair. About a week before it started, all show animals had to be brought to the fairgrounds to be inspected by a veterinarian, weighed and tagged. Jennifer and I showed up with our lamb in the back of our horse trailer at the appointed time and quickly learned how little we knew about the process. We did know that lambs were shown without a halter and that this required the handlers to maneuver them around with one hand on their chests and the other around their rear ends. To our surprise, everybody else at the weigh-in had a halter on their lambs and were leading them up to the veterinarian for inspection. Since we didn't have one, Jennifer had to wrestle her lamb from the trailer up to the veterinarian and on to the scale in front of a lot of giggling onlookers.

Our county fair lasted for over a week. The sheep were shown on the third day and the horse show was on the last, but the show animals had to stay at the fair the entire time. A good many of the parents whose children were participating in the fair parked campers at the facilities provided for this purpose on the fairgrounds. When Jennifer and I and her lamb showed up about midmorning of the day we were scheduled to arrive, most of the other animals were already in their stalls. A couple of Jennifer's friends in her 4-H group, who were also showing lambs, helped her get settled as I headed to my Alliance office. The next morning, I dropped Jennifer off at the fairgrounds on my way to work so she could feed and water the lamb, clean its stall and help the others in their building police the entire area. On the day she was to show her animal, I left the office in time to pick up Maxine at home and arrive at the grounds to help Jennifer lead her lamb over to where the judging was to take place. As I recall, there was one blue ribbon given to the winner, a couple of red ribbons and the rest of the class, which included Jennifer, got white ribbons. It turned out that nearly all lambs were still slightly wet from being washed early that morning, something that the judge said actually should have disqualified them. It turned out that only the three top winners had used blow-dryers, a necessity we hadn't thought of.

At the horse show over the weekend, Jennifer got another white ribbon in the Western Pleasure Class. She was embarrassed to be riding the only pony in the class, but Maxine and I thought she had done very well. I was about the only father helping his kid around the barn and appreciated the willingness of the other kids' mothers to help me learn the many arcane traditions involved in participating in 4-H activities at the county level. Jennifer learned even more, and at the end seemed to be looking forward to four more years of the same. I promised her we would try to talk grandma out of another horse for next year and said maybe she could consider showing a bred heifer in a year or two and perhaps a steer after that.

We borrowed a ram to breed to our two ewes and two females we had kept. In our first calf crop, from which I had kept eight replacement heifers, I didn't castrate one outstanding bull calf from one of Bill Jagger's cows. It had been bred to a Brink's three-quarter-blood bull, a Brangus, through artificial insemination. I grew him out with the replacement heifers to breed to our expanding cow herd. He was out of our best cow. I ended up using him for eight years, so he sired quite a few calves from his dam's own daughters, a practice I wouldn't recommend to anyone else, but our little line breeding program worked out fine for us.

It was almost impossible to make any profit in the cattle business during the mid-1980s. By taking advantage of some of the same income tax regulations that enticed so many outside investors to get into the cattle business, which I personally thought were hurting our industry, we were able to afford our little cattle operation. Using accelerated depreciation on our many outbuildings, we were able to charge off considerable losses against our cattle and farming expenses. Maxine kept scrupulous records not only for our taxes, but even on our household expenses. When we were selected for a random IRS audit in 1986 we came through it with flying colors. I was fully aware that most of our NSGA members weren't making a profit and had no income to purchase machinery or construct buildings to put on depreciation schedules during these hard times.

We sold our calves in the fall at the Crawford Livestock Auction and, of course, our first ones were Angus, except the few sired by Bill's three-quarter-blood bull. I was concerned that when we sold our first calf crop sired by the Brangus bull we had raised, they might be discriminated against. As it turned out, with only three-sixteenths Brahman they showed very few Brahman characteristics. In fact, they looked like good sized angus calves, a few of which had slightly droopy ears. About the only person who knew me who bought cattle at Crawford was the rancher who was in charge of the Box Butte County Fair livestock show, and he bought our calves nearly every year. His daughter later told me that some of the best mother cows they ever owned were the heifers sired by our Brangus bull.

Early in the fall after our first county fair, we hauled Jennifer's pony back to the farm during a visit to see Mom and returned to Hemingford with a twenty-eight-year-old registered Arab mare, Lucy, which was too old to breed, and a three-year-old sorrel Arab filly, Rosie, which needed to be ridden. Mom was letting a friend keep her Arab horse at the farm in exchange for helping with the chores. This lady had not only gentled Rosie, but had ridden her a few times. I had finished breaking White Wash and sold him to Nikki's mother, Joy Johannes, so I was able to direct all my attention to Rosie and Socks, who were coming along great. In spite of her age, Lucy was still high-spirited and was just the right size for Jennifer at thirteen-three hands tall (fifty-five inches).

At her second Box Butte County fair, Jennifer showed a fat lamb again and during the horse show rode Lucy in the Western Pleasure Class. This year we dried the lamb and Jennifer managed to get one of the blue ribbons. Although she and Lucy received only a red ribbon in the very large Western Pleasure Class, she felt more comfortable in the competition. Actually, poor old Lucy was a little too chargey to suit the judge. Her walk and trot were fine, but she would not canter on a loose rein, required in a pleasure horse. As usual, the Box Butte County fair attracted a top-notch western performer for the Sunday afternoon show the last weekend. Over the years when Jennifer showed, George Straight, Roy Clark, Charlie Pride and Ronnie Millsap filled the stands.

Jennifer decided to show a registered Brangus heifer at her third county fair. I had called my old friend and past IBBA President, Royal Buckley, and talked him into selecting one of his best calves for us. I hooked up the horse trailer, and Jennifer, Maxine and I headed for Royal's farm at Olathe, Kansas, just south of Kansas City. We stopped in Kansas City on the way to see our old friends, the Van Horne's, and drove out to look at the heifer the second afternoon. We were well pleased with the one he had picked for us and told Royal we would be out to get her early the next morning, as we were planning to drive all the way home in just one day, about a twelve-hour drive. When we arrived home after dark, I turned the heifer out in the corral with a few replacement heifers we had selected from our calf crop. Jennifer named her Lily and we halter broke her over the winter. She became quite gentle but was a little cranky. About June 1st, I turned all the heifers out with our Brangus bull. They had all grown nicely, but Lily was noticeably larger than the ones we had raised. After about six weeks in the pasture we brought Lily in so Jennifer could start grooming her.

The year after we got Rosie and Lucy, Mom gave Jennifer a yearling quarter horse colt out of the mare she and Dad had raced.

She was by Mike McGinley's stud called Old Felix, who was out of a great race mare called She Kitty and by the sire of many winning racehorses called Three Bars. Jennifer decided to show this filly in the halter class at the horse show and ride Lucy or Rosie, if she was well enough broke by then, in the Western Pleasure Class.

The fair manager didn't know quite what to do with Lily because they had no other Brangus, so he decided to stall her with the Angus, but he let Jennifer go ahead and show her alone. Jennifer was an old hand at showing by this time and didn't need much help from me except for one thing. Everyone used rope halters to tie the animals in their stalls. However, for the show most exhibitors preferred a fancy leather halter with a chain that went under the animal's chin connected to a leather rein. We needed to practice a few times with the fancy halter before the show, and since Lily made it difficult to change halters, we would lead her into what was called a grooming stall that had a head gate to make the swap. The second time we did this, just as I was starting to buckle the leather halter after removing the rope one I accidentally hit the lever that opened the chute gate with my arm, and as Lily escaped, the halter slipped off. I tried to get my arm around her, but in my panic, I lunged at her too fast and she trotted off through the fairgrounds. We were panic-stricken and people standing around the area started to cry, "Loose animal." Several of them joined us pursuing her. She never broke into a run but simply kept heading north until she reached the edge of the fairgrounds and came to an open field. I could see that we were going to have to find a way to get her into some kind of enclosure. Fortunately, Maxine was with me that morning and I told her to get in the pickup, drive west of the fairgrounds and then north to the county road beyond the field Lily was crossing.

Several people joined Jennifer and me following our escaped heifer across the field to the road, where we joined Maxine. I thanked them for their help and said Maxine, Jennifer and I could haze her to one of the nearby farms and into a corral. This may have been wishful thinking on my part, but we were embarrassed to death and didn't want anyone observing further the consequences of our carelessness. With Maxine driving down the middle of the county road and Jennifer and me on either side we were able to herd Lily, who had calmed down after the crowd following her dispersed. About half a mile west and another half north on another county road, we were able to turn her into the driveway to the farm of Gaye and Shorty Campbell, and finally into one of their corrals. The Campbell's son, Cory, was in Jennifer's 4H club and the whole family was at the fair. We moved Lily into a corner, where I got the rope halter on her firmly, tied her to the fence and shut the corral gate. Realizing we had finally captured our heifer, we couldn't decide whether to laugh or cry, but agreed that we hated the thought of going back to the fair to face the crowd who had observed our disaster.

It didn't take us long to find Gaye and Corey when we got back to the fair. They and several of the kind people who had been involved in the chase assured us that this was something that could be expected to happen every year. Fortunately, Jennifer and I couldn't foresee that this would not be our last embarrassing incident at the Box Butte County Fair. We did manage to get the show halter on Lily on the day of the breeding heifer show. The judge awarded them a red ribbon and explained to the onlookers that since there was no other Brangus to compare her with, he could not justify a blue ribbon, but he complimented Jennifer on her showmanship and indicated that based on his limited knowledge of Brangus cattle, her heifer was a good representative of the breed. She rode Lucy again at the horse show with pretty much the same results as the previous year, and thoroughly enjoyed the fellowship at the fair. I simply looked forward to the Ronnie Millsap performance the last day, which would signal that I had survived another Fair.

Brendan thoroughly enjoyed his three years at St. Agnes Academy. He graduated with a class of eleven, three boys and eight girls. Since he had such a good experience at the Academy, we decided to send Jennifer there for high school even though we had just moved to Hemingford. This turned out to be not the best idea, because all of Jennifer's country school eighth grade classmates went to school either at Alliance or Hemingford. Also, whereas Brendan's eight girl classmates had carried him high, the boys at St. Agnes often teased Jennifer. She did go out for volleyball and made the team in spite of her limited experience. They had an excellent coach, who taught her sound fundamentals that served her well when she transferred to Hemingford the next year. Ironically, Brendan remained an Episcopalian throughout his three years at the Catholic school and Jennifer joined the very active Catholic youth group in Hemingford. She was confirmed in that faith with her peers after they completed what seemed to be a much more abbreviated form of catechism than my friend Jerry Weinberger had described to me when I was in the fifth grade with him in Denver.

Brendan enrolled in the South Dakota School of Mines in Rapid City, having decided to follow his father's career as a civil engineer. He had enjoyed working in the summer during high school for the man who surveyed the acreage we had bought from Frank Dee.

Shaun had moved to Rapid City about the time it seemed we would be moving to North Platte, and we were not always sure what she was doing there.

Elizabeth graduated from San Marcus State College with a degree in marketing and went to work for Banana Republic in Austin as an assistant manager. When the ANCA convention was in San Antonio in the mid-80s, she took some vacation time and was able to join me at my hotel during the convention. I enjoyed the opportunity to introduce her to some of the many friends I always met at this event, and she got to see Les and Linda Davis, who had often seen her as a baby and small child when her mother and I had lived in New Mexico. We found time to drive up to Boerne and look at our old home in Friendly Hills, and she saw some of her high school classmates.

In mid-September 1985, when she was home for a weekend visit, Shaun took me down to her bedroom in the basement and told me there was something we needed to talk about. She said it was a serious matter and she needed me to tell "mama" for her because she would probably take it better from me. I said that she knew there was nothing she couldn't talk to either of us about and to just let me know what was going on. She simply said, "I'm pregnant." After a stunned silence I asked her who the father was and were they going to get married. She replied that he was a married man she had met at the bar where she worked and she wasn't interested in trying to work anything out with him because she believed he simply couldn't deal with it. I said if that was the case I didn't really need to know more about him and the only issue was whether she wanted to keep the child or put it up for adoption. She said she very much wanted to keep it. Both of our girls knew of our feelings about abortion and I don't think that option ever crossed Shaun's mind. I told her that we were looking forward to being grandparents some day, but weren't prepared for this. We both shed some tears before I told her I would talk to Maxine and then all three of us would talk.

Maxine and I sat down in the kitchen and broke the news to her. She took it better than either Shaun or I thought she might. She said she was afraid it might be something like this when Shaun herded me down into the basement. We agreed it would be better if Shaun tried to make it on her own up in Rapid City rather than move home and we would help her out in any way we could beyond that.

Shaun had already established residency in South Dakota and continued her job. She made an appointment with a doctor for a checkup and went on with her life as only Shaun could, probably losing less sleep less than either Maxine or I. We were on an emotional roller coaster for the next seven months. We had to tell Jennifer right away because she could tell that something was going on. I called Elizabeth and Brendan a few weeks later and soon was telling people that didn't need to know what had happened. This usually embarrassed the recipient of the news, but had the advantage of depriving those who prefer gossip to facts the opportunity to indulge themselves.

On March 17, 1986, Shaun delivered a baby girl with a full head of dark hair. Maxine said she was a beautiful baby, and within a few months I realized she was absolutely right. One of us went up to get Sarah—I loved the name—nearly every weekend for the first eighteen months of her life, by which time she was already entering her terrible twos. She was strong-willed, but extremely precocious and loving, when she wasn't throwing a fit.

The same summer we learned of Shaun's pregnancy I received a phone call from Frank, that he was going have surgery in Denver soon. He said he had been having some pain behind his left shoulder blade that he had assumed was a strained muscle. After it had lingered for several weeks he went to a doctor, who couldn't find anything wrong with his shoulder and had ordered an x-ray. He said they had discovered what appeared be a growth in his lung and he was going to have exploratory surgery. When Shirley called and told me they had found cancer, I immediately drove to the hospital and found most of Frank's family there. I learned they had removed a large growth from between his left lung and his ribs, which had proven to be cancerous.

When the doctor came into the room, Frank asked everyone to leave except Clay and me so we could discuss his options. The doctor told us it was mesothelioma, one of the least curable forms of cancer. He said it was possible to buy Frank some time with chemotherapy and radiation, and if he was willing, he could be involved in an experiment with a new form of chemotherapy. He said just the removal of the tumor would buy quite a bit of time to gain some weight and get through the treatments. We discussed the option of just forgoing the treatments and Frank quickly decided to sign up for the experiment and have as much time with his family as possible.

Frank's decision turned out to be a wise one because the chemo and radiation kept the cancer at bay for nearly eighteen months, and even though he initially lost his hair from the chemo, he dealt with it very well. His hair soon grew back as curly as ever and without a hint of gray. When the cancer finally reappeared, he was able to hold it off for several more months with radiation. He died at the age of 59 on April 1, 1987, a victim of a tiny bit of asbestos that had lodged in his lung when he was scraping insulation in the engine room in the destroyer he was helping decommission. His destroyer was heading out to join the invasion of Japan when the atomic bomb ended the war.

Frank never dwelt on the irony of his cancer, but felt fortunate when he learned he might be eligible to receive compensation from the fund the asbestos manufacturers had been forced to create. Frank hired a lawyer to look into the program and soon found that he easily qualified. Rather than join a class-action lawsuit, he asked his lawyer to negotiate a payment that he considered to be appropriate, and settled. He attended his county commissioners meeting the month of his death and drove the pickup while his two daughters threw hay off the back to the cows up till his last few days.

His funeral was held in a packed city auditorium in Laramie. Poor Mom, who never cried, quietly mourned the indignity of having to bury a grown son. I managed my emotions up until they played taps at the end of the military funeral. At that point, I let out one loud sob.

Elizabeth at 27

Jennifer and Mandy with trophy and ribbons
Fair 1986.

59

Sarah

Jennifer rode her black mare at several junior horse shows in the area around Alliance during the summer of 1988, after she graduated from Hemingford High School. She seldom placed less than second in the western pleasure class and won enough money to pay her expenses and collected several nice trophy halters. She was an excellent swimmer and had a job as a lifeguard at the Hemingford pool. In mid-summer she received an invitation to attend a swimming school at the University of Nebraska. We decided to take up the offer and make it into a family trip, with the outside hope she might be able to get a scholarship for the college swimming team. She enjoyed the opportunity, but quickly realized that she would have little chance of making the team competing against girls from much larger schools. She toured the campus and we told her we were willing to send her to college there if she wished. She quickly decided it was too far from home and much too big for her. She eventually decided to go to the junior college at Torrington not far from Scottsbluff, which is not far from Hemingford. They had a veterinary technician course she liked and we learned that most of the credits she would get there would be accepted by the University of Wyoming for her final two years of college. It turned out to be a good choice for her and we were delighted to have her that close to home.

Chuck Ball got off to a good start his first year by putting together what appeared to be a highly qualified staff in Lincoln. The first thing he did was move Deb to Lincoln as his personal secretary. Deb had been the best secretary I had ever had, with the possible exception of the few brief emergency periods when Maxine had filled in for that job. Chuck soon hired Mike Fitzgerald as communications director and magazine editor. I had run into Mike several times at cattlemen's conventions when he worked for the Drovers Journal and I actually had him in mind for the job if I were boss because I knew Troy would never move to Lincoln. Chuck then hired Shane Belohrad and Dean Settji, who, by coincidence, had graduated in the same class from a small town in eastern Nebraska. Dean had been working for the Colorado Cattle Feeders Association and had experience helping feedlots comply with environmental regulations, which had proliferated as feedlots grew ever larger. Shane had attended the Air Force Academy, but got his degree from the University of Nebraska. Perhaps Chuck's best move was hiring Hank Rogers, a Texas A & M graduate, who had been working for a large diversified operation in Idaho, which had a large feedlot. Hank led the organization of a market reporting service patterned after the one Chuck's father had so successfully created for his Texas Cattle Feeders Association. The last three of these new staff members were about twenty-eight years old, and Mike was in his thirties, like Chuck. Paul and I were pushing sixty.

One of the first things Chuck did when he started work was buy a fax machine for both offices, so we could send documents back and forth. A few days after we received our machine and were still learning how to use it, Cecilia called from the Lincoln office and asked us to fax the books to her. I was surprised, because Paul's wife had always done the bookkeeping for him and Cecelia had been his do-everything secretary; I didn't know she was a bookkeeper. I explained to her it wasn't all that simple to fax our books to her. I said we had a hybrid system that used our computer for billing magazine advertising and memberships, but Mary kept a traditional set of double entry books by hand. She said she didn't know what I was talking about and insisted I fax the books immediately. I said I'd see what we could do, called John Klosterman and explained the situation. He informed me he wanted the books kept in Lincoln and I should do whatever it took. I knew that Paul's bookkeeping system had been far simpler than ours and figured that John didn't really understand my problem either. I resigned myself to the fact that I wasn't going to be involved in any way with our budgets or bookkeeping, so had Mary pack up her ledgers and mail them to Lincoln. It appeared we were to continue sending out membership statements and solicitation letters, but with a return address to Lincoln.

When Chuck was first settled into his new office, he scheduled a two-day get acquainted and educational meeting for the staff of both offices. I drove our bookkeeper, Mary Broad, and communication director, Gerri Monahan, to Lincoln and we arrived in the late afternoon at the motel where rooms had been reserved for us. Chuck had told us to go ahead and have supper on our own because he had arranged that night for all of us, including spouses of married staff members, to be his guests at a local comedy club where we were all to meet. None of us from the Alliance office really knew what a comedy club was, but we were soon to get a rude awakening. Evidently Chuck thought this would be a bonding experience; however, the four of us were embarrassed by the crude, foul mouthed string of comedians who "entertained" us. Chuck and Cecelia thought the standups were hilarious and were disappointed that we weren't more enthusiastic. I lamely joked that I was of the wrong generation for that kind of humor and Gerri and Mary were noncommittal. We were to meet at the office at eight the next morning to begin a full day of training, which gave us an excuse to pass on an invitation to join the rest of the staff when they headed for a nearby nightclub. On the way back to the hotel, we agreed that we were headed for some culture shock under our new leader. I can't remember if Paul and Maxine were with us, however I think not, because they were both Baptists and neither drank a drop and wouldn't be caught dead at a comedy club.

When we got up the next morning, a freezing rain was falling and it was nearly impossible to even walk to the car. We had decided to drive home when the meeting ended that afternoon, so we had checked out of the hotel and struggled out to the car with our luggage. The staff was gathered around the big table in the office's boardroom and we all visited for a while over sweet rolls and coffee. When Chuck arrived, he proceeded to give us a pep talk about what he expected of the staff, working from several pages of notes he had written on a large flip chart. I couldn't help but be impressed with how well prepared he was as he gave us a presentation much like ones we often received during summer meetings of the affiliated executives officers of ANCA.

As the morning progressed, the freezing rain turned to snow and the wind came up. Cecelia sent out for box lunches and we continued our training through the afternoon. The snow was piling up and I was getting nervous about our drive home; I hoped that Chuck might turn us loose a bit early. The thought never occurred to him; we left the office after five p.m. when it was already dark and began our seven-hour drive back to Alliance.

By the time we got to Grand Island and headed northwest on Highway 2 the storm was intensifying. We should have found a motel and stayed there, but we all wanted to get home so I kept on driving. By the time we crossed the Dismal River at Dunning, the snow was getting deep, and between there and Thedford I had to stop a couple of times and kick snow out from in front of the car to keep going. The windshield wipers could barely keep up with the snow and I could drive only about thirty miles an hour over a road that I had driven many times. Somewhere between Thedford and Mullen, I caught up with a snowplow and followed it until we got to Hyannis. By that time, it was well after midnight and I was a nervous wreck. When I got to Hyannis, the snowplow driver pulled off the road at the only filling station, which was closed. I struggled through the storm and climbed in beside him. He said he was going only a few miles further west to the Grant County line, so I decided to spend the night at the old hotel in town. Fortunately the bar and grill was still open so we were able to get some cheeseburgers before we went to bed.

With the wind howling and the temperature down to zero, the furnace in the hotel was not able to warm upstairs hotel rooms enough to let me get much sleep under my two or three army blankets. I got up at about six the next morning and the women joined me shortly in the restaurant. Mary said they had slept together in a double bed to keep from freezing and I allowed I nearly had. After a hearty breakfast of hotcakes, eggs and sausage we headed west to Alliance as the sun was coming up. We soon found that the drifts were smaller and smaller as we proceeded. If I had wanted to I probably could have made it on to Alliance the previous night, but I probably would've run out of gas because I was on running on fumes when I filled up at the gas station that morning. I took the women home and told them to take the rest of the day off. Soon I pulled into the lane leading into the farm, which was only partly drifted over, and had no trouble getting up to the house. I had called Maxine before I left Lincoln and she had assumed we would spend the night on the way. I didn't get much sympathy when I told her of our difficulties driving as far as Hyannis and giving up when we were less than sixty miles from home. I did the morning chores, went into the office and spent the afternoon answering calls and contemplating my career as a cattle association executive, which was showing signs of ending badly.

I figured that if I was to keep my job, I had better get busy with what I had been told was my main responsibility, namely, signing up new members. In addition to our membership list, we had identified a large number of potential members from the state brand book, plus all the members that had dropped immediately after the merger, and the considerable number we lost during the difficult financial times of the mid-1980s. I knew the memberships we had lost during the merger would be hard to get back, so I planned most of our membership drives on the eastern side of the old Stockgrower's area.

Chuck visited our office shortly after he assumed his new duties, but rarely came to Alliance after that. I never had occasion to go to Lincoln unless one of our bi-monthly board of directors' meetings, at which I always had to give a membership report, was held there. I always carried a complete printout of our active members with me and provided a summary of new members signed up, along with members dropped after they were six months in arrears on their dues payment. The first year or two we had a substantial net increase in members, but never enough to meet the expectations most board members had for our newly merged organization. The first year was brutal due to the 800 plus members from the western half of the traditional NSGA who refused to renew. I had anticipated this, and my hope that losses would be made up by new members whose sales resistance had been greatly reduced by the merger, turned out to be well founded. Because of the disproportionate loss the first year, we had only a 400 member net gain; however it was considerably greater for the next several years.

The new members we received were fairly evenly distributed between our mail solicitations, membership drives—including my one-man efforts—and our ongoing sponsored area association meetings with Elanco. When I wasn't licking envelopes or attending meetings, I hit the road and made cold calls at ranch headquarters. I had been able to buy a useful directory that an enterprising firm had prepared for traveling salesmen, which gave the location of farm and ranch headquarters and the names of the current owners by township in every Nebraska county. I could check my membership directory to avoid calling on current members. Some days I drove all day without selling a membership, and other days I might sell several. Chuck also had instructed all of the staff to make at least ten cold phone calls to prospective members every night. He said he was working sixty hours a week and expected the rest of the administrative staff to do the same.

Chuck was obsessed with the idea of budgeting expenses in relation to staff time used. The idea of allocating costs to specific projects in agriculture was something Jim Gran and I had promoted. This was to support the University of Nebraska's Extension Service's Integrated Resource Management Program directed at cattle producers; consequently, the general idea resonated with me. But when he mailed us forms with his budget's line items listed to be filled out weekly, he asked us to indicate, first the number of hours worked each day, and then the percentage of that time dedicated to each of the items. I scratched my head as I tried to comply. Not having any input to the preparation of the budget I couldn't figure out the benefit of this exercise, but we all soon learned that these forms had to be in the hands of the bookkeeper before financial statements were prepared at the end of the month. Since I really had no say in management anymore and was primarily responsible for increasing our membership, I tried to report fifty to sixty hours of work each week and credited at least eighty percent of it to increasing membership. I divided the rest among the work I did with Jim for the Cow/Calf Council, meetings and other line items I can't recall.

My company car had gone to Chuck in Lincoln, but the number of miles I drove pursuing new members resulted in a large enough expense account to make the payments for a new one. I bought a little Dodge Dart, which got excellent mileage, and Maxine already had an American Motors Eagle with four-wheel drive, which she drove three times a week to her bookkeeping job in Lakeside.

That summer on weekends I didn't have to work, I replaced a couple of electric fences with permanent ones. I often got up early and rode one of our young horses before breakfast. Maxine loved to use the small chainsaw I had bought her to cut firewood from the abundance of dead branches that were scattered throughout our extensive shelter belts, and she walked three or four miles nearly every day with the dogs. Jennifer and I rode together occasionally and she always had our few ewes to feed along with caring for whatever animal she was preparing for 4H. Often, in the long summer evenings, we took the pickup out to the pasture to check our cows and calves just for the fun of looking at them. Sarah particularly liked riding in the pickup with me. Occasionally Jennifer and I found time to fish for blue gills on the little pond. Having the farm to come home to took the sting out of the fact that, for one of the few times in my life, I wasn't happy with my work. I had always craved responsibility, and just going to a board of directors meeting every two months to give a membership report didn't come close to filling that need. I did enjoy visiting my good friends on the board who represented our western areas and new ones I had made from the other councils.

When Sarah was about two years old, Shaun moved back to Alliance and got a job at the nursing home there. She soon discovered that she enjoyed working with older people and decided to become a nurse. She didn't think she wanted to make the commitment to become a registered nurse, so she enrolled

Grandpa and Sarah out looking at the cows in the old GMC Pickup.

in the two-year course at the community college in Scottsbluff to become a practical nurse. She sailed through the training with ease and we were happy to keep Sarah full-time instead of just on the weekends. She graduated, got a job at the hospital in Alliance and started dating Steve Heitz, son of Bill Heitz the filling station owner and U-haul dealer, who was the first man I had met when we moved to Nebraska.

When Steve and Shaun decided to marry, Maxine suggested that they have an outdoor wedding in our big yard at the farm. We talked them into having a fairly small wedding with just members of both families in attendance. It turned out to be a lovely affair and Sarah was the flower girl, spreading petals before the bride and groom when they stepped out of the house and approached the preacher standing under our blooming crabapple tree.

We saw quite a lot of Frank and Shirley while Frank was taking his cancer treatments. The doctor couldn't say that the cancer was in remission, but the radiation seemed to have stopped it in its tracks. The county fair was coming up and I mentioned to Frank that I wished Jennifer had a better horse for the horsemanship classes. He immediately insisted that he would like to buy a well-trained horse for Jennifer. I protested but he insisted, and within a week or so we had found a good one for sale. She was a good-looking eight-years-old black mare, about fifteen hands tall. Frank told us to spend up to $2,000 and we were able to finally buy her for that amount.

In the meanwhile, Charles Iodence had offered to let Jennifer use Mandy, the mare that his youngest daughter had used for pole bending and barrel run in 4H several years before, so Jennifer finally entered the fair with prospects for doing well in the horse show.

The previous year Jennifer had shown a steer we had raised that was out of one of our Angus cows and sired by the bull we had also raised. As I recall, she got only a red ribbon with him, however she had fitted and shown him well. At the end of the fair, all the market animals that were not headed for the state fair were sold at an auction that was well supported by businesses in the western part of the state. He brought well over market price.

That year we hadn't raised a steer that we judged was good enough for the fair, so we got Charles Iodence to help us buy one.

I felt completely inadequate to select a show steer and Charles's kids had always done very well at their county fair. He picked a black angus cross steer that looked like he might be a quarter Charolais. He turned out not to have a very good disposition and had a look in his eye that I had seen in untrustworthy horses.

While Jennifer was doing very well getting her horses ready for the fair, we were having problems with the steer. In the first place, he was not nearly as gentle as the cattle we raised, and in the second, he had an ornery stubborn streak. I had to give Jennifer a lot of help to get him halter broke and he never did lead as well as he should have. When I helped Jennifer lead him into his stall at the start of the fair, I had flashbacks of the problem we had had with her heifer two years previously. He didn't adjust to all the activity around the fair and wasn't drinking out of his water bucket, so the second day I decided to lead him to the big water tank in the middle of the fairgrounds when I was through with work that afternoon.

When I arrived Jennifer was nowhere to be found, so I untied the steer and headed for the water tank. He seemed pretty goosy, so I took a good two-handed hold on him. Just as we got to the tank someone walked up with a goat. The steer jumped sideways and I tripped over the step at the edge of the tank. As I fell, I thought, "Here I go again." I kept a tight grip on the halter rope as I landed flat on my back and the steer took off on a dead run directly away from me. I was bouncing along on my back and as I rolled over on my stomach, the 4-H moms standing in the area were all yelling, "Let go of the rope!" I finally did and joined half a dozen other people running after him. Fortunately, he slowed down at the edge of the grounds. A couple of people grasped the halter rope and we led him back to his stall. Jennifer managed to handle him on show day without any noticeable problems. She was happy to settle for a white ribbon and sell him in the sale a couple of days later.

The horse show turned out far better. Jennifer won the pole bending and finished second in the barrel race with Mandy. She wound up winning the western pleasure class on her new black mare. She had problems with her in the trail class and didn't place, but still won second all-around in her age bracket in the horse show, ending her last year in 4H on a positive note.

60

Bad Year

It soon became clear to me that even though I probably would not lose my job, the likelihood of ever getting a raise was remote. We had gone ahead and added two bedrooms and a bath to our little house, and even though we had no desire to move, Maxine and I decided that considering my frustration with my new situation, I should try to find a new job somewhere in the area. The problem was that there simply were not that many job opportunities in Western Nebraska. I did apply for the job of Director of Economic Development in Alliance, but was unwilling to take a cut in salary to get it.

On one of my membership drives, as I was driving by the well-known Ankony Angus Ranch about forty miles southwest of Alliance, I decided to drop by and visit their manager, Dr. Mac Cropsey, even though they were already members of the association. Mac was a well-respected veterinarian who had helped establish American Breeder's Service, the largest supplier of bovine semen in the country. I had used him to mouth (check the teeth) to confirm the ages of the cattle at our major Brangus shows when I was with the International Brangus Breeders Association. I had continued to keep track of him at the tradeshows during the National Cattlemen's Association conventions. I had also occasionally dropped in to see him at the American Breeder's Service headquarters near Denver when I was visiting Mom and Dad. Ankony was owned by Armand Hammer, who was best known as the owner of Occidental Petroleum Company. Mac was trying to talk Hammer into developing a vertically integrated operation that would encompass every step of the cattle industry, from planning the breeding program through selling high-quality steaks at white tablecloth restaurants. He was well acquainted with the owner of one of the country's biggest restaurant chains and was also trying to interest him in the project. Mac promised me that if he got the program going he would like to involve me in promoting it. This was an appealing idea if it could get off the ground, and quite timely because vertical integration in the feeding and marketing sectors was already underway.

When it became obvious to me that Cropsey's idea wasn't going to pan out, I approached Maxine with the possibility of applying for jobs that would require us to move, a prospect that did not appeal to either of us. We decided I had nothing to lose applying for some of the better jobs that came up from time to time, and if I got one that paid well, we could consider leasing the farm and returning to it when I retired. The American Gelveih Association granted me an interview and paid my travel expenses to Denver to meet their board of directors. The interview went well, but I could tell that they would like someone with a little more experience in performance testing, and of course probably the most damning was I was nearly sixty years old. I was disappointed when I didn't get the job, but my confidence had been bolstered by the fact I had gotten an interview, and I decided to keep trying. The fastest growing of the new, continental breed groups, the American Simmental Association, was also looking for an executive director, but I didn't get an interview for that job.

I was aware that the top position in the Santa Gertrudis Breeders Association was open, but I had been hesitant to apply because I had never been enthusiastic about their cattle. I finally decided to send an application and was invited to fly to Kingsville for an interview. I was in the strange position of personally knowing John Armstrong, who had recently been replaced as manager of the King Ranch by a younger family member, and knew his younger brother, Tobin, even better. I called Tobin and he told me that there had been a lot of changes in their breed association and he and John were no longer active. I learned later that there were not many applicants and the other person they interviewed was a Santa Gertrudis sales manager. Sometime during the interview, I expressed the opinion that I felt it was a conflict of interest for an employee to directly benefit from commissions for sales of members' cattle. The other guy got the job. I'm not sure I would have accepted the position if it had been offered, but the interview further bolstered my sagging self-esteem.

Since we had moved to Nebraska, we had tried to get to Colorado to visit Mom for a weekend every few months, and, of course we stopped to see her when we went skiing. By the winter of 1989-90, I thought she might be starting to fail. By late summer, when Elizabeth and her new husband Dave Askin, my brother Charlie, his wife Katherine, Maxine and I got together at Shirley's place south of Laramie for a picnic with her side of the family, I could tell Mom was not her old self. Chuck, who saw her nearly every day, said he had not noticed how quickly she had gone downhill. Over the years, I had made it a point to check up on the Kentucky Derby favorites in the spring and occasionally was able to visit her on Derby Day. When I had called her to discuss the race early in 1991, looking forward to finding out whom she was picking, it nearly broke my heart when I could tell she just wasn't interested in the race.

In spite of his slowly advancing multiple sclerosis, Charlie made it a point to drive over to the farm from their house in Thornton several times a week to check on Mom. He handled all her bills and had made arrangements for a neighbor lady to clean her house once a week and help Mom with her bath. He saw that she got to her long-time hairdresser for her monthly permanent. I knew that because Mom's balance had deteriorated over the previous ten years, she had stopped going downstairs. Charlie had bought a wheelchair for her and he kept it in his trunk to use when they went to the horse races in Denver. I was particularly concerned about Mom falling and breaking her hip, and wondered if Chuck was confident that he could continue getting her in and out of the house and into the wheelchair. He said he shared my concern about the seeming deterioration of both her physical and mental health, but was confident he could continue to look after her. When I shared my concern with her, it was obvious that she was quite happy with her current arrangements.

I continued to fret and worry about Mom living alone in her house and finally talked myself into a plan that worked out badly for all concerned. I told Maxine I didn't think it was fair for Charlie to have to continue looking after Mom, although he had never complained, but I knew that she would never consider moving in with Chuck and Katherine or us. She resisted the idea of finding someone to live with her or hiring at least a part-time nurse. I checked out the small nursing home in Hemingford, decided it had adequate facilities for her and talked Chuck and Mom into moving her into it. By the time I had helped her fill out all of the appropriate papers, I could tell Mom was having serious misgivings. I promised her I would come and have supper with her every night until she got settled. The first night, when I accompanied her to the dining room, she picked at her food for awhile and plaintively said, "I want to go home." I asked her to give it a try for a few days and left asking myself, "What have I done?" The next day I found her eating in a room by herself when I arrived at a little after five. The nurse on duty said she had been observed eating with her hands at lunch, which bothered the other people in the dining room. When I joined her at the table, she looked up rather listlessly and simply repeated that she wanted to go home. I couldn't stand the realization that I had pushed her into a situation so depressing, and told her I would make arrangements to get her back in her house.

    I immediately called Charlie when I got home and he agreed to get an incline built over the front steps of her house for the wheelchair, and would make arrangements to get her neighbor to look in on her more often. Charlie had not been too keen in the first place about my idea to move Mom, but was too decent to say, "I told you so." Mom immediately perked up when I told her she would be going home. I managed to get out of the agreement with the nursing home, but had to pay for one full month, even though she ended up being there about a week. I packed up Mom's few things and met Charlie at her house with the hope that things would get back to the way they were.

    A few days after I got home, Charlie called me at the office and told me Mom had fallen in the hall between her bedroom and bathroom and broken her hip. I drove back to Denver early the next morning and found her in the hospital where she had had a successful operation to repair the broken hip. The surgeon expressed confidence that she would fully recover, but I couldn't help recall her father had died on the operating table at age ninety-three while they were doing surgery on his broken hip. I soon learned that she was unwilling to even try to do any therapy. She had always been healthy, never having been to the hospital except to have her three boys, and to my knowledge had always had a strong heart. I tried to talk her into trying to use a walker as the therapist wished, but she never got out of bed again. She had simply lost the will to live. She finally went into a coma and died about forty-eight hours later. Either Charlie, his eldest son Charles or I were with her every minute those last three days. A few hours before she died, when I was holding her hand, she opened one eye for a moment, looked up at me and seemed to realize that I was there with her. I prayed this comforted her as much as it surely did me. She didn't let go of life readily. At the end she sat straight up in bed, took her last breath and fell back down on the pillow. I blurted out, "Oh Mom!" squeezed her hand for a few moments and she was gone.

Charlie had arranged Dad's funeral in accordance with his wishes, but Mom had never left any instructions about how she wanted her service handled. We decided to have a simple memorial at the mortuary before we buried her beside Dad at the Lilley Family plot at the Littleton Cemetery on Prince Street. We knew Mom would not want a minister conducting her funeral, so we settled on a fairly traditional service conducted by family members. I opened the service by reading her obituary. Next, Charlie talked briefly. Then Clay spoke on behalf of all of the nieces and nephews attending. I read a passage from the Bible selected by Katherine and followed that with a few anecdotes about Mom's love of horses, and I told the story about her joining the Daughters of the American Revolution—she was eligible through either of her paternal grandparents—in the 1930s. She had told me she thought seriously of resigning when Eleanor Roosevelt did after Marion Anderson was denied the use of the DAR Hall in Washington D.C. for a concert. She said she changed her mind when she considered that one of her grandchildren might want to join some day. Elizabeth did about twenty years after Mom's death. I then remarked that character was hard to define but easily recognized when observed, and that Julia F. Lilley had it in abundance. I closed the service by asking everyone to join me in saying the Lord's Prayer.

The mortuary furnished an organist, who sang three hymns that had been favorites at the Virginia Dale Community Church where mother had taught the adult class in the late 1930s: The Old Rugged Cross, I Walked in the Garden Alone and The Little Brown Church in the Vale. I asked the organist to change the words to The Little White Church in the Dale as we had always sung it. After the graveside ceremony, the family met at Mom's house and reminisced as we went through her things and some of Dad's, which were where they had been when he died thirteen years before, and tried to decide who might want what. We mostly selected items from Mom's overflowing china cabinet and several boxes of family photographs, including a couple of old albums, which Mom had stored in a large box. Katherine volunteered to conduct a garage sale to dispose of all the things that were left over. Shirley had the good sense to salvage a lot of pictures that no one wanted at the time, but which might turn out to be priceless to the next generation. Even though we had no place for it in our house, when no one else said they wanted it, I took Mom and Dad's antique solid mahogany bedroom set and stored it in one of the outbuildings on the farm. Uncle Luke had purchased it from Spiegel's Department Store in Chicago and had it shipped on the Union Pacific Railroad to his home in Cheyenne in 1883. As the family was enjoying visting at Mom's house, Maxine mentioned to Marian, Charie's daughter, that we should get together more often and the next time she would like it to be at our house.... Little did we know that this would be the case.

After Mom's funeral, things returned to near normal at the Lilley house. Jennifer and Brendan were both home from college for the summer. Steve, who had a good job at the new Burlington Northern Railroad facility, Shaun, Sarah and Steve's two daughters from a previous marriage were living in a house they had rented in Alliance. Maxine had finally been prescribed medicine that kept her occasional depression in check and was dealing with her other health problems without complaint, as usual. I had made peace with my new job situation and Maxine had made arrangements for Sarah and herself to visit Maxine's sister, Bev, in California the first week in August. In late July during Cheyenne Frontier Days, Shaun and Sarah joined the rest of us for a day trip to see George Strait, whom we first saw at our county fair. Following the show, we all spent an hour taking in all the activities scattered throughout the fenced area surrounding the rodeo arena. It was the first time we had all gotten together for quite a while, and as we drove home in the dusk, we remarked about how much we all had enjoyed the day. A few days after the Cheyenne trip, I had to flag for a team penning in central Nebraska, and Maxine and Sarah were to leave on their trip the next day. I had to start at about 6:00 a.m. to get to the penning by noon and Maxine had gotten up early to fix my breakfast. As I was telling her goodbye, she said she didn't feel very well, something you didn't hear from her very often. I kissed her forehead to see if she had a fever and felt her pulse. It was nearly 150 beats per minute. I knew she had worked hard all the previous day trying to get things organized for the trip and her asthma had flared up a little. We sat on the front steps a while and she assured me she would be fine. I should have insisted that she let me take her to the doctor, but I didn't know whom I could call to let them know I would be unable to flag the stupid team penning. What followed was a day that perfectly fit Murphy's Law, "If anything can go wrong it will."

Everything that could go wrong at a team penning did. After two teams had competed, a couple of the numbers glued on either side of the cattle fell off and we had to stop and replace them. The same thing happened a few more times and then a slow rain started falling. This caused the ink to run and made the numbers difficult to read, a significant disadvantage to the later contestants. Instead of being over a bit early as I had hoped, the contest lagged on until nearly dark because half the teams had to be allowed to run again after numbers were replaced. I wanted to call the whole thing off, but the contestants met during one of our delays and voted to finish the contest. When it did finally grind to an end, I jumped into my car, a nervous wreck, and headed home. By the time I got to Hyannis, I was so sleepy I had to pull to the side of the road and take a catnap at the wheel.

I woke up with a start from my troubled sleep just as it was getting light in the West. I pulled into the yard just as the sun was coming up and found Jennifer sitting on the step where I had left Maxine. She said she had taken Mama to the doctor late the previous afternoon and she had been admitted to the hospital. Naturally she was very concerned that I was not in the house and thought perhaps I was outside doing chores. We immediately drove to the hospital. Maxine did not look at all well, but said she was doing fine. She didn't seem to want to visit and soon turned her face to the wall and said, "Goodbye," something Brendan used to do when he was a little boy and didn't want to talk. I told her I'd let her get some sleep and went to the office for a while to check the mail and make some calls. In about an hour Shaun, who was working that day, called from the hospital and told me to pick up

Grandma Ilene and come to the hospital. When we arrived, we were taken to a private waiting room and found Shaun, Jennifer and Brendan already there. Evidently, when our family doctor arrived at the hospital at eight he had looked at Maxine's chart and immediately had her taken to the emergency room. After we had spent an anxious hour in the room the doctor came in and asked our permission to use the defibrillator to try to get Maxine's heart beating correctly, because she had a living will requesting no extreme measures be used it if she were unconscious. It finally dawned on me that we could lose her as I said, "Of course." A few minutes later "code blue" came over the public-address system and, when I looked at Shaun's face, I knew what that meant. After an agonizing period of time, the doctor returned and said that in spite of their best efforts they had been unable to stabilize Maxine's heartbeat. It had eventually stopped and they were unable to restart it.

The death certificate listed the cause of death as heart failure triggered by ventricular fibrillation. From what I have learned since, I am pretty sure that an asthma inhalant used excessively while getting ready for the California trip had triggered the fibrillation.

We were all in a state of shock for a few days and I buried my guilt and grief by immediately diving into all the details that had to be quickly dealt with. Charles Iodence showed up early the first morning with a breakfast casserole and for two days, neighbor after neighbor showed up with food. Elizabeth joined the family just as soon as she could get to Hemingford and stayed with us a week. We had the funeral at the Episcopal Church in Alliance and buried Maxine in the Hemingford Cemetery. After the burial service, the neighbors helped us host what resembled a family picnic at the farm. I had picked up four association board members and Chuck Ball at the airport.

Gary Glick and Bozo Simianer, who were both pall bearers, stayed a day and my kids, who were well acquainted with both, enjoyed listening to us reminisce about the old days. After everyone had gone, I sat down at Maxine's desk to see about paying the bills. Everything was in perfect order except for the pile of mail left by me over the past few days. I found an envelope with my name on it containing an outline of basically everything I needed to know to handle our affairs. I discovered another envelope with $700 in cash and the airplane tickets for her trip to California with Sarah. I got a refund on the tickets by sending the airline a death certificate. Our bills were all paid and I was not surprised to see how much money we actually had in our bank account. I had a separate account for our cattle operation and wrote all the checks on it, although Maxine always posted the bills and farm income. As I reviewed her books later, I found that she also kept a complete set of books on household expenses and depreciated our major appliances by saving money in escrow for their replacement. Other than our large monthly payment for the interest on the farm loan, we had no outstanding debt.

The association's annual convention was the third week of August, so I had a lot of office work to catch up on. I needed to help Jim with his Cow/Calf Council agenda, finalize my membership report and shake down merchants that sold products to the cattle industry for prizes to award at the convention to members who had sold the largest number of new memberships during the current year. This was one of my least favorite jobs, but it was important to recognize people who had given their time throughout the year to call on their neighbors and tout the advantages of belonging to Nebraska Cattlemen, Inc.

The primary responsibility that Chuck assigned me during the convention was something I had a lot of experience doing. I collected the resolutions discussed and approved by the committees and councils; worked with the staff, primarily Kathy, to get them typed using the word processor in Chuck's computer; and proofread and printed them for consideration by members at the business meeting the last day. The printer Chuck had hired to do the job had said they could have the several hundred copies back to us by 2:00 p.m. the following day, if we got the material to them by 11:00 p.m. At about 10:30, Chuck showed up and we stewed over minute details until after midnight, when I finally threw up my hands and went to bed. This was the third year in a row we were late getting the copy to the printer and I was at the end of my tether. I apologized to Kathy the next morning for running out on her and she said not to worry because there was nothing I could have done to change the situation.

After Jim Gran had given his Cow/Calf Council report and other council and committee chairmen were giving their reports, I asked Jim to come up to my room for a little break. As I recall, Jim simply mentioned to me that he thought I was holding up well for all I had been through recently. I started sharing some of the things that I had bottled up and soon I was simply babbling and weeping. At that moment, I really needed a friend, and although Jim was embarrassed, when I quit sobbing he simply put his hand on my shoulder and told me he understood what I had been through. With my short-lived breakdown over, I went back to my convention duties as if nothing had happened. At the social hour before the banquet, I was talking to Cecelia, who was in complete charge of all the convention activities, when she paid me a rather unsettling compliment. She said that I was, perhaps, the only man she had ever met who really loved his wife.

61

Reprieve

Brendan and Jennifer were both living at home when Maxine died. Jennifer was home for the summer, having completed her first year at the University of Wyoming following her two years at the junior college in Torrington. She offered to transfer to Chadron State College, which was only thirty-five miles north of the farm, but I encouraged her to continue pursuing her degree in education at Wyoming U. Brendan had gone to work for a surveyor in Alliance right after he got his degree in civil engineering from the South Dakota School of Mines and I enjoyed having him living with me at home.

I continued to put up the hay and look after the cows and appreciated Brendan's help on the weekends when I needed to haul in bales or build fence. I had finally completely given up on the job that Dr. Cropsey had been promising me. It was problematic that he could get Armand Hammer and his wealthy fast food mogul to finance his vertically integrated "Semen to Steak," a horrible name, concept. Since I was now sixty-one years old, I gave some thought to taking my Social Security at sixty-two and trying to either buy or rent enough farm and pasture ground to raise cattle full time. I had fun checking the real estate ads on weekends when I was out scouting for membership, looking at places I probably couldn't afford. I found one place that looked as if it might work just north of Scottsbluff. It had a year-round stream running through its pasture land and had a couple of good wells that irrigated quite a bit of terraced farm ground. The ditches were all cemented, which was good, but I knew it needed a better irrigator than I was. It had one good house on it that was currently rented and another small one that would work for me to batch in and I started looking into financing. By the time I was ready to make an offer, the place had already sold.

I still loved the farm, but it just wasn't the same without Maxine. I had left everything just the way it was the day she went to the hospital. Her clothes were all hanging in the closet and everything was on top of her dresser just as she left it. I hired a woman from Hemingford to clean the house every two weeks. Maxine had left it spotless and Brendan and I, particularly Brendan, were pretty neat bachelors. I got up early every morning to do the chores and often stayed at the office later at night than I needed to.

I still had the responsibility of the team penning, but managed to get the contestants themselves to do a lot of the work that Troy and Joyce used to do for them. A couple of years before the merger, the NLFA had taken up team penning and Paul Johnston had the good sense to let their contestants manage every aspect of the activity. They had slightly different rules than NSGA's and they fussed about things like a western dress code, which irritated NSGA old timers. Gradually fewer and fewer teams from the west competed, but the few that did were quite good.

When the newly merged organization had its first state-wide team penning finals, they were held in Broken Bow, which is in the middle of the state. I got Troy Smith to flag the event and help get it organized. All the staff from Lincoln attended and seemed to enjoy watching. Weirdly enough, my insecurity caused me to try to ingratiate myself with Chuck and I thought he would like to present the trophies from horseback to the winners. It was a bad idea and ended up looking a little silly. The board of directors of the newly formed Nebraska Cattlemen was not very enthusiastic about team penning and I certainly didn't push it, but there was one member from Saunders County that was actively involved and he single-handedly talked the board into keeping the event under the auspices of the organization.

I was called on occasionally at board meetings to help with some arcane point in the bylaws or Roberts Rules of Order, but I pretty much spoke when spoken to the rest of the time.

During the annual convention of the National Cattlemen's Association in January, 1992 I noticed that Chuck's relationship with the association's leadership in attendance had cooled a great deal. The previous two years he was with the officers and committee members constantly and coordinated all of their activities as I had when I was the Executive Vice President of the NSGA. I commented on this to my fellow staff members from Lincoln and they were rather guarded in their response, but I knew morale in the Lincoln office was not good. I still enjoyed the annual conventions and always attended our regional caucus, the executive officer's luncheon and my assigned committee meetings. Jim Gran and I were pleased about one thing that happened at the NCA convention that year. NC's Integrated Resource Management program was recognized as outstanding and received $2,500 from MSD Agvet, an agricultural pharmaceutical company for our efforts in Nebraska, which had already reached 2,000 producers in the state. Through the Cow/calf Council, Nebraska had been one of the states that pioneered the concept.

The second night of NCA conventions never had any scheduled activities so that those attending could socialize, and I was invited to join our officers and Chuck for a night on the town. We had dinner at a well-known steakhouse and then went to a nightclub that featured topless go-go dancers performing on tables. The five of us joined about seven other customers at the chairs set around one of the tables and enjoyed the view and more than a few drinks. I sat next to Chuck and found that I was the only one of our group inclined to visit with him. I had learned that he was good company in social settings when I had joined him, Shane, Hank and Dean on a few occasions in the evening after meetings when I had to spend the night in Lincoln. They were all bright young men and fun to be with.

We stayed at the bar long enough that a second dancer replaced the one who had been entertaining us. Like the previous one, she seemed quite young and certainly not hard looking at all. Anyone who watched Laugh In was acquainted with go-go dancing, but I had never observed it live before. As the girls danced around the table they often approached one of the customers who was holding out folded paper money so they could slip it into their panties. When I took my turn, I noticed quite a scar on our girl's thigh and when she bent over to receive my dollar bill asked her what had happened. She said she'd been in an automobile accident. Chuck had evidently observed this exchange and when we were all heading to the hotel in the taxi, he said I needed to think about getting married again. He said he had lost his mother just before he came to Lincoln and his Dad was just starting to date. I was somehow touched and said I had not given any thought to it, but perhaps I should.

I had developed high blood pressure in the last couple of years and had been told I should not drink alcohol while taking my blood pressure medicine. I had always loved my before dinner drink and soon learned that I could easily handle one drink, and in fact, enjoyed the fact that the one now gave me as much buzz as several might have previously. When I got out of the taxi I immediately realized that I had drunk too much. I walked unsteadily into the hotel lobby and bid my friends good night. Before I got into the elevator I ran into one of the NCA past presidents, whom I knew rather well. He was considerably further into his cups than I, and I visited with him and the equally inebriated executive officer from his state, sharing some gossip about association politics. I then managed to make it over to the elevator and as I was riding it up to my room, I got the giggles. I managed to unlock the door to my room, stagger over to my bed, sit down on the corner of it and fall onto the floor. I lay there for a while laughing, then managed to get up to get undressed and into bed, where I slept peacefully. I woke up the next morning feeling great and could remember every bit of what had happened the night before, actually quite fondly. I had always been able to hold my liquor until the time I threw up and knew I had not consumed much. It suddenly dawned on me that the only thing the alcohol had seriously affected was my balance and what had struck me as so funny the night before was my staggering around.

Sometime in the summer of 1992, I was asked to attend a special meeting of the board of directors in Lincoln. Chuck was not present and before it was called to order, President Delayne Loeseke asked me to take the minutes. Paul Johnston had resigned the previous year to be the Assistant Secretary of Agriculture in Governor Kay Orr's administration, and I had lost my best source of information from the Lincoln office. Consequently, I had little idea of what was going on. I soon learned that the only item on the agenda was a discussion of the possibility of asking for Chuck's resignation as executive vice president. As I recall, DeLayne looked at me and said something to the effect that he had told the executive committee there was a grey-haired guy in the Alliance office who could hold down the fort while this problem was being dealt with.

Ever since the National Cattlemen's Association convention, I had suspected that something was in the wind, and I appreciated having regained the confidence of the board. After the meeting was called to order, one of the directors moved that the board go into executive session to discuss a personnel matter, and the motion was seconded and passed unanimously. Being a state-chartered nonprofit organization, our minutes had to be published, however all that had to be recorded from an executive session was the action taken. The executive committee had put together a list of complaints concerning Chuck's performance, which among other things, included his contribution to low staff morale, his undecipherable budgets and financial statements and his role in ongoing feuds with the Nebraska Beef Council and the Nebraska Cattle Women. Several board members defended Chuck and others thought he should be given an opportunity to defend himself and be allowed to correct the problems. I was simply keeping the minutes and only entered the discussion a couple of times when some matter of record needed to be confirmed. They agreed that the board needed more time to think about these issues, and when we came out of executive session, a motion was approved to give Chuck an opportunity at the next regularly scheduled meeting of the board of directors to respond to these issues.

I was instructed to continue sitting in on executive committee meetings and asked to prepare the agenda and send out the notice for the next board meeting. At that meeting, they brought me up to date on the issues that led to the action concerning Chuck and asked if I had anything to add. I said that those of us in the Alliance office had very little contact with Lincoln except during the weekly conference calls, but could confirm that Chuck often procrastinated signing checks sitting on his desk, which caused complaints from our vendors. And when our paychecks arrived in the mail late, it caused staff members to be late paying their bills.

I knew nothing of the terms of Chuck's employment at the time he was hired, but he obviously thought he had cause to fight his termination. He came to the September 4, 1992 meeting fully prepared to defend himself. We once again went into executive session and, as I recall, Cecelia either presented some additional information to the board or had given it to someone who passed it on, and it was extremely significant to the outcome. In deference to my having been made privy to the discussion when the board was in executive session, I will relate only the action recommended. It stated that the association accept Chuck's immediate resignation in accordance with a mutually agreed upon non-disclosure document. Someone moved to approve the action coming out of the executive session and it passed with only one negative vote.

The next item of business was to hire a new permanent executive, and I was named acting executive vice president. When given the opportunity, I said I would very much like to have the job, but was not the least bit interested in accepting it on an interim basis. I was asked to leave the room, and when I returned I found that they had voted unanimously to hire me if we could agree to terms, although it had been suggested that I confer with Hank Rogers on matters affecting the Feedlot Council. I said I had no problem with that but wanted to have the final word and, of course, would consult with the board on other than day-to-day management decisions. I also said that I had no great desire to work beyond my retirement age three years hence. When the matter of salary came up, I asked for whatever Chuck was currently making, but was offered considerably less. I then said I would accept his starting salary—he had already received several substantial raises plus a large bonus, while mine had stayed constant—if they would pay for an apartment for me in Lincoln. I indicated that I would be traveling to the Alliance office more often than Chuck had, and when possible would be going home to my farm on weekends. A motion was made, seconded and passed unanimously to hire me as executive vice president according to the terms I had just outlined.

For the previous few months I had dared hope that this very thing could happen, and now I had to prove I could rise to the challenge.

Cattlemen Name Lilley Executive Vice President

LINCOLN — Roy Lilley was named Thursday by the Nebraska Cattlemen Board of Directors as Executive Vice President of the Nebraska Cattlemen association.

Lilley has spent his adult life working for cattle associations, starting with the American National Cattle Association (ANAC), predecessor to the National Cattlemen's Association (NCA). He then served four years with the New Mexico Cattle Growers and a 15-year term at the International Brangus Breeders Association as executive vice president prior to joining the Nebraska Stock Growers Association in 1979.

Lilley was born and raised on the Table Mountain Ranch in northern Colorado. He is a graduate of Colorado State University, formerly Colorado A&M, with a bachelor's degree in animal science and post graduate work in animal breeding and genetics.

In accepting the NC position, Lilley said he is glad to have been involved in the merger four years ago of the Nebraska Stock Growers Association, Nebraska Livestock Feeders Association and Nebraska Feedlot Council which created the Nebraska Cattlemen. "I am delighted to have an expanded opportunity to further the growth of the association," Lilley said.

The announcement follows the resignation of Chuck Ball on August 31. Ball had served as Executive Vice President since January 1989.

The Nebraska Cattlemen association serves as the spokesman for the state's beef cattle industry and represents nearly 5,000 cattle breeders, ranchers and feeders, as well as 54 county and local cattlemen's associations.

Roy Lilley

Clipping on promotion to Execv. V P. of the newly merged Nebraska Cattlemen.

62

Cleaning Up Messes

As soon as I was hired as executive vice president of the Nebraska Cattlemen, I had to find an apartment in Lincoln and make a decision about what to do with the farm in Hemingford. The first problem was solved shortly after the news of my promotion was announced in our weekly newsletter. Barb Marcy, who was a member of the Beef Council and had a family-owned registered Angus operation in western Nebraska, called to ask if I would like to take over the lease on her daughter's apartment in Lincoln because she wanted to move back home. I told her I would be happy to take a look at it. It turned out to be just what I wanted, a garden level, one-bedroom apartment not far from our office and in a price range acceptable to the board.

It took a few weeks to work out what to do with the farm. Fortunately, it was summer and I didn't have to worry about feeding any livestock, but I knew I would need to have someone living in the house come winter. Shaun and Steve were living in a rented house in Alliance and I asked them if they would like to live on the farm and look after it for me for the rent. I was confident this would suit Shaun and was pleased when Steve indicated he liked the idea very much. They gave notice to their landlord and soon moved in. Their son, Seth, had been born when they were in Alliance, and Katie was born about the time they moved to the farm, so the house was pretty crowded when I stayed with them during my visits to the Alliance office or came home for weekends. I continued to keep Hemingford as my legal address and couldn't help but dwell on the fact that if I had gotten one of those jobs I had applied for during my season of discontent, I would have dragged Maxine away from her beloved farm.

I had to deal with a problem the first week I was in Lincoln. Chuck had gotten crossways with a reporter from the Lincoln Journal who covered agriculture and was often critical of NC. He did have an abrasive personality, but I managed to get him off our back by killing him with kindness. By being evasive, Chuck had left the impression that we had some kind of hidden agenda on several legislative items, and when I told him more than he wanted to know about everything we did, he lost interest.

Another matter I had to deal with when I arrived in Lincoln turned out to be more difficult. About the time I got there, the governor announced an appointment to the board that oversaw the brand inspection system covering the western two-thirds of the state. For many years, the governor had named whomever the Nebraska Stock Growers Association had recommended, and it was possible that a recommendation had simply not been made during the turmoil of recent months. In any case, the man nominated was not a member of the Nebraska Cattlemen and, in fact, had often taken positions contrary to our policies when he served in the legislature several years prior. When I called the governor's office to register our objections, I was told that it was too late to make a recommendation and the appointment must stand. I was a little too candid with my reporter friend from the Lincoln Journal expressing my dissatisfaction with the appointee. When the paper came out with my comments I found it necessary to go see the newly appointed board member immediately to smooth things over as best I could. Our main objection to his being appointed was the fact that he was a registered lobbyist.

I was soon able to re-establish a good working relationship with two closely allied groups that we had managed to get crossways with over the previous several years. The first was the Nebraska Beef Council. Just as I had feared, Chuck Ball and Tom Scott had a strained relationship and, in fact, they eventually got to the point that they wouldn't speak to each other. We managed to get the problem with the Beef Quality Assurance Program straightened out, Tom Scott soon moved on to another job out of state and we resumed working hand in hand with them.

Another problem was that the NLFA and NSGA involved their wives in their activities in different ways and hadn't resolved the differences in the years since the merger. The NLFA had a women's auxiliary that had never been extremely active. The NSGA had always been closely associated with their women's organization, the Cow Belles, which were also affiliated with the national organization of the same name until they changed it into simply Cattlewomen. I had worked closely with the Cow Belles under NSGA and met with their officers soon after taking the job in Lincoln to see about bringing the two women's groups closer together. A joint committee was formed, and out of it grew an independently incorporated organization now also called The Cattlewomen. This effort took several years to completely gel; however, the feeling that the newly merged Nebraska Cattlemen wasn't supportive of the women's wishes was dispelled.

Soon after Logan McClelland was elected president to succeed Byron Eatinger at the November annual convention in Omaha, two internal matters that related to Chuck's tenure jumped up and bit us. Kathy and Cecelia had quit their jobs soon after I moved to Lincoln in the fall of 1992, and I was shocked when a summons was handed to us to respond to allegations filed by Kathy of sexual harassment by Chuck. I soon learned that we were made a party to the suit because, among other things, we did not then have a staff handbook for dealing with such things. I immediately called Logan and we contacted a lawyer. I knew Chuck was a good family man and told Logan I was confident we could defend ourselves. I called Kathy on the phone to see what I could learn from her, and asked Logan to get on the extension so I would have a witness to the conversation. Kathy said she could not talk specifically about the case; however, it became apparent that Cecelia was giving her a lot of advice. I was called to testify two different times during the proceedings and said only that the accusations did not ring true to me and I certainly could not corroborate any of them.

I felt the cost of defending ourselves was less than the amount we could be fined and the damages we might have to pay Kathy if we lost. Logan had immediately called a special board meeting to plan our strategy when I told him what faced us. A few members wanted to try to settle out of court, but Logan and I convinced a majority we could prevail. The board moved to let us handle the matter and authorized us to hire the lawyer.

Working with the law firm and testifying at the hearing were educational experiences. Some of the accusations were quite damning and had involved others in the association. I reported this to the board without any further detail. They expressed their appreciation for the way Logan and I handled the problem and told us they didn't need to hear any more about the matter. I locked the record of the proceedings in my drawer and to my knowledge no one but Logan and I ever read them. It turned out Kathy had no other witness than Cecelia and the charges were dropped.

A few weeks later we were visited by a workman's compensation auditor, who reviewed the last several years of withholding we had paid them. After several days of wading through our records, he told us he would be back in touch with us soon. About a week later we received a bill for around $10,000 for three years of under-payments and a substantial penalty. It seemed that non-administrative members of the staff were to have been paid overtime for all their hours worked over forty per week. The auditor had reviewed the detailed reports we all made each week as part of Chuck's accounting system and they had us dead to right. I called our lawyer once again and she managed to help us appeal the bill. We got several employees whom the auditor called hourly workers re-classified as having administrative responsibilities, reducing our bill by several thousand dollars. Hank Rogers and Mike Fitzgerald had already written what turned out to be a model employee's handbook covering procedures for reporting sexual harassment, detailed job descriptions, vacation policy and several other items relating to personnel matters. Unfortunately, we had shut the barn door after the horse had escaped.

I quickly came to appreciate the fact that Chuck had hired an excellent staff and I was more than happy to give them the opportunity to do their jobs. Dean Settje had already developed a reputation as one of the better-informed people in the state concerning the Nebraska Department of Environmental Quality's oversight of feedlots. Hank Rogers had put together a market reporting service for our unique Nebraska cattle feeding industry equal to that of the Texas Cattle Feeders. Shane had quickly straightened out our problems with the Nebraska Beef Council relating to the Beef Quality Assurance program and he became my go-to man for new projects. Mike Fitzgerald was a thoroughly professional magazine editor and communications director, and he soon took over the responsibilities of caring for our foundation. I had the good fortune to find an excellent young woman to replace Cecelia managing our conventions and planning and scheduling all our other meetings—and it was good to have Deb back as my secretary.

The five-man executive committee made up of the three current officers and two more members of the Board appointed by the Board, met every month, and was indispensable in working through the workmen's compensation issue and the sexual harassment hearings. Byron Eatinger, who also served on the Board of Directors of the Federal Land Bank, had obtained a copy of that large organization's employee's handbook that served as a useful guide for developing ours.

With our convention coming up, I was faced with the challenge of preparing a budget for the coming year. I had a hard time figuring out how to change the way we reported income and expenses so they could be compared with Chuck's complex budget of the previous year. I prepared a draft budget that made sense to me and ran it by Hank, our computer guru. He unraveled the mystery of Chuck's system, which had salaries buried in every line item so no one could tell how much any employee earned or even the total salaries paid without a lot of digging. We finally came up with a budget much like what I had been preparing for years, which was far less complex. At my first convention I had Hank give me a printout of the entire year's check register. This was so I could offer the extraneous minutia that had been in the previous several years' budgets for those who had grown used to suffering through a three-hour financial report. Part of our problem had been trying to work into our budgeting process the complications of crediting our income back to four different councils. Actually, this requirement was put in the by-laws only as a means of allocating board members to them based on their respective share of dues revenue.

We continued with our weekly staff meetings, but they lasted only about an hour instead of three or more. The whole staff no longer agonized over the details of every activity we were involved in. At one of my first staff meetings, when we were discussing our upcoming convention, I said that I really didn't care how some matter was handled because that's why we had a staff member to manage the convention. Hank chuckled and then they all burst out laughing. When I asked them what was the matter, someone said that he never thought he would hear that from the boss. Morale had gotten low from working long hours and not seeming to get much accomplished. I told them I saw no reason we shouldn't be able to get our work done during normal office hours and that non-administrative staff members would receive overtime pay when they worked over forty hours, but our goal was to not work such long hours in the first place. I hired an excellent bookkeeper, a personable woman closer to my age than the rest of the staff. Chuck had relieved Mary Broad in the Alliance office of that job and she asked for and received the opportunity to do the janitorial work there. When I moved to Lincoln, I had managed to rent the Alliance office to the Alliance Economic Development Council, reserving my old office, which I used from time to time, until we were able to hire a staff person to work in the west end of the state. I was fortunate to find Sarah Kettle, a recent graduate with a degree in equine science from CSU as well as a member of the first class to integrate a new leadership training program. She was well received and soon had our membership in that area growing again.

*****

Steve and Shaun got along fine for a while looking after the farm, but by summer it was obvious Steve wasn't working out as well as I had hoped. Also, he and Shaun were having marital problems. When Shaun married Steve, we didn't know much about him. As I mentioned earlier, his father was the first person I met when we moved to Nebraska and I had learned he and his family were well respected in the community. It wasn't until just before the wedding that we learned Steve had been married before and had two adolescent girls. We became apprehensive that Shaun had made a bad choice. Not long after they moved to the farm, Steve's ex-wife got into trouble with the law in another state and was thrown in jail, causing Steve to get possession of his two daughters and putting further strain on a marriage that was already shaky. Still, he seemed to enjoy taking care of the livestock and being a weekend farmer, and he and Shaun worked out some of their differences, so things straightened out for a while. Unfortunately, it wasn't long until Steve was put on probation by the railroad for a second time and Shaun finally filed for divorce after a few more failed reconciliations. Shaun, Sarah, Seth and Katie moved into a small house in Hemingford, which Maxine's sister, Beverly, purchased for them, and I was faced with figuring out what to do about caring for the livestock before winter.

In the meanwhile, I drove to the farm every weekend I could and on the ones Jennifer didn't come home from college, I often visited her there, staying with her at the little house that her Aunt Shirley was furnishing her. She had adapted well to college and had started dating some. In the spring of 1992, she began going steady with a ranch boy from Farson, Wyoming, named Marvin Applequist. Everyone called him Trip because his full name was Marvin Nathanial Applequist III. When the spring semester ended, Jennifer brought him home to meet me. I had met him a time or two when I was in Laramie and found him easy to like. He was quiet and obviously intelligent, and was taking pre-vet courses at Wyoming hoping to get into Veterinary School. The first time Jennifer brought him home with her, he asked me to take a drive out to the pasture in the pickup with him on the pretense of looking at the cows, and took the opportunity to ask me for Jennifer's hand. It was an old-fashioned gesture and I was touched. I told him I would be proud to have him as my son-in-law. Trip soon popped the question and they decided to get married in the spring of 1993, right after Jennifer graduated and Trip finished his junior year. As it turned out, Trip was accepted into vet school at Kansas State in Manhattan after only three years of pre-vet, which was quite unusual. His out-of-state tuition was to be paid under a multi-state agreement for land-grant colleges that did not have schools of veterinary medicine, such as Wyoming. They took a brief honeymoon, returned to Farson to work on the ranch for the rest of the summer and then moved to Manhattan.

Poor Jennifer had to plan her wedding with her father, typically a mother's job. Trip and his mother were Catholics, so we decided to have the wedding at the Catholic church in Hemingford. We had the reception and a dance at the American Legion Hall in Alliance.

There were several good stores in Scottsbluff where we could shop for wedding dresses. After Jennifer had tried on several, she came out of the dressing room in one in which she looked so beautiful I nearly cried. I had no idea what I was looking for, but I somehow knew that was the one. Jennifer seemed to like it so we had the first of the many things done that wedding planning demanded. A girl who had competed in horse shows with Jennifer when she was in high school had started a photography business and we engaged her for the wedding pictures. We arranged for a simple meal for invited guests at the American Legion, hired a western band to play for the dance that followed and, as was the local custom, the entire community was invited.

    Aunt Shirley and one of her good friends helped with the selection of dresses for the bridesmaids and ordered all the flowers. Trip decided what he, the best man and the other groomsmen would wear. The wedding went off beautifully except that I started crying the moment I started down the aisle to give Jennifer away and quietly wept during the ceremony. I had certainly never cried at a wedding before and was only glad that I didn't break into sobs as I usually did on the rare occasions when I cried. One of my friends told me that he thought it was probably a delayed reaction to the loss of Jennifer's mother. If it was, it was an unusual combination of happiness and grief.

63

Retirement

After Shaun divorced Steve and moved to Hemingford I decided to sell the farm. Before I moved to Lincoln, Shaun, Elizabeth and Jennifer had gone through the closet and picked out those items of Maxine's clothes that they could use; I hauled the rest to Goodwill. I still left everything on top of her dresser just as it had been, and I somehow found comfort sleeping in our queen-size bed. When I had to move to the basement when I visited home, I was forced to accept the fact that the dream of retiring to the farm was a shared one that was now shattered, so I decided to hold a farm sale in preparation for selling the place. I now had three pickups, including Brendan's little Datsun, two tractors, numerous farm implements, the welder, our boat with the outboard motor we used for waterskiing and a large shop full of miscellaneous tools. I also had about thirty-five 16-foot, 4-inch aluminum pipes, some perforated, and the fittings to connect them. I used them to flood irrigate our yard and the pasture next to the irrigation well. Unfortunately, the well had recently caved in so I could no longer irrigate with it or fill the cistern, which was essential for our complex alternate gravity flow water supply for both the house and stock water.

I contacted a local auctioneer to sell our accumulated farm equipment and listed the farm with a realtor. I spent a couple of weekends cleaning up the farm and helping the auctioneer organize everything for our little farm sale. My biggest job was digging the irrigation pipe, which carried water from the cistern to the yard, out of the grass that had grown around it over the many years it had been used before the well gave out.

The kids all came home for the Saturday sale, which cleared about $12,500 after I paid the commission. I managed to sell the cows and bull at private treaty to a nearby rancher, but still had to do something with the horses. I had sold the horse I had broke named White Wash to Joy Johannes three years previously, and had bred our Arabian mare, Rosie, to Joy's registered Arab stallion.

I had a two-year-old gelding from that mating. I named it Sham and started breaking it about the time Maxine died. Socks had recently died of old age and, to some degree, neglect, because I had not given any of the horses the care they needed the previous couple of years. I sent Rosie and Easter, a buckskin mare, to the ranch in Farson, Wyoming for Jennifer and Trip to use on the ranch. I had made friends with a lobbyist, whose family had a farm near Lincoln, and he agreed to let me keep Sham on their place. I was hoping I could continue to ride him on the weekends because he was not completely broke.

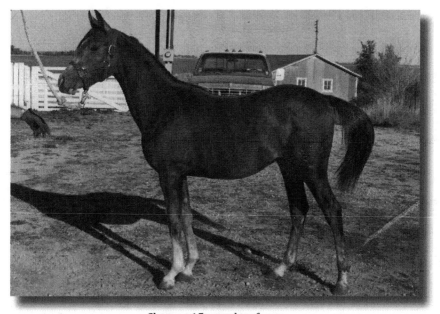

Sham at 15 months of age.

It took about four months to sell the farm. Land values had not yet recovered from the agricultural depression in the mid-eighties and I felt fortunate to sell it for enough to cover what we had paid for it after the commission. I paid Mom's estate, which had not yet been settled, the $65,000 that I still owed her. She had gifted Charlie and me each $10,000, which I applied back to the note. This still left me with a considerable amount of cash when added to the money I had received for the cows and the farm sale. I was now earning $60,000 a year instead of $40,000. Only recently I had barely been able to make the payment on the farm and meet all our other expenses. Now I no longer owned a home and didn't have any rent or farm payment, but I continued my frugal lifestyle. Still, the satisfaction I got in my new job meant a good deal more to me than the newfound wealth.

When the lease was up on my garden level apartment in Lincoln, I decided to move to one with two-bedrooms so the association's president could stay with me when he was in town. Shortly after the merger we had started paying our president's out-of-pocket expenses when he was on association business, but they rarely turned in an expense account. Byron Eatinger and Logan McClellan were the two who most often stayed with me. I put the antique mahogany bedroom set in the spare bedroom and told them both what a fine new mattress it had. I thought I had bought Mom a new mattress a few years before she died, but actually it had been much longer ago than that and I never learned until I was being roasted at my retirement party how uncomfortable it was.

In March I formally announced my intention to retire at the year's end. A seven-member executive search committee was chosen from the board to seek a replacement.

In August Greg Ruehle, Director of Private Lands for NCA, was selected to succeed me as executive vice president as of January 1, 1996.

At the November annual convention, I was honored for my seventeen years of service to both NSGA and NC, with a combination retirement ceremony and roast. I had told my staff that I was not particularly interested in receiving the traditional gold watch when I retired, so they surprised me with the gift of a pair of handmade spurs. They were decorated with raised gold letters of my reversed LIL brand and the letters NC, and were presented in a glass box with a bronze plate on it engraved with the words "World's Greatest Boss." They were not only a work of art but a useful pair of spurs, which I soon put to use. President Flaming, on behalf of the association, presented with me with the fender of a saddle—the large oblong piece of leather between one's leg and the horse—with the letters NC tooled in an outline of the state of Nebraska. I was thanking the association for the nice symbolic memento when outgoing President Flaming interrupted me to say that it was just a small part of a saddle they were having made for me, which could not be completed in time to present at the convention. He instructed me to drive to Arthur, Nebraska after the convention to tell the well-known custom saddle maker there named Rose, just what kind of saddle I wanted. I still had my dad's saddle and one of the two I had won during my rodeo days, but I couldn't have asked for a better retirement gift.

After the presentation of gifts, several of the past presidents took turns reminiscing about the many hours we spent together during their tenure. George Chilton related that we often came home from meetings quite late at night and I usually did all the driving. He said he could always tell when I was getting sleepy—I suddenly stopped talking—and he would have to make me pull over and let him drive. Byron Eatinger said he enjoyed staying with me when he was in town even though the mattress on the antique bed I was so proud of left him with a sore back. Logan agreed with George that I loved to talk and said he wished Byron had let me know about the bad mattress. He added that one advantage of traveling with me was that I knew all the small-town restaurants that had good homemade pie. Several other speakers mentioned my love of pie and my tendency to plan my meals around dessert. The last to speak was Jim Gran with whom I had worked not only as an NSGA president at the start of my tenure in Nebraska, but extensively during the merger process, and finally as chairman of the new organization's Cow/Calf Council. He managed to get in some good shots since he knew me better than anyone else. I responded to all these anecdotes with a few of my own and then briefly and candidly reviewed both the highs and lows of my time in Nebraska. I closed by expressing how thankful I was for the fact that the last few years had been by far the most enjoyable of my forty-five years in cattle association work.

Greg Ruehle reported for work two weeks before I left. The first week I had him at a desk in the basement reviewing our budget, last year's board minutes and our bylaws, among other things. The next week I gave him my desk, moved to the basement and kept out of his way while I wrapped up my affairs. The committee that was delegated the responsibility for picking my replacement was confident it had selected the right man because all of us had worked with him the last ten years in his various capacities at NCA. We had gotten many more applicants this time than when Chuck Ball was hired right after the merger, and it pleased me to think that Greg was taking the reins of a stable organization with an excellent staff.

I attended the NCA convention in San Antonio the next month, even though I had already moved to Manhattan, Kansas to live with Jennifer and Marvin. During the NCBA banquet I was presented a statuette created by well-known cowboy artist, Jerry Palin, a traditional recognition for executive officers of NCA affiliates when they retired.

In a short three-year period, my career as a cattle association executive had bounced from its lowest ebb to a climax even better than my optimistic nature could have imagined. After having attended all but four of the last forty-five conventions of ANCA, then NCA and finally NCBA, it was nice, for the first time, to just take in all the activities without any responsibilities.

From left to right: Gary Glick, me, Bozo and Ray Nauta at my second retirement in party in Alliance in 1996.

Roy Lilley lives in Fort Collins with his wife, Donice, who has two grown sons, one of whom is married and has two children. His children have blessed him with seven grandchildren and Sarah has added four great-grandchildren. He keeps track of his brood through Facebook postings that Donice monitors.